The Wizard of Odds

The Wizard of Odds

How Jack Molinas Almost Destroyed the Game of Basketball

CHARLEY ROSEN

Seven Stories Press
New York / London / Sydney / Toronto

First trade paperback edition: January 2003

Seven Stories Press
140 Watts Street
New York, NY 10013
www.sevenstories.com

In Canada:
Hushion House, 36 Northline Road, Toronto, Ontario M4B 3E2

In the U.K.:
Turnaround Publisher Services Ltd., Unit 3, Olympia Trading Estate, Coburg Road, Wood Green, London N22 6TZ

In Australia: Tower Books, 9/19 Rodborough Road, Frenchs Forest NSW 2086

Library of Congress Cataloging-in-Publication Data

Rosen, Charles.
The wizard of odds: how Jack Molinas almost destroyed the game of basketball / Charley Rosen.-A Seven Stories Press 1st ed.
p. cm.
ISBN 1-58322-268-5 cloth; ISBN 1-58322-562-5 pbk
1. Molinas, Jack, d. 1975. 2. Basketball players-United States-Biography. 3. Sports-Corrupt practices-United States. I. Title.

GV884.M63 R67 2001
796.323'092-dc21
[B]

2001041088

9 8 7 6 5 4 3 2 1

College professors may order examination copies of Seven Stories Press titles for a free six-month trial period. To order, visit www.sevenstories.com/textbook, or fax on school letterhead to (212) 226-1411.

Book design by Cindy LaBreacht

Printed in the U.S.A.

To Phil Berger (1942–2001) who, despite his nasty jump shot and ferocious drives to the hoop, was a sweet and gentle man.

Acknowledgments

In the spring of 1960, I had just concluded my initial varsity season playing center for the Hawks of Hunter College (it became Lehman College in 1972, but has remained in the same locale—Bedford Park Boulevard in the northwestern section of the Bronx). I stood six foot eight at the time, and because my statistics had been fairly impressive for a lowly sophomore (17.3 points and 13.2 rebounds per game), several basketball scribes who should have known better touted me as the latest "White Hope." At the urging of several friends who lived in the neighborhood, I undertook a pilgrimage to the Creston Avenue school yard to test myself against the legendary talents of Jack Molinas. The result was a massacre. Molinas ran me ragged, casually filled the hoop with hook shots from the most improbable angles, unleashed an old-time one-handed push shot, and defended me as though he was armed with a tennis racket. And he did it all with a mischievous gleam in his eyes and a dismissive curl of his smile that I've never been able to forget.

From there, I went on to register otherwise impressive numbers during my final two seasons at Hunter (peaking at 16.3 rebounds and 24.2 ppg), and I continued playing basketball for another forty years. I've played against a one-eyed high school All-American and several sad-eyed point-shavers and dumpers. I've played on a court built on top of a mountain and one built at the bottom of a swimming pool. I've scored forty-three points against Bridgeport University, fifty against Camp Lakowa, and zero points against Harlem USA (in a tournament game at Molinas's old stomping grounds in Haverstraw). I've played against drunken farmers at the Bavarian Beer Festival in Woodstock, New York, and against the likes of Wilt Chamberlain, Oscar Robertson, and Rick Barry. I've won some, lost some, hit miracle shots, and missed easy layups. But it was Jack Molinas who irrevocably confirmed my proper place in the basketball parthenon: a small-time big man.

Some thirty-eight years, six coaching jobs, two marriages, and nine published books later, I received a phone call from Julie Molinas. It seemed that he'd read several of my books (particularly *Scandals of '51* and *Barney Polan's Game)* and proposed that I write an authorized biography of his brother. Over the years, there have been several fictionalized versions of Jack's life (notably *The Great Molinas*, by Neil D. Isaacs; and *Big Time*, by Phil Berger) and several unpublished attempts at straight biography, but Julie had found these works to be either too speculative, too misleading, or downright inaccurate. Julie had at his disposal numerous scrapbooks, letters, photographs, and the core of his brother's story, 1,213 pages of transcribed dialogue between Jack and Milton Gross.

How could I refuse?

There are always innumerable pieces to the puzzle of anyone's life—some of them readily discernible, some of them hidden, and some forever lost. The sources, then, of this attempt to discover the truth of Jack Molinas's fascinating journey are varied.

For the family history, I am grateful for the fruits of Julie's own researches and his eyewitness testimony as well. Indeed, as the project developed, Julie's memory was stimulated and his imprimatur is stamped on almost every page. And the Molinas-Gross transcripts he provided obviously were invaluable.

I was also the grateful beneficiary of the generosity of two admirable men and accomplished writers—Phil Berger and Neil Isaacs. In late 1974, Berger and his late partner Stu Black were commissioned by *Esquire* to do an article on Molinas. Through an unfortunate series of misunderstandings that are commonplace in the workaday lives of freelance writers, the putative *Esquire* piece wound up in a truncated version in the pages of the *New York Post*. When I renewed a casual acquaintance with Berger, he was only too happy to share the notes, sources, and legal documents that he and Black had accumulated in their research. Accordingly, much of the testimony pertaining to Molinas's time in California comes from Berger's files. Specifically, these are the people interviewed by either Berger or Black some twenty-five years ago: Elliot Ableson, Clayton Anderson, Chuck Bernstein, Irving Binder, Paul Brandt Sr., Dick Brass, Linda Brauer, Frank Brian, Mike Cleary, Richard Crane, Dr. Richard Fishman, Larry Foust, Harvey Freeman, Hilliard Gates, David Goldstein (NYPD), Noelle Gordon (not her real name), Arthur Gould, William Green, Frank and Susan Guerrera, Stuart Gussoff, Bruce Hochman, Joel Horman, Mel Hutchins, Bruce Kaiden, Perry Knowlton, Leonard Kramer, Tony LaRosa, Leonard Martinet, Don Meineke, Harold Messing, Michael Minton (NYPD), Jim Mitchell, Phil Olofson, Andy Phillip, Burt Pugash, Allan Rabins, Harold (Rudy) Reiner, Red Rocha, Stu Segall, Al Seiden, Rev Shedlech (NYPD), Hyman Silverglad, Al Smith (Nassau County PD), Ellen Sohn, Louis Sohn, Sandy Solomon, Al Stein, Arnold Stein, Mark Tamboryn, Artie Tolendini, Stan Treitel, Ernie Vandeweghe, Dud Varney (LAPD), Steve Wallace, Marvin Weisman, Jack Wilson (LAPD), George Yardley, and Fred Zollner.

Likewise did Neil D. Isaacs graciously share his research materials. His wonderful novel *The Great Molinas* was immensely stimulating. His *Vintage NBA: The Pioneer Years*, an intriguing collection of first person narratives, was also invaluable.

I am indebted to Milton Gross, who conducted the original interviews with Molinas which were crucial to this writing. Were it not for Gross's persistent, clever pursuit of his subject, much of Molinas's story would have been lost.

In addition to the sources listed in the bibliography, the following New York newspapers were also consulted: the *Columbia Spectator*, the *Daily Mirror*, the *Daily News*, the *Herald Tribune*, the *Journal-American*, the *New York Post*, and the *New York Times*. Fort Wayne newspapers included the *Journal Gazette* and the *News Sentinel*. Also, from Williamsport, Pennsylvania, the *Sunday Independent*, and from Hazleton, Pennsylvania, the *Plain Speaker*.

The interviews that I personally conducted were with Red Auerbach, Johnny Bach, Albert Barouh, Irv Bemoras, Carl Bennett, Claudia Brandt, Paul Brandt Jr. (who also made available Molinas's letters to his father), Frank Brian, Hubie Brown, John Chaney, Stanley Cohen, Ed Conlin, Avery Corman, Ed Coyle (a longtime employee of Zollner Industries and frequent visitor to the Zollner household), Michael DeJacimo, Jerry Deutsch (one of the most devout hoop-o-philes in captivity), Robert Ellis, George Feigenbaum, Morty Freidman, Bert Garson, Al Geller, Marty Glickman, Arnold Goldstein, Robert Hacken, Ann Hemlock, Dick Kor, Sid Knuckles, Sam Messing, Ray Miller, Sue Nahmias, Lou Orlando, Harvey Persh, Andy Phillip, Bernie Reiner, Gene Rossides, Lou Rossini, Bob Santini, Dolph Schayes, Allan Seiden, Zeke Sinicola, Ellen Sohn, Zelda Spoelstra, Arnold Stein, Edwin Torres, Bill Tosheff, Whitey Von Nieda, Bernie Wincig, George Yardley, Bob Zawoluk—plus several ex-players and ex-coaches who agreed to be interviewed on the condition that they remain anonymous.

My thanks to them all.

The Wizard of Odds

Jack Molinas was at the top of his game. Only a rookie with the Fort Wayne Pistons, he was already a certified NBA All-Star who could score whenever he wanted to. Moreover, he was an Ivy League graduate with a genius-level 175 I.Q. Rich, handsome, young, charismatic, Molinas was irresistible to women. Ah, but Molinas could also lie with a sweet, buoyant smile, and he had a flair for larceny—he'd much rather swindle two bits from somebody than earn an honest dollar. Not even Molinas could guess how much money he'd gained by conspiring with gamblers to fix ballgames in high school, college, and in the pros.

For Jack Molinas, the real game was power—taming the unknown, manipulating people, odds, and possibilities, making the future dance to his own secret music. He just knew he was invulnerable, that he could always think or talk his way out of any predicament. "Don't worry" was his motto.

So, at six o'clock Saturday evening on January 9, 1954, when the Pistons' coach, Paul Birch, unexpectedly knocked on the door of the three-bedroom apartment on Monroe Street that Molinas shared with two of his teammates, Mel Hutchins and Don Meineke, there was absolutely no cause for alarm. Not even when Coach Birch said, "Mister Zollner wants to see the three of you at his house right away."

A Saturday night summons from the imperious Pistons owner? "What's going on, coach?" Meineke asked.

Birch was a stubborn man, a six-two backcourtsman on one of Fort Wayne's world championship teams in the pre-NBA dawning of professional basketball, and currently in his third season in command of the Pistons. He prided himself on old-fashioned values like hard work and uncompromising honesty. "Mister Zollner wants to talk about the upcoming All-Star game," he said, and his face flushed so much that his players knew he was lying.

"Well," Meineke said, "this is my second season in the NBA and, unlike my two roomies here, I haven't made the All-Star team yet, so I'm going to a movie."

"No," Coach Birch insisted. "I think you'd better come along too."

Meineke accompanied Coach Birch, and Molinas rode shotgun in Hutchins's car as they all drove eastward to Fred Zollner's home on 1601 Forest Park Boulevard near the corner of Vermont Avenue. And what did Molinas have to worry about? Absolutely nothing.

The NBA's fourth annual All-Star game was scheduled for Madison Square Garden in Molinas's hometown of New York City, just twelve days hence. Hutchins, a six-seven defensive stalwart, would be making his third appearance in the stellar contest, and the veteran analyzed the possible matchups. The Eastern Division squad featured Carl Braun, Harry Gallatin, and Dick McGuire from the New York Knicks; Ed Macauley, Bill Sharman, and Bob Cousy from the Boston Celtics; rookie Ray Felix from the Baltimore Bullets; Neil Johnston from the Philadelphia Warriors; and from the Syracuse Nationals, Dolph Schayes and Paul Seymour. The West was represented by Jim Pollard, Slater Martin, and George Mikan of the defending champion Minneapolis Lakers; Arnie Risen, Bobby Davies, and Bobby Wanzer from the Rochester Royals; rookie Don Sunderlage from the Milwaukee Hawks; and three of the Pistons, Hutchins, Molinas and Larry Foust. Hutchins would certainly be paired against the likes of Gallatin and Schayes, both powerhouse boardmen. While Molinas might certainly be required to take a turn against these two rough-and-tumble forwards, he'd most likely play most of his minutes opposite "Easy" Ed Macauley, a frail six-nine finesse player who couldn't guard his own shadow.

Hutchins warned the headstrong rookie about Macauley's unerring perimeter shooting, and the ferocity of All-Star competition, but Molinas couldn't wait to eat Macauley's lunch and be the hometown hero. "Don't worry," Molinas said. "Don't ever worry about me."

Fred Zollner was not only the high-flying owner of an NBA team, he was also the president of Zollner Machine Works, a corporation that employed nearly 1,800 workers and fashioned aluminum engine parts for most of America's automobile and aircraft manufacturers. As befitting his status as one of Fort Wayne's most influential citizens, Mr. Zollner's home was located in one of the city's most exclusive residential areas. The fifty-two-year-old Zollner lived alone in a three-story Tudor-style house built of red brick, decorated with thin white trim that resembled the frosting on gingerbread cookies, and set back thirty feet from the street. The spacious lawn was crusted with day-old snow, but the asphalt driveway was meticulously shoveled and sanded. The several cars parked near the garage aroused no undue suspicions in Molinas.

A black, uniformed maid opened the front door, and the three players were led into a large foyer that ended at the base of a long flight of carpeted steps. To the right, the foyer opened into a huge living room that Meineke remembered as being as spacious as "half a basketball court." The room was primarily furnished in luxurious leather couches and matching easy chairs; also blondwood coffee tables that showcased numerous gleaming glass ashtrays. The walls were hung with several boatside photographs of Mr. Zollner posing beside various outsized swordfish and tunas he'd caught, and a huge lacquered marlin was proudly fastened above the mantelpiece of a large redbrick fireplace.

Several men in business suits whom none of the players recognized were standing around the room in well-rehearsed casual postures designed to make them appear harmless. Mr. Zollner himself was seated in a leather easy chair and rose to his feet as the ballplayers were ushered into his presence. Dressed in black loafers, gray pants, a white shirt, and a neat blue necktie, Mr. Zollner otherwise ignored the players, walking over to the fireplace to place another thick log atop the already blazing fire. Casually, Zollner sat back in his chair and energetically puffed one of his favorite cigarettes, English Ovals. Zollner turned to the players and started talking about what specific transportation plans had been made for the All-Star game. He spoke about the departure time for the flight into LaGuardia Airport, hotel reservations, and per diem. His smooth face shone in the firelight, and his gray pompadour seemed to ripple like rising smoke. "As you fellows already know," he said, "it's a great honor to be chosen for an All-Star game."

The front doorbell rang just as Mr. Zollner finished his recitation, and the maid ushered another pair of ballplayers into the room—Andy Phillip and Fred Scolari. Several of the players traded uneasy glances, until Mr. Zollner suddenly said this: "There's been a lot of rumors around New York City that there's something funny going on with this team. Commissioner Podoloff is coming into town tonight and we're determined to get to the bottom of this mess. That's why I had you fellows come here."

None of the players dared move or make a sound.

"Okay, fellows," Mr. Zollner continued, "I know you've all been dumping ball games, so you better come clean."

As before, the players maintained a shocked silence. After a few moments, one of the strangers walked up behind the six-six Molinas, tapped the bigger man's shoulder, and flashed a police badge. "I'm Detective Captain Mitchell Cleveland," the man said, "and I want you to come along with me for questioning."

Molinas only shrugged and said, "Sure." Even as Detective Cleveland ratcheted a pair of handcuffs around his wrists, Molinas wasn't worried. Stupid cops. What did they know about anything? If Molinas's point-shavings at Columbia University had eluded the vigorous investigations of Manhattan District Attorney Frank Hogan, what could these rubes have on him?

While Molinas was being driven downtown to police headquarters, Mr. Zollner had two more visitors: NBA Commissioner Maurice Podoloff, arriving from the airport at about 8:30 P.M., and, several minutes later, the Pistons' All-Star center, Larry Foust. The big man was currently in the fourth season of an outstanding twelve-year career that would include eight All-Star games. He had been lured to Mr. Zollner's house by a phone call from Birch requesting the veteran's aid in drawing up an itinerary for an upcoming road trip. Mr. Zollner, who pulled out his wallet and pushed an honorary police badge into the player's face, let Foust into the house.

"Hi, Larry," Mr. Zollner said in a tone meant to be intimidating. He'd crack this case open all by himself. "Come on in. You're under arrest."

Foust couldn't help laughing, a bold reaction that greatly offended his boss. But Foust sobered up quickly enough when he entered the living room and saw several of his teammates, two men whom he instantly sized up as being cops, as well as Commissioner Podoloff. One of the detectives stepped forward and asked the players at large, "Do any of you have any knowledge that Molinas was betting on Pistons ball games?"

Almost in unison, Foust, Phillip, Hutchins, Scolari, and Meineke earnestly swore that they knew nothing about anything.

But Podoloff wasn't convinced, saying, "We know there's been fixing going on, fellows. And we know that one player on a ball club isn't enough to turn a game. Okay? So we're going to have all of you fellows take lie detector tests."

"Fine," said Phillip.

"That's okay with me," Scolari chimed.

"No problem," said Meineke, and Hutchins readily agreed.

"I'd be very happy to oblige," said Foust, "because I have absolutely nothing to hide."

The veteran players' agreeable responses were deemed sufficient to prove their innocence and the possibility of their submitting to lie detector tests was never mentioned again. Only the rookie, the obnoxious Ivy Leaguer from New York, remained under suspicion.

The entrance to the police station was at the rear of the building, just off the asphalt parking lot. Molinas was escorted into an interrogation room on the second floor, a bare, hopeless space with peeling gray walls, a barred window facing out on Berg Street, a small one-way spy window disguised as a mirror, and a hooded lightbulb dangling from a chain above the table. In the far corner, a rusted radiator occasionally clanged whenever the basement furnace was stoked. The meager furnishings included half a dozen wooden folding chairs, and a rickety wooden table whose surface had been scorched and blackened by a thousand carelessly handled cigarette butts. Molinas was pointed to the chair closest to the table and opposite the mirror, then his handcuffs were undone. Detective Cleveland was on hand, along with Chief of Police Al Figel and Detective Sergeants H. King, Edwin McCarthy, and Jack C. Lake.

Was Molinas worried yet? "Not a chance. I didn't give the whole operation two thoughts," he said many years later.

Then one of the cops said, "We're investigating point-shaving on the Pistons, Jack, and we've heard rumors that you're involved." "Then you heard wrong," Molinas said, "because I am not and never have been involved with point-shaving. I've done nothing wrong here." Then the cop said, "Isn't it a fact that you've bet on several of the Pistons games?"

And that's when Jack outsmarted himself and made the most idiotic mistake of his life.

When the detective brought up the question of his betting on the Pistons, Jack jumped to the conclusion that they were looking for the ballplayers who were turning tricks and dumping games. He knew that the Pistons games had already been off the boards for just over two weeks, meaning that no bookies would accept any bets on them up or down, and he figured the cops must have known this. At that time a lot of NBA players were out-and-out dumping. But, especially when the word was out that guys were going to play straight, just about everybody in the league went ahead and bet on their own team to win. This was such a common practice that when the detectives accused him of betting on the Pistons, Jack didn't think it was a big deal. He figured they were just sniffing around in an attempt to flush out the dumpers. So without thinking it through enough, he said, "Yeah, occasionally I make a wager on the Pistons. Whenever I think we're going to win, I bet one hundred or maybe two hundred dollars with a guy in New York. Maybe I've bet about eight or ten times."

They asked Jack next if the bets were made with a bookmaker, but Jack insisted that he was just an ordinary guy from the neighborhood. Stanley Ratensky, a student in the Brooklyn Law School. They called him Stanley the Rat. Molinas did it more as a favor to him than anything else. Stanley needed the money and Jack threw him some action. "Hey," Molinas said, "I bet a few times. That's all. I never dumped games or shaved points."

Molinas was then asked to dictate a statement, which Detective Cleveland transcribed. But Molinas objected to the initial copy Cleveland typed up and, after some haggling, signed the third copy, even though he still believed the statement to be inexact.

The final statement read as follows:

> I have been a member of the Zollner Pistons Basketball team since October 1953. After being on the team for approximately a month I called a man in New York by the name of Stanley Ratensky, knowing this man for a long period of time I called him on the telephone and asked him if he could place a bet for me. He said that he could and he would tell me the odds on the game either for or against the Pistons. After hearing the odds or points on the game I either placed a bet on the Pistons or else told him that the odds were to [sic] great and I did not want to place a bet. Several times I talked to him over the phone and odds or points were not mentioned and I told him that I thought on some occasions that we could win a particular game and I placed a bet. I did this about ten times.
>
> At no time was there a payoff to throw any games made to me by Stanley Ratensky. Nor was there any mention of the fact; however, the only reimbursement I received was for my phone calls which I made to

him. Also I received approximately $400.00 for the total times that I have been betting with him. This included the phone bill also.

There has [sic] been times during this basketball season when we lost games that I thought the ballclub as a whole were not putting forth their best effort. There was evidence that ill feeling existed on the part of the ball players toward the coach. This was shown many times during ball games when the players did not hustle or play the game they were capable of playing. A general let down was obvious. A couple of times this season I have heard mentioned on and off the court that if we could possibly lose the next game or the next couple of games it would become evident that a new coach was needed. The above statement does not necessarily reflect my own personal opinion since I was treated very well, by all concerned.

Q. Are you at this time under the influence of any alcoholic beverages, drugs or narcotics?
A. No.
Q. Has anyone promised you any leniency or offered you any reward or in any manner threatened you or put you in fear of your personal safety in order to obtain this statement?
A. No.

/s/ Jacob L. Molinas

By now it was nearly two in the morning, and after signing the statement, Molinas was told that Commissioner Podoloff wanted to see him. Then Molinas was handcuffed and taken to Detective Cleveland's office. Several others were waiting in the office along with Commissioner Podoloff—Mr. Zollner, Coach Birch, and six or seven people (undoubtedly policemen) whom Molinas didn't know. At Molinas's request, everybody else was asked to leave the room except for Zollner and Podoloff.

At age sixty-three, Maurice Podoloff was pudgy and barely five feet tall. With his prominent, rather gross facial features, he was by no means an attractive man. The NBA players privately called him Poodles, but the NBA commissioner had a dynamic personal presence that always commanded respect.

Podoloff had a copy of Molinas's statement and he asked him if he had indeed signed it. Molinas said yes, and Podoloff said that he would have to take some action against Jack, but first he'd like to ask some questions about the statement. Podoloff was concerned about the fact that the Pistons hadn't been playing well lately, and he picked out the part of the statement where Molinas had claimed to have overheard a teammate (or teammates) proposing that they shouldn't play as hard as they could because there was some bad feeling between the players and the coach.

"Is there any truth to this?" Podoloff asked. "Exactly who made these statements?" When Molinas hesitated for a moment, the commissioner leaned forward and said, "C'mon, Jack. We're both Jewish. Tell me the truth and I'll look out for you."

Molinas said, "It was only harmless locker room talk with no malicious intent on the part of anybody."

Then Podoloff said that since Molinas had violated an antigambling clause in his contract, he was going to be suspended.

Molinas was stunned. He was being suspended for betting on ball games? Why him? Why not the dozens of other players who were doing the same thing? He was tempted to tell Podoloff about all the guys on the Pistons and so many other NBA teams who were dumping. But all he said was, "How long is this suspension for, and do you really have to do it?"

The commissioner said he had not yet determined the length of the suspension. Because there was going to be a big furor over this, he'd have to wait and see how he could work it out. But Podoloff insisted that he did have to take some kind of drastic action. "There's too much pressure on me," he said, "especially from the newspapers, so I can't just let it go by. I could very well expel you, Jack, but I'm probably just going to suspend you, so as to leave the door open for your reinstatement."

Molinas pleaded that he hadn't done anything morally wrong, that he'd never done anything to harm the team. Then he turned to Zollner and asked if there was anything he could do. Zollner said the matter was completely out of his hands and was all up to Mr. Podoloff.

"I'm on your side, Jack," Podoloff said. "If there is any possibility of your playing again, why, I will represent your best interests."

By then Jack was desperate and even offered to play for nothing.

"Jack," Podoloff said. "Let's reverse our positions. You're the commissioner and I'm the player. What would you do?"

Molinas could only sigh, knowing the larceny in his own heart, knowing how glibly he could lie, knowing the truth. "There's no way I'd ever give you another chance," Molinas said, "because it would be too much of a gamble."

In his time, Jack Molinas was a world-class athlete, a lawyer, and master of the stock market, but he was also a big-time gambler and fixer in league with the Mafia, a double- and triple-crosser, a jailbird, a pornographer, a loan shark, and quite probably a murderer. In any event, Jack Molinas was much more than just another evil genius.

The generation that preceded Molinas was the one called upon to defeat Hitler and Hirohito and fight a righteous war. "Sacrifice" was their byword. Willingly, they forfeited their youth, their limbs, and too often their lives. And the good guys won the good fight and should have lived happily ever after.

But the atomic bomb vaporized more than the cities of Hiroshima and Nagasaki—it had also annihilated ideals. After the mushroom cloud and the firestorm, could anybody still believe in God? In morality, love, guilt, or innocence?

Jack Molinas was still an impressionable thirteen-year-old when the Atomic Age was born. Like his junior high school classmates, Molinas learned how to protect himself from the imminent atomic devastation by "taking cover." Along with his classmates, he learned to crouch under his desk and curl his arms around his head. Mere children, they were issued dog tags to wear around their necks so that their possibly charred remains might be identified. Total oblivion could occur instantaneously and without warning, a new reality that quickly put a desperate edge to every transaction, every interaction. Only chumps sacrificed. Even the Golden Rule was tarnished—*Do unto others before they do unto you.*

And nobody's been the same ever since.

In modern times, we've even made virtues of cynicism and partisan interests. So what if our leaders routinely lie and trample our moral codes? So what if a president is gunned down in public? Or another is impeached? Hey, so long as Wall Street is booming, and the job market is secure, and there's money enough to buy a new TV, well, then, who really cares?

Yes, there's no doubt that Jack Molinas was a crook. And, positively, he was more interested in strategy than in justice. But just as certainly, Jack Molinas represents something more than the paltry sum of the parts of his own twisted life. The terrible truth is that Jack Molinas was no less than the first modern man.

Jack's father, Louis Jacob Molinas, was a Sephardic Jew and proud of his heritage. In their ancient Iberian homelands, the Sephardim were attracted to the study of philosophy (as opposed to the Eastern European Jews, the Ashkenazim, who advocated the intensive study of the Babylonian Talmud), and developed the Spanish Cabala, a mystical interpretation of the Torah and the Ten Commandments. These were the Jews who were expelled from Spain in 1492 by Ferdinand and Isabella when they refused to convert to Christianity. The exiled Spanish Jews (followed in 1497 by Jews similarly evicted from Portugal) scattered across the known world, mostly settling in the Balkans, the Netherlands, Palestine, or the Ottoman Empire. The Sephardim considered themselves Jewish aristocrats and, over the centuries, have traditionally been zealous about protecting their religious independence. When a single boatload of courageous Sephardim fled from the religious persecution they'd been subjected to in Brazil and landed in New York in the middle of the sixteenth century, they claimed the distinction of being the first Jews in America.

Louis's forefathers were apparently millers who initially settled in Italy before moving on to Turkey. The original family name is believed to have been Molino, which is Spanish for windmill. The appellation was singular, but because the family was so extensive they were always referred to in the plural; therefore, "Molinas."

The second of three siblings (and the only male), Louis was born November 17, 1899, in Canakkale, Turkey, a small farming town southwest of Istanbul. Even in the relative obscurity of Canakkale, the Jewish ghetto was victimized by periodic pogroms, especially on Friday nights, the sabbath. His father was named Jacob Louis Molinas; his paternal grandfather, Louis Jacob Molinas (reputed to have been seven feet tall); and so on, the first-born sons alternating names in each succeeding generation. In 1914, Louis escaped from Turkey with his parents' blessing in order to avoid military proscription. From Istanbul, Louis boarded a freighter (he traveled in steerage) bound for New York City.

When he arrived, Louis moved in with his father's older sister, Clarisse Bernardo, her husband, Bahor, and their four sons, in a small tenement flat on the Lower East Side. Like most other immigrants, Louis was extremely industrious, quick to find menial employment (sweeping the aisles in a movie theater between shows) and also to enroll in an evening class (at PS 147) to learn the new language.

Louis's teacher was Julius Eisenstein, who turned out to be a pivotal figure in the young man's life. In addition to learning English, Louis also was taught many of the social amenities of this strange new country, and a lasting friendship was formed.

By 1916, his mother had remarried. Even so, despite the pittance he was earning, Louis sent money home every month. Louis eventually quit his job at the movie theater and began working in an uptown Manhattan candy store. His naturalization papers were dated July 7, 1920, and the document contains several bits of misinformation. His birth year is given as 1898, and he's listed as being five feet five inches tall, approximately five inches shorter than his actual height. At age twenty-one, Louis was a ruggedly handsome young man, his brown eyes coldly gleaming in his stern rectangular-shaped face. He'd already earned a reputation for shrewdness, impeccable honesty, and an impressive capacity for hard work. Louis was perhaps a bit introverted and rigid by American standards, but he'd been raised in the Old World, where such character traits were considered to be admirable. The only flaws in Louis's temperament seemed to be his volatile temper, as well as a brickheaded stubbornness. By the early 1920s, Louis was able to send for his two sisters, Esther and Clara, who each found a husband shortly after their arrival in New York. Soon after this, Louis and a well-to-do friend, Harry Azriel, combined their resources and bought a candy store on 110th Street and Lexington Avenue.

Sometime around 1927, Louis and Azriel got involved in another moneymaking scheme, buying bars of gold bullion in Toronto and selling them directly to the U.S. Treasury in Washington, D.C.—a practice that was legal until 1933. With Azriel supplying most of the up-front money, their first cautious venture into the "gold business" proved to be mildly lucrative. Louis used some of his newfound profits to establish another business—staffing coat-check rooms in various restaurants, ballrooms and nightclubs around New York. One of Louis's biggest accounts was the Mecca Temple on Fifty-fifth Street, an auditorium run by the Shriners.

Buoyed by their initial success, the partners made another trip to Canada, this time prepared to spend upward of fifty thousand dollars (mostly Azriel's) for the gold and expecting to at least triple their investment. Unfortunately this second load turned out to be gold-painted bars of lead. According to their agreement, Louis was accountable to Azriel for half the loss, a debt that would require nearly fifteen years of work to be paid in full. (One of the bogus bars of gold was donated to Roosevelt High School in the Bronx, where Mr. Eisenstein was now teaching, and placed in a display case in the chemistry department.) A much more significant result of this swindle was that from then on Louis could not tolerate any form of gambling or hazardous speculation.

In late 1928, the same Harry Azriel was the key figure in arranging a marriage between Louis and Benvenuta Grassian. Betty, as she was called, was born in Manhattan, but her parents were Turkish.

Abshalom and Allegra Grassian had been married in their hometown of Dardanelles, Turkey, in November 1895. They never learned English, even though seventeen years later they journeyed to America to "find a better life," and Abshalom opened a restaurant on Rivington Street on the Lower East Side. The old man's recipe for a long, happy marriage was a traditional Turkish one—"an obedient wife." Their daughter, Betty, was born March 14, 1910, and was trained to fulfill her role in the community. According to her, her parents had a perfect relationship: "What my father said, my mother did."

Unlike her older brother, Joseph, Betty graduated high school. She longed to become a schoolteacher, but she was dissuaded from continuing her education. After all, if she went to college, Betty might become too smart and nobody would want to marry her.

Betty was a dark-eyed Mediterranean beauty, noted for her gentleness and compassion. She and Louis were married in the Bronx on October 27, 1929, at the Temple Adath Israel, on 169th Street and the Grand Concourse.

The newlyweds settled into a cozy one-bedroom apartment in the Pelham Bay section of the Bronx, but Betty thought the location was too isolated. After two years, they moved into a two-bedroom railroad-style apartment at 2525 Grand Concourse, just a block north of Fordham Road. A luxury address, the Grand Concourse was the widest thoroughfare in the Bronx and was conceived as New York City's version of the Champs-Elysée. This bustling crossroads was serviced by several public bus routes, a nearby trolley line, an IND subway station, and just three blocks westward, the elevated trains that rattled and clanged above Jerome Avenue. The Molinases' neighbors were mostly Polish and German Jews, with a scattering of Italians, and they lived harmoniously in a sturdy line of classic Bronx apartment buildings—redbrick quasi-fortresses crowned with crenellated rooftop battlements. The Molinases themselves lived in apartment 5A, on the topmost floor, where every window opened onto the Concourse. Although the building lacked an elevator, the stairs were artfully crafted of white stone, and the prime location alone more than justified the hefty forty-three-dollar monthly rent.

The joint was always jumping: Children constantly called up to their parents to open the windows and throw down money for ice cream, or sometimes to "airmail" their forgotten mailbox keys. From time to time, itinerant peddlars would pause in front of the building and announce their services: A man with a pushcart would yell, "I cash clothes!" Another with a whetstone strapped across his back would loudly inform the housewives that he sharpened knives and scissors. Sometimes a lone fiddler would play plaintive, nearly forgotten songs from homelands faraway and be rewarded with pennies wrapped in scraps of newspaper tossed from opened windows.

Following Julius Eisenstein's interior decorating suggestions, Louis and Betty hung framed prints of old seascapes on the walls and furnished the apartment in the Colonial style. But Betty was especially fond of her luxurious kitchen, particularly the small dumbwaiter that so conveniently carried garbage into the basement, and also the newfangled electric refrigerator (still referred to as the icebox).

By now, Louis had expanded his business interests. While maintaining his coat-check concessions, he'd also joined with two partners and taken over the Glen Island Casino, a nightclub in New Rochelle. Louis always seemed to be either working or in transit, leaving Betty alone and forlorn. She halfheartedly cultivated interests in the theater and ballet, which she sometimes attended with her friends. But mostly she spent long, solitary hours reading popular novels.

Betty's life was brightened on April 16, 1932, when her first son was born in Mount Royal Hospital in Manhattan. In keeping with the Molinas tradition, he was named Jacob Louis, and to insure a lifetime of health, wealth, and good luck his parents sprinkled gold coins into his crib.

In many ways, Jackie was a difficult child, always active, getting into closets, climbing up on chairs, crying when he didn't get his way. As much as she loved him, Betty vowed never to have another child.

When Jackie was two years old, Louis began to notice that the boy's inclination was to pick things up with his left hand. In the legends of the Old World, the devil was believed to be left-handed, so a wrong-handed child was doomed to possess a "sinister" and devious nature. To remedy this alarming tendency, Jackie's left hand was tied behind his back until the situation was remedied.

Jackie was an intelligent, handsome child with shiny black hair and a dazzling smile. He could read English at three, and Spanish a year later. With his prodigious memory, he entertained his parents, their friends, and relatives with recitations of names, lists, and catalogs. His mother and his aunts repeatedly told him that "the girls will never be able to keep their eyes off you, or their hands."

Whenever Jackie disobeyed his father's commands, however, he would be spanked with either a bare hand or a strap. Betty was always horrified at her husband's severity with the child and continually voiced her objections. "Louis," she'd say, "he's just a little boy." But Louis was adamant: "The boy must learn discipline. It's the only way."

Even though Louis was rarely home, he was determined that his son would be raised properly. To that end, early one Sunday morning Louis took the four-year-old Jackie over to nearby St. James Park. Positioning the boy next to a particular tree, Louis told Jackie that he was going to leave him alone for a while, but that he'd better still be there glued to the spot when his father returned. Of course, Jackie cried some when Louis walked away, but he didn't dare budge until his father came back to fetch him two hours later. For years, Louis would brag about the incident as proof of his own prowess as a disciplinarian. So, too, would Jackie always remember his father's cruel obedience training.

Despite Jackie's restlessness and the strong will he demonstrated in his father's absence, Betty was utterly devoted to her son. The boy was always clean, well dressed, and fed only the healthiest of foods. Salads with feta cheese and Greek olives. Spinach and feta cheese *pastellas* wrapped in phyllo dough. Stewed tomatoes. Red rice. Potato pancakes with leeks. Desserts with almonds and sesame seeds. Beyond these material comforts, Betty also tried to override her husband's heavy-handed dominance and more gently nurture Jackie's emotional and psychological development.

When Betty discovered that she was pregnant again in the spring of 1936, she was distraught. Several friends and family members counseled her to have an abortion, but she refused. So it was that a second son, Abshalom Julian, was born to her on September 17, 1936, also at Mount Royal Hospital. He was named Abshalom in honor of his maternal grandfather, and Julian in remembrance of Julius Eisenstein, Louis's beloved friend and mentor who had recently died of complications during what was supposed to be routine hernia surgery. By then, Louis had become sufficiently Americanized that this time he took no countermeasures when Julian, like his brother, exhibited a proclivity to left-handedness.

When the boys were still young, the sleeping arrangements in the Grand Concourse apartment were somewhat unusual. Louis had the master bedroom and Betty the second bedroom, while Jackie and Julie slept on cots set up in their mother's bedroom. By the time both boys were in school, Julie's cot was moved into the master bedroom, while Jackie's remained in his mother's bedroom. Was this perhaps some stern and self-abnegating, yet foolproof method of birth control? "I don't understand the reason why these arrangements were made," Julie said some years later. "Maybe it was some kind of standard procedure practiced in the old country. It could be that my parents were having marital difficulties, but that would be hard to imagine. All I know is that my brother and I wouldn't dare question my father in any matter."

Of course, Jackie would tease and pick on his little brother, but only in a pro forma fashion. Increasingly, Jackie was becoming protective of Julie—most likely in an attempt to shield him from their father's unreasonable rigidities.

In September 1937, Jackie was enrolled in the kindergarten class at PS 33 when he was just five months past his fifth birthday. One of his classmates was Bobby Santini, who would become one of Molinas's most enduring friends. "Jackie was a very bright kid with a great sense of humor," Santini remembers, "but even back then he was always trying to grab an extra edge. For example, he'd fight everybody to sit in the highest seat in the classroom, and he'd also battle to be first on line. He was always very physical."

At age seven, Jackie was mentally evolved enough to solve complex mathematical functions and even algebraic problems in his head without resorting to pencil and paper. Flip him a penny or two and he'd gladly turn his tricks. But, all in all, young Jackie would rather be outdoors.

In the winter, he'd go "belly whopping" in St. James Park, wildly careening downhill while trying to maintain his grip on his top-of-the-line Flexible Flyer. Weather permitting, he competed in all the seasonal New York street games, from punchball to stickball, from flipping and matching baseball cards to putting marbles at risk in a game called Immies. While still in elementary school, he took a particular interest in playing poker for pennies or for comic books. Since both Jackie and Bobby were taller than their schoolmates, a keen rivalry eventually developed between the two. "Jackie was a good game player,"

Santini recalled, "with an intuitive sense of strategy. Sometimes we'd get so competitive that we'd wind up fighting. We were both big kids so we were a good match. He was strong in a wiry kind of way, yet he was never really ruthless or bloodthirsty. We'd push and shove and have little punch-outs but we never really hurt each other."

On weekends, Jackie and Bobby would take in a matinee at one of the several neighborhood movie theaters. In addition to the films, the theaters would regularly sponsor competitions in yo-yo twirling and top spinning, but Jackie was content to be a spectator. At the same time, Jackie developed a prepubescent crush on Ava Gardner and would never miss her latest movie. For the rest of his life, Ava Gardner would be Jackie's standard of what a woman should be, and the reason why sheer physical beauty would have such an overwhelming appeal for him. If an after-movie treat was affordable, the boys could go into any one of a number of local candy stores and order chocolate egg creams. If they were really flush, they'd have a snack at Bickford's Cafeteria on the Grand Concourse and 188th Street.

Upon entering Bickford's, the boys would walk through a small turnstile and take a ticket from a machine that rang with a chime when the ticket was removed. The boys would then pick up their trays, plates, and silverware at the beginning of the long food counters. Large platters of hot food were displayed on steam tables and portions were dispensed by uniformed servers, who'd also take the boys' tickets and punch out the appropriate price. Jackie was greatly impressed with the precision of the entire operation, and also the sense of overindulgence inspired by such huge quantities of greasy, salty, gloriously tasty and unhealthy food. Another counter offered pies, cakes, pastries, coffee, tea, and milk. Bickford's catered mostly to the weekend and after-work shoppers who thronged the area, but several locals also congregated there—including Joey Hacken, the neighborhood bookie who would soon become Jackie's guide to the underside of sports. Early in Jackie's tenure at PS 33, however, Hacken was just another familiar face.

One of the boys' summers was made more intriguing by the digging up of the Grand Concourse to facilitate some electrical repairs. The thoroughfare was closed to vehicular traffic and big ditches were spanned by thick planks so that pedestrians could cross the street, but Jackie proved to be the only kid in the neighborhood who dared to jump headlong across the ditches.

That same summer, Jackie was subjected to a short haircut that earned him a temporary nickname, "Cue Ball," and the unmerciful teasing of his playmates. Until his hair grew back, the taunts would often bring Jackie to the verge of tears, but he'd bite his lower lip until the urge passed because crying was for babies. Try as he might to deny this sensitive undercurrent in his otherwise carefully crafted daredevil personality, it was Jackie's basic vulnerability that (even as an adult) attracted so many loyal friends.

At home, Louis continued to rule with an unforgiving hand. Homework was done right after dinner. Bedtime was precisely eight-thirty for Julie and nine o'clock for Jackie. Anything other than instantaneous obedience was unthinkable, and while the boys respected their father, they also feared his wrath. One time, young Jackie had come into possession of a pea shooter and was firing away from one of the bedroom windows, aiming tiny pea pods at the heads of the passersby five stories below while Julie stood on the adjoining fire escape rooting his brother on. When one of the missiles struck an older woman in the cheek, Jackie ducked back inside but Julie had nowhere to hide, so the woman was able to pinpoint the apartment. Outraged, she immediately located a telephone and called the police. A patrolman soon came knocking on the apartment door and delivered a stern admonition to the youngsters. Jackie bravely endured the threat of being arrested and sent to reform school, but begged the policeman not to inform his father of the "crime."

Sue Nahmias regularly baby-sat for the boys at the going rate of fifty cents a night whenever Louis and Betty went out. "Mister Molinas would pick me up," she says, "then lay down the rules before he and his wife left. What time the boys had to go to bed and things like that. Then he'd drive me home later, but he never talked much. He never even asked if the boys had behaved because he couldn't even imagine that they wouldn't. And they did. They played quietly together—checkers or Chinese checkers—or they read comic books. They were very good with each other. When it was bedtime, they went off without a peep. Whatever the father said, they did to the letter. They were clearly afraid of having me give a bad report to him. It was an easy job."

Louis and Betty were fluent in English (which Louis always spoke with a slight accent) and Spanish, but they conversed mostly in Ladino, a variation of medieval Spanish adopted by Iberian Jews. In the written form, the vernacular was transliterated into Rashi, which was a modified version of Hebrew vowel lettering. In the spoken form, Ladino included Spanishized Hebrew words. Jackie pleaded with his parents to speak English in front of his friends, a request to which Louis reluctantly agreed.

In later years, Louis did express certain regrets about the way Jackie had been raised. "I was never wealthy," Louis said, "but there was always money in the house and food on the table. He never wanted for anything. Who knows? Maybe I gave him too much. Maybe I spoiled him."

On an emotional level, however, Jackie was stunted. Louis certainly loved his children but was never moved to come up to either one, put his arm around his shoulder, and just say something like, "How're you doing? Is everything okay?" Never. The only verbal communication between Louis and his sons was the lecture. Because Louis had listened intently to his own father's lectures, he assumed his sons would do the same. Betty constantly told her husband to try to be a friend to his sons, but Louis didn't know how to accomplish this. Only when Jack was an adult could he share any meaningful conversations with his father, and then strictly about business matters.

Years later, several of Jack's friends would place a significant portion of the blame for his felonies and malefactions squarely on Louis's shoulders.

"Jack's father was a tough, tough man," said Allan Seiden, a hoopmate of Molinas's. "He saw everything in extremes, either black or white. I think the old man's rigidity was instrumental in pushing Jack off the edge."

Ellen Sohn was Jack's girlfriend for many years, and she said this: "The father didn't know any other way to raise children and he did the best he could. But he was a mean old bastard who did everything by the book. The boys were afraid of him. And the mother was just lost in the shadows."

Week by week, Betty had to account for the "house money" Louis allotted her. Betty worked hard to keep the apartment spotlessly clean and she also insisted on cleaning up after the boys. Growing up, neither Jackie nor Julie had any daily household chores. No indulgence was too much for her oldest son. Afraid to demand that Louis desist from hitting Jackie for disobediences real or imagined, she would often protect her son by concealing as many of his petty misdeeds as possible. Later, when he was dating, Betty would wait up until three in the morning just to be able to show her son what snacks were available in the icebox. From the start, this gentle, affectionate woman was Molinas's only refuge.

Living in such a protected household and such a sequestered neighborhood, Jackie was virtually immune to the countless tragedies of World War II. Of course there were air raid drills, when the lights had to be switched off in the apartment and the shades tightly drawn and the tiniest "leak" would cause a white-helmeted air raid warden to come pounding on the front door. And there were ration books for sugar, paper, and gasoline, with paper bags from the grocery store being used over and over again. But the Molinas clan had no relatives or close friends killed or wounded in action.

Discarded metal pots and pans were routinely collected at the police station, and even at PS 33, the students were obliged to bring in string-bound bundles of newspapers for the war effort. Once every week, these bundles would be ceremoniously measured with a ruler and prizes awarded to the most patriotic students. As duly required, Jackie did bring in a perfunctory bundle every week, but to his mind the contest rewarded nothing more than sheer industriousness and thus had no appeal for him.

Then, in the fall of 1943, Jackie entered Creston Junior High School and began to slip away from his father's heavy-handed command.

4

Sometime in the late 1930s, Louis and his three partners sold the Glen Island Casino and purchased the Harbor Inn, also on Long Island. Then, in 1942, the four men moved on to their next, and final, cooperative business venture—the Famous Eagle Bar and Grill, on Surf Avenue and Twelfth Street in Coney Island. Eventually, this new enterprise would have disastrous consequences for young Jackie.

Coney Island was promoted by the local chamber of commerce as "The Playground to the World," and the Eagle was conveniently situated only two short blocks from bustling Stillwell Avenue, site of the turnaround station for the IND line, the Sea Beach line, the West End line, the Culver line, and the Brighton line.

When Louis took over the operation, the Eagle was situated near Luna Park, a popular amusement spot that featured a merry-go-round, a roller coaster, and a bandstand that spotlighted various well-known dance orchestras. Luna Park was billed as "the Eighth Wonder of the World," and its piece de resistance was a downsized re-creation of the Taj Mahal. For the first few seasons, the Eagle did a fast business selling food and beer to pedestrians on their way to and from Luna Park.

Cater-corner across Surf Avenue was the local institution Feltman's, an upscale dining spot. Also in the immediate neighborhood were Skeeball alleys, mechanical horse races, and pinball palaces. Passersby were further tempted by an abundance of freshly made popcorn, cotton candy, and corn on the cob for sale.

Then, in the winter of 1944, Luna Park burned to the ground, to be replaced by a huge paved parking lot, the essence of moneymaking vacuity. Mickey Zaffarano, a well-connected Mafioso who would later became another one of Jackie's mentors, rented a large section of the lot situated directly behind the Eagle Bar.

The Eagle had a small glass-windowed counter that opened directly onto Surf Avenue. From here, one of Louis's employees (or, once they came of age, one of his sons) would sell beer and summertime beach food—frankfurters, raw clams on the half shell, French fries, and hamburgers. Inside, there was room for fifty tables, each one surrounded by four round-back wooden chairs. Louis would tend the long polished mahogany bar, an imposing figure, tall, lean, and muscular, neatly attired in shirt and tie, and always standing ramrod straight. The Eagle was never a neighborhood bar but catered rather to the thousands of tourists, the transient, boisterous proletariats out to cram as much enjoyment as possible into a sun-drenched weekend. Louis's stern presence was always sufficient to keep the customers under control.

Even though he was repelled by the silly entertainment that appealed to these rough-hewn and rowdy Americans, Louis was also a determined entrepreneur who always kept a steady eye on the bottom line. So, every evening during the summer months, the Eagle featured cornball country-western bands—one favorite being Oklahoma Slim and the Okies. Jackie remembered "Wabash Cannonball" being wailed out into the night, month after month, year after year, projected through a loudspeaker and onto the street, where it could attract more customers.

During the season, Louis would work twelve hours a day all week long; to ease the strain, Betty and the boys would move to Coney Island as soon as school was out. In 1942, their initial seasonal rental was a ground-floor apartment in a private house on Mermaid Avenue and Twenty-ninth Street. One summer, Louis rented a small cottage in the exclusive Sea Gate section. But the boys were happiest when the family rented a suite in the Half Moon Hotel on the Boardwalk at Twenty-ninth Street. "I was ten years old," Julie said. "We lived on something like the twentieth floor, so we'd wake up every morning and see the ocean. It was a thrill that I remember to this day. After all, who ever heard of anybody living in a hotel?"

The bar would remain open from mid-April to early October. In the off-season, Louis would concentrate on his thriving coat-check concession. Louis prospered to the extent that by 1945 he had repaid Harry Azriel in full for his share in the gold-bar fiasco, and a year later he bought out his partners and was the Eagle's sole proprietor.

Yet there were some problems involved in sustaining the Eagle's profit margin. First off, the local Mafia underlings had to be paid off to insure regular delivery of beer and booze, and to avoid broken windows and fractured limbs. At the time, organized crime had a major presence in Coney Island, with its headquarters located in Joe Bananas's restaurant (Gargiullio's) on Sixteenth Street between Surf and Mermaid Avenues. Secondly, the Coney Island cops also had to be bribed. There was also some difficulty when the union tried to organize the Eagle's workers.

Of all the necessary kickbacks, the weekly payoffs to the police were the most painful. Every Friday night, Louis would appear at the 60th Precinct, meet a certain Jewish captain, and fork over a two-hundred-dollar stipend. On one busy Fourth of July weekend, Louis was too busy to rendezvous with the captain, and within hours he was arrested and booked for serving alcohol to a minor. Louis appealed the arrest and the resulting fine, and, months later, a local judge threw the case out of court and admonished the police for removing him from his place of business. But, it was a catastrophic event that young Jackie never forgot. The lesson he took away with him was that the good guys and the bad guys were in the same crooked business.

Back in the Bronx, Jackie made another startling discovery—the game of basketball. He was twelve years old and about five feet ten inches tall when he entered the seventh grade, class 7-A, at Creston Junior High School, which was on 182nd Street and Creston Avenue. His class team played in and won a seventh-grade tournament. From there he started going to the night center at Creston Junior High that was open on Monday, Wednesday, and Friday evenings. After school he'd play in the schoolyard, then go home to eat and do his homework, and then he'd come back to the night center and play basketball. He was tall for his age, but very thin and weak, so he shot from the outside and played away from the basket.

When Jackie was just starting out, the best players in the schoolyard were Eddie Roman from City College, and Joe Kaufman, Miltie Greis, and Dolph Schayes, all of whom played for NYU. But the star of the neighborhood was six-foot-three Joe Green, who would later become one of Jackie's accomplices. Joe was a tremendous athlete who'd had tryouts with the New York Football Giants, the Yankees, and the Knicks. All of these players were a few years older than Jackie, much bigger and more experienced, too, so he would just watch them and learn and then go play with the fellows his own age.

According to Bobby Santini, Molinas didn't have much of an impact in the schoolyard games. "Jack was a funny-looking, gawky kid," Santini said, "long and lanky and prancing up and down the court like a newborn colt. His game was nothing special. Just long one-handed push shots from the perimeter. Then all of a sudden he started growing. By the time he was fourteen, Jackie was six feet four."

Basketball was another mystery for Louis and Betty. They could deal with minor disobedience, with poor grades, with Jackie going out with the wrong girls. But basketball? It was something from another planet. Basketball also put Jackie in touch with people his parents could never hope to understand. One of these people was Joe Hacken.

Pincus Hacken was a lay rabbi in a small urban city in Austria-Hungary whose primary vocation was preparing young boys to be bar mitzvahed. Sometime in the early 1930s, Pincus was fed up with pogroms and low wages, so he decided to immigrate to America along with his wife, his son, and his daughter. Unfortunately, when the Hackens were subjected to a routine health examination at Rikers Island, the two women were discovered to have tuberculosis and were denied entry. Pincus and his thirteen-year-old son, Solomon, moved in with a cousin in a spacious apartment on Crotona Park North in the Bronx that boasted the great Jewish baseball player, Hank Greenberg, as a neighbor. After a few months, father and son found a modest one-bedroom apartment on the Lower East Side and set about to become productive American citizens.

Eager to learn the hows and whys of his newly adopted homeland, Solomon quickly Americanized his first name, changing it to Joe. A poor student, Joe would nevertheless read his lessons aloud to himself trying to eliminate his guttural accent. But he always felt that what he learned in the streets was much more useful than what he learned in the classroom. His father, who conducted his own affairs with well-mannered European gentility, frequently complained that Joe was hanging around with a wild crowd. After graduating from Seward Park High School and finding only menial employment, Joe carefully investigated his opportunities and dispassionately decided that the easiest way to make the most money was to become a professional gambler. Accordingly, Hacken weaseled his way into the trade and knew enough to bet on his first crooked basketball game when he was eighteen years old.

Because he always drove an old battered car (the better to fool the coppers into thinking he was just an ordinary Joe), Hacken's nickname was Joe Jalop and he prided himself on always appearing to be totally inconspicuous. That's why he was perpetually in need of a shave, habitually wore a dark sport shirt and a threadbare overcoat, and made it a point to carry four or five newspapers sloppily tucked under an arm.

Hacken first made his mark as a hanger-on in Blum's Pool Hall on 188th Street and the Grand Concourse, and soon had three runners working for him—Joe Green, Aaron Wagman, and Neil Kelleher. An honest bookie, Hacken gained the respect and trust of such important Mafiosi as Frankie Carbo and Blinky Palermo. Those who dealt with Joe Jalop lauded his sense of humor, his loyalty, his ability to tell a good story, and his high seriousness. The bookie was a stocky five foot eight with a pudgy face. It probably didn't hurt him that his full head of dark brown hair and dark, swarthy features easily convinced strangers that he was Italian. By the time Molinas hooked up with him, Hacken had graduated from the pool hall and was conducting his hot-line business from a candy store on 188th Street just off the Concourse. But his main office was the first table on the left just past the entrance to Bickford's.

Novelist Avery Corman (*The Old Neighborhood* and *Kramer vs. Kramer*) was also raised in the Fordham Road–Grand Concourse vicinity. Although he was a half-generation younger than Molinas, Corman likewise whiled away many youthful hours noshing on Bickford's serviceable coffee, cakes, and pies. "When I was growing up," Corman said, "New York was a patchwork of neighborhoods that were just like small towns, and each neighborhood had its own bookie. In those days, just about everybody in New York knew a bookie, and knew a place like Bickford's where the horseplayers, the wise guys, and the gamblers hung out. Fordham Road was a working-class neighborhood where there was always the notion of trying to get a leg up and somehow trying to make an extra buck. If you look back at the first- and second-generation Americans in the working class, you'll find a lot of horse players, numbers players, and people looking for quick money, free money, that are always the fantasies of the poor. It's quite ironic that when the building that housed Bickford's was torn down in the 1970s, it was eventually replaced by an Off-Track Betting parlor."

In warm weather, the action in Bickford's would overflow onto the sidewalk, and Jackie couldn't avoid being drawn into it because he had to pass by Bickford's on his way to and from Creston Junior High School. Sometimes after seeing a movie he and his friends would stop at Bickford's for a snack. And every guy for miles around who was interested in making a bet on anything would be there. "Even if you wanted to borrow money from a shylock, Bickford's was the place," Jack would say later. Most of the conversation was about sports and betting. Who would win the next prizefight, the next ball game. Who was the best at pitching pennies. Who was the best poker player. Who could throw a Spaldeen farther than anybody else. Anything you could talk about, you could bet on.

There was nothing surreptitious or unsavory about betting. Sitting at a table adjacent to Hacken might be the red-faced Irish cop on the beat, his jacket open, enjoying a cup of tea, studiously oblivious as Hacken booked his bets. Payoffs to the local police were just one of the necessary expenses for staying in business, as Louis Molinas also discovered.

Everybody in the neighborhood knew Joe Jalop. In fact, Hacken would build up his clientele by routinely picking up the tab for youngsters as well as down-at-the-heels gamblers, and by accepting one-dollar bets.

One particular time, Molinas was on the Concourse and fooling around with a rubber Spaldeen, trying to throw it as high as the roof of the Roman Gardens, which was a six-story apartment building, when along came Joe Hacken. Joe told him to move right up close to the building so that he was almost touching the wall and then throw the ball as high as he could. It seemed like a miracle, but the winds swirling around the upper floors of the building created a strong updraft and hurled the ball up and over the roof. Then Joe told him to throw the ball against the wall and act real casual just like he'd been doing before Joe arrived. After a few minutes someone that Joe knew happened to pass by, and after a lot of buildup, Joe bet the guy fifty dollars that Jackie could throw the ball over the roof. Whoosh! And there it went. Out of his winnings, Joe paid Jackie five dollars. For the rest of the day, Joe arranged bets on whether Jackie could do the same trick standing with his back flat against the wall, or crouching first on one knee, then two knees. Naturally, Joe won every bet and gave his new-found partner five dollars off the top. When Jackie asked him how come he did all the work but only got five dollars a pop, Joe told him this: "Always remember that the muscle does the work, but the mind makes the money." Jackie went home that day with twenty-five dollars in his pocket.

When Jackie was twelve years old he placed his first bet with Joe Jalop. His father gave him an allowance of five dollars a week every Sunday and Jackie had saved up another three dollars so he could bet a total of eight dollars on the Yankees game that afternoon. But Joe put him wise. He said the ball game was pick-'em, which meant that he had to bet eleven dollars to win twenty-one. Then he told Jack all about how the bookie got his cut, his vigorish, and he said that Jack didn't have to pay him the eleven dollars right away, that he only had to pay if the Yankees lost. Jack said okay. All day long he wondered how he could come up with another three dollars in case the Yankees lost, which they did. He wound up borrowing the money from a friend after promising to pay him back four for three. When he went back to Joe to pay his debt, he was told to keep his money. Joe told him he was too young to get involved with gambling, but stopped short of making Jack promise not to gamble again. Jack figured Joe just wanted to see if he would come up with the money if he lost. But Joe was a very shrewd man, and he was testing Jack's character.

Before long, Joe was teaching Jackie all about odds and point spreads, a betting device that had been developed after World War II and made gambling on football and basketball very appealing. Joe taught him about the "lox and bagel," which was also called "a split line." Say the split line for a basketball or a football game is 3–5. That means if you like the favorite, you have to give five points, and if you like the underdog, you have to take three points. If the underdog wins by four, it's called a middle and the bookie beats everybody. Joe took Jackie under his wing and was almost a second father to him.

Hacken certainly had his own agenda for nurturing a relationship with young Jackie Molinas. For years, Hacken had sponsored a powerhouse basketball team, the Hacken All-Stars, made up of local high school cagers. The All-Stars were arguably the most potent nonscholastic team in New York and regularly bested squads of collegiate players in various tournaments and exhibition contests. The All-Stars also comprised a ready-made talent pool of young players who might be inclined to join Hacken's stable of dumpers once they entered college. Hacken realized that someday Jackie would be good enough to be an All-Star, and among the neighborhood aficionados was later given credit for anticipating that Molinas would develop into an extraordinary basketball player.

Spending the summers in Coney Island did nothing to diminish Jackie's increasing interest in gambling. The best basketball games in the area were played at a playground in Kaiser Park on Neptune Avenue. In 1944, while Jackie was growing into his game, the dominating player was a twenty-two-year-old, five-foot-ten inch bully whose real name was Isaac Rosenman, but who was known as Cozzi because his hunched shoulders suggested Quasimodo, the Hunchback of Notre Dame. Cozzi had attended Lincoln High School but had not graduated, and he bragged that he'd played for two of Brooklyn's most outstanding barnstorming teams—the Visitations and the Jewels. When he wasn't hooping, Cozzi was a part-time pissant bookie in direct competition with the more respectable Shlombo, who operated full-time from a table set on the sidewalk in front of a candy store on West Twenty-ninth Street. Shlombo, in turn, answered to Mickey Goldstein, a high-ranking member of the Joe Bananas family. In fact, all of the bookies in Coney Island were Jews who worked for the mob.

Fresh from his brief experience with Joe Hacken, Jackie was now betting regularly—two or three dollars on a baseball game, a buck on which raindrop would run down the window first, five dollars on whether or not the Dodgers-Giants game would be rained out. Neil D. Isaacs, in his novel *The Great Molinas*, described the profound attraction that gambling had for young Jackie:

> Here was a game of transcendent competition, in which smartness could make you a winner. You invested a part of yourself, your stake, paying for the privilege of using your wits (or testing your luck—in either case part of your human essence) against the odds. If you were right (or lucky) you multiplied your stake and experienced an exaltation of ego. You were potent, stronger than fate or wisdom, above inexorable forces of nature and therefore—in a sense, for a moment—immortal. If you lost, you still had the excitement of the action, never mind the nifty ways of externalizing any sense of inadequacy or insecurity. There were things much worse than losing, like not playing.
>
> In a nutshell, to gamble was to feel alive.

Several months before his thirteenth birthday, Jackie began to study the haftorah in preparation for his bar mitzvah and had to suffer through after-school lessons at the Schiff Center on Valentine Avenue only two blocks away. The center was one of the most affluent in New York, combining a synagogue, a full-time Hebrew school, a gymnasium, and a pool. Jackie, naturally, would rather have been playing basketball in the schoolyard than memorizing the dense Hebrew words.

One day he did cut Hebrew school, but then had to figure out what to do about the absentee postcard the teacher would inevitably send to his home. Louis would take one look at the postcard and give Jackie the beating of his life. All the mailboxes for the tenants of 2525 were on the building's ground floor and were each secured by a small hinged copper-plated door. Jackie's solution to his predicament was to insert a flaming wooden match into one of the decorative spaces in the door of his family's mailbox. In a flash, the postcard, and all the other mail, was destroyed. Jackie played dumb and Louis never suspected anything more than a random act of vandalism. Jackie was delighted to have committed the perfect crime.

His bar mitzvah on March 23, 1945, was a gala event. But even though Jackie was now officially a man, Louis forbade him to leave the apartment on May 8 while the rest of the country was celebrating VE Day, which signaled the conclusion of the war in Europe. All of those screaming and joyously tumultuous people running riot in the streets were seen by Louis as a nightmare come true—the barbarians swarming and about to destroy everything he valued. It was a father's duty to protect his son from such a dangerous and undisciplined mob.

At age thirteen, Jackie also officially succumbed to the spell of "the devil's teeth," in Old World parlance, and was a regular at several schoolyard crap games. His uncanny successes earned him another nickname, the Mole. Jackie was unafraid to leave the neighborhood and test what he called "the luck of the Mole" in unfamiliar surroundings. One such crap game regularly convened in the schoolyard at the Bronx High School of Science. A lifelong friend and nongambler named Allan Stein was persuaded to accompany Jackie to this game to provide extra protection in the likely event of heavy winnings. The other players were in their late teens and they grumbled when Jackie walked away with most of their money. Stein was appalled. "You're only thirteen," he told his buddy, "but it's clear to me that you're either going to wind up a millionaire, or wind up in the electric chair."

Shortly thereafter, when Louis accidentally came across a sock full of Jackie's crapshooting winnings in a dresser drawer, a few strokes of a leather belt brought a confession, but no tears. Afterward, Louis delivered a stern lecture on the evils of gambling, and then donated the money to the Sephardic Old Age Home in Coney Island.

Harvey Persh was another of Jackie's junior high school chums. "In the seventh grade," Persh said, "there were a group of five or six boys who lived in the same neighborhood, were in the same classes, and played the same seasonal sports, and my mother suggested that we form a club, which we did—the Bronx Panthers. Our dues were ten cents a week and we used the money to buy blue jackets embroidered with gold letters and a gold panther on the back. Jackie was asked to join our club in the eighth grade. In addition to sports, we were very serious students and many of the Panthers went on to become lawyers, doctors, dentists, and engineers. Even so, our primary meeting place was the schoolyard where we played stickball, punchball, softball, and, of course, basketball. But since Creston Junior High was an all-boys school, we also socialized with a group of girls from Elizabeth Barrett Browning Junior High only a few blocks away. We'd all go to the movies together and have little parties at one of the girls' apartments, where we'd play Spin the Bottle. We used to tease him for wearing black shoes and white socks. But Jackie was very outgoing right from the start and was always the life of the party. He also called attention to himself by being a risk taker. For example, he couldn't pass a fire hydrant, no matter how high it was, without trying to vault over it. The only gambling we ever did was to play penny-ante games of poker, and Jackie always seemed to win. All of us remained lifelong friends."

In the spring of 1946, Jackie was fourteen and had sprouted to a height of six feet four inches. By now he was playing basketball on a much higher level than his classmates. Bobby Santini, who would top out at a sturdy six foot four was the only one of Jackie's age group who could battle him on equal terms. More and more, Joe Hacken would show up in the schoolyard just to watch Jackie play. After one pickup game, Hacken handed Jackie a ten-dollar bill and told him to buy a new basketball at Davega's Sporting Goods Store over on Fordham Road. More and more, Hacken would pick up the check when Jackie and his friends stopped by Bickford's or enjoyed an ice cream treat at Krum's across the street. "Here, guys," Hacken used to say as he snatched the check. "This is on me." While his buddies were totally impressed, Jackie would just shrug. Hacken's generosity was business as usual and nothing less than Jackie felt he deserved.

And the luck of the Mole still held. Jackie and one of the Panthers, Morty Friedman, went to see a movie, *The Locket*, starring Lorraine Day, at the RKO Fordham. The come-on that day was that every paying customer would be given a key and, after the movie, would be allowed to see if the key opened any one of three small lockets. The first opened locket would be worth fifty dollars, the second twenty-five dollars, and the third ten dollars. After the movie, however, both Jackie and Morty were in a rush to go back home so they wouldn't be late for dinner. When they were halfway home, Jackie noticed that his key was slightly larger than Morty's key, a difference that had to be significant. "I've got to go back and try my key," Jackie said, "because I know I'm a winner."

"Jackie," Morty protested. "We'll be late for dinner and our fathers will kill us."

Trying to convince his buddy to return to the theater, Jackie offered to split his winnings. But Morty refused, saying, "No chance you'll win." Jackie, however, wasn't the least bit surprised when his key was a perfect fit and he won the fifty-dollar jackpot. "You should've stuck with me, Morty," Jackie said later. "It cost you twenty-five bucks. I'm telling you, Morty, never bet against Jackie Molinas."

The neighborhood high school was DeWitt Clinton, but Molinas's aspirations always transcended the expected and the mundane. With his father's enthusiastic approval, Molinas's ambition was to gain admittance into the Bronx High School of Science, which (along with Stuyvesant High School) was one of New York City's most prestigious secondary schools.

He took the notoriously difficult competitive exam and scored very well. So he was all set for Science, which was within walking distance from his house. Then he got a letter from Samuel "Doc" Ellner, the varsity basketball coach at Stuyvesant. Molinas was thrilled that a famous high school coach would think so highly of him as to send a personal letter. Ellner's message was that he'd heard Molinas was interested in playing basketball and that the coach wanted him to come play for him. At the time, Stuyvesant and Science were on a par scholastically and the competitive exam Molinas had taken actually served for both schools. According to their own convenience, qualified students could opt to go to school in the Bronx or in downtown Manhattan. Aside from the geography, the only difference was that Stuyvesant had a superior athletic program. The letter turned the trick, so without even speaking to Ellner, Jack decided to go to Stuyvesant.

The school was located at Fifteenth Street and First Avenue, which meant a forty-minute subway ride each way. On top of that, Stuyvesant had so many students that they were forced to have a split session. Upperclassmen went to the morning session, which lasted from nine to one. Underclassmen, like Molinas, went to school from one to five. Unfortunately, basketball practice began at one o'clock and the ball games began at three, so that left him on the outside looking in.

Even though he couldn't play varsity basketball, and even though he intended to be a premed student when he went on to college, Molinas barely paid attention to his class work. He did the minimum amount of required work, but that was good enough to get A's and B's. His two best subjects were physics and chemistry.

In the fall of 1946, while Molinas was in his first year at Stuyvesant, the betting crowd at Bickford's was still buzzing about a college basketball gambling scandal that had been exposed in the newspapers the previous spring. Frank Hogan was the Manhattan County district attorney and his office had been tapping the telephone of a man who was suspected of receiving stolen goods. Quite by accident, Hogan's investigators discovered that the supposed fence was also involved in fixing college basketball games. Surveillance was stepped up and the full plot was quickly uncovered. Five members of the Brooklyn College basketball team were implicated along with several two-bit "unconnected" gamblers. The players were expelled in disgrace. One of them was Dave Budin, who was a sometime participant in the pickup games in Coney Island's Kaiser Park.

The city's lawmakers subsequently amended the bribery statutes to include gamblers who made bribe offers to amateur sportsmen. And Hogan made a public announcement that amused the Bickford's sporting crowd: "This unfortunate betting scandal is an isolated incident."

Molinas said later that "all the bettors in the neighborhood knew that college basketball games were still being dumped. Joe Hacken used to give me inside information about games involving several colleges—Kentucky, NYU, LIU, CCNY, Syracuse, St. John's, and Niagara. He would never come out point-blank and say that one particular team was dumping. He'd just say, 'Watch this team tonight. They're gonna win.' I'd say, 'How do you know they're gonna win?' He'd say, 'Don't ask. They're just gonna win.' I didn't bet the games but I followed them very closely and I was incredibly impressed by his predictions. During my first year at Stuyvesant, Joe gave me twenty teams and every single one of them was a winner."

On November 11, 1946, Molinas accompanied several of the Panthers to Madison Square Garden on his way to witness his first-ever professional basketball game. As Molinas approached the main entrance, gamblers were unabashedly trying to hustle up business. "Hey, kid," they even asked him, "you want to make a bet?" There were twenty-dollar bills being boldly brandished, and several shady-looking characters loudly debated the appropriate point spread. As in Bickford's, there was no concern about anything illegal transpiring. Betting on basketball games was just another normal pregame ritual.

The Basketball Association of America (BAA) was one of the forerunners of the NBA, and the contest that evening matched the New York Knickerbockers against the Chicago Stags. Molinas sat in section 325 and was enthralled as the game unfolded. The speed and the size, the skill and the savvy, the sheer physicality of the pro game was a revelation. Yes, he could envision himself not only competing with these superlative athletes but dominating them. Max Zaslofsky was high scorer for Chicago, but with Sonny Hertzberg leading the way, the Knickerbockers emerged victorious. "I'll be ready soon enough," Molinas told his friends. "That's the game for me."[1]

Because Stuyvesant was such a long way from the Grand Concourse, Molinas would sometimes take the subway out to Stillwell Avenue after classes and stay overnight with one of his Coney Island buddies. In fact, with the notable exception of Bobby Santini, most of Molinas's closest friends lived in Brooklyn and attended Lincoln High School. During Molinas's in-season visits to Coney

Island, he'd often seek out Cozzi and make informal bets on the Stuyvesant basketball games—always on the Peglegs to win.

Since his schedule of classes prohibited Molinas from playing on the Stuyvesant basketball team, he was delighted when, in March 1947, the Bronx Panthers signed up to participate in the junior division of the Mirror-Park Tournament. This citywide single-elimination competition was cosponsored by a newspaper, the *Daily Mirror*, and the New York Parks Department. That year, the tournament attracted 1,288 teams and lasted two full months, with the finals scheduled for Madison Square Garden.

Molinas had his one-handed push shot, his drive to the basket, and he was beginning to master what would become an unstoppable offensive weapon—a hook shot. (He was also learning a scoop shot, which acted as a countermeasure to the hook. It was Tom Cobb, a six-foot two-inch Creston schoolyard fixture, who taught Molinas the scoop.) In the meantime, the best player on the Bronx Panthers was Norman Tauber, who, at six four, was just as tall as, but much stronger than, Molinas. Tauber's greatest advantage was his jump shot, which was a rare sight in those days. "Opponents would see Norman shooting his jump shot," Morty Friedman recalled, "and they'd say, 'What is this? Is it walking, or what?' And Norman was unstoppable because nobody knew how to defend him."

Tauber is himself convinced that his own jump-shooting prowess greatly accelerated the development of Molinas's skills. "Our coach was Whitey Strauss," Tauber said, "and he put me at center and made Jack a forward because I was a more rugged and more mature player. One of the reasons Jack become such a fine, versatile basketball player is that in those formative years he learned the game as a little man and not as a center with his back to the basket."

The Panthers won the Bronx championship, and defeated interborough teams from Manhattan and Richmond, before narrowly defeating a Brooklyn squad (led by Solly Walker, who would go on to be a star at St. John's) in the city-wide championship game at Madison Square Garden.

"The Garden"—then as now, the Mecca of basketball. Molinas promised his teammates, and promised himself, that someday he'd return to the Garden as a pro and have the whole city eating out of his hand.

On the heels of their success with the Panthers, Tauber, Arnie Stein, and Molinas were asked to play in several local tournaments with the Ravens, a team of players who were one and two years older. Basketball had consumed Molinas's life and the more he played the more he wanted to play. At the same time, he was increasingly capable of playing up to the competition. Everything seemed to come so effortlessly and so gracefully to him. Like throwing a Spaldeen over a roof, like getting A's without cracking a book, like outsmarting everybody including his father. Playing basketball was a snap.

"We'd play an early game with the Panthers at the Creston Night Center," Stein said, "then we'd put our pants on over our uniforms and take a cab over to where the Ravens were playing. It was a wildly exciting time for us, and we could see Jackie getting better game by game." With the former Panthers making crucial contributions, the Ravens won a big-time tournament played in PS 70 on 170th Street in the East Bronx.

Throughout the summer of 1947 Molinas continued to hone both his basketball and his gambling skills back in Coney Island. By now Molinas was working the street counter at the Eagle, washing the dishes, and swabbing the floors. And there was Louis, wearing a necktie even when the temperature reached a hundred degrees. His son was such a hard worker that Louis readily rewarded him with lengthy periods of free time in the off-peak daylight hours so that Jackie could play ball.

As the participants advanced into their mid-teens, the games at Kaiser Park became more accomplished and much more physical. "Mostly we played three-on-three half-court games," Bernie Reiner said. "Disputed calls were decided by 'choosing,' where two opposing players called 'odds' or 'evens' and then at the count of three extended one or two fingers. Add up the extended fingers to get an odd or even number. It was largely guesswork, but there was also a semblance of psyching-out involved. Neil Isaacs, in his book *The Great Molinas*, quotes Reiner further:

> [Jackie] had extremely long hands, could palm a basketball by the age of fourteen, and he was the most proficient in the park at manipulating fingers at choosing, so that his team would always get the ball out after every call. This often infuriated Cozzi and occasioned a number of fistfights between them. Cozzi was several years older and had everyone else intimidated, but Jackie would say, "He can't do anything to me."
>
> Jackie had other memorable battles on that court. He dueled in basketball with Bobby Sassone, probably the only Catholic in the park, who went on to a fine career at St. Bonaventure... Then there were two kids I coached on a Recreation League team: Mark Reiner, a distant cousin who now coaches the Brooklyn College team, and Louie Gossett, the only resident black on our courts, who went from the park to NYU but is better known now as an actor.

In addition to wagering on basketball and baseball games, Molinas was still eager to place a bet on any and all disputable situations: who could throw a Spaldeen farthest, who could run backward fastest, could Jackie outrun a bus (no), could he shuck an oyster faster than someone could eat it (yes). Molinas's favorite game was to flip a quarter into the air, then step on it as soon as it hit the sidewalk. The opponent would then guess heads or tails, and either collect the coin in question or pay up. Molinas would always boast about his winnings, but whenever he lost a bet to Cozzi, the two would play basketball one-on-one for double-or-nothing and Jackie would usually win. Molinas was always a gracious loser, but every time he'd score, he'd taunt Cozzi, saying, "You can't stop me." Win or lose, Molinas was always so jovial and carefree that not even Cozzi could hold a grudge for long.

Back at Stuyvesant to begin his junior year in September 1947, Molinas initiated a friendship with Paul "Whitey" Brandt that was destined to endure for the rest of his life. "We were in an English class together," Brandt said, "and our teacher was trying to peddle a book of quotations that he had compiled. The teacher wanted each student in the class to buy the book for a buck. After class, Jackie came over to me and said that he knew of a store where he could buy the book for fifty cents. That was the first thing Jackie ever said to me and, typically, it revealed a slightly different point of view than anyone else had. Otherwise, Jackie seemed fun-loving and bright and perfectly normal."

Finally, as an upperclassman, Molinas had the opportunity to play high school basketball beginning in January. Stuyvesant's starting team consisted of junior guard Sal Mannino, and a quartet of fifteen-year-olds, Molinas, Brandt, Joe Caiati, and Stew Johnson, who usually played the whole game without substitutions and were nicknamed the Whiz Kids. Molinas quickly emerged as the team's third-leading scorer (behind Mannino and Caiati), averaging 12.7 points per game (ppg).

During the regular season, the Stuyvesant Peglegs finished second to Seward Park High School in Manhattan's Division I, and on March 4, 1948, they upset Franklin K. Lane High School at Madison Square Garden in the opening round of New York's highly regarded Public School Athletic League postseason tournament. Coach Doc Ellner's artful strategy stymied Lane's running game with an extended zone defense. Newspaper accounts reported that in addition to tallying a team-high fifteen points, Molinas "played the best game of his life" and "maneuvered beautifully under the boards." On March 13, despite twenty-three points by "the lanky" Molinas, Stuyvesant lost to Port Richmond, 45–40, in the PSAL's quarterfinal round before "ten thousand uproarious fans in the Garden."

A few weeks later, the *World-Telegram* published its "All-City PSAL Court Picks." Listed among the First, Second, and Third Teams were several notable players including Connie Schaff (who would later be involved in a point-shaving scandal at NYU), and five future CCNY point-shavers—Eddie Warner, Ed Roman, Herb Cohen, Al "Fatty" Roth, and Floyd Layne. Both Molinas and Mannino were named in the Honorable Mention category. At season's end, experts were already installing Stuyvesant as the favorite to capture next year's PSAL title, and Molinas was being touted as a future college All-American.

Not only was Molinas a great ballplayer and a good-time friend, but his sharp wits always kept him one step ahead of everyone else. Many of the players at Kaiser Park knew that Molinas had been betting on Stuyvesant games as an underclassman. They also knew that in Molinas's junior year, Cozzi or Shlombo would devise a point spread and Molinas would routinely bet against his own team. "He wasn't dumping any games," said Bernie Reiner. "However, he'd think nothing of blowing a strategic layup or throwing the ball away so that Stuyvesant would still win but would finish under the spread." Other Kaiser Park regulars swore that Molinas never bet on, or fixed, any high school games.

Molinas was both the muscle and the mind, and making more money than he could safely spend.

NOTE

1. *The Great Molinas*, p.53, Isaacs interview with Bernie Reiner.

Concurrent with his junior season at Stuyvesant, the fifteen-year-old Molinas was finally recruited to play on the Hacken All-Stars. Except for Joe Green, who was in his twenties, and Bobby Santini, the other All-Stars were from two to five years older than Molinas. They included Howie and Arnie Stein (who were not related), Lester Pape, and Eddie DeLeo. "We had fancy black uniforms and jackets trimmed and lettered in red," Arnie Stein recalled, "and we'd play against, and beat, the best amateur teams in the city. Hacken used to give us cabfare to and from the games, and then if he didn't personally take us out to eat afterward, he'd give us each ten or twenty bucks to buy our own post-game meals. We used to practice at City College because Bobby Sand was the assistant coach there and he was always trying to recruit the younger players. Sometimes we'd practice at NYU because Coach Howard Cann also wanted a shot at us."

In addition to booking bets on specific ball games in various sports, Hacken also distributed to his clientele weekly betting tickets for college football games. "Each ticket had about thirty of the top college games to be played that weekend," Stein said, "and the bettor would pick a minimum of four of those games and bet at least a dollar that all his teams would be winners. One loser would make the entire ticket a loser. We'd sell them to our friends and our classmates, and get a fifty percent kickback for every ticket we sold."

Betty Molinas approved of Jackie's involvement in sports, and since he wasn't yet interested in girls, she saw the games as acceptable outlets for his adolescent energies. On the other hand, while Louis offered no specific objections, he wasn't at all happy about his elder son's obsession with basketball.

By the spring of 1948, Louis had been informed by several of his friends exactly who Joe Hacken was and what was really on the menu at Bickford's. The All-Stars had reached the championship game in a tournament that was played in a YMCA downtown on Delancey Street. The game was so important that Hacken had recruited Ed Roman to play with the team. But when the fellows came to pick Molinas up, his father wouldn't let him out of the house. Louis told his son that Joe Hacken was a bum and a bad influence. He also said that the people who hung around Bickford's were a bunch of no-good gamblers. He did not want his son on a team that either used Hacken's name or was in any way affiliated with him. Jack pleaded that this was a championship game and that a lot of people from the neighborhood would be coming down to watch the team play, but Louis wouldn't budge.

Molinas was humiliated. Daddy didn't let his little boy go out and play. "The hurt went very deep," Julie said, "and all it did was push my brother further into Hacken's arms. Hacken was a substitute father who, unlike my brother's real father, let Jackie do exactly what he wanted. It was a situation my brother couldn't resist."

Molinas was determined never to let anything like this happen again. In the future, he gave his All-Stars uniform for Bobby Santini to keep and he would lie to his father whenever there was a game. Louis liked the Panthers because they were all nice *hamishe* Jewish boys from good families. So whenever Jack wanted to play with the All-Stars, he told his father he was going to play with the Panthers. It was the first time Jack ever told his father a direct lie.

Back in Coney Island for the summer, Molinas's circle of bookie acquaintances grew larger. The likes of Izzy the Bug, Frankie the Wop, and Looie the Greek boasted that they hadn't worked a "real" job since Pearl Harbor. Molinas also became friendly with Shpitz the Galitz, a harmless low-life racketeer, and his black sidekick, Pork Chop. These two earned their living by periodically enlisting for cross-Atlantic shifts on merchant marine ships, and then fleecing the rubes with loaded dice. The two con men were also instrumental in paying off the Coney Island cops so that a dice game could convene undisturbed on the handball courts till well past midnight. At every turn, Molinas seemed to be learning the same lessons. Suckers and their money deserved to be parted, and a little grease smeared on the right hands went a long way.

At Kaiser Park, the basketball games continued as before, and so did the betting. One particular game matched Hyman Silverglad and Rudy Reiner (who later evolved into a solid backcourtsman for the Newark College of Engineering) against Jackie and Julie, who was just short of his twelfth birthday. The gimmick was that the brothers Molinas would put up twenty dollars to their opponents' one dollar, but instead of playing a straight two-on-two game to twenty points, Jackie would pay if any shot taken by either Silverglad or Reiner so much as hit the rim. The final score was twenty to nothing and the Molinas boys earned fifty cents each. The real thrill came from being able to dominate an opponent to the point of humiliation. What could be better than the priceless insult or the scornful laugh?

Molinas was afraid to stash his serious winnings anywhere in his apartment, because Betty cleaned every room every day and was bound to discover it. That's when Molinas developed the habit of carrying large amounts of cash in his wallet. His load was lightened, however, when he lost another bet with Silverglad concerning how many Saltines Silverglad could eat. Otherwise Molinas would race buses in his loafers down Surf Avenue (and usually win) and bet twenty dollars a shot on baseball games (and usually lose). Molinas was a virginal sixteen, and the summer was also marked by his first interest in girls, a brief, hands-off flirtation with Gwendolyn Davis.

The Peglegs began the 1948–49 season with five consecutive wins before bowing to Metropolitan Vocational and their six-foot-eleven dreadnought center, Ray Felix, 53–48. After eight games, Stuyvesant was 6–2, and Molinas was scoring at an 11.6 clip, only a few digits behind Mannino. At that point, Doc Ellner moved Molinas into the low post and the youngster's game suddenly flourished. By midseason, Molinas was routinely scoring twenty or more points and was acclaimed as one of the leading centers in the city. A return match against Metropolitan Vocational saw Felix scoring thirty-five points, Molinas fouling out early in the second half, and Stuyvesant losing 49–46. The boys back in Coney Island speculated that Molinas was in the bag.

To Molinas, playing in a rigged ball game was more exhilarating than playing it straight. He had to be mindful of the score, the game clock, the point spread, and even the substitutions. Every sequence called for a quick decision. Should he make or miss his next free throw? Should he play all-out on defense and risk a foul? Was it time to kick a pass out of bounds, or get called for a three-second violation? Or should he go on a scoring binge to make his own statistics respectable? If he let Stuyvesant get too far ahead too early in the game, Ellner would empty the bench and Molinas would lose control of the outcome. Molinas loved the idea of playing so many secret games at the same time.

Sal Mannino and Paul Brandt were both January graduates, but Molinas became a one-man gang as the PSAL tournament got under way before five thousand "frenzied fans" at Madison Square Garden. Stuyvesant was the decided underdog in the opening game against Commerce High School, but pulled out a stunning 55–48 victory that wasn't resolved until the end of a three-minute overtime period. With his twenty-seven points, Molinas was the Peglegs' hero, thoroughly outplaying Charlie Whitman, Commerce's heralded six-foot-eight center, holding him scoreless in the first half and limiting him to a mere six points.

On March 12, Stuyvesant once again took on Ray Felix and his Metropolitan playmates, but this time the Peglegs prevailed, 53–48. The outsized Felix managed thirty-one points, but Molinas scored twenty points and controlled the boards.

Next up was a semifinal contest versus Taft High School, whose center, Shelley Thomas, was another veteran of the Creston schoolyard. Stuyvesant cruised to an easy win, 58–43, and Molinas was unstoppable. Molinas had already totaled thirty-five points late in the fourth quarter when Taft called a time-out. The public address announcer gleefully informed the crowd that Molinas had equaled the record for most points scored in a PSAL playoff game. Naturally, Molinas wanted the record all to himself—so he sidled up to Thomas as the players lined up to resume the game and asked if he'd heard the announcement. Thomas may not have been a very accomplished player, but he always knew the score. "Sure," Thomas said, "and you really ought to have the record. Tell you what, Jackie, next time you get the ball, make a good fake and I'll let you dribble past me. Just don't make me look bad." Molinas's record-breaking scoop shot rolled around the rim and into the basket just before the buzzer signaled the end of the game.

The New York *Daily News* referred to the Stuyvesant team as "Molinas and Co." and raved about Molinas's performance:

> He has an eye, height, generalship and more than a passing acquaintance with the baskets. He scored two shots from 35 feet out, which is sharp-shooting of a kind that makes men successful. Somebody should order a saliva test for Molinas. Or, maybe, his wires should be tapped.

Molinas's wires wouldn't be officially tapped, however, for another four years.

Meanwhile, New York's basketball fans were feverishly anticipating the PSAL title game in the Garden on March 19, which would pit the Peglegs against Lincoln High School. The "Honest Abes" were big, strong, deep, quick enough to run with Stuyvesant, and under the auspices of Coach Venty Leib, they also played inspired defense. Lincoln had won seventy-one consecutive games in regular-season PSAL competition only to succumb in the championship games in 1947 (to DeWitt Clinton) and 1948 (to Erasmus Hall). Stuyvesant's edge was the quickness and scintillating talents of Jack Molinas. Most sportswriters gave the advantage to Lincoln.

However, over the course of several summers at Kaiser Park, Molinas had competed against all of the Lincoln players and completely overwhelmed them—Bobby Sassone, Sid Youngelman, and especially the Honest Abes' center, Mark Solomon. That's why, in Coney Island, Shlombo established Stuyvesant as solid two-and-a-half-point favorites.

"Jackie didn't need the money," said a Kaiser Park regular. "He was the wealthiest guy in the park. But he was obsessed with gambling and with doing everything in the most devious way possible. So, Jackie approached Shlombo and arranged to dump the game for eight hundred dollars. And Jackie bragged about it beforehand. 'Bet on Lincoln and take the points,' Jackie told everybody in the park. 'I'm throwing the game. Guaranteed.' And that's exactly what he did."

According to another Kaiser Park veteran, Marvin Weisman, Molinas never said a word about fixing the Lincoln game. "As far as I'm concerned," said Weisman, "there's no doubt that Jack played the game to the best of his abilities. Any other opinion is revisionist history unduly influenced by what happened to Jack later in his basketball career." Julie agreed: "The only time I ever saw my brother cry was after the Lincoln game."

Nevertheless, under normal conditions, Molinas could have manhandled Solomon and torched him for at least thirty points. But Molinas played soft and small and weak. Doc Ellner screamed at Molinas throughout the game, "Low post, Jackie. Low post." But when his teammates passed the ball into him, Molinas just passed it back out to a guard.[1]

The game was tight from tip to buzzer, and Stuyvesant led by six at the end of the third quarter. But Lincoln regrouped, and with fifty-eight seconds remaining in the game, the 215-pound six-foot-three Youngelman lofted in a long two-handed set shot that gave Lincoln the lead, 41–40. Only eight seconds later, Molinas was fouled and his free throw that might have tied the game missed badly. The game ended with Arty Menaker, Stuyvesant's five-foot-three guard, in possession of the ball in the backcourt and being swarmed by three Lincoln players. Even as Doc Ellner screamed bloody murder at the two officials to call a foul, the final buzzer sounded with Lincoln winning, 41–40. Molinas, who had previously averaged twenty-eight points in the PSAL tourney, finished the championship game with only twelve.

Afterward, Ellner complained that his team had been robbed: "I never saw a worse job of officiating in my life. It was disgusting."

Despite his meager efforts in the title game, Molinas was awarded a miniature gold basketball by the *Journal-American* at a festive dinner in the Hotel New Yorker to symbolize his election to the First All-City Team. The award itself was a toy, a trinket that belonged on a charm bracelet, but Molinas added it to his growing collection. What Molinas was after, what he thought he deserved, was a trophy, all gleaming and gold-plated, the bigger the better. Such a trophy would be tangible evidence that Molinas himself was made of gold, and that he could fool all of the people all of the time.

NOTE

1. *The Great Molinas*, pp. 44, 55.

The basketball scouts were everywhere, eyeballing ball games, interviewing coaches, and spreading the word that Jack Molinas was the best high school hooper in the country. He received about seventy-five scholarship offers, which was a great deal back in those days. When the University of Kentucky found out that Eastern Kentucky offered him fifty dollars a week, a Kentucky assistant offered a hundred. Michigan also offered a hundred a week. Almost every school offered him a car and a set of new clothes. There were no NCAA rules restricting either the college coaches from making repeated home visits, or high school seniors from making recruiting visits to colleges, so Jack visited Eastern Kentucky and Muhlenberg. Because Stuyvesant was an honors school, his eighty-five class average was adjusted upward ten points. Ivy League schools were after him, too. Of course, none of the Ivy League schools offered anything under the table, nor were basketball scholarships available. He visited Yale and Cornell, but Princeton, Brown, and Pennsylvania also made big-time pitches.

Even the U.S. Military Academy at West Point tried to enlist Molinas's talents. Jack got special permission from Stuyvesant's principal to take a week off from school and go up to West Point to live the life of a plebe, but he wasn't crazy about all the regimentation.

Louis was in favor of accepting West Point's offer, feeling that Jackie needed more discipline. The West Point athletic department, however, could certainly read Molinas's dissatisfaction with their program and they found an easy way to retract their offer. The whole family was shocked when they received word from West Point that Jackie had failed the physical exam because of an enlarged heart. Louis and Betty had horrific visions of Jackie spending the rest of his life in a wheelchair, and they immediately took him to a cardiologist. The doctor reassured everybody that most athletes' hearts are enlarged as a matter of course and that Jackie was "as healthy as a horse."

At this point, Lou Rossini made a visit to 2525 Grand Concourse on behalf of Columbia University. Rossini had been the freshman coach at St. John's and had recently moved to Columbia to become Gordon Riddings's assistant. In lieu of an athletic scholarship, Rossini could arrange for Molinas to be awarded a physics and chemistry scholarship from the Charles Hayden Foundation, which would pay the full freight for three years. As a further inducement, Rossini offered to extend academic scholarships for three of Molinas's Stuyvesant teammates—Stan Maratos, Paul Brandt, and Mike Langol.

Louis was elated with Columbia's offer, but Jackie favored Michigan, for the money, the car, and the twelve hundred miles that separated Ann Arbor from the Bronx. And Jackie was not happy with the fact that at Columbia he'd have to pay his own way in his senior year. Even if he decided to transfer from Columbia after his junior season, he'd lose a year of eligibility. But Louis insisted, and Jackie reluctantly conceded.

Consider Jack Molinas at seventeen years old—prince of the playground, on his way to becoming first an All-American and then an NBA All-Star. And, with his long, triangular-shaped face, his pouting lower lip that framed a radiant, infectious smile, his sturdy Romanesque nose, his cordial brown eyes, and his neatly clipped shock of black hair, Jack was also heartthrob handsome. What did the future promise him? Riches, fame, eternal bliss. The intelligence to leverage all the secret wheels of power. What did he have to worry about? Nothing.

During the summer of 1949, Molinas grew to his adult height of six feet six and also became addicted to Cuban cigars. To celebrate his independence, Molinas wanted to leave the running of the Eagle Bar to Louis and Julie and spend July and August playing basketball in the Catskills.

In the early 1930s, the owner of a Catskill resort learned that several members of the recreation staff were college basketball players from New York. The players periodically organized their own games to stay in shape, and the owner, quick to see the possibility of an added attraction, let the guests watch them play. The idea caught on, and within a few years virtually all of the area's two hundred hotels were fielding a liveried basketball team. Ballplayers from all over the country jumped at the chance to earn some extra money, have a good time, and play some very competitive ball.

In any given summer, there were perhaps five hundred varsity basketball players employed in the Catskills. Each resort team usually played two games per week and practiced every day. There were no actual leagues, no standings, and no winner at the end of the season. But basketball games featuring the likes of Bob Cousy, Alex Groza, and George Mikan provided wonderful entertainment on a summer's evening.

Most often, the resort teams played each other, but sometimes all-star teams were imported to spice up the action. Johnny Bach was an All-American at Fordham and a defensive ace for the Boston Celtics. "Even when I was playing in the NBA, we'd go up to someplace like the Shawanga Lodge for a weekend of basketball," Bach said, "and they'd take great care of us. Great food, top-flight rooms, plus we'd get paid maybe a hundred and fifty bucks to boot. And the games were sensational."

Occasionally, Molinas, Brandt, and Maratos would pick up two neighborhood flunkies, drive upstate, and play one of the hotel teams for two hundred dollars, winner take all. Whatever the competition, Molinas and crew would invariably win, throw ten bucks each to the flunkies, and split the rest. But when Molinas expressed his desire to spend the entire summer playing basketball in the "Jewish Alps," Louis refused to give his permission. By now, Jackie was the Eagle's primary bartender and could not be spared. Betty pleaded her son's case. There were threats, rages, and dire predictions, but Louis never wavered. So once again, Jackie hooped and wagered away another summer in Coney Island.

Entering Columbia in the fall, Molinas found too many of his fellow students to be snobby, carelessly wealthy, and vaguely anti-Semitic. He was also amused to see the burning on-campus issues that regularly blazed across the editorial pages of the *Columbia Daily Spectator*. Four-eyed eggheads preening in print and trying to impress one another. College life was a joke.

For Molinas, the pompous in-house politics, the various branches of academe, even the shady glens, cobblestoned walks, bell towers, and abounding flying buttresses were only backdrops to the real business at hand—basketball.

Columbia had quite an extensive basketball program, including a freshman team, a freshman "B" team, a junior varsity, and a varsity team. In 1949, freshmen were ineligible for varsity competition—the idea being to allow new students to more easily make the academic transition from high school to college. In the same spirit, the frosh team's schedule was limited to just thirteen games, including an exhibition against the Halloran Hospital Wheelchair team. Molinas was elected captain of the freshman squad and was expected to be the star.

Molinas would often enliven the frosh practice sessions with his constant scheming. Like the time he was walking along 116th Street on his way to the gym when a car pulled up beside him. The driver was selling what he advertised as authentic cashmere sweaters made in India, and showing Molinas the labels, he convinced him to buy a dozen for five dollars each. Molinas then bolted into the gym and tried to sell the cashmere sweaters to his teammates for ten dollars. There were no takers, and when Whitey Brandt tore the label off one of the sweaters it was discovered that the cashmeres had, in fact, been made in Formosa. The con man had been conned.

The four best players on the frosh team had all played together at Stuyvesant—Molinas, Stan Maratos, Whitey Brandt, and Mike Langol. They were disdainful of most of the other players, and the four of them formed something of a clique. There were a couple of other outstanding players and together they were a very good team. Whenever they scrimmaged the varsity, they usually clobbered them. The only trouble with the team was the coach, Dave Furman, who didn't like the way the Stuyvesant guys hung together.

The "young Lions" opened the season by trouncing the Rutgers frosh team, 66–48. Molinas tallied thirteen points to lead both teams. Next up was a 67–52 triumph over Yale in which Molinas played with the Lions' second unit and scored twelve points, most of them coming in a second quarter surge that blew the game open. Even though Molinas sat out the initial eight minutes of a game at Fordham, he scored twenty-two in another Columbia rout. Molinas's twenty markers impelled the Lions to their fourth straight win, a 55–49 decision over St. Benedict High School.

But Molinas was also scoring off the court. Several of the frosh players were celebrating at a Tau Epsilon Pi smoker when their timbers were collectively shivered by the mere presence of a young Barnard student of exceptional beauty named Peggy Eisenhower. Paul Brandt immediately found a pay phone and called Molinas at home, saying, "Jackie, you've got to come over right now. There's a girl here who's so pretty that all the guys are afraid to speak to her. Jackie, she's waiting for you." Never one to shun a challenge, Molinas took a cab over to the fraternity house and indeed spoke to, and danced with, the lovely damsel from Reading, Pennsylvania. It was the start of a torrid romance that would last for five years.

Molinas was madly in love with Peggy—she was lovely, intelligent, and had a soft vulnerability that he couldn't resist. Peggy was the last jewel in his crown, and at one point he wanted to marry her. But Peggy was a gentile, and Louis not only forbade the marriage but commanded Jack never to see the girl again. There were furious arguments in which Jack's only viable threat was to elope. "Peggy was the love of my brother's life," Julie said, "but he didn't have the courage to marry her in the face of our father's opposition. I don't think Jack ever recovered from the whole situation. I'm convinced Jack's heartache over Peggy was the reason why he never did marry."

On February 10, 1950, the Lions had a close call against lightly regarded Horace Mann and actually trailed by sixteen points at halftime. Still not in the starting lineup, Molinas nevertheless scored twenty-five points and easily imposed his will on the ball game. His clutch left-handed hook tied the score with two seconds left in the fourth quarter to send the game into overtime, where Columbia finally prevailed 67–64.

Sometimes the disappointing level of the competition bored Molinas. The ball games themselves usually attracted only a few dozen fans, most of them related to the ballplayers. Worse, New York's newspapers published point spreads for only the varsity games. Molinas was trapped in Dullsville, U.S.A.

Joe Jalop, of course, was too slick to try and rig a mere freshman game. And back in Coney Island, both Cozzi and Shlombo were always careful not to leak privileged information about crooked ball games. Their aim was to limit one-sided betting and thereby keep the point spread under control. Even so, there were speculative rumors around Kaiser Park that Molinas had tanked "a couple of ball games" as a frosh.

On Saturday, February 18, the frosh were scheduled for a game at Princeton and the bus was to leave from in front of University Hall at twelve forty-five. Molinas had a chemistry lab class that ran from ten to twelve-fifty, and he rushed through his assigned experiment so he wouldn't miss the bus. In fact, Molinas arrived at University Hall at twelve-forty, but since he hadn't eaten since his eight o'clock breakfast and wouldn't have a chance to eat again until after the game (at about six o'clock), he informed Maratos, Brandt, and Langol that he was dashing over to a nearby deli to get a sandwich. The bus departed just as Molinas was returning.

Stan, Paul, and Mike had told Furman where Jack was, and if he'd waited another thirty seconds everything would have been fine. It seems Furman wanted to show Molinas up. Naturally they lost the game. Afterward, there was a big hassle at the school.

Editorials in the *Spectator* unequivocally defended Furman's action:

> Molinas never told Coach Dave Furman personally that he was going to get a sandwich. A manager who missed the same bus went down to Princeton by train. In the past, Columbia athletes, such as Gene Rossides and Leon Van Bellingham, who have missed buses have caught up with their respective teams by other means of transportation.... Molinas better show some hustle on the court, as well as in making the next bus.

Maratos, Brandt, and Langol wrote a letter to the *Spectator* (identifying themselves as "three of the four horsemen") to defend Molinas. "We have known Jack for quite some time including two seasons at Stuyvesant High School where last year he led us to the city finals. He has never let us down, not even for a moment, when we needed him most." And it was Brandt who convinced Molinas to remain at Columbia.

Still pouting, Molinas had inferior games as the Lions lost to Army, then beat Regis High School and Cheshire Academy. However, for the last game of the season (against Carteret Prep on March 8), Molinas held nothing back and scored twenty-eight in a closely contested 70–63 win. The frosh concluded their season with a record of 9–3 (not including a loss against the wheelchair team), and Molinas was the leading scorer at 16.6 ppg, and the team's second leading assist maker (2.0).

The varsity team had finished with an impressive record of 22–7, good for second place in the Ivy League. Its high scoring guard, John Azary, would be returning, but three other starters were graduating in June. When Molinas appraised the varsity's prospects for next season, he expected to be nothing less than the team's savior. However, the only public prediction that Coach Thurman would venture was that "Molinas has a fine chance to win a varsity berth."

Two weeks later, Molinas was back in action with the Hacken All-Stars. Their opponents were the CCNY varsity, a team that had recently astounded Sports America by winning two postseason titles, the NCAA and the even more prestigious National Invitational Tournament. Led by Ed Roman, Floyd Layne, Al Roth, Irwin Dambrot, Ed Warner and Norm Mager, the "Double Championship" City College squad was clearly the best undergraduate team in the country. The All-Stars were comprised mostly of inexperienced seventeen- and eighteen-year-olds, including two college freshmen (Molinas and Bobby Santini) and one sophomore (Danny Lyons from Fordham). Their most veteran player was twenty-eight-year-old "Jumping Joe" Green, a Creston schoolyard Hall-of-Famer.

The game was played at Taft High School in the Bronx to raise money for cancer research. "Joe Jalop was nominally the coach," Santini said, "but Jack and I made most of the important decisions. Anyway, it was a ferocious ball game and Jack was outstanding. We lost 77–76 to the best college team in America. Not only that, but Jack was clearly the best player on the court." The All-Stars also competed (and won) several classy tournaments, including the annual Don Bosco Tournament held in Haverstraw, New York.

Around this time, Joe Hacken became Jack's advisor. Throughout the college basketball season, Joe was giving him nothing but winners to bet on. He also warned the youth against hanging around with the wrong kind of people. There were a lot of corrupt people in this world, Joe said, and they could well be looking to corrupt him. Jack wasn't sure exactly who Joe was referring to, but he took his words to heart.

In spite of Hacken's crooked business, Bobby Santini retained a tremendous respect for the bookie. "He was a brilliant guy," Santini said. "Very personable and easy to be with. Hacken also had a deep understanding of other people's psychology. He knew I would never be interested in turning tricks, but he sounded me out once just to make sure. He did the same thing to Danny Lyons. Just a perfunctory question. Both of us turned him down and he never raised the subject to either of us again. But Hacken came hard after Jack, probably because he knew that Jack was so vulnerable. That Jack needed to please a father figure. Yeah, Hacken had it all figured out."

But, for the time being, Molinas also resisted. The games he'd already rigged at Stuyvesant and Columbia hardly counted for anything. The difference was that as a varsity player, Molinas would be in the national spotlight and his career as a pro might be at risk. "Thanks, Joe," Molinas said. "I'm flattered. But, no thanks." Hacken only smiled and said, "Okay, Jack. We'll talk about it next year."

Meanwhile, Molinas strode around the neighborhood with an undeniable majesty. "When he walked down the street," Avery Corman said, "all the younger kids would dash through the heavy traffic on the Concourse or Fordham Road just so they could walk past Jack and nod hello. If Jack was talking to you and one of your buddies walked by and saw it happening, then you became a celebrity by association. 'Hey, you know Jack? You know him well enough to talk to him?' Even when he was just walking along by himself, it was like he was on a stage." And because Jack never cursed—he'd berate friends for "using the 'F' word"—and was always polite, even the neighborhood adults admired him.

Molinas was also becoming a noteworthy presence among the resident wise guys at Bickford's. He said years later: "Every time I went to Bickford's I had a dozen propositions. 'Hey, Jack, we're all gonna make some money next season, right?' I mean I had every character in the neighborhood coming up to me with the same spiel. Of course, they'd make sure to keep everything light, all laughing and kidding around, but at the heart of it they couldn't have been more serious. I'd just laugh along with them and say nothing."

The games in the Creston school yard were better than ever. Ed Warner was a regular, so were Danny Lyons and Ed Conlin, both stars at Fordham, and Jackie Burns, a fireplug guard from Manhattan College. Irv Rothenberg was a six-foot-eight three-year NBA veteran who'd most recently played with the New York Knicks. But Molinas played rings around the bigger man, routinely embarrassing him with such ease that Rothenberg soon took what was left of his game elsewhere. Aside from Molinas, the dominant player was Dolph Schayes. A Bronx native and fresh from his first NBA All-Star season with the Syracuse Nationals, Schayes once amazed the school-yard regulars by knocking down 150 consecutive free throws.

Molinas and Santini also spent many hours playing ruthless games of one-on-one. "If there was a crowd watching," Santini said, "we'd play even harder. He was two inches bigger but I was somewhat stronger, so he'd want to back me into the pivot and I'd try to push him out. Once he got in close and went up with his hook shot I was pretty much dead." Come summer, Molinas once again pleaded with his father to be allowed to work in the Catskills. "No," Louis said. "It's a bad influence on your life for you to go there. No."

Back in Coney Island, Molinas spent extra time at Kaiser Park working on his outside shooting. After a ball game there he was approached by one of the players, a guy named Jack Matson, who asked Molinas if he was interested in earning some money next season. Molinas wouldn't have to lose games. He would just have to keep the points right. Matson said that all of the best college players in New York were doing it, and he mentioned several other schools, too. Toledo, Bradley, Kentucky, Holy Cross, Villanova, and lots more. Matson said that all the schools were making money hand over fist, so there was no reason why Jack shouldn't get a piece of the pie. Fifteen hundred a game to start and maybe twenty thousand bucks over the course of the season. In the back of his mind Molinas felt that if he ever decided to do anything along those lines he was already obligated to Joe Jalop.

Back at the Eagle Bar, Louis continued working sixteen hours a day and Jack still enjoyed working the counter window and tending bar. Molinas would entertain the clientele by holding in one hand six full glasses of beer at the same time. One evening, Molinas showed up at the Bat-A-Way range and proved himself to be a potent power hitter who wasn't intimidated by one particular machine that propelled baseballs at a hundred miles per hour. Coincidentally, a St. Louis Cardinal scout was on hand and he offered Molinas a tryout at Ebbets Field the next time the Cardinals were in town. But Molinas was committed to basketball.

Even though he'd turned down Joe Hacken and Jack Matson, Molinas hadn't quite convinced himself. According to one of the Kaiser Park regulars, Bernie Reiner, "Jackie bragged to us that he'd be doing business when he moved up to the varsity next fall and that he'd make sure to clue us in so that we'd all make a lot of money. Jackie just couldn't keep his mouth shut."

So Molinas loved to talk big. So what? He knew that he was smarter than anybody he'd come across so far. Smart enough to shave points, to dump ball games, to connive and manipulate and even steal. And what if he ever did get caught? Then he was smart enough to bullshit his way out of trouble. Hey, didn't his father pay off the cops? Didn't Shpitz the Galitz do the same? What about Joe Bananas and his boys? And none of them were nearly as smart as Jack Molinas. Right?

At the beginning of his sophomore year, Molinas moved into an eighth-floor room in Livingston Hall on Amsterdam Avenue at West 115th Street. Room 827 was a two-bedroom suite that he shared with Paul Brandt and David Love. Molinas missed his mother's cooking, but he was happy to get out from under his father.

Gordon Riddings was in his fifth season as head coach of the Columbia varsity and he preached the virtues of grind-it-out half-court basketball, a sloughing defense, individual determination, and team spirit. With last season's point guard (Sherry Marshall) and two dependable outside shooters (Norm Skinner and Al Kaplan) lost to graduation, the forty-four-year-old Riddings had modest expectations heading into the 1950–51 season. "There's no way we'll be as good as last year's team," he said before practice began. "Our battle this season will be for third place in the Ivy League behind Cornell and Penn."

The Lions' most important holdover was six-foot-three John Azary, whose credentials included All-Met and All-Ivy honors. Azary was Columbia's captain, most popular player, and he even coached a Church League team. Trouble was that, despite his size, Azary was most effective playing in the low post, the same position that Molinas preferred. As varsity practice began, there was no question as to which of the two pivotmen Riddings favored. "John is a terrific passer," Riddings said, "and he's the best pivotman in basketball."

Molinas was dismissed as merely a scorer and rebounder, a "colorful performer" who "is gradually finding out that there is such a thing as defense." Molinas, however, did have a significant early season edge over Azary. During the summer, the Columbia captain had been wounded (a machine gun backfired) while serving a brief stint in the National Guard, and in mid-September, had suffered a minor surgical procedure to remove two pieces of shrapnel from his right thigh. Accordingly, Azary was slow to round into shape and was frequently missing "soft shots."

Other members of the team were "three of the four horsemen," Whitey Brandt, Stan Maratos, and Mike Langol, none of whom was scheduled for significant playing time. And with the opening game only weeks away, Coach Riddings had this to say about his team: "We look lousy."

While the Lions were girding for what looked to be a difficult season, other events were galvanizing the campus. For laughs, there was the annual competition between the freshman and sophomore classes wherein practiced representatives climbed greased poles. But there was another incident that would eventually have a profound effect on Molinas's varsity basketball career: It seems that "an Amsterdam neighborhood gang of toughs" had appeared on the campus one Sunday night "obviously looking for trouble." As the gang passed by a sophomore dormitory, the residents obliged—bombarding the intruders with water-filled paper bags. A full-scale "brawl" was under way before the campus security officers appeared on the scene. No arrests were made and no serious injuries reported, but the *Spectator* called for an increased security presence, and also for the administration to "not look kindly" upon those "dorm residents who fail to keep their paper bags in their waste cans where they belong."

More juvenile pranks by jaded rich kids—and Molinas soon forgot about the whole silly business.

In a preseason poll of the nation's outstanding basketball coaches, City College was rated at the top of the list, with LIU seventh and St. John's ninth. The coaches also ranked Columbia as the country's thirtieth best team. But just two weeks before the season began, the Lions surprised Riddings by outplaying the highly ranked St. John's varsity in a scrimmage at University Hall. Molinas had not exhibited sufficient determination and team spirit to work his way into the starting unit, yet Riddings praised his prized sophomore for "fine displays of good basketball."

On November 27, Riddings addressed his team after practice. "You boys have worked very hard," Riddings said, "hard enough to force me to change my opinion. I've waited a long time to coach a team as hard-working and as talented as you boys are. Those of yous who've played for me before know what a pessimist I am, so I don't say this lightly.... But I'd be very surprised if we didn't go through the season undefeated." The juniors and the seniors were electrified by their coach's remark. Undefeated! Winning the Ivy League championship and qualifying for the NCAA tournament! The season of a lifetime!

Molinas was more casual about Riddings's announcement. Except when Molinas knew the desired result beforehand, he never expected to lose.

The next afternoon, a mere six days before the season commenced, Riddings suffered a massive heart attack. From his room at St. Luke's Hospital (where he would remain for the next eight weeks), Riddings called his twenty-nine-year-old assistant, Lou Rossini, and asked him to take over the team.

Rossini had a reputation for being a hard-ass, but his system, looser than Riddings's and featuring more off-the-ball movement, was more suitable to Molinas's quick and instinctive skills. Columbia's new coach also gave his players license to fire away whenever they thought they had a makeable shot. "Rossini was good for Jack," said Arnie Stein, "because he gave Jack an opportunity to play as many minutes as he could handle. I'm certain that Jack wouldn't have played nearly as much if Riddings hadn't gone down."

However, just three days after Rossini assumed command, Molinas was already in hot water with his new coach: Rossini had a prior engagement, but had required all of the Columbia players to attend a Saturday morning basketball clinic given by Clair Bee, the coach at LIU, down at the Garden. Early that same morning, Molinas was already on his way to Philadelphia to watch the Army-Navy football game and then participate in the postgame festivities. Molinas knew that Rossini would also be missing the clinic, so he asked Whitey Brandt to deliver the following message to Doc Barrett, Columbia's trainer: "Jack says he won't be here because he has to spend the day with his parents."

Molinas had several reasons to believe that his flimsy excuse was good enough. During Rossini's recruiting visit, hadn't he tried to cultivate a sympathetic relationship with Louis and Betty? Besides, Rossini had just gotten the head coaching job—he surely wouldn't want to raise a big stink over nothing. Right?

But Molinas didn't count on Whitey Brandt's inviolable sense of honesty. When pressed by Barrett as to Molinas's real whereabouts, Brandt quickly gave up the lie. Rossini was informed and ordered Barrett to slip a note under the door of Molinas's dorm room telling the young truant to appear in the coach's office promptly at eight o'clock on Monday morning.

"Jack Molinas had all the talent you could imagine," Rossini said. "He could run, jump, and shoot. He had wonderful flexibility and terrific moves with the ball. The only problem was that his personality wasn't that strong and he would always look for the easy way out. As soon as I took over for Gordon Riddings, I knew Jack would be a problem. And he sure was, sooner than I expected. When I saw him Monday morning I looked him dead in the eye and said, 'Jack, I know where you were, so if you lie to me, you're off the team.' I straightened him out right away. And he knew that he had a coach who was going to be right on his tail. So he told me the truth and I said, 'Well, you're not going to start the first five games and if there's one more incident you're off the team.' I never had any trouble with Jack after that because I knew how to control him."

Molinas's first appearance in a varsity uniform was in a December 4, 1950, exhibition game against the Columbia alumni—coming off the bench, he scored twelve points as the young Lions romped to a 90–40 victory. Molinas had nine in another lop-sided win (79–38 over Amherst), then scored nineteen while playing only seventeen minutes in a 91–42 pasting of the New York Athletic Club. Immediately prior to the game against Fordham on December 13, it was announced that Riddings would miss the rest of the season, and Columbia Athletic Director Ralph Furey formally promoted Rossini from assistant to acting head coach. The Lions responded by roasting the Rams, 70–47, with Molinas accounting for fifteen points. Even a hard-bitten sportswriter like Dick

Young was impressed: "Molinas, a skinny soph from Stuyvesant, looked like the classiest yearling in town as he rebounded ruggedly, handled the ball with surprising poise, and shot with precision from far out."

Chaffing under his five-game punishment, Molinas played halfheartedly in a 73–53 win over Rutgers. His total of six points and zero field goals would represent the most inept performance of his entire varsity career. Next up for the Lions was a three-game road trip to New Orleans and Houston. Starting at forward, Molinas totaled forty-one points as Columbia beat Tulane twice, and then Rice.

The Lions were undefeated in seven games, and the most recent Associated Press poll had them rated seventeenth—but there was much bigger news at the Morningside Heights campus. General Dwight Eisenhower, then president of Columbia, had asked for, and received, a leave of absence from the university to assume the position of Supreme Commander of the North Atlantic Treaty defense forces. Vice President Grayson L. Kirk replaced Ike. The general vowed that he would "reassume his duties as president of the university immediately upon his military release," but within two years he would be elected president of the United States.

Molinas, however, didn't give a hoot if Eisenhower was emperor of the world or campus dogcatcher. Having established himself as an indispensable member of the Lions starting five, Molinas cared only about the game at hand—the opening Ivy League contest against the similarly unbeaten Cornell Big Red.

Before every ball game, Hacken would call Jack and ask how he felt about the game. "The spread's five," Joe would say. "What do you think?" Jack would tell him if he thought the game would be an easy one or more of a struggle. Jack didn't feel there was anything illegal or immoral about what he was telling Joe. Jack was just giving his personal opinion to a good friend.

Molinas was also a frequent visitor to the neighborhood. Every so often, he'd bring home his dirty laundry for his mother to deal with. After home games he would head over to Bickford's for some coffee and cake and to see what else Hacken had to say. Joe was still giving Jack ball games to bet on and he hadn't given him a loser yet. All the guys who hung around there were all over Molinas like he was the Pied Piper. "Hey, Jack," they'd say. "You guys covered the spread again. That's great. But who do you like tomorrow?" A fellow named Stan Ratensky, whose father owned a candy store right next door to Bickford's, was the most persistent. "The number's twelve, Jack. Do you think you can cover? Who do you like, Jack? Tell me." Jack always gave the same answer. "Yeah, I like Columbia. I always like Columbia. Now go away and don't ask me any more questions. If you're so interested in how we're doing, then come over to the gym and see us play."

Columbia was favored by three over Cornell, and there was a lot of action on the Lions. Columbia didn't disappoint their backers, walloping Cornell 85–45, thereby establishing themselves as the team to beat in the Ivy League. Molinas was all over the court, rebounding like a demon, leading the fast break, and scoring seventeen points.

"I don't think we made a mistake all game," said point guard Al Stein. "And for the first time we began to realize just how good a ball club we were."

Meanwhile, Louis and Betty were mystified by the constant attention their son was receiving. Headlines and photographs in the newspapers. People asking for his autograph. And all because of a silly activity that featured grown men in silly uniforms throwing a ball at a basket. Neither Louis nor Betty ever missed a game, and both were constantly amazed at the vociferous enthusiasm of the other spectators. All of those people, most of the college students, getting so excited over a Jewish boy? Maybe they thought he was really Greek or Armenian or something.

More often than not, whenever they met new people, Louis and Betty were introduced as the parents of Jack Molinas! God bless America!

Early in the morning of Monday, January 9, 1951, Molinas and an unidentifed accomplice (probably Paul Brandt) broke into a wall-mounted case of fire-fighting equipment outside his room on the eighth floor of Livingston Hall and unwound several large water hoses. The nozzles were then hung over the staircase railing and the water was turned on. Not only was the entire eighth floor drenched, but the ground-floor lobby was totally flooded.

Within minutes, there were dozens of students splashing around in the lobby. Jack was wearing underwear and galoshes, but some of the fellows were naked. One kid showed up wearing water fins and a scuba mask. They were all laughing and clowning around, and it felt like the entire dormitory was going to float away. Finally, when they got word that somebody had called the security officers, they shut off the water and scurried back to their rooms.

The flooding caused extensive damage to the carpeting and a costly weakening of several plaster walls. After a while, a security officer showed up at Molinas's room. Jack answered the door still wearing his galoshes. "What's this all about?" he asked, the soul of innocence. Paul Brandt, his roommate, was frantically pointing to his feet, but Jack couldn't make sense of what he was trying to say. When the officer noticed the galoshes, he took down Molinas's name. He and Paul were eventually called into the dean's office. Jack told the dean he was wearing the galoshes because the floor was wet. That was all it took to get them off the hook. Another perfect crime.

Why did Molinas commit this childish act of vandalism? Was it just a classic case of supressed male rage? Or, caught between the extremes of his mother's pampering (which reinforced his latent narcisscism) and his father's humiliations, did Molinas need a palpable outlet for his burgeoning antisocial tendencies? Perhaps he did it just because he knew he could get away with it.

Bernie Reiner, one of the Kaiser Park crew, had a simpler explanation: "Jackie was a sick guy. He was a schmuck, a pathological liar, and he was totally amoral." Reiner went one step further about the next Columbia contest. "And, no matter what he said, I was positive that Jackie dumped the Princeton game, and I'm positive that Rossini knew about it."

Jack insisted later that he did not. "I knew the point spread every time we played, and we were favored by five for the first Princeton game. We won the game by one point, 53–52, only because Bobby Sullivan stole a pass, dribbled the length of the court, and scored a layup with less than a minute to play. The Princeton game was the first time all season that we hadn't covered the spread. I only scored thirteen points, but believe me, I gave it my best. The entire season was one hundred percent honest."

Whether or not Molinas bagged the Princeton game, he was certainly spreading the word about other fixed contests. "Hacken told Jack that St. John's was supposed to win a game at the Garden by under seven points to a team they could have beaten by more than a dozen," said an ex-NBA player from the Bronx who was also one of Molinas's gambling confidants. "So Jack opened his mouth and told every bookie in town that the game was phony, and because so much money was bet against St. John's, the spread went up to fifteen. I mean a lot of heavy hitters bet a lot of bucks on Jack's say-so. He wasn't trying to pull anything off. It's just that he had a big mouth, and wanted everybody to think that he knew everything. Jack was a star, so when he talked the moneymen listened. Turned out that the gamblers who had originally bought the game had to lay some money against St. John's to bring down the spread. Thank God the spread got down to ten and St. John's won by only nine. Otherwise Jack would have been dead meat."

On January 13, 1951, Columbia extended its undefeated streak to ten games by overwhelming Yale, 90–48, with Molinas netting sixteen points. Four days later, the Lions clobbered Penn, 68–50, to take sole possession of the Ivy League's top spot. In addition, Molinas's twenty-three-point outburst temporarily moved him ahead of the Quakers' brilliant sophomore Ernie Beck in their personal battle for Ivy scoring honors. Then, on January 18, college basketball was rocked by the first public revelations of widespread associations between gamblers and players—and Molinas narrowly escaped being arrested.

Hank Poppe had graduated from Manhattan College in June 1950 as the second-high scorer (1,027 career points) in the school's history. One of Poppe's teammates and best friends was John Byrnes. In early January 1951, Poppe had approached Manhattan's star center, Junius Kellogg, offering Kellogg a thousand dollars to "dump" an upcoming game against De Paul. Kellogg, however, informed his coach, Kenny Norton, of the bribe attempt and the police were called in. At 3:00 A.M. on January 17, Poppe was arrested in his home in Queens, and Byrnes was apprehended two hours later. Once in custody, Poppe and Byrnes confessed to having accepted three thousand dollars each from a trio of gamblers to make certain that Manhattan lost ball games against Siena (December 3, 1949), Santa Clara (December 29), and Bradley (January 12, 1950). Poppe and Byrnes earned an additional two thousand dollars each for helping Manhattan to *exceed* the point spreads against St. Francis; New York District Attorney Frank Hogan supervised the investigation because all the games had been played in Madison Square Garden.

The newspapers hailed Kellogg as an incorruptible hero, but the Bickford's boyos knew better. Several of them claimed to have firsthand knowledge of the true story: that Kellogg was himself involved in rigging ball games. That one of his telephone conversations with Poppe was overheard by a teacher. That when Hogan's investigators were called in, Kellogg was offered the choice of setting up Poppe and Byrnes or going to jail.

Three other men were also arrested, including Benjamin Schwartzberg and his brother, Irving, both of them bookmakers, felons and ex-cons. The front man for this tidy scheme was Neil Kelleher, who for many years had been a runner for Joe Hacken. Kelleher was arrested in his car, which was parked on 188th Street across the street from Bickford's. In fact, Hacken and Molinas had also been in the parked car, just shooting the bull and casually discussing spreads and dumps, but had left together barely thirty minutes before the police arrived to bust Kelleher.

Within weeks, Hogan's office had more bad news—between 1947 and 1950, a total of eighty-six games had been fixed at the Garden and in arenas in twenty-two other cities in seventeen states by thirty-two players on seven teams. In addition to Manhattan, the other teams implicated were LIU, NYU, Toledo, Bradley, Kentucky, and CCNY.

"All the coaches claimed that they had no idea what was going on," said one of the City College fixers, "but most of them were all full of shit. At Kentucky, Adolph Rupp's best friend was a bookie and he used to curse out his teams when they won but didn't cover. Clair Bee knew at LIU, and so did Nat Holman. I can remember one time when I'd been taken out of a game we were dumping and sitting right next to Holman. Bobby Sand, the assistant coach, walked over to Holman and said, 'Nat, they're dumping the game.' And Holman said, 'Mind your own fucking business.' What a laugh. The whole program was corrupt. Ed Warner was a great player, but he could barely read and yet Holman got him admitted into City College, which at the time was one of the top schools in the country. Be that as it may, I still maintain that an even bigger story than the guys who got caught is the guys who got away scot-free."

Frank Hogan was a decent man and a devout Catholic. He couldn't help breaking the Manhattan College story, but was subjected to irresistible pressure to lay off several other Catholic schools that were also heavily involved. Dozens of metropolitan area coaches and players (including several from Catholic universities), numerous bookies and sharpsters can all testify to the personal involvement of Cardinal Spellman, head of the archdiocese of New York. "It was simple," says one ex-coach. "Cardinal Spellman showed up at Hogan's office and gave him the word. That's why players from Holy Cross, De Paul, La Salle, Villanova, St. Joseph's, and St. John's went unpunished."

In addition, Hogan's office had several recordings of telephone conversations between a certain St. John's player and Eddie Gard, who was a one-time LIU star and front man for a gambler named Salvatore Sollazzo. In those days, the recordings were made on brittle celluloid platters. While the St. John's player was being questioned, and before the recordings were transcribed, "an appointed official of the City of New York" barged into the room and knocked the platter to the floor, shattering it into splinters.

Whereas the incriminated players from the local schools were all questioned individually and without benefit of counsel, St. John's was tipped off and their player was shepherded into Hogan's headquarters by a big-shot lawyer named Henry Urgetta, and a slew of priests. Urgetta wouldn't permit the DA's men to question the St. John's player in private, and without a confession, Hogan had no case. However, not only was the St. John's player doing business with Sollazzo, but was also sleeping with Sollazzo's wife, Jeanne.

None of this was a secret, especially among the knowledgeable betting crowds at the Garden. "I saw it happen many times," said a local college player. "As the St. John's player headed to the locker room after another disgraceful performance, scores of pissed-off bettors would be waving twenty-dollar bills and shouting, 'You ain't kidding anybody. The whole world knows you're fucking Sollazzo's wife and dumping ball games.' It was ridiculous. The St. John's guy was kicking balls out of bounds and missing shots he could have made with his eyes closed. Everybody knew everything."

Because Sollazzo was himself well connected, most of the apprehended players were paid off by the Mafia to keep their mouths shut. But the unfortunate trail of miscreant dealings goes even deeper.

Here's the testimony of one of New York's most distinguished coaches and an intimate friend of Frank McGuire, who coached St. John's from 1948 to 1952. "Frank was the son of a policeman," says Coach X, "and being brought up in Hell's Kitchen, over on the West Side of New York, he also knew Albert Anastasia and the entire Mafia crowd that operated there. In fact, Frank was the only guy that both the mob and the police felt they could trust. At the time, the mob had important members of both the police and the fire departments in their pockets and they needed a reliable, trustworthy bag man to make the payoffs. And Frank McGuire was the man."

Coach X's information is corroborated by an outstanding player who performed for one of New York City's Catholic colleges in the late 1940s: "Frank McGuire was always dressed in expensive clothes and was always flashing a ton of money. He drove a Cadillac, his wife drove a fancy car, they had a luxurious apartment in the city, and a large, well-appointed vacation home up in Greenwood Lake. McGuire never played the stock market or anything like that. His only discernible source of income was his coaching salary from St. John's, which only amounted to seventy-five hundred dollars a year. Everybody who wanted to know knew where McGuire's real income was coming from."

Coach X adds this: "After the basketball scandal broke and Senator Kefauver began to investigate the influence of organized crime, things were really hot in New York. To protect themselves and to protect Frank, the Mafia enlisted the aid of Ben Carnevale, an alumnus of North Carolina who was then coaching at Navy—and Carnevale got Frank the coaching job down in Chapel Hill."

In the aftermath of the scandals, Columbia's athletic director, Ralph Furey, piously announced that the Lions would not participate in the National Invitation Tournament in March in the event that a bid would be forthcoming. Furey decried Madison Square Garden, the scene of all the NIT games, as the "cradle of scandal." The only catch was that the winner of the Ivy League would automatically qualify for the NCAA's postseason go-round—and the first game was already scheduled against the Big Ten champion for March 20 in the Garden. Furey noted that while the NIT was "a commercial enterprise" sponsored by the Garden in conjunction with the Basketball Writers Association, "the NCAA tourney, on the other hand, is sponsored by the federation of colleges, and is fundamentally a playoff series to determine the best team in the country."

Meanwhile, the Lions (ranked seventh in the latest polls) did their best to keep the date with the Big Ten, routing Harvard twice, Dartmouth, Cornell, Army, Navy, and Brown, to set up another meeting with Penn that would decide the Ivy League championship. Despite a sensational performance by Ernie Beck (whose twenty-five points earned him the league's individual scoring title), the Lions squeezed out a 63–58 victory. A March 7 win at Princeton meant a 22–0 regular season for the Lions, a new record for Columbia, and only the sixth undefeated season in the history of college basketball.

The team celebrated with a "soda pop" party at Howard Johnson's on the way back to New York from Princeton. Then, at 2:22 A.M., when the team returned to Morningside Heights, some five hundred students were waiting for their heroes. Fire alarms were set off in several dorms, but the *Spectator* reported "nary a water bag."

Rossini flew out to Champaign, Illinois, and scouted a typically bruising Big Ten contest in which the scrappy Illini qualified for the NCAA tourney by thrashing Indiana. With their first-round opponent thusly determined, at noon on Friday, March 16, the Columbia team was feted at a "Beat Illinois" rally on the steps of Hamilton Hall. A huge bonfire was ignited, the cheerleaders sis-boom-bahed, the band played many stirring choruses of "Roar, Lion, Roar," and the president of the varsity "C" club presented a trophy, on behalf of its membership, to the "unsullied basketball team." An impressive list of speakers—from Dean of Students Nicholas McKnight to Athletic Director Ralph Furey—shouted rah-rah banalities at more than two thousand wildly cheering students.

The NCAA tournament included only sixteen teams, with Adolph Rupp's Kentucky Wildcats the odds-on favorite to cop the championship. Illinois, Kansas State, and Oklahoma A&M were considered to be Kentucky's only serious rivals. Even though Columbia finished the season ranked third in the AP poll, while Illinois ranked fifth, the records of Ivy League teams were considered suspect because of their "soft" competition. The Illini were paced by the hard-driving Don Sunderlage (a future NBA All-Star) and Irv Bemoras, and were a bruising, backboard-thumping ball club. On the other hand, the Lions were handicapped by a season-ending injury to third-string center Stan Maratos, and the fact that defensive standby Bobby Sullivan had been declared academically ineligible because he'd recently failed a chemistry test. Even worse, starter Bob Reiss was barely recuperated from a severe case of the flu, and John Azary was hobbled by a sprained ankle. Even though Columbia was the higher ranked team, the bookies installed Illinois as a three-and-a-half-point favorite.

Molinas had this to say about the Illinois contest:

"I thought we were in for a very tough game, but, nevertheless, I thought we could beat Illinois. Then, on the Thursday night prior to the game, I had a surprising conversation with Joe Hacken. We were sitting by ourselves at a table in Bickford's, when out of nowhere he said to me, 'Jack, if you're interested you could make a lot of money on this game.' He proceeded to offer me ten thousand dollars if I would make sure that Columbia lost by more than three points. Joe would also bet the ten thousand for me on Illinois, so the entire package was worth twenty thousand. This was the first time Joe had ever given me a dollars-and-cents proposition. Twenty thousand dollars was big money for a nineteen-year-old kid. The CCNY and LIU kids only got a grand or sometimes fifteen hundred each for throwing their games. I wasn't thinking in terms of compromising the morality of the situation, but I did turn him down. My main reason was that I simply didn't want the season to end. I also wanted the chance to prove myself against one of the best teams in the country, and to find out, once and for all, just how good a player I really was. Another reason I said no was because I really thought we could win the national championship. To back my own convictions, I withdrew fifty dollars from my savings account and bet another bookie that we would win. Unfortunately, my father found out about the withdrawal and the reason behind it, and he had a major temper tantrum. From then on, my father closely monitored every one of my savings account transactions."

At the start of the game, most of the Lions had the jitters, but Molinas took up the slack and Columbia stretched to a 45–38 edge at halftime. When Molinas missed four crucial second-half minutes because of foul trouble, the bigger Illini began controlling the backboards. Supersub Ted Beach came off the Illinois bench to score twenty-two points, mostly on long one-handers, and the Lions wound up on the short end of a 79–71 score.

As a matter of fact, the entire team appled up. John Azary shot only five for fourteen, Al Stein went four for twenty-one, Bobby Reiss was four for twelve, and Frank Lewis was two for six. Everybody choked except for Jack. He was hitting hook shots, push shots, and layins and scored twenty points. If Bobby Sullivan had been eligible, they may well have won.

A couple of days later at Bickford's, Molinas ran into Joe, who said, "See? All you had to do was say 'Yes' and you would've been twenty thousand dollars richer. The only difference was that the game wouldn't have been as close as it was."

The postseason honors started to pile up. Rossini was named Coach of the Year by both the New York and the Philadelphia Basketball Writers' Associations. Azary was chosen as the Ivy League's Most Valuable Player. Molinas (whose 14.4 ppg and 15 rebounds topped the team) was voted to the All-Ivy Second Team, the All-Metropolitan Second Team, and also the AP's Sophomore All-American Second Team. At a May 8 luncheon in John Jay Hall, Athletic Director Ralph Furey awarded gold medallions to all the varsity players to commemorate their extraordinary season. Senior John Azary was then asked to say a few words in farewell. "All that's left for next year's team," said Azary, "is an NCAA title. It's always good to leave room for improvement. After all, what could CCNY have possibly done for an encore after their double championship?"

Al Stein, the captain-elect, quipped, "Look what they did do."

After the laughter subsided, Furey suggested that the Lions hire a lawyer next season "just in case."

Just in case.

Molinas prided himself on being a fun-loving guy. He was always involved in pranks and kidding around. There was a fellow named Ian Brownley who lived right next door to Jack in the dorm. He was one of those stuffy, snobby Ivy League types that Jack couldn't stand. About five feet seven, but full of airs, Brownley was the fourth generation in his family to attend Columbia. He couldn't understand how the university could admit such lower-class boors as Jack and Paul. He used to snub them all the time and they always addressed him as "Sir Ian." Of course, Brownley took the nickname as a compliment. He was very wealthy and he had a very elaborate and expensive wardrobe, and so one day, Paul and Jack decided to get even with him. They jimmied open his lock, broke into his dorm room, stole all his clothes, and hid everything in their room. When Sir Ian came back to his room, he went wild. Soon enough, a security officer came knocking on Jack's door to investigate. Before the questioning could get under way, Jack took the initiative. He put his arm around Sir Ian and said, "We certainly wouldn't steal this man's clothes because we're the best of friends. Besides, I'm six six and Paul here is six four, and I'd need two of his jackets to make one pair of pants." Then he waved the rent-a-cop into the room and told him to go ahead and search the place. So everybody started nodding, no, no, that wouldn't be necessary, and Sir Ian said that they would never take his clothes, because, yes, they were the best of friends. As soon as Sir Ian and the cop left, Paul said, "Jack, we'd better do something quick or we'll both wind up in jail." Molinas told Paul not to worry, then they broke back into the room, returned all the clothes, and nobody was the wiser. The Mole strikes again.

However, on Thursday afternoon, May 29, 1951, Molinas's casual involvement in another harebrained amusement changed the course of his life. He later described what happened. "Our room was the center of much of the dorm's activity. Card games. Crapshooting. It was the end of exam week and everybody was celebrating, laughing, and kibitzing, carrying on, and tossing water bags out the window, and they were egging me on to join them. But I had one more exam that I knew I would flunk if I didn't study for, so I went into the smaller of the two bedrooms, closed the door, and hit the books. Still, they wouldn't be denied. They pushed open the door and kept bothering me to at least throw a water bag out the window. So I said, 'All right. I'll do it if you fellows promise to leave me alone.' And they agreed. So I reached out and grabbed whatever was at hand, which turned out to be a glass of water, and pitched it out of the window."

It just so happened that Mark Van Doren and his wife, Dorothy, were parked in their car on Amsterdam Avenue just below Molinas's bedroom window. Van Doren was a world-famous poet and a Full professor of English, who had been awarded a Pulitzer Prize in 1939 for his *Collected Poems, 1922–1938*. The glass shattered the windshield of the car, frightening both passengers.

"Van Doren was a very eminent professor, so trying to find out who threw the glass was the big mystery around the school. Paul and I had the reputation of being good-time-Charlies and it wasn't long before we were called into the dean's office. I was positive that somebody had ratted me out. Anyway, I wasn't worried. Nobody had been hurt, and I didn't think that what I'd done was such a big deal so I confessed and offered to pay to have the damaged windshield repaired. I said, 'I did it and I'm sorry. It was an accident.' Okay, next case, right? Wrong. The dean's name was Nicholas McKnight and he said that I had put him in a compromised position. Because of the water bag riot last October, he said that he had no choice but to take some kind of disciplinary action."

A few days later, Jack was called into the dean's office again and told that the appropriate punishment would be a six-month suspension. But rather than do that, the dean suggested that Molinas take a six-month leave of absence and said that he would review Jack's application for readmittance next February. So that's exactly what Jack did.

Molinas's statement to the newspapers was properly contrite:

> I was reprimanded by the Dean for my action and told to obtain employment while away from school. The Dean told me that if I did well at my job I would be favorably considered for readmission to the College. I am very eager to make up for my thoughtless action. I am deeply sorry for what I've done and am looking forward to returning to the team and all my friends at Columbia.

Privately, however, Molinas was seething. Coach Rossini had worked diligently behind the scenes to mitigate the punishment, but Molinas wasn't aware of this. All Molinas knew was that Ralph Furey, the athletic director, hadn't stood up for him. With all the other antics going on at the campus, Jack was furious that he'd been so severely, and so publicly, humiliated for what was essentially nothing more than a harmless schoolboy prank.

Other interested parties believed there was an ulterior motive for Molinas's harsh sentence. "Both Furey and Rossini suspected that Jack was dumping ball games," said a basketball insider who currently works for the NBA. "Of course they didn't have any proof, and they didn't want to simply expel him because Jack was too good of a ballplayer. All they wanted to do was to scare him."

One of the Coney Island bettors later became "a friendly acquaintance" of Rossini's and used to share a few drinks at Leone's after games at the Garden.

"Rossini never came out and said anything directly," reported the Kaiser Park alumnus, "but the New York City coaches formed a very tight community and Rossini made it clear that he knew exactly what was going on. What the hell, Jackie always had an entourage hanging around him, especially at the ballgames, and who were they? Guys like Aaron Wagman, Dave Budin, and Joe Green. Sometimes even Joe Jalop. Guys that every college coach in New York not only recognized, but knew were heavily into gambling. Rossini was a very smart man, and he knew damn well that Jackie was doing business."

As expected, Rossini furiously denied knowing anything about Molinas's tricky dealings. Years after the fact, Rossini said, "My God, if I had known about it I would have said something, right? And I hope that this whole conversation is going to be straight in what I'm saying, because if it isn't, I'm going to sue your [the author's] ass off."

During his six-month suspension, Molinas got a job at the Grumman Aircraft Company out on Long Island. Jack was furious. Had his name been Brownley or Vanderbilt or Rockefeller the entire incident would have been dismissed as an amusing example of youthful exuberance.

He considered transferring to Michigan, or to Eastern Kentucky, or any of the schools that had been so interested in him just two years before. The trouble was that if he transferred, he would lose a full season of basketball eligibility. If he returned to Columbia in February, he would only be losing half the season. He weighed all the pros and cons and finally decided that the best thing was to wait out the six months and go back to Columbia.

In late December, Jack drove down to Miami and enjoyed a week's vacation at a hotel on Collins Avenue. He hung around the beach and relaxed and dallied with the girls. His mother sent him some money on the sly and sometimes he'd go to the track and bet two dollars a race.

Every once in a while Jack got a call from Joe Hacken. Joe asked if he needed any money or any help of any kind, and Jack told him that everything was coming along fine. Joe was too smart to talk business over the phone, but when Jack told him he was planning on returning to Columbia, Joe just said, "Okay." And by the way Joe said it, Jack knew that Joe would help him get even with those bastards.

By late fall 1951, Molinas was back in the Bronx and playing in the Creston schoolyard, but there was something missing. Stanley Cohen, author of an intriguing memoir of the CCNY scandals, *The Game They Played*, remembered the change in Molinas's attitude. "One of the schoolyard regulars was a five-foot-eight buzzsaw named Bernie Grant," Cohen said, "who"d gotten a Section Eight discharge from the Marines and I guess you could say was certifiably crazy.

But Bernie was an extraordinary basketball player with a good two-hand set shot and lightning speed. Bernie and Jack would always be playing one-on-one games that always attracted a crowd and a lot of betting action. Bernie was giving away a huge amount of both size and skill, but he'd beat Jack like a rug because he played with such fury that his mouth would froth. I remember those games vividly, Grant driving around him and Jack laughing. Jack would also go head-to-head with Dick Kor. Now, Kor was a mere substitute on the NYU team and was nowhere near the same caliber of player that Jack was. Yet Kor would also outplay Jack, and again, Jack would break into that big, ingratiating grin. At first I thought, 'That's great. Other guys are scoring on him and Jack's so good-natured about it. What a guy!' Until I realized that Jack really didn't care that these lesser players were embarrassing him. There was an element in Jack's personality that somehow lacked commitment and intensity. As great a player as he was, he could have been an increment better. It was noticeable when he came back from Florida that Jack didn't feel that he *had* to win."

In addition to the regulars, a fellow named Aaron Wagman would sometimes play. Wagman was a large, brawny man with a shy, gentle manner who could rebound some but couldn't score with a pencil. In addition to selling betting tickets for Hacken, "Wags" worked in his parents' dry-cleaning store on Walton Avenue and sometimes sold hot dogs at Yankee games. Whenever he was working at Yankee Stadium, Wagman would always slip a free hot dog to anybody he recognized from the neighborhood.

One particular post-Florida episode convinced the school-yard habitues that Molinas was at least one step too close to the edge: Jerry's Grocery Store was fortuitously situated just across the street from the school yard, and between games the players would purchase and consume bottles of Mission Orange and Mission Grape sodas. The empty bottles would then be lined up along the base of a fence that ran parallel to one sideline of the basketball court. After playing in his newly accustomed desultory manner, and losing the game, Molinas suddenly started picking up the empty bottles and hurling them one at a time against the brick wall of a classroom building that flanked the other sideline. Crash! Crash! Methodically winding up like a baseball pitcher, he threw each and every bottle against the wall. Molinas was laughing and whooping, and yelling "yahoo!" as he tossed the next bottle. When all the bottles were destroyed, Molinas let out one more "yahoo!" then made an exit stage right and, as usual, left somebody else to clean up his mess.

In October 1951, Bill Tosheff was an NBA rookie with the Indianapolis Olympians. "We had just completed our last exhibition game," Tosheff said, "and we were on a train bound for Chicago to see the College All-Stars play the Royals. From there, we'd be traveling to Moline to open up the season against the Tri-Cities Blackhawks. The two best players on the team were Alex Groza and Ralph Beard, who had both been All-Americans at Kentucky and NBA All-Stars with the Olympians. Groza was my roommate, so I was sitting with him and Beard en route to Chicago. The morning's newspapers reported that Sherman White from LIU had just gotten nailed for shaving points, and everybody was a little antsy. I remember saying to Beard, 'You guys were playing when all of this stuff was happening. Were either of you ever approached by gamblers?' Instead of answering my question, Beard said, 'Tosh, if I ever thought I was going to be implicated in this I'd take my wife and my son and go to Mexico and never come back.' The next evening, both Beard and Groza were busted in Chicago, charged with shaving points while at Kentucky, and then booted from the NBA. Until Jack Molinas, Beard and Groza were the only players ever to be banned from the league for gambling, and all three of them were sacrificial lambs for a hell of a lot of other guys."

On January 8, 1952, at a basketball writers' luncheon at Mama Leone's restaurant, Rossini announced that Molinas had been reinstated at Columbia. Molinas would begin practicing with the team after the intercession break, and was expected to play in the team's next scheduled game—February 6 versus Brown at Providence, Rhode Island. During Molinas's absence, the Lions' record was 8–5, with all of their losses coming by a total of nine points. "Jack is bigger, stronger, and smarter than a year ago," Rossini told the scribes. "Had he been in the lineup, we would not have lost a single game. Not only will Jack start for us, but, with his ability to rebound, we'll be able to go back to the fast-breaking style of play that was so successful last year."

Except for fooling around at the school yard and the YMHA, Jack hadn't touched a basketball with serious intent in six months. The team took the train up to Providence; the morning of the game, Jack called Joe Hacken from the pay phone in the lobby of the hotel, ready to do business. Since Columbia was so much better than Brown, Jack suspected that the ballgame might be off the board, and that's exactly the way it was. That meant that the bookies wouldn't even quote a point spread. In the locker room before the Brown game, Molinas had the audacity to tell Joe McHenry, a reporter for the student newspaper, that he would score twenty-seven points in the upcoming contest. When the final buzzer sounded, Columbia had an easy 95–75 victory and Molinas had exactly twenty-seven points!

Jack called Joe the next morning from Worcester and learned that the opening line for Columbia's next game was Holy Cross minus two and a half. Holy Cross was a very good team and practically unbeatable on their home court. Their record at the time was 13–2, and although they weren't as big as Columbia, they were quick as a wish. Joe said that he'd be at the game and would let Jack know beforehand what was what. Jack told him he wanted the same arrangements that Joe had offered him for the Illinois game: twenty thousand dollars! Joe said he didn't think he'd be able to get that much, but he'd let Jack know.

At the arena there was no sign of Joe. Still no sign at the end of warm-ups. The game was just about to start, and still no Joe. Molinas figured he'd just go out and play it straight and maybe Holy Cross would beat them legitimately. Then all of a sudden Jack saw Joe standing right behind the Columbia bench. He needed a shave, as always, and he was wearing a dirty black raincoat, the same scruffy shoes, and beat-up hat. The only thing that was missing was the newspaper under his arm. Joe hunched over and shielded his hands like a catcher giving a signal to a pitcher, and the signal was one thumb down, which meant that Holy Cross should beat Columbia by more than the spread. Jack got the message loud and clear.

Jack picks up the action from there: "The game started and I was out there playing the way I usually play and I figured the spread was still two and a half. With the score tied at ten, Holy Cross called a time-out and I saw Joe casually signaling me to get myself a drink at the water cooler. While I was at the cooler, Joe walked by and said, 'The number went up to three and a half and the game's worth five and five.' That meant that my payoff was five grand and Joe would also bet five grand on my behalf on Holy Cross with the points. So now I knew that in order for me and Joe to win the money, Holy Cross had to win by at least four points.

"And the game continued and I knew I was scoring a lot of points, but, aside from letting my man, Togo Palazzi, drive past me a few times, I wasn't doing anything special to control the score. Then, with four and a half minutes to go, we were ahead sixty-eight to sixty. An eight-point lead with the game winding down to the closing minutes! And I saw Joe squirming in his seat and staring at me with a grimace on his face like he was in severe pain. Oh, my God. I thought I'd better start doing something quick. So I let Togo get by me again, and then once more. Then I stayed in the lane too long so the ref could whistle me for a three-second violation. I did this and I did that, and one of their guards, Ron Perry, went off on a streak, and things quickly got out of hand. The game boiled down to this: With forty seconds left we're losing by one point and I was on the foul line for one shot. And I had to make the correct decision in a hurry.

"If I missed the free throw, Holy Cross would have the ball and a one-point lead. Then I could maybe foul somebody, miss a shot at the other end, and foul somebody again to try and get their final lead up to four, but too many things had to break the right way for that scenario to work out. Of course, if I made the shot the score would be tied and Holy Cross would probably freeze the ball and take the last shot of the game, which, if successful, would mean they'd win by two and I'd lose the money. What to do? The only workable possibility was for me to make the free throw to tie the score and hope for overtime. Of course, there was no guarantee that I could make the shot even if I wanted to. But I shot it up and it went in and the score was tied.

"Now Holy Cross had the ball and I was in trouble because the game was out of my hands. So they were just passing the ball around to kill the clock, planning to take a shot with just a few seconds left in the game. Right? So what did I do? Damned if I didn't steal the ball. So I stole the ball and Rossini jumped up and immediately called a time-out. Now it was our turn to freeze the ball for the last shot.

"In the huddle, Rossini said that Holy Cross would undoubtedly expect me to take the final shot, so his plan was for me to set a pick on Bobby Reiss's man to free up Bobby for the shot.

"So we initiate the play with ten seconds left, and I set the pick and there's Bobby with a wide-open shot and only five seconds left in the game. And I knew he wasn't going to miss. Now, just as Bobby released the ball I raised my hands in the air just a little, but high enough to slightly deflect the ball and ruin the shot. And the buzzer went off and the game was sent into overtime."

Back in the huddle, Rossini gave Jack a strange look. "What was that all about, Jack?" he asked. Bobby was also looking at Jack, like he was afraid of something. Ever the conniver, Molinas immediately launched into the perfect excuse. "Coach," he said, "I had to raise my hands and jump a little bit because I had turned into Bobby's man when I set the pick and he was still coming, trying to run through me. If I would've held my ground, I was afraid the refs would've called me for an offensive foul, then they would've had a free throw and we would've lost the game by a point. We're on the road, coach, and as you well know, the refs are only looking for an excuse to screw us." Rossini bought it, hook, line, and sinker. Jack also apologized to Bobby Reiss.

When the overtime period was under way, Jack got a little bolder. "I let Togo get past me a couple of times, I let him take a couple of rebounds, and they finally won by five points, eighty-five to eighty. And lo and behold, I wound up scoring thirty-nine points!"

In the locker room, all of his teammates congratulated Jack for playing his heart out. Then the press came in. A reporter said it was the greatest performance he'd ever seen on a college basketball court. "I didn't know what to say. I'd made ten thousand g's to play less than my best and everybody was coming over and shaking my hand. I guess I realized then I could fool anybody."

Because of all the trouble he had gotten into at the dorm, Jack was living at home. Joe called him the next morning and the two conspirators arranged to meet that evening at Bickford's. When Jack got there, Joe told him that there was a problem. His banker didn't want to pay Molinas the ten thousand because he didn't believe that he'd done a tank job. How could he have scored thirty-nine points and still dumped the game? So Jack said that he wanted to meet the banker and Joe made an appointment for the following day.

Jack got all dressed up with a tie and jacket and his white bucks. Mister Ivy League. Then, precisely at 6:00 P.M., a big black Cadillac with Jersey plates came rolling up 116th Street and stopped in the middle of the block, right near the quadrangle. "I walked over to the passenger's side of the car with a smile on my face and whistling like I didn't have a care in the world. It was kind of dark, but as I leaned on the door window I could see a real tough-looking, ruddy-complexioned fellow behind the wheel, wearing sunglasses, a fancy suit with a silk tie, and a two-hundred-dollar overcoat. Joe's sitting in the backseat and there's a small package wrapped in brown paper sitting on the passenger's seat. All the car windows were open and Joe introduced me to Tony, and Tony said, 'Jump in the car.' I said, 'No, thank you. I'd rather stand out here.'"

It was clear that Joe was a little afraid of Tony, but Molinas wasn't in the least. Business was business. "Nobody said anything for a while, until Tony finally said, 'Jeez, that was some game.' As soon as he said that, I asked Tony if he'd made an agreement with Joe, and he said that he had. Then I asked Tony if he had, in fact, agreed to pay up if Holy Cross won by four points or more. Tony said, 'Yes.' So I said, 'There's no more conversation necessary. Just pay up the money.'

"Well, Joe started shaking, and Tony was completely flabbergasted. Finally, Tony said, 'I didn't think you'd cut it so close.'

"'You have absolutely no complaints,' I said. 'We fulfilled our end of the deal and that's that. Just pay up. Tell you what, though. In the future I'll make sure the games won't be as close.'

"Tony pointed to the package on the front seat and said, 'Okay. Go ahead and take the money.' But I wouldn't dream of reaching in and taking it, so he handed me the package. I said, 'Thank you.' Then I told Joe to call me, I put the package in my coat pocket, and I walked away.

"I treated myself to a cab and on the ride to the Concourse I tore open the edge of the package to make sure the money was there. I didn't count it in the cab, but I saw that it was all hundreds and fifties, so I had to go into my pocket to pay the cabbie.

"I walked into the apartment with my usual smile for my little brother, my mom, and my dad, then I went into the bedroom I still shared with my mom and closed the door. Yep, it was all there. Ten thousand smackers. More money than I'd ever seen in my life. The next problem was what was I going to do with all that cash. I couldn't very well spend it. And I couldn't hide it in the house because my mother was liable to find it when she cleaned up. That night I called Joe to make an appointment to meet him the next afternoon at Bickford's, then I hid the money in a shoebox that I shoved under the bed. And in the morning, I took the money with me to school.

"When I met Joe, I asked him to hold the money for me and I told him why. 'Okay, Jack,' he said. 'I'll hold your money just like you have a bank account. And I'm glad that you have such trust in me.'

"'Joe,' I said, 'if you can't trust your bookie, who can you trust?'"

The Columbia-Harvard game was considered too much of a mismatch to warrant a point spread, so, playing straight, playing bored, Molinas scored fifteen as the Lions rolled over the Crimson by 83–57. Playing at full throttle against a mediocre Navy team, Molinas tallied twenty points and grabbed twenty-two rebounds, as Columbia eked out a 65–61 victory. Against Princeton, Molinas's numbers were impressive—twenty-six points and twenty-four rebounds—but Columbia came up short, 70–63, and the *New York Times* called Molinas the "goat." It seems that Princeton's center, six foot eight Foster Cooper, incurred three personal fouls only six minutes into the ball game, all of which were the result of Molinas's driving hard to the basket. However, "Molinas's conception of fouling out Cooper was tossing outside one-handers or rolling away from him in the pivot."

Jack was a little afraid when Cooper picked up his third foul, because if he had fouled out Columbia would have beaten Princeton soundly. So he kept Cooper in the game by staying away from him. As the game got close to the wire, Jack began to play on the level. When Cooper finally did foul out of the game, there were four minutes left and Columbia was up by 56–55. The spread Jack was working with had his team favored by six and at that point he was trying his best, figuring it would be easy to win and still stay under the number. But Princeton got hot and Columbia had a dry spell and that was the ball game. After the Princeton game, Molinas's account with Hacken totaled twenty thousand dollars.

Instead of "dumping ball games," Molinas told himself that he was merely "manipulating the scores." And, of course, he never worried because he knew he could never get caught. As proof positive, Molinas asked Julie what he thought about all the point-shaving scandals that were still erupting in the newspapers. "Maybe I've been dumping, too, huh, kid?"

"No," Julie said. "You could never fool me, Jackie. If you were dumping, I'd know."

On February 20, Columbia was legitimately upset by Navy, 65–53. Molinas scored eighteen points but was unable to turn up the juice in a disastrous third quarter when the ball game was up for grabs. Similarly, Molinas's game was flat and he only managed ten points in a loss to Penn at the Palestra on February 23.

Molinas played for free in a home-and-home sweep of Dartmouth, scoring a two-game total of only twenty-four points. He then scored a dozen points and missed six out of ten free throws in a desultory 62–56 victory over Yale in New Haven. After the game, Molinas's teammates elected him captain for next year's squad.

The season concluded with a home game against Yale. Molinas most definitely did not play this one for free. "We were favored by nine and a half, and I had worked out a special grand finale deal with Joe. In addition to the regular price of ten thousand for the game, I also wagered the twenty thousand that Joe was holding for me. I scored fifteen points and tied the Ivy League single-game record with twenty-nine rebounds, and we won by seven. That made me a winner to the tune of fifty grand. Three tricks for fifty grand was a good season no matter what the team's won-and-lost record was.

"I still had no way to either spend or hide that kind of money, so Joe kept on holding it for me. Anytime I wanted all of it or part of it, I just had to say the word. That's the way we left off going into the summer."

He had averaged a modest 16.8 ppg, and the Lions achieved the same record with him (8–5) as they had without him. Because of his abbreviated season, Molinas's only postseason accolades were several Honorable Mention citations in various All-American lists.

On April 1, the *Spectator* published its annual April Fool's issue. A small column ostensibly highlighting the day's on-campus events carried the following notation:

> An Ivy League star for two years, Jack Molinas will appear on Morningside Heights today. His schedule for the day includes a visit to the Dean's office, a talk before the Disciplinary Committee of the Dormitory Council, and a lecture at McMillin Theater on "Glass: Its Role on Campus."

Under a close-up photo of Molinas was this caption: "I thought it was a paper cup."

Back in Coney Island for the summer, Molinas was promoted to "manager" of the Eagle Bar (Julie was in charge of the soft-drink department). Louis had also expanded his lineup of entertainers to include an accordion player, a "gay nineties singer," and an operatic baritone. Louis continued working twelve to sixteen hours every day, and the boys usually worked from 11:00 A.M. to 6:00 P.M. during the week, and longer on weekends and holidays. Long working hours were no problem for Jack—he'd just turn on the radio, listen to however many baseball games were broadcast locally, and turn a happy face to the customers.

In between listening to baseball games, and in honor of Peggy Eisenhower, Molinas would play one particular tune over and over again on the Eagle's juke box—the Harmonicats version of "Peg O' My Heart."

There were, of course, big-time ball games at Kaiser Park, and one of the featured players in the summer of 1952 was Eddie Gard, who had been the kingpin of the recent LIU scandals. Whenever Molinas felt he needed a more fast-paced game, he'd visit the black neighborhoods in Bedford-Stuyvesant. But more than working at the Eagle, and more than playing basketball, Molinas was becoming obsessed with betting on baseball games. "When he came back from playing ball," Julie remembered, "he'd ask me how'd the Cubs do, or did the Senators win. I knew that Jack was a Yankee fan so I thought that maybe one of his friends was a Cub fan and another friend was a Senators fan. I really couldn't figure out what was going on."

Increasingly, the money Molinas won or lost meant nothing. It was the gambling itself that appealed to him. "That was the summer," Julie said, "when Jack totally lost control."

He started out betting on baseball games, just to have something to do, and he soon wound up in a real rut. At first, jack bet a hundred dollars a game with Joe, the money to be added or subtracted to his account. Then he moved up to five hundred, then a thousand. By August Jack was betting as much as five thousand on a single baseball game. Over the course of the summer, he lost about ninety-eight thousand dollars (the equivalent today of about five hundred fifty thousand!). Joe never uttered a word of warning or caution. He was too smart. There Jack was, nineteen years old and forty-eight thousand dollars in the hole.

But in typical fashion, he wasn't worried because he figured that during the course of his senior year he could work a few more games and get back to scratch.

Bobby Reiss and Al Stein had graduated, and two of Molinas's Stuyvesant running mates—Paul Brandt and Stan Maratos—were expected to vie for playing time at the small forward spot. The Ivy League coaches predicted a second-place finish for Columbia, behind Penn, but if the Lions could count on "consistent play" from Molinas, they could easily cop the title. Molinas, however, was more interested in restoring his bankroll than in winning ball games.

On the morning of December 12, 1952, the early line posited Columbia as slight two-and-a-half-point favorites at home against the Fordham Rams. Up until then, Joe Hacken never once asked Jack for the money he owed, but when they rendezvoused at Bickford's on the day the season began, he said, "Jack, you owe Tony forty-eight grand and you're going to have to make it good." Jack had no problem with that and suggested they make a start as soon as possible. Like that night against Fordham. He told Joe that last season's money was not going to be enough. He was the captain of the team, the high scorer and leading rebounder, so he wanted ten and ten. No ifs, ands, or buts. Joe didn't bat an eye. "Okay," he said. "Go under the number tonight and your debt'll get cut in half."

Although Columbia had an apparently overwhelming size advantage, the Rams dominated the rebounds and controlled the game from baseline to baseline. Given Molinas's secret deal with Joe Hacken it was no wonder the Lions offense seemed haphazard and confused. The final score was 71–65, and Molinas netted seventeen points, tying Maratos for the team lead.

The only reason Molinas didn't work two nights later was because Trinity College was another cream puff team, and rather than establish a risky twenty-plus spread, the bookies disdained to accept any bets on the game. With Molinas cruising to a twenty-one-point and twenty-three-rebound performance, Rossini emptied his bench in a lopsided 75–55 win.

The Lions topped Rutgers, 64–55, before embarking on an all-victorious Christmas trip—handily beating Tampa, Georgia, and Miami. Molinas's game continued on the up-and-up, averaging nearly nineteen points and sweeping the backboards clean.

Here's how the *Daily News* described Columbia's next home game:

> Crack-a-Jack Molinas sank 26 points in 26 minutes of play to lead the Lions to an 82–57 rout of hapless Harvard in their Ivy League opener before about 800 at the sinner's gym. It was Columbia's sixth straight victory since their inaugural loss to powerful Fordham.

Even though Columbia edged Navy by 77–71, the Lions had been seven-and-a-half-point favorites, and so Molinas came away with eleven points and a clean slate in Tony's ledger. In the last seconds of the game, Molinas was on the foul line poised to shoot the first of two free throws. He was prepared to tank one of the two shots, thereby preserving an acceptable under-the-number margin of victory. Suddenly, a voice rang out from the stands, shouting, "Jack!" and Molinas turned to look. It was Jolly Cholly, one of the Bickford's crew who earned his living by driving his own taxi. "Jack!" the cabbie screamed again. "My shield's on the line! Don't do it!" Figuring that Jolly Cholly had bet Navy with only six and a half points, Molinas obliged and deliberately clanged both foul shots.

The Lions mauled Connecticut, Dartmouth, and Brown before Molinas agreed to work the Holy Cross game. Limiting himself to two field goals and only twelve total points, Molinas took no chances this time around, and underdog Holy Cross won big, 78–65. Molinas's account now showed a balance of twenty thousand dollars. The fix was also in against Penn in a February 4 game at the Palestra. Molinas's twenty-one points diverted almost everybody's suspicions and the Quakers prevailed, 63–56. He remembered the great lengths he had to go to in order to collect on his wager. "Ernie Beck was Penn's hotshot and we were both class of '53 and natural rivals. In our senior season, we were neck-and-neck for the league's scoring championship, which meant a great deal to me. But, I guess money meant more to me, or else winning a bet meant more, than winning the scoring title. So I wound up doing business in both of my showdowns against Beck and the first one was a crazy game.

"Penn was favored by six and a half, and with about a minute to go in the game, they were ahead by a point. I saw Joe in the stands squirming like he always did whenever a game was too close to suit him, but I also had thirty thousand dollars riding on the outcome. The trouble was that nobody on the Penn team, including Beck, could hit a shot to save his life. So I fouled a guy and he hit his two shots and they're up by three. Then I missed an easy shot and I fouled the same guy again and he made both and they're up by five. Then I missed again, we fouled them, and thankfully the guy missed this time. Fortunately I came down with the rebound. So here's the situation. We're losing by five and we needed to lose by six or I was out thirty big ones. And here's what I did: There was a little flare-up under the basket with elbows flashing all over the place and I put the ball behind my back like I was going to fancy dribble my way out of trouble. Right? But I knew exactly where everybody was, and what I actually did was to put the ball in a Penn player's stomach. A fellow named Bob Leach. He's standing right under the basket with the ball now in his hands and he gave me a strange kind of look, which I returned. Neither of us said a word, of course, but what I wanted to say was, 'Schmuck, shoot the ball!' Finally, he got the message, turned around, and laid the ball in. It was a little crude, I must admit, but I did collect my payoff."

Joe Hacken was famous for being closemouthed, so Molinas was never particularly worried about their schemes being uncovered. However, after the Penn game, Paul Brandt knew that something wasn't right. "I'm throwing easy passes that you're fumbling like the ball's got four corners," Brandt said to Molinas after practice the following afternoon. "And what the hell was going on at the end of the game, Jack?"

"Nothing I can't handle," said Molinas. "Let's go for a walk and I'll tell you what the deal is."

They walked from Morningside Heights down to Forty-second Street and Molinas made a full confession. "Where does it end?" Brandt asked when the tale was told. "They've got tremendous leverage on you, Jack. What else are they going to make you do?"

"Don't worry," was Molinas's ready answer. "Joe will always look out for me."

"Look, Jack, I know you trust Joe, but I don't know about that Tony character. Guys like him play for keeps."

"I know," said Molinas. "But I'm smarter then they are and I know I can beat them."

"I hope you're right, buddy," said Brandt. "Otherwise one bright morning you're going to wake up dead."

Molinas soon discovered that Brandt wasn't the only teammate who questioned his integrity on the court. He had moved back into the dorm for his senior year, and on the day before a game against Army, a teammate named Eddie Lehman came up to his room. "How is the team going to do tomorrow, Jack?" he asked. "What do you mean?" Jack shot back. "We're going to win." Then Lehman glared at Jack and said, "Are we really going to win? Are you going to be serious out there? Or are you just going to fool around again?"

Jack realized that Eddie had his number, so he called Joe and said, "Tomorrow afternoon we're playing up at Army, and I want to bet ten thousand dollars on Columbia to win." When Joe said the spread was two, he said, "Make that bet fifteen thousand. We're going to kill them." Sure enough, Jack went out and scored thirty-eight, got twenty-four rebounds, and Columbia won by twenty-six points. From then on, none of his teammates ever questioned his effort.

Three days later, Molinas was up to his old tricks. Columbia was a ten-point favorite to beat lowly Yale, but had to struggle to manage a 68–63 win. Molinas scored twenty-eight points to lead both teams and all the newspapers called him the "star of the game." Yet in order to keep the score under control, Molinas also missed ten free throws.

For the next two games, Molinas unleashed the full force of his excellence, scoring thirty in a rout of Harvard, and forty-one as Princeton fell. But he took another dive in a 76–74 double-overtime loss to Cornell—scoring twenty-seven before bricking a free throw that would have given Columbia the lead with thirty-two seconds left in the ball game.

Another game, another flop. This time he converted only two-of-six free throws in a 63–59 win over Dartmouth. With his game-high total of twenty points, Molinas also became only the fourth Columbia player to score over one thousand career points. Molinas next scored twenty-three points, but played what Rossini called "a sloppy game" as the Lions overcame Yale, 71–64, and once again failed to cover the point spread.

By now, Molinas had mastered the secret art of shaving points. An off-balance lunge on defense. A zig when a zag was required. Passes and shots off by mere inches. As he put it, "I could miss a shot off the front rim or off the back rim. I could even make a shot roll around the rim and curl out. I could hold a ball game in the palm of my hand. It was a great feeling."

On March 3, Columbia played a rematch against Cornell, the same team that had edged them in double-overtime just two weeks before. This time, Molinas felt he had something to prove. The Cornell players had big mouths, and they were bragging about how they were going to clean Columbia's clock again. But he was playing the game on the up-and-up and Cornell didn't have a snowball's chance in hell. With Molinas's eighteen points showing the way, the Lions roared to an amazing forty-five-point victory!

Only two games remained in Molinas's undergraduate career—Penn and

Princeton—and the Lions could virtually clinch the Ivy League title and a berth in the NCAA tournament by beating the Quakers. Jack had sprained a finger on his shooting hand in practice and it was all taped up, so he had a readymade excuse for having a bad game. The fix was in, and his focus on gambling had stripped any sense of personal pride that he had once had in his athletic ability. Jack wound up shooting only four for sixteen from the field and finished with eight points. The Quakers won, 59–45, and just about clinched the title.

By that point, Jack had absolutely no enthusiasm for playing basketball, and he couldn't wait for the season to end. He knew he was getting too careless for his own good, but because of all the recent disclosures of dumping at CCNY, LIU, and the rest, nobody on the local sports scene could ever imagine that any basketball player would be foolish enough to still be in cahoots with gamblers. He hoped that playing in the NBA would revive his game. Meanwhile, he had one more chance to make a killing, and the Princeton game was a real stinkeroo.

Molinas netted only one field goal and totaled a measly nine points as Princeton prevailed, 70–58. Leonard Koppett, in the *New York Times*, called Molinas's showing "the worst game he ever experienced at Columbia." And thus, Molinas's erratic career at Columbia ended with a dramatic thud.

New York Post sportswriter Milton Gross voiced the generally held view that "when Molinas failed so evidently against Penn and Princeton…the feeling was generated that Jack had dealt away any chances he might have had of playing professional ball." Molinas's response was that "no scout who is worth his salt will measure a player's potential by his performance in two or three games." Molinas further informed Gross that he was "making no claim on a future professional career," and that "the NBA draft next month will decide that for him." Molinas also announced that he was planning to make application to the graduate business school at Harvard.

In the immediate aftermath of his senior season, in which he averaged 21.6 points and 16.7 rebounds per game, Columbia's varsity "C" club awarded Molinas a trophy for being the most outstanding athlete in his graduating class. Moreover, the Metropolitan Basketball Writers granted Molinas (by one vote over Seton Hall's Walter Dukes) the prestigious Haggarty Award for being the best player in the New York area. Even better than the honors he received was the fact that he ended up the season not only paying Tony back his forty-eight grand, but also coming out with a hundred and twenty-five thousand of his own. He carried around about five thousand in his pockets and put the rest in a safety deposit box in a bank in Manhattan.

On March 28, Molinas was a starter for the East squad in the seventh annual College All-Star game, an exhibition primarily designed to raise money for the *Herald Tribune* Fresh Air Fund, which financed summer camp vacations for underprivileged New York children. The game at Madison Square Garden attracted upward of seventeen thousand fans, who delighted in the net-worthy hook shooting of Bob Houbregs, the long-range jump shots of Larry Hennessy, and the all-around excellence of native son, Jack Molinas.

A scant four days later, Molinas began a whirlwind cross-country tour that proved beyond question that he was the best college player in the country. The occasion was a grueling twenty-one-game series pitting the College All-Stars against the world-renowned Harlem Globetrotters in what was billed "The Third Annual World Series of Basketball."

The Globetrotters first saw the light of day in Chicago's Savoy Ballroom, one of many dance halls that booked basketball games when no dance was scheduled. The resident team was the all-black Savoy Big Five. In 1926 an enterprising twenty-five-year-old native of England named Abe Saperstein began booking the Savoy team around the Chicago area on their nights off. Saperstein had grown up on Chicago's North Side and despite his short stature (he was only five feet tall) had played on the "bantamweight" team at Lake View High School, then from 1920 to 1925 with the semipro Chicago Reds. When the Savoy Ballroom went out of business in 1927 (to be replaced by an ice skating rink), Saperstein decided to take the team on the road for good.

The team was called Saperstein's New York, which implied a well-traveled sophisticated organization, and their very first barnstorming game took place on January 7, 1927, in the small village of Hinckley, Illinois, for a purse of seventy-five dollars. From the start they played straight basketball and performed a pregame "circle" that featured passing fancies and other spectacular feats of tricky ballhandling. (Their "Sweet Georgia Brown" accompaniment wouldn't be added until the mid-thirties.) "When I booked them into Toledo for the first time in 1931—and gave them forty-three dollars—the circle wasn't that good," promoter Sidney Goldberg recalled.

Saperstein soon changed the team's name to just plain New York, then Saperstein's Harlem New York, and finally, in the mid-1930s, to Saperstein's Harlem Globetrotters. "'Harlem,'" Saperstein said, "because I wanted people to know the team was Negro, and 'Globetrotters' because I wanted them to know we'd been around." Even so, the team's bookings were still confined to small towns in Illinois, Ohio, and Michigan.

At the time, basketball was far from being a popular sport, and they were playing any team anywhere they could schedule a game, often contracting for a small percentage of the gate receipts as their only remuneration. The Depression years were difficult for the organization, but Saperstein persisted. In one of their first appearances in Chicago, the Globbies attracted twenty-seven fans and earned five dollars for their labors. Gradually, the team began to expand their range into more of the Midwest and Pacific Northwest. Like other barnstormers, they played in a variety of courts—high school gyms, armories, social halls, and even a drained swimming pool. Black men in a white world, they were forced to eat and sleep in segregated facilities and were subjected to constant racial epithets screamed at them by whatever fans came to see them play. Bernie Price, who joined the Globetrotters in 1936, remembered the impact the team had in so many outlying rural areas: "In some small towns the kids had never seen blacks before and they would rub our skins to see if the black would rub off."

Playing straight-up basketball and aiming to prove the prowess of black athletes, the Globbies were soon winning more than ninety percent of the 150 to 175 games they played every year. Saperstein soon saw the need to spice up the action to keep the fans interested in the often lopsided games, and the now familiar showboating routines gradually evolved. The first showman was Inman Jackson, whose standard trick was to roll the ball up one arm, across his shoulders, and down the other arm.

By 1939 the Trotters had never ventured further east than western Pennsylvania, but on the strength of their 148–13 won-lost record they were invited to the first World Tournament in Chicago, eventually placing third. The Globetrotters unequivocally established themselves as a legitimate team when they won the tournament in 1940.

In the mid- and late forties, the wily Saperstein realized that the unique appeal of his all-black squad would be seriously eroded should the fledgling NBA decide to integrate its lily-white teams. So Saperstein made a deal—the Globbies would agree to perform (for reduced compensation) in preliminary games to regular season NBA contests, thereby guaranteeing SRO crowds, if the pro teams would drastically limit the number of black players on their rosters. In those days, the NBA was a rinky-dink bus league and many of the fans would unceremoniously leave the arenas after the Globetrotter game was concluded. By 1953, there were only three blacks on NBA rosters—Nat "Sweetwater" Clifton with the New York Knicks, the Boston Celtics' Chuck Cooper, and Earl Lloyd of the Syracuse Nationals.

In 1948, the Globbies had defeated George Mikan and his NBA champion Minneapolis Lakers, 61–59, before a crowd of 17,823 at Chicago Stadium. The Globetrotters also won the highly anticipated rematch in 1949 to extend their winning streak to 114 games. Most basketball fans believed the Globetrotters to be the world's greatest team. Subsequently, the College All-Star series was followed much more closely than were the NBA playoffs, and was a huge moneymaker for Saperstein.

The Globbies' 1953 squad included Josh Grider, Pop Gates, and dribbling expert Marcus Haynes, all of whom would only be marginal NBA players. Elmer Robinson was the only player who could start for virtually any NBA team, but the Trotters' star attraction was Reece "Goose" Tatum, the so-called Clown Prince of Basketball.

The All-Stars carried a ten-man squad. The only players who were scheduled to play the entire series were Irv Bemoras and Jim Bredar from Illinois, Larry Hennessy from Villanova, Dick Knostman from Kansas State, Ron Feiereisel from De Paul, Richie Regan from Seton Hall, and Ken Flower from Southern California. To boost attendance, the team would pick up three new players as they moved to different parts of the country so that no matter what city they happened to be in, there would be a local favorite on the team. Originally, Molinas was only due to play in the initial seven games. The full-time coaches were Seton Hall's Honey Russell and Ray Meyer of De Paul, who likewise would be aided by honorary coaches in various stops along the way.

The twenty-one games were played on nineteen consecutive dates (from March 29 to April 16) in nineteen cities with day-night doubleheaders scheduled in New York and Chicago. The first contest was played in Madison Square Garden on Saturday afternoon. Molinas remembered: "I was looking forward to the games, I felt rejuvenated, and I'd played well in our practice sessions. But I'd had some trouble with Coach Russell. I was a nobody from the pussyfoot Ivy League and he didn't think I belonged on the All-Star team.

"We were getting ready to open the series in New York and, just as I was heading into the locker room, Lester Harrison came walking up to me. He was both the owner as well as the coach of the Rochester Royals. A very polite man, he told me that he was going to watch the way I played very carefully because he wanted me to join his team. Rochester had the sixth pick in the NBA draft and he hoped I would be available when their turn came. 'Well, Jack,' Harrison said, 'you know that you don't have to put out that much in these ball games. We all know that you're a really good player and that you'll make an outstanding pro. But if you play as good as you can play, why then you'll be drafted by one of the teams that picks ahead of us. Milwaukee, maybe, or Fort Wayne. And I'd hate to lose you. I want you to know that you'll certainly be a starter for the Royals. And you'll get all the money you're looking for.'

"I couldn't believe it. Here was the owner of an NBA ball club telling me to take a dive and sounding just like Joe Hacken! But I just listened and Harrison kept on talking.

"'We'll pay you top dollar,' he said, 'and a fifteen-hundred-dollar signing bonus besides.'

"Fifteen hundred dollars! I had well over one hundred thousand stashed away and I could light my cigar with fifteen hundred. All I said was, 'I'll think about what you told me, Mister Harrison. Thank you very much. It's been a pleasure to meet you.'

"Then, no sooner did Harrison leave, then who did I see waiting for me in the wings? Red Auerbach, the head honcho of the Boston Celtics. I remember he was wearing a houndstooth sport jacket and smoking one of his cigars. So now Auerbach called me over and said, 'Jack, we've got a funny situation here.'

"'A funny situation?' I said.

"'Yes. The situation is that the Celtics are interested in drafting you, but I'm afraid we'll never get the chance because we have the seventh pick in the draft, right behind Rochester. By the way, I noticed that Lester Harrison was just talking to you. Is he interested in drafting you?'

"'Well, he said he might be.'

"'You know, Jack,' Auerbach said, 'I think the wide-open way you play offense would fit much better with the Celtics. I'd put you on the starting team right away. I won't pull any punches with you, Jack, because I know you're a bright boy. I've scouted several of your games at Columbia and I think you're the best college player in the country. A lot of NBA people think you're a soft Ivy Leaguer, but I know better. And I'm afraid that after this tour everybody and his brother will know just how good you really are. And, don't worry, we'll pay you as much as any other team would. It's just a shame that we probably won't get a shot at you.'

"'Gee, Mister Auerbach,' I said, 'what do you want me to do?'

"'Just take it easy on the tour,' he said. 'You don't have to put out one hundred percent. It's a fun tour, Jack, so go and have yourself a good time. You don't have to score so many points, you know what I mean?'

"I knew exactly what he meant, but I thanked him and shook his hand and made no commitment either way. And I wondered what the hell was going on in the NBA."

Years later, Auerbach would deny that he'd ever spoken to Molinas under any circumstances. "I never ever talked to the kid," said Auerbach. "Never in my whole life. It's ridiculous. If anybody says I did, I'll hang 'em. Hey, the only time I ever saw any of the College All-Stars–Globbies games was in 1954 when Frank Ramsey was playing with the All-Stars. Nobody in the NBA had assistant coaches in those days, and nobody had scouts either, so most of my scouting was done through my former players recommending somebody. Very few of the college games were on TV, so that meant taking a train to see some kid play, or even worse, flying in a DC 3. But I would never even think of going to see an Ivy League game. Scouting is hard work, see? And the worst thing you could do was get on a plane and, say, fly to Chicago and both teams are using a zone defense and all the players are just standing around, and you'd want to shoot yourself. I mean, I was running the entire show up in Boston and I was so fuckin' busy I couldn't go anyplace."

Who was telling the truth here? A young man, soon to be a lawyer and then a convict, with a penchant for exaggeration? Or a gruff old man, also famous for manipulating the truth, trying to promote a spotless reputation?

In any event, as the first game got under way, the college boys were clearly intimidated by the Globetrotters, and trailed 42–24 at the intermission. Goose Tatum's long-armed hook shots and razzle-dazzle passes from the pivot did the most damage. Not only did Goose play with a smile, but he always initiated conversation with the player who was guarding him. Goose would plug the basket with another hook shot and then say, "How'd you like that, young white boy?" After the Trotters' gala halftime circus the All-Stars were much more competitive, narrowing their final deficit to 70–62. Molinas, indeed, maximized his limited playing time, scoring ten points and displaying remarkable poise.

"We had some lunch," said Irv Bemoras, "then hung around the Garden waiting for the night game. The more we talked to one another, the more we felt we could beat the Trotters. Coach Russell also made two important adjustments—playing Molinas more, and denying Tatum the ball in the pivot by fronting him."

Both moves paid great dividends. Because he'd been playing for so long against bogus teams that were part of the act, the six-foot-three Tatum was unable to cope with aggressive defensive tactics. He scored only two points in the nightcap and, in fact, rarely played for the duration of the series. Moreover, Molinas tallied six points in the final two minutes in pacing the collegians to a 69–65 victory.

The loss ended the Trotters' latest winning streak at 304 games. Over the twenty-six years of their existence, their total record now stood at 4,395 victories and only 261 setbacks. To reward his inspired play, Molinas was signed on at a thousand dollars per week for the duration of the tour.

The Trotters snuffed the Stars, 79–68, in Toronto the next evening. The collegians were offended when the Trotters resurrected several of their favorite trick plays in the waning minutes of the game. The Trotters also won in Philadelphia, and Molinas had his first subpar game—shooting only two for ten from the field and totalling thirteen points. Pat Kennedy was always one of the two refs and Molinas knew he was a very good official. The trouble was that he was also part of the Globetrotters' organization, so he called every questionable call their way. With a more impartial ref, Jack was sure they could have won all the close ball games.

As the tour progressed, each team's style became more discernible. "Both teams played man-to-man defense," Bemoras noted, "to make sure the game was wide-open and appealing to the fans. We were younger so we wanted to get out and run. When the fast break wasn't available, we'd pick-and-roll and play a passing game—spread the floor, pass, and pick away. Most of the Trotters were in their thirties, so they played a more deliberate style. They liked to pass the ball inside and cut off the pivot, and they also set strong picks for their outside shooters. Josh Grider and Pop Gates both had terrific two-handed set shots. And they all were very clever passers and rebounders."

Molinas only scored two points during the All-Stars triple-overtime victory in Raleigh, North Carolina. If Saperstein began to regret having signed Molinas for the entire tour, Harrison and Auerbach couldn't have been happier. The Globbies added NBA veteran Chuck Cooper to their squad and reeled off three consecutive wins—a single game in Indianapolis and a double-dip in Chicago—during which Molinas totaled only thirty-one points. Then Molinas exploded for twenty-two points in Laramie, Wyoming, keying the collegians to a 74–72 win.

"Both teams traveled together in a chartered airplane," Bemoras said, "and that was just about the only time we mingled. They let us into their poker games and they laughed while they won our money. But they were all really friendly to us, especially Josh Grider, who was a real quality person. Even when we chatted with them, we didn't discuss much except the ball games and the various cities we were headed for. We were an all-white team, of course, and because of the racial discrimination that still held sway in most parts of the country, the two teams stayed in different hotels. Sometimes both teams would go out in a group to a restaurant or a night club, and then they'd kid us about how sharp they dressed and how square we looked. They'd have their own retinues that would party with them after the games, so the most socializing we did with the Trotters was on the plane trips."

Molinas rarely joined the in-flight poker games and mostly kept to himself. "Jack and I were both Sephardic Jews," Bemoras said, "and that was our main topic of conversation whenever we got together. What were the foods both of our mothers cooked, and stuff like that."

The All-Stars' hotel accommodations were paid for, and each player also received fifteen dollars a day to cover his meals, as well as two free tickets to every game. As usual, however, Molinas always embraced any unusual challenge that might make his life more interesting. "A couple of times," Bemoras said, "we were in the locker room getting ready for our pregame chalk talk and Jack was nowhere to be found. When the coaches dispatched somebody to search for him, they'd find Jack outside the arena scalping his tickets. He really was quite a guy."

Molinas hit his stride on the West Coast swing, scoring twenty-two (including a crucial free throw in the final seconds) as the All-Stars nipped the Trotters, 77–74, in San Francisco. On April 8, a bonanza crowd of 35,256 thronged the Los Angeles Coliseum and Molinas's twenty-three points pushed the All-Stars to a five-point lead late in the game. However, during a rebounding scrum, tempers flared, especially when J. C. Gipson "took the starch and the wind out of Jack Molinas, the All-Star ace, with a well-placed elbow." With Molinas's ribs painfully bruised, the Trotters came on to win a fiercely contested game, 77–72. Clearly, Molinas was the best player on the court, and the local newspapers were "all agog" at "the brilliant play of the big New Yorker."

In Denver, Molinas posted twenty-four points in a 87-72 loss, once again impressing the locals. "Molinas is one of the sharpest all-around players to grace the auditorium boards in some time." For an encore, Molinas rang up thirty-four in a losing effort in Kansas City, Missouri. The next game was in St. Louis, and Molinas's twenty-five markers propelled the college boys to their fifth victory (against eleven losses) of the tour.

The next game was in Cincinnati. Jack remembered another encounter that would change his life. "A sportswriter came up to me before the game in Cincinnati. He told me that Fred Zollner of the Pistons had come to the arena to see me play. He also told me that Sweetwater Clifton was joining the troupe. Now, Clifton was a seasoned six-foot-eight NBA player, the starting center for the New York Knicks. He wasn't an exceptional offensive player, but he was one of the toughest defenders in the pros and a ferocious rebounder to boot. In fact, of all the NBA's big men, Clifton was the only one who could control George Mikan. I was still just a few days shy of my twenty-first birthday and this would be my first game-time test against a top-notch NBA player. Man, was I pumped!

"It was no accident then that I had a truly great game. I scored thirty-one points, had double figures in both rebounds and assists, and defended the hell out of Sweets so that he didn't score a single point. To top everything off we beat the striped pants off of them, 86–63. It was certainly the best game of my life.

"Afterward, a man by the game of Carl Bennett came up to me with a smile big enough to light up the whole city. He was the Pistons' general manager and I knew they had the fifth pick in the NBA draft. 'We liked the way you played tonight,' Bennett said. 'Jack, we're definitely going to draft you.' So that was it. After the game in Cincinnati, I knew for sure that I was going to be a first-round draft pick."

In Detroit, Molinas led the Stars with thirteen points, but Marcus Haynes bucketed several long-distance set shots and the Trotters held on to win a squeaker, 56–53. On April 15, Molinas outscored Clifton 29–21 and the collegians triumphed, 85–83, in overtime. The tour closed in Boston with Molinas scoring twenty and the Globbies posting an 87–83 win. The Boston newspapers expressed the hope that Molinas might wind up in Celtics uniform "if Red Auerbach decides he can play the corner position."

In the final accounting, the Trotters held a 14–7 margin over their opponents. But the biggest winner on the tour was Abe Saperstein, who grossed just over a million dollars.

As was customary, sportswriters from all the cities cast votes for the All-Stars Most Valuable Player and Molinas was the unanimous choice. The award—a four-foot-high trophy—was presented to Molinas at a luncheon at Toots Shor's restaurant that officially marked the culmination of the tour. Molinas hugged the big trophy as he discussed his plans with the assembled members of the press: "If it turns out that I'm too tall to be drafted into the army, I'd be interested in pro ball only if the price is right. Otherwise, I intend to enroll in the Harvard Business School." In truth, Molinas had no real interest in going to graduate school, but was making the first move in any future financial negotiations with whichever NBA team wound up drafting him.

In retrospect, the World Series campaign helped prepare Molinas for the rigors of NBA competition. "I learned a lot of basketball on the trip," he told the *New York Post*, "especially as regards physical contact." And the tour offered another, more lasting gift to basketball posterity—in 1954, Dane Clark starred as Abe Saperstein in a glossy, melodramatic motion picture, *Go, Man, Go*, which purported to represent the history of the Harlem Globetrotters. Most of the live-action shots were taken from the 1953 World Series games, and for a brief few seconds there's a clip of Jack Molinas (identified in the film as "Cameron") shooting a two-handed set shot—the only known footage of him still extant.

The 1953 NBA College Draft was held in Boston on Friday, April 24. The New York Knicks had the first pick and were faced with a dilemma. Walter Dukes, a seven-footer from Seton Hall, was their preference—a lanky player who could run and shoot like a guard and rebound like he was a pauper and the ball was made of gold. The only problem with Dukes was that he was considered to be a dangerously independent thinker, and was also being wooed by Abe Saperstein. The Trotters had offered Dukes a one-year contract worth fifteen thousand dollars, the Knicks would go no higher than ten thousand, and Dukes wanted twenty thousand. Ray Felix out of LIU, another seven-foot beanpole, was another option—the very same player who once played for Metropolitan High School. While Dukes was blessed with a sprightly mobility, Felix was more of a stationary pivotman. Also, Felix played with a certain stiffness and, in fact, had been out of school for a year and on the Knicks payroll while playing for a semipro team in Pennsylvania. Molinas was universally hailed as the most talented of the three, and, if he had shown to good advantage in the World Series tour, he was still believed by most NBA insiders to be an unproven Ivy Leaguer. In the end, the Knicks gambled on the player with the biggest reputation, Dukes, who indeed accepted Saperstein's offer and went off around the world with the Trotters. "Had we known for certain that Dukes was going to sign with the Globetrotters," moaned Joe Lapchick, the Knicks coach, "we'd have picked Molinas."

By some convoluted NBA logic, the Philadelphia Warriors had the next three picks—but only if all three of the players selected came from or played collegiately within a fifty-mile radius of the City of Brotherly Love. Their selections were Ernie Beck from Penn, and Jack George and Norm Grekin from LaSalle. The Baltimore Bullets then tabbed Felix, and the Milwaukee Hawks picked Bob "Hooks" Houbregs. Drafting in the fifth slot, the Fort Wayne Zollner Pistons tabbed Jack Molinas.

Louis Molinas wasn't in favor of Jack going into pro basketball "because when you give too much money to young boys you spoil their future." Nevertheless, Louis accompanied his son out to Fort Wayne to help in the negotiations.

Zollner's first offer was seventy-five hundred dollars, which Jack quickly refused. He repeated his inclination to enter Harvard Business School, a move his father supported, and then Zollner put all his cards on the table. "Well," he said, "you played in the Ivy League, Jack, and what kind of a player does that make you? The Ivy League is a baby league."

"Mister Zollner," Jack said, "You saw me play in Cincinnati so you know what kind of a player I am. And at home, on a special shelf that I built in my bedroom, I have a four-foot-high trophy with a big gold basketball on it that was given to me for being the most valuable player of the World Series of Basketball. That's the kind of a player I am, and you know it."

Then Zollner started talking about Jack's military draft classification, which was 2-AS, a classroom deferment that would automatically be terminated when he graduated in June. If he was taller than six six, he would get a permanent 4-F deferment. If he was less than six six, he would have to serve two years in the military. Zollner said that this uncertainty cast a cloud over Jack's future and made signing him a risk for the Pistons. But when Zollner wouldn't budge from his original offer, Jack told him he was going to school, and then he and his dad went back to New York.

Now more than ever, Molinas was a neighborhood god who walked the streets. All the wise guys at Bickford's were kibitzing him worse than ever. "Hey, Jack," they would say, "if you ever come across anything good in the NBA, let us know." Joe Green was always hinting around about the possibility of Jack's rigging games in the NBA. And so was Aaron Wagman. But Jack always said, "Nah, not me, go find somebody else." Another fellow that was always sniffing around was Stanley Ratensky, whose father owned a candy store in the neighborhood. Stanley the Rat was definitely small potatoes. His limit was maybe a hundred bucks a bet, and he said to Jack, "If you ever want to bet on any of the NBA games, please give me a call and I'll handle it for you. Please, Jack, I need the action and you'd be doing me a big favor."

All during this time, Joe Hacken was telling Jack that he had enough money salted away and that he should play it straight in the pros. "Play your best," he said, "and within two or three years you'll be in the All-Star game." But Jack told him not to worry, that he had no intention of doing anything shady.

In Kaiser Park, the Molinas boys had a standing bet. Any twosome who wanted to play them would automatically get ten-to-one odds. Throughout the summer, Jack and Julie remained undefeated.

"Jack spent a lot of time working with me to raise the level of my game," Julie said. "He taught me everything from basic footwork to subtle moves around the basket. Knowing that he was going to be away for so long, we were very close that summer. Besides helping me on the basketball court, he'd also be there for me through the countless awkward and confusing situations that all teenaged boys are constantly encountering. His support, his advice, and the positive slant he put on everything really boosted my self-confidence. We loved each other deeply and I absolutely idolized him. When I grew up, I wanted to be just like my big brother."

Somehow even the compulsion to gamble had abated, and Molinas was satisfied to place an occasional hundred-dollar bet on a baseball game. And he was not disturbed by the fact that nobody from the Pistons had called him all summer long. But there was no rush because Molinas knew he had Zollner's balls in a vise. Especially after the Knicks had squandered their number-one pick on Walter Dukes, Zollner simply could not come out of the draft with empty hands. So Molinas applied to Harvard Business School just to squeeze Zollner a little tighter.

Hey, at age twenty-one Molinas had a load of cash in the bank, a fat wallet in his pocket, a beautiful girlfriend, and the adulation of everyone who ever saw him play or saw him smile. All he had to do was wait for Zollner to crack.

The only fly in Molinas's ointment was the looming prospect of military conscription. He believed, he hoped, he almost prayed, that he had grown a half inch since the Globetrotter tour. Twice every day, Julie would carefully measure his brother, make the appropriate pencil mark on the bedroom wall, and also record the measurement and the time in a notebook. To Jack's dismay, he discovered that during the course of the day his height varied by as much as three-quarters of an inch. He was tallest in the morning, and when his chin was tucked in, and after he inhaled deeply. Wearing a pair of sweat socks also helped. How could he parley any, or all, of these factors into a 4-F deferment?

Right after Labor Day, Zollner finally called to ask Jack whether or not he had changed his mind about signing for the seventy-five hundred. Jack told him not only that he couldn't play for less than ten thousand, but that he had been accepted into Harvard, and that classes began in about a week. Zollner upped his offer to eight thousand, but Jack still held out.

"I'll never forget the date, September 10, 1953," Jack said, "because it was the day before classes started at Harvard. Mister Zollner didn't know it, but I was going to wait until it was almost five o'clock in Fort Wayne, then call him and tell him I'd sign for his last offer. But what happened was that he called me a few hours earlier to say, 'You blackjacked me, Jack, and I don't want to have anything more to do with you.'"

Right then Jack knew he had him. "Mister Zollner," he said, "I'm just trying to make the correct decision about my future."

"All right," he said. "I'll give you the eight thousand five hundred and I'll add a fifteen-hundred-dollar signing bonus. That's ten thousand, Jack. Take it or leave it." So he took it.

But the money itself really didn't mean anything to Jack; ten thousand dollarsseemed like pin money. For him, having Zollner meet his terms was all about respect.

Molinas flew out to Fort Wayne and barely scanned the contract before signing it on September 16. In so doing, he had only a dim comprehension of the contents of Article 15.

> It is severally and mutually agreed that any player of a Club, who directly or indirectly bets money or anything of value on the outcome of any game played for any National Basketball Association Club, shall be expelled from the National Basketball Association by the President after due notice and hearing and the President's decision shall be final, binding, conclusive and unappealable; and the Player hereby releases the President and waives every claim he may have against the President and/or the National Basketball Association, and against every Club in the National Basketball Association, and against every director, officer and stockholder of every Club in the National Basketball Association, for damages and for all claims and demands whatsoever arising out of or in connection with the decision of the President of the National Basketball Association.

Louis kept the bulk of Jack's salary and allowed his son a two-hundred-dollar weekly allowance. And Jack Molinas became an official member of one of the most storied teams in professional basketball, the Fort Wayne Zollner Pistons.

"The Zollner Pistons basketball team started out in a local YMCA league in 1939," said Carl Bennett, an early coach of the team, "and that same season we also played in an amateur industrial league. The next year I went up to Chicago and talked to Leo Fisher, a sportswriter for the *Herald American*, who was heading up and doing most of the work to keep the old National Basketball League alive. All I was after was to try and schedule some exhibition games with better teams. But Fisher said, 'Why don't you join our league, and you'd be playing the best teams on a regularly scheduled basis?' Fred Zollner thought it was a good idea and we were playing in the NBL by 1941. All of our basketball players were paid the same salaries—twenty-five hundred for playing ball, and an equal amount for working in some capacity for the company during the off-season. Fred was not interested in making any money from the basketball team, so at the end of the season, the players would also divy up any monies that remained from the gate receipts after all expenses had been deducted. Normally that meant another fifteen hundred or so for each player. I coached the team until we joined the NBA five years later, and then I became the general manager."

Fred Zollner was generally admired by the various sportswriters who covered his teams. According to sportswriter Myron Cope, "Zollner is short and stocky, a dapper man sporting peak lapels, a silk shirt, a constant tan, and an unruly coiffure that suggests he is about to mount a podium and conduct Beethoven's Ninth." Carl Biemiller, a local Fort Wayne journalist, saw Zollner as "a soft-voiced, friendly man with a taste for expensive striped suits and the engaging knack of making them look as if he'd worn them to bed."

Most of Zollner's basketball players, however, knew him to be an arrogant, self-involved playboy, and a thorough pain in the ass: Under the leadership of Bob Cousy, the NBA Players Association had been created in 1952 in an attempt to force the league's board of governors (the club owners) to raise player salaries and improve working conditions. Many of the players despised Zollner because of his insistence that any of his players who did join the union would be immediately cut from the team. Zollner also had a condescending attitude toward his players. Once, when Frankie Brian asked him a technical question about the pistons produced for airplane engines versus those meant for automobiles, Zollner's haughty answer was, "Listen, Frank, let's talk about the only two subjects you know something about—women and basketball." Moreover, despite a certain fondness that Zollner exhibited for his prize rookie, Molinas felt that his new boss was an anti-Semite.

Whatever the true nature of Fred Zollner's personality, along with Philadelphia's Eddie Gottlieb, New York's Ned Irish, and Boston's Walter Brown, he was certainly one of the NBA's most influential owners.

But, as the 1953–54 season was about to unfold, the NBA was on the verge of disaster: In the previous season, the Dumont Television Network had broadcast fourteen Saturday afternoon games. Now the National Broadcasting Corporation was interested in taking over and showing a much larger schedule of games. Yet as the season approached, Commissioner Podoloff was unable to finalize a satisfactory contract. Leonard Koppett, in his always fascinating history, *24 Seconds to Shoot*, explains the reasons why Podoloff's efforts were doomed:

> The individual owners couldn't look past their own selfish interests: Who was to get more money by having his team make more TV appearances? Who wanted to schedule a Saturday afternoon game when a Saturday night game would draw more at the gate? Instead of pulling together and making the television games as attractive as possible, they bogged down in bickering for small advantages.... Irish, with the Knicks now the most important feature of Garden basketball, had little interest in the small fees television could bring. He wanted the big live crowds. For the shoe-string operators in smaller cities, on the other hand, no fee looked small and every little bit of exposure was welcome. Podoloff, siding...with the have-nots, never succeeded in arranging a TV schedule that gave the uncommitted audience the best available games instead of the games particular owners wanted to sell.

The nine-team NBA was also plagued with weak franchises. When Ben Kerner had moved his franchise from Tri-Cities to Milwaukee in 1951, it was a major improvement, even though Milwaukee could hardly be considered a hotbed of basketball interest. Then, without warning, in March 1953, major-league baseball also began shifting franchises and the Boston Braves wound up in Milwaukee. Suddenly, Milwaukee was a big-league baseball town, wild about its new status and commercially committed to giving the baseball team every support. Just as suddenly, Kerner and the NBA were forgotten and ignored. Since the Baltimore and the Philadelphia basketball franchises were also struggling through lean years, the Milwaukee debacle meant that one-third of the NBA's teams were on the verge of collapse.

Money was scarce on all fronts: Norm Drucker was in his third season as an NBA referee and getting paid fifty dollars a game. When he decided to ask for a raise he arranged for a meeting with Podoloff, who made it clear that he had no idea what Drucker's name was. "What's on your mind, referee?" Podoloff asked. As soon as Drucker gave his pitch for a paltry ten-dollar raise, Podoloff jumped out of his seat, pounded the desk, and said in an anguished voice, "Are you trying to bankrupt the NBA?"[1]

George Mikan was the league's highest paid player, earning twelve thousand dollars annually from the Minneapolis Lakers. Cousy and Dolph Schayes each made an estimated seventy-five hundred. "All the rest of us," said an ex-NBAer who played from 1949 to 1953, "got paid about thirty-five hundred bucks plus seven bucks a day for meals on the road, and, believe me, it wasn't easy to live on that kind of money, especially if you had a wife and kids. Most of the owners had other sources of income besides their basketball teams and it's a good thing they did or they would've been as broke as we were. A lot of good players couldn't afford to play in the NBA. At the same time, a lot of us had no other choice. There were no other career options available. We had to make a living, you know? And that's why so many NBA players in the late forties and early fifties were doing business."

Like who?

"Like almost all the players on the Baltimore Bullets," said one veteran of that team (whose testimony is corroborated by several other veterans of what is now called "The Pioneer Era"). "There was another player, a big man, who occasionally also played to lose. When his teammates figured out what he was doing they were pissed. Oh, shit. There he goes again. Instead of throwing him catchable passes, they'd throw passes at his ankles just to make him look clumsy. Who else? A bunch of guys on the Knicks, especially the players who came from New York."

Whitey Von Nieda, who played for three seasons with the old Tri-Cities Blackhawks, recalled several teammates who studied the point spreads that were printed in the newspapers "like other guys studied the Bible."

In December 1951, the Manhattan district attorney's office arrested Sol Levy, an NBA referee, and charged him with conspiring with Salvatore Sollazzo to fix a total of six games during the previous season. For payments that varied between four hundred and five hundred dollars, Levy made certain that previously specified ballplayers were prematurely fouled out of those games.

Another one-time pro said this: "Levy wasn't the only ref doing business, not by a long shot. A ref named Chuck Soladare told me face-to-face that he was betting on ball games. The difference was that Chuck and a bunch of other refs would only bet on games that they weren't personally working. But the players were much worse. Even after the college scandals broke, there were plenty of games dumped in the NBA. One of my teammates was a famous superstar who had an unstoppable pet move to the basket. Whenever he was doing business, he would take three dribbles away from the basket and throw up a low percentage hook shot. We heard he was making half his yearly salary every time he fixed a game."

Besides Beard and Groza, Hogan's office uncovered the names of two other NBA players on another team (one being the ball club's primary gate attraction, the other a scrub) who had worked with gamblers as collegians. The district attorney's agents approached Commissioner Podoloff with hard evidence, and with demands that both players be booted from the NBA. But the owner of the team threatened to fold his franchise if Podoloff ever dared to even question his star player. The star remained in orbit, while the lesser player was quietly dropped from the league early in the 1951–52 season.

The unfortunate reality was that gambling had always played a significant role in the historical development of professional basketball in the United States. The very first pro league, the National Basketball League, was established in 1898 in Philadelphia and lasted for five years. The league's primary downfall was the unstable nature of the teams' rosters—a result of the better ballplayers auctioning off their services and frequently switching from one ball club to another before every game. An old-time barnstormer explained what professional basketball was like in the 1920s and 1930s: "We played about a hundred games a year. We traveled with six players and we'd hire a local kid to play with us in whatever city we happened to be. We'd play a game on Friday night and make sure to beat the yokels by a narrow margin. Then we'd get some bets down, play them again on Saturday night, and kill them. After we collected our money, we'd get the hell out of town. The Original Celtics were doing the same kind of thing. There was no other choice. Only we didn't call it point-shaving. We called it survival."

NOTE

1. *Vintage NBA*, p. 222.

By 1953, Fort Wayne was Indiana's third-largest city, a highly industrialized municipality with a population of approximately 175,000. Among its diversified manufactures were electrical and electronic equipment, trucks and truck trailers, and television and radio sets. The largest corporations were General Electric and International Harvester, which employed a total of nearly twenty-five thousand workers. There were several industrial parks on the outskirts of town replete with grimy factories and charred smokestacks that worked nonstop, spitting forth billowing ash-gray clouds that when the wind was wrong, blotted out the sun, the moon, and the stars. But the citizens quietly coughed into their hands and ignored the tiny pieces of grit that stung their eyes, because they knew where the money was generated that paid their mortgages and fed their children.

The Pistons played in the Coliseum, which seated ten thousand (at an average admission price of $1.75). Aside from an occasional sellout when the Harlem Globetrotters played a preliminary game, the average attendance was just over five thousand. The Pistons faithful took their basketball seriously and were fiercely loyal to their team and its players.

In addition to the pollution from the factories, there were other environmental dangers indigenous to Fort Wayne. "Since there were so many factory workers," said Johnny Bach, who made several excursions into the city as a member of the Boston Celtics, "there was a bar on every corner, and a lot of rowdy drunkards and unsavory characters roamed the streets, particularly on Friday and Saturday nights. It was a rough town and visiting ballplayers mostly stayed in their hotel rooms. In addition, Fort Wayne was well-known around the NBA for being a big gambling town."

Practice began on Monday, September 28, with a fifteen-member squad that was considered to be a significant threat to depose the NBA's reigning titlists, the Minneapolis Lakers. If the Pistons were hometown heroes, professional basketball remained a backwater sport in most sections of the country. There was nothing remotely glamorous or glitzy about being an NBA player. No endorsements were available to augment their mostly inadequate incomes, they had to buy their own sneakers, their faces and their achievements were unknown except to the most passionate hoop-heads, and they required full-time no-nonsense off-season jobs to make ends meet.

In the hardscrabble workaday world of the NBA, experience was everything—and the Pistons were blessed with an excellent core of veteran players. Chief among them was Larry Foust, a powerful, six-foot-nine, 265-pound, immobile pivotman from La Salle, a poor man's George Mikan. Heading into his fourth season with the Zollner Pistons, Foust was the team's high scorer and hungry for his points. "Foust would yell at all the guards," said Zeke Sinicola, a rookie from Niagara, "'Get the ball inside.' Over and over again, it was the same refrain. 'Get the ball inside.' And if you did pass him the ball in the pivot, when you cut off him, forget about it, you never got it back. Foust also had the worst hands of any center I've ever seen. You'd make a perfect pass to him, right on his fingertips, and he'd be catching it off his head. Thank God Foust had a big body so he could get inside and get some layups."

The Pistons' most noteworthy backcourtman was Andy Phillip, an NBA All-Star, a six-foot-two playmaker from Illinois, who would one day be voted into the Basketball Hall of Fame. As quoted in *Vintage NBA—The Pioneer Years*, an oral history compiled by Neil D. Isaacs, Zeke Sinicola had this to say about Phillip:

> Andy was a cold character, never greeted anyone, always looked at you narrow-eyed with his "Gasoline Alley" crew cut. It was like someone was stealing his food or something. I thought he was a bit overrated, even though he was from the Illinois Whiz Kids. He was good but not great. I guess he must have thought the same about me. He never said hello, never gave you a reassuring word when you made a good play. I would love to steal the ball from him. Quite a few times when he was dribbling I'd leave my man just to get the ball away from him. And then I'd be yelled at by the coach for leaving my man. But what could you do? You come in...and you're a rookie, the lowest thing down there, and you had to play the best way you knew how.
>
> I loved playing against Phillip [because]...he had a difficult time defending against smaller men. You could go around him, and after you did, he'd find some way to get back at you, set a hard pick or something.

Other players around the league considered Phillip a cheap-shot artist.

Phillip's best buddy was Freddie Scolari, a five-foot-ten scorer who hailed from San Francisco. Scolari who was another veteran NBA All-Star, did most of his damage with a low-slung one-hander. Phillip and Scolari hung out together and stayed apart from the rest of the team.

Frankie Brian was a six-foot one guard from Louisiana State who'd already been an NBA standout for six seasons. He was perhaps the Pistons' most popular player, described by teammate George Yardley as being "a real Christian attitude guy and everybody's closest friend."

Mel Hutchins, a six-six product of Brigham Young University, was a two-year NBA veteran and the toughest defensive forward in the league. At Carl Bennett's instigation, Zollner had purchased Hutchins from the financially strapped Milwaukee Hawks for an estimated ten thousand dollars. The Hawks owner, Ben Kerner, had promised Hutchins a percentage of the price but had not delivered.

As good as he was, there were certain elements of Hutchins's play that disappointed his new teammates. "Mel was too laid back," said Frankie Brian. "Whenever he was suiting up for a ball game somebody would have to remind him to tie his shoes. He had so much talent and he was so smooth that sometimes it didn't look like Mel was really trying. Heck, we'd always try and talk to Mel and psych him up, because if he had played hard on every play, he would've been a monster."

Foust's backup was Charlie Share, a hulking center from Bowling Green, and the NBA's tallest player. "Share was six eleven and about three hundred and fifty pounds," Zeke Sinicola said, "and he was a veteran so he was loyal to all the other veterans on the team. One day when I was guarding Phillip, Share stepped out and Phillip ran me into a vicious pick. Man, it was like getting hit by a truck. I remember Mel Hutchins and Frankie Brian running to my side and then shouting at Share, 'What the hell did you do that for? You could have killed him.' Then Share had this look on his puss like a kid caught with his hand in the cookie jar. 'Aw,' he said, 'I didn't mean it.'"

Don Meineke was a six-foot-seven finesse player who last season had been the NBA's rookie of the year. Meineke's game was similar to but not nearly as effective as Molinas's, and he would lose considerable playing time to the rookie.

Ken Murray was a 1950 graduate of Saint Bonaventure. A bull's-eye–shooting six-foot-two guard, he'd averaged an impressive 12.9 ppg in his rookie season split between the Baltimore Bullets and the Pistons. For the past two years, Murray had been in the army and Coach Birch criticized him for being "too porky."

A tremendous gulf of suspicion, fear, and disdain separated the veteran and the rookie players. No-cut guaranteed contracts did not yet exist and there were two foreseeable circumstances that threatened the livelihood of veteran players—a career-ending injury, and the young legs of a rookie who played the same position. Among the Pistons' newcomers, it was George Yardley (not Molinas) who came into training camp with the biggest reputation.

Yardley was a lean six-foot-six jump shooter who had broken all of Hank Luisetti's scoring records at Stanford and had originally been drafted by Fort Wayne back in 1950. From Stanford, however, Yardley had graduated into military service and a spectacular career with the Los Alamitos Naval Air Station team.

Yardley had also led Stewart Chevrolet to a national Amateur Athletic Union championship and missed making the 1952 Olympic team only because of a broken hand. He was indifferent to the lure of professional basketball—especially after Carl Bennett's initial salary offer was six thousand dollars. Yardley played volleyball on the beach while negotiations continued, and finally headed east when the bidding reached ninety-five hundred. "George was a gentleman all the time," said Frankie Brian, "one of the nicest fellows I've ever met."

Zeke Sinicola saw Yardley in a completely different light. "Yardley was the most snobbish man I ever met," said Sinicola. "The 'Golden Boy,' I called him, and I thought he was overrated. Jack Molinas used to eat him alive in practice. I even think Yardley feigned injuries to avoid going up against Jack in practice. Yardley was also one of the many guys on the team who looked down on New Yorkers. There were three of us, me, Jack Molinas, and another rookie named Jack Kiley, and we must've reminded Yardley of the Dead End Kids because he always acted like we were out to steal his wallet."

Emilio "Zeke" Sinicola was a high-scoring five-foot-ten guard out of Niagara who'd played three games for Fort Wayne in 1952 before being cut from the squad, and he was considered to be a rookie. Born and raised in Brooklyn, Zeke was sometimes too streetwise for his own good and was seen by his peers as being a malcontent. In any case, Zeke was a straight-shooter on and off the court.

Jim Bredar was a second-round draft pick from Illinois, an early cut who never got to play in the NBA. Other players on the bubble were Carl Oman from Carleton College, and two veterans, Dwight Eddleman and Don Boven, who'd only make the team if someone else was injured.

And what about Molinas? One of the Fort Wayne sportswriters derided Molinas's accomplishments in the "soft" Ivy League, as well as against the "showboating Negroes from Harlem." The prediction was that Molinas would have a "rough time making the squad."

As practice began, the ballplayers themselves quickly understood the exceptional range of Molinas's basketball talent, but many of them were repelled by certain aspects of his personal behavior. "I wound up with a nice seat on the bench because of Jack so I wasn't a big fan of his," said George Yardley. "But he was fantastic, more a finesse player than a banger. One of the reasons why he was so effective on the fast break was the way he ran, with a funny little shuffle. Actually, when a player is bounding down the court pell-mell, it's hard for him to change direction, but when a player shuffles, he can change quickly. Jack was much better on the offensive boards than the defensive boards because grabbing an offensive rebound usually led to an easy shot. And Jack sure loved to score. Aside from a certain selfishness, Jack's biggest defect was his inability to play defense. He was probably a worse defender than I was, and that's going some.

Jack was a smart guy, I'll grant you that, but he was also a manic bettor. He had to have two or three bets going all the time, and every third word out of his mouth had something to do with wagering."

Yardley also felt that Molinas disrupted the Pistons' game plan. "He had a monumental ego," Yardley reported, "and even though Larry Foust was our center, Jack would hightail it downcourt and get to the pivot before Larry did, leaving Larry to wander around the perimeter. Paul Birch was the coach, and since he'd been instrumental in drafting Jack, he had a stake in Jack's playing well. The upshot was that Birch let Molinas do whatever he wanted, and that really destroyed the other players' morale."

With Birch unwilling to put the rookie in his proper place, Foust resorted to bullying tactics. "I'd tell Molinas to get the hell out of there," said Foust, "because the pivot was the only place where I was effective and I didn't fancy the idea of a rookie running me off of my own turf. Molinas wasn't so easily discouraged, but eventually he got the idea."

Sinicola greatly admired Molinas but was somewhat confused by him: "Jack was a bit on the restless side, and he always had to have something going because well enough wasn't good enough for him. In fact, sometimes he didn't even know his own identity. I thought he was Jewish or Russian-Jewish, but every time you heard him being interviewed on a radio program in Fort Wayne, he kept changing his nationality. One day he said he was Irish, the next day he was Greek, or Spanish, or Turkish. Finally I said, 'Jack, tell them who you really are.' 'Naw,' he said. 'I make everybody happy.' That seemed like what he wanted to do, make everybody happy."

His mates respected Molinas's talent, but Frankie Brian saw a fatal flaw in the rookie's makeup: "Jack was a hell of a ballplayer, but he didn't have a killer's instinct. He didn't have the heart to fight you to the end."

Don Meineke saw Molinas as a new breed of player. "He was the first forward," said Meineke, "who could handle the ball on the run as well as a guard. Jack was the most versatile player in the league. He could play inside, outside, or in the corner. He could play fast or slow, wherever or however he could get his points."

Sinicola was Molinas's closest friend on the team and had his own opinion why so many of the Pistons disliked him: "The thing that a lot of people missed was that Jack was a great guy, but because he came on so strong, you really had to know him to like him."

Above all, Molinas had the respect of the players against whom he went head-to-head. "I would've loved to have played with Jack," said Bill Tosheff of the Milwaukee Hawks, "and you better believe that I would've given him the ball, too. Get the ball to Jack, and we're eating steak. Get it to Larry Foust, and we're eating hot dogs. That's the bottom line. Any other considerations are bullshit."

And just how good a player was Molinas?

Hubie Brown, a one-time NBA coach with New York and Atlanta, calls Molinas and Maurice Stokes the two most talented players of their era. "Molinas was a perfect player," said Brown, "and by that I mean he wasn't a specialist. He could handle and pass, play defense if he wanted to, and rebound in a crowd if he wanted to. He had a great assortment of head fakes and ball fakes. He was a savvy player with great timing, and his extra edge was his phenomenal hook shot, the best hook shot ever. There was nothing that Jack Molinas couldn't do on a basketball court."

Coach Paul Birch was a veteran of the Zollner Pistons world championship teams of 1945 and 1946. A sturdy defensive-oriented guard with limited ability, Birch's all-out hustle appealed to Fred Zollner. If Birch wasn't good enough to join the Pistons' advancement into the NBL, and then the NBA, his knowledge of the game convinced Zollner that he could be a successful coach. But Birch was from the old school, which believed there was only one acceptable way to mold a group of individuals into a cohesive team—abuse, belittle, and criticize the players at every opportunity so they'd be united in bitter hatred of their coach.

As the 1953-54 season dawned, Birch was in his third season at the helm of the Zollner Pistons and committed to the drill-sergeant approach to coaching. Stanley Frank, of the *New York Herald-Tribune*, said that "Birch operated with the grim intensity of a cop looking for his stolen patrol car and seemed to go out of his way to antagonize the players." Some of his players also considered their coach to be duplicitous: During training camp Birch glibly espoused the virtues of fast-break basketball to the writers who assembled after every practice, primarily because the promise of playing an up-tempo game would theoretically excite the fans and promote the purchase of season's tickets. The truth, however, was that Birch was a traditionalist who felt that running teams would eventually run right out from under the coach's control. Accordingly, Birch's favorite offensive strategies included various combinations of picks-and-rolls with his guards and forwards, as well as statuesque pivot play. Lumbering lead-footed players such as Foust, Share, Scolari, and even Meineke could thrive in Birch's system. But runners such as Yardley, Hutchins, Sinicola, and Molinas had nowhere to go. Dwight Eddleman neatly summed up Birch's problem thusly: "Birch didn't see eye-to-eye with anyone, not even himself."

Behind his back, the players used to make fun of the way Birch was constantly smoothing out his hair with his hand and sneaking looks at himself in any nearby reflective surface—a mirror, a car window, even a puddle of water. Because of the static puppetlike smile etched on his face, some of the players called him Mortimer Snerd. But the players lived in fear of Birch's high-strung temper. In a fury over mistakes real or imagined, Birch would curse, throw water bottles, or kick ball racks, basketballs, first aid kits, or whatever was within reach and wouldn't kick him back. Birch clearly favored Phillip, Scolari, and Molinas and screamed incessantly at the other players' slightest misstep. Because Hutchins was loathe to fully exert himself in practice sessions, he became Birch's favorite whipping boy.

Only forty-four years old and in tip-top physical condition, Birch would often scrimmage with the team. Charlie Share was also the recipient of much of Birch's scolding, and when the coach laced up his sneakers, the two used to go after each other. Whereas Share would steamroll his coach with colossal picks and prod his ribs with lethal elbows, Birch was forever banging the big man's knees. Birch was only about six two, but he was pretty strong and, to his credit, he never backed down from the much bigger man. Birch would call Share "a big piece of shit" whenever the big man made a bonehead play, and they would routinely threaten each other with mayhem. Birch finally eased up on Share only when the big man finally laid a ham fist up against his antagonist's face and said, "One more time, Coach, and I gotta go to your jaw."

But Molinas knew exactly how to handle Birch and his perpetual blustering. "Jack would always smile at Birch," said Meineke, "and stroke him whenever he could. Of course, the rest of us knew exactly what Jack was doing. Jack was a great one. What a charmer."

The rest of the Pistons feared and detested their coach. Every time one of them chanced to pass a birch tree, they'd make sure to give it a swift kick.

Even more than the personal tensions among the players, and the mutual bitterness with which the team and the coach regarded each other, the Fort Wayne Zollner Pistons had a much more serious problem. "At least four of the players were turning tricks," said a Fort Wayne insider. "Even Birch was betting on ball games. Jack Molinas in Fort Wayne was like a drug addict in an opium den."

With the exhibition season only seven days away, the Pistons had full-scale intrasquad scrimmages on October 9 and 10. Birch expressed particular disappointment with Don Meineke's play and made his first cuts. The practice games were also marked by the debut of a new step-through scoop shot that Molinas had taught to Foust. Although Molinas started for the "Blue" team in the first scrimmage, his performance was surprisingly stiff and uncertain and he was replaced in the second scrimmage by a veteran, Fred Schaus, who had arrived late to camp.

Throughout training camp, and even into the exhibition games and the beginning of the regular season, Birch deliberately neglected the development of his number-one draft pick. The suspicion was that Molinas measured a tad under the six-foot-six requirement that would excuse him from military duty. Birch simply didn't want to waste valuable playing time (and come to depend) on a player who might soon be unavailable.

The Pistons' initial preseason game against the Milwaukee Hawks on Sunday, October 18, was preceded by an exhibition tilt matching the Globetrotters versus the Toledo Mercurys. For the ocassion, Zollner scaled the house up to $2.50. The twin bill, however, was delayed for over an hour because the basketball court was much too slick for the safety of the players. The situation was remedied by liberally dousing the playing surface with gasoline, and then having a dozen maintanance workers get down on their hands and knees to scrub away the excess floor wax.

"Goose Tatum brought down the house with his antics" and the Trotters prevailed as expected. In the second contest, the visiting Milwaukee aggregation featured several interesting players including future Knick coach Red Holzman, rookies Bob Houbregs and Don Sunderlage, and veteran guard Bill Tosheff. For the victorious Pistons, Molinas played behind Meineke and had a poor game (zero for three from the field and a total of only three points). "Don't worry," Molinas told Sinicola after the game. "When the bell rings for real I'll be ready."

Because Hutchins, Meineke, and Molinas were the only single players on the team, they decided to share the expense of renting a house. "I had lived in the YMCA the previous season," Meineke told Phil Berger, "and besides being expensive there was absolutely no privacy there. So we found a nicely furnished six-room house on South Monroe Street that cost us each twenty-five dollars per month."

Each of the three beds were flanked head and foot with decorative wooden boards, so the long-legged players had to sleep diagonally. There was no shower in the bathroom, and since the tub was a scant five feet long they learned to bathe themselves in sections.

Eating out on a regular basis was too extravagant for their modest paychecks, but they occasionally frequented a Chinese restaurant on Main Street that served porterhouse steak dinners for only two dollars. When the trio first went grocery shopping, they filled their shopping cart with pretzels, potato chips, donuts, and, for Molinas's favorite breakfast, containers of sour cream and boxes of frozen strawberries. They also filled their freezer with sirloin steaks and their refrigerator with eggs, orange juice, bread, and potatoes. Meineke was put in charge of the broom and the dust cloth, and Hutchins washed and dried the dishes. Because of his experience at the Eagle Bar, Molinas was elected chef.

"Jack would fix bacon and eggs for breakfast," said Meineke, "and steak and potatoes for dinner. That was about the extent of our menu. While he cooked, Jack would wear an apron so he wouldn't get his pants soiled. Jack was a very personable guy who didn't smoke or drink booze, but he could drink soda pop all day long. His beverage of choice was 7-Up. Jack would also entertain us with stories about all the characters he knew in New York, and he'd show off his incredibly quick hands by catching flies in midair. Jack was a fun guy to be around and we all got along."

One day, Molinas received a letter from home addressed to "Jacob L. Molinas," and his roommates were surprised. Jacob? "Whenever Jack flirted with pretty girls," Meineke noted, "he was liable to tell them that he was French or Spanish or Italian or even German, but he definitely hid the fact that he was Jewish. Well, when I saw the letter, I asked him if he was, in fact, Jewish, and he said he was, but there was a funny expression on his face like he wasn't very comfortable with the question. I asked him if he was ashamed of being Jewish, and he talked about trying to avoid the prejudice that some people seemed to have against Jews. So Hutchins and I both said that Jack's being Jewish was no problem for us. Then Jack said that he'd appreciate it if we didn't call him Jacob, and if we didn't tell any of the other guys about that being his real name. Sure, Jack, no sweat."

Sometimes the roomies would accompany Hutchins to car auctions. "Mel was a motor head," Meineke explained. Or they'd play gin rummy, or go to the movies. When the Pistons were on the road, however, Molinas would abandon his roommates and go off with other friends.

The bachelors three would often host lively parties and invite a surplus of eligible young women. "Frankie Brian would stop by during the day," said Meineke, "and so did George Yardley. Zeke Sinicola was close buddies with Jack and he was around almost every night. But the married guys stayed away from our parties."

Immediately after the Pistons' first preseason game, Molinas and Jim Bredar left for Chicago to practice with a different incarnation of the College All-Stars in preparation for an annual game against the defending NBA champs. The All-Stars were basically the identical squad that had toured against the Trotters, with the notable addition of Walter Dukes, while George Mikan and his Minneapolis Laker playmates represented the NBA. Unfortunately, the collegians were once again coached by Honey Russell, who abhorred hook shooting in general and Molinas's in particular. No surprise, then, that Molinas scored zero points in limited playing time as the Lakers cruised to a 70–65 win.

The following night, October 24, the All-Stars were in Madison Square Garden to play the Knicks. Molinas was psyched to return to the Garden as a bonafide pro and conquering hero, but Coach Russell kept him nailed to the bench. The Knicks easily crushed the All-Stars, and Molinas scored only one point. Molinas felt that Russell had deliberately humiliated him in front of his family and friends.

In the locker room after the game, Joe Hacken offered Molinas some quixotic advice: "When you get back to Fort Wayne, Jack, just make sure to keep your nose clean." Pressed for an explanation, Hacken looked furtively around the room and refused to elaborate.

The Pistons breezed through the remainder of their preseason games, finishing as the only undefeated team in the NBA's "Grapefruit Loop." (Molinas was a spectator until the seventh game in Monroe, Indiana, when he scored seven points in a romp over the Hawks.) Red Auerbach was sufficiently impressed by the Pistons to predict they would usurp the Lakers.

In addition to the difficulties of poor leadership and vicious infighting, the NBA owners compounded their problems by agreeing to an unwieldy seventy-two-game schedule. Because of an expanded program of crowd-pleasing all-NBA doubleheaders, each team only played twenty-seven home games. And since Fred Zollner had a luxurious summer home in Coral Gables, five of the Pistons' "home" games were scheduled in the new Miami Beach Auditorium. That meant Fort Wayne would be playing fifty ball games on unfamiliar courts, a distinct disadvantage.

Nevertheless, spirits were high in Fort Wayne when the Pistons opened the season with two home-court wins, against Milwaukee (77–67) on November 2, and three days later against the Boston Celtics (83–79). Although Molinas never left the bench he could easily see how much more intensity the players brought to the regular season. There were a total of eighty free throws attempted in the first game, and sixty-five in the second, but despite the large number of fouls called, the games were so physical that they were almost brutal. Had the officials whistled every true foul, each team would have shot upward of 150 free throws per game. The refs operating principle seemed to be "No blood, no foul."

George Yardley was alarmed by the savagery of the competition. "Basketball players were a dime a dozen in those days," Yardley said, "so the referees let everybody whale on each other. I can remember one game later in my career when, in the middle of the second quarter, I took an elbow to my forehead and needed thirty stitches to close the wound. I'm sure I had a minor concussion as well, but the coach still forced me to take my regular turn in the second half. During the six seasons that I played in the NBA, I had over a hundred stitches in my face alone. Nowadays, the NBA players are much more valuable commodities, so the referees protect them. We were just meat."

Another problem with the referees was the lack of definitive direction from the league office. Sports journalist Leonard Koppett provided the particulars:

> Officials did not know whether to "let 'em play or call 'em close." Podoloff waffled. Chuck Chuckovits, who worked both NBA and college ball, recalled that the officials were reminded that the players had been All-Americans and the college rulebook would be used. Following this directive, Chuckovits and Jim Enright refereed a game ... with around 80 fouls. The following day, they received a telegram from Maurice Podoloff charging them with using a high-school standard and suggesting they need not be so technical. The following night they called only three fouls, which also displeased the higher-ups. Both Enright and Chuckovits eventually left for the more moderate world of the Big Ten.

Whatever their instructions from Podoloff, the referees knew enough to do their part to ensure good crowds by always favoring the home team.

After the two home wins, the Pistons next traveled to Rochester in upstate New York. Most teams traveled by bus wherever possible, or by train. They only rarely took commercial airplane flights. But the Pistons had a wonderful advantage over the other NBA teams because of Fred Zollner's private aircraft, a DC-3B with a heavy 220 engine and booster rockets to help lift it out of dinky airstrips. Since his team had use of the plane, "the Flying Z," Fort Wayne always had the worst schedule in the league. After all, the other owners reasoned, the Pistons weren't bound by the commercial airline's limited schedules.

Zollner frequently traveled with his team, and the Flying Z was divided into two equal sections, fore and aft. The luxuriously appointed front cabin was for Zollner's private use and it contained a bar, two reclining easy chairs, a sofa, and a picture window. The rear cabin consisted of three small cubicles, each with a small card table and four chairs, and was reserved for the coach and the players. "Fred Zollner was the biggest cocksman in the world," said a former player. "While all the guys sat in the back packed like sardines, he'd be up in the front with one of his blond girlfriends."

The standard procedure was for Zollner to be the first one to board the plane and the first one to get off, leaving his players to wait impatiently while he sometimes dallied.

Sometimes Zollner would venture into the rear compartment, point to one of the players, and invite him into the front for a "little talk." The fortunate player was then permitted to stretch out on the sofa and be overwhelmed with gratitude. "It was just another way of showing us that he had all the power," said Larry Foust.

Molinas spent most of the plane trips by himself, either snoozing as best he could or reading newspapers and magazines. Occasionally he played low-stakes poker with Foust, Hutchins, and Scolari.

The Pistons suffered their first loss in Molinas's NBA debut at Rochester on November 7. The game was a rout from the opening tip, with the Royals extending to a 47–25 lead just before halftime.

Lester Harrison was the Royals' owner and coach, whose first business venture was selling fruits and vegetables from a pushcart. Perhaps because of his humble beginnings, Harrison used to brag to his fellow owners that he could run his team for less money than they could run theirs. That's why teams visiting Rochester never got the traditional orange quarters to slake their thirst during halftime intermissions.

With the game clearly a blowout, Birch finally unleashed Molinas in the third quarter, and the rookie responded by scoring eight points. His tricky pivot work and drives to the bucket forced the Royals to repeatedly hack him, and Molinas's total included six free throws. In spite of the ferocious play and the bone-on-bone brutality, Molinas realized that his superior speed would allow him to avoid contact with the bigger, slower players who were assigned to defend him. It was as though Molinas and the guards were playing a different game than the forwards and centers—a quicker, smarter game, where skill and finesse could overcome brute force.

After the game, Les Harrison sniffed around the Pistons' locker room to make sure nobody had swiped any basketballs.

The Flying Z was grounded by bad weather, so Birch and his players were forced to take an overnight train back to Fort Wayne. They arrived in Waterloo, Indiana, at 9:00 A.M. on Sunday morning and were understandably not in top form for their afternoon game against the Knicks.

Before a meager crowd of 3,957, the exhausted Pistons couldn't piss in the ocean and shot only thirty-two percent from the field, losing 75–70. The Pistons had to laugh, though, at the Knicks' Al McGuire and his low-cut sneakers, a style no one had ever seen before. But the game was close, and with both Meineke and Yardley sluggish, Molinas received significant minutes. He responded with five points and an excellent floor game.

Next up was a crucial test for the Pistons—a matchup against the mighty Lakers in the first half of a doubleheader at Milwaukee. Mikan, the NBA's most potent pivotman, suffered a jammed finger on his shooting hand early in the game and was useless thereafter, shooting one for ten from the floor and scoring only three points. For the Pistons, subpar performances by Phillip and Scolari were offset by Meineke's nineteen points and the stout defense of Larry Foust. The Pistons won in a walk, 78–62, and Molinas scored two points in a cameo appearance. With their humbling of the champs, the Pistons seemed ready to take over the league.

On the road with the Pistons, Molinas gradually earned the respect, and even admiration, of an increasing number of his teammates. "Nobody could beat him at card playing," said Hutchins, "whether it was gin or pinochle. And he eased the pain of losing to him with all of his fast-talking patter. Jack was always on the lookout for action of any kind. When we stopped in an airport, he'd want to pitch pennies against the wall. Whatever the rest of the guys felt about him, they appreciated that Jack kept everybody loose and laughing."

His teammates were also impressed whenever Molinas picked up the check for a meal on the road. Molinas dressed well, and ate well, and seemed to have more money in his pocket than he was supposed to have. The other Pistons laughed indulgently when Molinas took every opportunity to be horizontal—lying down on the floor of the plane, or the locker room, or a basketball court, or even a restaurant. "I've got to stay stretched," the rookie said, "so Uncle Sam won't want me." There was a certain naivete about Molinas that disarmed even the most cynical veterans.

With a record of 6–3, the Pistons were in first place in the Western Division and a half game ahead of the Lakers. Their December 18 meeting with Minneapolis (in the first half of a twin bill in Buffalo) would be a critical contest for both the Pistons and their confident but as yet unproven rookie from Columbia.

Before the game, Molinas proposed a small wager to Meineke—five dollars on whether or not Molinas would score ten points. Not only was Molinas a rookie and a nonstarter, but he appeared to be buried deep on the Pistons' bench, so Meineke readily agreed.

Meineke, however, had an atrocious ball game, and his replacement (Yardley) quickly committed three fouls, so Birch dispatched Molinas into the game late in the first period. Guarding Molinas was Vern Mikkelsen, a six-foot-seven, 240-pound body cruncher, but the brash rookie ran rings around the veteran, and even had the gall to laugh at the ease with which he could score. Lakers coach John Kundla was forced to switch the quick-footed Jim Pollard onto Molinas, and the rookie's point parade ran into a temporary roadblock.

At the half, Minneapolis led 35–34, and Birch went off on one of his locker room tirades—inaccurate field-goal shooting being the topic that evening. Birch overturned a tray of quartered oranges and kicked a wastebasket across the room, all the while screaming about "concentration" and "being ready to play." Several of the veteran players, however, were fed up with their coach's hotheaded behavior and thought they'd teach him a lesson. Hustling into the locker room before Birch appeared, they emptied the ball bag and inserted a heavyweight cylinder filled with compressed air that was used to inflate the balls. When Birch got around to kicking the ball bag, he yowled in pain and nearly broke his big toe. But even though Birch limped for a week, he never once complained about the stunt nor tried to discover which cowardly bastards had done the deed. Birch would prove that he was tougher than his players.

Riding a ten-point spurt by Clyde Lovelette, the Lakers took control of the game midway through the third quarter, and Birch put his subs back on the court. Molinas always kept a running total of his points, and with his team trailing by seventeen with less than a minute to go in the game, he was fouled in the act of shooting and sent to the free-throw line for two shots. The first rippled the net and gave Molinas ten points. As he prepared to unloosen the second shot, Molinas suddenly turned to the Pistons bench and flashed Meineke a tooth-gleaming smile. The bet was for ten points, right? Not nine, not eleven. Molinas then proceeded to shoot his final (and to him superfluous) free throw high into the air and over the backboard.

Later, back in the locker room, Molinas smiled again as he accepted a five-dollar bill from Meineke. "I always know where I am," Molinas said. "Right on the money."

Money was also on Joe Hacken's mind when he spoke to Molinas the following morning after the Pistons had flown to Syracuse. Molinas was in the habit of calling Joe before every game just to let him know if anything unusual was happening. Maybe somebody had an injury that nobody else knew about. Maybe somebody was on a hot streak, or else couldn't hit the side of a barn. Joe would tell Jack what the point spread was, just checking with him to see if it was realistic or maybe out of whack. But that morning in Syracuse, Joe had a bulletin for Jack's ears only. It seemed that Joe knew one of Frankie Carbo's guys who had a contact on the Fort Wayne Pistons, and three of his teammates were doing business: Andy Phillip, Larry Foust, and Freddie Scolari. Joe said that the going rate for an NBA game was about twenty thousand dollars, and he told Jack that his teammates were each getting twenty-five hundred smackers plus whatever they bet for every game they worked. Joe's friend was over twelve thousand ahead before the game even started! Jack was not particularly surprised because there were rumors all over the league about a lot of teams. He had even had suspicions of his own. Even though Phillip was a great passer, every once in a while he would hit Jack square in his back with an intentionally errant pass and then blame him for screwing up.

Some forty-five years after the fact, Andy Phillip vehemently denied ever being in league with gamblers. "No," said Phillip. "No way. I was never involved. I don't know where a story like that could come from because I never knew Molinas that well to begin with. No, sir. Not me. Never, ever, ever."

Red Auerbach also debunked Molinas's testimony: "I don't buy that. You know what it sounds like Molinas was up to? 'Misery loves company.' Molinas was trying to give the impression that other players were doing what he was doing just to make himself look good."

On the other hand, Bill Tosheff reported, "The word was definitely out around the NBA that several of the Fort Wayne players, including Andy Phillip, were occasionally throwing games away." Several other NBAers reported hearing the very same word.

Maybe the truth is beyond recall.

Only this much is certain—the Fort Wayne Pistons played the Syracuse Nationals at the War Memorial Auditorium on November 18, 1953, before a crowd that was estimated at three thousand, in a game won by the home team, 79–76. Jack remembered the following:

"So Joe said to me, 'You're in a dump today, Jack, and there's no way you're going to win this game. The price is Syracuse minus five points, and they're laying the five till the cows come home.' Joe had one thing wrong: There was so much Syracuse money bet on the game that the price closed at eight points.

"Anyway, the game got under way and Birch put me in early because Meineke was laying bombs. Right away, I was out running downcourt on fast break when Phillip was at it again, throwing me a pass that hit me in the back of my head. A few plays later, he threw a pass off my foot. 'Andy,' I said to him, 'what the hell's going on?' But he didn't answer. Then another pass from Phillip bounced off my knee.

"That's when Birch pulled me out of the game, saying, 'Jack, what's the matter with you? You look terrible out there. You're slouching. You're not alert. I've never seen your reflexes so slow.' There was nothing I could say to him.

"So I sat back on the bench and watched. It was horrible. All the misplays were so obvious. It was like a slapstick game. We were down thirty-nine to twenty at the half. Twenty points in twenty-four minutes of play for what was supposed to be one of the best teams in the NBA. It was embarrassing.

"We were losing by about sixteen points going into the fourth quarter and the game was all but lost. And who was in the game? Phillip, Scolari, Foust, Meineke, and Hutchins. That's when Birch called me over and told me to go in for Meineke. And I really didn't want to play at all, because I knew that the other guys would only make me look like a jerk. So I walked over to my roommate, Mel Hutchins, and I said, 'Listen, Mel, it's two against eight out here. We're down by sixteen. Let's see what we can do. When you grab a rebound, forget about passing to anybody else except for me. Got it? It's just you and me against everybody else.'

"'What do you mean?' he said.

"'Just give me the ball, Mel. Just do like I said, and I'll draw you a picture after the game.'"

For the next ten minutes, Molinas received pass after pass from Hutchins and drove to the hoop. If Molinas couldn't create an acceptable shot, he'd pass back to Hutchins, receive a return pass, and then try again. "Hey," Foust shouted to Molinas. "Pass the ball!" The rookie could only laugh. "You want the ball, Larry?" he finally said. "Then go get an offensive rebound." But there weren't many offensive rebounds to be had as Molinas hooked, drove, forced the Nationals to foul him and unilaterally pushed the Pistons back into the ball game.

"He was just phenomenal," said Dolph Schayes. "It really looked like Molinas could score at will. But don't blame me. Earl Lloyd was guarding Molinas and I was guarding Hutchins."

With forty-eight seconds left in the game, Molinas maneuvered past Lloyd for a twisting layup that brought Fort Wayne within one point, 75–74, but that was to be their high-water mark. Schayes was fouled and converted his free throw; then, after Phillip missed a shot, Andy Kenville made a three-point play. A meaningless bucket by Foust at the buzzer produced the final margin.

Through the first three periods of the game, Molinas had totaled only four points. But he ended up with twenty-four, good enough to give the rookie a temporary line in the NBA record book (until he was supplanted by Wilt Chamberlain six years later) for most points scored in a single quarter.

After the game, Foust, Phillip, and Scolari all came over and shook Jack's hand and told him what a great game he had played. He had finally gained their respect and established himself as an outstanding professional player. But he could also see in their faces that they were furious at him—he had cost them their money.

Nearly twenty years later, when the record-breaking Syracuse game had become a blurry memory, and the truth had become a casualty of self-justifying lies, Molinas told a friend named Elliot Ableson about another postgame locker room conversation: "Jack rounded up Foust, Phillip, and Scolari and said to them, 'Hey, guys. I know you're dumping, and I want in.'"

Four days after the Syracuse game, the Pistons were scheduled to play the Rochester Royals in the second game of a doubleheader at Fort Wayne. When his customary pregame call to Joe Hacken revealed that there was no contract on the contest, Molinas had a brainstorm. As long as Foust, Phillip, and Scolari were going to be on the level, why didn't he bet a few dollars on the game and pick up some expense money? The problem was where to place the bet. Joe could have handled it, but Jack wasn't planning to wager enough to make it worth Joe's while. Then Jack remembered Stanley the Rat, and how he used to beg for something to be thrown his way. So, as a favor to him, Molinas called up Stanley the Rat at his father's candy store. Stanley told him that the Pistons were five-point favorites. "Okay," Jack said. "Just for kicks, put me down for two hundred dollars on Fort Wayne minus five points. And win or lose, we'll settle up at the end of the season." Stanley was extremely thankful and said that Jack could trust him through thick and thin.

With Meineke off to an uninspired beginning, Molinas played most of the game and scored fifteen points as the Pistons edged Rochester, 83–82. Fort Wayne failed to cover the spread and Molinas was out two hundred dollars.

On Thanksgiving Day, the Pistons were in Milwaukee to face the Hawks, losers of ten straight and a six-point underdog. On the road, Molinas often roomed with Sinicola, who knew there was something screwy with the team. "I remember one day," said Sinicola, "Jack walked into the locker room before a game and said, 'Okay, boys, how are we going to do today?' Man, you could see the terror in everybody's eyes when he said that. I pulled Jack over to one side and I said, 'What the heck are you doing?' He just shrugged it off and said, 'Don't worry about it, everybody bets.' And because I roomed with him, I'd hear him making telephone calls from our hotel room. He was betting on NFL games, college football, and college basketball, whatever he could bet he'd bet. He'd bet on a cockroach hitting the border of Mexico before the siesta set in. So one day up in the hotel room I asked him point-blank, 'Jack, you're not betting on any of the Pistons games, are you?' He said, 'No, and that's the honest truth.' But he was a chronic bettor and couldn't help himself."

By now, if Meineke didn't get off to a good start, Birch had no hesitations about yanking him in favor of Molinas—yet despite Molinas's twenty-two-point outburst, the lowly Hawks beat the Pistons 64–58. The *Fort Wayne Journal-*

Gazette reported that Molinas's "sensational play sparked a closing rally that made a potential rout into a rootin'-tootin' finish." Among them, Scolari, Phillip, and Foust combined for twenty-two points, which was eleven below the total number of points per game they usually scored. So, given the point spread, the loss, the subnormal production by three otherwise reliable players, and the fact that Molinas did not bet this game with Ratensky—could the game have been rigged?

The very next night, Scolari, Phillip, and Foust shared thirty-one points (and twenty assists), Molinas bet the Pistons minus eight points, and the Pistons trimmed Milwaukee 78–64. In addition to scoring eleven points, Molinas thrilled the hometown fans with his fancy passing and was credited with thirteen assists.

After the game, Hutchins, Meineke, and Molinas hosted another party that was attended by several of the visiting Hawks. "It was a wild night," said Meineke. "One of the Hawks was a guy named Bobby Harrison, who happened to be half Indian. Well, some of us were in our cups and we egged him on while Harrison stripped to his waist, turned over a bucket and beat it like a tom-tom. Then he did a war dance complete with all kinds of weird chanting. There was a lot of camaraderie between all the players in the league that doesn't exist anymore. And that camaraderie was one of the reasons why playing in the NBA was worthwhile."

The next morning, when the Pistons arrived at their hotel in Baltimore, Fred Zollner had arranged for a surprise. "We got in at about two in the morning," Andy Phillip told Phil Berger, "and there was a troupe of entertainers waiting for us in the lobby. A violin player, a guitar player, and a clarinetist. There was even a dancer there, too. In his own strange fashion, I think Zollner was trying to motivate us, or at least get our minds off of being tired. So he sat there with a big grin on his face while the entertainers performed right there in the lobby, and even though the players would've much rather been in bed, we had to sit there and make believe we were having a great time."

Molinas loved every aspect of life in the NBA. The fame, the women, and especially the constant traveling. A new city every day. A new restaurant every night. A new ball game. A new opponent to humiliate. A new group of hostile fans to stupefy into an awed silence.

On the other hand, most NBA players hated everything about playing on the road. Bill Tosheff still can't forget the hardships of trying to win away from home:

"The parquet floor at the Boston Garden had to be the worst floor in the league. Chasing Cousy and Bill Sharman around in that damn place, you'd get shinsplints because the floor was so hard. And whenever you fell, you'd get a painful floor burn. Madison Square Garden was a makeshift floor loaded with dead spots. Guys on the Knicks would try to herd you over to a dead spot and then snatch the ball while you were waiting for it to bounce back up into your hand. The courts in Baltimore and Philadelphia were also old portable floors that could unexpectedly kill your dribble. Add the courts, the mean-spirited fans, and the homer referees, and it's no wonder that visiting teams had to play good enough to win by twenty in order to escape with a five-point victory."[1]

Fort Wayne split its next two games—an 83–69 at-home thrashing of Philadelphia, and a 92–69 loss at Rochester—with Molinas totaling eighteen points. The Pistons' record was a disappointing 9–8 and they were tied with the Royals for second place in the Western Division, two games behind Minneapolis.

"Hello?"

"Stanley. It's me. Us against Boston tonight. What's the number?"

"You guys minus four."

"I'll take it."

"For how much?"

"A dime."

"You got it. Thanks, Jack. I really appreciate it."

"No problem. Give my regards to your father, will you?"

"Sure thing."

"Bye."

Molinas scored thirteen points and won his wager as Fort Wayne prevailed, 76–70. Then he tried to prepare for the showdown he'd been dreading all season long.

On December 4, Molinas was scheduled to undergo a physical examination to determine his military draft status. Fred Zollner had used his considerable influence to switch his prize rookie's draft board from Fort Wayne to Indianapolis, which had a higher rate of enlistees and therefore a much lower quota of draftees. On the morning of his appointment, Molinas visited a chiropractor to have his spine stretched.

The Pistons were scheduled to play the Knicks in Madison Square Garden that evening. The whole team flew to Indianapolis and waited in the airport while Jack went for the examination.

The limit for the army was six foot six, but this barrier had to be cleared by a half inch. Jack was six six and a quarter in his stocking feet, so he was right in the middle. He was prepared for the measurement. He wore an old, sagging pair of athletic socks that would conceal the fact that he was raising himself just a little bit on his toes. But one of the first things they did at the center was to make him take off his socks. He still did manage to raise his heels a little just as he was being measured. The verdict: six six and a half, and the doctor classified him 4-F. Jack's parting question was, "Doctor, is this classification subject to change?" It was, but only if Jack shrank.

All the fellows on the team congratulated him, although Meineke didn't seem so happy because he knew Jack would be getting more and more of his playing time. Jack was thinking the same thing—that he was now a full-fledged member of the team with no shadow hanging over his head, and that Birch would have to start playing him more.

"Sure enough," Jack said, "Birch called me into the front section where he'd been sitting with Mister Zollner and discussing strategy for that evening's ball game. 'Jack,' said Birch, 'Mister Zollner and I have been discussing your case, and we've decided that we're going to give you an opportunity to start the game tonight.'"

The Knicks' coach, Joe Lapchick, had already stoked the Pistons' ire by describing Fort Wayne as a "whistle stop" entry in big-time basketball. And Lapchick's game plan was to have six-foot-six, 230-pound Harry "the Horse" Gallatin guard Molinas and use his experienced elbows to raise some lumps on the rookie's chest.

Sticking to Birch's orders, Molinas began the game playing on the perimeter. But then, after connecting with two long push-shots, Molinas couldn't avoid the challenge any longer and drove headlong toward the basket. Gallatin tensed and prepared to blast the audacious rookie to smithereens, but Molinas deftly spun away and scored a layup. On the Pistons' next possession, Molinas smiled even as he dropped a hook shot through the basket over Gallatin's futile defense. More and more, Molinas began wresting rebounds away from Gallatin, until Lapchick had seen enough and sent Jimmy Baechtold—a smaller but quicker player—in for the Knicks hatchet man.

Jack remembered that night vividly: "Oh, was I happy. To play a good game against the Knicks in a packed house at the Garden? But I once again had some trouble with my teammates. When I took Baechtold into the pivot, Foust started yelling at me, 'Get out of there, Jack! I'm the pivot man on this team!' And when I grabbed a rebound and pushed the ball hard down the middle of the court, Phillip started screaming: 'You're not a guard! Give me the ball and get out on the wing! It's my job to lead the fast break!' Any place I went, there was a guy there yelling at me to go play somewhere else."

Molinas's fifteen points keyed the Pistons to a resounding 92–73 victory.

After the game, Molinas had a visitor in the locker room—Ray Miller, one of the Kaiser Park regulars who was a little down on his luck. "I asked Jack if he could help me out," said Miller, "and he reached into his pocket and pulled out a wad of bills. 'Sure,' he said. 'How much do you need?' I said that fifty bucks would tide me over. I was feeling kind of embarrassed anyway, and also doubtful that he could really help me out, because fifty dollars was a lot of money in those days. But he just peeled a fat fifty off of his roll and handed it to me without saying word one about when I would have to pay it back. Jack was always very generous whenever one of his friends got into a tight spot."

To celebrate Molinas's festive homecoming, several of the Pistons were invited to a late-night dinner at his parents' apartment in the Bronx. All of the players were impressed with Betty's cooking, Louis's good manners, and Peggy Eisenhower's graceful beauty. "What a wonderful family," Frankie Brian enthused. "With a background like that, it was no wonder that Jack was such a jolly fellow. I was also under the impression that Jack and his girlfriend were very much in love."

The hardened New York sports scribes were also taken with Molinas. They proposed that "the wise-cracking" Molinas was the best ballplayer to come out of the "big town" since Dolph Schayes, and the NBA's most accomplished rookie since Bob Cousy. Several writers also zapped the Knicks management for wasting their top draft selection on Walter Dukes, who, as Jimmy Powers noted in the *Daily News*, "has been anything but sensational with the Trotters, and has developed a little temperament."

The Knicks' front office was desperate to get Molinas into their lineup. A Jewish boy from the Bronx? The turnstiles would certainly spin out a merry tune. The Pistons were offered a neat package for the rookie—thirty-five thousand dollars plus Vince Boryla, a dependable set shooter and double-digit scorer. "We're not at all interested in trading Molinas," said Zollner. "Our plan is for him to remain in Fort Wayne for the rest of his career."

The Pistons, however, did make one roster move, waiving veteran forward Fred Schaus, who had been the team's insurance policy in the event Molinas was found fit for military duty. As Molinas's playing time increased, something also had to be done to stabilize the rookie's off-court behavior, and he was therefore assigned a new roommate for road trips, Frankie Brian.

Certain of Molinas's habits puzzled his new roomie. "He'd want to bet on anything," Brian said. "I can't even remember how many times he wanted to bet on which raindrop would reach the bottom of the window first. That seemed to be a favorite wager of his. The most unusual thing he did, though, was he'd talk to what he said was his girlfriend before every game and just about have the same conversation. Either he'd tell her, 'Well, heck, we're going to win tonight. Everybody on the team's feeling real good.' Or else he'd say, 'Some of the boys are feeling sick and we just can't get up for tonight's game.' It almost seemed like some kind of code, and until the whole deal fell through the floor, shoot, I couldn't rightly figure out what was going on."

With Molinas now in the starting lineup, the Pistons beat Syracuse at Fort Wayne. Molinas scored nine points and won another bet with Ratensky.

On December 9, the Pistons humbled the Warriors in Philadelphia, 83–69, and Molinas notched ten points. After the game, Molinas treated his old Columbia roommate, Paul Brandt, to dinner at a very expensive restaurant. "He was really spending money like a drunken sailor," said Brandt, "so I called him on it. 'Jack, where are you getting all this money?' Of course, the first thing he said was, 'Don't worry.' Then he said, 'I've been betting on the Pistons to win. Just penny ante bets, Paul, but they keep my interest level up. The bets help me jump higher and play a little harder. This way I can also send my whole paycheck home to my parents. It's no big deal, Paul. Believe me, there are dozens of guys all over the league that are betting on their own teams to win.'"

Fort Wayne next lost a home game to the Knicks (twenty points for Molinas and a hundred dollars lost to Ratensky), before flying to New York. If Molinas was, in fact, also dumping an occasional ball game, the Pistons-Celtics contest at Madison Square Garden on December 15, 1953, would have been a likely occasion.

The morning line favored the Celtics by three and a half, but as the game drew nigh, more and more bettors were backing Boston and the spread zoomed up to six and a half points before the local bookies stopped taking bets about an hour before game time.

Molinas started out like a house on fire, scoring eighteen points in the first half as the Pistons raced to a 40–29 lead. But the second half was another story. Later, Birch reported that "a stranger" had tried to enter the Pistons' dressing room during halftime, saying that he had to speak to Molinas. When the stranger was denied admittance, he scribbled a note and requested that it be passed to Molinas—the note read "Joe sent me."

Molinas played so poorly early in the second half that Birch had to put him on the bench. "Jack," said Birch, "what the hell's the matter?" Molinas informed Birch that he'd been out partying with some friends, that he hadn't slept all night long, and that he'd "run out of gas." In his absence, Phillip, Scolari, and Foust played slop-ball and the Celtics fought their way back into contention. However, Molinas consented to enter the fray with less than a minute remaining and proceeded to commit two fouls ("both of them crudely intentional," said a local sportswriter) against Cousy that brought the Celtics three easy points and boosted their final margin to 82–75.

Molinas had led Fort Wayne with twenty points, but his erratic performance was immediately suspect. As was his wont, Fred Zollner sat on the Pistons' bench during the game and couldn't help being suspicious of the rookie's performance. When questioned by Zollner, Molinas denied receiving any note, and claimed instead that a friend had contacted him to let him know that he had a date with a girl that evening.

The next day, Ike Gellis, sports editor of the *New York Post*, was clued in by several bookmakers who'd taken a bath in the game that henceforth the Pistons games were off the boards. The national betting syndicate bosses in Minneapolis were likewise convinced that the Pistons' recent effort against Boston was so unsavory that no further morning lines would be issued for any of their subsequent ballgames. Gellis tipped off Podoloff, who in turn informed a detective in

DA Hogan's office. As a result, wire taps were placed on the home telephones of all of the Pistons players.

The Pistons flew on to Boston, where they were massacred the next day, 91–74. Shut out in the first half, Fort Wayne's "fast-moving rookie from Columbia bagged sixteen points in the last two periods to lead the scoring." The Pistons then flew home for two days of hard practice sessions before heading to Milwaukee. During the Pistons' short stay in Fort Wayne, Zeke Sinicola had a profound epiphany:

"I wasn't stupid," Sinicola explained, "so I knew exactly what was going on. But I wasn't in any way interested in dumping games because I understood what the consequences were. And for me, playing professional basketball was like playing out a dream. The point is that the dream was strong for me, but it wasn't as strong for Jack, and that's why he got fucked up."

Molinas had a miserable game against the last-place Hawks, scoring only nine points as the Pistons won, 69–63, but didn't cover the spread. One of Milwaukee's substitutes was Irv Bemoras, who had been a teammate of Molinas's with the College All-Stars. "There was Jack on the free-throw line late in the game," said Bemoras, "and he shot the ball like he was heaving a shot put. Bang! The ball bounced high off the backboard. And I yelled out, 'Jack, what's going on?' He just shrugged and flashed me one of his 'don't worry' smiles. It was clear that there was something improper happening, and I remember being shocked. After the game, when I asked him about it again, he giggled like a little boy, shrugged his shoulders, and said nothing."

On December 20, the Pistons were 14–10 and trailing the Western Division–leading Lakers by two games, when they traded Charlie Share to Milwaukee for veteran guard Max Zaslofsky. At least one of the Pistons was less than thrilled by the deal: "Max was a fine ballplayer, but the only person he cared about was Max. The last thing we needed was another selfish player." On Christmas night, Zaslofsky scored fifteen points, Molinas had sixteen (plus a winning hundred-dollar wager), and the Pistons slaughtered the Celtics in Fort Wayne, 108–79.

The Pistons left for Minneapolis immediately after the Celtic game for the first of three consecutive contests with the Lakers. Zollner stayed behind in Fort Wayne to deal with a pressing business matter. The day after Christmas they beat the Lakers 77-71, with Molinas scoring sixteen points and limiting the muscular Mikkelsen to just five. The very next night, the Lakers won another grueling battle, 79–75, this time in Fort Wayne. Sealing the verdict was the miserable play of Phillip, Scolari, and Foust, who shot a combined seven for twenty-six from the field and totaled only seventeen points. Molinas wasn't much better, ending up with four points. After the game, the Pistons returned to Minneapolis, once again without Zollner.

Unfortunately, the Pistons were also battling among themselves. Zollner got wind of the team's discontent, flew up to Minneapolis, and called them together to hear their grievances: Meineke was sulking about losing his starting slot to Molinas. Fred Schaus had been reactivated and was similarly bitching about his lack of playing time. Yardley was out of action with a hyperextended elbow and studiously avoided any contact with his teammates. Foust was still shouting at Molinas to vacate the pivot, but had escalated the argument by throwing elbows at the rookie. And Andy Phillip, who'd often have a few postgame beers with Birch, was also complaining about Molinas. "One night Jack would get a lot of points and rebounds," Phillip said. "But the next time out he wouldn't do anything. His inconsistency was really hurting us." Phillip also voiced several of his teammates' disapproval of Birch's game-time substitutions.

After the players had their say, Zollner delivered a pep talk. It was okay for a player to be unhappy sitting on the bench, Zollner told them. Any player who was satisfied not playing wasn't worth his salt. Sure, Molinas was inconsistent and undisciplined, but he was, after all, a mere rookie. Zollner counseled patience and trust. Privately, however, Zollner also made a decision to fire Birch immediately after the season.

The team remained in Minneapolis for two days, practicing and preparing for their third tilt against the mighty Lakers. And on December 27, Zollner called Molinas into his hotel room for a heart-to-heart. Only ten days ago, Molinas had been quizzed by Zollner (and Birch) about his questionable conduct during the Celtics game in New York. Now, with all those awful yet persistent rumors of shavings and dumpings still ringing in his ears, Zollner asked Molinas point-blank if he had been betting on any of the Pistons' games. Molinas fervently denied doing anything that would dishonor himself or the team. "I'll take your word for it," Zollner said. "But I warn you, watch your step."

Meineke saw Molinas directly following this meeting and reported that the rookie wasn't especially upset. In truth, there are few if any warnings that can change the mindset of an addict. And while Molinas certainly loved playing basketball, he was totally addicted to gambling.

On December 28, the following item appeared in Ike Gellis's "Working Press" column in the *New York Post*: "Wonder what's going on in the Fort Wayne games? Most bookies won't deal with them."

Then, buoyed perhaps by Zollner's soothing words of encouragement, and undoubtedly determined to discredit the scandalous rumors, the Pistons played their best game of the season:

> MINNEAPOLIS, Minn., Dec. 30—The Zollner Pistons sparkled like the Northern Lights here tonight as they blasted the Minneapolis Lakers, 97–80, ending their own slump and snapping the Lakers' 16-game winning streak on the Auditorium floor.

> Eight of the nine Piston players who took part in the rout of the champions contributed to the scoring with rookie Jack Molinas setting the pace. He collected 17 points, one more than sharpshooting Max Zaslofsky.

But the rumors were not so easily dispelled. Before the Pistons took on the Philadelphia Warriors in a New Year's Eve game at Indianapolis, Zollner told the players that everybody on the team was being investigated. Molinas just smiled and shook his head. He knew that whomever the investigators were they were bound to be bozos, and wherever they looked they would find nothing. Foust, Phillip, and Scolari were probably shitting in their pants, but Molinas? What the hell did he have to worry about? A few pissant bets on the Pistons to win? Bah! What a joke.

> INDIANAPOLIS, Ind., Dec. 31—The Zollner Pistons welcomed the advent of the new year tonight with a ringing 83–56 victory over the Philadelphia Warriors. It was the Pistons' second straight road game triumph and moved them within a half game of second place in the Western Division of the National Basketball Association.
>
> The Zs were led by Larry Foust's 17 points, as well as 11 each for rookie Jack Molinas and veteran guard Max Zaslofsky.

The clock was running down on Molinas's NBA career: A January 2 overtime loss to the Royals at Rochester, wherein Molinas scored ten points. A January 3 loss to the Knicks in Fort Wayne in which Molinas went scoreless. That same day, the *Fort Wayne Journal-Gazette* published the results of a poll in which its readers had voted for the most popular Pistons of all-time—Larry Foust was number one, Andy Phillip number three, and the newest Piston of them all, Jack Molinas, was number nine.

On January 4, 1954, the *New York Post* received an anonymous letter that bore a Bronx postmark. The letter charged that Jack Molinas was telephoning bets to a friend in the neighborhood in which the ballplayer used to live. The newspaper turned the letter over to Frank Hogan's office, where the case was assigned to Chief Assistant DA George Tilzer. As a result, detectives set up a watch on the candy store owned by Stanley Ratensky's father, on a poolroom where the letter said Ratensky placed Molinas's bets, and on a neighborhood bar and grill.

Hogan's office also notified Podoloff, who immediately hired a private investigator. Podoloff next informed Zollner, who also hired his own private investigator and had Molinas's long distance-phone calls traced. Within hours, Zollner was able to report to Podoloff that Molinas had made innumerable calls to Ratensky's candy store, and several more to Stanley Ratensky's Bronx apartment.

On the afternoon of January 5, Zollner summoned Molinas to the Pistons' office in the Coliseum. "You're being watched very carefully, Jack," Zollner said. "In fact, your telephone at home is being tapped. If you were smart, you'd keep a very low profile." Molinas once more protested his innocence, but he was too smart to ever keep a low profile. As soon as he arrived home, he called Stanley Ratensky and bet a hundred dollars that the Pistons would defeat the Nationals that very evening.

Again, Molinas figured that Zollner was after bigger game than some piker who was betting spare change on his own team to win.

While Podoloff, Zollner, and Tilzer continued their respective investigations, Birch was instructed to continue to give Molinas his normal playing time as if nothing was wrong. On January 5, Molinas had twelve points in a 72–60 loss to Syracuse in Fort Wayne. The last bet that Molinas made as an active player was a losing one.

On January 6, Larry Foust, Mel Hutchins, and Jack Molinas were named to the Western Division All-Star team that would face off against the best players in the East on January 21 on the hallowed hardwood in Madison Square Garden. In Baltimore that night, Molinas celebrated by scoring eleven points in a 90–78 clobbering of the Bullets. Molinas played his last NBA game on January 7, 1954—a 79–67 loss to the home-standing Syracuse Nationals. Molinas scored only seven points.

At that point, the Pistons record stood at 18–17, which placed them third in their division, three and a half games behind Rochester and four games behind the Lakers. So far, all the preseason predictions of glory, all the expectations of competitive zest had been smothered in a rising tide of deliberate mediocrity.

At practice the next day, the team was buzzing over the rumor that it was under investigation. Larry Foust stopped Jack and said, "Word is that we're all going to be taken down to the police station and interrogated. Jack, what'll we do?"

Molinas told Larry there was nothing to worry about and kept on practicing. Nothing for *him* to worry about, but plenty for Larry and the others to worry about, right? Zollner had already warned Jack about one of his so-called investigations and what had come of it? Nothing.

NOTE

1. *Vintage NBA* p. 171.

NBA Commissioner Maurice Podoloff's insular world was all that mattered to him, and a war was raging, one that could destroy the integrity of his beloved league.

The biggest threat to the league's existence was the constant specter of gambling. So, despite his protestations of support to Molinas —"I'll look out for you, Jack," "I'm on your side, Jack," "I will represent your best interests, Jack"—Podoloff had no intention of ever letting him back into the NBA.

Molinas was released after signing the incriminating statement at Fort Wayne police headquarters, because, under Indiana law, it was not a crime for an athlete to bet on himself. Because of legislation enacted in New York after the collegiate scandals of 1951, however, Molinas's calls to Ratensky were in violation of the local antibribery codes. Bronx Chief Assistant DA Tilzer let it be known that he planned to take the "Jack Molinas wager-to-win" case to a grand jury in an effort to determine whether a widespread gambling ring was operating in the NBA.

The Pistons played the Nationals at home that Sunday night. Before the game, Phil Olofson, the team's publicity man, was told to inform the crowd of the day's events. "I used the microphone at the scorer's table," Olofson said, "and I made the announcement that Molinas had been suspended from the team pending a hearing. There had been several bulletins on local radio all during the day so most of the fans had already heard the news, but they were shocked nevertheless. Jack was a popular player and a hell of a gate attraction."

A statement issued by Podoloff on Monday morning claimed that Molinas had bet on a total of ten games, had won six of those bets, and had cleared a total of four hundred dollars. Molinas, said Podoloff, "was a crazy, amoral kid who doesn't know right from wrong." Podoloff emphasized that Molinas had never deliberately lost any games and that no other Fort Wayne players were involved. He also announced that Molinas's place in the upcoming All-Star game would be taken by Andy Phillip.

Zollner and Birch told the *Fort Wayne Journal-Gazette* that "while they were making no charges, they felt that several games might have been lost by failure of Molinas to exert himself sufficiently, citing a couple of games in which the rookie sharpshooter took only one or two shots at the basket in the entire game."

With the Pistons leaving Monday morning for a game against the Hawks in Miami, Molinas remained in seclusion in the empty house. "Don't worry," he'd told Meineke and Hutchins as they walked out the door. "I'll be back. You can bet on it."

An enterprising reporter for the *Journal-Gazette* rang the doorbell and, catching Molinas off-guard, elicited the following statement: "It's true that I bet on some of our games, less than a dozen, but I always bet on us to win. I've never done anything dishonest in my life." Molinas also said that he had not yet considered the matter of appealing Podoloff's verdict and wasn't sure if such a recourse was available to him. The brief interview was so painful that Molinas resolved not to answer either the telephone or the front doorbell.

For the first time in his life Jack was lost. Basketball was his whole life. He knew he'd have to get back to New York somehow. He was loathe to travel by air or by train for fear that he'd be recognized. On Sunday afternoon, he called up Al Hirschberg, an ex-teammate with the Bronx Panthers, and asked if he would drive his car out to Fort Wayne and pick him up. Hirschberg was glad to oblige, but there was a snowstorm blanketing the Northeast and he wouldn't be able to get out there until Tuesday night or Wednesday morning.

Molinas couldn't bear to call Peggy. But at eight o'clock Sunday evening, Molinas finally called his parents and apprised them of his suspension. "The main thrust of what Jack told my father," said Julie, "was that he didn't think betting a couple of dollars on his own team to win was dishonest. I remember that we were watching television, *The Colgate Comedy Hour* starring Dean Martin and Jerry Lewis, and, after my father got off the phone and relayed the bad news to me and my mother, we were all stunned into silence. We just stared at the TV screen and heard all the jokes and the canned laughter without saying a word. Later, my dad just clenched his fists and said, 'That gambling business. That's what started it. I knew it would turn out to be trouble.' My mother cried softly and, later on, she blamed what she called 'evil men' who had hypnotized Jack and forced him into doing things he wouldn't have willingly done. As for me, I was shocked and in total denial. I cried myself to sleep that night, and I didn't want to go to school the next day. How could I face my classmates? Or my teachers?"

Back in Fort Wayne, brooding and waiting for Hirschberg to arrive, Molinas finally doped out a likely scenario. Podoloff was no dummy. He had to know that other, more veteran players were dumping games. But to bust them would be to admit that NBA games hadn't been kosher for years. To extend the investigation would destroy the league. The only viable solution for Podoloff was to choose expediency over disaster and throw a rookie to the wolves. In a way, Molinas could even admire Podoloff's cold-blooded strategy. Sacrifice a rookie so that the NBA would live.

(Years later, other NBA insiders came to the same conclusion. "It was my understanding," said a Hall of Fame player, "that there was a tremendous list of guys who were doing business in NBA games. Some of the biggest stars in the league. It was a big, wide-open secret. The Manhattan DA, Frank Hogan, really wanted to do a big number and let everything out. It was Podoloff who persuaded Hogan to close the book on Molinas and keep the lid on. And it worked like a charm." This analysis was buttressed by Meineke, Sinicola, Tosheff, and several other NBA players.)

Now Molinas began to think about how to deal with the mess. He prided himself on being a pragmatist—accepting the reality of any situation and then figuring out a way to make everything come out right. And once he put his mind to it, a solution was simple. He'd go back to New York, demand a private meeting with Podoloff, and then blackmail the little jerk. Poodles Podoloff. Hey, Commissioner Poodles, Molinas would say, if you don't let me back into the league I'll hold a press conference and tell the world about all the other guys who were not only betting on their own teams to win, but who were actually dumping ball games. I'll give out the names and the dates. And I'll get my friend, Joe Jalop, as a witness.

Of course! What a great idea! And Molinas began to tell himself that Poodles would have no choice other than to readmit him. Before long, Molinas was convinced that his readmittance was a foregone conclusion.

On Monday afternoon, the reporters descended on the Molinases' apartment only to find Louis still dressed in a bathrobe and surprisingly calm. One reporter noted that Molinas's three-foot-high MVP trophy from the All-Stars tour was "enshrined in the living room, almost as a centerpiece amid the furniture." Louis was philosophical and stoic as he answered the questions they hurled at him. "I didn't expect either of my sons ever to do anything that's against the law," said Louis. "I myself wouldn't bet five cents on the surest thing in the world, and I don't approve of gambling in any form. What I don't understand is what makes kids do things like this. Jack always had a dollar in his pocket from the day he was born. He had no debts and he never borrowed. He has a nice job and he doesn't need the money, so there's no reason why he should be making bets. But I was never in favor of Jack going into pro basketball. When you give too much money to young boys you spoil their future."

Louis expected Jack to return to school and continue his studies, perhaps pursue his interest in dentistry. "Jack should never have done this," Louis said. "But at least there's one consolation. At least my son did his best in these games."

In the aftermath of what was being called "the Molinas Incident," the phones of all the Pistons players were tapped by the Fort Wayne police. "Whenever Mel Hutchins and I had something of importance to discuss," said Meineke, "we'd make sure to talk someplace on the street. In addition to the tapped phones, we also assumed that both the house and the car were bugged."

The next few weeks were a nightmare for Foust. "Most of the guys on the team were interrogated by the Fort Wayne police," he said, "but of course none of us knew anything. Then, when Andy Phillip and I arrived in New York for the All-Star game, we were met at LaGuardia Airport and interrogated right then and there by the DA's people. Wherever we went, we were under suspicion. I guess you could call it suspicion by association."

Frankie Brian was shocked by the news. "It was like I was hit in the face with a two-by-four," Brian said. Mel Hutchins was unforgiving: "Jack would bet on anything. But what he did had no influence on the way the games were played. No influence at all. Even so, I will never forgive Molinas for what he did to his teammates, the game, and the fans."

Paul Birch, encouraged by a public statement from Zollner saying that his job was not in jeopardy, tried to use the Molinas Incident to motivate his team. "I called a secret meeting of the team on the Sunday afternoon after the news broke," Birch finally admitted to the press. "The players were so grief-stricken and distrustful of one another that it looked like the team might disintegrate. Then I encouraged every player on the squad to give vent to his feelings. Andy Phillip and Fred Scolari did the most in helping to lift their teammates' spirits. The two of them have been around a long time and they helped steady the younger players." The Pistons responded with a hot streak, winning four of their next six games.

The Knicks coach, Joe Lapchick, reported an interesting self-protective reaction from his own players: "I broke the news to my players just before our game with the Royals. There was a long silence. Then one of the players, expressing the sentiments of the team, said, 'It's too bad it had to happen. But as long as it did, we're glad it was a punk rookie and not one of the old pros of the game.'"

Various politicians attempted to advance their careers by feeding on the Molinas Incident. In Albany, New York, State Senator Carlo A. Lanzilloti (R., Queens), demanded that the legislature investigate the "scandalous conditions" of collegiate and professional basketball. To that end, Lanzilloti proposed the establishment of a six-member committee (with himself as chairman) with a fifteen-thousand-dollar appropriation.

Dan Parker, in the *New York Daily Mirror*, charged that Podoloff had bungled the Molinas Incident. Parker's main argument was that Podoloff should not have conducted his own investigation and would have better served the cause of justice by "placing the matter entirely in Mr. Hogan's lap."

> Did Mr. Podoloff choose this rather strange course in order to "protect the game" instead of the patrons of pro basketball, fearing that an unhampered investigation by the New York District Attorney's office might have produced revelations that would wreck his league, whereas, actually, it would have helped it more in the long run by showing the public that he wasn't trying to cover up anything?

Most of the other sportswriters around the country, afraid perhaps to destroy professional basketball as they knew it, confined their comments to high-handed condemnations of Molinas. Arthur Daley voiced the majority opinion in the *New York Times*: "If a chap bets on his team, it can only lead to betting against his team eventually in order to make a bigger and surer killing. There can be no excuse whatsoever for Molinas's action." Daley also believed that "the disbarment of Molinas should have a wholesome effect in impressing on all athletes the impropriety of betting on themselves."

However, there were certain historical precedents where athletes who had bet on their own success were considered to be above reproach. Prizefighters, for example, would routinely bet their entire purses on themselves. Many jockeys either bet on themselves or allowed others to put up money for them. In 1946, a player in the National Hockey League, Babe Pratt, confessed to betting on his team while he was with the Toronto Maple Leafs. At first, Pratt was suspended, but after a hearing he was reinstated and merely warned not to do it again. In the past, baseball players had occasionally been suspected of betting on their own games. Tris Speaker and Ty Cobb were charged in 1927, but the commissioner of baseball, Judge Landis, quickly exonerated them, saying that neither player had played less than his best in the games under consideration.

At thirty minutes past midnight on January 13, Molinas and Hirschberg quietly slipped out of Fort Wayne and began the seven-hundred-and fifty-mile drive back to New York. By now, Molinas had regained his composure. His father's characteristic stoicism seemed to be a useful and necessary way of being. No one would ever see Jack Molinas cry, or whimper, or even complain. Any display of vulnerability would only prove his own weakness and provide his enemies with weapons to use against him. He wouldn't even accept the meager comfort of martyrdom. Jack Molinas was resolved to overcome Podoloff, to overcome the system, to overcome the squares who tried to limit the possibilities of his own free-ranging genius. "Don't worry, Al," he told Hirschberg a hundred times as they sped through the night. "I'm going to beat this."

Molinas, however, made certain not to tell Hirschberg about his plans to blackmail Podoloff. As they drove into Eastern Pennsylvania, a news report pulled in by the car's radio quoted Podoloff as saying that if Molinas were to request a hearing by the NBA Board of Governors it would quickly be granted. Podoloff added that, in any case, he doubted the suspension would be lifted. Podoloff said the suspension, now called "indefinite," would be made "for life" if there is no appeal.

Molinas had to laugh. Once he got through with Podoloff, once he threatened to blow the NBA right out of the water, there would be no need for any appeal or hearing. Poodles loved the NBA more than he loved his wife, and once Molinas mentioned the misdeeds of Foust, Phillip, and Scolari, the commissioner's resistance would turn limp. He'd teach Poodles the Putz to challenge the luck of the Mole.

Even so, as they approached the entrance to the George Washington Bridge, the radio news reported that the Molinas Incident was now being investigated by the Manhattan DA's office. Despite himself, Molinas panicked. He thought the news flash meant that the New York police were out to find him and arrest him.

Later, he would joke about his reaction, but Molinas was pale-faced and serious as he instructed Hirschberg to pull the car over to the side of the road. Then, opening the trunk, Molinas coiled himself inside and instructed Hirschberg to close and lock the trunk door.

And that's how the Golden Boy, the Prince of the Playground, the NBA's most Royal Rookie, came home to face his disgrace.

Molinas hid out at home for several days. When he finally did speak to Peggy, they had a row. He defended himself up, down, and sideways, and said that he'd gotten "a raw deal," but Peggy wouldn't buy his alibis. She didn't care how many other players had done the same awful things, and she didn't know if she wanted to continue their relationship. Perhaps they should each go their own way for a while.

Molinas was devastated. As much as he loved Peggy, she wasn't standing up for him in the clutch.

Aside from his intention to blackmail Podoloff, Molinas had no other game plan. Then he read a newspaper article that not only reported that he had repeatedly shaved points while playing at Columbia, but that his bets on the Pistons were as high as five hundred dollars per game, and that he'd won so often that the bookies finally refused to take his action. At that point, Molinas decided that he needed to take some steps to rehabilitate his public image. So he made a phone call to Milton Gross, a sportswriter from the *New York Post* who had been a rare partisan back when Molinas was booted from Columbia.

"What gets me," Molinas told Gross, "is all this talk about bookmakers. It's utterly preposterous. Stanley Ratensky is not a bookmaker. He's just a normal guy, like myself. I don't deal with bookmakers and, in fact, I don't even know any."

When Gross pressed him about the rumors that he'd been in some gambler's pocket at Columbia, Molinas said, "They're nothing but lies. I've never shaved points or dumped games. Not in college and not in the NBA. I swear it."

Later in the interview, Molinas told Gross that he probably would appeal the NBA suspension and asked the writer if he believed there was any chance of reinstatement. When Gross said no, Molinas seemed to lose his composure. "Who's the detective in charge of the investigation?" Molinas asked. "Who should I speak to? Who should I go and see?" When Gross gave him George Tilzer's name, Molinas said, "Can I call him? Can I call him now? Can you give me his number?"

Here was another side of Jack Molinas—a naive young man who had no idea how to survive once the bubble of his dream world was punctured. His know-it-all, smarter-than-thou persona was a fraud. Without basketball, Molinas didn't know who he was or who he was supposed to be.

Meanwhile, the resolution of the Molinas Incident was turned over to George DeLuca, the Bronx district attorney, who quickly convened a grand jury. DeLuca announced that he would be paying particular attention to reports that Molinas had been "playing games with the point spreads" in high school and college. "Our investigation is only in the embryonic stage," DeLuca said. "We'll get to the bottom no matter where it may lead." Podoloff responded by repeating his previous assertion that "the Molinas Incident is an isolated case."

Back in Fort Wayne, local prosecutor John G. Reiber was still unsure "whether Molinas's conduct was such as to warrant any criminal action in the light of Indiana statutes." Apparently, the only danger of indictment would come from DeLuca's investigations. But even DeLuca was doubtful that there were any legal grounds for prosecuting Molinas merely because he telephoned bets from an out-of-state location to Ratensky's candy store.

By January 15, Molinas had hired a lawyer, Jacques Mantinband, a leftist civil-rights advocate and former Bronx DA, who believed that DeLuca's hopes for a grand jury to issue an indictment was nothing more than whistling in the dark. Mantinband advised Molinas not to voluntarily submit to DeLuca's questioning, and certainly not to appear before the grand jury. "If they want him," Mantinband said on behalf of his client, "let them subpoena him. He has nothing to hide and he's willing to take a lie detector test."

The NBA's All-Star game, played in Madison Square Garden on January 21, 1954, was a rousing contest. Each player on the winning team would be awarded one hundred and fifty dollars, not an insignificant sum, while the losers would gain fifty dollars. The West was favored by two and a half points and, far from being one of the casual dunk exchanges that the latter-day All-Star exhibitions would become, the game at hand was taken seriously by all concerned and was played at full tilt.

With two seconds to play and the score knotted, Bob Cousy sank an arching one-hander that put the East ahead 84–82. The West called time-out and set up a play for George Mikan. Jim Pollard inbounded the ball to Bobby Davies, who then flicked a perfect pass to Mikan in the low post. Just before the buzzer sounded Big George swept to his left and was fouled by Ray Felix as his right-handed hook rolled off the rim. There was no time on the clock as Mikan stood alone on the court, needing to convert both free throws to send the game into overtime. A screaming capacity crowd of 16,478 raised a din that forced court-side writers to cover their ears. But Mikan was immune to the pressure. In a courageous performance that soon became the stuff of legend, Mikan actually laughed out loud as he dipped his hands and underhanded each of his free throws cleanly through the net. However, Cousy soon trumped Mikan's transcendent clutch shooting by scoring eight points in the overtime period as the East prevailed, 98–93.

After the game, Podoloff announced that the NBA's club owners had granted him the power to hire a full–time investigator whose duties would be "to protect the league against gambling."

Back in Fort Wayne, however, the events surrounding the All-Star game produced a much more intriguing story. On January 22, the following item appeared in Ben Tenny's column in the *Fort Wayne Journal-Gazette:*

> Let me draw a picture for you of recent developments. Though not on the All-Star squad, Don Meineke was taken to New York with Mel Hutchins, Andy Phillip and Larry Foust who were to play. Owner Fred Zollner and Coach Paul Birch were in two lengthy sessions with those four players Wednesday night and again on Thursday. The players would not say what it was all about and Zollner and Birch only said that the meetings were "morale boosters." Observers declare that the three Piston players on the West All-Star squad seemed tense and drawn and were far from their best for the action in that game.

The implications were unmistakable. Somehow Zollner and Birch had turned up hard evidence that Foust, Phillip, Hutchins, and Meineke were touched by the same scandal that had besmirched Molinas. But, as before, the lid was to remain firmly in place.

While all this was going on, Molinas wandered around the apartment with a bright smile and showed no signs of the emotional distress that raged in his soul. Whenever anyone inquired about his well-being, Molinas repeated his mantra, "Don't worry. I'll be all right." Molinas was gradually working his way into Peggy's good graces, and if his father barely talked to him, Betty nagged him constantly. "Of course, I want you to get reinstated into the NBA," she'd say, "but only to clear your name and not to play basketball. Basketball is over, Jack. We've all got to accept the truth of that, but you've also got to do something for yourself. You're only twenty-one years old. You can't just sit around and wait."

Since Jack studied Spanish at Columbia and could speak the language fluently, he thought he might try and get into some kind of training program for a job in a foreign country. He figured that there were plenty of companies that did a lot of business in South America, and that being a translator or liaison would be right up his alley. Getting away from the States also seemed like a good idea at the time. But there was nothing available that suited him. Paul Brandt suggested that he take the Law School Aptitude Test, which he did. Without ever cracking a book, Jack's score ranked in the ninety-ninth percentile. Peggy and his mom were as pleased as they could be. He contacted Brooklyn Law School to see if he could get in.

Fortunately, Brooklyn Law School was struggling to recruit suitable students and was eager to make a deal with Molinas. On the condition that DeLuca's grand jury failed to indict him, the school's authorities guaranteed that Molinas would pass the character examination once his classwork was completed.

Some of Molinas's Kaiser Park cronies also suspected that the Coney Island branch of the Mafia family tree was very instrumental in forcing the law school to accept him with a clean bill of health. And why would organized crime be so anxious to come to Molinas's aid? Because he had proven to be a good soldier by not giving up Foust, Phillip, and Scolari, thereby obliterating a trail that inexorably would have led to Frankie Carbo. However Molinas's application was processed, he was in fact admitted to Brooklyn Law School and was eager for the February 10 opening of the spring semester.

Since he'd been home, Molinas had taken Paul Brandt into his full confidence and, during the last week in January, his one-time Columbia roommate had finally arranged a face-to-face meeting with Podoloff. Here was Molinas's chance to squeeze the commissioner until he cried uncle. Louis insisted on accompanying his son and Molinas didn't have the heart to say no.

The NBA's office was situated in the Empire State Building and, besides Podoloff, the entire staff consisted of publicist Haskell Cohen and Connie Maroselli, who did everything else. Podoloff's standard procedure was to receive visitors while seated behind his large brown desk, but he stepped out from behind his fortress and extended his hand to greet Molinas. Here is Jack's account of their fateful encounter.

"Both of us were really friendly at the start of the meeting, and I was keeping my ace hidden deep in the hole. I started off by asking Podoloff if he thought it was possible for me to play with Fort Wayne next season. He told me that as far as he was personally concerned, unless I had any new evidence to offer, there was literally no chance that I'd be reinstated at any time. He gave me the impression that my hearing would come up before the board of governors sometime after the season and that the vote would most likely be cast against me. He was kind of vague as to exactly when the Board would be meeting.

"Then Podoloff began firing questions at me. 'You've admitted that you bet on games, isn't that right?'

"'Yes, sir.'"

"'Have you ever deliberately tried to lose a basketball game anywhere at any time?'"

"'No, sir.'"

"'Not at Stuyvesant, or at Columbia, or in the NBA?'"

"'No, sir.'"

"'Have you ever tried to hold down a score or control the margin of victory?'"

"'No, sir.'"

"Then he asked me about the Pistons-Celtics game played at the Garden on December 5. 'You scored eighteen points in the first half. Why, then, didn't you play much in the second half?'"

"With as much tact as I could muster, I told him to ask Coach Birch.

"When Podoloff asked me about the fluctuation of the point spread in that game, and about the bookies taking the Pistons' games off the board, I just shrugged and said, 'I don't concern myself with anything that has anything at all to do with gambling. But frankly it sounds like irresponsible talk by irresponsible people.'

"Okay, Podoloff had had his say, and now it was time for me to play my ace. But I was careful not to be either threatening or menacing.

"'Mister Podoloff,' I began, 'surely you must know that there are players on the Fort Wayne team that were shaving points and dumping games.'"

"'I'm aware of that,' he said.

"He knew! The sonofabitch knew all along!

"'Then how can you come down so hard on me just for betting on my team to win?'

"'You're a first-year player, Jack, and if I were to get anybody in trouble who's been playing in the league for several years, it might hurt the structure of the league.'

"'Listen, Mister Podoloff. You don't want to hurt the structure of the league any more than I do, but I still should be given another chance to play.'

"'All right,' he said. 'We'll see. We'll see.'

"It was clear that he was just trying to stall me, so I said, 'What if I held a press conference and exposed the names of all the players who were doing business with gamblers? What if I gave out specific names, and dates? What if I brought a big-time gambler to the press conference to back up all of my charges? I'm telling you, Mister Podoloff, I'm fully prepared to do this unless I'm immediately readmitted.'"

"'I will not make any deals, Jack. Be certain about that. And, yes, you could hold your news conference and tell your dirty stories and even bring in your so-called witness. But it wouldn't do you any good, Jack. First of all, it would put the absolute final seal on your dismissal from the league. Secondly, the league would certainly take a hit, but in the long run we would survive simply because the public likes our product. And thirdly, no one would believe you, Jack. You'd only be making a fool of yourself.'

"He was correct, of course, and I was right back where I started. Empty, confused, and without a game plan.

"'Let me give you some friendly advice, Jack," he said. "I understand you have an interest in the law.'

"'How do you know about that?'

"'You'd be surprised at how much we know about your comings and goings, Jack. Anyway, my heartfelt advice to you is to forget about basketball. For your own sake, don't ever touch another ball again, don't step foot on a court, don't go to a game, don't even watch one on television. You're about to start on another career, Jack. Give your whole heart and your whole mind to it.'

"I could see my father nodding his head, fully agreeing with everything Podoloff was saying. Me, I didn't say a word.

"And the last thing Podoloff said to me was this: 'Things aren't really the way they are, Jack. They're only the way they appear to be.'"[1]

NOTE

1. *The Great Molinas*, pp 124-132, based on an interview with Podoloff.

Molinas continued to root for the Pistons and whenever they were in town to play the Knicks he would go to the games. "I felt that Jack had gotten a bum rap," said Don Meineke, "and that he should've had another chance. But because of the political climate I had to be very secretive in my dealings with him. The way we worked it out was that Jack would call my room at the hotel and leave a telephone number. No name, just a number. Then, when the coast was clear, I'd call him back just to make sure he was in. If he did answer my call, I'd leave the hotel and call him again from a pay phone. The first time we connected this way, he asked if I could get him a comp ticket for the ball game, but I couldn't because he was persona non grata. So he'd have to stand in line at the box office and buy his way into the game just like your everyday civilian. But I was always interested in having dinner with him after the game. And he'd say, 'All right. I'll meet you on the corner of Fifty-second Street and Broadway an hour after the game.' And he would pull up in a big limousine with a good-looking woman sitting beside him. Then we'd go to a fancy restaurant and he'd always pick up the bill. Jack was a pistol."

According to Molinas, however, his relationship with Meineke was much more complex: "Not only were some of my teammates at Fort Wayne dumping ball games, there were also a couple of guys who were doing the same thing that got me in trouble—betting on the team to win. Mel Hutchins and Don Meineke. So, right after my suspension from the league, two interesting things happened as far as these fellows were concerned. There were times when Meineke and Hutchins would call me and give me the inside scoop on the next Piston game. They'd tell me to bet on Fort Wayne to win or to lose. And I would make bets on the basis of their information. I'd learned at least one lesson by now—not to bet with anybody other than Joe Jalop. And wouldn't you know that I won every bet? Every single one. The other thing that happened was that Meineke and Hutchins were continuing to bet on the Pistons to win and I was placing their bets for them."

Molinas's testimony is supported by a one-time NBA player: "Jack took the brunt of the whole thing, and the other Fort Wayne players had to make sure that he wouldn't rat on them so they kept him informed whenever they were doing business. The circus was in the Garden one evening so the Pistons were playing the Knicks at the Sixty-ninth Regiment Armory and me and Jack were sitting in the balcony and watching the game. New York was favored by two and a half, and Jack's ex-teammates had informed him to bet on the Knicks.

"Anyway, there's about two minutes left in the game, Fort Wayne was neck-and-neck with the Knicks, and I was shitting in my BVDs. 'Jack,' I said. 'We're losing.' And he said, 'Don't worry.' That was his famous saying. But nothing happened. The Pistons were still playing like they wanted to win the game. 'Jack,' I said, 'there's only one minute to go and we're going to lose.' 'Don't worry.' Now there's only thirty seconds on the clock, the score was tied and I was going crazy. I'd bet the rent money, the money for my car payment, the money for my electric bill. 'Jack!' I said. But he was still calm as he could be. 'Don't worry,' he said.

"Then all of a sudden, one of the Pistons—I'm not going to tell you who—was dribbling the ball in the backcourt all by himself. I mean his defender was about fifteen feet away and the guy just kicked the ball out of bounds. It almost looked like a football player drop-kicking the ball for an extra point after a touchdown. Now the Knicks had the ball and another one of the Pistons made a clumsy effort to steal the ball and instead committed an obvious foul. The Knicks made both free throws, they're up by two, the Pistons had the ball, and there seemed to be no way New York's going to cover the two and a half. The clock was ticking down…Ten…nine…eight…If the Pistons scored, I was a loser. If the Pistons didn't score, I still lost. 'Jack! I'm dying!' 'Don't worry.'

"There's five seconds to go when we heard somebody on the Pistons bench shout out loud, 'You motherfucking referee!' Bang! The ref called a technical foul, the Knicks made the shot and won the game by three points! And Jack turned to me with a big shit-eating grin on his face. 'I told you not to worry,' he said."

After conferring with Mantinband, Molinas decided to switch lanes and agreed to appear before the grand jury. Besides Molinas himself, a total of five witnesses were called: Lt. William Hyland of the Bronx DA's office, who presented the evidence; Stanley Ratensky and his father, Isidore; plus Morris Rosenzweig, a part-time bookie and manager of a Bronx poolroom, and Jack Israel, identified only as Rosenzweig's "runner."

Molinas appeared before the grand jury on two separate occasions—once for an hour and twenty minutes of harsh questioning, and later the same day for a stern fifteen-minute lecture by the foreman, Bernard A. Buge. Through it all, his main line of defense was that the bets he had placed on the Pistons to win "were incentives to make me play better."

On March 24, 1954, Assistant DA George Tilzer publicly announced the findings of the twenty-three-man grand jury:

> Despite painstaking and exhaustive investigation, we were unable to unearth any evidence of the commission of a crime. No evidence was unearthed involving any player being influenced by professional gamblers. The evidence was insufficient in the opinion of the Grand Jury to indict anyone.

Molinas was overjoyed. Facing the reporters assembled outside the courthouse, he began by being lighthearted and conversational. "I've been attending classes at Brooklyn Law School," he said, "and I've also been playing with the kids in the schoolyard, teaching them what I know about basketball." Then he was appropriately contrite and hopeful. "I'll never bet again," he promised. "I was silly. But I know in America you always get a second chance."

His hopes for immediate reinstatement were dashed, however, by Podoloff, who said, "The suspension is tantamount to life expulsion regardless of whether a crime has been committed. The relevant point is that betting by a player is a violation of his contract, and that's why Jack Molinas was suspended." Podoloff added that, as yet, Molinas had not taken advantage of his right to appeal the verdict.

Prompted by Milton Gross, the *New York Post* declared its support for Molinas: "While Molinas violated NBA rules by betting on himself, he was not a party to the kind of gambling conspiracy that did so much damage to college basketball a few years ago. In view of this, the *Post* asks the NBA to take Molinas back into the game. We're for giving him another chance."

Nobody—not Tilzer, nor Gross, nor Louis, nor Betty—ever asked Molinas where he'd gotten the money to pay Mantinband.

The Pistons finished the season in third place in the Western Division with a record of 40–32. In a screwy round-robin playoff situation, Fort Wayne lost twice to Rochester and once to Minneapolis. On March 27, just six days after the Pistons season was terminated, Zollner allowed Birch the dignity of resigning. Zollner's statement was terse: "I wish to compliment Paul for his all-out effort and for his integrity. I'm sorry that situations developed with which he was unable to cope." Zollner went on to describe a reorganization of the Pistons front office, one in which he would have greater control of the day-to-day basketball operations.

In due time, there were other changes in store for the Pistons. Red Rocha was a nine-year veteran of the NBA who finished his playing career in Fort Wayne in 1956–57 before becoming the Pistons coach. "What I heard," said Rocha, "was that as a result of the Molinas deal, all of the players on that team were put under heavy surveillance by the Fort Wayne police. For the rest of that season and the season after, their phones were tapped. Scolari was sold to Boston, and within the next few seasons, Zollner dismantled the team, trading or selling players in their prime. I think the old man became suspicious of any player who became a star. In Zollner's eyes, to become a star was to become suspect. That's why Meineke was eventually dealt to Cincinnati, Hutchins to New York, Phillip to Boston, and Foust to Minneapolis." In 1958, the season after George Yardley scored 27.8 ppg and became the first NBA player to total over two thousand points in a season, he was unceremoniously traded to Syracuse.

Law school was a snap for Molinas, leaving him plenty of time to play basketball. On weekends and holidays, he played on several barnstorming teams. Finn's All-Stars, the New Jersey Titans. The name of the team would change according to whoever they could get to sponsor them. They traveled around Pennsylvania and the New England area and would play other barnstorming teams for the gate receipts. They also played for various charities and benefits. But they never played for free.

In April, Finn's All-Stars were in Lennox, Massachusetts, to play the Lennox Merchants, a solid squad that had won twenty-four and lost only twelve games against high-quality touring teams that often included NBA players. The sponsor of Molinas's squad was Bronx-born Danny Finn, a guard who had recently finished his second season with the Philadelphia Warriors—but Finn was bothered by a torn ankle ligament and did not make the trip. The All-Stars were an iron-man-five consisting of Molinas; six-foot-six Boris Nachamkin, a senior at NYU; six-four Richie Surhoff from LIU and the Milwaukee Hawks; six-three Gene Beliveau, a veteran of the semiprofessional Eastern League; and George Feigenbaum, a six-one guard from LIU who'd also played with the Milwaukee Hawks. The game was played at the State Armory and attracted a near-capacity crowd of eight hundred fans. Finn's All-Stars emerged victorious, 90–85, and although Molinas "missed several soft shots," he set the pace with thirty points.

The manager of the State Armory, Bill Gregory, was so impressed with Finn's All-Stars that he booked them for another game a few days later against the McGuire All-Stars, a team featuring five members of the New York Knickerbockers. Al and Dick McGuire, Carl Braun, Connie Simmons, and Buddy Ackerman would be joined by the sensational rookie center of the Baltimore Bullets, Ray Felix.

Molinas was primed to play against a team of outstanding NBAers, and on game day he was at the wheel of his father's car—the 1954 Buick Special—driving twenty to thirty miles per hour faster than the local speed limits allowed. Somewhere in Westchester County, he was stopped by a motorcycle cop. "Don't worry," Molinas told his teammates as the cop dismounted and approached them. "Just sit quietly and let me handle this." When asked to show the policeman his license and car registration, Molinas complied, saying, "My name is Jack Molinas. Maybe you've heard of me. I played basketball for Columbia University and also in the National Basketball Association with the Fort Wayne

Pistons. I'm heading up to Lennox, Massachusetts, with my buddies here, to play in a benefit game for crippled children." The cop was suitably impressed and let Molinas go with just a warning.

Fuzzy Levane was a recently retired NBA player who was doing some part-time scouting for the Knicks. "I went up to see the game in Lennox when I heard that Molinas was scheduled to play," said Levane. "When I actually saw Molinas on the court, I told the Knick players that they couldn't play against him. I didn't want them to get involved in any incident." Carl Braun later testified that his refusal to be on the same basketball court as Molinas was his own idea, and that he had no instructions to boycott the game.

Spurred by the embarrassment of the McGuire All-Stars walking off the court, Molinas hired another lawyer, Maurice Knapp, and on April 22 demanded that Podoloff supply a written notice of charges. When Podoloff refused, Molinas filed a motion in the Bronx Supreme Court seeking to enjoin the NBA for keeping him on the ineligible-to-play list. Molinas argued that since the grand jury had failed to indict him, Podoloff had no legal grounds for prolonging the suspension. Moreover, Podoloff's refusal to provide a written notice of charges was a "denial of plaintiff's legal rights." The McGuire All-Stars' action was cited as proof that the NBA suspension had prevented Molinas from earning a living.

Additionally, Molinas argued that his $8,500 contract with the Pistons would not expire until October 1, 1954—and since he had only received $3,362, he was entitled to the remainder of his annual salary. Molinas also wanted court costs plus $50,000 for his "emotional distress."

For Molinas, the highlight of the hearing was when Podoloff was called to the witness stand and Knapp's sharp line of questioning easily dismantled the commissioner's decorum. "Jack Molinas is a cancer," Podoloff was soon shouting, "and he has to be amputated to save professional basketball as we know it!" But Bronx Supreme Court Judge Samuel Joseph ruled that Molinas's betting had violated his contract with Fort Wayne and had therefore rendered it null and void.

In issuing his ruling, the judge also took the opportunity to deliver a lengthy polemic describing the far-reaching and malevolent influence of Molinas's gambling. "When the breath of scandal hits one sport, it casts suspicion on all other sports. It does irreparable injury to the great majority of players, destroys the confidence of the public in athletic competition, and lets down the morale of our youth." Judge Joseph concluded by declaring, "I am constrained to say that the plaintiff's conduct was reprehensible."

Rebuffed in the court, Molinas next instructed Knapp to contact Podoloff and initiate the mechanism of a formal appeal. "We feel the contract clause that deals with betting is ambiguous," said Knapp. "We feel that Molinas wasn't given notice of charges and a hearing as provided for by NBA laws. And we feel that Molinas did nothing morally wrong. His unwise actions may merit censure but don't warrant so drastic a measure as expulsion."

One of Molinas's most memorable barnstorming trips took him to Montreal. "This wasn't such a good team," said Lou Orlando. "It was just a bunch of guys who played together in a recreation league in Greenwich, Connecticut. Jerry Deutsch and I had both played for the University of Connecticut, and the other players were no better than average. Well, one of the guys was a kid named Jerry Rappaport who was a good shooter but who took too many shots. Anyway, Rappaport's father-in-law came from Montreal and he arranged a weekend of exhibition games for us up there. A game Saturday night and another one on Sunday afternoon. Since Jerry Deutsch and I were from the Bronx, we both knew Jack Molinas and we invited him to come along with us. And he agreed."

On the drive up, Molinas and his brand-new Buick were stopped for speeding somewhere in Westchester County. "Sit tight, you guys," he said. "Let me handle this." Molinas proceeded to identify himself to the policeman. "Maybe you've heard of me. I played basketball at Columbia and also with the Fort Wayne Pistons in the NBA. Me and my buddies here are on our way up to Montreal to play in a charity basketball game for the benefit of some crippled kids."

"Oh, yeah," the policeman said. "I sure have heard of you. You gave me the same story when I stopped you a couple of weeks ago. Now you can tell the story to the judge."

The deal in Montreal was that, win or lose, the visitors would get a lump sum of money to cover expenses and wages for the seven players who made the trip. Since Jack was by far the best player on the team, he was deeded two hundred dollars, Orlando and Deutsch each received seventy-five, while the rest got fifty each. To save money, the seven players checked into two hotel rooms. "Naturally," said Orlando, "everybody started scrambling to see who's going to sleep on the bed, or on the couch, or on the floor. Everybody except Jack. He didn't give a shit where he slept. While the rest of us were fighting for position, Jack was on the phone talking to a bookie. 'Yeah, okay,' Jack said. 'I'll take that ten times. Give me that five times. Give me that one twenty times.' Jack always had his own itinerary."

The Saturday night opponents were the Quebec All-Stars and the home team led by six points at the half. "Everybody was swearing and cursing in the locker room," said Orlando, "because we should have been killing those guys. And Jack kept on saying, 'Relax. Relax. Relax.' Then Jack found a pencil somewhere, wrote something on one of the lockers, then covered it up with a strip of adhesive tape. 'I just wrote the final score,' he said. 'So there's nothing to worry about because the game's already decided.' So we came back out and we're playing pretty good. Jack, of course, was gangbusters. Nobody could stop him. The game came down to the last minute and we're a point behind and we had the ball. Jack called a time-out and he said, 'Deutsch, you take the ball out of bounds, pass it to Louie, then stay away from everybody. Louie, you dribble around the court. They're ahead by a point so they're not going to bother you. Right? You just dribble around, then pass it to me when I call for it.'"

The game resumed with Deutsch passing to Orlando as ordered. "I was dribbling around like crazy," said Orlando, "and there's Jack standing in the left corner with his legs crossed at the ankles and his hands on his hips. And we're both looking at the clock and it's down to thirty seconds and I was getting nervous. 'Jack!' I said. 'Relax,' he said. Then it's down to fifteen seconds. 'Jack!' 'Relax.' Then I swear the clock was down to five seconds and all of a sudden Jack took a step along the baseline, then came flying up to the foul line, and just before he gets to the foul line he shouted, 'Now!' And I threw him the ball and he caught it right at the middle of the free throw line while he was still moving away from the basket—and up went the fadeaway hook shot. The crowd was absolutely silent, and while the ball was still in the air, Jack shouted, 'It's history!' and kept running off the court and right into the locker room. Naturally, the shot was good and we won the game. And naturally, when Jack peeled the tape off the locker, his prediction was perfect."

An even bigger crowd showed up on Sunday afternoon to see the Americans take on the Montreal All-Stars. Before the game, Molinas received a large trophy for being the outstanding player the night before. "Oh, how he loved trophies," Orlando said. "But right after he got the trophy the rest of us were warming up, shooting layups, and we saw Jack hugging the trophy and talking to the promoter, Jerry Rappaport's father-in-law. Jack was as calm as a clam, but the veins on this other guy's neck were bulging like he's about to have a heart attack. So what's it all about? There was a standing-room-only crowd and Jack said they've all come to see him play, but he's not going to take the floor unless he got another five hundred bucks. Not to be split among the team, but just for himself. And the guy had no choice but to fork over the extra money. Then Jack goes out, scores fifty points, and we won again."

Right after the game, with two trophies in hand, Molinas wanted to make a quick exit. "The only trouble with that," said Jerry Deutsch, "was that I always took a real long shower after a ball game. By the time I was dressed everybody was long gone. I was left in Montreal with three bucks in my pocket and I had to borrow bus fare from the promoter. It was a big joke to Jack and, I must confess, as pissed off as I was when I found out they'd left me, I couldn't stay mad at Jack for long. Nobody could. He was as playful as a little kid, and just about as harmless, too. With everything that eventually went down, one of Jack's saving graces was that he only hurt himself."

That spring, Joe Hacken made a move on middleweight boxer Bobby Jones, offering him fifteen thousand dollars to blow a fight. Jones told D.A. Hogan and the cops hit Joe Jalop from four sides. Jack spoke right away to Joe's wife, then went to see his attorney, Frances Kahn, and took care of everything. Jack put up the ten thousand dollars bail and Joe was only in jail for a few days.

In mid-October, Molinas made a trip out to Champaign-Urbana, Illinois, to visit Julie, who was a candidate for the freshman basketball team. While he was there, Molinas scrimmaged with the Illinois varsity and easily overwhelmed George Bon Salle, the Illini's All–Big Ten center.

"It was good to get reacquainted with my brother," said Julie. "He had apparently accepted his suspension and was still a happy-go-lucky type of person, always laughing and minimizing the importance of everything that everybody else worried about. Charismatic, confident, and cynical. That was Jack. He tended to do almost everything to an excess, and he was most secure when he could control a situation. But even then, after his golden dream had been so cruelly shattered, I doubt if my brother ever really explored his own feelings."

By now, Louis was getting weary of the family's summer routine—looking for a new place to live in Coney Island every summer, then shlepping everything from the Bronx. Julie was off at college, Jackie was going to law school in Brooklyn, so Louis decided to give up the apartment on the Grand Concourse and move to Brooklyn into a three-bedroom apartment at 2310 Ocean Parkway, only a ten-minute drive to the Eagle Bar.

In July, Molinas had petitioned the Office of Committees on Character and Fitness of the New York Supreme Court Appellate Division for a "preliminary determination" as to whether or not his ouster from the NBA would prevent him from being admitted to the Bar. Several months later, Molinas was pleased to receive the following ruling:

> On the assumption that the petitioner has honestly and completely disclosed all of the facts in connection with the incident referred to in his petition, the preliminary determination of the Committee, by memorandum dated October 11, 1954, that the incident described in the applicant's

petition...would not, in and of itself, preclude his ultimate admission to the Bar, has been approved.

This conditional acceptance surprised several of Molinas's fellow students. "The basic constant in Jack Molinas," said Edwin Torres, "was his incredible arrogance. Despite all of his legal troubles, Molinas still retained that NBA glow, and he had a large contingent of jock-sniffing admirers who always followed him around from class to class and ran errands for him. Nobody could deny that Molinas was a superbly talented man, but we were all astounded when the Committee on Character and Fitness gave him their preliminary approval. Normally, if you had a traffic ticket the committee would turn you down. I knew a guy who got a thumbs-down from the committee because he had once gotten a ticket for going into a segregated saloon somewhere out west with an Indian. The word we got was that Molinas's dad had some kind of political connections through the ownership of a bar and grill he owned in Coney Island. It was all very vague, but what was clear was that the normal protocol had somehow been short-circuited."

In addition to his full-time load of classes, Molinas was also able to scratch his basketball itch by playing on weekends in the Eastern Basketball League (EBL). Basketball had been considered a significant morale-boosting activity during World War II, with every military base sporting its own team. When the veterans returned home, they brought with them an increased interest in watching and playing the game, and a number of minor leagues were soon created. Foremost among these was the Eastern Pennsylvania Basketball League, which was originally chartered in Hazelton on April 23, 1946, and included the Allentown Rockets, Hazleton Mountaineers, Lancaster Red Roses, Reading Keys, Wilkes-Barre Barons, and the only out-of-state team, the Binghamton (NY) Triplets. (Through the years other notable franchises included the Berwick Carbuilders and the Lebanon Seltzers.) The EBL (the name was changed in 1947) preceded the NBA by six weeks and was therefore the oldest professional basketball league in the country. Games were played mostly on weekends in high school gyms, and the players (who were paid by the game) drove in from their homes in (mostly) Philadelphia and New York. In time for the 1954–55 season, the EBL decided to try and boost attendance by signing two outstanding players whose gambling activities had resulted in their being banned from the NBA—Sherman White and Jack Molinas. (As the season progressed, the Scranton Miners signed Ed Roman and Floyd Layne.)

Molinas turned down offers from Hazleton, Carbondale, and Wilkes-Barre to sign with the Williamsport Billies (who advertised him as "one of the finest gentlemen in the game"). Molinas said that his participation in the EBL would "go a long way in the process of clearing my name." Maurice Podoloff said that Molinas's desire to play in the EBL was "encouraging."

Molinas was the league's highest-paid player—earning about one-hundred and fifty dollars a game—but finances were always iffy in the Eastern League. That's why veteran players would either ask to be paid in cash or else take their postgame paycheck and race to the box office and demand payment there and then. Quite often, players who'd just played sensational ball games would be cut from the team because another player who'd work for less had suddenly become available. John Chaney was an Eastern League fixture who went on to become an outstanding coach at Temple University. "Many times we were paid according to the number of people in the stands," said Chaney. "There might be fifty cents for every paid admission put into a pot that the players would split. There was also a team in Lancaster, Pennsylvania, that was sponsored by a meat company, and the players used to get paid off in tubes of baloney."

Molinas would usually drive down to the Friday night game, leave immediately afterward, and drive to the next city where he'd check into a hotel, play on Saturday night, then return to New York. But sometimes, if he was detained by a double-overtime session in the law school library, he'd simply take a plane.

Peggy would often accompany Molinas on the Eastern League weekends and on one occasion they were driving to Wilkes-Barre on a snowy night when the car spun out of control and grazed a guardrail. Molinas was barely scratched and Peggy suffered only a mild neck injury, but for years thereafter Molinas would brag about the big score he'd made by convincing the insurance company to pay him top dollar.

Almost everybody who knew Molinas had a favorite narrative of some sort of adventure en route to an Eastern League game. "I went down to Williamsport with him once," said Marvin Weisman, a boyhood friend from Coney Island. "I remember that Louis and Betty were also along for the weekend. It was a foggy night and Jack was driving my car and speeding as usual. 'Don't worry about it,' he told us as he followed the white line. Sure enough he got pulled over by a cop. While the cop was approaching us, Jack asked me to give him my license. Which I did, and the speeding ticket was made out to me. Okay, a few weeks later, I got a letter from the motor vehicle bureau in Pennsylvania saying that since I hadn't paid the ticket they were issuing a warrant for my arrest. A short time later, Jack was driving his own car and he was stopped at a roadblock near the gym in Williamsport. A cop shined his light in Jack's face and said, 'Hello, Mister Weisman. You're the guy we've been looking for.' Then Jack showed the cop his own license and they had to let him go. Sure, Jack got himself in plenty of trouble, but he also got himself out of plenty of trouble, too. Oh, yes. Eventually, the owner of the Williamsport team paid the ticket."

Whenever Molinas drove he was constantly fiddling with the car radio trying to find a ball game in progress. "We were coming back to New York from a game in Allentown," said Jerry Deutsch. "It was around midnight and Jack was doing his usual thing with the radio dial, when suddenly he stomped on the brake and the car came to a screeching halt near a phone booth. After Jack jumped out of the car and made a phone call, I asked him what the hell was going on. 'There's a bookmaker in Brooklyn,' he said, 'who really is in over his head. The game I was listening to just ended, but I was able to bet it because the bookie was confused about the time zones.' Jack sure did love to beat bookies."

There were many past and future celebrities toiling in the Eastern League: Jim Luisi, a clever shooting guard, who became an actor with such credits as the Broadway version of *Sweet Charity* and several television series, including *The Rockford Files*; Hubie Brown, a longtime NBA coach and TV colorman; Jack Ramsey, who'd later become the Hall of Fame coach of the Portland Trail Blazers; and Jack McCloskey, the EBL's Most Valuable Player in 1953 and 1954, and later the general manager of the Detroit Pistons. Some ot the EBL's best players in the 1954-55 season were Jimmy Brasco from NYU; George Feigenbaum, Molinas's teammate from the Finn's All-Stars; several CCNY fixers, including Floyd Layne, Ed Roman and Ed Warner; and another one-time teammate of Molinas's, John Azary from Columbia.

"Remember," said Hubie Brown, "there were only eight teams in the NBA and only ten players on each team. That adds up to only eighty players. Guys played in the Eastern League because there was no place else for them to play. I'm telling you the truth here, that many of the guys in the Eastern League would be NBA All-Stars if they played today."

Aside from the NBA, the competition in the Eastern League was the finest in the world. "The difference," said one veteran of the EBL and the NBA, "was that there were no point spreads issued for Eastern Leagues games and every one played on the up-and-up."

"The Eastern League was a hell of a league," said Hubie Brown. "Everybody played a cerebral kind of game with a lot of motion. It was a form of a passing game before anybody gave it a name. A lot of the old guys, especially from the Northeast, called it Jew basketball."

Even the referees were sensational. "The majority of the guys who became great officials in the NBA," said Hubie Brown, "all learned how to referee in the Eastern League. I'm talking about guys like Earl Strom, Jake O'Donnell, and Mendy Rudolph, whose father, by the way, was president of the league." One of the early EBL referees was Tommy Lasorda, who later traded his whistle for a baseball and wound up as the beloved manager of the Los Angeles Dodgers.

The Williamsport Billies played their home games at Roosevelt Junior High School and in his debut Molinas scored thirty-four points in a win over Hazelton. Molinas missed two games in early January 1955, when his father was bedridden with influenza, but the Billies remained in first place for most of the season.

Molinas was chosen to play in the EBL's All-Star game, but even there his cocky attitude easily set him apart from his colleagues. "The deal was," said John Chaney, "that the winners of the game were to get sixty percent of the pot and the losers the rest. Guys were running around and lobbying for the losers and the winners to have equal shares and everybody had a loud opinion. Except for Jack. He wasn't worried about what the split was going to be because he knew he was going to win."

Williamsport's regular season record was 19–11, good enough for first place, but the Billies were upset in the first round of the playoffs by Hazelton. Molinas played in only twenty-four games, yet his scoring total (610 points) was second to EBL leader Sherman White.

But the EBL games failed to fully satisfy Molinas's Basketball Jones, so on Sundays, and occasionally on weekdays, he'd also play in the Connecticut League. According to George Feigenbaum, playing in both leagues required some doing: "If we played an Eastern League game on Sunday afternoon, we'd drive like mad up to Connecticut, change our uniforms in the car, and hopefully get to the gym in time for the tip-off. On many occasions we'd jump from the car right into the ball game without any warm-ups. Sometimes we were late because Jack had to stop off and phone in his bets for that night's college and NBA games. He'd bet as much as a thousand a game, which was a whole lot of money in those days. Jack also tried to get me involved. 'Don't worry,' he said. 'It's easy money.' But I saw firsthand how much his life had been ruined by gambling and I wanted no part of it."

The Connecticut League featured franchises in Danbury, Torrington, Bridgeport, and Hartford. "Every player got the same salary," said Feigenbaum. "Thirty-five bucks per game. But the Eastern League didn't want any of its players to doubleup, so, in Connecticut, we played under phony names. Jack's pseudonym was Jake Miller."

If Molinas played basketball just for fun, he had other, more dependable ways of earning his living. As he put it: "I had a very good read on the pro games and I was also a fairly good handicapper of college games. While I was going to law school and playing in the Eastern League, I started to take a very deep interest in betting on basketball games. I had been doing this for years, but now I was really devoted to it. Sometimes I'd bet as many as twenty ball games a night. I would say that my hobbies were law school and playing ball, but my occupation was betting on basketball games."

In addition to his own opinions, Molinas also had impeccable inside information: Robert Ellis was Molinas's classmate at Brooklyn Law and is now a successful attorney in New York City. "Jack was part of our study group," said Ellis, "even though he never studied all that much. I say one of his biggest contributions to the group was his conviviality. In a more material sense, however, Jack made a lot of money for us, and this is the way it happened: My brother and I ran a candy store as a way of paying our way through law school, and since I worked the night shift, our study group would often meet there over coffee. Well, every Saturday night at a certain time Jack would get phone calls in the candy store. The calls were from NBA players informing Jack about the games they were working. These guys were so good that they could make or miss a spread by a single point, and they never gave Jack a bum steer. I'd say there were about five or six players who called on a regular basis. I was always amazed by how many NBA ball games were rigged. In a three-game playoff series only one game would be for real. What these players were doing was paying for Jack's silence. They were vulnerable, but they'd take care of him if he kept his mouth shut and didn't snitch on them. We did a great business on Saturday nights because every tinhorn bettor and bookie would be there to get the inside dope. Jack was always generous with his information."

At age twenty-two, Jack Molinas was already caught in several traps of his own devising. Ultimately, the pain that throbbed so deeply in some black-blooded chamber of his heart had been created by his willful addiction to gambling. At the same time, the only way he knew how to allay that pain was to up the ante and gamble more and more. Nor could Molinas bear to let anyone see his pain, much less detect that pain slowly transmuting into anger. No, Jack Molinas instead wore the mask of an enchanted warrior. He could easily deal with whatever injustice fell from heaven and landed in his lap. He could smile at the mirror image of his own shame. Watch him as he laughed and threw money to the wind. Hear him as he swore that the hand hidden in his pocket grasped a golden key. Believe him when he said that appearance and reality were two faces of the same gold coin.

In the new Ocean Parkway apartment, Jack and Julie each had their own bedrooms for the first time in their lives, and Jack was thrilled to be able to move his ever increasing collection of trophies (which eventually totaled thirty-three) into his room. Even though his mother dusted the trophies in her normal housecleaning routine, Molinas would periodically inspect them, looking to scrape away the slightest sign of tarnish or rust. From time to time, Molinas also pored over the scrapbooks of newspaper articles (including reports of both his glories and his abasement) his brother had assembled. Molinas also littered his desk and dresser with assorted curios from the Globetrotter tour. In the privacy of his bedroom, Molinas seemed like an old man wistfully teasing himself with memories of his long lost youth.

During the course of his relationship with Peggy, Molinas never addressed the possibility of their getting married. Whenever Peggy pressed the issue, he'd resort to the same kind of vague evasions that Podoloff had used on him. Finally, just before Christmas in 1954, Peggy realized that she had no future with Molinas and broke off their connection. Molinas was devastated emotionally, but as always he kept his true feelings in a very private section of his psyche. "There's more than one fish in the sea," he told his friends.

Despite his seeming stoicism and the bravado he often employed in public to dismiss his inner anguish, there was a definite difference in Molinas's behavior. His self-image constantly needed reinforcing and he became even more manic than usual. When one of his friends bought a flashy black-topped white Bonneville, Molinas immediately went to the same car dealer and traded a Chevrolet he'd previously purchased for a black Bonneville with a white top. (Whatever his current automobile of choice happened to be, there was always a basketball in the trunk along with a pair of white Converse sneakers threaded with gaudy orange laces.) Also, Molinas began to cruise the Lower East Side in search of prostitutes, bragging to his friends about how much his "fancy women" truly loved him.

In truth, women were either instantly attracted to or repelled by Molinas's brash public demeanor. His laugh was giggly and shrill, the kind that made strangers turn around and stare. In the company of civilians, he was always shy about his size and responded to inquiries about the high-altitude weather with mute embarrassment. Molinas was a witty conversationalist, even if his jokes often fell flat. His personal charisma was such that most people were eager to please him and readily talked about subjects—like basketball, the law, cars, food, and movies—with which he felt most comfortable. Molinas was also interested in the theater, and was particularly fond of musicals. He once paid the unheard of price of seventy dollars for a pair of tickets to *My Fair Lady*. He'd often approach an attractive girl and boldly place an arm around her shoulders. Yet he was also polite to women, raising himself from a chair to greet one, gallantly taking off his hat in a woman's presence, and always holding doors open for them.

Molinas was also a great lover of what he considered to be gourmet food, especially Italian cuisine and the fare at top-notch steakhouses. When dining in Brooklyn, he favored a Northern Italian restaurant named Carolina's. In Manhattan, he'd frequent either Broadway Joe's or the Pen and Pencil. "A good meal," he used to say, "is better than good sex." A scant two years after his banishment from the NBA, Molinas weighed two hundred thirty pounds and took pains to try and conceal the slight paunch that drooped over his belt.

A much more serious problem involved the increasing difficulty Molinas was experiencing in placing his bets. Bookies were simply refusing his action because Molinas rarely lost a wager, and they were afraid that every game he'd bet on was rigged. True, Joe Hacken could be counted on to lay off a few thousand bucks here and there, but even Jalop's action was being shunned because of his association with Molinas. More and more, Molinas was forced to place his bets through a "beard," a neutral third party that was paid a small percentage of any winnings.

Additionally, Molinas was making a bad name for himself among the local bookmakers because of his growing propensity for paying off his bad bets late or sometimes not at all. Hey, he was Jack Molinas. Right? Any time he lost a bet it was always somebody else's fault—some player who had miscalculated and made a free throw he should have missed, some referee who had coughed up a toot instead of swallowing the whistle—so why should he have to pay?

Molinas had minimal problems on the basketball court, however, as he led the Williamsport Billies to the EBL's regular season title. In a tight basket-for-basket competition, Molinas averaged 27.3 ppg and barely overcame Sherman White to cop the EBL's scoring crown. (John Azary averaged 7.3 ppg.) Both White and Molinas were selected to the EBL's All-Star team (along with Ed Roman, Bud Haabestad, Danny Finn, and Zeke Sinicola), with Molinas voted the league's MVP. In the postseason battle for the President's Cup, Williamsport swept Sunbury in two games before losing in the final round to arch-rival Wilkes-Barre.

Meanwhile, Molinas was still in touch with several of his Fort Wayne buddies. In the previous season of 1954–55, the Pistons had advanced into the championship round against Syracuse and had taken three of the first five games. Needing only one more victory to claim the NBA title, the Pistons lost to the Nationals, 109–104 in Game 6, before falling in the deciding game by a single point, 92–91. According to George Yardley, "The end of Game Seven was very weird. We were inbounding the ball with a one-point lead in the final seconds when one of our players practically threw the ball into the hands of the other team. Syracuse scored in a hurry and they were the champs. From then on there were always unwholesome implications about that ball game."

A year later, the Pistons once again fought their way into the NBA finals, this time to oppose the Philadelphia Warriors. Paul Arizin was the Warriors' leading scorer, a long-range bomber who was matched against the Pistons' defensive ace, Mel Hutchins. Philadelphia won the initial two games, with the Pistons rebounding for a victory in Game 3.

Game 4 was played in Fort Wayne and, although Hutchins's smothering defense limited Arizin to only three points, the Warriors prevailed, 107–105. In Game 5, however, Arizin notched twenty-seven points and Philadelphia won the game, 99–88, and with it the NBA championship. At least three NBA players had the same take on the deciding contest: In Game 4, Hutchins was in Arizin's pants. In Game 5, Hutchins never came within ten feet of Arizin; the wise guys in Coney Island were convinced he was taking a dive.

Was it a mere coincidence that Molinas made a bundle betting on Syracuse? Hardly.

On June 12, 1956, Jack Molinas graduated in the top ten percent of his law school class.

Molinas still enjoyed playing weekend basketball in the EBL and the Connecticut League, although a certain competitive edge was missing from his game since Podoloff had sandbagged his NBA career. Similarly, even though the prospect of someday becoming a lawyer only made Molinas yawn, he dutifully enrolled in a bar review course. Worse, more and more bookies were wise to his "beards" and he could barely get down a measly two hundred bucks on a sure-thing game. Meanwhile, if law school had cost him a bundle, so had his new cars, his flashy wardrobe, and all the high-priced restaurant tabs he picked up night after night. The legal bills alone from his various petitions, defenses, and appeals were enough to make his wallet flatter than a pancake. In truth, not only was Molinas bored with his life, but he also needed a quick infusion of big-time bucks.

With only eight franchises, the pro game was limited to a maximum of four games a day, and his steady supply of inside tips was rapidly diminishing. Also, honest bookies knew how crooked NBA games were and would only handle small-time courtesy bets for their regular customers. So, as the 1956–57 basketball season got under way, Molinas decided that the only future exciting enough, indeed the only one available to him, was studying the college games like a broker studied the stock market. If he scrutinized every team and every game, eventually he'd find a mismatch and a careless point spread.

The newsstand in the lobby of the New York Times Building in Times Square sold newspapers from virtually every city in the country. Molinas would buy dozens of newspapers every day and take more notes than he ever did in law school. He would also pay a legitimate Associated Press reporter for the use of his name and call the public relations guys at the colleges. "Hello, this is Mister So-and-So working for the AP out of New York and I'd like to do a feature article on your school. Had the team played up to par in their last game? Or below par? Was somebody in foul trouble? Did the other team play man-to-man or zone defense? Was there any dissension on the team? Was any key player likely to become scholastically ineligible?" Information on injuries, of course, was very dynamic. Throughout the course of his investigations, he always kept meticulous records.

From time to time, Molinas would drive up to the Bronx and check in at Bickford's to see what he could see. On one of his visits, he hooked up with

Shelly Thomas, the one-time center for Taft High School who'd allowed himself to be faked out so that Molinas could score a record-breaking basket in a PSAL playoff game at the Garden.

It turned out that Thomas was doing the same kind of research that Molinas was. When Molinas questioned him, Shelly said that he was working for a guy in Miami and assisting him in the making of the morning line.

This is how the process worked: At that time, the line was made by three people—Shelly's guy in Miami, Abe Hershfield in Minneapolis, and another big-timer in Biloxi, Mississippi. Now, what does making a line mean? It means that on just about all of the ball games played on a particular night, each of these three guys would pick the team most likely to win—the favorite—and also determine the number of points he thought would constitute an appropriate line. For instance, if Duke was playing Clemson, Duke should be the favorite. Let's say one of the line makers says that Duke should be favored by eleven points, one says Duke by twelve points, and the third guy says Duke by thirteen. What they'll do is get together and find the mid-position of the three lines—which would be twelve points—and that would be the opening line for that particular ball game. Of course, they'll add or subtract a half a point just to make sure the game isn't a tie, or, as it was called, a wash. Now, the reality may be that each of the three line makers really believes that Duke should beat Clemson by twenty points, but that doesn't justify making Duke a twenty-point favorite simply because twenty points is too much. With a twenty-point line, everybody and his mother would bet on Clemson and take the twenty-point spot. The twenty points is the true handicap, but the line is always less. The line must be a number that will encourage betting action on both teams. The outcome of the game is of no consequence to the line makers. They just want to create a number that will protect the bookies. If a bookie takes fifty thousand dollars on Duke minus twelve and a half points and fifty thousand on Clemson plus twelve and a half, then his ten-percent cut of the handle—or his "vigorish"—is ten thousand dollars and he doesn't care who wins.

The guy in Miami that Thomas was working for was himself working for a Mafioso who ran a bookmaking syndicate in Harlem. Shelly's job was to help the bookie in Miami determine the proper line and also to place bets for both of his bosses. In addition, Shelly would advise them which teams they should be betting on. From time to time, Shelly would ask for Molinas's opinion and Jack would give him maybe five games a night just as a favor. Well, Jack ran into a hot streak and Shelly's bosses asked him where his information was coming from, so he told them it was Jack. The next thing Molinas knew he got a telephone call asking him to meet with the Harlem mobster in a candy store on the northeast corner of Second Avenue and Ninety-sixth Street. His name was Joey Raos and he made Jack a proposition. He was going to give Jack a bunch of games every day and ask him to figure out a morning line by 8:00 A.M. They would then float the line around the country and see how the bookies reacted.

Jack picks up the story: "Shelly and I would always compare notes. He'd make up his lines and I'd make up mine and then we'd get together and sort things out. I'd speak to Shelly the night before a game, the afternoon before, even a week before. I'd give all of my picks to Shelly, who'd relay them to Joey Raos, and Shelly would bring me any money that I had coming to me.

"Occasionally, the line makers would conspire to issue a bogus line. If the handicap was fifteen points and the line that would bring in action on both teams should be eleven points, these guys would open the game at seven. Why would they do this? So that they could make their own private bets on the favorite, but giving seven instead of fifteen. It was a form of larceny. Bookies all over the country were paying for the service, were paying to have a knowledgeable source establish a morning line. Right? Sure, the money that they'd lay would up the line eventually, but they'd still be in at seven. What they were doing was stealing money from their customers.

"I worked through Shelly for the entire 1956–57 season, and my picks were winners sixty-two percent of the time. That may not seem like a big deal, but it meant a profit of thirty-eight thousand dollars for every hundred bets. Over the course of the season, I made around eight hundred picks. So my own profit was just over thirty thousand dollars. I also picked up another few thousand by having Joey Hacken place two-hundred-dollar bets here and there with local bookies."

In addition, Molinas was privy to certain information that also brought him five extremely lucrative paydays: Mike Parenti and Billy Crystal, both products of New Utrecht High School in Brooklyn, had received basketball scholarships to St. John's University. They were seniors in the 1956–57 season, the two best players on the team—and they were also doing business with the old Trick Master, Joe Hacken. The contract called for each player to receive one thousand dollars per game for bagging a total of five ball games. When all the dealing was done, the latest St. John's fixes netted Molinas approximately twenty g's.

At age twenty-four, Molinas was at the peak of his physical prowess and he continued to play brilliantly in the EBL. On November 12, 1956, at halftime of the Williamsport Billies opening game, Molinas was presented with the Tommy Bell Memorial Award for being the league's most valuable player in the previous season. Despite his twenty-six points, the Billies fell to Hazelton, 102–92. The game seemed to set the tone for the rest of the season. The Billies struggled to make the play-offs (finishing the regular season at 13–17 before being quickly eliminated in the first round of postseason play), while Molinas kept making the scoreboard light up like a pinball machine. His average of 26.5 ppg ranked him third in the EBL, behind Hal "King" Lear and Sherman White.

Approximately fifty-two percent of law school graduates pass the New York State Bar exam on their first attempt, and in January 1957, Molinas joined this slim majority. With an endorsement from the Character and Fitness Committee already in his pocket, Molinas was invited to become a senior partner in an otherwise prestigious law firm, Levy and Harten.

Molinas's first case involved Sherman White, his EBL rival who'd been implicated while at LIU in the scandals of 1951. It seems that when White was first picked up for questioning, the detectives had confiscated his bankbooks. Under Molinas's guidance, White eventually had his money returned.

Otherwise, Molinas was too busy playing basketball, gambling, and devising point spreads to devote much time and energy to his legal career. He estimated that his first year's income at Levy and Harten was only eight thousand dollars.

After his breakup with Peggy, Molinas started going to NBA games at Madison Square Garden. He was there to watch the ball games, to study the players, and to imagine how he would have thrived in the new fast-paced game legislated by the introduction of the twenty-four-second clock in 1954–55. Trying to keep a low profile, he'd walk with a hunched posture and hold a hat to shield his profile from passersby. Occasionally, fans would spot him and offer their wistful encouragements: "You belong out there, Jack." "You would've been the best, Jack." "You got screwed big-time, Jack." He'd thank them and try to fade back into the crowd.

Nothing that Molinas was doing seemed to satisfy him. He was increasingly unhappy and restless. And then Shelly Thomas introduced him to Dave Goldberg, and Molinas finally discovered a calling that could fulfill all of his needs.

During one of their telephone conversations, Shelly Thomas said to Molinas that he wanted to introduce him to someone who could do him some good. "The guy operates out of St. Louis," Shelly said, "and he's one of the biggest players in the country. I can also vouch for his intelligence because he bets the same teams as all the people in Harlem bet. He's a great guy and I think you should have a talk with him. Do it, Jack. You have nothing to lose."

"If this guy is so terrific and such a big shot," Jack said, "then why don't you do something with him? What do you need to involve me for?"

"I can't make any deals with him, Jack, only because I'm plugged in so tightly to New York. But you're more or less a free agent."

Shelly was a good friend, but he wasn't supposed to be introducing Molinas to anybody who might, in any way, be in competition with his Harlem people. But all the same Jack agreed to meet this hotshot from Saint Louis.

About two or three days later, he got a call from Shelly telling him the guy was in town, so they set up an appointment to have cocktails at five-thirty on a Friday night at the Peacock Alley in the Waldorf-Astoria hotel. The man in question was Dave Goldberg, and after they were introduced, the first thing he said was, "I hear you're doing rather well, Jack, and I hope we can do something together."

Jack was more than willing to make a deal. "We quickly reached an agreement whereby I provided Goldberg with the same plays that I was giving Shelly to turn over to his guys in Harlem. The difference was that I didn't have to give Goldberg the numbers until ten o'clock, which was two hours later than my deadline with Shelly. The significance is the Harlem bettors and their partners in Miami would be placing their bets at around ten o'clock Eastern time, when the bookies around the country opened for business. Most bookies wouldn't take large bets from public sources until about half past twelve so they could balance out the lines if there was too much money bet on one side or the other. But with Goldberg having the original lines at ten o'clock, he could get his bets down in a Chicago clearinghouse before the lines changed too much. It was an enormous advantage that could save anywhere from two to four points a ball game. Because of his connections, Goldberg was also able to carry some of my own bets. In addition to whatever money I won for myself, Goldberg paid me a hundred and fifty dollars for every winner that I gave to him.

"I found out later that Goldberg was not only booking action on his own, but he also had a 'sheet' with another Chicago betting service. Having a sheet meant that Goldberg had a string of customers—I'd say it was fifteen or twenty—who habitually bet several thousand dollars every night. But since he didn't have the bankroll to cover them, Goldberg was essentially subcontracting these customers to the betting service. Goldberg's payoff was fifty percent of what his customers lost. On the flip side, he was totally responsible for whatever his customers won. So Goldberg had a twofold operation going for him, his own bookmaking operation plus a very substantial sheet with the Chicago service. It was a sweet deal. Anyway, it turned out that my winning picks went up to sixty-four percent while I was dealing with Goldberg and he was very impressed."

Impressing Dave Goldberg was no easy business. He'd grown up in a predominantly upper-class Jewish neighborhood in St. Louis and was a gym rat, a self-made athlete who practically lived in the local YMHA. Football, baseball, and basketball were his sports and he trained as hard as a boxer preparing for a title fight. By his senior year in high school, Goldberg was six feet tall and one hundred and eighty pounds—a superbly conditioned athlete. He lacked the basketball genius of a Jack Molinas, but he was one of the finest schoolboy backcourtsmen in St. Louis.

"And he was an excellent fighter as well," said Jake Samuels, a longtime family friend. "Dave would fight you at the drop of a hat. Not a troublemaker or a bully. Just a tough kid who would never back down from anything."

Goldberg was too restless to consider going to college, and shortly after graduating from high school, he stumbled across the opportunity to purchase a gasoline station in his neighborhood. He knew little about servicing automobiles, but it was a chance to own something and he grabbed it.

The gas station soon became a kind of informal social club for Goldberg's high school friends. Some of them worked for him and others merely "hung out" there. In addition to heated discussions about cars, they talked about the girls they had and had not conquered, and they talked not any less feverishly about sports. Inevitably, the gas station discussions with his friends led to arguments about sports and then to wagers. Goldberg began booking these wagers and the gas station soon became a drive-in bookmaking establishment. Like Molinas, Goldberg was a quick learner who easily grasped the subtleties of bookmaking and prided himself on his own handicapping abilities.

Nobody was surprised when Goldberg's nascent bookmaking service eventually became hugely successful. And since St. Louis was one of the country's major sports betting centers, it was likewise inevitable that Goldberg came to the attention of major gambling interests in the city. By the time Molinas and Goldberg met, the gas station was long gone and Goldberg was well connected with every significant gambling operation in the United States, Canada, and Mexico. And like Molinas, Goldberg was eager to expand his own possibilities.

Goldberg would periodically come to New York on business, and after the success of their first season working together they met again at the Peacock Alley—it was in mid-February of 1957—and he had another proposition in mind. "Listen," Dave said to Molinas. "We're making a ton of money, but you're not fully capitalizing on your position. You're playing in the Eastern League. You must know the referees, Jack, and some of them must also officiate college games. Am I right, or am I right?"

In fact, Jack knew most of the referees who worked within two hundred miles of New York.

"That's what I'm saying, Jack. Why don't you get a little friendly with the refs? If you want, tell them that I'll gladly wager twenty-five hundred dollars on their behalf on either side of whatever college game they're working. They pick the team, I make the bet and take all the risk, and they get the winnings. Naturally, they'll have to blow the whistle once or twice to help us out."

Then Goldberg told Molinas about a "beaver" he had in his pocket. (That's a colloquialism for a basketball official; beavers have stripes on their back just like referees do.) "The guy worked in the Missouri Valley Conference, Jack. He has since been expelled from the league, but I had him. He was mine. The guy called me up thirty-three times, and we had thirty-two winners, one push, and no losers. I couldn't begin to tell you how much money we both made. When a beaver tells you he's got the game, Jack, that's the surest winner you can ever have. It's even more of a sure thing than having a player. Say, Jack. I know you play ball with plenty of pros, but do you play with any college players?"

"Sure. After the college season is over, there are a lot of open tournaments that I play in all around New York. A handful of pros from the NBA play in these tournaments, a bunch of us from the Eastern League, and most of the players are college kids, the best in the area."

"Okay," Goldberg said. "Now we're talking. Maybe some of these college players could use a little extra cash, you know? Listen, Jack. Why don't you pal around with these guys, take them out to dinner, slip them a C-note just to make them feel obligated to you. Spend as much money as you want to, Jack, and send me the tab. If any of these players happen to ask a leading question, well, then, find out if they're willing to do business during the season."

"Suppose I spend a thousand dollars fishing after them," Jack said, "and nobody bites?"

"No problem. I'll cover expenses. You just tell me what you spent it on."

"Fair enough," Jack said, and they shook hands.

The Mole was back in business!

Goldberg knew all along that in order for his vague schemes to be actualized he needed a significant bankroll behind him. One phone call to the Chicago operation elicited an enthusiastic response. There was only one catch—the Chicago bigwigs wanted to meet Molinas.

On the flight out, Molinas realized that this meeting could be his passport into the top echelon, so he concentrated on getting his act together. He was dressed like a businessman, wearing a gray suit and horn-rimmed glasses, and even carrying a little attaché case. These guys were the big boys, backed by all of the Chicago hoods and the Chicago Family, and they didn't take any prisoners, so whatever arrangements they made would have to be spelled out very carefully. Any misunderstandings could be very dangerous for Molinas. He couldn't come off as being humble, nor could he be a tough guy.

A black limousine was waiting for Molinas when he arrived at Chicago's Midway Airport. After a twenty-five-minute drive into the suburbs, the car pulled up in front of what an overhead sign described as THE CICERO HOME IMPROVEMENT COMPANY. Molinas ducked through the front door and found himself in a small reception room where a gorgeous young woman was sitting behind a desk and pounding away at a typewriter. The chauffeur led him through the front room and into a much larger room that was divided up into nineteen doorless cubicles that were each bounded by opaque Plexiglas walls. In each of these numbered spaces a clerk sat on a swivel chair in front of a small desk that was cluttered with writing pads, and boxes of sharpened pencils, along with a telephone capable of receiving as many as four incoming calls. Above each cubicle was a light that flashed red whenever the clerk was speaking on the phone. Near the front of the room was a larger desk set on an elevated platform, and that's where the supervisor was stationed. Equipped with a special phone that could plug in to any of the calls happening in any of the cubicles, the supervisor could easily discover whether any of the clerks were actually writing up legitimate bets or trying to steal a few bucks on the side. Obviously, none of the clerks had any way of knowing exactly whose phone the supervisor was tapping.

Behind the supervisor's desk a large blackboard was fastened to the wall and tended by another supervisory clerk. All the games available for betting were written on the blackboard along with the current point spread. It was the blackboard clerk's job to keep a record of how much money was being wagered on each of the games they were handling, and then to change the line if need be. For instance, if one team is a six-point favorite and everybody is laying money on the favorite, the guy at the blackboard would ring a little bell to alert the clerks in the cubicles that a change was coming, and then change the six-point line to seven or seven and a half or whatever. This happened frequently because the house was booking about five thousand dollars on every incoming phone call. The whole place was as efficient as any Wall Street brokerage house.

In addition to laying straight bets, this particular office was one of the central layoff offices in the country. That meant that other bookies around the country would hedge their overloads there. Say a local bookie somewhere receives a thousand-dollar bet on one team and three thousand on the other team. If he stays with the action he's booked, then he becomes a gambler himself, hoping that the team carrying the thousand wins the game. Obviously, that's a tremendous risk, one that any right-minded bookie would rarely take. So what does he do? He contacts a layoff bookie, or a hedge bookie, and tries to bet the two-thousand-dollar difference so his own books are even-Steven and he's got three thousand riding on each team. And whenever the hedge bookie gets overloaded, he in turn lays off his overload with the Chicago office. The Chicago office is so big that they can always even out their own books by betting bits and pieces here and there all over the country.

Of course, you could bet on a variety of action in the Chicago office. Horse races, prizefights, anything. The biggest action, however, was on basketball and football. It's very hard to beat baseball over an entire season because baseball is almost always a straight statistical bet. Good pitching almost always beats good hitting. A short left-field wall in Fenway Park. A short right-field porch in Yankee Stadium. Ground-ball pitchers against fly-ball hitters. Righties pitching to righties. Lefties pitching to lefties. There are no point spreads, or run spreads, in baseball. Just straight odds, and odds are hard to beat with any consistency. But football and basketball are opinion bets where a hardworking gambler like Jack can find an edge. He was very much impressed with the entire operation.

"I was introduced to the boss of the office, Norman Rosenthal, whom everybody called Lefty. This guy had white hair and very fair skin and he looked Scandinavian. He was very soft-spoken, and he had a very light Southern drawl, but he was sharp as a tack. Lefty was wearing a slick sharkskin suit and he had a Piaget watch on his wrist—that's like a three-thousand-dollar timepiece with big diamonds instead of numbers. Standing next to Lefty was a guy named Tony Dicci, who needed a shave and wore dark glasses and a black leather Eisenhower jacket. After we were introduced, Tony invited me to touch his jacket because he was so proud that it was made of the softest kid leather. I'd say Tony was just about the toughest-looking guy I ever saw. Even if I was a priest I wouldn't cross him."

Lefty showed Jack around and explained the nuts and bolts, and then he said that while they were doing a bang-up business, sometimes the action was slow. "Dave tells me," Lefty said, "that you can get a couple of college kids to maybe do business with us. Is that true?"

"Probably," Jack said, "but I don't know for sure because I haven't made a move on anybody yet.

"So we talked and we dickered and we eventually came to an agreement as to how much money they would make available so I could buy a game, how the word would be passed along, what my cut would be, and how the money would be delivered. I was more than satisfied with the arrangements. Except for a few minor points, my main stipulation was that I would get paid in nothing larger than one-hundred-dollar bills. Lefty was also agreeable, so we had a deal. I'd bill them for my expenses, try to get some kids involved during the spring and summer, and we'd hopefully start buying ball games next season.

"Back to New York there was a guy named Spook who was always hanging around the high school games and the postseason money tournaments—like St. Anthony's in Jersey City, and Don Bosco in Haverstraw, New York. Spook's job was to hook up high school players from the metropolitan area with college coaches who were looking for a playmaking guard, or a rebounding center, or what have you. Spook knew everybody everywhere and I was very friendly with him. He would come by my law office and ask me for ten or twenty bucks to buy some needy kid a meal and I'd always lay it on him. I was still in pretty good physical shape and I'd usually play in the most competitive of the money tournaments. In addition, I'd also put up a hundred bucks or so to sponsor a team and buy uniforms and I'd ask Spook if he could get me some good players who wouldn't mind passing me the ball. So I'd play and coach these teams, and I also took my cue from Joe Hacken, giving the kids twenty bucks for dinner just to romance them.

"I still considered Joe to be my mentor, so I let him know exactly what had transpired between me and Rosenthal. Joe thought it was a good idea. 'Listen, Jack,' he said. 'What if we do it this way.... When you come across a player who you think might do a trick, let me know and I'll be the one to approach him. That way you won't get into any more trouble.' Good old Joe, always looking out for me. So that's the way we worked things.

"I was playing in a tournament in Saint Francis Xavier on President Street in Brooklyn and Spook had arranged for this black kid from somewhere in the neighborhood to play on my team. I was scoring thirty-five or forty points a game, but the kid was hanging in with me. Passing me the ball in the right place at the right time and making most of the leftover shots that I didn't take. His name was Vinnie Brewer and he played at Iowa State. I was doing my regular routine, slipping him money after games and getting friendly with him. And the kid had a real hungry look whenever the money was flashing, so I sicced Joe on him. Vinnie Brewer was our first recruit."

Molinas hadn't been so excited since he first started playing with the Pistons. It was the spring of 1957 and he was counting the days until the beginning of basketball season in November. *That* was something he hadn't done since the end of his freshman season at Columbia.

Columbia. Fort Wayne. Those days seemed like they were a million miles away.

During the summer, Molinas bided his time and concerned himself mostly with familiar pursuits: playing basketball at Kaiser Park and working in the Eagle Bar. Whenever Molinas was tending bar, the radio was switched on—tuned either to a popular music station or, even better, a baseball game. If the latter was available, Molinas would eagerly solicit bets at large. For a hundred dollars, would the next pitch be a ball? a strike? hit fair? or foul? As usual, Molinas had an edge. He knew that the odds were six to five that a three-two pitch would be fouled off.

With his smile clenched around an expensive Cuban cigar, Molinas would swab the counter with a damp towel and offer a cheerful greeting to every customer. "Hey, champ. What'll you have?" Another familiar opener was, "Let me ask your opinion..."—which was always a preface to a betting proposition.

Yet his closest friends were able to discern that in spite of his obsessive gambling, Molinas was a compassionate person. "He had a very tender side," said Ellis, "and was a soft touch for everybody with a sob story. For example, when my daughter was three years old she'd walk around with a sad, droopy face because she had no sister or brother to play with. So what did Jack do? He went out and bought her a little Scottie dog, Tinkerbell. It was her best friend for the next seventeen years. And when that little girl first saw the puppy and her face lit up like a Christmas tree, I swear that Jack had tears in his eyes."

But Molinas never outgrew his adolescent taste for mischief. "My wife and I used to spend our summer vacations up in the Catskills," Ellis said, "at Kate's Bungalow Colony, and Jack would often drive up to spend a weekend with us. It was all pretty low-key. If we didn't go to Monticello Raceway to bet the Trotters, we'd usually spend Saturday nights in the recreation cottage they called 'the Casino,' just drinking sodas, eating hamburgers or grilled cheese sandwiches, playing the jukebox or playing cards. Well, on the Fourth of July weekend, Jack came up from the city with a huge bag of firecrackers, and he was looking for trouble. After a few beers, he stuffed the whole bag into the crotch of a big tree and set everything off. Bang! The vibrations blasted the light fixtures from the walls of the adjacent bungalows and people were running around screaming bloody murder. Jack realized immediately he'd made a mistake. He was very contrite and not only did he pay to have the light fixtures repaired, but he paid the tab for an impromptu party in the Casino."

With his summer revelries over, Molinas settled down to business, teaming up with Joe Hacken and putting the word out on the street that they were interested in being introduced to money-hungry college basketball players. Financial incentives were offered for consummated introductions, and should any of the players eventually agree to turn tricks, the go-betweens could also earn very liberal commissions.

In early November, Molinas's and Hacken's underground advertising found a couple of takers. Aaron Wagman was twenty-five, a small-time hustler who lived in the Fordham Road area of the Bronx. He was a manager for Harry F. Stevens, who ran the food concessions at Yankee Stadium. During the baseball season, and during prizefights or football games, Wagman sold hot dogs in the grandstand. In the off-season he worked on inventory, counting peanuts, pretzels, and Cracker Jacks. Wagman boasted that he was close friends with several members of the New York Yankees, but nobody in the neighborhood believed him. Mickey Mantle? Yogi Berra? Whitey Ford? According to Wagman they all called him "the Big A" and frequently treated him to steak dinners. Molinas remembered later that Wagman used to be a runner for Joe Hacken when Joe worked out of the poolroom, and that he was a bit of a shylock, pushing money out on the street, six for five.

Joe Green was another neighborhood fixture who was one of the most ferocious rebounders in the Creston Avenue school yard and a one-time teammate of Molinas's with the Hacken All-Stars. An outstanding basketball player at Taft High School, Green had received bona fide scholarship offers from several reputable colleges but had declined them all simply because he never qualified for a high school diploma. He bragged that he'd had tryouts with all of New York's professional teams in basketball, baseball and football, and that he'd also trained as a professional boxer, but like Wagman, nobody took his claims seriously. Whatever the season or the weather, Green wore the same dirty pair of sneakers, a filthy sweatshirt cut at midsleeve, and greasy chino pants. From time to time, Green worked in the stockroom at Macy's, and it was said that he could live on forty cents a day and gain weight.

"Joe Green always played with us against the hotel teams up in the Catskills," said Paul Brandt. "He would take out his false teeth before a ball game, then play like a tiger. He was about six foot two and very strong. Joe was belligerent and if there were any problems, he'd be the first one to start throwing punches. He was our hatchet man and he used to say that fisticuffs were like Christmas presents—better to give than receive."

Central to Green's madcap reputation was the time he walked in uninvited to a practice session of the University of Tennessee varsity basketball team and asked the coach for a tryout. Maybe because Green was dressed in his habitual wardrobe, augmented for the occasion with a straw hat and a corn weed dangling from his mouth, the coach was understandably dubious. But the varsity players thought it would be a laugh riot to embarrass the hayseed and the coach reluctantly consented. Of course, as befits a fairy tale, Green proved to be the best player on the court. The coach was amazed that such a fine talent had not previously come to his attention, and he asked Green where he'd been hiding himself. "Well now, Coach," Green said in a stagy drawl, "I've been very busy on my father's farm tending the mules." Whereupon Green tipped his hat and walked out of the gym.

Wagman and Green were both accomplished pool sharks and had formed a close friendship hustling rubes in the local billiard parlor. They both had lofty ambitions of becoming influential bookies and fix-masters, but were chronically short of cash. Then, during the previous summer, Green had hooped with two college players whom he believed were willing to throw basketball games. Green informed Wagman and they began searching for a well-heeled backer. Several bookies turned them down, including one who offered to back them in fixing football players instead. "We don't know any football players," Wagman told him. Not yet.

Of course, the two erstwhile fixers also spoke to Joe Jalop. Joe squeezed them until they gave up the name of their main player, Richie Hoffman from South Carolina, and also Jerry Alaimo from Brown University. Joe said that he didn't think Hoffman was a strong enough player to carry a game, but he'd think about their proposition.

Naturally, Joe called Molinas and they agreed that Wagman and Green might be telling the truth, that they might very well be able to deliver Hoffman and Alaimo. They decided to sit tight and see what Wagman and Green would do next.

Within a few days, Wagman and Green approached Molinas, calling him at his law office and making an appointment. Wagman did all the talking, saying that they had one player interested in dumping games, and maybe another one as well. At first Wagman wouldn't divulge the names, but he said that both players played for major colleges whose games were on the board, and both of them were starters. Of course, through Joe, Molinas already knew exactly to whom they were referring. When he asked Wagman how much money would be involved, he said one thousand for each of the players and another thousand each for him and Green. A total of four thousand per game. After Wagman gave the players' names, Molinas told them that he was interested.

"But," Molinas said, "I need to have an agent. Somebody to talk to the players face-to-face." Molinas was thinking of Joe Hacken, and of course neither Wagman nor Green had any idea that Joe and Jack were already in cahoots in this deal.

"I understand," Wagman said, "but we don't want Joe Hacken to be involved in this at all."

"Why not?"

"Because he has a bad reputation in the neighborhood," Wagman said. "He doesn't hang around Bickford's so much anymore, and he left owing a lot of guys a lot of money."

It was true that Joe was operating out of Manhattan more and more, but he never welched on a bet in his life. He'd certainly paid Molinas every penny he had coming and all of it right on time. It is more likely that they didn't want Joe involved because he'd already turned them down. Molinas subsequently made an appointment to meet Wagman and Green at the Bickford's cafeteria on Fifty-seventh Street. He wanted them to think that they had fooled him.

Since Joe Hacken told him about the two players Wagman and Green were promoting, Molinas called Dave Goldberg in St. Louis to explain the situation. He told Goldberg that he wanted to bring Hacken in on the action and Goldberg gave him the go-ahead. Goldberg promised to put up all the bribe money and reimburse Jack for whatever expenses he would need. Molinas assumed that Goldberg would also cut Lefty Rosenthal and the Chicago operation in on the deal.

Jack picks up the play-by-play from here: "The Bickford's on Fifty-seventh Street was L-shaped, and I had Joe wait out of sight while I sat down with Wagman and Green. It was a question of strategy, of not antagonizing them right off the bat and having them leave in a huff. We said our hellos and I told them that I was now going to produce the fellow who'd be my agent and they said fine, go get him. Which I did. There were some very puzzled looks passed between Wagman and Green, between Green and Joe, between Wagman and Joe. Every possible combination you could think off. I knew that they didn't know. They thought they knew that I didn't know. It was a pisser. Even after Joe sat down and we began to talk in earnest, I never let on that Joe had already clued me in. Once Wagman and Green understood that either Joe was in or the whole deal was a no-go, they tabled their objections.

"When we finally got down to the nitty-gritty of it, I played dumb and asked Wagman who the teams were and which players he had. Richie Hoffman at South Carolina, whom Green had played against in the Catskills. According to Wagman, Hoffman was a sure thing. The other player, Jerry Alaimo from Brown University, had never been asked outright if he'd be willing to do business, but Green was pretty sure that he'd be happy to be cut in.

"I was aware that Wagman and Green had first approached Joe Hacken, and I also knew the other four or five bookies they'd gone to. 'Have you told any of this information to anybody else?' I asked Wagman, and he swore I was the first he'd spoken to. Right off the bat, then, I knew I couldn't really trust either of them.

"In any case, I agreed to work with them and we talked about the possibility of sending Green down to South Carolina to speak to Richie Hoffman. Then we looked at the schedule and saw that South Carolina would be playing NYU at Madison Square Garden in just a few days. All of this happened in early

December of 1957. Green called Hoffman down in South Carolina and confirmed that his team would be coming into New York the day before the game and that we could make our arrangements at that time.

"Goldberg wired the money in my name to a midtown hotel, and everything was all set and ready to go. Richie Hoffman was supposed to get a thousand, Wagman and Green a thousand each, and there was two thousand for me. That meant a five-thousand-dollar contract. Wagman, Green, and I had planned to bet our payoffs. Joe Jalop wasn't in for a payoff, but he'd bet his own money on NYU.

"The South Carolina team was staying at the Paramount Hotel over on Forty-sixth Street and Eighth Avenue, and the plan was for Joe Green to go over there and talk to Hoffman as soon as the eight A.M. line was set. At an appointed time after the game, Green would return to the hotel and pay off Hoffman his grand in tens and twenties. What happened instead was that Joe Green's brother, Chris, said that he'd heard something about the district attorney's having found out that the South Carolina game was fixed. According to the brother, the whole thing was a trap and we were all going to get nabbed. Green believed it and ran over to Wagman's apartment to say he was pulling out.

"Well, both Joe Hacken and I thought it was a figment of Chris Green's imagination, or if anything, the brother was trying to keep Joe Green out of trouble. So, we spoke to Joe Green, pleading with him to get hold of Hoffman and not to worry about silly rumors. But Green was shivering in his boots and the game never came off. It sure didn't help my credibility that I had to call Goldberg and report the bad news.

"By the way, South Carolina lost and didn't cover, so even with Hoffman playing straight, we would've won our bets.

"Okay, so I still had all of Goldberg's money. Right? What to do next?

"As it turned out, the morning after the NYU game, South Carolina flew up to Buffalo to play St. Bonaventure, so I decided to put the same deal together a second time. I called up Goldberg in St. Louis, and, yes, he was okay with the new deal. He even wired me another two hundred and fifty bucks to cover the extra expenses. Wagman, Green, and Hoffman were also on board. Meanwhile, I was on the phone for days, absolutely neglecting my law practice. Anyway, Green was going to fly up to Buffalo with Hoffman's money and we'd be in touch the morning of the St. Bonaventure game to relay the spread.

"So right before Green was set to leave for the airport, we're all sitting around a table in a hotel coffee shop and going over our last-minute arrangements. It was a snowy Saturday morning. We would bet Wagman's money with this bookie, Green's money with that one, mine with another one. I told Wagman and Green that my backer was registered in a room at the same hotel and that I'd have to go upstairs and get the money. Of course this wasn't true, but I wanted them to believe that somebody had flown in from out of town this time so there'd be no shenanigans like Green had pulled before. Somebody with a gun who'd blow a hole in Green's head if he chickened out again. So I diddled around, then came down with the money, and we were finally ready to roll.

"But guess what? The snow was really coming down and it was even worse in Buffalo. So much so that all flights out of New York are cancelled. Obviously, Hoffman's not going to do business without someone there to put money in his hand after the game. And we were stuck a second time.

"When I called Goldberg, he wasn't amused. 'Don't you guys know what you're doing?' he wanted to know. 'Whom do you have working for you, Jack? A bunch of clowns? Are you just wasting my time, or what?' The only thing that mollified Goldberg at that point was that I was still picking winners for him to bet on.

"So now we went in for the third time. South Carolina versus Georgia in the Gator Bowl Tournament down in Jacksonville, Florida. We met again at the Bickford's on Fifty-seventh Street and I said to Wagman and Green, 'Listen, I don't know for sure if Hoffman's jerking me around, or if you two guys are jerking me around, but my reputation's on the line here and this one's got to work. Now this is what we're going to do. Joe Green, I'll tell you what...I'm going to give you my car and you'll drive down to Florida. Me and Joe Hacken will fly down on the day of the game and meet with you to get the line and the money straightened out. Wagman, you stay in New York. Let's not foul this up again. Let's be professionals and take care of business.' It was like a little pep talk to a team.

"All right. So that's the way it worked out. Green drove down to Jacksonville and Joe Hacken and I flew down and everything looks kosher this time.

"Now, my own private scheme was to bet my two-thousand-dollar share with Goldberg and also to bet as much as I could with my own people. I had a line of credit that must have run to twenty thousand dollars and I had maybe ten or fifteen bookies that I still could bet with. I also knew that back in New York, as soon as Wagman got the word that the deal was set, he'd also be betting his ass off. So I said to Joe Hacken, 'Listen, we can't let Joe Green call Wagman, because if he does that, Wagman's money is going to screw up the point spread.' And Hacken agreed. So we told Green that after Hoffman got paid and the deal was set, he wasn't permitted to make any phone calls. Green agreed only because he had to, but he wasn't too happy.

"So there's Wagman waiting in a phone booth in New York for the word from Green, and Green was making all kinds of excuses so he could sneak away and make the call. We drove and walked around Jacksonville, just looking to kill time before the game. Every step that Green took, I was on one side of him and Hacken's on the other side. I even followed Green into the bathroom just in case there was a telephone in there.

"The morning line had Georgia favored by two and a half points, and I had to place my bets before I called Goldberg and told him that the deal was set and that South Carolina was going under. If I had called Goldberg first, the bets he would have laid would have jacked up the line to four and a half or even higher, and I'd rather stick him with the higher line than stick myself with it. For myself I bet a few nickels with one bookie and a few dimes with another for a total of about seven thousand dollars. By the time I called Goldberg, the line had moved up a half point and he was a little concerned that there might be too much activity on Georgia. I told him, no, that people just felt that Georgia was a better team than the morning line indicated. Of course, since the Chicago operation was the biggest hedge office in the country, all the money that local bookies were laying off on South Carolina eventually showed up in Chicago.

"With the volume of action that the Chicago office was handling, it took about fifty thousand to move their line a half point, and a hundred thousand to move it by a full point. So if I had bet seven thousand on Georgia and the line moved up a half point, there was another forty-three thousand being bet on Georgia. That could have been the total of a lot of small bets, or else a couple of big-timers had gotten the word that the game was rigged. Anyway, I bet seven thousand of my own plus the five thousand that I'd received from Goldberg. I'd say Goldberg himself bet around thirty g's and who knew how much Lefty Rosenthal and his boys had wagered. But the final line was Georgia minus four and a half, which meant that there was two hundred thousand dollars more bet on Georgia than on South Carolina.

"The game itself was a comedy of errors. First off, Hoffman didn't even start the game. About a half hour before the game began, I saw a tiny article in the local newspaper saying that Hoffman had a bum ankle and might not be playing. This, of course, was after all of our bets were in. Then, when Hoffman finally got into the action, he was so nervous that the first time he touched the ball he threw a pass to nobody. His second touch resulted in a missed layup, then on the ensuing trip downcourt, Hoffman misstepped, reinjured his ankle, and had to be taken from the game. That was it. Hoffman played a total of one minute. Now we had a dead-even game with nobody working it for us. On top of that, the basketball coach at West Point, John Mauer, showed up in the seat next to mine. Years ago, he had recruited me big-time, so I had to chat with him while the game was being played. I was sweating bullets because I was in danger of losing my own money, and I had to talk about what this fellow was doing, and do I remember so-and-so. Fortunately, Georgia won and easily covered the spread.

"After the game, Joe Hacken and I met up with Hoffman to pay him off. I had a thousand bucks in my pocket for Hoffman, but because of the injury Hacken talked the kid into taking only six hundred.

"Meanwhile, back in St. Louis, Goldberg saw zeroes beside Hoffman's name in the box score and had no idea the kid had only played one minute. So Goldberg was happy because his money won, and he wanted to know if I had any other games that he could buy.

"Now we were in business. Fixers, Incorporated had its first credit on the balance sheet. We were one for one and eager to play again.

"Okay. So Joe Hacken and I had our return flights booked and Joe Green was supposed to drive my car back to New York. A couple of days later Hacken, Wagman, and I were sitting around in the cafeteria and talking about maybe doing an upcoming South Carolina–Maryland game. But Wagman was bitching like crazy because Green never showed up in New York. Not only that, but after we won the Georgia game, I had given Green his thousand bucks and also Wagman's thousand. So with Green AWOL, Wagman still hadn't gotten paid. Green's reputation was that money in his pocket gave him a certain sense of power and he loved to blow whatever money he had on prostitutes. We're all very concerned about Green's whereabouts, but there was nothing we could do about it. We couldn't very well call the police or the Missing Persons Bureau.

"Three days later, I got a phone call: 'This is the Miami Beach Police Department. Are you Jack Molinas?' Oh, my God! We're all going to get busted! But they'd called to tell me that my car had been left in the airport parking lot six days ago. A black-and-white Chevy with a red interior? The license plate? Yes, that's my car. So I had to fly down to Miami Beach, pay a fifty-buck fee because the car had been towed away and impounded, and then drive back to New York by myself. And still there was no news from Joe Green.

"The day after I got back from Miami, I finally got a person-to-person collect call from Miami. 'Hello? Hello, Jack? This is Joe. How are you?'

"'Joe!' I said. 'Where the hell have you been? Are you crazy or something?'

"'I flew to Havana, Jack, and I had the time of my life. I was dancing, and drinking, and screwing the señoritas. I'll be back in New York as soon as you wire me fifty bucks for my plane fare.'

"'Fifty bucks! What happened to the two thousand?'

"'I spent it all, Jack. Gambling, drinking, and screwing. Like I said. I lived, Jack! I'm happy! Smile, Jack! Don't worry about a thing!'

"'Tell that to your partner. He's asking for his thousand dollars.'

"'Yeah,' Green said. 'That's a problem. Does he know that you gave me the two thousand?'

"'No.'

"'Good. Then you can do me a favor, Jack, and tell Aaron that you only gave me six hundred, since Hoffman got hurt and barely played. That way I'll only owe Aaron three hundred. Otherwise, Aaron'll blow his top and take a powder. I'm telling you, Jack, Havana is heaven.'

"So I wired Green the fifty, he met us in the cafeteria, told Wagman that I only paid him six hundred and that he'd repay the three hundred from our next job."

Molinas was forced to take a hard look at his new partners. He knew that they'd lie to him in a minute, and that Green would cheat Wagman whenever he could. And Molinas knew that Wagman wasn't quite as smart as advertised.

Fixers Incorporated. What a motley crew.

The shadow of the Molinas Incident continued to darken the NBA. "It was early in the 1957–58 season," George Yardley remembered, "and Zollner had moved the Fort Wayne franchise to Detroit. Red Rocha was the Pistons coach and he called a team meeting in his hotel room on the morning before a game against the Lakers at Minneapolis. Rocha read to us what he said was an edict from the league. In essence, the edict said that the NBA had continued its surveillance of several players, tapping phones and bugging hotel rooms. The league knew that there were certain players who had been, and still were, doing business with gamblers. Rather than expelling these players and giving the league another black eye, the NBA suggested that the players in question should quietly retire at the end of the season and nothing would be made of the facts at hand. There was a lot of kidding that no matter what happened over the summer months, even if you broke both legs, you'd still play at least one game the following season so you wouldn't be implicated. But at the end of the 1957–58 season, a lot of players who seemed to have plenty of game left retired prematurely. Among them were Mel Hutchins, Don Meineke, and Andy Phillip."

At the same time that Commissioner Podoloff was so successfully finessing the NBA's suspected dumpers into hanging up their sneakers, Molinas was tearing up the Eastern League. True, Molinas was not (and never would be again) in the same kind of game-hardened physical condition demanded by his coaches at Columbia and Fort Wayne, but his game had matured during his four-and-a-half-year forced absence from the NBA, and he was a more potent scorer than ever before. The highlight of Molinas's 1957–58 season was a fifty-point effort against Scranton in early February. All told, Molinas averaged 32.2 ppg (second to Larry Hennessy's league-leading count of 32.4), the high-water mark of his EBL career.

If the numbers in the box score were impressive, there were also signs that Molinas was losing his edge in the shadow of the basket. Molinas was still only twenty-five years old, but a new generation of big men showed him little respect. Rugged players like Stacey Arceneaux, Wally Choice, and Roman Turman would routinely rough up Molinas and force him out of the pivot. Molinas's rebounding totals were down, and increasingly he was becoming a perimeter player. More telling was the fact that the Billies finished out of the play-offs for the first time since Molinas's tenure in Williamsport.

Even with all of Molinas's game-fixing schemes and multiple trips to Florida, he only missed three of the Williamsport Billies total of twenty-nine games. Arriving on time was another matter. As Mike Bernardi reported on January 26, 1958, in the *Williamsport Beacon*:

> The "Late Mr. Molinas" might be an appropriate title for the Billies' all-star performer. I know of no statistics on how many times Jack has been late for Billies games since he joined them several years ago. But if such figures were kept he'd probably rank as high in that division as he does annually in the point-producing race.
>
> It was Molinas' tardiness Saturday night that caused the Bills to be without him, Jimmy Brasco, Zeke Sinicola and Angy Lombardo until nearly a half hour after the scheduled starting time of 8:30 for a game against the Scranton Miners. All were traveling together by auto from New York.
>
> Bill Pickelner, president of the Billies, read the riot act to Molinas before and after the game. He questioned him as to why, on nights when he knows the weather to be bad, he doesn't start earlier from New York.
>
> Molinas offered the excuse that he was stopped and ticketed by a policeman for exceeding a 35-mile per hour limit on a section of the Turnpike.

Playing only the second half against Scranton, Molinas's lowly total of fifteen points certainly cost him the EBL's scoring title.

Meanwhile, Fixers Incorporated sought to parley their initial success into bigger and better paydays. But there were problems. Jack picks it up again:

"Our little family continued to meet in the same L-shaped cafeteria on Fifty-seventh Street and we all came to the same conclusion: Richie Hoffman was not a strong enough player to work by himself. Besides that, even after his ankle healed he still wasn't starting, and the general feeling was that Hoffman was not trustworthy. So we decided not to have anything more to do with Hoffman unless we could get another South Carolina player lined up. Since Joe Green was the contact with Hoffman, we had him make the call to South Carolina and explain the situation. 'Well,' Hoffman told Green, 'I could speak to my room-mate, Bob Pericola. There's another player named Mike Callahan who also might be interested.' The way it was left was that we wouldn't do anything until Hoffman got back to Green about his two teammates.

"We were still waiting to hear from Hoffman when South Carolina played a game against Maryland. For some reason, Maryland opened as only a four-and-a-half-point favorite, and there was an awful lot of money bet on South Carolina. What probably happened was that the handicappers suspected that South Carolina had taken a dive against St. Bonaventure and that they'd make up for the down game by playing their balls off against Maryland. All of the pin-headed bettors just jumped on the bandwagon. Well, they all got cremated when Maryland won by twenty points.

"Wouldn't you know that for their next game, against Virginia, South Carolina opened as a big underdog—seven or eight points that eventually moved up to ten points. There was so much money wagered on Virginia that the game was taken off the board. Virginia also won big, by close to twenty points. Now, even though the games against Maryland and Virginia were dead honest, everybody in the country was swearing that South Carolina was dumping.

"Dave Goldberg called me in a frenzy. 'What are you guys doing?' he screamed at me. 'I lost all the money I made in the South Carolina–Georgia game in the next two games. Are you guys double-crossing me? What gives?' He didn't believe me when I told him we weren't doing anything with South Carolina either up or down.

"It was crazy. There we were, sitting out a couple of games and there were fourteen different crosscurrents at work. Worse, South Carolina was now a worthless team for us. Hoffman never called Joe Green back and I figured that was the end of our involvement with him."

Molinas continued to earn his livelihood by betting, and by handicapping point spreads for bookmaking operations in St. Louis, Harlem, Miami, and Biloxi. Fixing games was still a sidelight. But with Richie Hoffman and South Carolina out of the picture, Fixers Incorporated honed in on Joe Green's other connection, Jerry Alaimo from Brown.

Green spoke to Alaimo in New Haven the day before Brown was set to play Yale, but Alaimo turned him down. Jack figured that just being approached with an offer to dump a game would be enough to shake up Alaimo, so he bet two thousand dollars of his own money on Yale. Sure enough, Alaimo had a terrible game. Alaimo was Brown's best player and without him playing effectively, Yale cruised. Jack won his wager.

However, Alaimo was so outraged by Green's proposition that he made an anonymous telephone call to the Manhattan district attorney's office reporting the putative bribe attempt. As a result, the DA placed both Green and Wagman under surveillance. But the two poolroom pals were tipped off and immediately went underground until the DA's investigation was aborted. As soon as Molinas got wind of the situation, he shut down Fixers Incorporated for the duration of the season.

No tears, no recriminations, and absolutely no regrets. Always the pragmatist, Molinas simply stepped up his search for the next edge in the next arena. "The mob used to operate horse rooms all over New York. These places were basically modest-sized betting parlors protected by payoffs to the local police precincts. You could walk in, put your money down, and then leave, or you could hang around and spend an afternoon there, wagering on any race on any track anywhere in the country. Some of these horse rooms were in the backs of legitimate stores. Others were in apartments. Whatever the location, all the windows would be closed and the shades drawn and sealed. There was a big clock with a sweep hand on the back wall, a time-stamp machine to validate betting tickets, and there was only one telephone in the whole joint. In the back room, accessible only to the big cheese. The place was run by the mob, right? So nobody in his right mind would try any funny business. Well, I guess I wasn't in my right mind, then, because a fellow came to me with a system and I bought right in.

"This is how the scam worked. The fellow, let's call him Red, was tight with an electrical engineer that was an ex-employee of Con Edison. This engineer had the ability to open a manhole cover somewhere on a side street and put himself underground where all of Con Edison's cables were. I don't know how the job was done, but this engineer could tinker with a certain cable and reduce the amperage available to a certain neighborhood. He'd go underground just before noon and make his adjustments so that the official clock in the horse room would lose maybe two seconds every minute, which would amount to about two minutes every hour. There would only be small, almost insignificant signs that something was haywire—the lights would be dimmer, the normal volume on the radios would have to be turned up, or the bread in a toaster might come out lighter than usual. After an hour or two, Red's engineer would return everything back to normal and nobody would know the difference.

"It was a highly complicated process and Red and I had to seriously dicker over what the payoff would be. Originally Red wanted fifty percent of whatever money I won, but we finally settled on twenty-two percent.

"The rest was a cinch. All I had to do was find a horse room in which none of the clerks wore a wristwatch, then I'd give Red the high sign, and an hour or so later, I'd had some beard waltz into the room and bet on an out-of-town race that had already been run. Past-posting, the practice was called. I'd have to pick my spots carefully, and I only ran the scam for a couple of weeks, but I wound up making a daily profit of about five thousand bucks."

There were other means by which Molinas past-posted horse rooms. "I'd set up a deal with a guy who was stationed outside the room right next to a public telephone. For a certain fee, you could call certain bookies and get the results of any given race within seconds of its conclusion. So that's what my guy on the outside would do.

"Meanwhile, I'm inside this sealed environment with what was known as a "buzzer" attached to my leg and concealed by my pants. A buzzer consisted of a small piece of metal, a flashlight battery, and an elastic band. The guy outside had the sending end of the buzzer and when he pressed a button, I would get a small electrical shock on my leg. We'd have it all arranged. One initial buzz, or shock, meant Aqueduct, two buzzes meant Laurel. Three subsequent buzzes meant the third race. Two more buzzes meant the Number Two horse.

"Now, if I was a good customer of this particular bookie or this particular room, this is what I was permitted to do. As close to post time as possible, I'd approach the boss of the room and say, 'I really want to bet this race, but I'm still not sure which horse I like. Would you clock the ticket for me and let me bet it? I'm not going anywhere. I'm just going to sit here and study the racing form for a couple of minutes more.' Since there's no apparent way for any outside information to reach me, the boss would invariably go along. So I'd sit still and stare at the racing form. My head didn't come up. I didn't look here. I didn't look there. All of my sudden my leg is getting pinched. Four times. And I knew that the winner of the fifth race at Hialeah was the four horse, and that's the way I'd fill in my ticket. Of course, I couldn't run this deal more than one time in one place.

"By the way, the same setup also works very well in a high-stakes card game. All you need is a code that identifies cards and your guy standing on the other side of the table."

Always questing after the invincible past-posting edge, Molinas also hooked up with "the Tip-Off Time Man." "His name was Marvin, he was about five foot four, three hundred pounds, and he walked with a limp. Marvin was a typical Brooklyn individual, speaking with the 'dems' and the 'toidy-toids.' He always wore a little pointy hat, but never a necktie, and I made an awful lot of money with Marvin.

"For a fee of thirty or forty bucks a week, it was Marvin's job to provide his clientele of bookmakers with accurate starting times for college basketball and football games. He'd call up every school that was on the board just to make sure the starting time hadn't been changed. But sometimes he'd deliberately give out a wrong starting time so a game would be an hour old before he placed his own bets.

"There are a lot of edges in this area alone. For example, for many years the starting time of Purdue basketball games was legitimately listed as being eight o'clock, when in actuality the opening tip-off was at seven-thirty-five sharp. By the time he lays his bet at eight, a smart bettor can just about figure out how a game is going. I can remember betting a Purdue-Iowa game that was pick-'em. But by the time I laid my bet just before eight o'clock, Purdue was already leading by twelve points and I made a bundle.

"There's a college down in Danville, Virginia, where the time-zone line runs right through the middle of town. So when half the town switches to daylight savings time, the other half doesn't. It caused a lot of confusion to everybody except Marvin.

"The point is that you never know where you can find an edge."

If he perpetually teetered on one edge or another, Molinas never expected to fall. None of his past-postings at Mafia operations ever frightened him. When friends asked how he could so cavalierly cheat the mob, he'd just shrug. He was looking after his own ass. Period.

For over four years, Paul Brandt and Molinas's attorney of the moment had been telephoning, writing letters and petitions, and generally pestering Podoloff, trying to get the commissioner to introduce the possibility of Molinas's reinstatement to the Board of governors. But Podoloff kept stalling and making excuses. The NBA had more important matters on the table—expansion, television contracts—than to rehash old business. In reality, Podoloff was patiently lobbying the league's owners and wasn't about to call the Molinas Incident to a vote until he was positive that he could control the result.

In March 1958, Molinas took his case to the newspapers and the controversy became public. Milton Gross of the *New York Post* printed a series of sympathetic interviews. Gross quoted Molinas as saying this:

> I can sit back and think that when I was with Fort Wayne George Yardley was my sub and now he's the leading scorer in the league. I can think how I'm averaging 32 points a game with Williamsport in the Eastern League. I know if they'd let me, I could move into the NBA and help out some team. That's important, sure. That's what I want, but what I want even more is to have nothing hanging over my head any longer. It can hurt me in my profession. I may want to go into politics where my suspension could be especially damaging.
>
> The only way to avoid it, is to clear it all up. I don't want reinstatement and then for them to tell me that I can't play. I want to show them that I can. I'd even play for nothing. I love what I'm doing now. I also love basketball. The way it is now only half my life's my own. I want the other half. I've paid for it in the last four years. I don't owe anybody anything anymore. It's time my rights should be considered.
>
> I appreciate the gravity of my act and the ramifications of it. What I did was wrong but it happened so long ago. This is another lifetime.

Gross canvassed the NBA owners and discovered that after initially excoriating Molinas, Fred Zollner had changed his outlook. "In industry," Zollner told Gross, "we don't hold the mistakes a boy makes against him when he's a man. There should be a chance for rehabilitation...."

John Kundla, the coach and general manager of the Minneapolis Lakers, was impressed by Zollner's change of heart: "If Zollner said okay, I'd bet that everyone would go for Molinas's reinstatement. Now that Molinas is a lawyer I'd be tempted to give him another chance.... I wouldn't want to feel responsible for ruining anybody's life, but there's another consideration, too. If Molinas had a bad game, the fans would get on him. He could take a bad beating that way."

Attorneys advised Molinas that his four-year indefinite suspension had abrogated the reserve clause in his contract with the Pistons and would in the event of his reinstatement make him a free agent. Kundla even went on record to say that the Lakers would be interested in signing Molinas should his suspension be revoked. On the other hand, Zollner insisted that the Pistons would fight to retain Molinas's rights.

Several NBA owners, however, were dead set against Molinas's readmission. "When baseball takes back those Black Sox fellows who were banned in 1919," said Walter Brown of the Boston Celtics, "then basketball will take back our fellows, and not until then."

Eddie Gottlieb of the Philadelphia Warriors similarly cast his public vote against Molinas: "Being a lawyer now has nothing to do with it. Molinas didn't do anything wrong in the eyes of the law. He did it in basketball and basketball has to protect itself."

The St. Louis Hawks owner, Ben Kerner, raised another objection: "If we're going to condone something a man did, then what's to prevent somebody else from doing the same thing and then expecting that he too would be forgiven?"

The matter raged in the press for weeks. Gross reported that the mail he'd received at the *Post* favored Molinas by better than nine to one. Even Bob Cousy said he'd welcome Molinas back into the NBA.

Finally, in mid-April, the NBA owners convened in New York and were asked to consider once and for all the question of Jack Molinas's reinstatement. After a brief discussion, four votes were cast against lifting Molinas's suspension: Ben Kerner of the St. Louis Hawks, Ed Gottlieb of the Philadelphia Warriors, Walter Brown of the Boston Celtics, and Ned Irish of the New York Knickerbockers. Four voters were cast in favor of reinstating Molinas: Danny Biascone of the Syracuse Nationals, Lester Harrison of the Rochester Royals, John Kundla of the Minneapolis Lakers, and, of course, Fred Zollner. In the event of a deadlocked vote, the NBA bylaws required the commissioner to decide the issue—and Podoloff voted to sustain Molinas's suspension.

Jack was devastated. "I really thought with all my heart and soul that I would be reinstated. It was interesting that none of the Jews—neither Kerner, Gottlieb, nor Podoloff—voted for me. And I was furious that, after stringing me along for over four years, Podoloff turned me down. He would have been perfectly justified in voting for me. As a matter of fact, in 1961, Paul Hornung and Alex Karras, two outstanding players in the National Football League, were charged with betting on their own teams to win. Hornung with the Green Bay Packers and Karas with the Detroit Lions. The truth of that situation was that both Hornung and Karras had, in fact, made several bets on their teams to lose. Pete Rozelle was the NFL commissioner and he very well knew what the real deal was. Despite all of this, Hornung and Karras were only suspended from playing for one year. One measly year! And later, when Hornung was reinstated, he was treated like a hero. Well, I certainly wasn't looking to be a hero. I was just looking for another chance to play basketball in the NBA, a chance I was never given. Not getting that second chance really turned me around. I was angry and I was bitter, and a part of me couldn't help hating the NBA."

Prior to the summer of 1958, Molinas was already making plans for getting Fixers, Inc. off to a good start in the upcoming basketball season. In fact, he wanted to expand the operation. The big question was how could they get more recruits? Since Joe Green was a pretty good ballplayer, they even thought they could fix him up with a bogus high school diploma and get him into a college. In the end, however, they decided to send Green to Camp Winnado in New Hampshire for the summer because it had always attracted some of the best college players in the New England area. Through a contact of Jack's, Green got a job as a counselor, but in reality he was there as a talent scout.

Green soon met up with several players who said they'd be willing to dump games. Jerry Vogel from Alabama, plus players from Temple and Lafayette. With Richie Hoffman still eligible to play for one more season at South Carolina, Fixers Incorporated felt they were in real good shape going into the 1958–59 season.

Aside from this, Jack and his cronies also had a network of close to fifty reliable bookmakers from Philadelphia, New York, Boston, and Baltimore who would either take their play directly or accept their bets through a beard. They had bookies that were backed by the five Mafia families in New York. They were capable of betting a total of a hundred thousand dollars a night. Jack felt certain that they would be making a million dollars or more once they got under way.

With all of these possibilities, Joe Hacken and Molinas decided to increase their options. So without telling either Wagman or Green, they decided to line up several more backers. When the season started on December first, in addition to Chicago, they had backers in Brooklyn, Boston, Manhattan, Miami, and Cincinnati. Joe and Jack also decided not to give more than one game to a backer on any particular night, because if they gave the backer two games and one of them was a loser, he might say that the loser cancelled out the winner and they wouldn't get paid.

In early September, Molinas invited some of his old friends from the Bronx Panthers (and their wives) to spend an evening with him at Yonkers raceway. "The implication," said Arnie Goldberg, one of the Panthers, "was that the races were fixed and that Jack knew the winners. We all pooled our money and gave it to Jack, who personally placed the bets on each of the races. Amazingly, we won every race. With only one more remaining, Jack insisted that we bet all of our winnings on a particular horse in that last race because 'it was a lock.' Naturally, the horse lost and we were cleaned out. Jack told us that he had also lost his entire stake, but I for one didn't believe him. In fact, to this day I'm certain he took our money and unbeknownst to us bet it on the winner. There is no question in my mind that this whole deal was a well thought out swindle."

Was Molinas, then, just a hard-core gambler who thought nothing of deceiving his friends? Did loyalty mean anything to him?

"A lot of people said that Jack was a prick," George Feigenbaum observed, "but these were either people who didn't really know him, or else people who couldn't get any inside information from him. I knew Jack as well as anybody. For God's sake, I even lived with him for a while. And he was always a nice guy. He'd never get into any type of power trip with his real buddies. I mean, he'd go along and do whatever everybody else wanted to do. He never drank more than an occasional beer and he never did drugs. He was never a nasty type of guy. In fact, he was more like a baby than anything else. Always upbeat, always supportive, always with a smile on his face. At the slightest excuse always breaking into his high-pitched giggling laugh. And he never, ever withheld any information from his inner circle. I'm telling you, Jack Molinas was a beautiful guy. The only problem he had was an uncontrollable urge to gamble. But in those days, nobody ever heard of a gambling addiction."

Before the season started, Joe Green informed Molinas that Wagman had unilaterally contacted a Mafia-backed bookie in Pittsburgh named Frankie Cardone and offered to sell him fixed games. Green always kept Jack posted on what Wagman was doing because he had covered him for the two thousand dollars he'd spent in Havana. Molinas was annoyed that Wagman was making separate deals behind his back, but he bided his time, waiting to utilize this information to his own best advantage.

At the same time, Molinas was preparing for the season by studying newspapers from every major city, reading what the local sportswriters had to say and trying to assess the strengths and weaknesses of all the major teams. "I knew the proprietor of the out-of-town newsstand in the Times Building and I would give him five bucks a week to put aside the newspapers that I wanted. Then I'd go down there two or maybe three times a week and pick up my stack. I'd guess that my weekly newspaper bill came to about three hundred dollars. So I was doing my homework one late November night about a week before the season started when I read a short article in a newspaper from Columbia, South Carolina, that Richie Hoffman has been suspended from the team for the entire season because of some undisclosed rule infraction. Man, it seemed like we'd had nothing but bad luck with Hoffman.

"So the season started and we were making out like bandits. In the beginning of the season, all of our business was done on out-of-town ball games. On most business nights, Hacken, Green, Wagman, and I would split up and each of us would handle a different game in a different city. Our procedures were identical—calls only made to and from public telephones, a designated player bending over to tie his left sneaker during pregame warm-ups to indicate that everything was set, and the payoff delivered afterward. We had everything covered.

"Anyway, a few weeks into the season, Green tipped me off that Wagman had been in touch with Richie Hoffman, and that another South Carolina player, Mike Callahan, had already turned a few tricks. Wagman's banker for the South Carolina games had been Frankie Cardone in Pittsburgh. So we all had a meeting and Wagman made a full confession, including the fact that Cardone had already bought an upcoming game between South Carolina and Georgia Tech. Hacken and I thought about selling the game to Goldberg, but we knew that Goldberg would tip off Chicago and all that extra money in the betting pool would jack up the point spread. What we did instead was to give Green five hundred dollars for the information, and then bet on the games with our own money. Sure enough, South Carolina took a dive and Hacken and I cleared more than ten grand. It was like a Christmas present.

"To make things even better, I was approached by an old friend of mine, Dave Budin, who said, 'I know what's going on, Jack. I know that there are games being fixed, and I think I can help you, because I have a bunch of players who are ready to go along.'

"I wasn't really afraid of being set up, but I always took every precaution to keep my name out of any business that I didn't know from A to Z. 'Wait a minute,' I said. 'I don't want to have anything to do with you. If you've got players, then go and speak to Joe Jalop. Whatever you want to do, you do with him.'

"Budin had players ready to go, but not enough dough to ring the bell. So Budin and Hacken made an appointment and that was a marriage."

Molinas had known Dave Budin from playing ball in Coney Island and Manhattan Beach and everywhere around the city. After his involvement with the point-shaving scheme in Brooklyn College, Budin had gone back to school and eventually got his degree. At the time, he was a junior high school gym teacher somewhere in Brooklyn. He was a bright guy who only cared about making an easy buck.

Budin was also good-looking, a dapper dresser, and routinely dated showgirls. In other words, Dave Budin was Molinas's kind of guy. And he could deliver the goods. He had Wichita, NYU, Connecticut, Seattle, Colgate, Seton Hall, Bradley, Iowa State, and Colorado in his pocket. That brought Fixers, Inc.'s stable to a total of thirteen teams.

"The first game we worked under Budin's auspices was Wichita versus Cincinnati. It was a trail run to see if Budin actually had the players he said he did. Budin got nothing up front, but we'd come up with a few thousand if he could deliver the goods. Most often, Budin made his own payday by betting his own money on a game he now knew for sure was rigged.

"Wagman wanted to sell the game to Frankie Cardone in Pittsburgh for nine thousand dollars. Half of that would go to the two Wichita players and the one Cincinnati player whom Budin had given to us, while Wagman, Hacken, Green, and I would split the remaining forty-five hundred. Before the deal with Cardone was sealed, Wagman and Green went to Wichita to handle the details. As for me, I was down in Knoxville organizing the dumping of a Tennessee game. The morning line in the Wichita game favored Cincinnati by five and a half points and we were selling Cincinnati to lose. But Wagman ran into some trouble with Cardone.

"What happened was that Cardone said he couldn't handle the contract at nine thousand. It was too much money. So Cardone offered to bring in another bookmaker named Gil from Cincinnati and they'd split the nine thousand ice money. Well, Hacken and I discussed the situation and we felt that Cardone and Gil would be betting upward of three hundred thousand on the game, which would throw the line out of whack. So we thought we'd sell the game to another backer and only tell Wagman that we were going to pass on the game. Of course, when Wagman told Cardone that we were out, Frankie blew his stack.

"Meanwhile, I got a backer in Philadelphia to buy the game for nine thousand and to limit his own wagers to fifty thousand. The other difference was that we were now selling Cincinnati to win, and we had Green tell the Wichita players and the Cincinnanti player that the fix was still on but flip-flopped. I was still pissed at Wagman for working with Cardone behind my back, so I called up Joe Green and asked him to double-cross his buddy Wagman, which I knew he'd do in a flash. So Green told Wagman that the Wichita-Cincinnati game was a bust. No fix. No ice. No action. Green, Hacken, Budin, and I bet all we could on Cincinnati and they won the game by fifteen points. Okay, so now we knew that Budin's contacts were legit. We paid him five thousand for the game and went on from there.

"But Budin could never make enough money to stay ahead of himself. Right after we hooked up with him, Budin found himself in a hole and tried to run a little game on Lefty Rosenthal from Chicago. Budin claimed that he had the quarterback of the Columbia football team and offered the Columbia-Brown game to Lefty for ten thousand—five for the quarterback and five for Budin. Lefty was interested, and he'd buy the contract only if one of his agents, Joe Hennessey, could meet the quarterback in person because ten thousand was a lot of money, and Chicago also intended to bet a ton on the game.

"This Hennessey guy was a football expert who was supposed to know everything. So Budin was in big trouble because, in reality, he didn't know the Columbia quarterback from Adam. But Budin was also resourceful. He got a picture of the quarterback from a magazine, then went out and found some kid who looked just like the quarterback and was built just like him. There was a meeting in a hotel, Hennessey was satisfied and forked over the ten grand. Unfortunately for Budin, the real quarterback had a great day and Columbia won the game.

"When Budin spoke to Lefty, he said that the quarterback had tried his best to mess up but it just didn't happen. If Lefty suspected that he'd been had, he didn't let on. He just wanted Budin to return the ten grand. Budin said that he'd already given the quarterback five thousand as promised. "Okay," Lefty said, "then give back your five grand and I'll deduct the rest from any future earnings." All in all, Budin was lucky he wasn't counting fish at the bottom of the East River.

"Around this time, I also found myself involved in fixing a football game. The bankroll came from the Harlem Mafia and the game involved two teams in the National Football League. There were seven players involved, and the night before the game, the players were crammed into a limo with the Harlem boss and told what the script was. The home team was favored by nine and a half points, which meant that they could only win by nine or less. The boss emphasized that there would be a lot of money bet on the outcome and that the mob didn't take too kindly to being double-crossed. Just to make sure their interests were protected, the mob would have an emissary stationed behind the home team's bench. And that bulge in the emissary's jacket wouldn't be his lunch.

"Okay, with twelve seconds left in the game, the home team was winning by nine. The trouble was, though, that they had possession of the ball on the ten-yard line and it was fourth down with seven yards to go for the first down. The coach called for a field goal attempt and in came the NFL's best kicker. Ordinarily, a ten-yarder was a piece of cake. A good kicker would make maybe ninety-eight percent from there.

"I was seated in the stands next to a real loudmouth fan who bet me ten bucks that the field goal would be good. When the kick went wide, I thought the game was over and we'd won the bet. But the opposing team was offside on the play and the home team had another chance to kick, this time from the five-yard line. The nudnick sitting next to me welched on our bet because of the penalty, so I bet him a hundred that the next kick would be botched. Of course he agreed, laughing all the while. Normally, a five-yard field goal would only be missed once in every two hundred attempts.

"There were seventy thousand fans in the stands screaming their lungs out because most of them had bet the game at nine and a half. What happened on the second field-goal attempt was that the holder fumbled the snap and tried to run the ball into the end zone before being tackled on the ten-yard line. The fans went nuts and threw every piece of garbage they could find down on the field."

Because he had to orchestrate and oversee so many rigged college games, Molinas was only able to play in nineteen of the Williamsport Billies' twenty-eight ball games. His points per game average remained commendable (26.1), but the Billies' record fell to 9–19 and the team missed the play-offs for the second consecutive season. Even so, Molinas considered his fifth EBL season to be an unqualified success. Most of the referees in the Eastern League also worked college games, and Jack went out of his way to be friendly toward them. No scowls when they whistled him for a foul he didn't commit. No discouraging words when he got hacked in the act and they silently sucked on their whistles. Just some good-natured banter and a few beers shared after a game. And it came about that two of the refs said they'd be willing to fix any of the college games they happened to be working for fifteen hundred bucks a pop.

Zeke Sinicola was in his last season of active competition, and whenever the two old friends shared a ride down to Williamsport, Sinicola would always lecture Molinas on the perils of the path he'd chosen. "You're a hell of a ballplayer," Sinicola would say, "you're a good person, and you're also a reputable lawyer. Jack, look at your future. You're going to be rich someday anyway. So why the hell are you fooling around with all of those gangsters? You can't win playing with those guys." Then Jack would get soft and say, 'Yeah, Zeke, I know you're right.' But he never changed his ways."

As much as Sinicola admired Molinas and enjoyed his company, trust was never part of their friendship. "It was in December of 1958," Sinicola remembered, "and I was driving down from New York to an Eastern League game with Ed Warner, Carl Greene, and Bobby Sand. The weather was bad and the roads turned icy as we reached Pennsylvania. Suddenly the car went into a skid and the next thing we knew we went off the road, busted through the guardrail, and plunged fifty-five feet over a cliff. It was a miracle that none of us was killed. That was the end of basketball for me in the Eastern League. In any case, Jack got wind of our accident and hustled over to interview us, pushing himself to be our lawyer. 'We'll sue the state,' he said. 'We're gonna collect a hundred thousand dollars apiece.' That was Jack all right—bragging about something that had no link with reality. I wound up with fifteen hundred bucks, and I have no idea how much Jack made. Jack was a wonderful guy, but he was first and foremost a trickster."

Molinas worked plenty of college games that season.

"There was a problem later that season, however, with a game between Mississippi and Alabama. It seemed that Joe Green told me that an Alabama player named Jerry Vogel was in the bag and that Alabama was a cinch to dump the game. Green had his hand out, because after I had given him the five-hundred-dollar tip for telling me about the Wichita–Cincinnati game that Wagman had sold to Cardone, I told Green that I"d give him a grand for the next tip I could use. Green also informed me that Wagman had sold the Alabama-Mississippi game to Frank Cardone in Pittsburgh.

"It sounded good to both Hacken and me, and we decided to sell the same game to Dave Goldberg in St. Louis. So I put my ass on the line by calling up Goldberg and telling him that we had the game. All I needed from Goldberg was fifteen hundred dollars for the player, a thousand for Hacken, and a thousand for me. In addition to the thirty-five hundred, we also wanted to bet an extra five thousand on Mississippi. Goldberg agreed to back us. In addition to the eighty-five hundred we had coming from Goldberg, Hacken and I also bet another ten thousand around New York. The total we had riding on the outcome was eighteen thousand five hundred. When Mississippi did, in fact, crush Alabama, I had a large payday. Nobody checked the box score because we won and didn't care about the specifics.

"To nobody's surprise, Green took the thousand I gave him, flew to Las Vegas, and disappeared for a couple of days. It later came out in the wash that Vogel had scored over twenty points and was never even approached by either Green or Wagman. Green had merely handicapped the game and thought that Mississippi was a shoo-in. I had wound up betting eighteen big ones on a dead legitimate game!

"And here's the kicker. Eventually Vogel did come aboard and do business with us. Then in February of 1959, Vogel quit school and joined the air force. As a kind of going-away present to Fixers Incorporated, Vogel gave us the names of Dan Quindazi and Lenny Kaplan, two of his teammates who he was sure would work with us.

"We certainly had the magic touch. And the Mole was the undisputed underground king of college basketball!"

In late February, Molinas had an unexpected encounter with a pair of strong-armed associates of Bobby Kraw, a Brooklyn bookmaker with marginal mob connections. Covering Molinas's informed wagering had been very costly to Kraw, and the bookie was resolved to even his accounts by any means possible.

On Monday nights, Jack used to make the rounds of the various bookmakers with whom he had bet ball games over the weekend. He would visit all the five boroughs and either pay or collect what was due. On this particular night, a friend of his telephoned. Ray Leone was a very imposing figure at six foot two and two hundred eighty pounds, who had at one time been a professional boxer and was currently working as a private detective. Ray called to say he was going through a tough time and asked Jack if he had any work for him. Since he'd be collecting a great deal of money that night, Jack said, "Sure. You can come along on my rounds and act as my bodyguard and I'll give you a hundred bucks."

"Great," he said. "Should I pack?" Meaning a gun. Jack said sure, he might as well.

The two men drove around the city for several hours while Molinas collected something like nine thousand dollars. He was driving a brand-new black Oldsmobile Starfire with a red interior and bucket seats. It was a two-door model so there wasn't much room in the backseats. The weather was unseasonably warm, so all of the windows were rolled down.

Molinas had just made his last pickup and they stopped for a red light on Avenue W in Brooklyn, just about a block from his apartment. They were third in the line of cars waiting for the light to change, when suddenly two fellows came out of the car right behind them and walked up to the car. One fellow came up on Jack's side and one on Ray's, and each of them had a gun. This was the first time the Ivy League grad had ever had a gun pointed in his face. The fellow on Jack's side said, "Put the car in park and both of you climb into the backseat."

Jack scrambled around and crawled into the backseat. Then the fellow got behind the wheel, locked the door, pointed his gun at Ray, and said, "Now it's your turn." But Ray was too big to climb into the back, so he had to get out of the car, fold down the front seat, and then stuff himself into the rear with a great deal of huffing and puffing. By now, the whole business was starting to get out of hand.

After his partner took Ray's place in the front passenger seat, the first fellow said, "All right, give us the money. We've been following you around and we know you collected a big score."

"As a matter of fact, I don't have any money," Molinas said, "because I had to pay it all to the last guy I saw."

They started to search Molinas, but couldn't find anything because he had the money in his shirt pocket right next to his heart. Now the two fellows were getting frustrated. They threatened to shoot Molinas if he didn't come up with the cash. He looked hard at the two of them and saw that they were obviously professionals. No itchy trigger fingers, Jack figured. "I don't have the money," he shrugged. "There's nothing I can do about it."

Now they frisked Ray and quickly found the gun. "Who's this guy supposed to be?" one of the holdup men said. "A cop?"

They took Ray's gun, together with his wallet and his keys. Then one of them put his gun right up against Molinas's forehead and said, "I'm going to count up to three, and if I don't get the money by then, I'm going to shoot you."

Then he started counting. "One."

"You can count to a hundred," Jack said, "but I still don't have the money."

"Two."

"Shooting me isn't going to get you something that I don't have," Jack said.

Then the fellow who was counting said, "Listen, if I have to shoot you, I'm also going to have to shoot the fat boy because we can't have any witnesses."

With that, Ray started crying. "I'm a father!" he said. "I have a family! You can't shoot me! Jack! Jack! Give him the money! Please, Jack!"

What could Jack do? He reached into his pocket and handed the money over to them. "You're lucky your buddy cracked," one of the fellows said, "because we probably would have shot you."

"I believe you," Molinas said. "But listen, I have a little bit of a problem here. I've got a hot date tonight and now I don't even have a dime to make a phone call. The least you can do is leave me a couple of bills."

"Yeah, that's a pretty good story," the fellow with the money said, then he peeled off two hundred-dollar bills and handed them over to the ever resourceful Molinas.

All of a sudden, there was a vile odor in the car. Ray was so frightened that he had crapped in his pants. Luckily, that caused the two gunmen to clear out of the car in a hurry. Molinas then drove Ray back to his car, gave him his hundred, and drove his car straight to a carwash to have it cleaned.

About two months later, Jack was in a neighborhood bar having a drink with a girl when the bartender came over and put four glasses of Scotch in front of him. "Who bought these?" Jack asked him. The bartender pointed to a guy down at the end of the bar.

After a while the guy who bought the drinks walked over and shook Jack's hand. He looked very familiar. "Where do I know you from? Your face is so familiar," Jack asked.

"For nine thousand bucks," the enforcer said, "it ought to be familiar."

Molinas recalled the encounter and asked him who had tipped him off. The man hesitated just a bit before saying, "Nobody tipped me off. I just knew that you were beating all the bookmakers in Brooklyn pretty good. Your reputation precedes you."

Jack knew that Bobby Kraw had put him up to it, because Kraw was the one Brooklyn bookmaker that he had been beating like a drum.

They shook hands again and Jack left the bar with his date. He never saw the fellow again. Kraw, however, would eventually become a very important influence in Molinas's life.

With so many rigged games in his pocket, Molinas wasn't too worried about losing a measly nine g"s. "What was also happening was that Wagman and I made a deal. We would double-back any of the games that either of us had. I'd sell his games to Chicago via Dave Goldberg in St. Louis, and he'd sell my games to Cardone in Pittsburgh. We'd also make sure that both Goldberg and Cardone believed they each had exclusive rights to the ball games in question. That way we'd each wind up with a few thousand extra because the players involved would already be iced with the original backer's money. But we did take a few more chances than we should have.

"Wagman and Green were down at the University of Alabama meeting players through Dan Quindazi. One of the players they were introduced to was Lenny Kaplan, the star of the Alabama team. But Wagman wasn't convinced that Kaplan was ready to do business, so he held off making a proposition. Wagman did say, however, that Kaplan was a big fan of mine, that he'd followed my career with Columbia and then with Fort Wayne. Wagman was positive that Kaplan would gladly come on board if I were to speak to him.

"Meanwhile, Quindazi was suspended from the team for two games for getting into an argument with the coach. The first game Quindazi would be missing was Alabama versus Georgia. From hanging around with Quindazi in his fraternity house, Wagman and Green discovered that the other Alabama players didn't think they had much of a chance to beat Georgia even with Quindazi. So Wagman decided to sell the game to Cardone, telling him that three Alabama players wanted to do business, which was a bald-faced lie. But I was reluctant to sell another legitimate game to Goldberg like I had with the Alabama-Mississippi game because I didn't want to press my luck. Anyhow, even though the game was straight, I bet a bundle, Georgia mauled Alabama, Wagman collected money for nothing from Cardone and split it with me. And abracadabra! There was my nine grand back safely in my pocket."

The 1958–59 season was a bonanza for Fixers Incorporated with only a few minor glitches along the way. One situation with serious and long-lasting consequences occurred with a St. John's–St. Joseph's game for the championship of the Holiday Festival in Madison Square Garden. Dave Budin swore to Molinas that he had St. John's' high-scoring guard, Allan Seiden, willing to dump the game. Jack knew that Seiden was straight, because he had tried to get to him many times and had been rebuffed. So he told Budin that he was passing on the game. But Budin quickly turned around and sold it to Goldberg on his own. The line opened with St. Joe's a six-point favorite, and by the time Goldberg and the Chicago gang got their money down, the spread went up to ten. But Seiden had a sensational ball game and St. John's won by thirty.

Lefty Rosenthal called Molinas from Chicago, wanting him to check out whether or not Budin really did have Seiden. That certainly put Jack in a bind. If he told Lefty the truth, that Budin was lying to him, they would have fitted Budin for cement Florsheims. He wound up telling Lefty that Seiden had, in fact, agreed to dump the game, but the kid was too point-hungry to be reliable. When it came down to missing a shot, Seiden just couldn't do it. Lefty was satisfied and Budin was off the hook. But poor Seiden. Even though the kid was always one hundred percent honest, the word got around that he was a dumper.

There was a game against Niagara later that season when several of the St. John's players were doing business. The line favored St. John's by eight points and they were winning by two with two minutes to go. The St. John's coach, Joe Lapchick, was shouting out to his players to freeze the ball and preserve the win, but Seiden couldn't help himself. He scored twelve points in a row and St. John's didn't cover. The kid was addicted to scoring points and was incapable of missing shots on purpose. "The worst thing Seiden ever did," said Molinas, "was bet on St. John's to win a game. A lot of his teammates did the same thing."

Molinas's report to Lefty Rosenthal soon became common knowledge in the New York gambling community, and Lapchick received an anonymous telegram announcing that Seiden was in league with a Chicago bookie. "We went down to D.C. to play George Washington," Seiden remembered, "and I was the hero, winning a close game with a flurry of points in the clutch. On the train ride back to New York after the game, Lapchick told me that I was going to be thrown off the team for shaving points. Needless to say, I was shocked. I had no idea what Lapchick was talking about. Who could have told him such a crazy lie? It took me a long time, but I finally convinced Lapchick that whatever he'd heard wasn't true. After the season, I was the number-one draft pick of the St. Louis Hawks. Even though I thought I was the best guard in training camp, I sat on the bench for the entire exhibition season. I was so fed up that I quit the team. I'm sure my not being given a chance in the NBA had something to do with the phony rap that Jack Molinas laid on me."

The next significant game for Fixers Incorporated was Alabama-Tulane, a contest played on February 14, 1959. Quindazi had been reinstated by his coach, and Molinas, ever the optimist, told Wagman that he had already spoken to Alabama's other star, Lenny Kaplan. Even though he had not yet done so, Jack felt he had a lock on the game. The plan was for Wagman to sell the game to Cardone and for Jack to sell it to Goldberg. When he offered the contract to Goldberg, he jumped at it. "But don't let anything go wrong," Goldberg told him. "Me and the Chicago crowd want to bet the mortgage on the game, so make extra certain that everything's going to go right. One other thing, Jack. Keep a tight lid on this deal because I don't want anybody else's money screwing up the line." The price agreed upon was a thousand each for Quindazi and Kaplan, plus another two thousand for Molinas. Wagman's deal with Cardone was identical—a total of two grand for the players and two more for the setup.

But then Goldberg himself screwed up. He happened to be in town at the Hotel New Yorker and he was supposed to leave the two grand for the players in an envelope marked with Joe Hacken's name at the front desk. But when Hacken and Molinas got to the hotel, the envelope had been addressed to a fictitious name that they didn't know about. That meant they had to pay the players' ice out of their own pockets. As it turned out, they never did get their hands on that two thousand.

In addition to the missing two grand, the fact remained that Jack still had not spoken to Kaplan, Alabama's high scorer and best player. So he and Wagman flew down to Tuscaloosa the day before the game to try and get Kaplan involved.

To complicate an already complicated deal, Wagman had his own agenda. He wanted to eliminate Quindazi, pocket the money designated for him, and go with just Kaplan. Which was fine, except that they still hadn't spoken to Kaplan.

When they got to Tuscaloosa, Molinas put in a call to Kaplan and arranged to meet him at the hotel. Molinas had never seen Kaplan before and thus was a bit surprised that he was such a little fellow, about five foot seven. He was also well-dressed, immaculately groomed, and very articulate. Jack was really under the gun, so he wasted no time in getting into his spiel.

"What do you think of the game?" he asked him.

"It'll be a real tough one."

Then Jack paused for effect and said, "Well, Lenny, I'd like to make a little wager on the game as long as I'm down here. Just to cover my expenses, you know? Who do you think I should bet on?"

He just shrugged and repeated, "It'll be a real tough game."

"Listen, Lenny…why don't you pick the team I should bet on? Alabama? Or Tulane?"

"How much money will you bet?"

"If you think you like your team," Jack said, "then I'll bet two hundred dollars for you on Alabama."

"Suppose I tell you that I like Tulane?" Kaplan asked.

"Well, then I'd bet a thousand for you on Tulane."

"Jeez," Kaplan said. "That's a lot better than two hundred. But if you bet on Tulane that would mean that I'd have to play less than my best."

"You're a pretty bright fellow, Lenny. I guess that's exactly what it does mean."

"What would I have to do?"

"Alabama should be favored by five or six points," Jack said. "All you'd have to do was win the game by less than that and I'd bet a thousand dollars for you."

"Could I get in trouble?"

"Only if you go around like a blockhead and tell everybody that you're dumping the game."

"You're a lawyer," he asked, "aren't you?"

"Yes, I'm a lawyer."

"Well," he said, "I guess you can respect a confidence."

"Absolutely."

"I'll tell you what," he said. "I'll do it for fifteen hundred."

"You got it."

Molinas handed him fifteen one- hundred-dollar bills and then told the kid to call him back later in the day for the final point spread.

Next Molinas met with Wagman and told him that Kaplan wanted fifteen hundred and that they didn't need Quindazi after all. Since it was still before noon, and a little too early to get a read on the line, Wagman and Jack went out for lunch.

While they were eating, Molinas was thinking that Wagman was about to sell the game to his guy and Molinas would be selling the game to his guy, and there was going to be a ton of money bet on Tulane. A short while later, he called Hacken in New York and found out that the opening line favored Alabama by six and a half, so he bet ten thousand on Tulane through several New York bookies, expecting the line to go down to about three after the Chicago and Pittsburgh money showed up. At that time, neither Goldberg nor Cardone had been given the final okay.

He conferred again with Wagman, who reported that the line had gone down to six, so Jack told him to call Cardone and say that they were off to the races. Bet Tulane with six points.

He knew Cardone was also betting a ton and that it would take a while for him to lay all of his wagers, so Jack had to wait a bit longer before calling Goldberg—

otherwise there'd be too much money bet on Tulane in a short period of time and the game might be taken off the board. Meanwhile, he and Wagman walked around Tuscaloosa and killed some time in a Cadillac dealership. In anticipation of their winnings, Wagman even went in and took a car for a test drive.

At about two o'clock Molinas finally called Goldberg, who said the line was four points. "Looks like the game is getting hot," Goldberg said. "Are you sure nobody else knows about it?"

"Hey, Dave. If I'm lying, I'm dying."

Goldberg decided to wait and see what happened with the line before he laid his own bets.

Jack called Goldberg every half hour. At three o'clock, the line was down to three and a half. Of course, Goldberg had an eye on the Chicago ledgers and was able to watch the flow of money from all around the country because Chicago was the ultimate layoff operation. That meant that the money Cardone had been betting here, there, and everywhere would eventually show up in Chicago. Goldberg thought that three and a half was too tight a spread, that the Alabama players (even though they only had Kaplan) wouldn't be able to dump the game unless they had at least four points to work with. "I don't like what I'm seeing," Goldberg said. "In fact, if the line continues to go down, I want the Alabama boys to go out and try to win. You can tell them that I'll give them the same payoff either way. Let's see what happens."

At four o'clock Kaplan called to get the line. "Look, Lenny," Jack told him, "the line is moving down rapidly and I don't know yet what we're going to do. Just sit tight and call me back at six o'clock."

"I'll be at my fraternity house at six," he said. "Why don't you call me there?"

Molinas then turned around and told Wagman that he had already given Kaplan the line at four points and that he was going to dump. Furthermore, that he wouldn't be having any other contact with Kaplan until after the game. This, of course, was a lie. So Wagman called up Cardone and the Pittsburgh wagers were appropriately adjusted.

When Jack called Goldberg again at around five o'clock, the bookie said, "The game is flying downward and the line is now two.... Hold on, Jack. I just got a flash.... The game is now pick 'em. Everybody in the country seems to be betting against Alabama. Tell Kaplan and Quindazi to go out and win." Jack told Goldberg to hold off for a while until he made contact with Kaplan.

Always quick on his feet, Molinas had delayed Goldberg because he knew that when he told Rosenthal to bet the game at pick 'em—which was a straight-up wager with neither team spotted any points at all—the line would quickly go back up to two. He next called Joe Hacken in New York and told him to bet ten thousand on Alabama at as close to pick 'em as possible before Goldberg's money raised the line.

At a quarter to six, Jack called Goldberg and told him the deal was on and that he should bet Alabama at pick 'em. Fifteen minutes later, he called Kaplan at the fraternity house and spoke to him in a code because he was always wary of his phone calls being taped.

"We'll go less than four o'clock," Molinas told him, "but I understand it's zero now. But if it falls one, two, or three o'clock, you figure on a double. You'll wind up with thirty fruits instead of fifteen."

What he was saying was that the kid could dump the game, but, if it were possible, Alabama could also win by either one, two, or three points. The option was his. If Alabama won by three or less, they would double his payoff.

Kaplan was a really smart kid. All he said was, "That's wonderful. I'm a hell of a fruit eater."

As expected, Alabama closed minus two points. But Goldberg had gotten most of his bets down on Alabama at pick 'em, one, and one and a half. Molinas figured that Goldberg must have bet at least two hundred thousand to move the game from pick 'em to two.

Then he called Hacken, who said he'd been able to bet eight grand at pick 'em and two grand on Alabama minus one.

So here's the way the line moved. It started with Alabama favored by seven, then down to four, where it paused for an hour or two, then down to zero, and then back up to two. The average bettor who saw this price movement wouldn't know what was going on with the game and would probably pass on it. That meant almost all of the money wagered on that particular game was laid by professional gamblers. Cardone had Tulane with seven points and also with four. Goldberg and the Chicago crowd had Alabama at anywhere from pick 'em to two. Molinas had ten thousand on Tulane with seven, eight thousand on Alabama at pick 'em, and two thousand on Alabama at minus one.

Come game time, he and Wagman bought general admission seats at opposite ends of the court. At the half, Kaplan had eighteen points and Alabama was leading by one. Wagman was very upset. "What the hell's the kid doing?" he asked Jack. "Why is he playing so good?"

"Don't worry," Jack said.

During the halftime break he called Goldberg to say they were winning by one and Kaplan had eighteen points. "That's terrific," Goldberg said. "How's Quindazi doing?"

"Terrific."

At the start of the second half, Kaplan started making mistakes—missing shots, throwing the ball out of bounds, committing silly fouls—and Tulane took a fourteen-point lead. But then with about ten minutes to go, Kaplan started playing like an All-American. With twenty seconds left, Kaplan intercepted a pass and threw a perfect lead pass to a teammate whose basket tied the score. Now Tulane had possession, but they wound up making a bad pass and the ball was turned over to Alabama. They worked the ball to Kaplan, who dribbled to the top of the key, stopped, and threw up a jump shot. The buzzer went off while the ball was in the air, and the ball came down through the basket. Alabama won the game by two points, 74–72, and Kaplan had scored twenty-six.

It was a perfect ending. Everybody was a winner. Molinas had won all of his bets. Twenty thousand dollars' worth. Plus two thousand each from Goldberg and Cardone. Cardone had won with Tulane at either seven or four points. Goldberg won with Alabama at pick 'em, one, and one and a half. The worst Goldberg had done was tied at two.

Kaplan was the hometown hero and the fans carried him on their shoulders all around the court. Plus, the kid had also earned himself three thousand dollars. As a further reward, Jack promised Kaplan that after he graduated he could play for the Williamsport Billies in the Eastern League.

But there was one fly in the ointment. Goldberg had told Chicago that the last word he'd gotten from Molinas was that Alabama was out to win the game, and Lefty Rosenthal from Chicago had sent an agent to Tuscaloosa to eyeball everything. Goldberg informed Jack that he would have to come to Chicago to pick up his two thousand from Rosenthal, plus some other money that he was still owed for the Alabama-Mississippi and Alabama-Georgia games.

The following day, Molinas flew to Chicago and met Goldberg in the bookmaking office in Cicero. Lefty was also there, as well as two or three tough-looking guys with suspicious bulges under their jackets. Lefty was the spokesman, and there was a menacing edge to his words.

"This is the deal," Lefty said. "Because we bet so much money on Alabama to win, I sent somebody to scout the game and his report indicated that this kid, Lenny Kaplan, wasn't playing his best, especially in the third quarter. My opinion, Jack, is that there was something wrong with the contract you sold us. Like possibly you were actually double-crossing us. I just want to check and make sure everything was on the up-and-up, just to ease my mind. What I want you to do, Jack, is to get on the phone and speak to Kaplan right now. I'm going to be listening in on the extension and I want you to ask him why he scored that last basket."

Actually, that was not the right question to ask Kaplan because the last basket he scored enabled the Chicago operation to win their bets. Had Kaplan missed that shot, the game would've gone into overtime and who knows what would have happened. Lefty undoubtedly thought that Molinas had instructed Kaplan to dump the game, and that this particular question would cause the kid to come up with some lame-brained excuse. Whatever motive they may have had, Jack was afraid to have Lefty overhear anything Kaplan might have to say about the game. After all, he had in fact given Kaplan the option of either dumping or winning by less than three points.

"You bet a lot of money," Molinas said to Lefty, "but you won the money.

What's your complaint? And anyway, I'm not going to make the phone call. I just want the money that you owe me."

Then one of the strong-arm boys pulled out a gun and held it tightly against Jack's forehead. "Listen," the guy said, "you get on the phone and call the kid or else. Forget about the money you're supposed to collect from us. We're talking about the only way you're leaving here is inside a cement box."

Jack had no choice except to dial the phone, knowing that if Kaplan made the wrong statement he was a dead man.

"Hi, Lenny. It's me, Jack. How're you doing?"

Fine. Great. He was still the campus hero.

"Just do me a favor, Lenny, and answer one quick question. At the end of the Tulane game? Why did you make that last shot?"

"Are you kidding?" he said. "To win the game, of course."

Everybody was happy when he hung up the phone, and even the three head-breakers left the room. Then Goldberg opened a desk drawer, pulled out a slim envelope, and handed it to Molinas.

"Here's your money," Goldberg said.

Inside the envelope was a single thousand-dollar bill. "First of all," Jack said in a huff, "I told you that I want to be paid in hundreds. And more importantly, this is three thousand dollars short. Our deal was for four thousand. For the time being I'm not even talking about the other money you owe me. What gives?"

He knew that when he first told Goldberg the game was set the line was pick 'em, and by game time the line was Alabama minus two. That meant the Chicago boys had bet at least two hundred thousand on the game. And now they were shortchanging him like this?

"Take the thousand," Goldberg said. "That's enough."

"But..."

"But my butt," said Goldberg. "We're holding the rest just to make sure that you'll be selling us more games in the future. You're lucky that you're getting the thousand. Now beat it, Jack, before we change our minds."

Fixers Incorporated was still in business and the three-thousand-dollar loss was chicken feed. In all, the group was making upward of fifty thousand dollars a week, money that was bet as fast as it was earned. And Molinas's eyes got bigger and bigger. He wanted more players from more teams. He wanted to sell "exclusive" contracts to a dozen backers. Next season, he'd be much better prepared. And if at all possible, Molinas wanted to cut his ties with Aaron Wagman, mainly because Wagman's primary bankroller, Frankie Cardone, was a thief.

Molinas learned this difficult lesson on the evening of February 28, 1959, when contrary to Joe Hacken's dictum, Fixers Incorporated sold two games to Cardone—Alabama versus Auburn, and Temple versus Lafayette.

Jack remembered the game: "Auburn was favored by eleven points, which was a hefty spread. But Kaplan did a good job of laying down and Auburn won by eighteen. That was a win. As far as the other game was concerned, Cardone told Wagman that the line he was working with had Lafayette as a six-and-a-half-point favorite, and he wanted to bet Temple. No problem. We had players on both teams, so we could just about name the final score.

"Okay, then. When Lafayette won the game by seven points, we figured we had another winner, right? Wrong. After the game, Wagman called up Cardone to settle up, and Cardone said that he'd made a big mistake. The line that he had bet was Temple plus seven and a half, not six and a half. Which made his Temple money a loser. According to Cardone, the loss had offset the win and he couldn't pay us the money for either contract.

"Wagman tried arguing with him. What about all the ice we owed to the players? Like fifteen hundred to Lenny Kaplan. No dice, Cardone said. I even got on the phone to plead with Cardone, but I didn't get anywhere either.

"Starting next season, we'd have to get the players' ice from the backers in advance of the ball games. And never, ever would we sell more than one game to one backer."

When Kaplan asked Molinas for the fifteen hundred due him from the Auburn game, Molinas gave him five hundred. Kaplan contacted Molinas again in June just before the young man was set to marry his college sweetheart. "I need the thousand you owe me," Kaplan said.

"I don't have it," Molinas said. "All my money's tied up. I can only spare a hundred."

To Molinas, the unpaid debt seemed like small change, but it turned Kaplan against him.

In the summer, Molinas made a moderate effort to gear up his legal practice. At the same time, an electrical engineer named Sandy Solomon happened to move into a bachelor's apartment on Ocean Parkway directly across the street from where Molinas was still living with his brother and his parents. Coincidentally, Solomon also had a legal problem, and a mutual friend (Marvin Weisman, Solomon's brother-in-law, and one of the Coney Island crew) connected him with Molinas. The resulting lawyer-client relationship gave Solomon a disturbing insight into exactly how Molinas operated.

"I was working for a contractor," Solomon recalled, "and I lent him some money on the basis of an oral agreement that we'd thereby become business partners. But we never signed anything and the contractor not only reneged on our oral agreement, but also claimed he didn't have the money to pay back what I'd lent him. So Jack agreed to take the case. 'Don't worry,' Jack told me. 'I'll take care of everything.'"

What Molinas did, however, was to farm Solomon's case out to another lawyer. "Jack was the kind of guy who knew a lot of people," said Solomon. "As an attorney, his style was to flash his personality to get the cases, then give the paperwork and the legwork to other attorneys and split the fee. He was more of a finder than a working lawyer."

But, hey! Why should Molinas care what anybody thought of him? The facts were irrefutable:

Molinas was just rolling in dough.

He was outsmarting everybody, including several big-shot Mafia bosses.

He was still kicking ass in the Eastern League and was certainly good enough to be an NBA All-Star.

He was sleeping with the most gorgeous showgirls in New York. "Jack was blessed with an enormous penis," said one of his old flames, "and he was absolutely wonderful in bed."

He was the ultimate realist who did unto others before they did unto him.

And he lived in a duplex penthouse apartment on the sunny side of Easy Street.

So who needed the NBA? Playing for lunatic coaches. Ruining his knees for peanuts.

Being the all-powerful trickster was a lifetime better than the NBA.

Right?

As the summer progressed, Molinas, Hacken, Wagman, and Green held a "board of directors" meeting at the Bickford's cafeteria on Fifty-seventh Street to plot their strategy for the upcoming basketball season. Since several of their players had graduated, they decided that they needed to recruit new players and more teams. Joe Green was the best recruiter, so they agreed that he should spend the rest of the summer at a hotel in the Catskills called Klein's Hillside. Despite all the money he'd won, Green was broke, as always. Wagman still didn't know that Green had been telling Molinas and Hacken everything that he had done last season—all the games Aaron had double-backed, all the contracts he sold to Pittsburgh, every bet, and every edge. So Wagman drove Green up to Klein's unaware that Jack had slipped Joe three or four hundred bucks to cover his expenses and to keep Molinas informed.

Through a contact of Hacken's, Green got a job on the athletic staff at the hotel. He wasn't a great social animal, but he got along very well with the fellows he played with. Molinas kept in touch with him during the summer and spoke to him privately when he came back to New York. The list of players Green had talked into turning tricks was impressive. There was Dick Fisher from Tennessee, a nice kid from a stable home who was majoring in business administration. Jack was surprised that Fisher wanted in because he was more of a straight-up kind of kid, not the streetwise, smart-alecky type who usually fell for their pitch. Green had also gotten Jerry Graves, the high scorer and captain of Mississippi State. Graves was a coup because he was a bona fide All-American. Also Lou Brown from North Carolina. For every game that one of Green's recruits worked successfully, Green got a thousand dollars.

One of Lou Brown's teammates at North Carolina was Doug Moe, a six-foot-five bruiser out of Erasmus Hall High School in Brooklyn. Moe was an easygoing young man who was easily led by his buddy Brown. When Brown introduced Moe to Green, Moe firmly refused to participate in any fixed games, but was foolish enough to accept a seventy-five-dollar "gift."

"I didn't see anything wrong with taking the money for not doing anything," Moe said, "but I guess I was involved, wasn't I? And I never even entertained the possibility of reporting either Green or Brown to the police, or to my coach at North Carolina, Everett Case. Lou and I were good friends and I didn't want to be in any way responsible for sending him to prison."

After graduating from North Carolina, Moe was unofficially barred from playing in the NBA, but went to enjoy an All-Star career in the American Basketball Association. From there, Moe became the first American to play professional basketball in Italy. When knee surgery ended his playing days, Moe finally reached the NBA, first as an assistant coach (with San Antonio) and then as the widely respected head coach of the Denver Nuggets.

Another fellow that Green set up at Klein's Hillside was Gary Kaufman, who played at the College of the Pacific. Molinas had played ball with Kaufman a year or two before in a summer camp, so he had a relationship with the kid. But Wagman dished the dirt on Jack to Kaufman, saying that he shouldn't do business with Molinas because he had a reputation of not paying players. Kaufman called Jack later to tell him all of this, and eventually he wound up working for him instead of Wagman and Green.

Of course, Molinas did a lot of recruiting that summer himself. Joe Green would call and tell him about a very good playground game up in Riverdale in the Bronx where there might be a possibility of meeting some college players. Molinas would then drive up in his black Pontiac convertible, knowing it was just flashy enough to catch the eye of a college kid.

When Molinas went to meet a potential dumper on a social level, he would never show up wearing a suit and tie or a diamond watch. His standard recruiting outfit was a pair of sneakers, chino pants, and a plain T-shirt. He might have been five years older than they were, but he always came on like he was a player, like he was one of them.

One of the kids he met that summer was Billy Reed from Jamaica High School in Queens. Reed was going to be a sophomore at Bowling Green and he was a pretty good player. They just chatted about Billy's background and his prospects of starting in the upcoming season, and Jack enticed him with an occasional twenty-dollar bill. Through Joe Green, Molinas knew that another Bowling Green player, Tom Falantano, had already agreed to dump games. But he sat tight with Reed and waited for the right moment to pop the question.

Jack also sidled up to a pair of New York City high school seniors who were guaranteed to become college All-Americans and surefire NBA players. They were Connie Hawkins and Roger Brown. He played with both of them and was generous with his cash. They were both two years away from being eligible for college varsity ball, but Molinas felt sure that they'd both eventually be turning tricks for him.

College basketball practice started in late October, and so that was when Molinas sat down with Joe Hacken to go through their list. They discussed each kid in depth, trying to decide on a few prime candidates. What was a kid's family background? How good a player was he? Good enough to control a ball game? Did the kid need money? Would he sacrifice the glory for the money? Did he have any other weak spots in his personality? Might the kid be influenced to join us if we hooked him up with a whore? Was he interested in clothes? Cars? Since Molinas was the one who had played with these kids and mingled with them, Hacken usually went along with his judgments. They had fifteen possibilities and ultimately they reduced the list to ten.

The softening-up process worked like this: Hacken and Molinas would travel from city to city, and Jack would call up a particular kid and say that he was just passing through town. "I can't shake free from a business meeting," he would tell the kid, "but my partner is also in town and he'd love to take you out to dinner." All of these kids loved to get a free meal, so they'd agree to meet Joe Hacken. Then Joe would start off with the usual spiel: "Jack and I are betting on a couple of games and we'd like to get your opinion on such-and-such a game." If the kid was agreeable, Joe would continue: "If you think your team is going to go over the point spread, then we'll make a little wager for you." If the kid was still agreeable, Joe would go on from there. If the kid hesitated in any way, then Joe would cut off the line of questioning. At that point, no laws had been broken, no bribes offered, no nothing. Amazingly enough, about two-thirds of the kids were raring to go.

Just before the 1959–60 season got under way, a Coney Island bookmaker who said he had players to offer approached Molinas. The bookie's name was Bobby Kraw, the same gentleman who had commissioned two torpedoes to shake down Molinas for nearly nine thousand dollars. Kraw was about six two, two hundred and eighty pounds. He had a pudgy face and the pushed-in nose of a boxer. He was bald, but he had more hair on his body than a gorilla. At first glance, Kraw looked like a hired killer, very hard-looking with nervous, menacing eyes. But he was actually a sweet-talking fellow whose heart was as soft as butter. He was also very smart and he knew what an edge was. Kraw had a buddy named Charles Tucker, a fairly good school-yard hoopster, who knew of a bunch of players ready to take a dive. On Tucker's list were Freddy Portnoy from Columbia and Sal Vergopia from Niagara. Molinas was thrilled to have an opportunity to make everything come full circle with the tilting of a Columbia game.

In November, Molinas signed on for his sixth season with the EBL's Williamsport Billies, determined to lead the team back into the play-offs. For the first time since his NBA days, Molinas spent long preseason hours working on his game—increasing the range of his one-hander, perfecting his left hook, and even doing wind sprints. The Billies coach, Bobby Sand (who had been Nat Holman's assistant during CCNY's glory years and scandalous years), informed the Williamsport newspapers that "Molinas is bearing down all the way and is ready to go all out this season."

New on Williamsport's roster were the likes of Joe Holub, former NBA standout with Syracuse and Detroit; Julius McCoy, the EBL's rookie of the year in 1959;

former Globetrotter Carl Green; one-time CCNY point-shaver Floyd Layne; and Allan Seiden. At the beginning of the season, Seiden usually traveled from New York to Pennsylvania riding shotgun in Molinas's car. Incorrigible as always, Jack would try to break the tedium by dealing hands of poker to Seiden as he drove.

Seven games into the season, with the Billies' record at 6–1, Molinas (along with Tom Hart, more of a high-jumper than a polished hooper) was traded to the last-place Hazelton Hawks for former Niagara star Tommy Hemans. The word out of Williamsport was that coach Bobby Sand believed Molinas to be "over the hill." According to Seiden, the real reason Molinas was traded was because "Jack wouldn't kiss the owner's ass." But in his premier performance with Hazelton, Molinas scored forty-five points in a victory against the Scranton Miners.

Molinas received "a warm reception" in his first appearance in Williamsport wearing an enemy uniform, and proceeded to outscore Hemans fifty points to twenty as the Hawks pulled an upset, winning 123–112. "The Billies fans were outraged," Seiden reported, "and many of them boycotted the Billies games after the trade." In his second game against his old team, Molinas netted twenty-eight points in leading the Hawks to another unexpected victory. With Molinas in the lineup, the Hawks home attendance doubled and the team made an honest (albeit unsuccessful) run at a play-off spot.

Molinas showed up for most of the Hawks games, missing only five of twenty-seven. The only poor outing he experienced was the Sunday morning he showed up in Hazleton without his sneakers. Molinas wore size fourteen, but a frantic search around town only turned up a pair of size tens. So the team's trainer cut out the part where the toes were and Molinas paddled around the court like some cartoon character and scored only ten points.

Even though he was becoming increasingly distracted by his point-shaving business, Molinas's per game average of twenty-five points ranked him ninth on the EBL's scoring parade. "Flat out," said Hubie Brown, "Jack Molinas was one of the greatest players to ever play the game of basketball."

In the fall of 1959, Molinas fell in love again, if only briefly. She was Gwendolyn Davis, a teacher at Mark Twain Junior High School in Coney Island, and while some of Molinas's friends thought she was square, he was entirely enchanted by her innocence and her vulnerability. Gwendolyn had no reason to doubt Molinas's representation of himself as being a full-time attorney, so she was never suspicious of the numerous phone calls (both made and received) that continually interrupted their privacy. They dated steadily for several months and even discussed the possibility of becoming engaged.

Toward that end, arrangements were made for Molinas and his parents to meet Gwendolyn's parents at the latter's Brooklyn apartment. On his way to the dinner party, however, Molinas decided to try his luck at a high-stakes crap game convened at a friend's house in Coney Island. Molinas vowed to leave after either winning or losing a thousand dollars, or at six-thirty, whichever came first. He was ahead by about five hundred dollars with his self-imposed time limit rapidly approaching when the local police raided the game. As a result of the bust, Molinas spent the entire night in a jail cell, and Gwendolyn broke off their relationship.

Immediately prior to the commencement of the 1959–60 basketball season, Dave Goldberg put enormous pressure on Fixers Incorporated to start the ball rolling with a surefire winner because all of the big-heeled guys from Chicago wanted to attend whichever game they came up with. West Virginia was determined to be the closest thing to a lock that they could find.

Molinas, Hacken, Green, and Wagman held a preseason meeting at Bickford's on Fordham Road, where they drew up their itinerary for the first few weeks of the season. They discussed the various teams they controlled, who and where they would be playing, the relative strengths and weaknesses of the matchups, and then decided on the specific games they were going to work. Among the other games they settled on were Bowling Green versus Michigan State, North Carolina State against Wake Forest, South Carolina against North Carolina, also a Wichita game and a Temple game. The total was eight games in the first week of the season. Of course, they focused on the West Virginia–Tennessee game they all had figured the same way: Jerry West and his boys could win by as many points as they wanted to. Twenty, thirty, or even more. So an opening line of thirteen to fourteen didn't scare them. They also decided that since the Chicago bosses would be on hand, Hacken, Wagman, and Molinas would make the trip down to Morgantown, West Virginia. Meanwhile, Green was off to Toledo to give Bowling Green's Tom Falantano a five-hundred-dollar down payment to dump the opening game against Michigan State. After the West Virginia game, Hacken, Wagman, and Jack would rendezvous with Green in Toledo to zero in on the Bowling Green–Michigan State contest. After that, Green was scheduled to fly down to take care of a couple of North Carolina and North Carolina State games. Molinas would fly back to Pennsylvania to play a weekend series in the Eastern League, and Hacken would fly back to New York to take care of the betting. Wagman would also return to New York and get a head start on handicapping any future action.

After Green and Wagman left, Joe Hacken and Molinas set up their own schedule. The deal was that they were partners with Green and Wagman on their teams, but Green and Wagman were shut out from the games that Hacken and Jack set up. Neither Green nor Wagman knew that Hacken and Jack were also involved with Dave Budin, and nobody else except Hacken knew about the two Eastern League refs that Jack had who also worked college games in New York and Philly.

Since everything was getting bigger and more complicated, Hacken suggested that the two of them divide the workload. "I'll take charge of Budin, Wagman, and Green," Joe said. "I'm real friendly with Green so I can keep tabs on him and his buddy and find out if they're trying to go behind our backs on anything. You take care of the money, Jack, and the bookmakers. Also, we know there's going to be plenty of arguing and hassles with our backers about collecting what's due us. You're a lawyer, Jack, and an expert arguer, so you take care of the backers too."

They hired a couple of runners named Bosco and Barnard to help out, and they scouted out several banks of public telephones around the city where they could have some degree of privacy but also be able to communicate with each other. Hacken gave Jack his list of about twenty-five bookmakers and the code he was supposed to use. Sometimes his code name was Bobby, or Harry, and sometimes it was Jack.

Their little operation had blossomed into a national conspiracy with tentacles reaching all over the country. They had nearly twenty teams under contract and ready to do business, and they also had backers in Brooklyn, Philadelphia, Chicago, St. Louis, Boston, New York, Miami, and Cincinnati. By the end of December Hacken and Molinas expected that they would have lines on every team in the country, lines that would be more accurate than any bookmaker's or handicapper's.

Jack picks up the play-by-play: "As the season got closer and closer, our various backers would call me every day wanting to know what the first action was going to be. I'd just tell them not to worry because we'd be ready with the right games in plenty of time. So I had a lot of reasons to be careful with the opening game, and since the Chicago guys wanted to eyeball the game for themselves, I really couldn't sell the game to anybody else.

"Anyway, Wagman confirmed that Fisher was ready to lay down, so we drove all night and arrived in Morgantown the morning of the ball game. We decided that I would be the front man, so Hacken and Wagman checked into a hotel and began to jockey the telephones. I met up with the Chicago contingent at their luxurious two-bedroom suite in a different hotel. Lefty had made the trip south, along with a guy named Tony DiChiantini, and an older man named John who was the boss of the entire Chicago syndicate. There were two bodyguards with them, big bruisers armed with enough hardware to win the battle of Gettysburg. Tony was also accompanied by a beautiful redhead. Right off the bat, John and Tony wanted to have a little party to put everybody in a good mood while we were waiting to find out what the price on the game was going to be. 'Sure thing,' I said. 'Yeah. Let's go.' So I called room service and ordered food and booze, but I also sneaked a call to Wagman and told him, 'Let's not let anything happen to screw up this game or else we'll all wind up getting killed.' Wagman told me not to worry, that the game was a snap. Even so, I was starting to have second thoughts—maybe West Virginia wouldn't be very sharp for their opening game, maybe Fisher wasn't good enough (or wouldn't play enough) to influence the score—so I hadn't made any personal bets on the side.

"Suddenly John asked me where everybody was going to sit to watch the game. Did I have enough tickets for everybody? Jesus! I had forgotten all about it. But I called up the coach of West Virginia, Fred Schaus, who'd been a teammate of mine with the Pistons, and he said that he'd gladly leave me six tickets even though the game was a sellout. Little did he know that his guests were the biggest Mafia bosses in Chicago!

"Meanwhile, Wagman was periodically checking in with Fisher, and at about six o'clock, the latest bulletin was that Showalter's ankle was going to get heavily taped and there was the possibility that he was going to start the game, which would mean limited action for Fisher. Naturally, I told Tony and John exactly what the situation was just so they wouldn't think we were trying to pull a fast one. Tony said that because they didn't know much about basketball they'd defer to Lefty. 'I like the game anyway,' Lefty said, 'but just to protect ourselves, we should only make half a bet. Everybody on your end, Jack, will get the same amount of money.'

"That was fine with me. Lefty called Chicago to let us know what the line was that he'd be betting. In the meantime, Tony counted out ten hundred-dollar bills, gave them to me, and told me to tell Fisher to take a dive. Ten minutes later, Lefty reported that the line they'd bet was West Virginia minus eighteen and a half. That meant Tennessee would have to lose by at least nineteen for us to win the money. I called Wagman to inform him about the extra thousand for Fisher and also for him to let Fisher know what the final line was, and that was that.

"The freshmen game had just finished when we all took our seats behind the West Virginia bench. John and Tony were dressed real sharp with their brand-new wide-lapel suits. Tony's redhead wore an expensive dress and all kinds of jewelry and was easily the most striking girl in the entire gymnasium. There were about thirteen thousand fans packed into the place, and since most of them were students, just about everyone else was wearing dungarees and sneakers or some other kind of casual clothing. Even Fred Schaus did a double take when he turned around and said hello to me. I introduced him to Lefty, Tony, John, Wagman, Hacken, and the redheads, and everybody stood up real formally to shake hands all around. John was very much impressed that I knew the coach and he figured that the game was in the bag.

"Turned out that Showalter's ankle was still too sore, so Fisher started and the kid played a great game—fouling, making errors, and missing easy shots. West Virginia was having an easy time controlling the game and when Fisher fouled out with two minutes left, Tennessee was losing by thirty-one points. Schaus had long since taken out his first team and was in the process of taking out his second team. Me and Wagman and the Chicago crew were laughing and joking and having ourselves a good time, right?

"Unfortunately, West Virginia's third team was so bad that they couldn't even bring the ball safely upcourt. Suddenly, Tennessee started intercepting passes and making every shot they took and the lead began to shrink in a hurry.

"Tony nudged me in the ribs and said, 'Jack! Why don't you tell your buddy Fred to put his starters back into the game?' I said, 'No, that would be impossible.' Then John spoke up and also asked me to speak to Schaus about putting his first team back into the game. 'No, no,' I repeated. 'That wouldn't be proper, and besides, it would give me away as having bet on the game.' As the margin kept getting closer and closer, Tony and John kept nagging at me, but there was nothing I could do.

"Finally, the game ended with West Virginia winning by fifteen points, which made us losers. After the buzzer, Schaus turned around with a big smile on his face. 'Hey, you guys,' Schaus said merrily, 'don't be so glum. It was a great game, wasn't it?'

"Yeah. Sure. A terrific game. See you later, Fred.

"What happened then was that Wagman got the thousand dollars back from Fisher and returned it to Tony back at the hotel. 'Even though we lost,' Wagman told Tony, 'the kid did a good job, you know? Making all those turnovers and missing all those shots. Maybe you should give the kid something anyway just to keep him on the line in case we want to work with him again.' So Tony peeled off a hundred for Wagman to give to Fisher. Afterward, Tony said that he and the redhead were planning to rent a car and drive to Pittsburgh to visit with some friends and then fly on to Chicago. John was all set to fly straight out to Chicago.

"'Hey,' I said to Tony. 'Me and Hacken and Wagman are driving to Toledo to see if we might work a Michigan State–Bowling Green game, so it would be easy for us to drop you off in Pittsburgh.' What I was really angling for was to spend some time with Tony to mend some fences and make sure he knew we were on the up-and-up.

"I drove and Tony rode shotgun, so we had plenty of time to talk. Tony said that he'd only lost five grand on the game. 'I don't blame you at all, Jack,' he told me, 'but next time let's make sure we have a stronger game so I can at least get my money back.'

"Now, I was all set to double-sell the Bowling Green–Michigan State game to at least two other backers, but I decided that I had to get the Chicago boys in the black before I started double-crossing them. It was more a question of staying alive than of doing the honorable thing.

"After we dropped off Tony and the redhead, Wagman, Hacken, and I hooked up with Joe Green in Toledo. We had a little meeting and came to the conclusion that we absolutely needed a winner and that Falantino was not good enough to get the job done. Billy Reed was also on that Bowling Green team and I'd played with him in various tournaments around New York. Of course I'd been careful to try and cultivate Reed by giving him extra cash for expenses and the usual stuff I did, but Green and Wagman egged me to go straight after the kid. 'You can get him, Jack. He's such a big fan of yours that he's bound to say yes. He respects you too much to turn you in. The worst the kid can do is say no, so what's the risk?'

"There was some degree of conflict in my mind about this situation because, up to that point, Lenny Kaplan was the only player I'd ever approached and offered an incriminating proposition. Anyway, I was so bothered by how the West Virginia–Tennessee game had turned out that eventually I decided to arrange a meeting with Reed and pop the question myself. The way it worked out was that Green and Wagman had Reed perfectly handicapped and the kid was ready to go. The thousand dollars I offered seemed to him like all the money in the world. Reed's only hesitation was his fear that the spread might be anywhere from ten to twelve points, which he felt would be unworkable. When a call to Goldberg in St. Louis revealed that the line was only six, Reed couldn't have been happier. The weird thing about the Bowling Green situation was that because Falantano was dealing only with Green and Wagman, and Reed was dealing only with me, the two teammates were unaware that each of them was dumping.

"I still wasn't one-hundred-percent sure about the game until about an hour and a half before tip-off. By then the Chicago money had jumped the line up to eight and a half points, but Goldberg told me that he had some good news—one of the referees was on board and would be favoring Michigan State. Well, that was enough for me to bet five thousand with a couple of bookies back in New York.

"The Bowling Green team flew out to East Lansing on December second, the afternoon before the game, and we drove there the next morning through a snowstorm. The game was played in another one of those huge field houses that looked like a mausoleum. Falantano only played for a few minutes and he was not a factor in the game, but Reed certainly was. In the first half, Reed scored too many points, got too many rebounds, blocked too many shots and Bowling Green was only six points behind. During the intermission, Green, Hacken, and Wagman insisted that I try and get a hold of Reed and tell him to take it easy. I had to fight my way through the crowd just to get near the locker-room door as the Bowling Green team came back out to start the second half. I couldn't get close enough to talk to Reed but I did manage to catch his eye and give him a quizzical look. He responded with a wink, so I knew that everything was under control.

"Sure enough, Reed started the second half with a couple of botched shots, a three-second violation, and a poor job of trying to seal his man off the boards.

The referee that Goldberg owned called about four times as many fouls on Bowling Green as he did on the home team. In no time at all, Michigan State's lead swelled to seventeen points and the game was out of the woods. At one point, the lead extended to forty and the final score was ninety-six to sixty-seven.

"A few days after the game, when Green called Falantano to see if he wanted to work a game against DePaul, Falantano refused. 'I've got the five hundred dollars that you gave me right here in my pocket,' Falantano said. 'Not only am I not interested in working any more games for you, but I want to see you again so I can return the five-hundred.' And guess what? Reed worked four more games for us that season—versus DePaul on December 10, Bradley on December 12, Loyola of Chicago on February 29, and Detroit on March 5 (the only game that didn't come out right for us), and Canisius on December 3 of the following season—and Falantano never returned the money.

"Who cared about a measly five hundred dollars? The important point was that the West Virginia–Tennessee fiasco was redeemed and the Chicago boys were happy."

In fact, the Chicago bosses were so pleased with Molinas that they offered him another tool to use in his work—the Perfect Drug.

Developed by a Canadian chemist especially for the Mafia, the drug was an odorless, colorless, and tasteless liquid that was supposed to take effect only twenty minutes after ingestion. One drop would reportedly raise the victim's body temperature to 104 degrees for three or four days and thereafter cause diarrhea and nausea for another forty-eight hours. Even after the symptoms had disappeared, the victim would be too weak and sore to compete effectively in any athletic endeavor for at least a week.

The whole drug business came about because there was an organized crime family in Brooklyn that was always after Molinas to sell them a rigged game, and as often as they asked he would refuse. The Chicago people were well aware that the Brooklyn Mafia was itching to get a piece of Jack's action, so they wanted to do something that would keep him happy and insure his loyalty. The drug was a token of their appreciation, a bribe to keep the always-enterprising con man in the fold.

A pint of this nameless drug was delivered to Molinas's apartment on Ocean Parkway, and he was eager to discover exactly how it might be utilized to fix sporting events. The same day he received the shipment, Molinas put a few doses into a small plastic bottle he had emptied of eyedrops. Then he took the bottle with him to Rand's Bar in Coney Island. By chance, Bobby Kraw was also on hand for his evening meal and the two men shared the same table. As always, they kidded each other over the robbery that Kraw had sponsored.

"Your bodyguard was very impressive, Jack. 'Put your guns down or I'll shit in my pants.' Very impressive."

"It worked, didn't it? But tell me, Bobby, where'd you get those guys? The unemployment office?"

"Hey, Jack. I needed the money more than you did."

They both laughed and toasted their continuing friendship. Then Molinas told Kraw about the drug, and about how eager he was to see how it worked.

"The best way," said Kraw, "is to test it on yourself."

"No, thanks. But since you need money so badly I'll give you a hundred bucks to take a dose."

"Forget it, Jack. Look, there's a dozen guys in here tonight. Let's pick one of them."

Maybe that guy? No, he's a friend of Kraw's brother. How about that guy? No, he's too nice. One by one, they eliminated all the neighborhood hangers-on. Then the front door opened and in walked Jackie Jensen. Molinas and Kraw exchanged a conspiratorial wink. They had found their guinea pig.

Jackie Jensen was about nineteen years old. He never did a day's work and never told the truth. He would walk around with two hundred-dollar bills in his wallet and when it came time to pay a check, he'd say, "Well, I only have a hundred." And somebody else would wind up paying for him. He thought he was the best-looking guy in the world, the smartest guy in the world, the best athlete, the best card player, and so on. Nobody could stand him.

Jensen came over to Jack and Bobby's table and gave them his typical glad hand. "How are you fellows doing?" he asked. "Who's buying the drinks?" Bobby said the first round was on him, and he also offered to buy each of them a steak dinner. As soon as Jensen left the table to visit the men's room, Jack put a drop of the drug in his drink.

Jensen was about halfway through his steak when he said, "I don't feel so good. I think there's something wrong with my steak." Then he started moaning and holding his stomach. Meanwhile, Jack and Bobby couldn't stop smiling, just imagining how much money the drug was going to make for them. Jensen staggered into the men's room.

About then another guy came walking into the bar, a local bully named Bobby Narder. Right away, Bobby Kraw and Jack traded another mischievous wink. Twenty minutes later, when Narder went to the men's room, Jack doused his drink. Narder came back to the table laughing his head off. "You gotta see this," he said, then he led a bunch of them back to the men's room. And there was Jensen, his tie off, his shirt unbuttoned, on his knees with his head in the urinal. His hand was on the lever and he was alternately puking and flushing, puking and flushing, with the water hitting his head and splashing all over the floor. Naturally they all started laughing at him, but Kraw and Molinas were also laughing because Bobby Narder was up next.

Now that Molinas knew how the drug worked, it was time to formulate some kind of scheme. He thought that the easiest mark would be a prizefighter, so he enlisted Joe Hacken's help and they picked out a light heavyweight named Harold Johnson, who was fighting in Philadelphia. Because of Joe's connections with Blinky Palermo and Frankie Carbo he had no trouble getting into Johnson's dressing room before the fight. It was Johnson's routine to suck on an orange just before leaving the dressing room and Joe managed to use a syringe to inject one drop into each half of the orange. Two drops were used because they needed the drug to work faster than usual. Sure enough, Johnson sucked the orange dry and then went into the ring.

Johnson was a terrific fighter who would later become the light heavyweight champ, but by the third round he was starting to get weak. Then his head began to ache and in between rounds he was throwing up. Right in the middle of a round, Johnson got hit with a solid right to his stomach and proceeded to shit in his pants. The next thing fight fans saw was Johnson pushing his way into a clinch and throwing up on his opponent's shoulder. As soon as that happened, Johnson's trainer threw in the towel and it went into the books as a TKO. Jack and and Joe Hacken and the Chicago boys made an awful lot of money that night.

In another attempt to buy Molinas's loyalty, Lefty Rosenthal informed him of a much more ambitious scam—drugging an entire football team. Oklahoma was rated the top college team in the country was scheduled to play the second-rated team, Notre Dame, in Chicago's Soldier Field. On the Thursday night preceding the Saturday afternoon game, the Oklahoma players were taken to a nightclub in Chicago called the Chez Paree for a meal and an evening's entertainment. Because the outing had been prearranged, Rosenthal was able to place his bets on Wednesday (on Notre Dame with six points) and also to contact an assistant chef at the nightclub who did part-time muscle work for the Mafia.

Molinas is on record about what transpired next. "There were thirty-five players on the Oklahoma team, plus two assistant coaches, a trainer, and Bud Wilkinson, the head coach, and they all ordered steaks. The assistant chef put a single drop on each of the players' steaks but left the other steaks alone. The unused portion of the drug was flushed down the kitchen sink and the empty vial was washed thoroughly and dumped into the garbage. After about thirty minutes, some of the players began to show signs—headaches, the runs, stomach cramps, the whole deal.

"By the time they got back to their hotel, Wilkinson was in a panic. A doctor was called in and his diagnosis was Asian flu. Once the news became public, the spread went down to two, and there was even some talk that the game might be cancelled. At one point the game was actually taken off the board. Lefty was worried about this, but I put him straight. 'Oklahoma will play even if they only have eleven healthy players,' I said. On Friday night, Wilkinson made a statement that Oklahoma would play even if he had to suit up the junior varsity team. His statement was so inspirational that many of the Oklahoma fans started betting on their team to win. The game was back on the board and the line went up to three and a half before the Notre Dame money bet it down to pick 'em.

"Because the football players were in such great physical shape, many of them shook off the effects of the drug and were able to play. Of the thirty-five who were drugged, only nine missed the game. The final score was Notre Dame thirty-five and Oklahoma seven. I'd only bet two thousand, but the Chicago syndicate won over a hundred thousand. The headline in the newspapers said 'Flu Bug Bites Sooners.' Incidentally, this same drug was used on college football teams for the next four or five years. The Mafia would send their people to get jobs working in the kitchens at campuses all over the country, and when they worked on the training table they would drug the football players. It took at least six months of preparation just to put someone in the right spot at the right time. And the headlines were always the same—'Flu Bug Visits USC,' or Washington, or New

Mexico. There was one season where Lefty and his crew worked their drug act fifteen times. There were vaults full of money made on this particular scam.

"Aside from the Harold Johnson fight, there was only one other time that I used the drug to fix an athletic event. Dave Budin convinced me to try and drug the Bradley University basketball team during a game against St. Bonaventure at the Garden. Through Budin's contacts we already had a handle on Bradley's second-best player, a six-foot-seven jumping jack named Al Sanders. Chet Walker was Bradley's All-American and they were a really tough team, one of the best in the country. Bradley was a six-point favorite over St. Bonaventure and we felt that if we could get Walker doped up, then the Bonnies would be a lock. Sanders, by the way, was Walker's roommate, and he insisted that he also be doused with the drug so nobody would suspect him of anything crooked.

"So on the afternoon of the game, Budin hired this black kid named Rufus, dressed him up in a waiter's uniform, gave him a tray and a pitcher of doctored orange juice, then drove him to the Paramount Hotel, where Bradley was staying. It was a funny scene with the passersby trying to figure out why a waiter was climbing out of a car balancing a pitcher of orange juice on a tray. Anyway, Rufus walked right through the lobby without being challenged by anybody, got on the elevator, found the right room, and knocked on the door. When Sanders opened the door, Rufus said, 'Here's your orange juice.' Sanders then grabbed the pitcher and poured a glassful for himself and one for Walker.

"'What's this all about?' Walker asked. 'We've never had orange juice before.'

"'Coach's orders,' Rufus said. 'You can call him and ask him about it, but I don't think he'll appreciate that you're questioning his decision. The coach told me he wants everybody to drink orange juice to give them extra energy for the ball game.'

"So Sanders and Walker each gulped down a glass of the juice, then gave the empty pitcher back to Rufus. 'No tip will be required,' Rufus said, then he left the room, put the pitcher and the tray down on the floor right outside the door, took off his uniform and laid it right next to the pitcher, took the elevator down to the lobby, walked calmly into the street, jumped back into the car, and off he went.

"We all laid our bets on St. Bonaventure with six points. I bet about two thousand and Budin must've bet ten thousand. The game was close from wire to wire. Walker would play three minutes, then a substitute would be sent in while he ran to the bathroom. He'd come back to the bench a few minutes later and be sent back into the game for another short stretch, and this went on all game long. It's ironic that Sanders didn't seem to be affected at all by the drug. I figured that the drug had sunk to the bottom of the pitcher and since Walker drank the second glass, he got the heavy hit.

"Long about the end of the third quarter, somebody handed me a copy of the next morning's *Daily News*, the early edition. The headline on the back page said that the Bradley players had been drugged and there was a picture of the pitcher, the tray, and Rufus's discarded uniform! Anyway, Walker wound up with twenty points, Bradley won by eleven points, and we lost our wagers.

"Afterward, there was a big investigation by the Manhattan district attorney, who believed that Walker had dumped the game. Sanders, who was dumping, was never suspected, but the shadow of scandal hung over Walker's career even after he became an All-Star player in the NBA."

As the season unfolded, Molinas and Hacken continued to scout the college ranks for likely players to be recruited. They soon found an easy mark in Ray Paprocky, a six-foot-five forward for NYU. Paprocky had been an outstanding player at Grover Cleveland High School in Queens, but was a poor student and left without graduating. Later, after a hitch in the army, Paprocky attended night school, earning sufficient credits to be admitted into NYU's School of Commerce, where he majored in hotel management. Paprocky's athletic scholarship was limited to free tuition with no allowances for room, board, or books. And Paprocky was besieged by a battery of personal problems that left him desperate for money.

Paprocky was married, his wife was expecting a baby, and the projected hospital expenses would be over four hundred dollars. He was taking sixteen credit hours, commuting by subway three hours a day between his home in Queens and the NYU campus in the Bronx, and also working eight hours at night in a fruit cannery. In addition, Paprocky had no money in the bank and his father had just died. Paprocky had pleaded with the NYU athletic department to find him a substantial summer job, but the only job he was offered was to referee intramural basketball games at three dollars a contest.

Paprocky's financial distress was well known to both Hacken and Molinas, and Hacken was selected to make the move. Hacken's opening gambit was to ask Paprocky to get him six tickets for an upcoming NYU–St. John's game at the Garden no matter what the cost. Paprocky came up with his own two free tickets plus four others badgered from his teammates, and he sold them to Hacken for sixty dollars. Eventually, Paprocky agreed to shave points in five games for Hacken. But the first game that Paprocky worked proved to be a disappointment.

NYU was favored by eleven and a half points against St. John's and Paprocky was going to make sure they went under the spread. Molinas and his cronies were so confident about the outcome that they sold the contract to Rosenthal. NYU was winning by ten points with two seconds left in the game, Paprocky had the ball deep in the backcourt, and they were already counting their money. Then Paprocky passed the ball to a teammate who threw the ball at the basket from at least fifty-five feet away. Bang! The ball went in, NYU won by twelve, and Molinas's bets were lost. Paprocky was distraught, but Hacken gave him a couple of hundred dollars in good faith.

By now, Fixers Incorporated had gained such notoriety in the basketball underworld that players began approaching them. One of these guys was another NYU player who was all over them, pestering them to let him earn some money. They also had a third player on that NYU team, a guard who had to make a shot in the wrong basket in order for a game to come out right.

Players were coming out of the woodwork. Jerry Vogel at North Carolina, was brought into the corral by the team's sixth man, Lou Brown. It was not uncommon at all for one player they had in the bag to tell them that a couple of his teammates wanted in. That's exactly what happened with the North Carolina State team.

Joe Green had recruited Don Gallagher when they'd worked together during the previous summer at Klein's Hillside. Gallagher was married and had a baby boy, so he had a lot of financial responsibilities. As soon as the season started, Gallagher got in touch with Green to say that three of his teammates had volunteered to dump games.

Anton "Dutch" Muehlbauer's parents had separated when he was young and he was always easily led by his peers. His affability helped make him a popular young man, but he was a very poor student at Abraham Lincoln High School in Brooklyn. Inferior grades, however, were no obstacle for an outstanding basketball player to gain admission to North Carolina State. A mediocre total of 750 in the College Board aptitude tests was acceptable, and the school's admissions office was satisfied if an athlete's combined high-school transcript and college boards score predicted a D-plus average. Muehlbauer majored in recreation and parks administration (another name for physical education), but still required special tutoring to maintain his athletic eligibility. Indeed, once the season was over, Muehlbauer was expelled from the college for failure to attend classes.

Stan Niewierowski, from Bishop Loughlin High School in Brooklyn, also majored in recreation and parks administration. Unlike Muehlbauer, Niewierowski was reasonably articulate and a competent student. But, aside from the free room, board, tuition, and books provided by the school, Niewierowski found that the allowable fifteen dollars a month for incidental expenses to be a hardship. He was also described by a teammate as a "fellow who would gamble on anything. Throw a feather in the air, and he'd bet whether it would hit the floor." When Niewierowski was introduced to Joe Green, the young man said simply, "I need the money."

Terry Litchfield was from Louisville, Kentucky, where his father was the statewide director of the YMCA, and was scarcely the type who might be expected to seek out involvement with gamblers. Pronounced by one doctor as blind when he was six years old, Litchfield overcame severe nearsightedness to become an outstanding basketball player. Litchfield, however, was very unhappy with his lack of playing time and developed a severe dislike for coach Everett Case.

With four players doing business, Molinas expected that any game involving North Carolina State would be a sure thing. But, as ever, there were always unforeseen problems. A guy who said his name was "Ricky" showed up in Winston-Salem to watch a North Carolina State–Wake Forest game. The guy said that he represented the Chicago syndicate and he bought the game in their name from Wagman and Green. It was an easy game, with the underdog North Carolina State team losing by fourteen points, well over their seven-point spot. Then it turned out that Ricky's real name was Steve Likos and that, rather than working for the Chicago group, he was Dave Goldberg's partner. So there was Goldberg working Lefty Rosenthal's blind side and setting up his own deals. Afterward, Likos told Wagman and Green that the next time they had a game they could call Goldberg or Likos directly and avoid dealing with both Molinas and Chicago. Jack was told about all of this by Joe Green, who was still acting as his spy.

From Winston-Salem, Green and Wagman moved on to Columbia, South Carolina, to speak to Richie Hoffman about the prospects for fixing a South Carolina–North Carolina State game to be played on December 8. Hoffman had already graduated from South Carolina, but he swore that he could arrange for two of his ex-teammates to do business—Larry Dial and Bob Franz, who split the center position. Dial and Franz were subsequently promised five hundred dollars each to dump the game, Hoffman was given seven hundred and fifty for being the contact man, and just to make sure the game was under control, Green gave North Carolina State's Don Gallagher a hundred dollars to play extra hard and win the game. Fixers Incorporated went ahead and sold the game to Chicago. No payoffs were made, however, because although Gallagher scored twenty-one points and Dial and Franz stunk up the court, South Carolina still managed to win, 72–71. This marked the second game in eight days that had backfired. Naturally, the Chicago consortium wasn't overjoyed.

Two days later, on December 10, they were working a pair of ball games—Bowling Green against DePaul, and South Carolina versus Georgia Tech. Both contests were sold to Goldberg, and as part of the deal he was supposed to make a pair of bets for Molinas and Joe Hacken. Two thousand on DePaul and two thousand on Georgia Tech. But every time Jack asked Goldberg if he'd laid the action, he just kept stalling. When it came time to cash in all the chips, it turned out that Goldberg had reneged on his agreement and had not made any of the bets. It was a good thing that the cunning Mr. Molinas had also sold both games to his Boston backer, so he wasn't hurt too badly.

Richie Hoffman was also playing games with everybody else's money. For the South Carolina–Wake Forest game, the payoff was the same as it was supposed to be for the South Carolina–North Carolina State game—Franz and Dial would get five hundred and Hoffman's share was seven hundred and fifty. But

Hoffman told Green and Wagman that he had a third South Carolina player who would also have to be paid five-hundred. In truth, there was no third player and Hoffman pocketed the extra five hundred.

To make matters worse, Goldberg had Wagman and Green fly out to St. Louis to butter them up and convince them to cut Molinas and Joe Hacken out of the loop. It was clear that Fixers Incorporated was falling apart.

Even so, the group held together for at least one more successful fix—Georgetown at Niagara on December 17—another game that Molinas double-sold to Boston and Goldberg. Both of the Niagara fixers—Sal Vergopia and Lenny Whelan—hailed from the Bronx and were veterans of the Creston Avenue schoolyard. For a thousand dollars each, Vergopia and Whelan were obliged to ensure that Niagara either lost or won by less than the eight-point spread. The final score was Niagara 87, Georgetown 86. But Wagman became quickly disenchanted when Goldberg withheld a large portion of the contracted payoffs for both the Bowling Green–Wake Forest game and South Carolina–North Carolina State. As a result, the next game on the agenda, South Carolina at Maryland, was a Gordian knot of double- and triple-crosses.

Molinas sorts out the complexities: "We had three players in the game—Dial and Franz with South Carolina, and Tom Callahan with Maryland. The opening line favored Maryland by fifteen points and I figured with three key players doing business, Maryland was a lock to cover the spread. What happened, though, was that Wagman was angry at being shorted seven hundred dollars by Goldberg, so before he even approached Goldberg about the game, he sold it to Frankie Cardone in Pittsburgh—Maryland to win and cover. Goldberg was still sitting on the fence, not wanting to make a final decision because he thought fifteen points was too much to give. But when the betting wave caused by the Pittsburgh money reached Chicago, the fifteen-point spread had moved up to eighteen. Goldberg was irate and told Wagman that Hacken and I had obviously sold the game to a backer in Pittsburgh, and he cursed the two of us for being double-crossers. So then Goldberg turned around and asked Wagman if it was possible for South Carolina to beat Maryland.

"'Sure,' Wagman said.

"'Here's what we're gonna do,' said Goldberg. 'We're gonna take South Carolina and the eighteen points. Give Dial and Franz five hundred bucks a piece and tell them to go out and win the game. Then give Callahan another five hundred to dump.'

"As soon as Wagman told Green what the new deal was, Green called me up. So I started laying money on Maryland at the same time that Goldberg was betting on South Carolina. Hacken and I wound up getting fifteen thousand down on Maryland.

"The upshot was that Hacken and I had contracted to pay the three players to make sure Maryland won, and Goldberg had Wagman pay the same three players to make sure that South Carolina won. Before the game started, however, Hacken approached Dial, Franz, and Callahan and told them that all bets were off, that they should play the game straight. But all of them were still confused once the game began, and passes were being thrown to the wrong team, easy shots were being missed, and the first quarter was a comedy of errors. When things settled down, Maryland just ripped South Carolina apart at the seams. The final score was eighty-five to fifty-two. Hacken and I won big, and Goldberg lost even bigger. After blowing his cork and vowing to get to the bottom of everything, Goldberg never did figure out exactly what had happened."

On January 12, 1960, Molinas got involved with a ball game that had dire consequences both immediate and long-term. He had played ball several times in Coney Island with Gary Kaufman, a kid from Brooklyn. Some of the Kaiser Park regulars also told him that Kaufman loved to bet on college basketball. Jack did his usual grease-the-palms routine and by his reaction knew that Kaufman was hot to trot. In fact, some time in late December, he had flown out to Utah to watch Kaufman play for the College of the Pacific and see if he was good enough to turn a game by himself. The College of the Pacific was an eighteen-point underdog in that game and Kaufman had told Jack beforehand he was so sure Utah wouldn't cover the spread that he'd already bet a few hundred with a local bookie on his own team plus the points. Molinas told Kaufman that he had also bet on COP and would give him two hundred bucks if they got in under the spread. Sure enough, the kid played brilliantly and Utah won by only fifteen. Jack was impressed with Kaufman and also with a big rebounder on his team named Leroy Wright.

Hacken and Molinas had just won about fifteen grand on the South Carolina–Georgia Tech game, the one where Dave Goldberg took a bath by backing Georgia Tech. That meant Hacken and Jack were looking for a can't-miss game to sell to Goldberg and heal the breach. So, shortly after New Year's Molinas made a call to Kaufman at his campus dormitory in Stockton, California, just to ask him if he was interested in making a few extra bucks. "You bet," Kaufman said. "And not only am I interested, but I've got three of my teammates, including Leroy Wright, who would love to do business with you. It's a fantastic situation, Jack. We're playing Saint Mary's in a couple of days and with four of the starting players we've got a stranglehold on the game. You've got to fly out here, Jack, and set us up."

What could be better?

Kaufman picked Jack up at the airport in his sporty red Triumph, then demanded ten thousand dollars to dump the St. Mary's game. They haggled a bit and agreed that six thousand would be a fair price—fifteen hundred for each of the players, payable in advance. Molinas didn't care about the other two players but he insisted on meeting Wright and confirming that he was ready to dump the game. Kaufman agreed.

By now, Jack knew that the game was a lock. St. Mary's had a great player named Tom Mescherey, who would later become an NBA All-Star, and the game was to be played on their court. So he decided to bypass Goldberg and sell the game directly to the big boys in Chicago. Lefty was very eager to buy the game but insisted on sending someone out to California to speak directly with Kaufman and Wright. That was fine with Jack, especially since he had already arranged to speak face-to-face with Wright anyway.

Wright told Molinas that he'd been promised a thousand dollars to fix the game and that was fine with him. So, right away Jack knew that Kaufman was working an angle on his own teammate and planning to pocket the extra five hundred. He told Kaufman that the Chicago office wanted to send an emissary to check things out because they wanted to bet an awful lot of money on the game. Wright had no problem with that.

The next scene was a hotel in San Francisco. Molinas was there, along with Kaufman, and Wright, who was a black fellow, about six foot nine and wearing a funny-looking suit that made him look like some kind of character out of a Li'l Abner comic strip. And representing Chicago was one of the Mafia chieftains, Tony DiChiantini, and a pistol-packing bodyguard. Both Kaufman and Wright said there was no way they could beat St. Mary's even if they played straight, and they'd make sure they would lose by more than whatever the line turned out to be. Tony was more than satisfied. He handed Jack the six grand to ice the players and an extra thousand for his own expenses. Because of Goldberg's deal with Chicago, Goldberg would eventually be billed for this money.

As soon as Tony left for the airport, and before he got the final okay from Chicago, Molinas called Hacken in New York and told him to line up the bookmakers because they were going to shoot the moon on this game. So far that season they were a hundred thousand in the black and Hacken agreed to bet it all. So, the game opened with COP as a seven-point underdog and the twenty-five thousand that Hacken got down only moved the spread up to seven and a half. At that point, Jack called Goldberg in St. Louis and told him that the game was under contract. He did this so he could get his own action laid on the game and also erase any hard feelings he still had from the South Carolina–Georgia Tech game. Fifteen minutes later, Goldberg called back to say that he'd bet sixty thousand and the line was now up to thirteen points!

Meanwhile, Chicago was already bitching about all the St. Mary's money that had shown up and they'd taken the game off the board. So Jack called Lefty and asked him what he thought they should do about the game. Lefty said that they'd put the game back on the board at eleven, but they were now changing their bets to COP with the points. Now, once the Chicago office put the game at eleven, everybody in the country would follow suit. Before long, enough COP money showed up from back east to reduce the line to eight points, which is where it stood as the game began.

So what did they have going on? Hacken had bet the rest of their treasure chest on St. Mary's minus eight points, Goldberg had sixty grand on the same team at the same price, and Chicago wound up with two hundred thousand on COP plus nine and a half. Only if St. Mary's were to win by exactly nine points would everybody Jack was dealing with be happy. Somehow he had crawled out on a limb that was in danger of being cut off.

St. Mary's College was located on top of a mountain in Southern California. The gym seated only about three hundred fans, and when Jack scouted the environs he discovered to his shock that there was no public telephone in the building. In fact, the nearest phone was ten miles away. But the really bad news was that Kaufman had gotten into an argument with his coach at the Utah game and wouldn't get off the bench all night long. In fact, Kaufman's coach, Van Sweet, was so furious at the kid that he never played another minute for the rest of the season!

At the half, St. Mary's was leading 35–12, so Molinas got in his rented car and drove like a madman through the mountain hills to the gas station where the phone was. He called Hacken in New York, Goldberg in St. Louis, and Lefty in Chicago and told them that everything was happening right on schedule. Then he raced back to the gym for the second half.

With two minutes to go, the third and fourth COP players that were working the game had both fouled out, but St. Mary's was still ahead by fifteen. Then a minute later, the lead was down to thirteen when Wright collided with another player as they chased a loose ball and had to be taken from the game. Now there were five honest players on the floor for COP and they were playing like gangbusters. It was nail-biting time. With only eight seconds left on the clock, St. Mary's had the ball and a nine-point lead. Everything looked right as rain. Everybody was a winner. Molinas and Hacken, Goldberg and Chicago. It was the perfect game at the perfect time. Except that a COP player stole the ball and raced down the court. The buzzer went off to end the game about half a tick before the player scored the bucket, but the referee signaled that the two points counted. That last score cost Jack Molinas and Joe Hacken one hundred and twenty-eight thousand dollars!

Jack drove back to the phone at the gas station at about five miles per hour, still in a state of shock. He called Joe Hacken and told him the bad news. Joe was just sick and had nothing to say. Jack would be back in New York the next day and they would try to figure out some way to recover. Then Jack called Lefty in Chicago, who couldn't have been happier. Lefty even promised Jack a fifteen-hundred-dollar bonus. The last call Jack had to make was to Goldberg, but he did not have the heart to do it. It wasn't until one o'clock in the morning that he worked up the courage to call Goldberg.

"Hi, Dave," he said. "This is Jack. Did you find out the score yet?"

"No," he said. "I've been calling every newspaper in the country but nobody knows the score. I know that since you didn't call me before this that we lost the game, but tell me what happened."

After Molinas supplied the painful details, Goldberg began cursing and screaming. "Do you know how much I bet on this game?" he yelled. "Between this game and the South Carolina game I owe my life! I'm in so much trouble that I don't know whether to shit or go blind! Son of a bitch! We shouldn't be losing like this! The least you can do, Jack, is to go and get the money back from those double-crossing players of yours! There's going to be an investigation, Jack, and for your sake, I hope you're clean."

So Molinas drove back to the St. Mary's campus, but nobody was there. He then got back in the car and drove the forty miles to the COP campus, arriving there just as the players' bus arrived. He immediately approached Kaufman and asked for the money back.

"No," he said. "We dumped the game and we're entitled to all of the money."

"You're entitled to nothing because you didn't even play."

"No, I didn't play," he agreed, "but I'm responsible for lining up the others."

Molinas didn't feel like arguing with him, so he said that he needed the money back from Wright and the other two players.

"I already spoke to Leroy about this very possibility," Kaufman said, "and he feels that he went out and played poorly enough to satisfy his end of the bargain. The fact that you didn't win your bet is your tough luck."

"Okay," Jack said. "You do whatever you want as long as you are prepared to face the consequences." Then he reported the latest development to Goldberg, who blew his stack. He believed that Kaufman had double-crossed them from the start and that none of the COP players were dumping. Goldberg also said he was going to have a pair of head-breakers fly right out to California and have a talk with Kaufman. Molinas was supposed to meet them at the airport and take them to Kaufman's dormitory. When he told Kaufman that he was about to have some visitors, the kid wasn't at all impressed. So Jack met Goldberg's goons at the airport but wanted no part of fingering Kaufman.

He called Kaufman the next day from New York to see if he was still alive and Kaufman couldn't stop laughing at what jerks the two enforcers were. Not only had Kaufman, Wright, and the other two players been allowed to keep the money, but they also talked Goldberg's goons into convincing their boss to fork over ten thousand dollars so they could dump COP's next game! Thankfully, that game was a complete success, so all of them recouped their money.

But all of that was still in the future, and when Molinas returned to New York the day after the St. Mary's game, Wagman told him what Goldberg was really thinking: that Wright had played a good game, as had the third player involved in the erstwhile fix. That the entire deal was a setup initiated by Molinas. That he was a double-crossing rat.

When Jack called Goldberg to protest his innocence, Goldberg said that he didn't have time to argue. "I'm going to be in Pittsburgh tomorrow," he said. "I'll be registered under the name Gregory Dodge in room number 743 at the Pittsburgh Hilton Hotel. Bring Joe Hacken with you because I also have some questions for him. Just make sure you're there, Jack, and then we'll sit down and have a pow-wow."

Molinas wasn't crazy about the idea, but he really had no choice. Anyway, if Goldberg wanted to have his legs broken, he already knew where Jack lived. Jack was dating a model named Tootie at the time and asked her if she'd like to take a mini-vacation. She was all for it. So Tootie, Hacken, and Molinas flew down to Pittsburgh the very next day.

As soon as they got there, Molinas sent Hacken to find Goldberg while he checked into a room with Tootie. He put some soft music on the radio and soon they were having a session between the sheets. By the time Hacken came walking into the room, Tootie was taking a shower and Jack was cooling down with a highball.

"You must be nuts," Hacken said. "Here you are, about to be killed, and you're gallivanting with this girl?"

"Let me tell you something, Joe. I'm only gonna live once, and if this is the end, then I'm gonna go out in style. That's my philosophy of life, my friend."

"You're crazy, Jack. I never realized just how crazy you really are."

Jack just laughed and said, "All right, Joe. I'll get dressed and be right with you." Then he told Tootie that he had a business conference and for to her to sit tight until he returned. So he showered and shaved and kept Joe waiting for forty minutes.

As soon as Molinas walked into Goldberg's room, he was right on Jack's case. "That's real nice, Jack. We lose around a hundred grand in two games and you come here with a blond? Not only that, Jack, but you have the balls to keep us waiting here while you're getting laid?"

"One thing has nothing to do with the other," he said. "You said you wanted to have a meeting? I'm here. Here's the meeting."

"All right," Goldberg said. "Let's go into the other room. There's somebody I want you to meet. Joe, you wait for us here."

Molinas followed Goldberg into the next room. It was a large bedroom with a balcony overlooking the street. Two little guys with big shoulders and no necks were waiting for them. A pair of professional bone-breakers. One of them pulled out a gun and motioned for Jack to go out onto the balcony. "What should I do with this jerk?" the guy with the gun asked Goldberg. "Should I throw him off the balcony, or should I shoot him?"

Cool as a cucumber, Jack knew that this was just another bluff designed to scare him. They were not going to throw him off the balcony and they were not going to shoot him. He wasn't alarmed or frightened in any way. As a matter of fact, he thought the whole thing was rather amusing.

Molinas had no idea that Goldberg had also summoned Wagman and Green to Pittsburgh and had them stashed in an adjoining suite. After cooling their heels for nearly an hour, Goldberg's partner, Steve Likos, entered the room and began peppering Wagman and Green with questions.

"Which one of you two guys sold the South Carolina–Maryland game to a backer here in Pittsburgh?"

Both Wagman and Green denied selling the game to anybody.

"Well," said Likos, "the Goon and the Midget are in the next room, and if everybody's answers don't match then tomorrow morning somebody's gonna wake up dead."

Again, Wagman and Green insisted they hadn't sold the game in question to anybody other than Goldberg.

"If what you say is true," Likos said, "then it was Molinas and Hacken who gave the game away."

Wagman shrugged and Green said, "I don't know anything about what anybody else did or didn't do."

Likos then left the room and went next door, where Goldberg and two henchmen were grilling Molinas and Hacken. When Likos returned several minutes later, he began talking about the COP–St. Mary's game: "From reports that we have received, we know that Leroy Wright played a bad game. We know that he scored only six points and made a lot of mistakes. That's good. We also know that Gary Kaufman didn't play at all. That's bad. The third guy who was supposed to be doing business had a terrific game. That's also bad. There was even supposed to be a fourth player doing business, but we were never told his name. That's even worse. What we really believe is that Molinas only had Wright and that he was bullshitting about the other players. If this is true, then your buddy Molinas, and his midget of a sidekick, are both in deep shit. Tell us what you know about the situation, and you guys better not even think of lying."

"All I know," said Wagman, "is what Jack told me—that he had four players on the College of the Pacific team."

"Me too," said Green.

Once again Likos disappeared into the adjacent room, but when he returned this time he had an envelope full of money—three thousand dollars that the

Chicago office owed to Wagman and Green. "Here," Likos said as he handed Wagman the envelope. "We've decided that you two guys have been straight with us. So take your money and take a hike."

Wagman and Green dashed from the room, happy to be uninjured, ecstatic to be alive.

Another reason why Molinas always claimed he wasn't scared was that he hadn't done anything wrong. He didn't double-cross Goldberg on the Maryland game—all he did was bet his own money. It wasn't his fault that Goldberg bet on the wrong team. And he didn't do anything wrong with the College of the Pacific game, either. If Goldberg was going to bitch about losing sixty grand on that game, Molinas could sit down and prove to him that he had lost a hundred. He had to respect a gun pointed at his head, but he wasn't going to let Goldberg bulldoze him. Jack looked at Goldberg and gave him a smirk. It wasn't a smile, he later said, it was a smirk.

"What am I gonna do with this guy?" Dave asked his two boppers. "He thinks everything is a joke. Put the gun away and get out of here." So the two boppers left and Goldberg and Jack sat down and hashed out their differences.

This is Molinas's version of events, but Molinas's testimony was not always accurate. According to numerous friends, bookmakers, girlfriends, members of the New York betting community, and even police officers, rather than so casually dismiss his hired muscle, Goldberg commandeered the gun and ordered the henchmen to grab Molinas by his ankles and dangle him off the edge of the balcony. Molinas's immediate reaction was to say this: "You can't do this to me! I'm Jack Molinas!" For several minutes, Molinas hung suspended seven stories above the concrete sidewalk. And he was held there until he swore he would never cross Goldberg again, until he promised to make restitution for the losses, and until he acknowledged that another mistake would be fatal. Molinas never denied nor confirmed this version of his "Interview in Pittsburgh," but whenever the subject was raised he would respond by erupting into his familiar high-pitched giggle.

The next game on Molinas's agenda was Temple at Lafayette down in Easton, Pennsylvania, where the visitors would be a four-point favorite. He had the best player on the Lafayette team through one of Joe Hacken's connections and, without letting either Wagman or Green in on the deal, he sold the game to his Brooklyn backer for twenty-five hundred. Then he and the backer drove to Easton, got to the Lafayette campus at about four o'clock the day of the game, called the player in his dorm, sat in the backer's car—a gray coup de ville with New York plates—and made the deal. The whole thing was a bit too much out in the open, but they paid the kid a grand and nobody was the wiser.

Before the game, Jack called Goldberg and told him that he liked Temple over Lafayette and that he should make a bet. Goldberg pushed Jack to try and find out if he had a contract for the game, but Molinas just said that he was handicapping the game straight up. Goldberg was reluctant to bet on an honest game, but he did. Although Jack was back to even for the current season, he still had about two or three hundred grand stashed away. But he didn't want anybody to know just how flush he was, so he thought it appropriate to limit his bet to five thousand. Temple won by a large margin and he was now just over six thousand ahead for the season. He didn't know how much Goldberg bet, but he did give him a winner as a kind of restitution and felt that they were back on the right footing.

Right after the Lafayette game, Joe Hacken took a ride up to Boston to speak to a kid who'd gotten the word to them through an intermediary that he was ready to dump. The kid played for MIT and when Joe met him, the kid was wearing an ROTC uniform. Joe turned the kid down. He told Jack that the kid looked so good in his uniform that he didn't have the heart to corrupt him. Joe was always different that way. He had a sentimental streak that Molinas never possessed.

On February 13, 1960, Molinas sold a successful contract to Goldberg—Maryland (plus five points) at North Carolina State. With Molinas's stable of players—Niewierowski, Muehlbauer, Litchfield, and Gallagher—all doing business, the home team won by two points and the Maryland money collected.

A few days later, Molinas sold another winner to Goldberg—Seton Hall–Dayton at Madison Square Garden. The fixers were Arthur Hicks and

Hank Gunter of Seton Hall and they'd both worked several previous games for Molinas and Hacken. The fact that Hicks and Gunter were accredited students at a reputable school like Seton Hall was another indictment against the reprehensible tactics used by powerhouse basketball programs to recruit, and then admit, blue chip ballplayers.

Hicks had been an All-State player at St. Elizabeth's, a Negro Catholic high school on Chicago's South Side. In his senior season, 1956–57, he scored a total of 1,151 points, as Elizabeth won forty-eight games in a lengthy fifty-one-game schedule. Hicks came from very poor family circumstances in the South Side slums and was a poor student, with little aptitude and less inclination for schoolwork. Even though he was certainly not college material, Hicks was enthusiastically recruited by fifty universities, including Notre Dame and all the Big Ten schools. He finally chose Northwestern, one of the Midwest's most prestigious academic institutions. The admissions office at Northwestern seriously debated the wisdom of accepting Hicks, but they finally welcomed the young man after deciding that his pitiful academic performance at St. Elizabeth's was primarily due to the basketball team's time-consuming fifty-one-game schedule.

In his first academic quarter at Northwestern, Hicks took two courses in physical education, one in geography, and one in English. He failed two, withdrew from the third with a failing grade, and didn't attend the fourth frequently enough to receive a grade. One Northwestern source later admitted that Hicks should have been dismissed at that point. But he was given another chance. In the second quarter, Hicks attended even fewer classes and was failing all four courses when he was finally advised to leave the school. After this, Hicks hung out in New York, played in various summer league tournaments, and caught the eye of Joe Hacken.

Seton Hall had originally been Hicks's second choice after Northwestern, and in the late summer of 1958, he was accepted there as a matriculated student. A faculty member at Seton Hall who requested anonymity said, "All of the credentials required by the admissions board were supplied by Hicks. This included transcripts of his work at St. Elizabeth's and Northwestern."

At Seton Hall, Hicks became friendly with Gunter and eventually introduced him to Hacken. Hicks also brought Hacken together with Al Saunders of Bradley University, against whom Hicks had played at St. Elizabeth's. Gunter, who had attended Samuel Gompers Vocational High School in New York, had been out of school for a year before entering Seton Hall. He was described by a local sportswriter as "quiet, easygoing, with some intelligence, but easily led." Both Hicks and Gunter found themselves in constant trouble with the school's authorities. They had been disciplined for a number of serious infractions of campus rules including drinking and late-night carousing in the dorms.

For the game at hand, Dayton was favored by six points, and Hicks and Gunter agreed to guarantee that Seton Hall would lose by more than the spread.

Indeed, with both players having atrocious performances, Seton Hall lost by thirty-five points. After the game, even though all of the Seton Hall players had been instructed to return to the campus via the team bus, Hicks and Gunter went looking for Hacken to collect their fees—a thousand dollars each. When Hacken failed to show up at the appointed place, Gunter rushed back to the Garden and caught the team bus just before it left. Hicks continued his fruitless search for Hacken and ended up spending the night in New York. When he returned to Seton Hall the next day, Hicks was expelled.

Oh well, Molinas was back in Goldberg's (and Chicago's) good graces, he'd already squeezed five or six winning games out of Hicks and Gunter, so it was time to move on to the next item on his itinerary.

In an attempt to replace his Seton Hall connection, Molinas once again took an unseemly risk. He had played in several summer tournaments with Jerry Deutsch, an outstanding guard from the University of Connecticut. Deutsch had stubbornly resisted Molinas's pitch many times and had easily forgiven Molinas for so cruelly stranding him in Montreal, and the two remained good friends. "I was still playing at UConn," Deutsch said, "and, one night, we were on our way out of the locker room heading to the court for pregame warm-ups. There was a public telephone right outside the locker room and it rang just as I was passing. It was Jack, saying that he wanted to speak to another player on the team, Jimmy Ahearn. Now, Jimmy was a wonderful ballplayer and totally, totally honest, but none of this was any business of mine, so I called Jimmy over to the phone. The game was going to start in about ten minutes and there was Jack making Jimmy an offer to shave points. Of course, Jimmy refused. But we were all amazed at Jack's guts, and also at how desperate he must've been to take a chance like that."

Molinas won a few more games but failed to come up with a blockbuster deal that would completely recoup his losses. And despite providing a string of winners for Goldberg and his pals, Molinas was still upset that the Chicago connection continued to withhold significant sums of money. "Their shorting me was a deliberate policy designed to force me to keep doing business with them. But with the season almost over, they owed me about eight thousand dollars. By the end of February, I was increasingly PO'd at what was going on, so I decided to get even with all of them regardless of what the personal consequences might be. It was a question of self-respect. I decided to pick a game, tell them I was using the Perfect Drug, and then not use it. Since Lefty was ultimately responsible for holding back my money, I also wanted to deal with him directly.

"The game I locked in on was Brown at Columbia with Brown installed as an early-line four-point favorite. I told Lefty that I was going to arrange for three players to be drugged and that I'd call him again and identify the players when the deed was done. When I made the final A-OK contact with Lefty, I made sure to call him from a pay phone in Morningside Heights, so if he had my call traced he'd have proof enough to believe that I was right on the case.

'Okay,' I said to Lefty. 'Everything's all set. I got someone working the training table to douse three of Columbia's best players.'

"'Who were the guys you drugged?' he asked.

"I had the newspaper right there, glanced at the rosters, and read three names—A, B, and C—and instructed Lefty to bet the mortgage on Brown. Which he did. The price quickly went down to Brown minus two points and that's where Lefty and his boys laid their action.

"After that, I drove over to Coney Island and dropped in on Bobby Kraw's house on Twenty-ninth Street, looking to watch the game on TV with him. It was about six-thirty when I got there and Bobby was just finishing his dinner. 'What do you think about the game?' I asked him, and he said, 'It's a real tough call. In fact, it's so close that I don't want to bet it.'

"'Do you think that Brown can win?'

"'Sure,' he says. 'If A has a good game, if B rebounds, and if C plays good defense, then Brown will take it.'

"That's when I realized what a huge mistake I'd made. It hit me like a ton of bricks. Instead of giving Lefty the names of three players on the Columbia team, I'd inadvertently given him the names of three players on Brown. Sooner or later he'd realize this and was bound to believe that I'd swindled him, that I'd drugged three players on the team I was telling him to bet. If that didn't get me killed, then I'd live forever.

"So I hurriedly called Lefty and asked him which team he'd been betting. 'Brown,' he said. 'Just like you told me.'

"Naturally, we were speaking in a prearranged code just in case the lines were bugged, and the message that I conveyed was that he'd misunderstood me. That players A, B, and C were on Brown and that, in fact, I'd told him to bet on Columbia. By now it was seven o'clock and bookies would only be taking action for another fifteen minutes. 'My God,' Lefty said. 'We're gonna have to wash the game!' Which meant that he'd try to at least get as much money bet on Columbia as he'd previously bet on Brown. Eventually, the Chicago office laid their money this way: forty-four thousand on Brown minus two points, and eighty-four thousand on Columbia at pick 'em. Unfortunately, this meant that if Brown won the game by one point, they'd lose all of their bets.

"Sure enough, one of the Brown guards made a shot at the buzzer and Brown won by a point. So Lefty and his backers lost over forty grand one way and over eighty grand the other way. And the three Brown players that I'd told Lefty I'd drugged? A was the game's high scorer, B was the second high scorer, and C was the top rebounder.

"After the game, I got Lefty on the phone and said, 'Well, I guess we lost.'

"To my surprise, he said, 'What's the difference? We'll get it back the next time.'

Two days later, Molinas was in his law office when he received a call from Lefty, who was in Miami seeing to some kind of business deal. "Hello, Jack," he said. "How are you?"

"Gee, Lefty, that was a tough game you lost on Saturday night."

"Yeah," he said very casually, "but that's how it goes sometimes. But, hey, if you have anything else working, why don't you give me a call and we'll get together later in the week."

"Sure thing, Lefty." Then they hung up.

If Molinas was immersed in the day-to-day minutiae of his gambling obsession, he was also determined to play the rebel in every aspect of his life, no matter how trivial that rebellion might be. For example, Molinas scandalized the other celebrants when he performed his role as best man at Paul Brandt's wedding decked out in the obligatory tuxedo but also daring to wear a straw boater.

In the early spring, Molinas and some of his Coney Island buddies would meet for a friendly game of softball on Sunday mornings. "After the softball game," said Bobby Kraw, "we'd have a neighborhood crap game down in somebody's basement. On this particular Sunday, one of the guys invited us to have our crap game in his basement. The guy happened to be a cop assigned to the vice squad, so we thought we were as safe as we could be. The jerk even watched us play for a while, then after about a half hour, he called his pals from the vice squad and had all of us arrested. Of course, Jack was there, and when he tried to escape by crawling out of the basement window one of the cops slapped him and threatened to shoot him. Well, they took us down to the station house and booked us. I remember there were thirty-seven of us arrested. They had us all in one huge detaining area while we waited to be taken to the courtroom and to while away the time we started playing craps again. Finally they got all of us fingerprinted and photographed and when we got to the courtroom there must have been fifty people from the neighborhood waiting to take us home. Everyone of us pleaded guilty except the very last one to be arraigned, who, of course, was Jack. And I'll be damned if the son of a bitch didn't beat the rap."

Meanwhile, the Chicago office continued to owe Jack the eight thousand dollars and he was wracking his brains trying to think of a way to get it back. He called Lefty back on Wednesday. They chatted about what the prospects were for the weekend's games, and then Jack said, "The season's just about over, Lefty. Do you think you could send me the money you're holding for me."

"Sure, Jack. No problem. In fact, why don't you catch a plane and come down to Miami tomorrow. I'll definitely have your money for you, but I also have to speak to you about something I'm sure you'll find very interesting."

"Sounds good to me, Lefty. See you tomorrow."

Both Bobby Kraw and Joe Hacken advised him not to go. "Don't worry," Jack told them both. "Those guys are not going to do anything harmful to me. I'm the goose that lays the golden eggs."

Lefty was waiting for Molinas at the Miami airport with a pair of henchmen and a black limousine. Lefty drove and Jack got into the front with him while the two goons sat in back. Lefty said they were going over to a hotel on Miami Beach to meet with Tony DiChiantini, then he started talking about the Brown-Columbia game. "Jesus," Lefty said. "What the hell happened with that game, Jack? First you tell us that the three players you drugged played for Columbia, then you tell us that they played for Brown. But look at the stats, Jack. None of them were drugged at all."

So Jack started making lame excuses. "Maybe something happened and the drug was weakened. I haven't used it in such a long time. Maybe it has a short shelf life. The drug was put on the players' pregame steaks, but maybe they didn't eat their steaks. A dozen things could've gone wrong, Lefty."

While this was going on, Molinas took a comb from his pocket, lowered the sun visor to look in the mirror, and made a show of combing his hair. In reality, he angled the mirror so he could see out the back window, and sure enough, there was a pink Cadillac obviously following them. What was really frightening, though, was that he could also see the occupants of the Cadillac—a bunch of bullet-headed goons. And sure enough, instead of heading toward Miami Beach, they were driving in the opposite direction, toward the Everglades.

Molinas knew they weren't going to kill him because the arrangements were too elaborate—you don't need seven or eight yeggs to kill one guy. By the same logic he also knew they were planning to give him a beating. His only course of action was to pretend that he didn't know what was going on, but as soon as they stopped for a red light he was going to open the door and run out. It was just his luck that Lefty drove through side streets where there weren't any stop signs or traffic lights. He even thought about trying to jump out of the car while it was still moving.

"You're in a lot of trouble, Jack," Lefty said. "Something suspicious happened with the ball game and we have to find out exactly what went wrong."

"Okay," Jack said. "Fine. Just tell me where we're going."

"It's going to be resolved," he said. "We're going somewhere and we're going to make a decision."

Jack didn't really believe that this thing was going to be settled so rationally, but he thought that maybe, just maybe, he'd have a chance to talk his way out of this mess.

Finally, they came to a stop in a very desolate area. The pink Caddy pulled right up beside them and six guys jumped out and formed a semicircle around Jack's door. Two of the guys had blackjacks, two had brass knuckles, and the last two were armed with billy clubs. One of them said, "All right, Jack. Get out of the car."

"Are you crazy?" he said. "I'm staying right here."

So Lefty turned to him and stuck a gun in his ribs. "You'd better get out, Jack."

Without pausing to think about what he was doing, Molinas grabbed the gun and pushed it to the side. "Don't point that thing at me, Lefty. It's liable to go off. Put that thing away. You're a bookmaker, Lefty, not a gunman." To Jack's surprise, Lefty shrugged and put the gun back into his pocket.

That's when one of the guys in the backseat pulled out his gun. The guy's name was P.J. and he was from New Orleans. He was short and stocky and a very rough customer. "My name isn't Lefty," P.J. said, "and I'm not Jewish so you can't bullshit me. The first thing I want from you is your coat." So Jack took off his coat. "The next thing I want you to do is empty out all of your pockets." So he gave him his wallet, his credit cards, and even his spare change. "Now get out of the car."

Molinas gave Lefty another look, but he said, "This guy is serious, Jack. You'd better do what he says."

That's when Jack got scared. Either P.J. was going to fracture the back of his skull with the butt of his pistol or he was going to shoot him. So he decided that he had no choice but to get out of the car. As soon as he did, the six thugs started to close in on him and he made up his mind that he would have to fight his way out. One guy hit him in the shoulder with a billy club, then out of the corner of his eye Jack saw somebody on his left coming down with a pair of brass knuckles. He was wearing his Columbia ring on his pinkie and the blow from the brass knuckles shattered both the ring and the finger. The ring actually prevented a much more grievous injury to his left hand. Jack instinctively reacted by punching his assailant in the gut with all his might and the guy sagged. There Jack was, six foot six and weighing two hundred and twenty pounds, all adrenalized and feeling no pain. So he slugged the guy again and this time he fell to the ground, and that's when Jack ran through the break in the circle. The other five goons took off after him. Lefty and the driver of the pink Caddy jumped in their cars and also gave chase.

Before long Jack came to a barbed-wire fence that must have been about five feet high. There was a flower garden on the other side of the fence and Jack realized that he had one shot at jumping over the fence. If he didn't make it, he would be hanging on the barbed wire and they'd catch him and really give him the beating of his life. He had never been a high jumper, but he leaped like a gazelle and just flew over the fence and kept running.

Molinas's shirt was ripped, so he took it off and threw it away while he tried to figure out what to do next. Here he was wandering through the streets of Miami, shirtless and not quite sure how he got there, but he wound up in a hospital where they treated his finger and put it in a cast. He stayed there overnight.

The next morning Jack started walking the streets, shirtless, penniless, trying to bum a dime so that he could make a call and have somebody wire him some money. He had a couple hundred thousand dollars stashed away in New York but he didn't have a dime for a phone call. People were giving him dirty looks and treating him like some low-life panhandler, until one guy finally took pity and gave him a quarter. Two bits never looked like such a fortune. He immediately found a candy store, changed the quarter into two dimes and a nickel, and made a collect call to Goldberg in St. Louis. He called Goldberg because he felt that since he had originally hooked him up with Lefty and the Chicago operation, he was responsible.

Naturally, Goldberg had already heard that Jack was due for a beating and he tried to defend Lefty and his goons. "Jack, they lost way over a hundred thousand on the game and it was obvious that you didn't play straight with them."

"That's no reason for them to do what they did. They should've trusted that I'd make up for whatever they lost on the next game. They short me and do everything wrong and now, all of a sudden, they do this? The hell with them, Dave, I'm never doing any business with them ever again."

"Don't get so hot, Jack. How much did they hurt you?"

"I got a broken finger, that's all."

"Do yourself a favor, Jack. Call up Lefty and apologize. He's staying at the Flamingo Hotel."

"Me apologize to them? It'll never happen, Dave."

After more of this back and forth, Goldberg agreed to wire Jack some money at the airport. As soon as he was finished with Goldberg, Jack called Lefty at his hotel, but certainly not to apologize.

"You son of a bitch!" Molinas said. "Any time you want a piece of me, you leave your eight goons and your gun behind and we'll have it out man-to-man. You're a coward, Lefty!"

Jack had to go to the bathroom, then he called Goldberg again just to make sure there'd be no foul-up with the money he was sending. He always used the code "red-white-and-blue" whenever there was money left for him and he wanted to double-check everything so that he wouldn't be stranded.

By the time Jack called Goldberg, the bookie had also talked to Lefty. "Jesus, what'd you do?" Goldberg said. "Lefty's really angry. He said you threatened him. That was a crazy thing to do, Jack. These people are very bad, Jack. You can't be threatening them if you want to keep your head in one piece. The only way to get out of this alive is to put your tail between your legs and apologize. I can help you, Jack, but you've got to make the first move by yourself. Otherwise, you're a dead man."

Eventually, Molinas was convinced that Goldberg was right, so he called Lefty again. "I'm sorry that I got so hot, Lefty. I'm sorry about screwing up the Brown game, too. I'm sure I can make amends for that if you give me another chance. You know you hurt me enough as it is. You busted my head open, my hand's broken, my arm's in a sling, I've got a concussion, my entire body's bruised, and I just spent the night in a hospital. It'll take me months to recover."

Lefty seemed to be somewhat gratified when he heard how badly Jack was hurt. Then Lefty muffled the receiver and had a short discussion with whomever else was with him—obviously some big shots such as John or Tony. "All right," Lefty finally said to Molinas. "Go back to New York and we'll see what's what."

Jack called Goldberg next and brought him up to date. "That was a smart thing to do, Jack. I'll take it from here."

So Jack hitchhiked to the airport, then picked up the two hundred bucks that Goldberg had wired to the American Airlines counter. They gave Jack the money on the basis of the code phrase and his signature and he was on his way, another hairsbreadth escape in the record book.

The season was just about over. Just the NIT and NCAA tournaments had to be played out. But Molinas kept an uncharacteristically low profile, making only small wagers on the championship games. And it was good riddance to a bad season.

As much as he tried to dismiss the injury to his finger as only a mild annoyance, the pain was considerable and Molinas sought the help of an orthopedic specialist, Dr. Myron Isaacs, who had been a marginal member of the Bronx Panthers. The injury was diagnosed as a comminuted fracture, and Dr. Isaacs was forced to perform a minor surgical procedure before resetting, and then recasting, the finger.

If the injury kept Molinas off the basketball court, there were other games he continued to play—like finding ways to cheat bookmakers. "There was a bookie in Coney Island named Willie who used to operate out of a candy store. I was mainly interested in betting basketball games, but I'd bet horses with him, too, just to fool him into thinking I was an ordinary run-of-the-mill bettor. Willie's system was to have his customers write out a ticket that he would time-stamp and stash in the freezer underneath the ice cream. Willie didn't want to be bothered with balancing his accounts during the day, so he'd take all the tickets home with him and have a clerk figure out who owed what to whom. And I came up with the idea of using invisible ink to postdate my tickets.

"I'd get a ticket from Willie, then using regular ink I'd write down the name of a horse or two that I liked in a race that had, let's say, a two o'clock post time. But I'd always leave an empty space between the horses. Then I'd hand the ticket to Willie a few minutes before post time, he'd time-stamp it, and give it back to me in case I wanted to bet on any other subsequent races. I'd hang around the candy store studying the racing form, and I'd arrange for a buddy of mine to come into the store after the two o'clock race was won and give me the name of the winner. Then, using the invisible ink, I wrote the name of the winner between the horses I'd already picked in the two o'clock race. I'd return the ticket to Willie, saying, 'There's nothing else that I like,' and he'd put the ticket in the freezer. That evening, Willie would take all of the tickets from the freezer, put them in his pocket, and go home. The next morning, he'd give the tickets to his clerk to tally the results. By then, of course, the invisible ink would appear and I'd always have a winner. I worked Willie for about a year and beat him out of more than fifteen thousand dollars.

"Eventually, Willie got suspicious. He shut me down because I was winning too much, so I sent a beard into the candy store to work the same trick. But when Willie took the ticket from the beard, he didn't put it in the freezer. 'I want to watch this ticket,' Willie said, then he put it on the counter. When he saw the ink appear out of nowhere, Willie went berserk. He signaled to a strong-arm guy who'd been waiting in the back room and the beard wound up with a black eye and a broken arm. I had to give the beard money to cover his hospital bill."

In addition to trying to swindle bookmakers, Molinas was reluctant to pay his own bills. There were dozens of bookies in every borough who had chits for Molinas and not a prayer of collecting. Paying his debts was always a last resort and Molinas became adept at wriggling out of obligations or arranging favorable compromises. Most bookies knew that he had some kind of marginal connection with organized crime and were hesitant to lean on Molinas and force him to ante up. Not everyone let Molinas welch, however.

Jack was betting the horses, and also booking somebody else's action with a bookmaker from Coney Island, a guy named Bunnie. He had run up a tab that amounted to eighty-three hundred dollars. The fellow whose action Jack was betting with Bunnie had run out on him, so in reality, half of the debt wasn't strictly his. Jack had several meetings with Bunnie and explained that because he had been stiffed for four thousand he didn't have the wherewithal to pay him. In truth, Molinas had more than enough to pay Bunnie, but he thought he could finagle the situation without coughing up a dime.

"Well," Bunnie said, "I'll have to go to my boss and find out what should be done about this."

It turned out that Bunnie's boss was Joey Gallo, aka "Little Joe." And a few days later, Little Joe called Jack in his law office and said this: "Listen, Jack, there's a little matter of a couple of dollars that you owe to Bunnie and I'd like to have it straightened out. Why don't you come down to my place on President Street and we'll find an agreeable solution."

"When?" Jack asked.

"How about tonight at six o'clock?"

"I don't know, Joey. I have an appointment with a client and I'm not sure that I'll be free."

"Okay," he said. "I'll be in touch." Then he hung up the phone.

About two hours later, a pair of head-breakers came walking into Jack's office. "Hey," one of them said, "you have an appointment with Little Joe."

"I don't know what you're talking about."

"Yes, you do. And you'd better come along peacefully if you know what's good for you."

He didn't have to be told twice. One of them drove Jack and the other followed in a big black Cadillac, and they went down to President Street to see Joey Gallo, one of the most powerful Mafia bosses in New York. Once again Jack insisted that he really wasn't worried because he knew to the letter all about the mob's silly codes of honor, and he knew there was a loophole. It all depended upon whether Bunnie would lie to save face, or tell the truth and reveal himself to be a fool. But the greatest foolishness was being untruthful to a big-time chieftain like Little Joe.

Gallo was very friendly when Molinas was brought into his office. "Well, Jack," he said, "what're we going to do about this matter of the eight thousand dollars?"

"Nothing, Joe," Jack said.

The word was that Jews didn't have the same kind of courage that Italians did, so Gallo was impressed by this rather rude answer.

"You've got a lot of balls coming in here and speaking to me like that," Gallo said.

"I'm protected," Jack said. "You invited me here so I figure that I'm as safe as if I was in my mother's arms."

Gallo got a big laugh out of that, but Jack did have to explain himself. "I didn't know that you were in the picture," he said. "I asked Bunnie before I started playing who he was involved with and he said nobody. He said he was alone, so I took a shot at him. That's what I do. Take shots at bookmakers. If I knew you were involved, I would never have tried to hold out on Bunnie."

Then Gallo called Bunnie into the room and asked him, "Did you tell Jack here that you were working for yourself."

Bunnie said, "Yes. That's the way it was."

Now Gallo was disgusted with Bunnie because the guy had probably been shortchanging him, and he ordered Bunnie out of his sight. Since Gallo's name was never mentioned by Bunnie, Little Joe had no right to collect the money from me.

"Listen, Jack," Gallo said, "you're a pretty smart Jew. As I'm sure you know, I can't touch this situation. But by the way, I understand that you get off pretty good in baskets. Why don't you give us a call sometime and let us know what's happening?"

"I'd be happy to give you every game I have," Molinas said, "but I'm involved with some people in Chicago. I'll give you their phone number, and you can get their permission for me to give you the games. That's the only way it can work."

Gallo huffed and puffed and said, "Ah, forget about it. All right, Jack. As far as I'm concerned I'm going to choke this one off. Nice to meet you."

"Same here," Jack said. They shook hands and out walked Jack, the winner once again on a mere technicality.

Betting the horses may have been an off-season hobby for Molinas, but his quest to find the perfect edge was a full-time obsession. Working with two associates (B.C. and a horse groomer), Molinas found a way to fix races at Aqueduct. A miniature electrical receiver was inserted into the chosen horse's anus, and B.C. was stationed in the grandstand near the clubhouse turn with a transmitting device. When B.C. pushed the appropriate button, the resulting shock would cause the horse to spurt forward and hopefully win the race.

In addition, there were dozens of small-time gamblers who were anxious to curry favor with Molinas in hopes of being let in on his lucrative basketball fixes. One of these guys was a little Italian named Nicky, who was about sixty-five years old and was always trying to beg his way into Jack's basketball action.

Nicky had come across another Italian fellow—Vinny—who owned a racehorse but was in a lot of trouble because he owed a shylock a bundle. "I got a wife and a kid," Vinny told Nicky. "I'm not a heist man, I'm not a burglar, but I gotta do something because I just can't make the payments."

"Tell me about your horse," Nicky said. "Can it win a race?"

"No, but it can lose."

"That's no good," said Nicky. "We gotta make it win."

Both of these guys were from the old school—wearing conservative suits with the wide lapels, felt hats with the front brim turned down, pinky rings, alligator shoes, the works. They both had deep hoarse voices and spoke with heavy Italian accents. And they were straining to figure out some way to make the horse a winner.

"I got an idea," Vinny finally said. "If you can get hold of some kind of narcotic, we can hit the horse and win a race."

Nicky thought it was a great idea, so he paid a visit to his boss, Don Sforza, to ask his permission, but Sforza backed off.

"If you can win the race," Sforza said, "that's beautiful, but you can't touch narcotics because narcotics is banned by the Mafia."

So Nicky came to Jack, who hooked him up with a nonnarcotic stimulant. Nicky and Vinny started borrowing money left and right to bet on the horse, and they came up with about three grand between them. Like the good soldier that he was, Nicky went back to Don Sforza to make a gift of his information.

"Listen," Sforza said, "if you give me this horse and you tell me that it's drugged and it can't lose, the horse better win or you'll be in big trouble."

"The horse is positively gonna win," Nicky swore. "I'm going to be there to personally supervise the hitting of the horse."

"Okay," Sforza said. "My advice is not to do this around here and not to make your bets at the track. Call me when everything is ready and I'll have someone make your bets for you."

Nicky was appropriately grateful.

So, Nicky and Vinny got the horse into a race at a track in New Hampshire, and the day before the race they drove up there to make the play. The horse was ten-to-one on the morning line and they were both going to be rich. Their plan was to sneak into the paddock area before the race and make the hit nice and easy. Sure enough, early the next morning, they walked into the paddock area just like they belonged there. The only other people around were grooms, jockeys, trainers, other horse owners, and racetrack officials. And there's Nicky wearing his Damon Runyan Broadway outfit, and Vinny's wearing a black leather coat, a black cap, dark slacks, and they're both smoking smelly cigars. Everybody's staring at them, wondering who they are and what their business was, and Nicky and Vinny were strutting around like they're about to pull the coup of the century. The two of them were glad-handing everybody in sight, imagining to themselves that they are totally inconspicuous. "Hello? How are you? How's your horse feeling today?"

Once they found out where the horse was stabled, they realized that they had no idea how to administer the drug to a horse. Nicky was the lookout while Vinny tried to figure it all out.

"You've got to inject the drug into the horse's ass," Nicky said, but Vinny was too short and couldn't reach that high. So they switched positions—Vinny became the lookout and Nicky was going to find a spot to hit the poor horse. While Nicky was walking around the horse with the hypodermic needle in his hand, the horse dropped a huge turd on his shoe.

Now they forgot about drugging the horse and they concentrated instead on something far more important—getting the shit off Nicky's shoe.

After fifteen minutes or more of this Laurel and Hardy routine, Vinny finally took up the needle again and bang! He hit the horse in one of its haunches. Beautiful. The horse was officially hit. But as they were walking away from the paddock, Nicky had second thoughts. "Maybe we ought to hit the horse again," he said. "All the bosses are going to be betting and if it loses, then I'll really be in the shit." Okay. So they returned to the paddock, refilled the needle, and Vinny hit the horse again.

Nicky next found a phone and called Don Sforza to let him know the deed was done. Sforza bet two thousand on the nose. Then Nicky and Vinny called up their wives, their friends, and everybody they wanted to impress. When Nicky called Molinas, Jack bet five hundred on the horse to win. At post time the price on the horse was down to five to two.

The race got under way and the horse went right to the front and even opened up a four-length lead. Nicky and Vinny were jumping for joy and already counting their money.

But at the halfway mark, the horse suddenly stopped, threw the rider, and fell down. The entire field passed and the horse didn't move. Vinny and Nicky started cursing the jockey. The stupid jockey must've hit the horse in the ear!

An ambulance drove up to take the jockey to the hospital, and of course the horse was dead. When the subsequent blood test revealed that the horse had died from an overdose, there was holy hell to pay.

Don Sforza called for a sit-down, which meant that all of the big shots in that particular family met to hear the evidence and issue a judgment. It was eventually decided that Nicky didn't really do anything devious, just that he did a poor job. So they fined Nicky a thousand dollars for being so stupid, and that was that. Nicky had to borrow the thousand from a shylock, which meant he had to pay back thirteen hundred. But Nicky was happy that he got off so easily.

In June, Molinas filed an antitrust suit in the state supreme court in Kings County against Maurice Podoloff and the NBA, asking for reinstatement into the league plus three million dollars in damages. In the action, Molinas's attorney, Joel H. Weinberg, charged that his client's having been blackballed from the NBA in 1954 constituted an illegal restraint of trade. Molinas also claimed that the reserve clause in the standard NBA players contract was, in fact, an illegal instrument that prohibited him from dealing with any team other than the Fort Wayne Pistons. He charged that the NBA, by "actively eliminating him from organized basketball, has effectively placed all basketball players within their control in a condition of bondage, through the use of the player draft and the uniform contract." Molinas's suit asked that the court rule that the defendants "combined and conspired to restrain unreasonably and have conspired to monopolize organized basketball in violation of the Sherman Antitrust Act."

The only other antitrust action in sports that had gone to trial was *Bill Radovich v. the National Football League*. Radovich had jumped from the Detroit Lions of the NFL to the Los Angeles Rams of the newly formed All-America Conference in 1939. When the AAC folded, Radovich tried to get back into the NFL, only to discover that he was barred not only there but also from playing in another pro league (the Pacific Coast League) as well. He sued, lost in two lower courts, took his case to the supreme court, and eventually won a $105,000 judgment against the NFL. Radovich's suit was the basis, and the hope, of Molinas's action.

Molinas's motion was accepted and a nonjury trial was ordered to commence in early January 1961. "I've no doubt what will come of this action," said Maurice Podoloff, president of the NBA. "The same thing that happened before will happen again. We will be upheld. It will just cost us additional legal fees." The NBA nevertheless offered Molinas twenty-five thousand dollars as an out-of-court settlement, but Jack was so sure that he would win he turned them down.

By early May, Molinas's finger had healed sufficiently for him to get back on the basketball court. Molinas's primary running buddy was Allan Seiden. "We played in summer leagues all over the place," Seiden said, "New Jersey, the Brownsville Boys Club, upstate in Haverstraw, down in Greenwich Village, in Harlem. Anywhere there were trophies to be won, Jack was there."

Seiden recalled a memorable tournament game—this one at Haverstraw against Snooky's Sugarbowl, a traditionally high-powered squad from Harlem. "The guy who sponsored the team gave Jack five hundred dollars to get players," Seiden said. "He gave me fifty bucks, brought three of his friends for free, and kept the remaining four hundred and fifty. Since all of his friends were stiffs, Jack and I took almost all of the shots. We lost the game in double-overtime, one hundred and thirty-one to one hundred and thirty. Jack scored fifty-nine points and so did I. Even with a mangled finger, Jack could still shoot the lights out."

After the games, Molinas and Seiden would inevitably wind up at the Playboy Club. "Jack was great with the ladies," Seiden said. "We'd get there at closing time and he'd always find a little bunny for me to take home for the night."

But Molinas was also busy setting up players for the 1960–61 season. "I was up at Yonkers Raceway betting on the trotters," Molinas recalled, "when this big kid came up to me and introduced himself as Freddy Portnoy, a basketball player from Columbia. Of course, I knew exactly who the kid was but I played dumb. 'What can I do for you?' I asked him. Portnoy shrugged and said, 'Gee, I'm just about broke and I really need a winner.' So I told him to bet the six horse in the eighth race and the five horse in the ninth race and the kid won a couple of hundred dollars for himself. From there it was easy talking the kid into turning tricks once the season began.

"Lou Brown was also a big help to us that summer, bringing several guys whom he knew from Jersey City into the fold. Brown did a real good scouting job because all of the guys he brought to us were not only outstanding players but also in financial difficulties."

Brown's first recruit was Ed Bowler from LaSalle, who had attended three different high schools in his hometown of Jersey City before finally getting his diploma. Bowler attended Virginia Tech briefly and left there because he was dissatisfied with the coach. Soon after that, his mother died and his family was plunged into deep financial woes. A guidance counselor at LaSalle claimed that Bowler was admitted more as a hardship case than for his basketball ability, but he was awarded a full athletic scholarship. After his freshman year, Bowler got married and had to live off campus. When Bowler's wife became pregnant, the anticipated costs threatened to be overwhelming, until Brown stepped in and offered a foolproof solution.

Brown's next contact was Frank Majewski, who played at St. Joseph's College. A graduate of St. Anthony's High School in Jersey City, Majewski had originally accepted a basketball scholarship to Holy Cross but left there because of academic difficulties. His grades improved considerably in an industrial-management course at St. Joseph's. When Majewski's widowed mother became ill and was unable to work, he also turned to Brown for aid.

After Brown introduced Bowler and Majewski to Wagman, the two players were told that in addition to earning money for shaving points, they could also qualify for bonuses if they could induce any of their teammates into doing business. Bowler drew a blank, but Majewski came up with two other St. Joseph's players. Jack Egan, from Bethlehem Catholic High School in Bethlehem,

Pennsylvania, was the best player on the team. He was also majoring in industrial management and was an average student. However, Egan was married and the father of two young sons. Early in the summer, his wife suffered a miscarriage and the player was swamped with medical bills. Vince Kempton hailed from Chaminade High School in Mineola, New York, and was a political-science major. He had been dropped from St. Joseph's because of excessive absences but had gone to night school and regained his eligible status. Kempton was forever complaining to Majewski about some vague personal financial urgency (which Molinas suspected had something to do with gambling).

Egan, Kempton, and Majewski were the heart of the St. Joe's team, and with them Molinas & Company had a lock on every game. The contact man was Majewski and they offered him a three-thousand-dollar package per game—a thousand for each player. Majewski countered by asking that they give him two thousand and give Kempton and Egan only five hundred a piece. When Wagman said that five hundred was a lowball number, Majewski said they'd gladly work for that. Ultimately, they arranged to give Kempton and Egan seven hundred and fifty dollars for every contract, and fifteen hundred to Majewski. They also put in an incentive system—they would pay them each another two hundred and fifty for every successful game. These bonuses were also incremental, so that for the second successful fix they'd each get an extra five hundred, then seven-fifty for the third game, and so on. All the parties were agreeable and the deal was struck.

Because Molinas had been roughed up by Goldberg and his cohorts, he also insisted way before the season even began that they sell the St. Joseph's and the LaSalle games to a new backer—a guy named Barney from Brooklyn. His motion was unanimously adopted. It turned out to be beneficial for everybody, because all of the St. Joseph's games they worked were winners.

In early July, Molinas met a young woman named Shirley Marcus. She would ultimately become an eyewitness to the most tragic event in Molinas's life. But in the carefree summer of 1960, Molinas saw Shirley sitting by herself at a table in the Mermaid Bar in Coney Island and asked if he could buy her a drink. Shirley was a beautiful young woman, still living at home with her mother and working at a drab secretarial job in Manhattan. At the time, Molinas's hairline was rapidly receding, but at age twenty-eight he was still trim, handsome, and bursting with vitality, and they were immediately attracted to each other. The initial installment of their relationship lasted for nearly a year, during which Molinas squired Shirley about town, took her to the most expensive restaurants, theaters, and nightclubs, and even took her to see a basketball game in Philadelphia.

Molinas was also doing his own scouting during the summer of 1960, and there was one particular player whom he'd been romancing for three years—Connie

Hawkins. Molinas began investing in Hawkins while the young man was a sophomore at Boys High School in Brooklyn. Hawkins, whose nickname was "Goose," was astonishingly poor. He lived with his mother in a cold-water flat, he had only one acceptable shirt and one pair of pants that he wore to school every day, and his shoes were held together with rope and wire. Not only was Goose illiterate, but he was also well-known in Bed-Stuy for his lack of intelligence. However, the young man was six foot seven and still growing, he had the largest hands anybody had ever seen, and he could almost jump high enough to touch the moon.

"The kid was maybe fifteen years old when Jack started working him," Bernie Reiner recalled. "Jack used to hoop with Hawkins in the school yards and the kid was in awe of Jack's hook shot. After the games, Jack would give him ten bucks and tell him to go buy himself whatever he wanted. The kid barely had shoes on his feet and here was this smooth-talking, well-dressed guy showering him with money. Ten bucks here. Twenty bucks there. Until he met Jack, Hawkins had never even seen a twenty-dollar bill before. And Goose was way too stupid to realize what was really happening."

Hawkins remembered the first time he ever played against Molinas: "It was up in a place called Kelly Park, near Kings Highway in Brooklyn," he once told a reporter, "and all I knew about him was that he was supposed to be a great player. He came up to me and said, 'Hawkins, I'm Jack Molinas.' I was impressed that his hands were almost as big as mine. I saw Jack a lot after that. Manhattan Beach, Rockville Centre, wherever there were games he was playing in them. One time he told me he knew how hard it was for poor kids and if I needed help or money, just let him know. He said he liked me. A few years later, I also remember seeing Jack once at a Knick game in Madison Square Garden. I was there with Roger Brown and our girlfriends and after the game Jack took us all to dinner at a real fancy restaurant. Then when we wanted to go home it was raining and we thought we could take a cab. Jack says why take a cab. Take the girls home nice. He had a lot of credit cards and he said he'd get us one of those Hertz cars to go home with. He was going to get a Lincoln, but they didn't have one, so we got a Chrysler Imperial instead. Man, we impressed those girls good!"

By the time Hawkins was a senior at Boys High School, he'd matured into a talented, high-flying sensation, the most recruited New York schoolboy ever. Whichever college Hawkins chose would become (after his obligatory year playing freshman ball) the odds-on favorite to win the national championship.

Molinas also stepped up his own recruiting efforts, periodically arranging "dates" for Hawkins with high-priced prostitutes. Then, one night in August, before a summer league game to be played in Bed-Stuy, Molinas invited Hawkins to his law office. Also invited was Roger Brown, a sweet-shooting forward from Brooklyn's Wingate High School, considered by college recruiters as New York's second-best prospect. Molinas handed each of them a ten-dollar bill for transportation to the game and dinner afterward. "That's when Jack introduced us to a man named 'Joey,'" Hawkins recalled. "Jack said that Joey was a client of his. Then Jack and Roger left the room and Joey started talking to me about basketball. Who did I think was better, Wilt Chamberlain or Bill Russell? Then he asked did I know any good college players? I told him Wilky Gilmore of Colorado, Vinnie Brewer of Iowa State, and some others. Then he asked could I introduce him to them some time. I said, 'Sure.' I thought he was just another New York basketball nut."

Hawkins had spent recruiting weekends at Indiana, Iowa, Colorado, Michigan State, Ohio State, Illinois, Kansas, Northwestern, and Seattle. "I was offered two hundred and fifty dollars a month under the table to attend Seattle," he said. At the end of the summer, Hawkins finally selected the University of Iowa. "I went for the money," he said. "About three hundred dollars a month."

When asked how Hawkins qualified for admittance to Iowa, school authorities said "it was on the basis of our entrance examinations—a procedure which we have been using with a great deal of success for a great many years." Even though his subpar academic record at Boys High School prohibited Iowa from awarding him an athletic scholarship, the rules governing the Big Ten conference allowed for Hawkins to be admitted on probation if he paid his own way. Arrangements were made through an Iowa alumnus to provide a job at a filling station with the unspoken understanding that Hawkins would only have to make a weekly appearance there to collect his paycheck. The athletic department also planned to surround Hawkins with tutors and hope for the best. The Iowa varsity coach, Sharm Scheuerman, predicted that Hawkins would be a three-time All-American and then move on to an illustrious, and lucrative, career in the NBA. Hawkins, still very naive and easily impressed, couldn't believe his good fortune. When he was a ragamuffin youngster hanging around the school yards, everybody used to tease him and even beat him up. But now, everybody loved Connie Hawkins.

Brown was a smoother player than "the Hawk," a better outside shooter and defender who also played with a certain arrogance and belligerence that Hawkins lacked. Brown's home was comfortable and neat, but there were problems. His father and mother were separated, and she, with the help of Brown's uncle, had to support five children, the youngest of whom was afflicted with cerebral palsy. If Brown was more streetwise and cynical than Hawkins, he also had his hand open whenever Hacken or Molinas pulled out their wallets.

On the Labor Day weekend, Hawkins and Brown (who had committed to Dayton) were scheduled to play in a basketball tournament in Rockville Centre and Molinas had lent them his Pontiac convertible. At 3:00 A.M. on the morning of September 2, 1960, Mrs. Rose Sweeny stopped for a red light in midtown Manhattan when her rear bumper was lightly struck by the Pontiac, which was driven by Brown. After Mrs. Sweeny and Brown emerged to inspect the minor damage, Brown abruptly returned to the Pontiac and drove off. The license number was noted by an alert cabdriver who'd stopped to survey the accident, and the ownership was traced to Molinas. Eventually, Molinas represented Brown at the hearing and Judge Ludwig Glowa let Brown off with a suspended sentence. The incident proved to both Hawkins and Brown, however, that Molinas was a mover and a shaker who could take care of business.

Once Connie Hawkins introduced Vinnie Brewer to Joe Hacken, Molinas took over. He wined and dined Brewer all summer, buying him clothes and giving him a hundred-dollar bill every time he saw him. In all, Jack must have spent fifteen hundred dollars on Brewer. And once the season started, Brewer was looking forward to turning some tricks and making big money. Jack and Joe Hacken were already planning which Iowa State games they would be working. Then what did the kid do? As soon as he went back to school he stole a car and was suspended from the basketball team! All he had to do was pick up the phone, call Molinas, and say that he needed five hundred dollars or whatever to buy a car. Jack would have given him the money in a heartbeat. Anyway, that was the end of Vinnie Brewer's basketball career.

As early as the fall of 1960 there were unmistakable signs that Molinas's entire gambling operation was doomed. On September 24, Aaron Wagman was arrested in Florida for trying to bribe a University of Florida football player, fullback John McBeth, to fix a game. Phillip Silber, a UF undergraduate from New York, was also arrested for serving as a liaison between Wagman and McBeth.

When interrogated by the local police, Wagman revealed that Dave Budin was in Ann Arbor, Michigan, trying to get a halfback from the University of Oregon to blow a game. Because the initial contacts between Wagman and Silber had taken place in New York, the case was transferred to the jurisprudence of the Manhattan district attorney. Wagman was subsequently released on twenty thousand dollars' bail but was put under surveillance.

What Wagman did then was very interesting. He had over forty thousand dollars put away, but once he returned to New York he contacted all of the money men behind the fixes and asked for money to pay his lawyers' fees. Barney from Brooklyn agreed to give him fifteen hundred provided that Wagman would supply an exclusive option on any games he had for sale. Frankie Cardone in Pittsburgh made a donation. Goldberg and Lefty Rosenthal gave a thousand dollars each. Phil LaCourt up in Boston also sent Wagman some money. When the dust cleared Wagman had much more than the five grand he was asking for.

Molinas confronted Wagman about why he was wheedling money from everybody. "I may have to go to jail," Wagman said, "and I'll need as much money as I can get to support my wife and my family." Jack was so impressed that he contributed another thousand himself.

At about this time, Joe Hacken and Jack were meeting to discuss the upcoming season. They certainly felt the pressure of Wagman's arrest and knew they had to be careful on two counts—to keep an even tighter lid on all of their gambling activities, and to avoid telling Wagman anything that might incriminate them. But even with an indictment hanging over his head, Wagman was working harder than ever before to make as much money as possible before he got tossed into the slammer.

Once the season was under way, however, it was strictly business as usual. On December 10, 1960, St. Joseph's played Dayton at the Palestra in Philadelphia, and the fix was in for the Hawks to go under the points. St. Joe's was favored by three points, but Majewski thought they had no chance to win the game under any circumstances. Majewski, Egan, and Kempton played the game straight, St. Joe's lost 67–65, and all three players got paid.

Of course, there was always the possibility of an occasional glitch. That same night, LaSalle played at Niagara and Bowler was to see that LaSalle lost by at least eight points. Niagara did win, but the final score was 77–71. Even though Bowler had made plenty of deliberate mistakes, Wagman forced him to return eight hundred of the thousand dollars that had been advanced. "In order to get paid," Wagman told Bowler, "the game has to work out right. Trying isn't enough."

As the official intermediary who had introduced the Philly fixers to Wagman, Hacken, and Molinas, Lou Brown was also supposed to get a set fee (usually a thousand per game) for the tricks his players turned. But Wagman balked at paying Brown after the LaSalle-Niagara contest went sour. "Before you get any payoff," Wagman told him, "a loser has to be made up with a winner. If you have two losers in a row, then you'll need three consecutive winners before you get paid."

"Nothing doing," Brown said, holding his ground. "If you mess with my cut, then I'll take my guys and do my business elsewhere."

Wagman quickly relented to the extent of sending Brown the full thousand for the St. Joseph's–Dayton game and five hundred for the unsuccessful LaSalle game.

Molinas was thrilled to have Freddy Portnoy in his clutches, because he continued to believe that the Columbia athletic department had failed to support him during the glass-throwing incident that had led to his suspension after his sophomore season. But Molinas was cautious enough to let Joe Green be the front man for Portnoy's fixes.

Of all the shavers and dumpers who ever worked for Molinas & Company, Freddy Portnoy was the least likely candidate. At DeWitt High in the Bronx, Portnoy was not only an outstanding basketball player, but maintained a 90 scholastic average. He also came from a family that was stable, loving, and comfortably middle class. Portnoy's many scholarship offers included an appointment to West Point. He finally selected a modest thousand-dollar-a-year academic scholarship to Columbia because of the school's reputation and proximity to his home. Why, then, did Portnoy agree to fix ball games? "Sheer stupidity," he said. "It all seemed so simple that it was easy for me to overlook the seriousness of what I did."

The first game Portnoy worked was at Rutgers on December 13, 1960. Green and Portnoy had previously met in the lobby of a movie theater on Fordham Road, where the player agreed to do his worst so that Columbia lost by at least twelve points. When, in fact, Columbia lost by thirteen, Green gave Portnoy a thousand dollars.

A week later, Portnoy agreed to work another game, this one at Pennsylvania, and Molinas sold the game to several backers. The winning number was Penn by thirteen, but at halftime Portnoy's hot hand had kept the Lions within four points. Portnoy was the last player out of the locker room as his team headed up the stairs that lead to the court, and Green jumped out of the shadows at full scream: "What are you doing? This is business! The way you're playing, my backers'll think that I don't have you and then we'll both be in deep shit!"

To start the second half, Portnoy unloosed a half-ass jumper from beyond the bounds of propriety, but to his surprise the ball dove through the hoop. In the stands, Green exploded with a series of loud maledictions that startled everybody in the small gym. Portnoy didn't take another shot for the rest of the game and Columbia lost by well over the spread, but Green withheld Portnoy's payment.

Green also suckered Portnoy at least once by deliberately misinforming the young man about the point spread. Columbia was an eight-point underdog to Princeton, and for Green to win, the Lions only had to lose by nine. But Green told Portnoy that the spread was twelve and Columbia would have to lose by thirteen. When the Lions lost by nine, Green collected, but Portnoy was shut out. (When Molinas eventually discovered this particular swindle, he was convinced that Green had simply pocketed Portnoy's payment.)

Through contacts made by Charlie Tucker, Molinas and his gang were also party to fixes perpetrated by Charlie North and John Morgan, players at the University of Detroit. Molinas sold most of the rigged games in the 1960–61 season to backers in Brooklyn and Boston, and only occasionally to the Goldberg-Rosenthal partnership. Wagman made his own private deals with Goldberg and Frankie Cardone in Pittsburgh. But, increasingly, Bobby Kraw was horning in on everybody else's play, even going so far as to make separate deals with players whom the Wagman-Molinas axis had originally recruited.

Lou Brown described for *Look* magazine the complications surrounding the LaSalle–North Carolina State game played at Philadelphia on December 21:

The game had more angles than a geometry examination, with Wagman putting over an involved double cross on Bobby Kraw. Kraw had made deals with Anton Muehlbauer and Terry Litchfield of North Carolina State. They had failed previous games with George Washington and Georgia Tech, so they received only a small part of the $1,000 each that Kraw had promised them. A third North Carolina State player, Stan Niewierowski, the team captain, was working for Wagman and his partner, Joe Green. Kraw suggested to Wagman that they should pool their "shavers." (Litchfield was not involved in this particular game.)

Wagman agreed, and it was decided to rig the next game, N.C. State–LaSalle, with N.C. State to go under the points. Wagman, however, did not tell Niewierowski to work the game, and he didn't tell Kraw that he had Bowler of LaSalle.

The line on the game opened with N.C. State favored by one point. Wagman didn't bet a penny, but the big gamblers (in Chicago), to whom Kraw had sold the game, sent it in heavy for N.C. State to lose. The volume of the Chicago money caused the line to shift five points the other way, with LaSalle now a four-point favorite. This meant that Kraw's backers had gambled close to a quarter of a million.

With LaSalle now a four-point favorite, Wagman was in the driver's seat. He instructed Bowler to see that LaSalle won by less than four. This was an easier assignment than making certain a team loses. Wagman's group (Cardone from Pittsburgh) placed their bets—well over $250,000 —on LaSalle to be under the four points by which it was now favored. As a result of this heavy action, the line shifted drastically again, so that N.C. State once more became the favorite.

By now, the two emphatic shifts of the line had convinced Kraw that there was something more going on than he had bargained for. He tried to balance off his first bets, but couldn't cover all the money, so he got word to Muehlbauer not to work the game. Kraw lost all the money he couldn't balance off, but Wagman's group cleaned up.

Strangely, even though Bowler was trying to make mistakes, he didn't have a bad night. He told me that one time he tried to throw the ball out of bounds, but a teammate made a remarkable save. Bowler actually made baskets he was trying to miss. Once, he did not jump for a rebound, but the ball came right into his hands. LaSalle fans congratulated him on his performance.

Although Wagman's Pittsburgh backer cleaned up, he realized that when two different groups had players from the same team, the confusion was dangerous. When Muehlbauer went home for Christmas, Wagman got him away from Kraw, by convincing him that he could make more money that way.

On most weekends, Molinas continued playing in the Eastern League, functioning as player-coach for the Hazleton Hawks, and for his double duty he was paid two hundred dollars per game. The highlight of Molinas's season was a forty-three-point performance that paced the Hawks to a 132–125 victory over Williamsport, the team that had dismissed him as over the hill a year before. At that point, Hazleton's record was a respectable 8–7, good enough for third place in the league standings. Unfortunately, Molinas's gambling activities limited him to twenty-two appearances in the team's twenty-eight games, and despite his valiant on-court efforts (30.0 points and 9.5 rebounds per game), the Hawks finished the season in last place with a record of 10–18.

The Christmas holidays brought some goodies to Molinas but also some portents of trouble to come. Before Connie Hawkins came home for the Christmas vacation, Coach Scheuerman gave him two hundred dollars to pay his dormitory fees for the spring semester. But when Hawkins arrived in New York, he quickly spent all of the money on Christmas presents for his family and his friends. At a Knick game at Madison Square Garden, Hawkins came across Molinas, who treated the young man to dinner at a nearby restaurant and cab fare home. As always, Molinas repeated his generic offer to "help" Hawkins out of any kind of jam.

"I felt I couldn't go back to school without the money," Hawkins said. "I was real desperate. Then I heard what Jack said, about if I ever needed help. He was the only person I knew who had that kind of money, so I called him up and asked him for a loan. He brought the money to my apartment the day before I went back to school. A hundred-dollar bill and two fifties."

Molinas was positive that the young man knew the score, and that by next season when he was eligible to play varsity ball, Hawkins would be happy to do business.

Another of Molinas's old friends, Paul Brandt, got in touch prior to the Christmas holidays with some news that he hoped would frighten Molinas into going straight. "I was in the navy and stationed in Philadelphia when Jack was in the NBA," said Brandt, "so we'd see each other whenever the Pistons came to town. After my discharge, I went to work in New York and I'd sometimes visit Jack in his law office. I never was particularly fond of his clientele. They seemed to be a bunch of sleazy guys on the fringes of organized crime. Not really true mob types, but more like somebody's stooges. Anyway, I'd been told by a friend in the Manhattan district attorney's office that their surveillance of Wagman had alerted them to the possibility that Jack was deeply involved in fixing ball games. I was told that if I could get Jack to cease and desist right away, then the DA probably wouldn't have enough evidence to build a case against him. In the past, when I'd tried to dissuade Jack from fixing, he'd shrug it off in his typical fashion. 'Don't worry,' he'd say, 'they can't get me.' Then when I relayed the tip I had gotten from the DA's office, Jack said he couldn't get out of the racket because he was too committed. He said that he had double-crossed some dangerous people and now he had to perform. He said that he would tell me all the gory details some other time, but he never did."

After Wagman was arrested in Florida, Molinas had an inclination that he was going to be followed by detectives and that the phones he usually used were going to be tapped. "I knew it was only a question of when the DA was going to pull me in for questioning. So Paul's information was not really a news bulletin. A few days later, I also made my own connection with somebody in the DA's office, somebody who was assigned to the Wagman case. This was a guy who liked to bet basketball games and owed a lot of money to a bookie friend of mine. The guy told me that I was under twenty-four-hour surveillance, that the detectives woke up with me, put me to bed, and followed me everywhere in between.

"The detective also complained about the way I drove. 'Jack,' the guy said, 'you have to slow down or you'll get both of us killed.' Since I expected that I was being tailed, I would weave in and out of traffic, and if a green light was just about to turn red, I would pass the car in front of me and make a quick right-hand turn. Anybody following me would have a hell of a time keeping up. The detective told me that the only way they could catch up with me after I shook them was by guessing which one of my favorite hangouts I'd show up at.

"A couple of weeks later I was driving down to an Eastern League game. I had a Bonneville convertible at the time with special tires and I was doing a hundred and five miles per hour. All of a sudden, there's a car right up behind me, an unmarked car with a blue light flashing on its roof. So I pulled over to the side of the road and sure enough a guy came over and said, 'Jack, my job is to follow you. We both know where you're going, okay? You've got a game in Scranton tonight and there's plenty of time for you to get there so you don't have to drive like a maniac. I've got a wife and two kids, Jack. So do me a favor, please, and slow down.'"

In his book *The Great Molinas*, Neil Isaacs imagines an encounter between Molinas and one of the state investigators on his case:

> Molinas is having a drink with big Sid Youngelman in the Left Bank across from the old Garden. They are at the bar talking, in a preliminary way, about setting up a sure thing on an NFL football game. Molinas gives Youngelman a cigar, takes one himself. From his other side a man resembling a New York version of Christopher Plummer reaches across with a lighter and lights both cigars, looking Molinas straight in the face. It is Vinny Richter, one of Hogan's chief investigators, who helped crack the Carbo boxing case and would now be instrumental in breaking the basketball fixes. Neither man shows a flicker of recognition.

This all happened in the last week of December, while a grand jury was meeting to hear evidence against Wagman. So Molinas got together with Joe Hacken and told him everything that was going on. They discussed the possibility of getting out of the fixing business altogether. After batting the subject back and forth, Joe said, "I think if we're careful nothing's going to happen to us," and Jack agreed. They also tried to figure out all the legal implications, and it was clear that in order for the DA to arrest them some kind of corroboration would be essential. Some player or other would have to agree to testify against them. Joe wondered if the Manhattan DA had the jurisprudence to investigate games that they had fixed in places like North Carolina, Pennsylvania, California, Michigan, and elsewhere. Of course they were making telephone calls from New York, but even if the DA had incriminating wiretaps they couldn't be used as evidence in a court of law. Molinas's opinion was that they should refrain from working any games in New York until things cooled down.

The Holiday Basketball Festival was under way at the Garden and they had made preliminary arrangements for Majewski and the other St. Joseph's players to work a game against St. Bonaventure to be played on December 27. In light of the recent developments, Hacken and Molinas thought it best that Wagman inform the players that they wouldn't be working the Saint Bonnie's game after all. Majewski was thrilled at the opportunity to play all-out in a high-profile tournament in New York.

Jack and the others also decided to be even more discrete than they had been before. They were going to avoid using any one particular phone booth for more than a day. This was especially crucial for Wagman, who was obviously the focal point of the DA's surveillance. Wagman got in the habit of alternating between phone booths in a Bronx candy store, midtown hotels, a Greenwich Village drug store, and the East Side Airlines Terminal. But amazingly enough, there was still no feeling that the circle was closing in on them. It was still a game of wits, and Molinas, in true keeping with his lifelong ways, did not feel, or could not allow himself to believe, that he was in imminent danger.

During Molinas's brief hiatus from the gambling scene, he began to renew his friendships with some of his boyhood chums in the Bronx Panthers. "Jack started showing up to the social parties we were still having," said Harvey Persh, an original Panther. "Sometimes he'd come alone, sometimes he'd come with a beautiful girl on his arm. To show you the devil-may-care kind of guy Jack was, when he couldn't find a parking spot in a hurry, he'd always park next to a fire hydrant and never worry about getting a ticket or having his car towed away. We were all still sports fiends and ninety percent of our conversation dealt with sports. Jack was always very gregarious, but none of us ever brought up the subject of the betting scandal that got him booted from the NBA. I don't recall Jack ever discussing anything about his own personal life."

Molinas's three-million-dollar suit against the NBA was finally brought to trial on January 3, 1961, before Judge Irving Kaufman, the same judge who sentenced the Rosenbergs to die in the electric chair. Several witnesses were called, but much of the testimony was a rehash of the damage plea trial conducted seven years before. Molinas claimed that while with the Pistons he never placed a wager involving "so-called point-shaving" and that his wagers were "always placed on my team to win, and realized me a net profit of approximately four hundred dollars, on which I paid income taxes." Molinas further complained that not only had the NBA blackballed him for employment as a professional basketball player, they had also refused to allow the league's players to appear in exhibition games in which he was scheduled to play. Podoloff stoutly maintained that Molinas was guilty of more than a mere "technical violation" of NBA rules and was responsible for "destroying the public's confidence in the game."

On January 11, Judge Kaufman ruled against Molinas on the basis of these conclusions:

(1) It was understandable why the league barred an admitted gambler.
(2) Molinas failed to establish an NBA conspiracy to blackball him in pro basketball; coaches and players refused to play against him because they thought it unwise to participate in a game with an admitted gambler.
(3) NBA refusal to let a member team hire Molinas was due to his suspension for gambling, and not the reserve clause.
(4) Molinas failed to sustain the burden of proof as required by law.

Kaufman also summarily dismissed Molinas's attack on the NBA's reserve clause by noting, "It does not appear that Molinas was in any way displeased over playing with the Pistons and, were it not for his suspension, it is likely that he would have continued to play for them without complaint."

Podoloff was overjoyed. "Judge Kaufman's decision," he said, "establishes the principle that any reasonable means taken to keep the sport above reproach and criticism apparently is recognized as a necessary exercise of my authority as league president."

Of course, Molinas was extremely disappointed, but the adverse ruling was not unexpected. He was smart enough to realize that the courts were unwilling to interfere with the activities of private sports organizations.

On Saturday night, January 7, Fixers Incorporated was back in business with a vengeance. "We had Columbia versus Penn in Philadelphia with Freddy Portnoy in the bag. Jerry Graves was working to make sure that Mississippi State went under the spread against Auburn in Montgomery, Alabama. Vanderbilt was at Tennessee with Dick Fisher turning the trick. And Stan Niewierowski and Anton Muehlbauer were contracted to sink North Carolina State against Duke. Joe

Green was handling the payoffs for this one, and since Joe was an avid fan of Batman and Captain Marvel, he mailed the money for Niewierowski and Muehlbauer inside comic books. In addition to our own lineup, Bobby Kraw had a St. Joseph's game, Charlie Tucker had a Detroit University game, and Dave Budin also had a game. There must have been five or six backers involved.

"By now I was making a conscientious effort to drive out to Nassau County or to New Jersey to make my phone calls. I advised Wagman to take the same precautions, but he said that he was moving around so much that it was impossible for the DA to tap his calls.

"One Friday night, Paul Brandt and I were having a late-night snack at Bernie's Diner at the corner of Avenue U and Coney Island Avenue. We were having scrambled eggs and talking about the DA's investigation. The word that I'd received from my inside man was that Hogan was going to start questioning all of the players in about two months, just as soon as the NIT and NCAA tournaments were over. I was a little concerned that some of the players might crack if they were called in for questioning. There were only four that I'd been dealing with directly—Billy Reed, Lenny Kaplan, Gary Kaufman, and Leroy Wright—and at some point I'd have to get back to them and coach them how to act if and when the DA's detectives ever got to them. But these kids couldn't implicate me without also implicating themselves, and I thought that would never happen. I thought that if Hogan wanted to go on a fishing expedition he'd call me in for questioning and that would certainly embarrass me and damage my law practice. But I believed there was no chance that I could be arrested, and if I were, I'd have solid grounds to sue Hogan for false arrest.

"While I was talking, I noticed that our waiter was making unnecessary trips to our table and giving us the kind of highfalutin service we could expect at the Waldorf-Astoria. Even when he wasn't refilling our water glasses or brushing crumbs from the table, the waiter was hanging around too closely. It was clear to me the waiter was an undercover detective. Just as a test, I bent closer to Paul and spoke in a real low voice like I was communicating some kind of top-secret information. And the lower I would talk, the closer the waiter would come to the table. This went on for about fifteen minutes.

"The check came to five dollars and as we got up to leave I dropped a ten-cent tip on the table. Paul was shocked. 'You can't leave the guy a lousy dime,' he said. 'Since when are you such a cheapskate, Jack? Leave him at least a dollar.'

"'Don't you worry,' I said to Paul. 'Our waiter makes more money than we do.'

"Paul gave me a funny look because he didn't understand what was really going on."

By now, the DA's men had accidentally zeroed in on Molinas's operation. The detectives were tapping a bank of public telephones on Fordham Road, directly opposite Alexander's department store, hoping to gather incriminating information of several Bronx bookmakers. In the past few weeks the weather had turned nasty and Molinas was too lazy to drive out to Long Island or New Jersey to make his business calls. It was much easier to take the subway up to the Bronx and not have to worry about snow or ice on the roads. Imagine the detectives' delight when they heard Molinas making deals with players and backers from coast to coast.

A few days later, he was having lunch with Joe Hacken and they were going round and round about the DA. Joe had been arrested on bookmaking charges about twenty times already and had beaten the rap in at least half the cases. With his police record, though, Jack thought Joe should get out of the city. Maybe go to California, or even someplace in Europe. That way he could avoid being questioned and not give the DA any more ammunition that he'd already collected.

"Not a chance," Joe said. "I've got too much business going on in New York. Besides, I can take care of myself. Maybe if enough time passes and the players can keep their mouths shut, Hogan will forget about the whole thing and leave us alone. But until then, what about you, Jack? Maybe you're the one who should take a vacation."

"No way, Joe. Look, I've got it all figured out. They're tapping our phones, right? That means that they're tapping into our action. They hear us talk about a few games that are in the bag. They check them out. Whenever we mention a game I guarantee you that they call their friendly neighborhood bookie. You think cops don't bet, Joe? You know how sports-minded Hogan's office is. They're playing in softball leagues, in basketball leagues, even in bowling leagues. I've gotta be right on this, Joe. If I take off and we cut back on our action, we'll also be cutting down on the extra income for the cops. I've got to keep on operating, Joe, to make it worth their while to let me stay in business."[1]

Molinas also met with Wagman and gave him the same advice he'd given to Hacken. Get out of town so a grand jury can't get their hooks on you. "No," Wagman said. "I'm living here, I'm married, and I'm renting an apartment. It would be ridiculous for me to run away, Jack."

"Well, at least contact all the players you've been talking to and tell them to clam up when they get called in because unless they confess, the DA has no case against them and no case against us. All the evidence he has is wiretaps and you know what that's worth in court. Zippo." Wagman agreed to get in touch with his players and tell them not to incriminate themselves.

While all this was going on, a detective out of Hogan's office by the name of Campbell managed to strike up a "friendship" with Wagman. They soon worked out a deal in which Wagman would bet money on fixed games for Campbell, and in return, Campbell would furnish Wagman with relevant information from the DA's office. Wagman would brag about his new buddy and the inside dope he was getting. Of course, Campbell was just setting Wagman up and every conversation the two of them had was taped. None of the information that Wagman got from Campbell was worth a thing.

The DA's guys had all of Wagman's habits down pat: where he would go, how he would get there, what he liked to eat. His days were numbered.

When the grand jury handed down an indictment, even though Detective Campbell's tapes constituted overwhelming proof of his crimes, Wagman pleaded innocent. The subsequent trial lasted only four days, and on January 22, 1961, Wagman was convicted of paying a bribe to John McBeth and sentenced to five years in prison and fined ten thousand dollars. Wagman was released upon payment of a twenty-thousand-dollar bond while he appealed the verdict.

Once Wagman had been sentenced, Molinas felt secure enough to resume his fixing operations. But the season was coming to an end, the local bookmakers were still wary of accepting his action, and opportunities were scarce. "I was fortunate to find out about a bookie with deep pockets in Oregon who would accept large bets as long as they were in cash. So I called the bookie, whose name was Jerry, gave him a cock-and-bull story, then flew out there with a bodyguard who carried my thirty thousand dollars plus a .45 in his pocket. After we arrived, my man chauffeured me around in a rented Rolls Royce. I was supposed to be an heir to a copper fortune, so I dressed the part—a Harris tweed suit with a vest and a pocket watch in the finest New England tradition. When I hooked up with Jerry, he had a gorgeous redhead for me, and I played the role of a real sucker going for the girl head over heels. There was much intrigue the evening before the game as to which team I was betting on and it was easy to figure out that the redhead was Jerry's spy. Neither of them knew, however, that the game was fixed and I had three players in the bag. We all had dinner together and I goaded Jerry into taking a much larger wager than he had originally intended. In the end, I walked away with thirty thousand dollars more than I had when I got there. I left the girl a thousand, which led Jerry to believe that she had double-crossed him."

The last rigged game of the 1960–61 season was set up by Jerry Vogel and Dan Quindazi, former Alabama basketball players working for Wagman. The captain of the University of Connecticut football team, Bill Minnerly, introduced Vogel and Quindazi to three UConn hoopers: Glenn Cross was a physical-education major and an average player, not on an athletic scholarship and paying his own way with GI Bill funds, and commuting from Willimantic. He was an indifferent student and enjoyed little social rapport with the other students. Two years before, Cross had dropped out of school for two semesters because of lack of funds. Jack Rose, also a physical-education student, came from an underprivileged family in South Windsor, Connecticut, and was attending UConn on a partial athletic scholarship. Pete Kelly came from a comfortable Garden City, New York, family. Kelly was an average ballplayer on a partial scholarship, doing well in his business courses, and a popular campus figure. Teammates said, however, that Kelly was usually suffering from the "shorts" and frequently hit friends for small loans. For $750 each, Cross, Rose, and Kelly agreed to have UConn lose to

Colgate by at least eleven points. If the scheme succeeded, Vogel and Quindazi would earn five hundred dollars each and Minnerly seven hundred and fifty.

The day of the game, somebody calling himself "Kelly" called Wagman collect, saying he was at Hamilton, New York, the site of Colgate. Wagman took the call in one of his "offices," a phone booth in the New York West Side Airlines Terminal, but when he had to pay only forty cents for the call he became suspicious and tried unsuccessfully to cancel his bets. "Kelly" was, in fact, one of Frank Hogan's detectives.

Colgate won the game by twelve points, making Wagman, his partners, and his backers winners. Kelly scored thirteen points, a good night for him. He played well in the first half, was pulled while his team was ten points behind, and never got back into the game. Later, Kelly wrote a friend at school: "Nobody will believe this now, but I didn't try to shave points in the Colgate game. I played my best."

Hogan now believed he had sufficient hard evidence to ask a grand jury to indict Wagman for bribing basketball players. The DA also discovered that Wagman had applied for a passport and was preparing to leave the country. His hand forced, Hogan had Wagman arrested on March 16 and charged with thirty-eight counts of bribery. Wagman faced a maximum sentence of 380 years in jail and $380,000 in fines. Bail was set at $60,000, but even though Wagman's recent gambling frenzies had netted him over $100,000, he refused to dip into what he referred to as his family's "secret nest egg" and chose to remain in jail, hoping that either Molinas or Hacken would post his bond.

As he had done in his testimony after his arrest in Florida, Wagman once again implicated Dave Budin. This time, Wagman also gave Hogan's detectives the names of two other accomplices: Joe Green and Joe Hacken. (Green was in Mexico when he heard the news and had just mailed a postcard to Wagman that included his return address. Green rushed back to the mailbox and waited there for several hours until the collector came by and he could retrieve the card.)

"The district attorney told the newspapers that Aaron was the mastermind behind dozens of fixes," said Stanley Cohen, "which was totally ridiculous. Everybody in the neighborhood knew that Jack Molinas was the only person in that whole crew who had the kind of demonic intelligence it took to hold a network like that together. If there were two guys involved in stealing a candy bar from a store, Wagman would not be the mastermind. Wagman couldn't mastermind his way around the block."

Molinas had to keep tabs on Wagman while he was locked up in the Tombs, so he went to Wagman's attorney, Joe Weinberg, and asked if he had any objections to Jack's acting as cocounsel. With Weinberg's permission Jack met with Wagman and easily convinced him to sign a retainer. Once he was signed on as one of Wagman's attorneys, Jack could visit him as many times as he wished and thereby keep him up to date about everything that was happening on the outside. Over the next two months, he met with Wagman at least two or three times every week.

What Molinas was doing was obvious: He wanted to build up Wagman's morale and convince him not to turn state's evidence. At first Wagman said he could hold out and that he wasn't a snitch. But as time went on he started to waver. "I can't face three hundred and ninety years, Jack. The DA's promised that if I cooperated, I'd only be prosecuted on one bribery count and face a sentence of five to ten years. So you'd better get me out of here if you know what's good for you. I can tie you and Hacken into this mess in dozens of places."

Hacken and Molinas even discussed the possibility of putting up Wagman's bail, but they were convinced that he'd leave the country and sixty thousand was too big a chunk to be stuck with. Wagman's various backers had already sent him some money, but they weren't about to post a sixty-grand bond either. With Wagman already in jail, none of those guys wanted anything more to do with him. But Molinas kept working on Wagman, trying to get him to take the fall by himself. He told him that if he ever incriminated any of his business partners, his life wouldn't be worth a plugged nickel even when he did get out of prison. Slowly but surely, however, Molinas could see that Wagman was going over to the DA's side.

In mid-May, even though the special tutors provided by the Iowa athletic department were writing all of Connie Hawkins's term papers, the young man was struggling to maintain a D-plus average. By then, Wagman had given Hogan enough information for Budin to be called in for interrogation. Budin readily admitted his part in several fixes and then began reciting names—one of which was Connie Hawkins. Budin reported that Hacken had told him, "Molinas has Roger Brown and Connie Hawkins in the bag."

Budin had never met Hawkins and he provided no specifics. In truth, Hacken had never even mentioned either Hawkins's or Brown's name in Budin's presence. Later, the suspicion in the gambling community was that Budin would have given up his mother's name to save his own hide. In any event, Hogan's office dispatched one detective to Iowa City and another to Dayton to bring the two players back to New York for questioning. "When they picked me up at my dorm room," said Hawkins, "they wouldn't even let me bring any clean clothing along."

Brown admitted accepting a total of two hundred and fifty dollars from Hacken, but swore "it was only date money and free dinners" and that he was "a victim of circumstances." According to Brown, "it was fairly common for fans to give me entertainment money even while I was a senior in high school. The same thing happened at Dayton, too. Once in a while fellows who followed the freshman team would give me a couple of bucks for a date." What return did Hacken get for the money he gave to Brown? "He'd see some kid he didn't know in the playground," said Brown, "and ask me if I'd introduce the kid to him. And I would."

Hawkins reiterated that the two hundred dollars he'd accepted from Molinas was merely a loan: "The police put me and Roger in a hotel for two weeks, and every day, for eight hours, we had to go to the district attorney's office. They asked me so many confusing questions that my head began to spin. They didn't believe it was a loan. They didn't believe that I knew nothing about crooked ball games. They didn't believe me when I didn't even know what a point spread was. Those people wouldn't believe me if I told them my own name. They said I was trying to protect Molinas. I was frightened. I thought they were going to put me in jail if I didn't say what they wanted." (One detective told a sportswriter that with his testimony Hawkins "really buried himself.")

On several occasions, Molinas informed friends that both Brown and Hawkins were innocent of any wrongdoing. At other times, Molinas claimed that both players "knew what was going on" and had tentatively agreed to turn tricks once they were eligible for varsity competition.

On May 15, Hawkins was expelled from the University of Iowa.

On May 23, Joe Hacken was indicted on one count of conspiracy and seventeen counts of bribery. (Hacken's twenty thousand dollars' bail was paid by Molinas, still the loyal disciple). Fourteen players were mentioned in the indictment, with Hawkins being named in four of the forty-one overt acts in the conspiracy count. Among other charges, Hawkins and Brown were described as being "intermediaries" in recruiting prospects for bribe offers.

Dayton expelled Brown on June 1.

After Hacken was indicted, Hogan had the grand jury's term extended to December in anticipation of more arrests. And finally, despite his routine claims of infallibility and his insistence that all cops were clucks, Molinas felt moved to try to protect himself. His idea was to meet with the four players whom he had directly approached about fixing games: Billy Reed from Bowling Green, Lenny Kaplan from Alabama, and Leroy Wright and Gary Kaufman from College of the Pacific. The names of all four had leaked out of Hogan's office as witnesses who would certainly be summoned to testify before the grand jury. For starters, Molinas drove out to Toledo, Ohio, to confront Billy Reed.

"Jack drove me out into the sticks," Reed said, "and he told me that it wasn't a difficult thing to appear before a grand jury. He said that he knew a number of players who'd already been questioned, had talked their way out of trouble, and were back in school without their names ever mentioned in the newspapers. He mentioned one player, Tony Jackson from St. John's, who he said 'made a monkey out of the grand jury.'"

(Jackson was never accused of bribe taking—only of failure to report a bribe offer. For that, Jackson was refused admission into the NBA.)

"Jack also told me," Reed continued, "that when I was brought to the witness stand I should be indignant and act as if I had been accused of robbing the First National Bank. Whatever the questions might be, Jack said I could always use the phrase, 'I don't remember.'"

According to Molinas, the conversation was much more inclusive: "I felt that Reed was a little weak and that he might crack once he got in the clutches of the DA. My main effort was to tell him that he had nothing to worry about. Then I asked him what his major was and he said he wanted to go on to teacher's college. I asked Reed if he had any money and he said he'd saved up about five thousand dollars. 'If the DA does call you in,' I said to him, 'and if you do stand up, I'll tell you what I'll do. I'll pay all of your expenses in graduate school. A full scholarship. As a matter of fact, if anybody from the district attorney communicates with you, you should call me immediately. An even better idea is if you sign a retainer and officially make me your lawyer.'

"'That's a great idea,' he said.

"So I whipped out a blank retainer form and filled everything in except the fee. 'Don't worry about the money,' I said, 'because you don't have to pay me anything.' And then he signed it.

"Another player I had to take care of was Lenny Kaplan, who had graduated from Alabama and was working as a maitre d' in a restaurant at the Pimlico Hotel in Baltimore, which his parents owned. To protect myself as much as possible, I went down there with a private detective I had hired. The detective's main job was to wire me with a tape recorder. Well, the restaurant was packed when we got there but we were shown to a small table off to the side. After a while, Lenny came over and we had a little chat, at which time I asked him, 'Lenny, did you ever fix a college basketball game?' He said, 'No.' Then I asked him if I had ever approached him about fixing a game, and his answer was the same. 'No.' Then we had a general conversation in which he absolved himself of all guilt and never admitted that he'd done anything wrong. 'Wonderful,' I said. I had everything down on tape, I had a good meal, and I was very happy.

"However, when I replayed the tape the following day in my law office, the conversation was just about inaudible. There was the sound of silverware being rattled and dishes banging against the table. Later on, Kaplan said he suspected that I was taping him and had deliberately tapped a fork against a plate all during our interview. But I don't think the kid was smart enough to do something like that. The tape recorder was simply too sensitive."

The last players Molinas interviewed were Kaufman and Wright. "I flew out to California and met with both of them and they were very agreeable. They claimed they would deny the fact that I'd offered them a bribe, and that they'd both agreed to do business. They understood exactly what the situation was. All in all, the only guy I was still worried about was Billy Reed."

While Molinas was "very concerned" about what Wagman was (or would be) telling the DA, he knew that Hacken would never rat on him. And given that Reed, Kaplan, Kaufman, and Wright held the fort, Molinas believed that he had plenty of time to figure out a way to outsmart Hogan. What Jack didn't realize was that Hogan's investigation had also fingered Lou Brown, taped a microphone to his chest, and instructed him to call Molinas and arrange a meeting. "When we did get together," Brown said, "I told [Molinas] that the police had questioned me but I hadn't told them anything, and I asked for his advice. He told me to keep my mouth shut and not to worry about anything because Wagman would never talk. Then he began to ridicule the DA's men. When the tape of this conversation was played in Hogan's office, the detectives there were more eager than ever to get hard evidence. I arranged a second meeting with [Molinas] at Second Avenue and Twentieth Street. While we were talking, I saw a couple of detectives walking in front of us. I told [Molinas] that Wagman had told me many times that he was mixed up in it. Although [Molinas] is a cocky man, he was a little nervous at this.

"'You could fight a war,' he said, 'with all the men who are involved in the fixes. But they will never get me for one reason. Between me and jail is a stone wall, and the name of that stone wall is Joey Hacken. We have been through a lot together, and Joey will never talk.'"

Whatever else was threatening his workaday life, Molinas was still a great basketball player. "Jack continued to dominate top-notch tournaments like the one in Haverstraw, New York," said Lou Orlando. "The teams up there always had open rosters so that any NBA players who chanced to be in the area could be hired for the championship game. Anyway, in the spring of 1961, Jack had agreed to play with a team that I was on. Jack was usually late so we weren't worried when he wasn't around as we took the court for the pregame warm-ups. But, son of a gun, there he was on the other end of the court wearing the uniform of the host team. Jack had gotten a better offer and that was that. Nobody was surprised when Jack's new team won the championship and he won another trophy as the tournament's most valuable player."

If certain things hadn't changed, others had, and his fellow hoopers began to disbelieve Molinas's routine avowals of his own innocence. "Even if Wagman and Hacken hadn't been arrested," said Orlando, "we all knew that Jack was deeply involved in all of that fixing shit. After my team lost to Jack's in the Haverstraw tournament, we went out to a restaurant where he showed me a letter he had just received from Wagman in the Tombs. Wagman was upset because Jack had posted Hacken's bond. He told Jack that he'd better get his ass over to the jailhouse and get Wagman out or he was gonna blow the whistle. But Jack just laughed. 'Is he serious?' Jack said. 'It's just unbelievable how these guys make up these stories. I swear, Lou, Wagman's got nothing on me.' When I suggested that he not take Wagman's threat so lightly, Jack just laughed again."

While Joe Hacken was out on bail he was always under heavy surveillance. That meant that Joe and Molinas couldn't communicate with each other. They certainly couldn't meet anywhere and they knew that all of their phones were bugged.

Through a mutual friend, Joe did manage to get a short note to Jack:

"Everybody's singing like canaries. But you'll be okay as long as your fellows dummy up."

To celebrate the Fourth of July weekend, Molinas drove up to Rhode Island with a lovely blond actress named Helene. But changing girlfriends was even easier than changing basketball teams. "This Helene was sort of a floozy type," said Ann Hemlock, "while I was very straightlaced in those days, all dressed in Bermuda shorts and knee-high socks. As soon as we saw each other that was it. Jack totally ignored Helene and spent the entire weekend with me. Afterward, he drove me back to my apartment in Manhattan and just left Helene in Rhode Island to find her own way home. I knew right away that Jack was manipulative and devious, but he was a wonderful lover and we ended up having a wild romance for about five months."

Anne was also impressed with Molinas's high-stepping lifestyle. "Jack was always a big spender," she said, "and he took me to the best restaurants in New York—the Chambord, Broadway Joe's, the Persian Room. A normal meal for him was a big bowl of soup, a couple of baked potatoes, and at least two steaks. Jack wasn't much of a drinker, but the bill for the two of us would easily come to a hundred dollars."

And if Molinas's idea of a good time was often reckless, Anne didn't really object. "He was partial to fancy convertible cars," she remembered, "and his favorite stunt was to drive down Park Avenue with his hands clasped behind his head while he was steering the car with his knees. It was great fun, but the man was wild."

On the flip side of Molinas's appeal was his unpredictability. "He was always dating a lot of girls," Anne says. "He even dated Helene again after he'd ditched her in Rhode Island. No matter how much fun we had together, I was never sure if he was going to keep our next date. And even when he did show up, some of our dates were bizarre. Like the time we had a late dinner, then he drove over to a really bad neighborhood in Brooklyn at two o'clock in the morning. He said he had to pick up some money that was owed him, and he left me waiting in the car for about two hours. After a while, a bunch of creepy-looking guys came out of the shadows and surrounded the car with baseball bats and tire irons. God knows what they were preparing to do, but Jack came out of the building just in time. He gave each of the guys ten bucks and they backed off."

For Anne's birthday on August 28, Molinas presented her with an expensive bracelet adorned with diamonds and pearls. "He said the bracelet was worth a thousand dollars," Anne said, "and there was an engraving on the back—'Love always, Jack.' When he gave it to me, he said, 'That doesn't mean that I'll always love you. It means that you should always love Jack.' Life was never dull with Jack Molinas."

Late in the summer, Gary Kaufman called Molinas to say he had something very important to discuss. Molinas agreed to visit Kaufman at his parents' house at 2108 Fifty-eighth Street in Brooklyn. Molinas expected that Kaufman was getting nervous about the DA's continuing investigation and needed to be reassured that no harm would befall him if he feigned ignorance. What Molinas didn't know was that Kaufman had already agreed to cooperate with the DA's office. Detective Nat Laurendi was stationed in one of the upstairs bedrooms, monitoring a small transmitter that had been taped to the back of the TV set in the basement.

Kaufman led him down into the basement and before they started talking Jack walked around the room just to see if he could find anything that looked out of place. This was the kid, after all, who had taken money from a pretty crafty con man knowing that he'd been suspended by his coach, spent the St. Mary's game on the bench, and refused to return the money. So Jack had good reason not to trust him. Instinctively, he walked over to the TV and turned on the switch because that would ruin any bug that might have been placed anywhere in the room. But the TV didn't come on.

"It's broken," Kaufman said.

"Is there a radio down here?"

"No."

So Jack just shrugged and asked him what he wanted to discuss. Just as he had expected, Kaufman was getting worried about the DA. Jack told him there was nothing for either of them to worry about because he hadn't actually thrown the game.

MOLINAS: I'm warning you, though, it could be very dangerous if you ever implicated me or any of the fellows who put up the bankroll.

KAUFMAN: You mean the higher-ups?

MOLINAS: That's right. If anyone ever identified them, they'd get shot, they'd get killed. I'm not kidding.

KAUFMAN: They're really that type of guys? They'd kill people?

MOLINAS: That's right. Yeah, you know what crew this is? I'll tell you now. But if you ever repeat this…

KAUFMAN: I'd get killed. Hey, I wouldn't say anything.

MOLINAS: It's the old Capone mob from Chicago. That's why it's advisable for you to deny everything.

Molinas left there convinced that he had scared the kid half to death, and that Hogan's boys wouldn't get a word from him.

Shortly after Labor Day, Molinas met Ellen Sohn, who would turn out to be the only other woman besides Peggy Eisenhower he seriously considered marrying. "I had a girlfriend who was very much into meeting eligible men," said Sohn, "and was dying to get married. She lived in Los Angeles, where she was dating one of Jack's friends, Myron (or as he called himself, 'Mike'), the doctor who treated Jack's broken finger. So my girlfriend fixed me up with Jack on a blind date. I was twenty years old, stood only five foot three, and had a very young appearance. When I answered the doorbell and we saw each other for the first time, he was taken aback. 'Are you Ellen,' he asked, 'or is your sister home?' He took me out to dinner and on the way to the restaurant he stopped in front of an apartment building in a crummy neighborhood and said, 'I'll be right out.' He was gone for about a half hour and he never gave me an explanation. Jack did tell me, though, that there was some kind of investigation and that he expected to be indicted. But, see, I didn't understand all that. All I knew was that Jack was always laughing and carefree and we had a lot of fun. Being with Jack was always exciting."

Ellen understood that Anne Hemlock was Molinas's "special girl," but before long, they were seeing each other twice and sometimes even three times a week. For the most part, Ellen wasn't fond of Molinas's friends—"a bunch of poor-ass Mafia minor leaguers who lived in the shittiest parts of Brooklyn." Molinas would always be involved in one scam or another with this particular crew, and Ellen frequently came along for the ride. "There was a used-car lot on Jerome Avenue," she said, "that was supposed to be a clearinghouse for stolen cars. There were various real-estate deals. There was another scam that had to do with setting up machines in apartment buildings that would dry-clean clothes. There was always a bunch of stolen goods in the trunk of Jack's car. Booze, fur coats, dishes, TVs, radios, air conditioners. God knows what he was doing with that stuff. There was also some kind of deal that Jack was working on that had to do with some Las Vegas hotel and that was supposed to involve Frank Sinatra. I couldn't keep up with all of Jack's operations."

Ellen did like "the Panther bunch." They were solid citizens and, like Ellen, most of them were Jewish. "The only times that Jack would take me to the theater," she said, "was when we were out with his Panther friends from the Bronx. Otherwise, it was 'You wait in the car. I'll just be a minute,' and then out to some fancy joint for dinner. Jack liked me to wear flashy clothes with plenty of sequins, and we'd always go to the restaurants where the waiters knew his name. Voison. The Copa. The Plaza. He had an American Express card, which was a big deal in those days. The funny thing was that no matter which restaurant we went to, Jack always insisted on being placed at a table where he could sit with his back to the wall. He never admitted to any kind of wrongdoing, but there was a definite fear factor working on him."

As their relationship continued, Ellen would be forced to "wait in the car" for as much as three hours before Molinas reappeared. "And he'd never even apologize," Ellen said. "I was very masochistic back in those days, but one time after I'd been waiting for over two hours, I just drove off. Jack was very pissed off about that. His idea of rectifying with the situation was to drop me off at some restaurant and have me wait there while he went off on his errands. I remember that I once took a cab and went looking for him. I found his car parked near the Golden Gate Motel in Brooklyn, where he was shacking up with some girl. By the way, the only time I ever saw Jack cry was at the funeral of his friend Stuart Silverstein, who'd died in a freakish car accident, and who at some point owned the Golden Gate."

Molinas even brought Ellen to Ocean Parkway ostensibly to meet his parents, but after a perfunctory exchange of greetings, he escorted her into his bedroom to show off his trophies (one of which was taller than she was). As might be expected, Betty sensed that her son could get "serious" about Ellen and withheld her approval. "Jackie," his mother said, "if you ever married Ellie you'd have to make a lot of money to keep her happy." Molinas only laughed and said, "Ma, I'm not planning on marrying anybody, so don't worry about it."

Molinas always spoke fondly of his mother but would never talk about his father even if Ellen broached the subject. "He'd just dismiss any talk of his father with a wave of his hand," said Ellen. "The way I saw it was that the old man had been much too strict in the way he'd tried to discipline Jack, and when Jack finally had the chance to get out from under his father's authority, he just went crazy. Joey Hacken came along and taught Jack the virtues of making the easy buck and the poor kid couldn't resist the temptation. I always thought that much of what happened to Jack was his way of releasing all of that suppressed anger he felt for his father. I also think that what sustained Jack through all the ups and downs was his vision of the perfect life and how close it always seemed to be."

NOTE

1. *The Great Molinas*, p.146.

Midway between his twenty-ninth and thirtieth birthdays, Molinas's body began to thicken and lose flexibility. His weight gradually increased to upward of 230 pounds (the inevitable result of his gargantuan appetite for steaks), and on the basketball court he was no longer capable of riding the crest of a fast break. But he was now a wily veteran who compensated by creating favorable angles for himself and anticipating the development of a play a heartbeat before the other players. Playing ball was actually more enjoyable than ever before as Molinas became more dependent on outsmarting the foe. In truth, Molinas thought he was as good as ever.

Prior to the 1961–62 Eastern League season, Molinas was relieved of his coaching responsibilities and replaced by Stan "Whitey" Von Nieda, who'd played in the NBA (and its forerunner, the National Basketball League) from 1947 to 1950. Von Nieda was an old-school coach whose only loyalty was to winning, and, EBL icon or not, he had little patience with Molinas's arrogance and casual training methods. "We had a couple of practice weekends before the season began, " said Von Nieda, "and Jack would show up with a beautiful girl on one arm, while in his other hand he had a suitcase full of liquor. It was clear that Jack had other things on his mind besides basketball. Although he had certain disdain for his teammates, he wasn't at all mean-spirited. But the main trouble I had with Jack was his lackadaisical attitude toward practice. When the other guys on the team were running wind sprints, Jack would just jog along. 'I'm getting in shape slowly,' he'd say."

Von Nieda had several pep talks with his erstwhile star player. "You can't live on your reputation," Von Nieda said. "And you can't play for me if you're not in shape."

Molinas's response was always the same: "By the time the season comes around I'll be in great shape."

Von Nieda ran out of patience after the Hawks played a preseason exhibition against the Camden Bullets in Philadelphia. "I played him the entire first quarter," said Von Nieda, "and even five minutes into the second quarter. He had totaled one rebound and two points and he looked like he was about to keel over and die. 'Jack,' I asked him, 'are you in game shape yet?' He couldn't even catch his breath enough to give me an answer."

After the game, Von Nieda had dinner with an old friend, Eddie Gottlieb, the owner of the NBA's Philadelphia Warriors. "Get rid of Molinas," Gottlieb advised. "He's nothing but bad news and, besides, from what I hear it's only a matter of time before the cops grab him for fixing ball games." The very next day, Von Nieda traded Molinas to the Wilkes-Barre Barons for what he jokingly described as "an old basketball and a pair of sneakers."

The beautiful girl on Molinas's arm was Ellen Sohn, and she continued accompanying him once the season was under way. Ellen enjoyed watching Molinas play, and even more, enjoyed his good moods before and after the games. But Molinas played in only seven games for Wilkes-Barre before he voluntarily retired from the EBL in mid-December. Even though he struggled getting up and down the court, Molinas still managed to average 17.7 points per game.

However, one week after leaving the EBL Molinas decided that he had enough game left to play in a new professional league (the American Basketball League) that the Harlem Globetrotters owner, Abe Saperstein, had founded to compete with the NBA. Saperstein was angry when the Minneapolis Lakers moved to Los Angeles and he was not offered the opportunity to buy into the NBA and situate a franchise in San Francisco—after all Saperstein had already done to keep the NBA solvent in those early years, from scheduling his crowd-pleasing Globbies as preliminary games to selling Sweetwater Clifton to the New York Knicks. With eight new teams to stock, Saperstein was desperate for marquee ballplayers, even (or especially?) one with a notoriously tainted past. Accordingly, Saperstein agreed to meet Molinas in Pittsburgh and discuss the possibilities.

The meeting with Saperstein proved disappointing—Molinas was too risky even for a fly-by-night operation like the ABL (which lasted only for a season and a half). While in Chicago, Molinas stopped in at a strip joint that got raided by the police just as he finished his first drink. Molinas used some legal "double-talk" and was released.

On November 30, 1961, Wagman made a deal with the district attorney, pleading guilty to lesser charges in exchange for testimony that totally implicated Hacken and Molinas. Even so, Molinas wasn't unduly alarmed. He knew that by the tenets of New York State law, a conviction could not be based solely on the testimony of a coconspirator. Without additional corroboration, Wagman's confessions couldn't touch Molinas.

Meanwhile, Molinas and Ellen were becoming increasingly intimate. "I lived with my parents and my younger brother Stephen in a house in Kew Garden Hills in Queens," said Ellen, "and Jack practically lived there, too. Stephen had an IQ of one hundred and sixty-five and was always a sports fan, so he and Jack really got along. Jack was so charismatic and so intelligent and he could talk about anything. Everybody loved being with Jack. My mother was especially impressed because he could finish the Sunday *New York Times* crossword puzzle as quickly as if he were writing a letter. My parents believed that when Jack stayed overnight he slept in my brother's room, but he used to sneak out and come to bed with me. I was madly in love with Jack and told him so. But when he told me that he loved me, I wondered if Jack was really capable of loving anybody. And when he swore that he wasn't in love with Peggy Eisenhower anymore, I wasn't sure about that either because he still had all of her letters and talked about her constantly. I think that maybe Peggy was the one girl whom Jack really loved. Another time, Jack admitted that sports came first in his life and that I was number two. He meant it as a compliment, but I wasn't at all comforted."

To prove that Molinas was serious about Ellen, they'd often have dinner with Joe Hacken. "Joe was polite and very thoughtful," Ellen said. "I could tell by the way he mispronounced some words that his formal education was limited, but he always understood everything that was said in his presence. Joe also had a photographic memory. I've seen him leaf through a newspaper and then recall every article and every advertisement on every page. He was probably nice-looking when he was younger, but by the time I met him most of his teeth were missing. Joe said that he was married to a woman named Fosca and they'd had two children together, but they had been estranged for some time. Fosca was living with a cop named Fred in a house that Joe owned in Levittown. Joe and Jack never talked business when I was with them. One of the reasons why I was impressed with Joe was that he treated people much nicer than Jack did."

For Christmas, Molinas presented Ellen with a diamond heart pendant. "Does this mean that we're engaged?" Ellen asked.

"I can't get engaged and I can't get married," was Molinas's response. "I can't make any long-range and lasting commitment because of the probability that I'm going to be indicted."

Ellen didn't know if Molinas was making a convenient excuse or if his reluctance was sincere. As close as she was to Molinas, Ellen never quite knew what was really on his mind. "It was that macho basketball attitude," she later decided. "A man isn't supposed to admit that he's vulnerable or indecisive."

The DA's men seemed to be ubiquitous—lurking in every shadow, privy to every telephone call, just waiting to pounce with subpoenas in their hands. And the core members of Fixers Incorporated weren't the only ones to be subjected to this round-the-clock surveillance. Dave Budin was also aware that he was being tailed by detectives, and for a while he decided to get out of the racket. But Budin missed the easy money and, like Molinas, found it easier to simply ignore what he saw in the rearview mirror and hope that somehow his involvement would get overlooked.

While all of this was happening, Molinas continued rigging ball games, swindling unwary bookies, and worrying about losing his hair. As long as Reed, Kaplan, Kaufman, and Wright kept their traps shut, the good life would last forevermore. Then, on the morning of January 12, 1962, Molinas received a troubling telephone call from Billy Reed in Toledo.

"I'm in the college president's office with two detectives from the Manhattan district attorney's office. They want to take me to New York and question me there, but I told them that I had to speak with my lawyer before I could agree to anything."

"Just tell them that you refuse to go with them," Jack said.

"I can't very well do that because the college president said I should cooperate with them or else I'll get expelled from school," said Billy.

"Fine," Jack said. "Tell me what flight you're coming in on and I'll meet you at the airport."

They were due into Newark at seven that same evening, and as soon as Reed got off the phone Jack placed a call to the New Jersey sheriff's office. The sheriff was an avid basketball fan, and through the years Jack had played on teams he'd sponsored in the various tournaments. So Jack told the sheriff that he needed a favor. "I have a client arriving at Newark from Ohio," Jack said, "and I anticipate having a little problem with Frank Hogan's office. If Hogan's detectives attempt to take my client into New York against his will, I'd like to be able to press charges against them. Do you think you could help me out?"

"Sure," the sheriff said. "I'd rather not get too heavily involved in something like this, Jack, but if you and your client will sign an affidavit I'll make the arrest if the detectives try to take him away against his will."

Armed with this, Molinas felt he was in a pretty good position. And sure enough, when he got to the airport, there were two men from the sheriff's office waiting for him. Before long, two of Hogan's men showed up with Billy Reed in tow.

"What's the problem here?" Jack asked.

When the detectives said that they were taking Reed in, Molinas resisted. He was Reed's attorney and if they wanted to question his client, they would make an appointment and he'd bring him in tomorrow. They objected, so Jack stepped between them and Reed, put his arm around Reed's shoulders, and told them once again to stay away.

"We're taking him in, Jack," one of Hogan's men said, "and that's the end of it."

"No, you're not."

"You know that we carry guns, Jack."

"Take your guns and shove them up your ass."

They were flabbergasted. "Is that your final word?"

"Absolutely," Jack said. "You're out of your territory here and you've got no legal right to take this man against his will. If you try to take him, there are two men here from the sheriff's office and I'll have you arrested for kidnapping, which is a felony."

The officers had never encountered anything like this before and they didn't know what to do. Finally, one of the detectives called his office and said that one of Hogan's assistants, Pete Andreolli, wanted to speak with Molinas. Once again, Jack explained his position, and Andreolli was very accommodating. They made an appointment to bring Reed to the DA's office the following morning at ten and that was that.

Jack drove back to New York with Reed. The kid was frantic. "There's nothing for you to get upset about," Jack told him. "All you have to do is deny what happened and that will be the end of it. I'm certainly not going to let you incriminate yourself, Billy, because that would also incriminate me." Reed seemed to calm down a bit.

They checked into a room with twin beds at the Hotel Martinique and Jack stayed with Reed all night. They had wine, women, and Chinese food. They had more discussions in the morning. By the time they had to leave for the meeting, Jack felt he had complete control of Reed.

Before Molinas took Reed to Hogan's office, they stopped at the law office to sign a retainer that officially made Molinas Reed's attorney of record. Reed also signed a statement (which he didn't read) stating that Molinas had never bribed him. The statement was witnessed by Evelyn Henry (Molinas's legal secretary) and Richard Tolchin, and notarized by Carl Harten, two lawyers who shared space in the same office.

When they got to the DA's office the next morning, they were ushered into Albert J. Scotti's office, another one of Hogan's right-hand men. "We want to examine Reed outside of your presence," Scotti said. Naturally, Jack refused. Then Scotti said they'd subpoena Reed to a grand jury.

"That's your prerogative," Jack said. "If you have a subpoena to hand my client, give it to me and I'll see that it's honored."

With that, Scotti got very indignant and red in the face. Then he took Molinas and Reed into the court of jurisdictions to meet with Judge Dickens in his chambers. Andreolli met them there, and he told the judge that there was an obvious conflict of interest at work. Since Jack was under active investigation by the DA, he couldn't represent Reed. The judge said that he didn't think it advisable for Jack to represent Reed.

"The fact is," Jack said, "that no charges have been brought against me. And furthermore, it isn't in the purview of your jurisdiction to issue such a ruling on this point. This man is entitled to counsel and he chose me."

There was nothing the judge could do, so they left his chambers and walked out into the corridor. Then the same two detectives who'd tried to take Reed at the airport suddenly appeared, put their hands on the kid, and started to take him away. Molinas jumped in between them and shouldered them aside. "You can't take him!" he said, and there was a little scuffle.

"Don't force us to get rough on you, Jack," one of them said.

"The only way you're going to take him is over my dead body," Jack said. "You're going to have to pull out your guns and shoot me."

"You know, Jack, that we can take him away bodily."

"I know no such thing. All I know is that I'm not surrendering my client." Then he turned to Reed and said, "You don't want to go with them, right?"

At this point, Reed started to waver. When they noticed this, the detectives were all over him. "You've got to come with us, Reed. We're going to arrest you and also arrest your lawyer."

"Don't let them bullshit you," Jack warned Reed. "If they wanted to arrest us, they would have done it already. There's no charge under which they can arrest either one of us. You have the right to stay with me, Billy. You don't have to go along with them."

Then the kid folded like a house of cards. "You know what, Jack?" he said. "Let me go with them. You don't have to worry about anything, Jack. I'll come back to your office afterward. Just let me go with them and see what's what."

Once Reed said that, Molinas was powerless to keep him from going. So they took him away. Jack could only wonder how this trembling kid would hold up under their questioning.

The DA's men questioned Reed for several hours. They even manacled him to a radiator until he finally cracked. It was Andreolli who suggested to Reed that the only way he could absolve himself of the sins he'd committed would be to allow them to tape a mini-phone to his chest, then come to Molinas's office and record their conversation.

Reed returned to Molinas's office later that afternoon. Reed said to him, "You can't represent me, Jack, because that would be a conflict of interest."

Molinas asked him if he wanted another lawyer and Reed thought that would be a good idea, so Jack drove him to the office of Joe Panza, another attorney located about six blocks away. So far Reed and Jack hadn't said a word about the case. After Jack briefed Panza about the circumstances and the possible conflict of interest, he declined the case.

Reed and Molinas returned to Jack's office and then Reed started asking questions. The whole thing made Jack feel uneasy, but he never suspected that the kid was bugged. Reed showed him a pink slip, a subpoena from the grand jury for the next morning. "What am I supposed to say to them, Jack?"

"You're supposed to say that you don't know Joe Hacken and that you've never dumped games for me."

"You know that's not true," Reed said.

Molinas just answered, "Yeah, yeah, yeah," like he wasn't even listening to him. The conversation continued:

REED: The more I look at it, it seems that they know you gave me money.
MOLINAS: See, they're only guessing, only guessing to the extent that they just keep adding up all little bits of information. They draw a pattern and they guess, that's all they do.
REED: I'm afraid that if I follow your advice, they'll get me for perjury, too.
MOLINAS: The only way they can get you for perjury is if you make a false statement as to a fact. Now, what exactly is a fact? A fact is something that they can't controvert. If they ask you if I ever gave you money to fix a game, the answer is no.
REED: Still, when they ask me things like that I'm afraid to answer because I think maybe they already know that you gave me money.
MOLINAS: How can they know about it? Tell me how. Do you think I told them?

The next day, January 18, Andreolli told Judge Dickens that the DA's office was officially instituting an investigation aimed at connecting Molinas with the fixing scandals. Before the judge, Reed disavowed any intention to retain Molinas as counsel. They assigned him a Legal Aid lawyer, and the kid went before the grand jury to testify against Jack. This information was made public, and as soon as Jack read it in the newspapers, he realized that Reed had been bugged. At that point he also surely knew that within six months he would be indicted. Meanwhile, in the face of everything that was going so horribly wrong, Jack continued living his normal life—practicing law, going to court, trying his cases. Even though he knew deep down that time was running out, that one day he was going to pick up a paper and read that he was under indictment, he continued betting on games. His one concession was that he stopped fixing them.

Jack was also playing in the usual round of tournaments. He and Allan Seiden were cosponsoring a team in the Mount Carmel tournament in Jersey City. The St. Joseph players also had a team entered—Frank Majewski, Vince Kempton, and Jack Egan—and sure enough Lou Brown came up to Jack in the locker room and introduced himself. Jack knew who he was, although he had never met him face-to-face. They had just won a semifinal game and Jack had scored forty-two points, so he was feeling pretty good. But then Brown tried to engage him in an incriminating conversation that connected him with Wagman and Green. Jack wasn't going to be dragged into anything like that, but all of a sudden Allan walked over. He said hello to Brown and then he motioned for Molinas to follow him to a quiet corner.

It seemed that before Brown came into the locker room he'd taken off his jacket just for a moment—long enough for Allan to see a microphone taped to his chest. But even as he told Jack what he'd seen, Allan couldn't quite figure it out. "What is he," Allan asked, "some kind of sportswriter? Or a reporter for a radio station?"

"No, Allan. It's a private thing."

"Does it have something to do with what the newspapers are saying about Hogan investigating your involvement in fixing basketball games?"

"Something like that. The less you know about it, Allan, the better off you are."

Then Jack walked over to Brown and said, "Listen, I don't know who you are, and that's the end of it."

By now, several ballplayers had been arrested on the basis of Wagman's testimony—including Hank Gunter and Arthur Hicks of Seton Hall, Ray Paprocky of NYU, and Freddie Portnoy of Columbia. The vise was drawing tighter and tighter.

If Ellen truly loved Molinas, she was also appalled (and sometimes even frightened) by his occasional fits of mindless cruelty. Ellen's father was a well-to-do owner and operator of a Manhattan printing business and owned a summer home in northern New Jersey's Morris County. "Jack and I were there by ourselves one weekend," Ellen recalled, "and we had a fire going in the fireplace. It was a cozy scene. But then we started to run out of firewood and Jack didn't want to go outside and get some more from the shed in the back. My father loved to play softball and he kept his favorite bat there because of the weekend games during the summer. So what did Jack do? He picked up my father's prized softball bat and threw it into the fireplace. I was screaming, crying, and totally outraged, but Jack only laughed. To him it was a big joke. That's when I first realized that Jack had serious psychological problems."

As far as Molinas was concerned, a more distressing problem was the greediness of the detectives who were tapping his phone. "These guys were listening to the discussions I was having with Joe Hacken about which teams we were planning to wager on, and then getting their own action down. The trouble was that the detectives were betting too much money too soon. Plus, they didn't have the resources to wait until game time and then spread their bets around. Of course, these fellows didn't have the wherewithal to drastically shift the lines, but they were obviously telling all their family and friends about the sure things I was into. The result was that the lines were changing before I could get my own action down. On several occasions, this shift in spreads cost me a lot of money. One time, I was so furious that I dialed Hacken's number but spoke directly to the detectives: 'Listen, you sons of bitches. I'm giving you fellows valuable information and you don't know how to handle it. Keep the information to yourselves and don't make your bet until just before game time. Don't you know anything about how this business works? How dumb can you be? You fellows are cutting my throat. You better wise up or your source of information is going to dry up in a big hurry. Talk about killing the golden goose!'

"When the situation didn't change, I felt I had to do something drastic. North Carolina State was playing LaSalle in Philadelphia and I decided to fix one last game to teach those dumb cops a lesson they'd not soon forget. Bobby Kraw had control of three players on North Carolina State—Stan Niewierowski, Anton

Muehlbauer, and Don Gallagher—and also Ed Bowler on LaSalle. What I did was to warn Joe Hacken beforehand that I was going to pull a fast one, then I called him up from my home phone knowing that the cops were listening in. 'Joe,' I said, just bursting with enthusiasm, 'we've got an all-time lock on this game! We've got three players on North Carolina State, one on LaSalle, and also one of the officials. The early line has LaSalle favored by four, but we're going to the bank on North Carolina State. This looks like a triple bet, Joe. We can't lose. This is going to be our biggest score ever!'

"We hadn't spoken to any of our backers, but before we knew it, the cops' money had moved the game to pick 'em. So Joe and I arranged with Kraw to have his North Carolina players take a dive. In fact, our instructions to all parties was to keep the game as close as possible until the very end. And then we started betting heavily on LaSalle. It was LaSalle, LaSalle, LaSalle with every New York bookie who'd take our action. We wound up getting about twenty-five thousand down on LaSalle. Only then did we sell the game to Dave Goldberg, who happened to be in New York at the time. Naturally, he was worried about the way the line was fluctuating, but when I told him it was all natural action he calmed down.

"So we all took the train down to Philly to watch the show. Me, Goldberg, and Joe Hacken traveled together, and Joe Green went by himself.

"I recognized a handful of plainclothes cops from New York in the crowd. I found out later that one of them raised his betting money by taking a second mortgage on his house. As the game started, I was more interested in watching the expressions on the cops' faces than on following the play. I felt like I was a general in charge of a huge military campaign. What a thrill."

The score was tied at thirty-all at the half, and it remained tight until LaSalle put on a surge with about five minutes to go in the game. "LaSalle won the game by fifteen and everybody won their bets except the cops. After the game, a detective came up to me, gave me a dirty look, and then walked away. I'd say this game was the most enjoyable fix of my entire career."

Like Adelaide and Nathan Detroit in *Guys and Dolls*, Ellen and Molinas spent much of their vacation time at various racetracks. "I saw every flat track along the eastern coast," said Ellen, "from Rockingham Park to Hialeah. When we were down in Florida we also went to the dog tracks. Jack would bet on anything that moved. He also liked the trotters because he said it was easy to fix the races. At Roosevelt Raceway Jack would be invited to sit in George Raft's private box. Jack was very impressed with how slick Raft was."

Ellen herself was impressed by how easily Molinas ignored the gathering storm clouds. "Indictment or no," she said, "he still focused on what I considered to be trivial things, like amassing the largest collection of basketball trophies in the history of Western civilization. After one particular tournament, the awards were distributed in Small's Paradise, a famous nightclub in Harlem. We were the only white people there and I felt scared and terribly out of place. But Jack loved it, especially the loud cheering that broke out when he went up to the dais to receive his latest trophy."

And even though Molinas had sworn his undying love for her, Ellen knew he continued dating other women: "Jack used to say that I should get the Dick Tracy award because I was always able to find out what he was up to. And believe me, it was surprisingly easy to do. 'Jack,' I'd say, 'who was that girl my brother saw you with last night?' Then he'd get all flustered and say, 'Where did he see me?'"

On March 16, Molinas flew down to Washington, D.C., to deliver a speech at a Touchdown Club dinner. "I recognized one of Hogan's detectives on the same flight," Molinas said later, "and I saw him again sitting in the audience taking notes while I was speaking. I'd agreed to make the speech earlier in the year and the topic I'd selected was 'The Integrity of College Basketball.' My main point was that just because there are a couple of bad apples in the barrel doesn't mean that every apple is bad. In spite of all the scandals and rumors of scandals, college basketball was basically an honest game."

Molinas was finally arrested two months later on Thursday, May 18, on five counts—three bribery charges stemming from Billy Reed's testimony of rigged Bowling Green games (against DePaul on December 10, 1959, Bradley on December 12, 1959 and Canisius on December 3, 1960), as well as two counts of "attempted subornation of perjury and conspiracy to fix twenty-five other games involving twenty-two players from twelve colleges." Hogan further informed the media that the perjury charge was a result of "Molinas's alleged effort to induce Reed to lie before the grand jury." Hogan emphasized that because of his cooperation Reed was not arrested and would not be charged with any crime.

Other players were named but likewise granted immunity: Thomas Falantano from Bowling Green; Gary Kaufman and Leroy Wright from College (now University) of the Pacific; Sal Vergopia and Lenny Whelan from Niagara; Lenny Kaplan from Alabama; Don Gallagher, Stan Niewierowski, and Anton Muehlbauer from North Carolina State; Richie Hoffman, Mike Callahan, Robert Franz, and Larry Dial of South Carolina. Most but certainly not all of the fixers.

The indictment also named ten coconspirators: Joe Hacken, Aaron Wagman, and Joe Green; Frank Cardone and Morris Heyison, who were described as "Pittsburgh gamblers"; David Goldberg and Steve Likos from St. Louis; Lefty Rosenthal from Chicago. Other persons named as coconspirators "because of financial interests" in the deals were: Anthony DiChiantini, alias Tony Dicci, alias Tony Dee, "an ex-convict from Chicago"; Ralph Gigante, "a brother of Vincent (the Chin) Gigante, who was acquitted some time ago of a charge of shooting underworld kingpin Frank Costello." Hogan was "highly pleased" with the fruits of his office's lengthy investigation and promised to "keep the ball rolling."

Like Wagman, Hacken and Green were quick to plead guilty and were scheduled to be sentenced on May 24. Molinas retained a woman, Frances Kahn, as counsel, pleaded not guilty before General Sessions Judge Irwin D. Davidson, and was released on five thousand dollars' bail pending trial. If convicted, Molinas faced prison sentences of more than thirty-five years and fines of more than thirty-five thousand dollars. "When this matter is finally resolved," Molinas told United Press International, "my innocence will be fully established."

In truth, Molinas was worried sick. He'd never anticipated that all of the players would be such easy marks for Hogan, nor that Hogan would give them free passes for cooperating. What did Molinas have going for him? An almost inaudible tape recording of Gary Kaufman exonerating him. A signed and notarized statement from Billy Reed also clearing him of any wrongdoing. And his peerless intelligence. In the clutch, Molinas trusted that he'd come up with a winning strategy.

At the same time, he still didn't quite believe that he had done anything wrong. After all, in a hundred years would anybody care if North Carolina State lost a game it should have won? Hey, there were murderers and rapists walking around scot-free. There were Nazi war criminals still at large. Why bother with a gambler who was simply trying to find an edge?

Louis and Betty Molinas were heartbroken—again. They left their telephone off the hook and stayed in the apartment until after dark. Louis even stopped attending services at the small Sephardic Center that he frequented on Sixteenth Street and Cropsey Avenue.

Julie had recently graduated from Illinois and was living at home and teaching science at a local junior high school. Whereas his older brother (even when he was an adult) always tiptoed around their father, Julie had learned to tune out his father's constant carping and found refuge in his room. A year before, Julie had met and fallen in love with a young schoolteacher named Jennie. The trouble was that Jennie was Catholic, and when the young couple began planning their wedding, Louis and Betty strenuously objected. Ellen Sohn remembered Jack siding with his parents and trying to dissuade Julie from marrying a shiksa. But perhaps noting how Jack's life had nose-dived ever since his breakup with Peggy Eisenhower, Louis and Betty eventually accepted Jennie into the family.

Shortly after Molinas was arrested, Julie was granted a job interview at a newly opened junior high school in Uniondale, Long Island. "I realized that Uniondale was a small community," Julie said, "and I wanted everything to be out in the open. So when I arrived in the principal's office for the interview, I reached into my briefcase and took out a copy of the *New York Post* that featured a screaming back-page headline of my brother's arrest, complete with a picture of him. 'That's my brother,' I said to the principal. He studied the picture for a moment, then said, 'I'm hiring you, not your brother.' And I wound up teaching in the Uniondale school district for over thirty years, most of them on the high school level."

It was Ellen's father, Louis Sohn, who put up Molinas's bail. "I didn't want him to do it," Ellen said, "because I knew by then that Jack had absolutely no conscience. I certainly didn't love him anymore. But like the masochist that I was, I kept thinking that somehow things would get better. My father, though, really believed that Jack was innocent."

In late June, Molinas agreed to be interviewed by Jimmy Breslin for an article in *Sport* magazine. Stoutly maintaining that he was being tried in the press and found guilty by "innuendo," Molinas scoffed at the charges as set forth in the indictment:

> "Everything I did they tried to make something big out of. They brought one kid into the district attorney's office who used to play for Louisville. What's his name now? Mantel, that's right. Red Mantel. Well, they say, 'Did Molinas ever buy you anything?' He says yes. They jump off their chairs. 'What?' they say. He tells them, 'After a game we went out and he bought me a soda.'
>
> "I was always around playing ball. After the games we'd go out and get a sandwich someplace. Well, who is going to pay, some 19-year-old kid? I'd pay. What would it cost, three, four dollars? Now, I'm through with that. The other night I'm playing in the schoolyard at Grover Cleveland High School and they say that this little fellow who used to play for George Washington, Jon Feldman, that's it, well, he wanted to meet me. I said, 'Please, don't introduce me to anybody anymore.' From now on, I just go home after the game. I won't even buy a soda."

Breslin was one of the few writers who reserved judgment: "We'll wait until the final returns on this thing come through. There may be more names to use before this thing ends. And there is also an awful lot of blame to pass around. We're going to try and place it where it belongs."

Just as they had done in the wake of the scandals of 1951, the NCAA, several individual conferences, and many colleges announced that they were taking salutary steps to make sure undergraduate basketball would regain its lost virginity: The NCAA tightened transfer rules, eliminated organized summer basketball leagues, and recommended on-campus sites of games whenever possible. There was also considerable support for the NCAA to unilaterally institute a minimum academic grade average for intercollegiate eligibility. The Eastern

College Athletic Conference tightened every rule on its books. The Western Conference upgraded its academic standards. The University of North Carolina and North Carolina State both curtailed their respective schedules, abolishing the Dixie Classic tourney in Raleigh, restricted the number of players who could be recruited from outside Atlantic Coast Conference territory to two a year, and barred summer-league competition. Dayton reduced its freshman schedule from forty-one to fifteen games. Even Madison Square Garden trimmed its college schedule to the traditional Holiday Festival and ten regular-season doubleheaders. Of course, the politicians competed with one another to introduce bills that would make fixing ball games a federal offense.

But the general consensus seemed to be that most of the guilty ballplayers should never have been in college to begin with. The latest panacea was more effective screening procedures that would deny college admission to academically unqualified athletes. Coaches, athletic directors, alumni groups, and booster clubs all washed their hands. The most convenient villains were the admissions officers.

On the morning of October 4, Joe Green made a telephone call to Assistant District Attorney Pete Andreolli, to say "I'm no good to anyone" and to announce that he'd just swallowed a bottle of sleeping pills. While Andreolli kept Green on the phone, the call was traced to a Manhattan drugstore and two detectives were sent to bring Green into custody. Green was taken to Andreolli's office, where he proceeded to take a razor blade from his pocket and severely slash his left wrist. Green's bail was revoked and he was remanded to a prison hospital in the Tombs. Andreolli expressed his disappointment, not because of Green's pain and obvious psychological distress, but because the attempted suicide might hinder the DA's plans to use Green as a star witness in Molinas's trial, which was scheduled to begin in six days.

Molinas bounced from one lawyer to another, searching for someone who could devise an airtight defense of the indefensible. In late August, Molinas finally landed in the law office of Jacob Evseroff. Even though he told Molinas that "the prosecution has a blockbuster case," judgment day was nigh and Evseroff was hired. At one time, Evseroff considered himself to be "a great basketball fan" who'd watch two or three ball games every week at Madison Square Garden, but who lost his interest in the game after the scandals in 1951. Evseroff was not intimidated by his famous client. "I don't treat Mister Molinas as I would an ordinary client," said Evseroff. "He's a lawyer and I consult with him and I respect his opinion. But I'm the captain of the ship. If we have a disagreement, I make the decision and we sink or swim by that decision."

The rackets bureau had the reputation of doing their homework, and if they went to the trouble of securing an indictment, the defendants usually conceded defeat and made the best deal possible. Molinas was the only person indicted in the case who chose to stand trial, but at least in the beginning of their relationship, Evseroff believed his client's avowals of innocence. When pressed, Molinas named Bobby Kraw as the principal force behind all of the fixes.

After the usual delays, the jury selection began on October 30, on the thirteenth floor of the criminal court building. The presiding officer was Supreme Court Justice Joseph Sarafite, a soft-spoken, silver-haired man, who'd spent ten years as Hogan's right-hand man. Of all the judges available, Sarafite was considered the most pro-prosecution, and his sentences were the most severe.

Assistant DA Peter Andreolli was in charge of the prosecution—a plodder, with a colorless courtroom presence, who nevertheless had been working on the case for two years and had an encyclopedic command of the evidence. Andreolli questioned each prospective juror on their feelings about "eavesdrop evidence." However, Judge Sarafite said that he had not yet determined if a series of wire and tape-recorded conversations proposed by Andreolli as the backbone of the prosecution's case would be admissible evidence. The jury that was finally selected was composed of eight men and four women.

From the very beginning of the proceedings, Molinas's discomfort was evident. Unable to fit his lanky legs comfortably under the counsel table, he sat at an angle and nervously drummed his fingers on the tabletop. From time to time, he hunched forward and scribbled notes on a yellow foolscap pad. But there was still some of that crazy chutzpah in him, too. On the very first day of the trial, Molinas sidled up next to District Attorney Hogan and said, "I'll bet you ten thousand dollars that you won't convict me."

Before the trial commenced, Molinas was offered a deal—admit that he'd masterminded several fixes in exchange for having his license to practice law revoked and serving a six months' sentence. Molinas refused.

In his two-and-a-half-hour opening statement on the morning of November 1, Andreolli recited a catalog of what the people would prove. He further charged that Molinas had tried "to frighten off prospective witnesses from testifying against him."

Defense attorney Evseroff delivered a much briefer and more impassioned speech. In his fifteen-minute address he said the defense would prove that this was a case of nothing more than guilt by association. He called Wagman, Green, and Hacken "parasites" who used their friendship with Molinas to contact college basketball players who could be bribed. Evseroff said the witnesses against Molinas would be "crooks, thieves, and corrupt college kids who would say anything to save their own skins."

The prosecution's initial witness, Aaron Wagman, had already been convicted in Florida of attempting to bribe a football player. He'd been sentenced to five to ten years and was out pending appeal. Wagman's deal with Hogan's office specified a suspended sentence of three to five years only if Molinas was found guilty. Wagman was on the witness stand for seven full days and seemed to be enjoying himself immensely—eagerly describing the several meetings at the Fifty-seventh Street Cafeteria, at Bickford's on Fordham Road, and at several candy stores and luncheonettes all over the city. Consulting notes and several NCAA yearbooks, Wagman enumerated all the hows and wherefores of the ball games he and Molinas had "worked" together. Wagman lied when he claimed that he'd "made about ten thousand dollars" fixing games in the 1959–60 and 1960–61 seasons. "But I didn't come out ahead in any year," he said, "because I gambled away what I made."

During his testimony, Wagman also mentioned Joe Hacken's name dozens of times, usually referring to him as Molinas's "errand boy." Suddenly, on the third day of Wagman's testimony, Andreolli paused in his questioning, turned to the rear of the courtroom, pointed his finger at a man about to leave, and asked Wagman: "Is that the man you have been referring to as Hacken?"

A sorry figure in a worn red lumber jacket, Hacken was ordered to the front of the courtroom and ordered to identify himself for the record. But Molinas never glanced at him.

Later, during the luncheon recess, Molinas and Evseroff were conferring in the courthouse lobby when Hacken walked over. Molinas waved his friend away, saying, "It wouldn't look good for the jurors to see us talking."

Hacken sighed and said, "Nobody wants to be seen talking to me anymore."

In his cross-examination, Evseroff asked Wagman when he'd first heard about fixing games. "I heard it in the neighborhood," Wagman answered.

"From whom?" was Evseroff's next question.

"From Molinas."

Evseroff hammered at Wagman for three days without finding a loophole in his testimony.

Andreolli next called on Billy Reed, who had recently joined the army. Reed was flustered and nervous, but he impressed the jury by appearing on the witness stand wearing his military uniform. His mumbled words were barely audible as he also cited dates and payments for fixed ball games. The prosecution then moved to support Reed's testimony by playing the incriminating tape.

In his fascinating account of several influential modern-day trials, *What the Hell Is Justice?*, Paul Hoffman summarized the controversy over the tapes:

> Only by playing and replaying the tapes for hours were two detectives, assisted by Reed and armed with a knowledge of the subject under discussion, able to piece together what was said and provide a transcript for the jury to follow.
>
> Evseroff protested that the transcript was merely one man's or two men's version of what was actually on the tapes. He had his secretary, Maxene Richter, listen to the tapes when they were played in court, transcribe what she heard and offer her version for the jury's consideration. It was part of his effort to show that the tapes were unintelligible, but Justice Sarafite barred it.
>
> After three days of legal wrangling, the 42-minute tape was played to a jury armed with the detectives' transcript.

Evseroff, however, scored a three-point play when he produced the statement that Reed had signed in Molinas's law office. In the paper as read to the jury, Reed contradicted his own sworn testimony by stating that he never had accepted money or the promise of money from Molinas or anyone else "not to do my best in any athletic contest in which I participated." The statement also claimed that various sums that Molinas paid to Reed were, in fact, loans. Carl Harten testified that he had notarized Reed's signature on the statement, and Molinas's other law partner, Richard Tolchin, testified that he had witnessed the signing. Reed's version was that he had signed the statement without reading it, had signed a carbon copy, and didn't recall having his signature notarized. Justice Sarafite ruled that the jury would have to decide for themselves whether the statement was actually an affidavit.

Next up were Gary Kaufman, Leroy Wright, and Lenny Kaplan, who recounted the specifics of proposals, rigged games, and payoffs. Andreolli also played the tape that had been made during Molinas's visit to Kaufman's home. Molinas's warning Kaufman not to implicate him or his backers under threat of death was, to Andreolli, the coup de grace.

Despite the mounting evidence against his client, Evseroff attempted to show that Molinas, as player-coach of the Hazleton Hawks, was only trying to recruit talent for his Eastern League team. The money that Molinas paid to these and other players were merely "bonuses" to that end.

Andreolli even called Fred Schaus to the stand to testify that Molinas's performance with the Fort Wayne Pistons had been inconsistent to the point of being suspicious. Evseroff reduced Schaus's complaints to sour grapes when he brought out that Molinas's outstanding play had, in fact, caused the Pistons to cut Schaus.

The prosecution finally rested on November 29, after presenting thirty witnesses and sixty-two exhibits (including three tape recordings of conversations between Molinas and players he allegedly bribed).

After a brief adjournment, Evseroff initiated Molinas's defense by questioning ten character witnesses in less than an hour. Among these were Carl Green, who played with Molinas in Williamsport, and Louis Sohn, who said, "I'd be proud to have Jack as a son-in-law." Zeke Sinicola appeared as a substantive witness—testifying that he'd been in Molinas's car on December 21, 1957, en route to an Eastern League game during a snowstorm, thereby contradicting Wagman's claim that on that same date Molinas was in a New York hotel room plotting a bribe scheme. (Andreolli countered by producing a Pennsylvania weather report showing no snow that day.) Private Detective George Palosik was called to the stand and testified as to the accuracy of a transcript made of the largely inaudible recording of the conversation between Molinas and Kaplan in the restaurant in Baltimore in which Kaplan denied any shady dealings.

By the fifth week, attendance had dwindled to the ever present Ellen Sohn, Louis and Betty Molinas, as well as a dozen law students and bored senior citizens. Stan Isaacs of the *New York Post* wrote that the trial should be attended by "college presidents, the parents of all the future basketball players and all those who have contributed to the atmosphere which has produced the revelations in the courtroom."

During the trial, Molinas continued practicing law and betting on football games. "I recall going over to Jack's house over the weekends to discuss our strategy," Evseroff said, "and he had three different TV sets tuned to three different football games. My impression was that Jack was still a heavy gambler."

Edwin Torres, who knew Molinas at Stuyvesant High and later at Brooklyn Law School, happened to see his one-time classmate during a break in the trial. "I was a lawyer myself in those days," said Torres, "and I had a lot of business in the courthouse. One day, I saw Pete Andreolli and his entourage of lawyers and clerks come walking down the corridor, headed for the courtroom. Jack was standing there with his big shoulders flexed and talking to Evseroff. When Jack saw Andreolli, he dashed over to grab the front door. Then he made a deep bow as he pulled the door open, and he swept Andreolli into the courtroom with his arm extended. Always the grand gesture for Jack."

On November 30, the trial was unexpectedly recessed when Judge Sarafite suffered a kidney ailment and had to be hospitalized . The jury was sent home for three weeks and only called back to witness several minor arguments and proceedings that took place before various substitute judges.

On December 6, Molinas appeared in the "cafeteria court" on the first floor of the criminal courts building to settle a traffic ticket he'd been issued for a parking meter violation. After paying a five-dollar fine, he lit a cigar and reached for a reporter's newspaper. "I want to see what happened in North Carolina," Molinas said. He was referring to the trial of Dave Goldberg and Steve Lekemetros, who'd been charged with bribing four North Carolina State players. "They were found guilty," said the reporter, "and their sentencing is tomorrow."

"They sure do things fast down there," Molinas said. "I hope my jury doesn't read about this case."

The following day, Judge Herman Clark of Raleigh, North Carolina, sentenced Goldberg and Lekemetros each to five years in prison and fined them a total of thirty thousand dollars.

Molinas's trial was resumed on January 3, 1963, and Evseroff argued that the lengthy time during which the jurors were sent home legally constituted a dismissal of the jury. Even though Justice Sarafite denied Evseroff's motion for a mistrial, Molinas was convinced that the long delay would constitute legitimate grounds for appeal should the verdict go against him.

"I had lunch with Jack and his father every day," said Ellen Sohn, "and Jack never said a word to either of us. No bragging. No bluster. But also no sign that he was afraid of anything."

During one short recess, a detective named Irving Benson came over to Molinas and said, "You're supposed to be so smart, Jack, but we were following you all the time and you never even suspected anything."

Jack just laughed in his face and said, "Oh, yeah? Do you happen to remember a ten-cent tip you got one Saturday night in Bernie's Diner?"

With that, Benson scowled and walked away in a huff.

"The only way I can win this case," Evseroff was heard to say during another intermission, "is for the defendant to get on the stand and lie his head off." Indeed, the press was informed that Molinas would take the stand in his own defense, but he backed out at the last moment. "I believe we would have won the case," Evseroff said, "had Jack testified. I thought that the tapes of him and Reed could have been attacked and shown to be ambivalent. Also that Wagman was clearly an unreliable witness whom I'd easily discredited. But Jack said that he had too much information buzzing around in his head and was afraid of making mistakes under cross-examination. That was the only time I ever saw Jack lose his nerve."

In his six-hour closing argument, Andreolli presented Molinas as a money-hungry, conniving gambler who used his law practice as a means for furthering his evil motives. Andreolli presented letters, documents, and hotel bills placing Molinas in various cities from Tuscaloosa, Alabama, to Bowling Green, Ohio, for the express purpose of paying off players for their parts in a fix. "The law is a noble profession," said Andreolli, "but that doesn't make every lawyer an honest man." Throughout Andreolli's presentation, Molinas never changed the fixed expression on his face—not even when the prosecution referred to him as a "goon."

Molinas's law school classmate, Robert Ellis, was irate at Andreolli's closing argument. "Andreolli was a self-righteous and highly vindictive man," said Ellis. "His version of events was that Jack went into the playgrounds and school yards and corrupted these young men, when the truth was that most of them came looking for Jack. I've always felt that Jack was victimized by a backlash from the scandals of 1951."

Evseroff suggested that Molinas himself deliver the defense's summation. "I thought it would be very, very effective for him to speak in his own behalf," said Evseroff, "and advance the arguments I had prepared without the district attorney having the opportunity to cross-examine him. But Molinas didn't want to do it. I think he was afraid to do it. I think he was so emotionally involved that he couldn't handle it." And in his closing argument, Evseroff painted a picture of Molinas as a victim of everybody else's greed.

The case went to the jury on January 7 and the verdict was reached in eight hours. Guilty as charged on all counts.

Several of Molinas's law school buddies were aghast at the verdict. Under present-day practice, Hogan's wiretaps and entrapment tactics would force a judge to direct the jury to find the defendant not guilty. And there was a persistent rumor that U.S. Attorney General Bobby Kennedy was directly involved in the outcome, wanting to make sure that Molinas would serve as a negative example to anyone who tried to corrupt the youth of America.

In the corridor outside the courtroom, Molinas cornered Nat Laurendi, one of the detectives who'd lost a bundle on the North Carolina State–LaSalle game. "It doesn't matter that I'm going to do time," Molinas boasted, "because I'm going to be okay, anyway. And you can bet on it!"

In the four weeks between the verdict and the sentencing, Molinas frantically conferred with Evseroff and his partner, Bill Sonenshine, to determine the strategy for filing an appeal. They quickly decided to focus on Sarafite's illness and argue that the trial should have terminated rather than allowed to lapse. As ever, Molinas was confident that a mistrial would be declared and he'd have another chance to beat the rap. Next time, he would follow Evseroff's advice, take the stand, and lie like a rug.

Molinas was also optimistic about the expected sentence. Hacken had drawn seven and one half to eight years; Green (who was currently under psychiatric observation) would get six to seven; and Wagman, three to five suspended, since he was already serving his five-year sentence in Florida. The most severe sentence Sarafite could impose would be thirty-five years, but Molinas expected that the penalty would be comparable to Hacken's—even less, because of Hacken's previous arrests.

On February 11, Andreolli asked Sarafite to impose the maximum sentence, arguing that "the defendant has not exhibited an iota of change, not a bit of penitence." Evseroff pleaded for leniency. Then Jack Molinas stood while Justice Sarafite rendered his decision: "In my opinion, you are a completely amoral person. You are the prime mover of the conspiracy, and you were the person most responsible. You callously used your prestige as a former All-American basketball player to corrupt college basketball players and defraud the public. It is also unfortunate that you were ever admitted to the bar because you have perverted your office as an attorney. You were sworn to uphold the law but you sought to hinder and impede the district attorney's investigation. I concur with the verdict because the evidence in the trial left the jury no choice but to find you guilty as charged."

Jack remembered what happened next: "In my heart I really anticipated a sentence of about two years. After all, I was an educated man, a lawyer, and my so-called crimes hadn't hurt anybody except some bettors and some bookies. Ten years before, Salvatore Sollazzo had only gotten three to six and that was considered to be a really long sentence.

"Then the judge said that since the conspiracy charge was a misdemeanor, there'd be no penalty, but I had expected as much. For bribing Reed, the judge sentenced me to five to seven and a half years in a state prison. I was stunned, but he wasn't finished. For the subornation of perjury charge, the judge said the same thing—five to seven and a half years. Then instead of saying 'concurrent,' he used the word 'consecutive.' I thought I was hearing things. I couldn't really believe that he'd said consecutive. For the first time in my life, I was a little unsure about what I had heard. My total sentence was ten to fifteen years in prison! The judge went on to say that the first time I'd be eligible for parole would be two-thirds of the way into the minimum sentence, which would be six years and eight months, but I barely heard him. All I could think of was that he'd said 'consecutive' instead of 'concurrent.' Or did he? Fifteen years behind bars! The most severe penalty ever imposed in New York for a crime of this nature!"

There was an audible gasp from the gallery, but everybody was impressed by Molinas's reaction—standing impassively and not even blinking.

"The sentence," said Justice Sarafite, "is to begin immediately." Then, with blind Justice looking on, Molinas was abruptly handcuffed and led away by two armed guards.

What follows below, with a few interruptions, is the prison narrative of Jack Molinas.

"The Tombs was the largest detention prison in the world and prisoners were held there pending trial or shipment to a state prison. It's a maze of bars and screens and locks. The keys were six inches long and looked like lethal weapons. Everything was through a locked door and every guard had a key. I walked ten feet and there's another guard unlocking another door. Another ten feet brought me to still another guard unlocking another door. The word of my sentence had preceded me and all of the guards thought it was too high and expressed their sympathies. Moving from section to section, I got processed, fingerprinted, and showered. But I remained in a state of shock. I remember long narrow corridors, about ten feet wide and eighty feet long, with cells lined up on both sides. Some of the prisoners were shouting at me, asking what my sentence was. 'What's your bit?' is how they phrased the question. 'What's your bit?' Those who were awaiting their own sentence wanted to discover what kind of mood the judge was in that day. Then one of the inmates yelled down the corridor, 'He got five to seven and a half wild!' 'Wild' was a term meaning consecutive sentences. So in addition to all my other woes, I had to learn a new language.

"Fifteen years! Fifteen years!

"They put me in a cell, slammed the door, and locked it. There was a cot, a chair, a sink, and a toilet. My new house. Since it was around midday, I was also handed my lunch on a tray—one piece of baloney between two slices of white bread, and a plastic cup of very weak tea. This is my new life, I thought. No more steaks. Just baloney sandwiches for fifteen years.

"I stayed awake that first night, sitting on my bed and staring at the walls. I found out later that I was the subject of a suicide watch, but I wasn't at all aware of the guards' constant presence outside my cell.

"What was I doing there? Here's the Ivy League boy wonder with all his possessions taken away, sitting in a jail cell, staring at the bare walls, looking forward to fifteen years of this. Fifteen years was an eternity. I'd be forty-six when I got out. I couldn't believe the severity of the sentence. Fifteen long, slow, agonizing years. Why did the judge think he had to make an example of me? I cried, I moaned, I suffered. It was too painful to think about what my family was going through. I couldn't even think about the possibility of parole. Fifteen years. Had I cooperated with the DA I'd have gotten only six months.

"I couldn't squeeze myself between the bars. I didn't have a key to unlock the door. This was it. Even though I was in shock, I began to make up my mind that the only thing I could do was to adapt to my new life. Aside from trying to kill myself, adapting was the only option I had. The only viable option. I'd simply have to make the best of it, of the next fifteen years! By the next morning, I knew that I was going to survive. And not only survive, but find some way to beat the system."

While Molinas was coming to terms with the rest of his life, Martin Keene wrote this in the *Brooklyn Daily*:

> Molinas is a product of the civilization that produces Cadillacs and B-Girls and the summer house in Westport. He knows that money can buy these things because our culture tells us that these are what makes a man count. He is a resident of a world that has surrendered to all that is weak and egocentric in man, and forgotten the meaning of self-discipline and self-control.
>
> Molinas is a lot of people named Jack, and the difference between him and a great many others is only opportunity.

Dave Budin received a suspended sentence. According to Andreolli, "This defendant's involvement stems from the fact that he's an inveterate gambler. It's almost a disease with him." Andreolli also noted that Budin cooperated "one hundred percent." Phillip LaCourt, described as "a professional gambler from Boston who helped finance the ring," was sentenced to two to five years. Charles Tucker, "a minor figure," also received a suspended sentence.

Louis Brown, Jerry Vogel, and Dan Quindazi were sitting on a bench outside the courtroom waiting for their lawyers to finish up some details relating to the suspended sentences and lengthy probation they had each received.

"What do we do now?" Brown asked Vogel.

"I don't know," said Vogel. "Shoot ourselves, I guess."

"I was still awake when a gong sounded at six o'clock in the morning and after a few minutes a guard brought me breakfast: some bitter dark-brown liquid that was supposed to be coffee, two slices of white bread, and a little plastic cup of jelly. Then an announcement was made over the loudspeaker about which prisoners were going to be shipped to Sing Sing that day. My name was called and another guard slipped a brown paper bag into my cell just before the voice on the loudspeaker told us to put all our belongings in the bag. All I had was my toothpaste, toothbrush, and a change of underwear.

"Then I was escorted into a room where I was stripped naked and searched. They looked in my hair, in my ears, my nose, my mouth, they spread my cheeks and looked up my anus. They looked into every crevice in my body where I could possibly hide something. Then at about seven-thirty, I was loaded into a big department of corrections bus with bars on the windows and a metal gate separating the inmates from the driver and two armed officers.

"There were about thirty of us there and the trip up north to Ossining took about an hour and a half. For a while, nobody spoke. We had to make a stop at the Bronx County Court on One hundred and sixty first Street right off the Grand Concourse to pick up a few more inmates. And I was sitting in the rear of the bus where I could look out the back window as we passed my old neighborhood. There was Pete's Pool Room. The Creston school yard was just down that hill. The memories were very painful as my past floated away. Now I had to look forward to living in a hellhole where I felt I didn't belong. I pretended to wipe my nose with my sleeve so that none of the other guys could see the tear leaking down my face.

"Then everybody suddenly got lively and the questions started flying: What's your bit? Has anybody ever been to Sing Sing before? What's it like? How's the food? The old-time cons were the centers of attraction. They said that Sing Sing was a 'reception center,' which meant everybody sentenced to a state prison in the metropolitan area had to go to Sing Sing first. Once there, the prisoners would be classified according to the crime and their personal background and then either shipped to another institution or kept at Sing Sing. Most of my fellow cons knew who I was, and I asked one of the old-timers if he thought I'd be staying at Sing Sing.

"'You're a basketball player,' he said, 'and there's always outside teams coming in to play the Sing Sing varsity. That means you're a lock to stay there.'

"The old-timers also said that Sing Sing was one of the oldest institutions in the state, that it was very spacious, and had a good athletic program. They promised that we'd all be eating at lot better there than we had in the Tombs.

"'You're in the big time now,' one experienced con told me. 'What a hell of a way to make the big leagues.'

"'Don't get disheartened, kid,' another veteran said to me. 'It's just another way of life and you'll soon get used to it. You're big and strong and you have a good head on your shoulders so you should have no trouble.'

"Some of the other guys obviously knew that I was a lawyer, so they pestered me with questions about their cases. About writs and appeals and a hundred different possibilities for them to regain their freedom.

"In between all the talking I was wondering what kind of life I could have in prison. Will I read a lot? Will I play sports? How will I kill so much time? I was certainly more than a little scared because I didn't know which way my life would turn. My future was full of surprises—all of them unpleasant. But I guess I felt more despair than fear.

"Finally we got in sight of my new home. It was situated high on a hill and overlooking the Hudson River. As we got closer all I could see was a big stone wall and huge gates. Then I saw the turrets on top of the walls and the machine guns mounted on the turrets. And there were armed guards everywhere I looked. It looked like a fortress.

"The bus pulled up and it seemed like there were a thousand eyes watching me as my left wrist was manacled to the right wrist of another prisoner. He was a short little fellow named Jim, who'd held up a drugstore with a shotgun. The guards were carrying rifles and they looked like they would've been happy to shoot one of us. I half-expected someone to appear with a whip and start whipping us. It felt like I was entering Devil's Island. And we walked in columns of two into one of the buildings.

"We were led into a reception area where we were seated in folding chairs. After a while, we were issued our 'prison grays,' which consisted of dark gray pants and shirt, gray socks, gray underwear, a gray jacket that fastened with clips instead of buttons or a zipper, and a round gray cap with a short brim. The shoes were very unusual—wide and circular at the toes so that it was just about impossible to walk faster than a quick shuffle. Then we were instructed to shave because we had to have our pictures taken—we were given one razor blade for about twelve inmates and instead of shaving cream, we had a small bar of soap. The guards watched every move we made. After our pictures were snapped we were taken to our cells. We were locked inside, but there were trustees who seemed to have free run of the corridors. The next thing I knew, I had a visitor, a guy who said he'd played ball with me in one of the Haverstraw tournaments. He gave me some toothpaste and a bar of some sweet-smelling soap. He came back later with a jug of coffee and a ham sandwich. 'I hope you'll feel better,' he said before he left for good. I don't remember his name and I certainly didn't remember playing against him, either.

"All of the new inmates had been placed in an isolation area where we weren't allowed to have any contact with the general population. For the next two weeks, we were scheduled to go through an extensive testing routine. We took IQ tests, also tests to measure our skills in physics, math, and reading comprehension. We were given physical examinations by a doctor and psychological exams by a psychiatrist. Most inmates have no profession except forgery or lock-picking or whatever their criminal expertise might be, so they also gave us aptitude tests with the aim of trying to teach the new cons some sort of trade.

"While I was still in isolation, several other trustees also visited my cell. A few of these fellows were onetime Mafiosos who were running a bookmaking operation. They befriended me and gave me other toiletries that I lacked, also underwear and socks. And they'd always ask me who I liked in upcoming basketball games. 'I like Texas Tech plus five points against SMU,' I'd say, and they were impressed with the accuracy of my handicapping. But this particular group also had a very effective gimmick.

"It was all based on the fact that prisoners were allowed to raise homing pigeons, and also to give them as gifts to members of their families. So, when a wife or a child came for a visit, they would take home a pigeon in a cage. Then the wife, say, would be instructed to contact the local bookmaker, get the line on Saturday night's games, and find out about any injuries that went with the hot games. This information would then be written on a little sheet of paper and attached to the pigeon's leg. Then the pigeon would be thrown in the air. And sure enough, it would return to its cage in Sing Sing, where the guards would inspect it for contraband. And presto! These bookies behind bars would have point spreads to work with.

"All the inmates had to listen to the same radio station and which one it would be was strictly at the discretion of a controller in the radio tower. This guy was also an inmate and he was free to chose a news station or a rock-and-roll station or a ball game. One night, a pigeon returned with the news that San Francisco was an eleven-point favorite over the Knicks but that their star player, Wilt Chamberlain, would be out with an injury. Everybody in the joint bet against San Francisco and the controller was pressured to play the station that carried the Knick game. The unit of betting was a carton of cigarettes, which was worth about two dollars and fifty cents in trade. Considering that the cons worked in the prison laundry or kitchen or whatever and earned only ten cents a day, a carton of cigarettes represented a lot of money.

"These particular bookies also used the homing pigeons to get the scores of games that the other bookies wouldn't get until the news broadcasts that evening. Which was an enormous, can't-lose advantage.

"I got another visitor at my isolation cell who recruited me for the Sing Sing basketball team. They had a beautiful indoor gym that was as good as any of the courts the pros played on. Even though I was in 'protection' for two weeks it was possible for me to get permission to play with the team on Sundays. 'Don't worry, Jack,' the guy said. 'I'm sure the athletic director will take care of it because you're such a good player.' The next day he showed up to say everything was all set. I was being released on Sunday to play against some outside team. He even brought me a pair of sneakers and a white T-shirt that said SING SING in black letters. I was psyched to play ball again.

"But at five o'clock on the following Friday morning, a guard stopped by my cell to tell me that I'd just been 'boated out to Attica.' I was totally dismayed. I had only been in Sing Sing for eight days and I'd believed all the old-timers on the bus when they said I'd be there for the duration. Even from my isolation situation, I could sense that Sing Sing would have been an okay experience for me. The word was that Attica was for the most hardened criminals, killers and rapists, certainly not for guys like me. But I had to return the sneakers and the T-shirt and pack up my belongings.

"When it was time to go, my wrists were manacled and leg irons were fastened around my right ankle, then one wrist and the ankle were connected with chains to another con—a fellow who was about five foot six and had killed a cop with a rifle. The two of us had to move very slowly and in perfect tandem to avoid injury. With my free hand, I had to carry a brown box secured with a string that held my personal belongings. In addition to the two guards, there were two other cons making the trip—another murderer and also a fellow who specialized in armed robberies. It was Washington's Birthday and the weather was freezing cold—maybe five degrees—and we were taken by car to the Ossining train station. We were escorted by one police car riding in front of us, and one trailing us.

"The car pulled up to the front of the station and one of the guards jumped out first. He stood there with his handgun held at a forty-five-degree angle to the ground, the safety catch off, and his finger on the trigger while the four cons struggled to extricate ourselves from the car. The station was very crowded with commuters as we were paraded through the central entrance. I felt completely humiliated—unshaven, wearing my prison grays, and shackled like a mad dog. I pulled my cap over my eyes and hoped I wouldn't be recognized by anybody I knew. I felt like crawling into a hole and dying.

"We had to sit down in the main waiting room and wait for our train. There was a little boy nearby about five years old wearing big fur mittens and bouncing a ball up and down on the floor. Suddenly, the ball bounced away from him and came rolling over to where I was sitting. The kid came over to retrieve the ball just as I tried to bend over and pick it up for him. But his mother came running over, grabbed the kid, and pulled him away. And I felt stripped of every last bit of human dignity that I was clinging to.

"When the train finally arrived, we were put in a private car hooked on to the end of the commuter train. We were seated together and our handcuffs were removed while we ate baloney sandwiches for lunch. All of the other fellows had been to Attica before, so I kept firing questions at them: What time do we get up in the morning? How's the food? Will we have a job? What's the daily routine? How tough is the parole board? How strict are the guards? Do the prisoners beat each other up? How hard is the time?

"They told me that Attica was the most severe of all the maximum-security prisons in the state. Attica was reserved for incorrigibles, mostly violent inmates considered to be impossible to rehabilitate. And I wondered why I was being sent there. Because I was considered to be a wiseass lawyer? Because I had cost some cops a lot of money by the way I fixed the North Carolina State–LaSalle game?

"Attica is about thirty miles south of Buffalo and there was snow covering everything that wasn't moving. Again there were two police cars to escort us from the train to the prison, which was only about a five-minute drive. And the place was amazing to see, with gun turrets and barbed wire and revolving spotlights. The walls were two feet thick and twice as high as they were in Sing Sing—towering thirty feet above the ground and, to discourage any prisoners from trying to tunnel their way out, extending another twelve feet below ground level.

"We had to pass through four gates and several metal detectors just to get inside the walls. Our boxes of personal belongings were also inspected four different times. Then we were put into a similar isolation situation as we'd been in Sing Sing. The number that I was given was one that I'll never forget as long as I live—18896. That was who I was. Not Jack Molinas, but number 18896."

The entire complex consisted of eighteen buildings that included the four main housing blocks—A, B, C, and D. Together the four cell blocks enclosed a large open area that was divided by narrow corridors into four separate exercise yards. These corridors intersected at a common point known as "Times Square," and a complex system of manned gates allowed for the sealing off of any cell block within minutes. Each cell block was home to approximately five hundred inmates and each was divided into 12 "cell groups" or "companies."

"What followed was two weeks of the same kind of tests I'd taken in Sing Sing—physical, mental, vocational, et cetera. When I appeared for my interview with the placement board, they asked about my education and previous job experience. They told me that, among the two thousand prisoners incarcerated in Attica, all of the academic and intelligence tests had ranked me in the one hundredth percentile. Then they asked me what type of a job I would like to have. This was an important issue because I could very well be doing the same job for the next fifteen years. So I said that some kind of secretarial or administrative work would suit me fine. They also asked if I'd be willing to teach any of the classes that were offered to the inmates. Sure, I'd love it.

"Two days later, a notice was delivered to my cell informing me what my job would be—a porter in the tailor shop. I would be sweeping and mopping floors for fifteen years! The tailor shop was particularly noteworthy because most of the prison's homosexuals worked there! In other words, I was the smartest prisoner in Attica and I had the lowest, most humiliating job in the entire institution.

"Then I spoke to the fellow in the cell next to mine and he said, 'You've never been in an institution before, Jack, and they're only trying to test you. Just stay cool and do what you're told. They're only fucking you around.'

"The day before I was scheduled to go into the population I was called in to see Deputy Warden Myers. He was a tall, slim German type who reminded me of nothing less than a Nazi. All the minor prison officials wore blue uniforms, but the top brass wore blue pants and white shirts.

"'Jack,' he said, 'as you already know, you've been assigned to the tailor shop and I want you to do a good job there. And I'm giving you one warning, Jack. You're only the second lawyer in the prison population. The other one's name is Burt Pugash. If I ever find out that you're preparing legal writs or giving any kind of legal advice to any of the other prisoners, Jack, then you're going to find yourself in a strip cell.'

"I'd already been told that being sent to a strip cell was the worst punishment that could be meted out to an inmate. It was usually reserved for an inmate who hit an officer, killed another inmate, or started a riot.

"'Yes, sir,' I said. 'I understand, sir.'

"I'd also been informed that I should never talk back to or question any prison official. Doing that would brand me as being 'a wise guy' and that's one of the worst reputations for an inmate to get. There was a certain routine for voicing any discontents—writing a memorandum to my guidance counselor, who would then process it through the proper channels. But writing one of these memos was usually a futile gesture, anyway. So I never even hinted to Myers that I was unhappy with my work assignment.

"So, the next evening after I had dinner in my isolation cell, I was allowed to go into the A Block yard for the first time. I was there for about five minutes when I saw two colored fellows square off for a fight. They were both around six foot two and I found out later that they were both ex–prize fighters—one used to be a professional and the other was a Golden Gloves champion. One of them punched his rival in the face and knocked him out cold, then jumped on top of him and started banging his head hard into the concrete floor. The guy on the bottom was unconscious, his head was split open and bleeding all over the place, while the guy on top had a glazed look in his eyes as if he was half crazy. Without a second thought, I rushed over to the two fighters, put my arm around the guy on top, and said, 'You're the winner, pal. You're the winner.' Then I pulled on his arm to get him off of the guy on the bottom. The winner just walked away without a word, so I called out to a guard to get the loser to a hospital quick, and then I also walked away.

"After another ten minutes I was totally surprised, and even a little scared, when a bunch of fellows came crowding around me and started asking all kinds of legal questions. Could I help this one prepare his appeal? Would I help that one prepare a writ? Until then I didn't understand the implications of the warning Myers had given to me. Should I help these fellows or not? It was a very ticklish situation. If I didn't help them, somebody might get all riled up and I could easily get killed. If I did help them, I could end up in a strip cell. I was kind of overwhelmed by the situation and I didn't know what to do or what to say, when suddenly, somebody came to my rescue.

"It was Joey Gallo, who was serving time for extortion. The crowd around me instantly dispersed when Gallo came over and shook my hand. 'Welcome to Attica, Jack,' he said. 'You remember that eight grand you never paid back to Bunny?'

"Oh, oh. Now I was in worse trouble than ever.

"'I just want to tell you, Jack,' he said with a big laugh, 'that you're the first Jew who ever beat me for money. And I respect that, Jack. I really do.'

"I also think that Gallo was well-disposed to me because when I was booted from the NBA I'd never given up the names of the other NBA dumpers who were doing business with bookies sponsored by the Mafia. Over the years, I got a lot of mileage out of that situation.

"'By the way, Jack,' he continued, 'one of the main rules in here is that you never interfere when two guys are fighting. If you do, you're liable to get your own head bashed in. It's even worse if a white guy interferes with spades, or vice versa. Something like that could trigger a widespread riot.'

"'What do you mean?' I asked. 'The guy on the top was going to kill the other guy.'

'It's none of your goddamn business, Jack. All you'll do is make yourself a mortal enemy. The right thing to do is just turn your back and walk away.'

"'I didn't know.'

"'Don't worry about it, Jack. I'll take care of it. But I hear you're in the tailor shop. C'mon, let me introduce you to the queen bee.'

"Then he walked me around the yard until we found a colored fellow about six foot three and two hundred and thirty pounds. This guy was one of the strongest human beings I'd ever seen. (I later found out that when he was a cab-driver in Brooklyn he'd killed two of his passengers and was doing twenty to life for murder.)

"'Edna,' Gallo said, 'I'd like you to meet my friend Jack. He's going to be working with the girls in the tailor shop and I'd appreciate it if you could look out for him.'

"'*Edna?*'

"'Sure thing, Mister Gallo,' Edna said, and he almost crushed my hand as he shook it.

"After Edna went on his way, Gallo told me not to worry about my work assignment. If I behaved myself, they'd eventually move me to something more appropriate. Then he asked if I had any questions, so I told him about Myers's warning and the crowd of inmates who were seeking legal advice from me. What should I do?

"'Anybody who wants you to do any legal work,' Gallo said, 'you should send them to me. That's one of my many operations in here, Jack.'

"And before we parted, Gallo said to me, 'Who's the boss here, Jack?'

"'You are.'

"That same night, a guard came to my cell. 'You were a witness to a fight in the A Yard this afternoon, right?'

"'Yes, sir. That's right, sir.'

"'Well, the report we got is that one of the guys had a razor and slashed the other guy's face.'

"'No, sir. No, no. It was just a fist fight, sir. There was no knife.'

"And, after that, whenever I found myself too close to even a loud argument I took a powder.

"The next day, however, some guy I never saw before walked up to me in the yard and said, 'Joey Gallo sent me, Jack, and he wants you to come along with me.'

"Of course I had to trust this guy because nobody would dare to use Gallo's name for any kind of a setup. So the guy led me over to the winner of yesterday's fight.

"'Jack,' my guide said, 'this is Paul. Paul, this is Jack. You know, Paul, Jack just got here and he didn't realize what he was doing.'

"Then me and Paul shook hands. 'Never do anything like that again,' Paul said. 'Not to me, not to anybody.' He was very polite and respectful to me. I mean, I hadn't hit him or said anything that was remotely insulting. All I'd done was save the other fellow's life. But it was obvious that Gallo had arranged our little meeting.

"In fact, it turned out that the fight had actually been instigated by Gallo. Both the fighters were friends of Gallo's and were involved in the operation of a betting ring. There was a dispute over the payment of some cigarettes, and Paul was selling the other fellow a ticket. That's prison lingo for making a threat. The other inmate was buying a ticket, which meant he accepted Paul's challenge.

"My address was A Block, Thirty-eighth Company, Cell 36, and it turned out that Company Thirty-eight was comprised of all the 'girls' who worked either in the tailor shop or the kitchen. So the next morning, the alarm woke us at five-thirty and we had to line up in a double column to walk to the mess hall, which was in C Block, about a mile away. We were lined up according to height, so I was at the head of the entire procession. Several guards accompanied us as we walked through the various corridors. Talking on line was strictly forbidden and would be punished by a 'keep lock,' in which you'd be confined to your cell for a period of time. Every few hundred yards or so we'd come to an intersection controlled by guards called 'traffic cops,' who would hold up one line to let another line through.

"As we walked into the mess hall everybody on my line started wiggling their asses in a very suggestive manner. And the inmates already there started calling out, 'Hello, Edna.' 'How are you, Susie.' 'You're looking fine today, Barbara.' And I said to myself, My God, what are these people going to think of me? What do I do if someone makes a pass at me? And the same thing happened after we finished breakfast on our way out. But my embarrassment wore off in a hurry and I decided to have some fun, so when the other girls started wiggling their asses, so did I. Everybody had a good laugh about that.

"There were about forty workers in the tailor shop (about half of them black and half white) and their job was to make clothing for the entire inmate population. Most of them worked the sewing machines or did the handwork, and my job was to constantly sweep up the threads and scraps that fell to the floor. I was doing my work very conscientiously because I wanted to be considered a good worker and promoted to something more suitable.

"At one time or another, just about everybody in the shop made some sort of overture to me. 'What's your real name? Is it Jack or Jacqueline?'

"'When are you gonna be indoctrinated, Jack, and become one of the girls?'

"'Hey, Jack. Would you like to make it with me?'

"'Do you like to sew, Jack? Is there anything else you like to do that girls like to do?'

"'Oh, Jackie, Jackie, we love you.'

"Most of this was done in a laughing, teasing kind of way, but I always gave them straight answers. But no matter how suggestive their come-ons were, it was unthinkable for one inmate to ever touch another without first asking permission. That's because you never know if someone wanted to touch you with a malicious intent, or if someone didn't want to be touched and would react in a violent fashion. Another primary rule was that in the mess hall nobody ever touched somebody else's food or even passed his hand over somebody's food. The fear was, of course, that the food could be poisoned. In prison, people held grudges for years and years over imagined insults, so everybody was very conscious about protecting themselves from everybody else in every possible situation.

"In any event, after a few days I started developing a good rapport with most of the girls in the tailor shop. They accepted me as an outsider, as a man. They knew that I was only there because the authorities were out to reprimand me and to break my spirit. Even so, no matter how friendly they were and how much they teased and flirted with me, I never lost sight of how dangerous most of the girls were. Despite their feminine characteristics, their crimes were serious and a lot of them were very vicious people. One of the sewing-machine operators used to dress up like a woman, cuddle up to men he'd pick up in a bar, get them drunk, then maneuver them into some dark alley and steal their money. When three of his victims discovered that he was a man, he killed them with a knife. There were several other murderers there, too, so I could never relax in the tailor's shop. But as careful as I was, it didn't take me long to get into serious trouble.

"The shop was a huge room with the smaller sewing machines in the front area, the big industrial sewers in the middle section, and the cutting machines in the rear. My job was to keep sweeping all day, and later, when everybody else was finished working, I'd sweep up again and then mop the whole room. Well, there was one particular officer stationed there who didn't like me. Part of this was probably because I was Jewish and a New York city slicker. This officer wasn't a very intelligent person and everybody knew that he was going to night school to get his high school diploma. In fact, all the inmates in the shop looked down on him because of his obvious stupidity. So his plan was to take all of his resentment out on me.

"One afternoon, when everybody else had gone back to their cells, this officer came up to me, pointed to a broom, and said, 'Jack, I want you to sweep up the room.'

"I was going to do just that anyway, so I said, 'Yes, sir.' Then I took the push broom and spent about fifteen minutes sweeping the floor clean.

"After I was done, the officer came over and said, 'You're under arrest.'

"I couldn't believe what I was hearing. 'What do you mean, sir? What's this all about?'

"'I'm locking you up because I told you to use the straw broom and you used the push broom. You didn't obey a direct command and that's insubordination.'

"He called somebody with his walkie-talkie and within thirty seconds, another guard came and escorted me to my cell, which was about a half mile from the shop. Then he posted a sign on the outside bars of my cell that read KEEP LOCK. That meant I had to remain in my cell until I was summoned for a trial. A keep lock could be a dangerous situation if an inmate had any enemies in the population, because all of your meals were brought to your cell. Since the specific trays of food were designated for specific cells, it wasn't difficult for the meal to be poisoned. The only inmate who maybe had a grudge against me was Paul, but I didn't think he'd risk offending Joe Gallo, so I wasn't at all worried about the safety of my food.

"The next morning at eight o'clock, a guard appeared to say that my trial was on and to escort me to the deputy warden's office. I was searched twice, then taken to a big room where several other inmates were also waiting for their trials. Now, what were these fellows charged with? One had hit another inmate, one had punched a guard, another had started a riot in the B Yard. And there *I* was, charged with using a push broom instead of a straw broom. While we were waiting, I asked the others for some advice. The deputy warden was both judge and jury, and I was to treat him with the utmost respect and refer to him as 'Your Honor.' And all of the inmates told me never to plead not guilty. None of them could remember an inmate being found not guilty. And the reality was that a plea of not guilty always resulted in a punishment that was twice as severe as a guilty plea would have brought. It was funny because in a normal court of law the best advice is never to plead guilty.

"I was waiting there for several hours when finally a guard called out my number—18896—and it was my turn. The office was a long room with a long table and the deputy sat at the far end of the table in a high chair that looked like a throne while I stood at attention. There were armed guards flanking the deputy, a guard beside me, and an American flag in each corner of the room. The deputy wore a blue uniform with a white shirt and he had eagle bars on his epaulets that signified that he was a colonel.

"The first thing he said to me was, 'How do you plead?'

"'I don't know what the charges are, Your Honor.'

"So he read the complaint, which simply charged that I had disobeyed a direct order from an officer and that I was cited for insubordination. That was all the report said. There was nothing about a broom. 'How do you plead?' he repeated.

"'If it would please the court,' I said, 'I would like to offer this explanation...' Then I just started talking. While I was talking, my posture kind of drooped and the guard kept poking me with his elbow, reminding me to stand at attention. So I told the deputy about the brooms: 'If I had used the straw broom, the dust would only have been stirred up and my work would have been for naught. The push broom was the only one that could have gotten the job done.'

"I thought that I presented my argument very well and that I didn't come off as a wise guy. My thoughts were reinforced when the deputy smiled a little after I was through. Then he gave me a little lecture: 'It's a very serious thing to be cited for a rules violation, whatever the circumstances might be. This citation of insubordination, for example, will go on your record and may be a factor in determining whether or not you'll be granted a timely parole.'

"'Yes, sir. Thank you, sir.' And I was taken back to my cell thinking that I had done the best I possibly could.

"Two hours later, the disposition came. It was delivered by an inmate, the last in a series of runners who relayed the message from the deputy's office to me. Even though the slip of paper was still sealed, the runner knew the result. 'You got two days lockup, Jack, but your sentence is suspended. You'll be out in ten minutes.'

"The next time I walked into the yard, I was treated like a hero because I hadn't pleaded guilty and I'd beaten the system."

"After a while I got used to the girls in the tailor shop and I began to take notice of how differently homosexuality was regarded inside the walls. I'd guess no more than five percent of the population were fairies, but some of them were very aggressive and there were frequent rapes. Marriages were also commonplace and I witnessed more than one. Another inmate would play the role of a minister, and the happy couple would hold hands and kiss each other at the wedding ceremony. After a marriage took place, everybody in the yard knew that the girl belonged to the husband, so you flirted with her (or even had an affair) at great risk. In fact, I would say that most of the deaths that occurred while I was in Attica resulted from some form of adultery. Gambling disputes caused arguments, but the real violence came from the homosexuals.

"The prison administration did more than tolerate homosexuality. Many times the administration rewarded a particular shop for doing outstanding work by placing a girl to work with them, knowing full well what the outcome would be.

"There was one fag there who'd had silicone injections and had actual breasts—like a 36C bust. He also had long blond hair, slim hips, his legs were long and slim, and his face and his legs were hairless. He walked and talked like a woman. And he kept coming up to me and saying, 'Jack, I'd like to make it with you.' And despite myself, sometimes I'd look at him and I'd want him to be a real girl so badly that I'd get an erection. Because I thought it might get a little out of hand I backed away from the situation.

"After I'd been in Attica for a while, I wasn't sure that I wouldn't be capable of making love to a man. Nobody can actually say, 'No, I'll never do it,' because psychologists believe that everybody is a latent homosexual. That means there's a little bit of this kind of drive in each of us, but it's normally suppressed. Out in the real world, there are so many women available that this desire can remain dormant. But the question is, in an all-male enclosed society, at what point does your latent homosexuality break out? Who knows? I never had a homosexual episode during my prison time, but if I'd been there for fifteen or twenty years, maybe I would have.

"There are some prisons that allow inmates with good records to have cohabitation privileges with their wives. Some of the other inmates—the bachelors, for example, or the ones who can't stay out of trouble—do get jealous and it does create a lot of dissension, but I still think it's a good idea. Face it, men who are incarcerated build up a tremendous sexual drive no matter how much saltpeter is put in their food. Sometimes this drive manifests in positive ways—like reading, or painting, or taking classes—but most often the energy gets perverted. People on the outside have no idea how difficult it is to live inside a prison and keep your soul intact."

As soon as he felt fairly comfortable in his new environment, Molinas sought out the lawyer whom Deputy Warden Myers had identified—Burt Pugash, who had blinded his girlfriend, Linda, by splashing acid in her face. (After his release from Attica, Pugash married Linda, but then was accused of threatening to throw acid into another woman's face.)

"Even in prison," said Pugash, "Jack was a con man. He tried to ingratiate himself with me not with a 'Hi, how are you? My name is Jack Molinas.' The first thing he said to me was, 'Hey, Burt. We have things in common. In fact, I even met your girlfriend at a party once.' I knew this was a lie, but I went along with it because there was something very likeable about Jack. Sure, he could also be ruthless, but even so he was never malicious. And Jack was right, we had much in common. We both were lawyers (my specialty was criminal law), we both were Jewish, and we were both originally from the Bronx. Immediately, the two of us became tight. On the other hand, Jack also developed a tremendous camaraderie with the prison's gambling community. The one weakness that he had, behind bars or out in the real world, was gambling."

"Of course, gambling was against the rules. And when I first got to Attica I was too scared to intentionally do anything illegal. I was afraid of everything, everyplace, and everybody. There was nobody I trusted. Not Joe Gallo. Not Burt Pugash. I walked around half-expecting somebody to sneak up behind me and hit me. The whole day-to-day routine was frightening.

"During certain hours on Saturdays and Sundays everybody's cell doors were opened and we were free to walk around the gallery and socialize. I did this very reluctantly, until I got involved with a very unusual card game.

"The preface to this story is that inmates were allowed to have certain kinds of pets and some of the guys had either birds in a cage or fish. But there was this one fellow whose cell wasn't far from mine and who had a pet chipmunk. I'd never heard of a domesticated chipmunk before, but this one used to run freely around this fellow's cell. Not only that, the chipmunk would be the lookout whenever we had a card game there.

"A guard would periodically patrol the gallery during this open-door time. He'd start at the One Cell and work his way up to the Forty Cell and back. Up and back. Then he'd disappear for a while before showing up unexpectedly to walk his route again. The guards weren't really interested in keeping perfect order—which was impossible, anyway—but they were out to catch and arrest any inmates who were doing something blatantly illegal. The card game was in Cell Twenty, which was about midway along the galley, and while we were playing, the chipmunk would run down to Cell One and hang around there. When the guard appeared at Cell One it would take him about forty seconds to reach Cell Twenty, but in the meantime, the chipmunk would run into the cell and start chattering away. With that, we'd fold up the game and pretend we were having a conversation—usually about sports because that was the safest subject. When the guard made his rounds and left through the galley door near Cell One, the chipmunk would take up his post again and the card game would resume.

"'That's amazing,' I said to the chipmunk's owner the first time I saw his pet in action. 'How does he do that?'

"'It took me three years,' the fellow said, 'but that's what I trained him to do.'

"The stakes in the card game, and in all the other gambling activities, were cigarettes. They were the means of exchange for anything and everything. You could get your shoes spit-shined for two packs of cigarettes. You could get your shirts ironed and the collars starched for five packs. On the street cigarettes cost about fifty cents a pack, but because we weren't required to pay any tax in a state prison the cost to us was two bits a pack. Even though I never smoked cigarettes, I quickly got interested in trying to accumulate as many of them as possible for the same reason that everybody else did—to pass the time. And why did I gamble? The same answer—to pass the time.

"It was a friendly little card game with the big winner coming away with maybe a carton. The relatively low stakes, however, didn't prevent one fellow from trying to cheat. He was actually very crude, fumbling and dropping his cards on the floor, and while he leaned over to retrieve them, he'd slip another card out of one of his socks. The other players were pretty sharp and they easily figured out the cheater's routine. Threats were made and the cheater hightailed it out of the cell. As soon as possible, he petitioned the deputy warden for a transfer to another institution, but his request was denied. Two weeks later, the cheater was found 'piped' in a bathroom in one of the metal shops. The word 'piped' means being hit with a hard object in the head and seriously injured. This guy went to the hospital with a fractured skull and only then was his request for a transfer granted. Obviously, card cheats were not tolerated in Attica.

"All this time I was reading the newspapers that circulated among the inmates and paying close attention to the basketball games, both college and pro. I was getting copies of the *New York Post*, the *New York Times*, and the *Herald Tribune* through the mail. A few of the other guys were getting the newspapers from their hometowns. Of course, all of the papers arrived a few days late but we didn't care. And there was a system by which each newspaper that came into A Block was passed along. There was literally a list—Bob got the *Post* after I was done with it. Then it went to Harry, then Milt, and so on. I was twenty-seventh on the list for George's *Albany Times-Union*. (Magazines made the rounds the same way.) All of the inmates in Attica had been convicted of crimes that were committed in New York, but many of them hailed from other cities scattered from coast to coast. This system, then, allowed every interested inmate to read almost every newspaper in the country. With such plentiful resources, I was able to track the fortunes of all the important teams.

"Now, there were several operations issuing betting tickets where you'd get nine-to-one odds if you picked at least four-of-four winners. The tickets came out either Thursday or Friday when the newspaper published lines for the weekend's games. This was the same kind of thing that Joe Jalop was running when I played with the Hacken All-Stars. The main difference was that the lines on the tickets in Attica were sometimes way out of whack. Even so, I knew how difficult it was to dope out a winning ticket, and I was also determined to keep a low profile, so I refrained from betting.

"Then I got lucky and the quality of my life in Attica changed dramatically."

After working in the tailor shop for about a month, I sent a memorandum to the deputy warden saying that I was extremely dissatisfied with my job and that I'd like to be transferred to another position, possibly as a schoolteacher. It was kind of a shot in the dark, but a few days later I received word that my request was approved and that I'd been assigned to the school. The shift also meant that I had to move to the D Block, which was another blessing.

"Inmates were housed strictly according to their job assignments. All the teachers, plumbers, metal-shop workers, and certain porters lived in the D Block. The law library was also there. The inmates there were somewhat more intellectual than in the other blocks. Most of them had some sort of formal education and they could relate on a more rational basis, and consequently I felt much more relaxed there. Instead of living with murderers and thugs, I was now mingling more often than not with swindlers and fellows who were doing time for grand larceny—men who could use their minds to steal instead of their bodies. Definitely my type of people.

"When I first walked into the D Yard I was lost, just wandering around aimlessly. Then a little fellow came up to me and said, 'Hi, my name is Mike. I'm from New York and I'm sitting in Five Cell. How're you doing, Jack? Is there anything I can do to make you more comfortable here?' It wasn't a homosexual come-on, just a fellow who was out to be a friend of mine. In prison, when somebody is solicitous of someone at their first meeting it's a signal they're interested in developing a friendship. And it was important for me to have a trustworthy friend in prison, especially someone who'd already been there a while, as Mike had, and could teach me the ropes.

"Mike was Italian. He had very dark bushy hair and heavy eyebrows. He was about five foot four and a hundred thirty pounds, but really tough. He was accused of robbing a dress shop at gunpoint, but he was a really nice fellow and he turned out to be a wonderful friend.

"In prison friendship was an entirely different sort of relationship than it was outside. In society, the average guy was married with a well-developed home life and also a steady job. In the course of a normal week, he might see his best friend for a couple of hours. In prison, you're with a friend all day, every day, except when you sleep. You're with him in the mess hall, in the yard, and sometimes where you work. You saw each other in times of unusual stress, so you got to know each other very well. Moreover, if a fellow was your friend, you were responsible for his actions. If he got into an argument or a fight, you'd have to take his side.

"Also, the only thing you ever said about yourself was your name and where you were from. Eventually, you'd mention what kind of crime you'd committed and what your bit was. That's it. There's no other pedigree that was worth talking about. There were, however, certain kinds of crimes that were looked down upon—mostly child molesting and things like that.

"I was in Three Cell, and later that afternoon Mike started talking to me. There was only one cell between us, so we were practically neighbors, but still, just about everybody in the cell block could hear our conversation. 'Hey, Jack,' he said. 'Could you use a sandwich? I've got an extra one here. And I'm making some coffee. Would you like a nice hot cup of coffee?' He said the word 'nice' in a much lower voice, which was a big message to me because there were two ways to make coffee.

"The sinks in the cells only had cold running water. All of the inmates had thermos bottles because when everybody returned to their cells from dinner—which was about six-fifteen—the runners who serviced your gallery would make their rounds and fill up your thermos from a hot-water tap at the end of the gallery. Naturally, the water in the thermos didn't stay hot for very long, so if you wanted really hot coffee or tea you'd have to make it right then. There were some old-timers, however, who had what was called a 'dropper.' This was a piece of metal attached to two pieces of carbon and an electric wire. You could plug the wire into the outlet, put the dropper in a cup of water, and heat it to a boil. Being caught with a dropper was illegal and was punished by a seven-day lock-up. But the screws never bothered the old-timers, who knew exactly where to hide it anyway. So when Mike said 'nice' in a kind of secret way, that was the clue that he had a dropper.

"Really hot coffee was always a special treat, so I passed my thermos to the fellow in Four Cell and asked him please to pass it on. The protocol was that everybody was required to pass things on from cell to cell. Sandwiches, coffee, newspapers, magazines, anything that wasn't outrageously contraband. Sometimes this was inconvenient because you had to get up off your cot, or you were on the toilet, but if you didn't do it for them, they wouldn't do it for you.

"Gradually, Mike became my friend and my confidant. And that certainly made the time much easier to take. Mike was a student at the school where I'd be teaching and was even registered in one of my classes. He'd introduce me to other interesting fellows and generally made me feel less alone and alienated than I had in A Block.

"One of the fellows I met through Mike was named Basil, a chunky guy of about five foot three. A Jewish kid originally from Cleveland, Basil's crime had something to do with embezzling money from his boss. Basil had a malformed hip that caused him to walk with a limp. His body was tilted and to see him walking, especially when he was in a hurry, was a funny sight. In the outside world, he probably would've been stuck with a nickname—Gimpy, maybe—but in prison inmates referred to each other only by their legitimate first names. That's because everybody lived under such a high degree of tension that guys were just suddenly snapping all over the place. Just losing control, flipping out, and more often than not getting violent. So you wanted to make sure that nobody had any reason to hold any kind of grudge against you, and you had to pick your friends very carefully. In fact, you consciously made an effort to make friends only with guys who were very even-tempered.

"Anyway, both Mike and Basil were extremely poor and smoked only raggedy-looking handmade cigarettes (as opposed to 'tailor-mades' that could be purchased in the commissary and were the accepted medium of exchange between all prisoners). They'd been good buddies for many years and had a friendly rivalry where they'd bet whatever tailor-mades they could afford on sporting events. Basil was a gin player. Mike was like me, always looking for an edge. Before long, the three of us started hanging out—two midgets and one semi-giant. We were 'the gruesome threesome.' We had a good time just bullshitting with each other, and because we stayed out of trouble the screws never bothered us. Actually, the screws usually let the teachers get away with small violations, anyway, because the inmates who were attending classes would get really irate if a class was cancelled because the teacher was locked up for some silly reason.

"School was in session from nine to eleven in the morning, then came a break for lunch, and there were more classes from one to three in the afternoon. As a teacher, my daily salary was doubled from five cents a day to ten cents. I taught American history and chemistry, maybe two or three forty-minute classes a day. But sometimes I only had one class a day, so I'd get to hang out in the teacher's lounge reading, trading the latest prison gossip, or just bullshitting about sports.

"It was while I was teaching that I began to get deeply involved again in gambling. At the outset, it was Mike's idea. 'Why don't we run our own pool?' he said. 'We could put our tickets out on Monday and get a big jump on all the other pools. You're as good a handicapper as anybody in here, Jack, and the lines you gave would be trusted. All you'll have to do is tell me what numbers to put next to what teams and I'll do the rest. I'll do the distributing, the collecting, and I'll also keep the records. We'll put Basil in charge of D Block and I'll take care of the rest. I've been in here for ten years, Jack, so I know everybody in the four blocks.'

"'I just came here,' I protested, 'and I don't want to get in any trouble.'

"'I'll take all the risks,' Mike said. 'We'll go partners—fifty-fifty. But if anybody asks you if it's your pool, you have to say yes because you're the one with the reputation. Believe me, Jack, we'll wind up with all the money in this joint.'

"I thought about it for a couple of days, and I asked Joey Gallo if he had any objections to my starting up another pool. Only after I received Gallo's permission did I give Mike my okay and instruct him how I wanted the operation set up. The minimum bet was one pack on four games and the maximum bet was ten packs. Four-for-four winners paid ten to one. Five for five was fifteen to one. Six for six was twenty-five to one. Seven for seven was fifty to one. Eight for eight was a hundred to one. And nine for ten was two hundred to one. On Mondays, Mike would come up to me with a list of the following weekend's football and basketball games and I'd figure out a line for each game. There were no half-point lines and we'd win a tie (or a 'push'), which was a huge advantage for us. Mike had already organized a network of runners and bankers in each block. Then he'd hand-print about two dozen tickets and get them to the runners. And the first week we were in business we had a tremendous play.

"Mike also used the same method of delivering cigarettes to the winners as the other pools did. Since the mess hall was in C Block, everybody had to go there at least three times every day—except on Sunday mornings, when we could skip breakfast if we wanted to. There were institutional rules that forbade certain kinds of clothing in the mess hall, nor could an inmate carry a package into the mess hall. The last corridor leading into the mess hall was a half mile long, and inmates would routinely leave packages on the floor anywhere in that corridor. Another prime rule among the inmates was that you'd never dare pick up someone else's package on pain of at least a terrible beating. So it was a failsafe system.

"What happened, though, was that by Thursday we had about fifteen cartons worth of bets. That's when I started to get worried. 'Mike,' I said, 'if a couple of players were to hit it big, we'd never have enough cartons to pay off. Plus, each inmate is only allowed to spend ten dollars a week to buy cigarettes. Even with you, me, and Basil buying up our quota, we could still come up short.'

"But Mike had everything figured out. 'Could you raise enough cash on the street to cover what we might need?'

"'Sure.'

"'Okay, then it's simple. I can make arrangements with people in the street to mail a money order to the account of whoever breaks our bank. No problem, Jack.'

"But we did have another problem in due time because of the large number of cartons we had accumulated. Each inmate was only allowed to keep five cartons in his cell. If he tried to hide more than that, one of the periodic shakedowns would easily turn them up and he'd be busted. What we did was pay certain inmates a pack a week to store five cartons for us. On top of that, runners got a pack a day, the guy who delivered the cartons also got a pack. The bankers who collected the scraps on which the bettors wrote their bets had to get paid. Mike and Basil were also on a salary.

"That first week, we paid our debts promptly and cleared a profit of six cartons. By the second week the operators of the other pools were playing our tickets because my lines were different from the newspapers' lines and they figured that mine had to be wrong. After the second week's action, our profit was two hundred cartons. By the third week, we'd put all the other pools out of business and I was one of the richest men in Attica.

"It was around that time when I got arrested again: Because I was the tallest inmate there I was always first on line whenever we went to and from the mess hall. One morning, we were on our way back from chow when a short dumpy little screw came running up to me and said, 'You're under arrest for speeding.'

"'Under arrest for speeding?' I said. 'What does that mean? Sir.'

"'You were walking too fast and the rest of the line couldn't keep up with you.'

"I still couldn't believe it. 'I've been walking at this same rate ever since I got here. Sir.'

"'Well, today you were walking a little faster than normal.'

"So I was in keep lock for the rest of the day. The next morning, I was taken in to see Deputy Warden Myers. 'Jack,' he said, 'you're amassing a terrible record. You've only been here for a few weeks and you've already been arrested twice.' Then he started getting a little hostile. 'This is a very serious situation, Jack. We can't tolerate your happy-go-lucky attitude. You got off easy the last time, but if this happens again, I'll have to send you back to the tailor shop. How do you plead?'

"'Guilty, Your Honor, with an explanation.'

"'Let's hear it.'

"'I'm significantly taller than most of the other fellows, Your Honor, and when I take a step it's a little longer than everybody else's step so it takes more of an effort to keep up with me.'

"'Then it's your responsibility, Jack, to take shorter steps.'

"I saw that he was in a grouchy mood so I didn't say anything else. When I got my sentence, I was PO'd. It was seven days in keep lock. That meant my meals would be brought to me, I couldn't go to the Saturday night movie, I couldn't go to the yard, and I couldn't teach my classes. I began to understand that this was part of my continuing harassment by the administration. This was an important realization because it got me geared up to show them that I was tougher than they thought I was."

Once every two weeks, Julie would visit his brother, sometimes in the company of his parents, and frequently with Bob Ellis or Ellen Sohn. For years afterward, Julie was still haunted by these visits.

"Attica was about an eight-hour drive from the city," he said, "and I'd drive all night so I could be there at nine in the morning. By the time I got to the toll booth I was in a terrible mood. When I drove through the town, I'd see kids going to school, people going to work, just like any normal day. Except that I was up there to visit my brother in jail. Then I caught my first sight of the prison walls and its dead gray stones. Once inside, they gave me a form to fill out and the final humiliation was being fingerprinted. The routine never varied—I'd get searched several times, walk through the metal detector, and marvel anew at how green the grass was inside those dead walls. Doors opening and closing behind me with loud clangs. Doors and more doors. I was afraid to move a step out of line in the event that someone would put a hard hand on my shoulder and tell me that I had committed a serious violation and would have to stay there. I was finally directed to a small cubicle in a long room and told to sit in a very small, very uncomfortable wooden chair. There was an armed guard sitting on an elevated chair so that he could see everybody at one glance. Then Jack came in dressed in the usual prison garb, but what always caught my attention was the fact that he, like all the inmates, wasn't permitted to wear a belt. We were separated by a table and he had to stand while we talked. If we wanted to shake hands or embrace we had to look at the guard, who'd give us permission with a nod or else shake his head to say no. Jack always tried to be cheerful and tell me that everything was okay and that I shouldn't worry about him, but he always looked thin and pallid and I could tell his happy face was an act. A bad act. We'd talk for about fifteen minutes. Did he need anything? Did he have enough money? Was he eating well? Was he getting enough exercise? Yes, Mama was fine and sends her love. Yes, Papa was fine and also sent his love. Whenever I took my parents to visit, everything was much more difficult and more emotional. Then the guard would say it was time to go and I could never stop myself from crying. My poor brother."

Most of the letters Molinas wrote in prison were addressed to Ellen. "He'd write about how much he loved me," Ellen said, "and how much he wanted me to wait for him. He also gave me instructions for some things that he needed. He was always vain about his thinning hair and there was a certain hair cream that he liked, Shontex, but it had a certain oily base that was forbidden in prison. So I'd be instructed to unwrap the bottom of a tube of toothpaste, then use a rubber spatula to scoop out all of the toothpaste, and refill the tube with his hair oil. I'd do that about once a month and it took me at least four or five hours each time."

When Ellen visited Molinas, she was even more distressed. "Jack looked so thin," she said, "and most of our time together was spent with him trying to cheer me up. One time I brought Jack a rug for him to put in his cell and that really brightened him up. But the only good thing about those visits was that I got to know Julie much better. Julie was a very kind person, a nice man who lived in the shadows."

On March 11, 1963, Molinas was officially disbarred in New York. At the same time, Jacob Evseroff and his associates were hoping to secure a "Certificate of

Reasonable Doubt," hoping that the presiding judge (Supreme Court Justice Samuel Hofstadter) would be convinced that a subsequent appeal might have a reasonable chance of reversing Molinas's conviction. The basis of the brief filed by Evseroff's partner, Bill Sonenshine, was that the trial should have been terminated rather than allowed to lapse during Justice Sarafite's illness. Should the certificate be granted, Molinas would be eligible for bail while his appeal was being considered. Hofstadter was "dismayed to observe the same lawyers appearing repeatedly on behalf of defendants charged with gambling and related crimes. Such regular repetition strongly suggests that these attorneys are mouthpieces selected not by the defendants but rather by the overlords of the gambling rackets."

Despite expressing no doubt that Molinas's guilty verdict was appropriate, on April 1, 1963, barely ten weeks into Molinas's sentence, Hofstadter reluctantly ordered his release on thirty-five thousand dollars' bail (provided by Julie, Louis, and other members of the family) while his appeal began its journey through the courts. "Such a long suspension [of the trial]," said Hofstadter, "would seem to require the granting of a certificate." Nine days later, Molinas was released from Attica.

"At the age of thirty-one I'm completely settled down," Molinas told Milton Gross of the *New York Post*. "I've come a complete cycle—student, professional athlete, lawyer, and now I hope I can become a businessman. They say three strikes and you're out and I've had two as an athlete and lawyer. But I'm trying to live a normal life. I'm helping to prepare my appeal. I'm also setting up an organization to go into business selling a steam-cleaning machine that will clean, press, and deodorize up to a dozen garments in ten minutes for fifty cents. About the only normal thing I can't do is get married now with this thing hanging over my head. My girl wants to get married. She's stood by me."

The dry-cleaning machine was merely a reprise of an old idea that Molinas had explored years before and rejected for being technologically unreliable. Fresh out of prison and Molinas was already up to his old tricks.

While his lawyers developed their strategies, Molinas thoroughly enjoyed his freedom. Artie Tolendini was a stockbroker who often handled Molinas's business. After an unexpected meeting at a party in February 1964, Molinas and Tolendini decided to drive down to Miami to witness the second Cassius Clay–Sonny Liston heavyweight championship fight. The car belonged to Tolendini—a 1962 Starfire—but Molinas did all the driving, mostly at excessive speeds. By the time they reached South Carolina, Tolendini had fallen asleep. "I was rudely awakened," said Tolendini, "to find the car off the side of the road and stuck in a huge haystack. 'Where are we?' I asked Jack, and he said, 'In heaven.' Some locals on a tractor appeared after a while and pulled us back onto the road. What with the accident and all, it took us twenty-three hours to reach

Miami, and even though Jack was driving like the devil was chasing him, he never got a ticket."

There were no tickets for the fight, either, and precious few hotel reservations in Miami, so Molinas bet a bundle on Clay and found the action he craved at the dog tracks. "Eventually," said Tolendini, "we ended up at the Castaways Hotel, where we hung around the pool all day. Jack would kill time by playing mah-jongg with the old ladies. He'd beat them out of fifty cents and they loved him. Jack would put his arms around one of them and say, 'I was born too late. If you were only a couple of years younger, I'd fly you down to Puerto Rico and we'd have ourselves a party.' Then he'd pinch another old gal on the cheek and say, 'Your husbands are crazy to leave you girls alone like this.' What a charmer he was."

Road trips were infrequent, however, and Molinas was happy to spend most of his reprieved time at one racetrack or another. During the basketball season, he confined his efforts to simple handicapping and bet more than ever before. For the first time in nearly twenty years, however, he refrained from playing basketball. By now, Ellen had moved out of her parents' house and had an apartment in Queens, where Molinas spent the majority of his evenings. Fearing that his phone at home was still tapped, Molinas called in most of his action from there. Whenever anybody asked about the possibility of his appeal being denied and of his being returned to Attica, Molinas would laugh and say, "Don't be silly. I'll never do another day in jail."

Gus Newman, another of Jacob Evseroff's associates, wasn't so sure. "Molinas got the idea that someone else besides Evseroff or Sonenshine should argue the appeal. His choice was O. John Rogge, an elderly attorney who was well known for defending a variety of left-wing causes. Molinas felt that Rogge's prestige would help the case. My opinion was that Rogge's undeniable prestige would have an adverse effect. The judges in the appellate division would think that we were bringing in somebody to talk down to them and that we were trying to unduly influence the court. But Molinas was adamant."

On June 16, the appellate division ruled unanimously that the five-week lapse in the trial, in itself, was not grounds for reversal. Molinas would have had to prove that the jurors had been prejudiced during this time. The court did find Molinas's sentence to be "unnecessarily excessive" but did not reduce it.

"The next step," said Newman, "was to get leave to go to the court of appeals and, of course, Molinas had his own stubborn ideas about how this should be handled." At the time, leave to appeal to New York's highest court could be granted by any one of seven judges, the most liberal being Chief Judge Charles Desmond and Judge Stanley Fuld. According to Newman, "There was an unwritten law that the judge who granted leave couldn't write the majority opinion. Molinas was so concerned with the ultimate, so preoccupied with who was going to write the majority opinion reversing his conviction, that he didn't want to go to either Desmond or Fuld, because that would preclude them from writing the majority opinion. Instead, Molinas picked Judge Adrian Burke, one of the court's most conservative members. Molinas figured that leave would be pro forma and that would make Fuld and Desmond available. Again, Molinas was stubborn about this and we couldn't make him see reason." On July 9, Burke refused the petition and ordered Molinas back to Attica.

The night before he was scheduled to surrender himself to the authorities, his mother stayed overnight at a friend's house and the only chance he had to bid her farewell was in a letter that he left for her. (If his sorrow seems sincere, and even touching, note the addict's strong denial of his addiction.)

7/10/64
To my dearest mother,

As fate might have it, the only night you don't come home turns out to be the eve of my surrender to commence serving my term—

Please forgive me for not telling you sooner as I should have done, but I kept putting it off to spare your feelings—

First of all, I want you to know how deeply & truly sorry I am, not because of the situation I'm in, but because of the position I have placed you in, & really, you deserved a much better fate & a whole lot more. I have nothing but praise & the deepest respect for the way you have brought me up; the unselfish & constant giving of yourself to me; the depriving of yourself of life's many pleasures so that I might be more comfortable & have more. Believe me, even though I have never let you know it, & even though I have been ungrateful, selfish, etc., deep down I really appreciate everything you've done & I'm sorry I took so long to let you know it. I'm sorry you couldn't be proud of me—

I guess everything turned out wrong, & who knows what the future holds for us all—I should have been married at several junctions in my life & had many kids (I'm really sorry for that) but I guess it wasn't in the cards—

Another thing, don't for a moment think that any of this is due to gambling because it's not so;—it's a lot more than that—You should only know how really insignificant it really is in my life. I couldn't begin to tell you all the complicated & complex reasons for all this but then again I'm not a professional analyst but I have a fair idea—I blame no one but myself for my dilemma & I only hope things turn out a little better than they appear at the present time.

Presently, I have Bob Ellis working on my case & I'm sure he can do something to remedy this current state of affairs—If anything comes up of any importance, he will contact you; or should you want to speak to him, you may call him at his office XXX-XXXX. Also note Ellie's new number XXX-XXXX.

I packed the suitcase & when I need it she will pick it up and bring it to me—She'll return the suitcase—

There's nothing more I can say except that I believe in God & since I really hurt no one but myself I have faith he will help me in part out of this situation.

I will write to you soon

Your loving & devoted son,

//Jack//

P.S. There is one other thing I wanted to tell you, & that is how swell Ellen has been through all this—She is another person I'm sorry for;—that she has all this trouble. She's a good girl & I'm sorry I never married her & had some kids but maybe the future will be brighter—One thing you should know by now is that I'm an optimist—

When Molinas went off to prison, he stuck Ellen with over three hundred dollars' worth of telephone bills—and although he promised several times to repay her, he never did.

Back in Attica, Jack once again picks up the narrative: "I decided to get back in shape and the best way to do that was to play basketball. The one thing that hit me, though, was that there was absolutely no integration of any of the sports at Attica. It was white against white and black against black.

"The best games were played between the block teams and there was a system whereby they would play against each other every Saturday and Sunday. Obviously the A Block basketball team, for example, consisted of the best players in A Block, but a lot of guys who weren't such good ballplayers desperately wanted to play on their block team. There were several reasons for this: the opportunity to travel to the various blocks to see their friends and/or their girls, and the chance to smuggle contraband items from block to block. I started off by playing pickup games in the yard to get my legs back. I was an ex-NBA player and every half-baked hooper in the yard wanted a shot at me, so the games were very rough.

"The court we played on was in pretty bad shape. The floor surface was just packed dirt and both baskets were about two inches too low. Anyway, I had been playing only for a couple of days when one of the fellows who was guarding me kept submarining me. That meant every time I jumped for a rebound or a shot, he'd either hit me in my stomach or hit my legs. That's the most dangerous thing you could ever do to another player, but when I complained to him he just brushed me off. He was a big guy, about six foot five and two-twenty, and I swore the son of a bitch was deliberately out to hurt me. And I knew exactly what was going on—it was considered a big accomplishment among the inmates if you hurt somebody else in a ball game. After that, I forgot that I was inside a prison. I was simply a basketball player in a highly dangerous and competitive situation.

"The next time he went up for a rebound, instead of jumping with him, I hit his legs with my right knee. That caused him to lose his balance and land flush on his back. When the dust had cleared he was unable to move, and the orderlies had to bring a stretcher and take him away to the hospital. I didn't feel particularly bad about it either because the guy had brought the whole thing on himself.

"After the game, Basil came over and said, 'Jack, you better dig yourself. From now on, every nut job in the joint is going to want to play against you and mess you up.'

"He was right. And except for playing HORSE or other spot-shooting games, I never touched a basketball again as long as I was there. But as it turned out, I wasn't at all done with athletics.

"There was a guy from Brooklyn named Fat Charlie who stood six six and weighed about two-thirty. Fat Charlie used to be a shylock on the street, but now he was a defensive tackle and captain of the D Block football team. One day, Fat Charlie asked me to come out for the football team. 'Jack,' he said, 'you'd make a great pass receiver.' And I decided to do it.

"The football field was littered with small pebbles and rocks the size of golf balls, so getting tackled was a risky business. All the football players had bruises, welts, and gashes from head to toe because of the field. Their makeshift uniforms didn't give them much protection either. Guys had helmets made of plaster of Paris or even tin cans, and shoulder pads made of cardboard. And they played like Roman gladiators ready to sacrifice their lives to gain an extra yard. Neither piling on nor punching were considered to be fouls. What a team we had. The two tackles were enforcers. One linebacker was a rapist. The left guard was a murderer. The fullback was a cat burglar. And I was a fixer. They tried to rough me up during the tryout but I was one of the heaviest players out there and I knew how to protect myself. I was also surprised at what terrible shape the rest of them were in. It was easy for me to outrun all of them. After a couple of practice sessions I proved Fat Charlie to be a wonderful scout and I was the best pass catcher on the team.

"So I had Ellen go to a sporting goods store and buy me a complete uniform. She spent a hundred and fifty dollars and I had a white satin uniform with green trim complete with hip guards, elbow pads, steel cleats, a helmet with a steel face guard, also ankle supports and a boxer's mouthpiece. And I was ready to face the war. It was raining like crazy for the first game I played and the field was a mud hole, but in my fancy store-bought uniform I certainly stood out from my teammates. The fellows on the other team were laughing at me and one of them said that they were going to teach me a lesson. Sure enough, I lined up at the right end position and three guys came at me and knocked me facedown in the mud. I had to come out of the game to scrape the mud out of my mouth. But I said to myself, if this is the way they want to play, then let's play.

"But no matter how rough the game was, no matter how badly a player might be hurt, everybody tried to walk off the field under their own power. The only time it was okay to be carried off in a stretcher was if a player had a broken leg or was unconscious. It was also true that the medical staff was so incompetent that guys were afraid to go to the hospital.

"There was one particular doctor who prescribed the same remedy for every ailment—two aspirin. The right linebacker on my team had something wrong with his knee, but this doctor wouldn't send him for an Xray. Every time the linebacker went to see him the doctor gave him two aspirin. Again and again.

Meanwhile, the guy's knee was getting worse and worse. Finally, the linebacker came back to the doctor with the last two aspirins taped to his sore knee. 'Doc,' the linebacker said, 'the aspirin you gave me didn't do any good.' The linebacker got fourteen days in keep lock for being a wise guy.

"There was another memorable game that featured a forty-four-year-old player named Dash. He'd been on the A Block team for ten years and was on the verge of being released on parole. But Dash insisted on playing one more game before he got sprung. He was a quarterback, and on the one and only play he was in, he got hit in the chest and was knocked out. It was a very hot day, and I yelled at the nearest officer to get some oxygen. The guard wasn't too happy about having to go fetch the oxygen on such a hot day, but he went and got it. Meanwhile, I was feeling Dash's pulse and it was getting weaker by the second. Finally the oxygen tank came and the officer put the plastic mask over Dash's face. I could feel the pulse start to get stronger, but after about a minute, the oxygen tank ran dry. I told the officer to go get another tank of oxygen, but the officer said it was too hot to go through the routine a second time. Then he started arguing with me—I was only an inmate and I was supposed to take orders, not give them. If I didn't shut up, I was going to be busted for insubordination.

"Sure enough, Dash's pulse gradually disappeared and he died right there in my arms."

"Things got interesting when the warden challenged an all-star team to play against a team of screws that was supplemented by a couple of ringers. We figured we'd have to deliberately blow the game or else the screws would make life miserable for us, but meanwhile we'd get some satisfaction out of beating up some of them. As the game progressed, however, we saw that we could win and it was a battle between being humiliated for the sake of survival and satisfying our pride. We decided to play to win, and using only one play we went the length of the field to beat them. I'd fake a post and go down and out, the ball would be there, and I'd step out of bounds. We ran the play seven straight times and covered eighty-four yards for the winning touchdown. Christ, they ought to make a movie about it." (They did—*The Longest Yard*.)

If playing basketball and football were too risky, Molinas next tried baseball and wound up getting arrested for the third time. "In the spring, I went out for the D Block baseball team and I proved to be a pretty good hitter. I played first base and in my debut I hit a home run over the prison wall that won the game and I was the hero of D Block for the day. We were scheduled for another game right after lunch the very next day against what was supposed to be the best team in Attica—and even though inmates bet heavily on all the interblock sporting events, this particular game set a record for cigarettes wagered.

"The mess hall rules were very strict. You couldn't come in there with a coat, or with a package. While eating, the talk had to be minimal. For security coverage there were turrets set up in each corner of the hall, and there were tear-gas canisters attached to the ceiling that could be released by a guard pressing a designated button. The inmates selected their own food and their own portions from a cafeteria-style setup. Another one of the mess hall rules was that an inmate had to eat every last bit of food that he took. Leaving any leftovers was considered to be wasting the taxpayers' money and was treated as a serious offense. So, I'd made sure to finish up my lunch to the last morsel and I'd returned to my cell to get ready for the baseball game. I was putting on my uniform, lacing my cleats, and banging my fist into the first baseman's mitt that Ellen had sent to me, when a guard came by and snapped a key lock on my cell door.

"'What's going on, sir? I've got to go play in a baseball game.'

"'You're locked up, Jack. The call came down from the mess hall.'

"The guard didn't know the particulars, but within a few minutes I found out the reason for my latest arrest—one of the mess hall guards, who'd been watching me through a pair of binoculars, claimed that I'd left a piece of bread on my tray. I knew that was a lie because I'd made sure that my tray was clean. The whole thing sounded like a setup.

"The next day I was hauled into Deputy Warden Myers's office. 'Here you are again, Jack,' he said. 'Wasting food is a very serious offense. If all the inmates did this, before long there wouldn't be any food left. I have to make an example of you, Jack.'

"'Can I ask a question, Your Honor.'

"'Go ahead.'

"'How did the guard who reported this know which tray was mine?'

"'That's not the issue here, Jack. He says it was your tray and that's that. How do you plead?'

"'Guilty, Your Honor.'

"'With no explanation?'

"'No, Your Honor.'

"My punishment was being locked in my cell for seven days. I missed the game, of course, which was won, three to two, by A Block. The way I figured it was that some guard had made a large wager on A Block and wanted to insure his bet by getting me out of the lineup. Well, it sure did work. I had to hand it to the guard, whoever he was, for doping out the perfect fix."

On November 10, 1964, the New York State Supreme Court reduced Molinas's sentence to seven to twelve and a half. At the same time, Joe Green's sentence was reduced to four to five and Joe Hacken's to six years. Molinas was disappointed that the reduction was so minimal and he resolved to submit another application in the near future. In a letter dated November 11, Molinas wrote the following to Paul Brandt:

> ...As far as my conviction is concerned, I'm petitioning the U.S. Supreme Court to be heard—& should I fail here I have many further remedies—
>
> Aside from all the legal hogwash, I'm still in relatively good spirits except for the fact I have a real swell girl in Ellen all involved with me—She has visited me each time she's allowed to (once a month), prepared a monthly food package (15 lbs.), & in general is the absolute best. This makes me feel quite bad & at present I still haven't decided what to do, since it still is a long time to wait. Can't get that feeling out of me that I don't want to be a burden to her....

Molinas needn't have worried about being a burden to Ellen. For her part, she'd been closely reexamining their relationship and discovering it to have been extremely unsatisfying even when the going was good. She was distraught that Molinas was in Attica, but at the same time Ellen was more than half-glad that he was out of her life.

Upon his reentry into the prison population, Molinas reactivated his betting operation which had been suspended during his absence. "While I was gone, the other pool operators had reopened their businesses, which was fine with me. I still had the advantage because I could make my own lines on the games while they had to wait to see the lines in the newspapers on Thursday. In fact, to maintain good will I even played their pools on a regular basis. Since I had the biggest bankroll, I'd also act as the hedge man so that the other operators would have a place where they could even up their books if their action got top-heavy on any one team. Again, I did this to make sure there was no animosity between us and them. So there I was, the bookmaker's bookmaker.

"Now, none of this very complicated gambling activity could go on without the administration's being aware of it. It would've been easy for the warden to put all of the betting operations out of business in about fifteen minutes. But, in truth, they couldn't completely stamp out gambling any more than they could've stamped out homosexuality. The administration's attitude was that there was usually no violence involved in organized betting as long as everybody got paid in a timely fashion. It was also thought that gambling even kept some inmates out of trouble. But, as soon as word got out that certain operators weren't paying their debts, or that certain bettors were stiffing the operators, then the threat of some kind of violence became real and the administration was quick to bust the guilty parties.

"That's why welching was taken so seriously by the inmates. If somebody didn't pay up, then the entire system was in danger. And welchers were piped by total strangers. Of course, if a guy was going through hard times most of the operators would take his marker. The only compromise I ever made was to take markers for a maximum debt of one pack. Otherwise my policy was that a bettor had to put up cash to bet. Just about all the other operators employed enforcers to collect their money, but that was something I refused to do. Cash on the line led to no misunderstandings, no hard feelings, and no beatings.

"As we became more and more successful, it became increasingly difficult to stash all the cartons. Sure, I paid rent to just about all the inmates in my gallery to store five cartons in their cells, but I also had to find other hiding places. There was a guard who was taken ill and forced to spend six months in the hospital. By hook and by crook I arranged to store fifty cartons in the guard's clothing locker while he was away. We also worked out a deal with the officers on duty in the gallery so we could put twenty-five cartons in their lockup drawer. After a while, we had to branch out and rent cells in the other blocks as well.

"We also began to look for ways to spend the loot we had. The only clothing inmates were forced to wear were the institutional pants. The only restrictions on any other apparel were the colors. Any kind of shirt, sweater, hat, coat, gloves, scarf, or any other outer garment had to be either gray or white. Underwear and socks could be any color. None of the clothing the other inmates were selling would fit me, but Mike and Basil bought things like cashmere sweaters and mohair coats. For me, there were watches, caps, earmuffs, pipes, tobacco, and cigars. Finally I devised an even better idea—we would buy food!

"On Sundays, when the cells were unlocked and everybody promenaded around the gallery, there were lines in front of my house with inmates trying to sell food that they'd received from their friends and families. I had made it known that I'd pay twice the street price for authentic gourmet food. Guys would come to my house with their food, we'd agree on a price, then Mike would handle the deliveries. Of course there were occasional arguments when inmates would try to tell me that a can of fruit cocktail was gourmet food, but nothing ever got out of hand.

"There was a fellow named Tiny who stashed cartons for me who used to be a chef in a ritzy restaurant in Chicago and was serving a twenty-year bit for killing his wife. Tiny had a hot plate in his cell and I would give him all the food I bought so that he could make a buffet in my house every Sunday morning. Almost everything was canned, of course, but we'd have tuna fish, salmon, sturgeon, chicken, goose, various pates, crackers, finger sandwiches, puddings, fruitcakes, cookies, the works. We'd get salamis and baloneys, once we got a fifteen-pound turkey, and we were also able to buy several hams at Christmastime. It was a weekly feast that I threw open to everybody, including the guards. It was the guards who took any of the leftovers that were perishable.

"Naturally, the whole situation upped my standing in the entire prison community. This, plus the money I had at my disposal, allowed me certain comforts and amusements. For example, many inmates had pet fish but the legal limit for the tanks was five gallons. I had a special eighteen-gallon tank built to my specifications from various glass and metal scraps, a job that required the connivance of perhaps thirty inmates. Ellen sent me several books on raising fish and I became an accomplished ichthyologist. The inmates who also kept fish would sell me babies—three packs for a cardinal fish, et cetera. Of course, the oversized tank was illegal, but the screws appreciated the tasty Sunday buffets, so aside from stopping by to admire my fish, they left me alone.

"I also had a small device made in Germany called a 'melita,' which essentially was a mechanism for percolating coffee in a single cup. And the only coffee I ever drank was Martinson's, which was a very fancy brand in those days. I'd go through about ten pounds of coffee every month."

> 12/11/64
> Dear Paul,
>
> I received your letter of November 22 and like you was quite happy to hear that we can correspond even though it's only once a month—I guess we can be happy for little things—and speaking about little things I was really elated to learn that Claudia is expecting—Christmas just came a little early for you this year— You know I really got a laugh when you refer to yourself in your letter as an "old guy"—We aren't that old yet, are we? I wonder how long it will be before I'll be able to make that statement "my wife's pregnant." If you're old now, I'll be ancient…
>
> As far as my case is concerned, I'm still appealing & just hoping somewhere along the line I'll get a break— Well, we'll see—
>
> Everything else is fine & I'm in good mental spirits at present—Teaching is quite interesting but just as it is outside teachers are underpaid…. But then again we get free room & board which is certainly worth something…
>
> Fondly,
> // Jack Molinas 18896//

If Molinas was high on the list of Attica celebrities, the most glamorous inmate was certainly Willie Sutton, renowned for breaking out of numerous high-security prisons. "I would see Willie in the yard, but he was a private kind of guy who was more interested in doing his daily walking exercise than in conversing with his fellow inmates. A few times, however, he motioned for me to join him in his walk and we became very friendly. He was in his early sixties and was a scholarly type with an extensive knowledge of the law. That's what we'd talk about—law, law, law—and we were both impressed with each other's command of the subject. In his heyday, he'd stolen a great deal of money and lived an easy life, but Willie freely admitted that his time behind bars wasn't worth the fruits of his crimes. Nevertheless, he felt that crime enchanted him. He'd always felt that he could outwit the law and trying to do just that was an appealing challenge. The two of us had a lot in common, especially our prison grays.

"But even in prison, there were guys who were still trying to prove that crime was a profitable way of life. We ran into a couple of them in the operation of our pool.

"One day, Mike returned from collecting some bets and he handed me a pack of Kent cigarettes, which was perfectly sealed and seemed to have the same consistency and weight of a regular pack. 'This pack feels a little funny,' he said. 'I'm gonna open it up.' He discovered that the package was filled with soap shavings.

"Now, most of the inmates worked for five cents a day, which meant that a pack of cigarettes cost them a week's wages. A lot of them were supported strictly by their prison jobs and had no outside help whatsoever. So if a low-income inmate could swindle somebody out of a pack a week, that's really a big deal. The trick was to find out who the swindler was.

"We kept track of the situation and discovered there was that one counterfeit pack coming from B Block every week. There were five hundred inmates in B Block and every one of them was some sort of a crook, but Mike did his own detective work. First off, he found which shops used soap and by questioning various inmates he was able to locate the particular shop that used that particular kind of soap. Then he spoke to one of the inmates who worked in that shop and got the word out that there was a one-carton reward for any information that would lead to the identification of the culprit. Because my pool was the one involved, everybody knew there'd be no violence, so Mike had dozens of spies working for him. We made sure that the investigation was very light hearted.

"It took about two weeks to crack the case. Someone reported to Mike that a certain inmate was taking an abnormal amount of chips from the soap box in one of the laundry shops. The suspect was immediately put under surveillance. Mike paid five packs to the inmate in the cell adjacent to the suspect's and that's how he was finally caught. His punishment was that he was not allowed to bet in our pool anymore. It was all very good-natured. I even offered to give him a carton if he showed me how he'd rigged up the counterfeit pack.

"We only had one other fellow try to cheat us and this turned out to be a much more touchy situation: There was a colored fellow who when he'd filled out a ticket had only picked three games. The discrepancy involved the fourth game, which was Michigan–Michigan State, and he'd told the runner that he wanted Michigan. However, when Michigan State won, the fellow claimed that he'd taken Michigan State. I spoke to the runner again and he swore that the fellow had picked Michigan. Okay, that settled it—we absolutely couldn't pay the guy, because if we did everybody else would shake us down the same way. When the bettor came to me to plead his case, I said that I had to take the runner's word against his. This whole thing simmered for about two months until I got word that the fellow was looking to come after me and kick my ass. Sure enough, he found me getting ready for baseball practice and he approached me with a menacing look in his eye.

"'Well, Jack,' he said, 'what're we gonna do about the ticket?'

"'We're gonna do nothing,' I retorted, 'because the runner said you had Michigan and that's what you're stuck with. I think you should forget about the carton of cigarettes and stop making a big hassle out of this. It's your friends who are razzing you and getting you so worked up that you want to fight me. And believe me, you're certainly not going to get the best of it if we do fight. I'm going to hurt you and you're going to hurt me, and we're both going to get in serious trouble. And what for? Some cigarettes? I know that you're a big-time guy, the type of guy who wore fifty-dollar alligator shoes in the street. Right? So I think this whole situation is too petty for either of us to be concerned with.'

"'You're right,' he said. Then he walked away and that was the end of it.

"Mike was always scheming for a way to make life either easier or more profitable for us, and with that in mind he became a Jew. And here's why: Normally, Jewish services are on Friday nights and Saturday mornings, but the rabbi who was assigned to Attica had other commitments and was only available on Wednesday nights. Unless an inmate was in keep lock or solitary he couldn't be denied the opportunity to attend the religious service of his choice. Besides me and Basil, there were about fifteen Jewish inmates in the entire prison and most of them were high-rolling bettors. So Mike signed something that identified him as a Jew and made him eligible to attend the Wednesday night services. There was an officer in the back who was very bored and paid no attention to what the congregation was up to. And the rabbi was also busy reciting the prayers. The rest of us would occasionally mumble like we were praying, too, but what we really were up to was making payoffs and booking bets.

"'O sanctuary of our King, O regal city,' intoned the rabbi.

"'What are the weekly totals?' I asked in a whisper.

"'Bless ye the Lord Who is to be blessed.'

"'We're up forty cartons in A,' said Mike, 'sixty-five cartons in B, and forty-four cartons in C.'

"'Blessed art Thou, O Lord our God.'

"'We're running out of storage space,' I hummed.

"'Amen.'

"'Amen!'

"The synagogue was one of the few places where there was a sense of peace, and where any personal differences could be dealt with in a rational fashion. If you accidentally stepped on somebody's toe in there you'd just say 'Excuse me' and there were absolutely no repercussions. If you did the same thing in the yard, you were liable to wind up in the hospital.

"There were makeshift knives everywhere—scraps from the metal shop that, for a price, had been filed to a sharp edge. Some fellows hid their knives in their cells, which was an enormous risk because the periodic shakedowns were sometimes done with metal detectors and having such a weapon could land the inmate a strip cell for a long time. Most inmates were smart enough to hide their knives somewhere in the yard. The code, of course, was that nobody would dare steal somebody else's property unless he was willing to fight for his life. And if the knife was discovered by one of the yard screws, they'd have no way of finding out to whom it belonged."

So many of the inmates were constantly on the verge of violence that crackups were commonplace. "One time an inmate had been coerced into umpiring a pickup softball game that I was playing in. It was just a fun type of game with absolutely nothing on the line. Well, in the very first inning when the umpire called a close pitch a strike, the batter just turned around without saying a word and smashed the umpire flush in the face with the bat. I also witnessed a friendly low-stakes card game that suddenly erupted into a vicious knife fight. The constant tension—of being watched, of having to be careful about where you stepped, about every word you said—just made guys snap."

1/23/65
Dear Paul,

I'm sorry to have been so remiss in answering your last letter but believe it or not I've been quite busy with my case—Presently my chances to receive bail from the U.S. Supreme Court are excellent— Should all go smoothly I should be on the street before the end of the month— Boy, would that be great—...

I'm in good shape down to 205 & feel in good spirits—
Always,
//Jack Molinas 18896//

In late January, Molinas was busted again. "I came back to my cell after mess and there was another keep lock sign hanging on the bars. As far as I knew, I hadn't done anything wrong and I was so disgusted that I didn't even ask the guard what the charge was. An hour later, a runner showed up to tell me that an anchovy can had been found in my toilet trap and I'd been charged with obstructing the passage of water in the block, which was a very serious complaint. I was called before Deputy Warden Myers once again and I was put through the same routine—Myers sitting on his throne, the long table between us, the American flags in each corner of the room, and the inevitable scolding about my being an intelligent man yet persisting in breaking the law. But this time I was indignant. When Myers asked for my plea, I said 'Not guilty, Your Honor.'

"This was unheard of at Attica. The guards raised their eyebrows in surprise and Myers wasn't sure that he'd heard me right, so I had to repeat my plea. 'That's right, Your Honor. Not guilty.'

"'What's your defense?'

"'Well, Your Honor, before I present my defense I'd like to confront the man who issued the charge first.' The guy was a civilian plumber, so I got a postponement until he could come to the prison.

"My plea was the talk of the block. 'Jack pleaded not guilty!' All the inmates knew that if I didn't beat the rap my punishment would be especially severe.

"The next day, the plumber showed up and testified that the anchovy can had been found eighteen inches below my trap, where it was blocking the flow of water to the entire gallery. There was another witness against me—a guard who worked in the mail room saying that I had received six cans of anchovies in a food package delivered two months previous. After hearing their testimony, I asked the deputy warden if I would get the benefit if I could prove a reasonable doubt. Myers thought about it for a moment, then said, 'Yes.'

"So I posed just one question to the plumber: 'Isn't it possible that if somebody else in a higher cell flushed the anchovy can down his toilet that the can could wind up stuck in my trap?'

"'Yes,' he said. 'It's a possibility.'

"Then I asked the mail-room guard if anybody else in the gallery had received canned anchovies in the last two months. Of course he didn't know if they had or had not.

"Then I made a statement in my own defense: 'Your Honor, one of the points that you constantly make whenever I'm called up before you is that I'm an intelligent person. And it's true. I was a college graduate and also a lawyer. I'm certainly intelligent enough to know that an anchovy can is not water soluble and that if I flushed one of them down my toilet the chances were great that the toilet would back up and flood my cell. That would have been a very unintelligent thing for me to do. Also, given the possibilities that someone else might have been in possession of a can of anchovies, and that someone else might possibly have disposed of the anchovy can down their own toilet, I believe that more than a reasonable doubt exists, Your Honor. And I ask you to uphold my plea of not guilty.'

"Myers barely waited for me to conclude when he issued his judgment—'Not guilty!'

"When I walked out into the yard, I was the hero of the century. Not even the oldest con could remember any inmate having a not-guilty plea upheld."

"Shortly thereafter, I encountered a situation which was much more dangerous than a not-guilty plea could ever have been. I was in the teachers' lounge playing a word game called GHOST with several other teachers. One of them was a fellow who had bilked the president of Nedicks out of a hundred grand. Another teacher was serving time for murdering his mother in a dispute over a multimillion-dollar inheritance left by his father. A third teacher had killed a cop when he was sixteen years old. Now, I was very good at word games and nobody could beat me at GHOST. The game was played by trying to fill in blank spaces with letters and then guessing the mystery word. Once you accumulated a total of five incorrect letters, the game was lost.

"Besides the teachers, there was another person in the room. His name was Jimmy and he was the school principal's secretary. Now, this Jimmy wasn't the smartest fellow in the joint. He was a compulsive gambler who would rob a bank and steal ten thousand dollars, then go to Aqueduct and lose it all by about the fifth race, then rob another bank the following day and return to the racetrack. In fact, he'd been originally busted for robbing two banks in the same day.

"So Jimmy challenged me to a game of GHOST. We'd actually played a few times before, but this time he was primed to beat me. What he'd done was write up a crib sheet that listed several obscure words that he thought he'd catch me with. He was actually very clumsy in the way he tried to hide the crib sheet, but I didn't say anything at first. And, in fact, I had already given four wrong letters before I finally figured out what his word was—PSALM. Then it was my turn and I beat him four consecutive times.

"He seemed to be very upset about the results, and I was foolish enough to rub it in. 'Jimmy,' I said, 'the only reason why you almost beat me in the first game was because you obviously looked up difficult words in a dictionary and wrote them down.'

"Jimmy didn't respond. He just walked over to his desk and started typing. I could see that he was angry—not only because I'd beaten him but because I'd implicitly insulted his intelligence. Then out of the blue, he took a key, opened one of the desk drawers, took out what I thought was a pencil, palmed it inside his right hand, and then started walking toward me. When he was about twenty feet away I realized that what I thought was a pencil was actually a small sculptor's knife with a razor edge, like the kind used to carve clay. I glanced quickly at the other teachers but they were preoccupied and didn't notice anything wrong.

"I figured I was in for a fight and I had about five seconds to come up with an alternative. There was a two-foot length of pipe within my reach on the window ledge and I considered grabbing that as a weapon. What went through my mind, though, was that he could slash me pretty seriously but it was unlikely that he could kill me. On the other hand, if I hit Jimmy with the pipe I'd probably kill him and then I'd be in Attica forever. And if I hit him but didn't kill him, he'd wait for the right time and then someday try to kill me. It was literally a life-and-death situation. My hands were sweating and I didn't want to stand up and make a move because Jimmy obviously wasn't aware that I'd seen his weapon and any sudden movement on my part would've undoubtedly precipitated an attack. But I did turn my back on Jimmy to reach out and lift the pipe from the windowsill. My hands were so wet, though, that the pipe slipped out of my grip and wound up back on the windowsill.

"It was amazing how much went through my mind in the five seconds it took for Jimmy to stalk across the room. Without formulating any specific plan, I stood up and placed a hand on Jimmy's shoulder in a very reassuring manner. 'Oh,' I said, 'you came back for another game. That'll be fun, won't it, Jimmy? You're a really good player.'

"He still wore a very grim look, but he didn't know what to make of my friendliness. My entire chest was exposed and he could've slashed me in a heartbeat. When he hesitated for a moment, I began talking really fast. I apologized for what I'd said about the crib sheet. 'I was only kidding, Jimmy. You and I are still friends, right?' I also made sure to move between him and the three teachers so that nobody else could see that he was armed. If the word got out that Jimmy had come at me with a razor-sharp weapon but hadn't used it, he would have been ridiculed from one end of the joint to the other. 'What do you say we play another game, Jimmy?'

"I could see the anger drain from his face as he said, 'You shouldn't have accused me of that. I always play fair and square.'

"I apologized again and we played several more games of GHOST, none of which I won. I'd say that those games were the most important that I'd ever fixed."

On March 1, 1965, the Supreme Court issued a list of actions taken. The following notice was published under the heading "Criminal Law":

> Refused to review New York State court conviction of Jacob Molinas, a New York lawyer, for fixing college basketball games between 1957 and 1961 (No. 725, *Molinas v. New York*).

The highest court's failure to consider the case shocked Molinas and plunged him into a free-falling despair. Burt Pugash, Attica's other attorney, was also distraught. "It was incredible," said Pugash, "that the Supreme Court didn't recognize that the biggest part of the prosecution's case were illegal wiretaps. Why were they illegal? Because they were recordings of privileged conversations between an attorney and his clients. I took note of how many convictions of crooked union officials and cutthroat Mafioso had been reversed and I realized that there were political overtones to Jack's case. I suspected that somebody high up in the Justice Department was pulling the strings. Jack was entitled to a reversal and the reinstatement of his attorney's license. The whole thing stunk."

Molinas was so tormented by the Supreme Court's unjust decision (and so emboldened by the outcome of the anchovy trial) that he began to freely offer legal advice to his fellow inmates. "I was teaching a class in government and the Constitution and my friend Mike was one of my students. Just before the class got under way, Mike spoke up: 'Jack, one of the guys here is having a little problem with his lawyer. He's got the papers his lawyer sent him right here and it sounds like some kind of legal double-talk. Anyway, we were wondering if you could explain it to us.'

"I thought, what the hell. Treading the straight and narrow had only got me shafted. We were in a ground floor classroom and the library was next door—so to protect myself I hustled into the library and took out a book on Constitutional law, then returned to the classroom and put the book on my desk. Mike closed the door and I proceeded to do what Deputy Warden Myers had explicitly warned me against doing.

"Before long, I was totally involved in the point of law raised by the inmate's papers, and I was careless enough to start writing some salient information on the blackboard. I was at it for about fifteen minutes when, wouldn't you know it, a sergeant suddenly pushed open the door and walked into the room. This particular sergeant had very poor eyesight and wore very thick spectacles, and as soon as he entered the room, I immediately started talking about the Constitution. The sergeant was sniffing around, looking over inmates' shoulders and listening to me for all he was worth. Inevitably, he made his way up to the blackboard, and moved up so close that his eyes were about three inches away from what I'd written.

"'This is law!' he finally said. 'I'm locking up this entire class!'

"Then he herded us out into an anteroom and put a keep-lock sign on the classroom door. We were just sitting there and waiting for the deputy warden to come over and inspect the evidence. Everybody was moaning and complaining. They'd get locked up for sure, but I was worried that Myers would put me into a strip cell. All at once, another inmate poked his head into the room and whispered to Mike, 'Everything's taken care of.' Then Mike gave me a broad wink.

"Just then, the sergeant came blustering into the room. 'All right,' he shouted, 'who erased what was on the blackboard?'

"We just shrugged because we'd been sitting in the anteroom all along. Obviously, by some signal that I wasn't aware of, some inmate had gotten the word to pry open the classroom window, climb inside, and erase the incriminating evidence.

"When the deputy warden arrived on the scene to question me, it was easy to blabber about how I'd been teaching the class about the Fourteenth Amendment. Because there was no evidence, and because the sergeant's eyesight was questionable, we all got off scot-free. And I became even more determined that, from then on, I would give as much legal advice as I could.

"When the word got out, I was swarmed with inmates with all kinds of questions. I figured out a system whereby I refused to write anything and I refused to read any kind of legal papers. The only advice I would give was face-to-face and verbal. That way, the administration couldn't prove anything against me, but I could also make the inmates happy.

"There was a fellow named Greg who was from a small town in upstate New York. One day Greg approached me with a very interesting case. He'd been charged with conspiracy to commit grand larceny, paid a lawyer five hundred bucks, took a guilty plea, and received three and a half to seven. Anybody who'd passed the Bar would know that conspiracy to commit grand larceny was a misdemeanor that carried a maximum sentence of only one year. A mistake like that never would have happened in New York City.

"I told Greg that, yes, there had been an error. The guy had already served eighteen months and when I explained what the mistake was, he just blew up and threatened to have his lawyer killed. Sure enough, he followed up on my advice and he was set free a couple of weeks later.

"A guard spotted me talking to Greg in the yard, and I was subsequently called into Myers's office. 'Jack,' Myers said, 'I hear that you've been giving legal advice. If we find out it's true, I promise that you'll wind up in a strip cell.'

"'I'm glad to say it's not true, Your Honor.'

"Then he asked me what went on between me and Greg. The report was that we'd had a conversation in the yard that caused Greg to jump up and down in celebration.

"'The fellow merely asked me if conspiracy to commit grand larceny was a felony or a misdemeanor, Your Honor, and all that I told him was that it was a misdemeanor. Obviously, when he contacted his people on the street he discovered that he only should've gotten a one-year bit.'

"Myers had no proof that I was lying, so he let me off."

Through all the vicissitudes of prison life, Molinas never stopped trying to find a way out:

> 5/17/65
> Dear "Pops,"
> ...It was really a pleasure to learn of the birth of your new baby girl—I hope it doesn't make you feel too old, although it should make you feel younger—...Incidentally I was pleased to learn you & Claudia liked the gift Ellen sent; she does have good taste, even though she chose me—
>
> ...Oh yes, I was wondering if you could do me a favor— As you might know the N.Y. Legislature has been working at revising our Penal Law &

> has set up a Law Revision Commission—They have submitted their recommendations & I was wondering if somehow you could get your hands on a copy of this report—I'm especially concerned with that position relating to the new laws proposed on entrapment- If the Commission report is not available in its entirety, try to get just the latter portion—I would sure appreciate it.
>
> ...I've also been thinking about your idea to do a book about my life & it just might be a good idea...
>
> Fondly,
>
> // Jack Molinas 18896 //

"With the word out in the yard that I was giving legal advice, the administration was determined to catch me. Everybody's cells were periodically shaken down with a lot of fuss and fanfare, but the administration would also do mine in a sneaky way. Of course it was no trick for me to find out what they were up to. I'd arrange my papers in a certain way—maybe have the third page from the top lap over the edge. Or I might put a ruler on top of my papers and position it exactly one inch from the bottom edge. That's how I discovered that they were going through my belongings about three times every week. They seemed to be desperate for a reason to bust me. And eventually they found one.

"Basil came up to me one day to say that he had made parole and was scheduled to be released in a few days. Naturally, I felt very happy for him and everything was hunky-dory. 'By the way, Jack,' he said, 'could you do me a favor? I have a good job waiting for me, but I want to write some letters to several other potential employers. Could you get me a couple of sheets of carbon paper?'

"No problem. Since I was a teacher I had unlimited access to various school supplies, so I gave him five sheets of carbon paper. Unfortunately, an officer happened to see this and, sure enough, I got arrested again, this time for misappropriation of state property. Now that they had a legitimate charge against me, I was afraid that the deputy warden would sentence me to a strip cell. This was a gruesome punishment that had been ruled unconstitutional by the Supreme Court but was still being administered in Attica.

"The inmate would be put in a special cell that had no windows and no light. The walls and ceiling were metal and the floor was marble. There's a big metal door with a small peephole for the guards to look in, and a small slot at the bottom through which your food was passed. There's no furniture inside the cell, no bed, no toilet. The inmate was stripped naked and given some newspaper to clean up his mess, but the stink lingered for the duration of the sentence—which was a minimum of thirty days. The inmate was given a blanket at ten o'clock at night and it was taken away at six in the morning. There was no heat in the cell and in the winter the marble floor was frosty, so an inmate had to keep walking the entire day. There were only two meals a day shoved through the slot—a slice of bread and a cup of tea for lunch, and half the normal ration for dinner.

"Inmates who'd been in strip cells came out all screwed up. It took several days before their eyes would stop watering and they could tolerate daylight. In addition, they'd be thin, very submissive, and very insecure. I saw plenty of guys who went completely berserk after being released from thirty days in a strip cell. One guy just lost it during mess—he threw his tray in the air, started screaming and running around the room. None of the other inmates paid him any mind. We just kept eating our food while the guards chased the poor fellow around. It was important to get the meal down in case the officers had to clear the room or unleash the tear-gas canisters. There must've been ten officers trying to nab the guy. And none of the inmates cheered. None of us laughed. We just kept our heads down and minded our own business.

"Because the carbon paper arrest was my fourth, I was positive that I would suffer a similar fate.

"I told the deputy warden that I'd given Basil the carbon paper so that he could find a better job once he got out, but Myers wouldn't buy it. 'That's no excuse,' he said. 'You wasted state property, Jack, and that's a flagrant violation of the trust that we placed in you when we allowed you to be a schoolteacher.'

"Uh-oh. I cringed as he pronounced my punishment.... But it was only a keep lock for fourteen days.

"I say 'only,' but fourteen days was a long time without any exercise. Any keep-lock time was also potentially very dangerous because it presented any inmate who held a grudge against me a perfect opportunity to have me poisoned.

"When an inmate was keep-locked his meals were brought to him on a tray, right? So what someone bent on revenge would do was get a piece of glass from somewhere and pay somebody in the machine shop to grind the glass into a fine powder. The ground glass would then be taken over to the C Block, where the mess hall was, and for a fee or a favor one of the cooks could easily mix the glass into the food designated for a particular keep-locked inmate. Jello was a favorite because when the ground glass was mixed in, it was invisible. Once the doctored Jello was ingested, there was nothing that medical science could do to save the victim. Ground glass could also be mixed into meat loaf, mashed potatoes, or any kind of gravy.

"So being keep-locked could be a deadly situation. In fact, if some fellow was a good prisoner but had accidentally offended some other inmate, the aggrieved inmate would get somebody to pick a fight with him. In that case, there's an automatic lockup while awaiting trial.

"All the time I was in keep lock I wondered if anybody had their sights on me. Maybe Paul, the fellow who was in the fight I'd broken up my first day in the yard? Or the colored fellow who'd said he'd picked Michigan State but hadn't filled out the ticket? Perhaps the fellow who'd put soap shavings in the cigarette pack? Or Jimmy, the GHOST player? Or friends of the basketball player I'd low-bridged and maybe paralyzed? The more I thought about the possibilities, the less appetizing Jello became."

Soon after his release from his latest keep lock, Molinas was unexpectedly presented with a way out of Attica.

Just before Molinas had been sent back to Attica in July 1964, he'd approached Robert Ellis with a problem. "Jack told me," said Ellis, "that a lot of money was owed to him through some loan-sharking he'd done. He asked if it was okay to tell the people who owed him the money to bring it to me. I was glad to help him out. Jack was very happy and said that we'd decide what to do with the money later on. I was connected with a very staid law firm at the time and within two weeks a total of over two hundred and seventy thousand dollars in one-hundred-dollar bills was brought to my office."

Ellen Sohn had a similar experience: "Before he left for his second stint in Attica, Jack gave me instructions to meet some guy named Rinny every week at a certain time on the corner of Madison and Fifty-ninth Street. Rinny would give me envelopes full of cash and I was supposed to keep them until Jack got out of jail. I had no idea where the money came from or what the deal was."

Coincidentally, Ellen read a newspaper report concerning Mays Department Store and a multimillion-dollar swindle. "Jack had left me his car," Ellen said, "and there were loose scraps of paper scattered all over it, each scrap scrawled with a different name and number. I went through all of the scraps and was surprised to find that many of the names matched some of the names of suspects in the Mays case. That's when I realized that I'd been a bag woman for Jack. I was used to his idiosyncrasies, but being an accessory to a crime was too much. I called Bob Ellis and when we compared notes, we decided to visit Jack in Attica and find out exactly what was going on."

Molinas quickly fessed up. Operating in a partnership with Herman Witt (who was married to pop singer Fran Warren), Molinas had come across a mechanical device that could flawlessly reproduce anybody's signature. Molinas and Witt decided to duplicate the signature of the president of the J. W. Mays Department Store. They then made up dummy invoices for dummy corporations—like the "XYZ Toy Company"—and paid themselves with counterfeit Mays checks. Eventually, the store unearthed the swindle and alerted the district attorney's office. Several runners and middlemen were arrested, but the masterminds had thus far eluded detection.

"When I learned about the scam," Ellis said, "I contacted the Brooklyn District Attorney, at Jack's direction, and turned over to them the money that had been delivered to my office. I advised Jack to testify in the Mays case, in the hope that his sentence in the basketball fixing case would be reduced. And that's just what happened."

Ellen wasn't quite as tactful. "If you don't talk," she told Molinas, "I'm going to talk for you. You're a sick son of a bitch, Jack, and you deserve to spend the rest of your life in jail." When she returned to New York, Ellen immediately placed a call to Aaron Koota, the Brooklyn district attorney. She identified herself as Jack Molinas's girlfriend and said that Molinas had something important to say about the Mays case. The next day, two detectives appeared at Attica to question Molinas.

"I really didn't give them much information, but I did make several broad hints that I knew enough to break open the case. The detectives advised me that, sometime in the very near future, I would be subpoenaed to a grand jury and brought down to New York City to testify. Two weeks later, an order came instructing me to pack my belongings because I was being transferred to the Tombs. Sure enough, accompanied by two detectives, I was taken on the nine-hour train ride down to the city on November 4, 1965. I had just enough time to bequeath the cigarettes I'd been accumulating to Mike, Basil, Tiny the chef, and several other faithful friends and employees.

"After speaking with my lawyer, I agreed to testify in return for a waiver of immunity. But, honestly, I didn't tell them anything that the DA didn't already know."

Others involved in the case swore that Molinas's deal with the district attorney involved his squealing on Herman Witt. One participant also claimed that Molinas convinced the DA's office that he had inside information about a coterie of gamblers and drivers who were fixing horse races at Yonkers Raceway. In fact, there was a fixing ring, but Molinas knew nothing about it except what he read in the newspapers. A boyhood friend gave this reason as to why Molinas cooperated with the DA: "Witt had double-crossed Jack and stiffed him out of a couple of hundred thousand dollars in the Mays deal." Whatever Molinas's arrangement was, several inmates back in Attica considered him to be a "stoolie."

To her dismay, Ellen Sohn was also called before the grand jury. Her testimony was that in their several meetings Rinny had given her a total of ten thousand dollars. In truth, the sum was closer to sixty thousand dollars. Of the rest, Ellen spent some on what a friend called "niceties." She'd also make trips to a racetrack in order to safely cash the one-hundred dollar bills. Some of the money was presented to her brother Steven, who invested it in the stock market. Later, when Molinas demanded that his money be returned, Ellen refused.

"The Tombs was a hot and dirty place and about ninety percent of the fifteen hundred inmates were in there on narcotics busts. The only time I could see the sun was when I was allowed up on the roof to play volleyball. I never did testify before the grand jury, but every couple of days a pair of detectives would escort me over to the district attorney's office, where I'd be interrogated. What I didn't know about the Mays case I pieced together and told them as if I really knew the score. What they got from me was a detailed account that substantiated everything they had from other sources—but nothing new.

"My very first week in the Tombs I was chatting in a rec room with some inmates. I have a deep voice and I was talking too loud to hear one of the guards tell me to keep it down. The guard called me into a small area that was ordinarily off-limits to inmates. 'Didn't you hear me tell you to keep your voice down?'

"'Not at all,' I said.

"He was about five foot seven and a hundred and sixty pounds, and at one time he'd been a professional boxer. While we were talking he started putting on a pair of boxing gloves. 'Well,' he said, 'I don't care how big you are, you and me are gonna go at it.'

"It was always the runts with their Napoleon complexes who thought they could make themselves taller by picking fights with big guys. I wish they'd all leave me alone and buy themselves a pair of Adler elevator shoes.

"'I'm not fighting anyone,' I said.

"'I'm gonna hit you then, and if you don't defend yourself I'm gonna knock you out.'

"'If you put a hand on me,' I said, 'I'll have you in court tomorrow. Hey, I didn't do anything to you, so why are you fucking with me? I'm very sorry that I didn't hear you tell me to pipe down. All right? I apologize.'

"He mumbled and grumbled, but let me go back to my cell. As it turned out, within a few months we became the best of friends.

"I also met a couple of old pals back at the Tombs. Burt Pugash, the lawyer. And the guy who'd gotten his head split open in the fight I'd broken up in Attica. He must've thanked me a thousand times for saving his life."

On December 14, Molinas won a small victory in the federal courts when U.S. District Judge Harold P. Burke agreed to review his conviction. The brief drawn up by Molinas's newest attorney, Thomas H. Newman, had complained that Billy Reed's clandestine taping of his conversation in Molinas's law office was a violation of the defendant's rights under the Fifth and Sixth Amendments.

"Reed steered the conversation to topics suggested by the prosecutor, which were designed to elicit incriminating statements by Molinas," said Newman. The brief further claimed that the testimony of an alleged conspirator—Reed—against Molinas would not have been enough to convict the defendant. Then Newman quoted the prosecution: "These taped conversations provided the major portion of the corroboration needed..."

Newman based his argument on a recent landmark decision by the U.S. Supreme Court that a defendant must be given the "guiding hand" of a lawyer when the purpose of interrogation shifts from investigation to accusation. When questioning focuses on the accused and is aimed at getting a confession, a defendant must be permitted to consult with a lawyer. Newman asserted that Molinas didn't realize he was being "questioned" through the tape recording and was therefore illegally deprived of legal counsel.

In response, the state stressed the fact that Molinas was a lawyer himself. Also that instructions given by Molinas to Reed during their conversation were an attempt to get Reed to perjure himself—a crime for which Molinas was convicted. The state concluded that to apply the Supreme Court's decision to Molinas's case would mean that Molinas was entitled to legal counsel during commission of a crime itself.

Newman was optimistic: "This is the first time since my client's conviction that any judge has heard the arguments on the merits of his case." Molinas, of course, believed that Judge Burke would certainly rule in his favor and overturn the conviction. That's why Molinas was in rousing good spirits as he began his bizarre stint in the Tombs.

"In my free time, I developed a new hobby—the stock market. We were allowed to read the *New York Times* and the *Wall Street Journal* every day. I was also receiving literature from the various brokerage houses and I studied everything I could get my hands on. The rabbi at the Tombs also liked to play the market, and during morning services he'd let me use his telephone to call my broker, Sandy Solomon. It didn't take me long to start making a lot of money. Soon enough, I was advising some of the inmates as to what stocks they should be buying. The natural progression was that I began investing money for the guards, too. One time I was locked in my cell for seven days on a minor infraction and the guards made sure that I got copies of the *Times* and the *Wall Street Journal* so that I could keep everybody up to date.

"And my stay at the Tombs was prolonged under very unusual circumstances. A very high official in the criminal justice system heard about my expertise on the market, and he decided to put me to work. Twice a week a limousine would pick me up at the Tombs, one of those hideaway jobs with a bar and stereo and TV and thick curtains in back, and I would be chauffeured to Wall Street. I was playing with about two and a half million dollars and was doing very well for him. The limo picked me up at ten in the morning and I had to be back by midnight. The only stipulation was that because I was a prisoner two officers would accompany me wherever I went—Otto Kohl and Don Harding—a pair of terrific fellows. They used to call me 'Little Cinderella' because I had to be home by midnight.

"A few of the cons thought that I was getting sprung every week only because I was turning state's evidence against some of the other inmates in the Tombs. So some of them avoided me at all costs. Not even the Tombs bigwigs knew what was going on. They thought that I was some kind of undercover agent investigating how the joint was being run. That's why a lot of people in the Tombs were afraid of me.

"After I did my work on Wall Street for the judge, I had the rest of the day free. So me and Don and Otto hung out in bars and restaurants. Of course, I'd also invest a little money on the side for Don and Otto so that they'd be kindly disposed to me.

"One night we were dining at Patty's Restaurant when who should walk over but Lefty Rosenthal! He said that the bosses were happy with the way I'd taken my punishment without ratting on anybody. We shook hands and Lefty said, 'Good luck, Jack, and let's let bygones be bygones.'

"Being on the street took getting used to. Everything in prison happened very slowly and I was unnerved by how fast people walked, and how fast they talked. All the noise of passing traffic was almost unbearable. Even the food required an adjustment because of the spices and the oils. The first time I crossed a street I was paralyzed by the speed of the traffic and Don had to pull me back to the safety of the sidewalk to keep me from getting run over. I'd only been incarcerated for about a year and I couldn't even imagine what kind of adjustment would be necessary for someone who'd been sprung after ten years or more. But I quickly recovered my civilian frame of mind.

"I'd sometimes have dinner with Ellen, but she was acting a little weird, like she wasn't at all happy to see me. I mean, I was horny as I could be, but Ellen seemed to recoil every time I pecked her on her cheek.

"Anyway, one day I was sitting in my cell talking with my next door neighbor, a guy named Al who was somewhat of a ladies' man. 'Listen,' he said, 'since you've got all this street time, how'd you like a date with a really good-looking girl?'

"'You bet.'

"He gave me her telephone number and said that I should mention his name when I called her. So I called her from the rabbi's office, used Al as a reference, and told her that I was tall, dark, handsome, and an inmate in the Tombs. Of course she didn't believe me, but she was intrigued enough to make a date to meet at an expensive restaurant called the Penguin. I had Julie bring me some fresh clothes from home and I was dressed to the nines—a black silk suit, a white silk shirt, a silk necktie, black patent leather shoes, a cashmere topcoat, fancy leather gloves, the works. I made arrangements for a limo to pick up me and my two shadows and off we went.

"The girl's name was Nan and she was very attractive and too intelligent to believe that I really was a con. So I had Don come over and open his coat to reveal a pair of handcuffs and a handgun. We had a great time and she gave me a little kiss when the limo dropped me off at the Tombs. 'I'd love to do this again sometime,' she said.

"When I got back into my cell, I started thinking that I hadn't gotten laid in about a year and a half and something should be done about it. I decided to make a date with a girl whom I knew I could have a good time with. So the next morning I called up an old girlfriend named Jean and explained where I was and what I wanted. That was fine with her.

"The next time I was out on the town, Don and Otto and I met Jean at a seafood restaurant, Sloppy Louie's on Fulton Street, and we ate like royalty. Then it was getting close to nine-thirty and all I could think about was getting laid. 'Honey,' I said to Jean, 'would it be all right for us to come over to your apartment?' She must've thought I was into some kind of kinky sex, so she resisted at first, but she finally agreed.

"Jean lived in a small one-room efficiency in Jackson Heights. When we got there, she took off her coat and, man, did she look good. I fixed Don and Otto up with a few drinks, put on the TV for them, and then desperately looked around for someplace where Jean and I could have some privacy. By then it was about ten-fifteen and I was really hot to trot. We tried getting together in her walk-in closet, but the smell of camphor and the heavy coats were too overwhelming. We tried the bathroom next because there was a soft rug on the floor. But my head hit the sink and my leg banged against the commode. No good. In total frustration I sat on the toilet seat. That was it! And it was the best sex I've ever had!

"I worked hard to make peace with the other inmates who were understandably jealous of my freedom. I'd take orders to bring back little goodies for them—candy bars, coffee, a bunch of White Castle hamburgers—small packages of stuff that I could sneak in past the guards. After a while, my goings-on became a standing joke among the other inmates, and I'd have to tell them all about my various adventures.

"Meanwhile, I was making a fortune for my judge and for myself, too. I had the golden touch and everybody made money, including Otto and Don, the few inmates who had the money and the interest to play along, the guards, and my buddy Paul Brandt. Not even an adverse ruling by Judge Burke could completely damper my good spirits.

"This went on for about three years. The only break in the action came when I was shipped back to Attica for July and August because living in the Tombs was like living inside an oven. My angels were really taking care of me."

8/31/66
Dear Paul,
...Since my arrival back here at Attica, everything is going along just fine—I got my old job back teaching American history here at the school, & I'm active as always in our sports program— I finished out the baseball

season batting around .250, which isn't too good, but when you consider that I was locked up in the Tombs for eight continuous months without any recreation whatsoever, I guess it isn't too bad—...I must also confess that I struck out the first five times I came to bat—I guess that's nothing to brag about, but I finally did get my timing back.

...You know, I was thinking of going into the trucking business when I eventually get out & intend to buy some heavy equipment to do long-distance hauling for various companies on a leasing arrangement—Do you know anything about it, & if you do I invite your opinion—Now don't get any ideas that I'm going to do any driving, 'cause it just "ain't" so—...

Always,

// Jacob Molinas 18896 //

Back in the Tombs in the fall, Molinas continued beating the stock market and living a privileged life. "Whereas the year before," said Burt Pugash, "Jack used to sneak in candy bars for the other prisoners, things were much different when he returned from Attica. Jack used to come back from what we used to call his 'furloughs' with a shopping bag full of corned beef sandwiches and turkey sandwiches and all kinds of similar delicacies. What made this most startling was that in the Tombs inmates were not permitted to have any outside food come in. In Attica, you're entitled to have a food package one a month, but not in the Tombs. And of course whenever an inmate came into the Tombs, no matter where he'd been he was subjected to an absolute strip search. Even a candy bar or a jelly bean was contraband. I'd say, 'Jack, how do you do it?' And Jack would say, 'I've got the authorities in the palm of my hand.'"

"Except for the food situation," Jack remembered, "everything was much more relaxed in the Tombs. There were no restrictions on what we could wear, so most of the inmates dressed in blue jeans and sweat shirts. Also, because most of the inmates in the Tombs had not yet been convicted of anything and were, in fact, there awaiting trial, there was no prohibition against someone like me giving legal assistance to the other fellows. There was one little Puerto Rican kid who barely spoke English and, even though he'd been charged with homicide, was intent on trying his own case. He came to me one day and asked if I could help him prepare his summation. So I listened to him and made corrections in his argument and we practiced for several days. Because of the language problem, it was one of the most difficult things I ever did. But the kid wound up with a hung jury and I counted it as a miracle.

"My continuing success playing the stock market was another miracle. After a while, I became involved with an informal investment group, which consisted of three lawyers, two doctors, and Paul Brandt. The way we operated was that they'd put up the capital and I'd make the investments. While I was in the Tombs, I must've made about thirty thousand dollars a year for myself.

"This little group was doing so well that I said to them, 'Why should we have to pay commissions to registered brokers every time we want to make a deal? Why don't we buy a seat on the stock exchange for ourselves?' So I had Don and Otto take me down to the mercantile exchange and I spoke to one of the board of governors. The price was thirty-six thousand dollars, which was no problem, but it was very difficult to get a seat because every aspect of an applicant's personal background and financial situation would be subject to scrutiny. Our plan was to have my kid brother, Julie, buy the seat and then nominate me as the on-the-floor trader. The guy who interviewed me had no idea that I was a convicted felon and the whole thing was a farce to begin with. But I loved the idea of being a party crasher into this little clannish group of millionaires.

"Julie, of course, was clean as could be and we actually got well into the approval process without the board of governors ever suspecting who I really was. But, ultimately, I decided to pull back because if it ever came out that I had a seat on the mercantile exchange when I was supposed to be doing time, the resulting scandal would have turned the entire prison system inside out, and I'd have to serve my entire sentence without the possibility of parole. I was also concerned about jeopardizing Julie's teaching career."

Even though Ellen no longer had any warm feelings for Molinas, she'd meet him every Thursday night in front of the Brooklyn Borough Hall and then go out to dinner. "Jack really sickened me at that point," she said, "because he still didn't know right from wrong. Over dinner all he'd talk about was how he was an innocent bystander in everything that had gone down. He had no respect for anything and he had no fear of anything, either. He was smart enough to know, however, that I was over him. I used to hate having to meet him on those Thursday nights. I'd pray that I'd get sick so that I couldn't go. It was the Mays thing that really turned me off to Jack. But I still hung on because I felt it would be wrong to abandon him while he was still in jail. Isn't that disgusting?"

In the spring of 1966, primarily to get away from Molinas, Ellen moved to Los Angeles.

> 11/29/66
> Dear Paul,
>
> ...About that book we've been talking about doing. It sounds like a great idea. My life has certainly been interesting enough, hasn't it? But you & I will have to give a little thought to its theme & and what type of tone to present.... In the meantime, I agree that we should have a contract between us that authorizes you to approach potential publishers on my behalf. Just don't get bogged down with it—The simpler the better—If you wish I could draw up one that would also suit our purposes. I'll leave it up to you. As we also agreed, my main job is to write out a brief outline.

Will await your next word—
Always,
// Jacky //

"The Tombs was a different kind of place than Attica with a different kind of tension in the air. Normally, the guys in the Tombs would have to wait a month or two until their trials came up, but because the court calendars were so jammed up, some of the inmates had to wait for periods of up to two years. It was understandable that trivial events would cause certain guys to crack up. This happened one more time while I was there. Sure enough, it was another little half-pint nut case who attacked me for no good reason.

"It was in late June, just before I'd be sent to Attica for the summer, and it was close to a hundred degrees in the Tombs. Sometimes the guards would deliberately keep the windows closed on a hot day as a punishment if there'd been any hassles in a particular section. The windows were situated about ten feet above the floor and the only way they could be opened was if a guard climbed up on a catwalk to do the job—which involved a lot of huffing and puffing because the climb wasn't all that easy and the windows were usually jammed. So we were all sweltering and it was hot as blazes in the cells and the gallery. After the guard on duty made his rounds and went into the next gallery, I climbed up onto the catwalk and pried open every single window. Most of the inmates were very appreciative of the risk I'd taken, and about four minutes after I'd done the deed we were locked in our cells.

"About two hours later, we were released from our cells and freed to roam the gallery. Just as I came walking out of my cell, the guy in the cell next door—with whom I'd been on very friendly terms up until then—came sneaking up behind me. The everyday tension was so high in prison that inmates are always very alert and their senses were unusually acute. So I heard something out of the ordinary and when I turned to look I saw this fellow coming at me with a very strange weapon—he had a full can of Babo Cleanser in a sock. It was a makeshift blackjack and he was just about to crack me on the back of my head when I turned around. The can came down on my shoulder instead and I had no choice but to start punching him. 'I like the heat,' he said as we fought.

"And how tall was this guy? About five foot nothing!

"Before long, the riot squad came racing onto the scene. A riot squad was comprised of six to ten of the toughest cops in the joint. They were armed with lead-weighted billy clubs and they'd be swinging from the heels right out of the box. Their motto was 'Break bones first and ask questions later.' They were on the verge of waylaying both of us when they unexpectedly pulled back and just grappled us apart.

"Another guard subsequently told me why the riot squad hadn't unloaded on me: 'They know you go out once or twice a week, Jack, and they don't want to fuck with you because your patron is some big-shot federal judge. If they'd have hit you, they surely would've marked you up, and since you weren't at all aggressive toward them, they just wanted to avoid making explanations to some bigwig.'

"Anyway, I was called down to the dep once more. 'Can't you stay out of trouble?' he asked me. 'You're obviously highly intelligent, Jack, and you have yourself a great deal here. So why are you constantly getting in fights?'

"I told him how I'd been attacked from behind, but I didn't mention the homemade blackjack—which had disappeared from the scene, anyway. The result was another seven-day sentence in the box. I was locked up immediately even though it happened to be my day to go out on the street.

"When Otto and Don located me, I begged them to get me out of there. 'I'll tell you what,' Otto said. 'We can come and get you every day this week except Sunday.'

"Their regular job assignments were to deliver subpoenas and various paperwork all over the city, so for six days of my sentence I rode around with them in their car. When they had to make a delivery, I'd just sit in the car and read the newspapers. The only day I was in the box was Sunday. After that, some of the other inmates would jokingly genuflect whenever they saw me."

Molinas didn't get nearly the same kind of respect during his summer sojourns back in Attica. With Mike already out on bail, his betting pool was terminated—and so were his popular Sunday morning buffets. There was another, more ominous reason why his fellow inmates were cool to him. They'd heard through the grapevine about his princely privileges in the Tombs and many were convinced that the only explanation was that Molinas was squealing to the district attorney.

At the same time, there were no overt hostilities directed at him because Molinas continued offering verbal legal advice at large. No one would dare put Molinas out of commission and thereby inhibit the theoretical possibility of another inmate's regaining his freedom.

July 29, 1967
Mr. Paul Brandt
38 Shadey Terrace
Wayne, New Jersey

Dear Mr. Brandt:

This letter will confirm the agreement we have reached for the production of one or more works, including any and all versions or derivatives thereof, based upon, or using any incidents relating to my life and career in basketball, including, but not limited to, the criminal proceedings in which I was personally involved several years ago (any and all of such work or works being sometimes hereinafter referred to as the "Work").

We have agreed that the tentative title of the Work shall be "Around the Rim and Out." …

Your signature at the foot hereof will constitute this a binding agreement between us.

Very truly yours,
// Jacob Molinas //

Accepted and agreed to:
// Paul Brandt //

"There were so many long, empty hours that even my gambling and playing the stock market couldn't fill. There were card games all over the place—whatever game suited your interest. Bridge, poker, casino, hearts, gin rummy. Burt Pugash was in the Tombs for quite a while waiting for a writ of appeal to go before the court and I played a lot of gin with him. I also taught myself to become a pretty good chess player—good enough to work out all the chess puzzles in the *New York Times*."

Molinas also amused himself by befriending some of the Tombs' colorful characters. Foremost among these was Larry Shupack, a "degenerate gambler" originally from California. Shupack's father owned a furniture business and put him on a liberal allowance, but Shupack would lose every cent after two or three days at the nearest racetrack. His first brush with the law occurred in Los Angeles, where Shupack was arrested for breaking open a machine that dispensed loose peanuts (he claimed he was after the peanuts, not the money). Instead of appearing in court and paying a small fine, Shupack jumped bail and journeyed to New York City. In so doing, Shupack crossed state lines and his minor offense instantly became a felony. Shupack was quickly arrested in New York for panhandling and sent to the Tombs, where he met Molinas.

Chronically destitute, Shupack would earn money to buy his favorite food (pie and coffee) by singing and dancing in the mess hall or the gallery. Standing about six feet tall and weighing nearly two hundred and sixty pounds, Shupack appeared to be clumsy, although he was surprisingly very light-footed. Molinas tolerated Shupack more than did the other inmates because of their mutual fascination with gambling. Even so, Molinas knew that Shupack was a "loser" and otherwise kept his distance.

David Stein was another offbeat inmate with whom Molinas developed a genuine friendship. "David was a remarkable artist whose specialty was forging Marc Chagall paintings. He got caught because one day Chagall himself was walking along Madison Avenue when he saw a painting in the window of an art gallery that bore his name. He walked into the gallery and asked the proprietor, 'How much do you want for that painting?'

"'Fifteen thousand dollars,' was the answer. 'It's an original Chagall.'

"'This is not a Marc Chagall,' the artist exclaimed. 'This is a forgery!' Then Chagall, who was eighty years old at the time, proceeded to tear the fraudulent painting to shreds. The proprietor summoned the police, the old man's identity was discovered, and the 'dealer' who'd sold the putative Chagall painting to the gallery was apprehended.

"David had started out as a piano teacher, but he loved art so much that he eventually opened up the Trianon Gallery on Park Avenue. In addition to counterfeiting paintings, David also did the same with sculptures. When he lived in France he had done a copy of some famous Greek sculpture, placed it outside on a lawn, then went there every day to urinate on the statue. David explained that urine eats into marble at a very rapid rate and can age a statue ten years in a month.

"When his trial came up, David eventually made bail but had no money at his disposal, so I had Julie post a six-thousand-dollar bail. To show his appreciation, David gave me two of what he called his 'original forgeries.' David used that term to describe an original painting deliberately done in the style of a particular artist. One of these was a face of Christ that could pass as a work by Rouault. The other was a large checkerboard abstract in the style of Paul Klee."

9/2/67

Dear Paul,

...I understand that you called Don Harding yesterday and told him that one of the largest publishing houses in the country is interested in securing the rights to the JM story & that they also think it will be have good commercial value—What wonderful news—Who do think might play me in the movie? Paul Newman is too short. Maybe Elliott Gould?...

Fondly,

// Jacky //

The Manhattan district attorney's investigation into the Mays swindle had procured the desirable indictments and there was no longer any excuse to keep Molinas detained in the Tombs. However, the Brooklyn DA, Aaron Koota, had reprised his investigation into the Mafia's attempts to fix races at Yonkers, Roosevelt, and Monticello. Carmine Lombardozzi and several of his henchmen from the Sheepshead Bay area near Coney Island had already been arrested and Koota was hungry for more inside information.

"It proved to be a very fortuitous situation for me. What happened was that on one of my days out Don and Otto had to deliver a couple of subpoenas to some of the drivers at Yonkers Raceway. I was dying to go into the track with them, but they refused. Convicted felons were not allowed inside racetracks and if I got spotted, there'd be hell to pay. So I waited outside in their car while they took care of business. Quite accidentally, a reporter from the *Daily News* chanced to see me in the car and there was an article in the newspaper the next day to the effect that I was a key figure in the DA's investigation of rigged harness races. There was also a report on the local NBC-TV evening news broadcast to the same effect. Well, apparently the federal judge who was my patron prevailed upon Koota to keep me in the Tombs and interrogate me about fixed races. As before, I parroted information that I'd picked up in the newspapers, but that was enough to keep me out of Attica a while longer.

"It was also a wonderful opportunity for me to go before the grand jury, tell them what they already knew, but get credit for being a public-spirited citizen who was risking the vengeance of the Mafia. This had to have a beneficial effect on my parole hearing, which was scheduled for the following June."

Molinas continued to have stimulating adventures in the company of Don and Otto. "One time we were in Manhattan without a car and it started raining very heavily. There was a subway station on the corner and Don suggested that we make a run for it. Now, Don and Otto were middle-aged men on the hefty side, while I was still in good physical shape, so I easily outdistanced them. When they finally caught up to me in the station, Don was in a panic.

"'Don't ever run away from us like that,' he said, 'because, God forbid, if one policeman recognized you and also recognized me and Otto, why then he's liable to shoot you. And if he shot and killed you, it would be legally justified. It's no joke, Jack. It's always better to be wet than to be dead.'

"Words to live by."

4/22/68

Dear Paul,

...As you know I was *36 years old* last Sunday (4/16) & while that number does sound horribly old, I must confess I feel like 21. Must be my clean living! Anyway I'm sure I'm adding years to my life's expectancy by my present clean, healthy & "disgusting" way of life— I guess when you get drunk, you need a little time to sober up!...

Always,

// Jacky //

With a federal judge beholden to him, Molinas had quite a bit of leverage for a convicted felon. He also bragged to Paul that four Central Intelligence Agency bigwigs and three Security Exchange Commission officers were also the beneficiaries of his stock market expertise. (Otto Kuhl and Don Harding had sufficient funds to retire from the force and open a nightclub in Hempstead called "Jack's Lounge.") Even when his usefulness as an informant in the racetrack conspiracy ended, Molinas sat back and waited for his favors to be returned. On May 9, Judge Sarafite further reduced Molinas's sentence to six to nine and a half, which meant that he'd be immediately eligible for parole.

Four days later Molinas was returned to Attica and placed in protective custody. "This was a restrictive situation," said Burt Pugash, "with a separate gallery and separate yard. Cons in protective custody ate in their own cells and were subjected to an increased security presence. Jack was there because his life would be in danger if he'd been in the general population. Prisoners didn't care who he'd informed on or how relevant his informing was. In their eyes, the fact was that Jack was a rat and would have to be eliminated. I think it was his supposed cooperation in the investigation of the harness race fixes that turned the prisoners against Jack. I used to try and argue with the prisoners, demanding that they tell me of anybody who went to jail because of Jack's testimony. Of course, they couldn't but that didn't deter them from thinking that Jack was a rat. In truth, Jack did a number on the DA. He stretched it out for two years and he certainly did an easy bit. The other thing Jack accomplished by conning the DA was creating a situation where his life really was in danger up at Attica. This was something that the parole board would consider when Jack was eligible to appear before them. Given what he faced when he first was sentenced, Jack did a remarkable job of beating the system. The man was a genius!"

The parole board was scheduled to convene on June 4 and Molinas spent his time preparing his presentation. "The all-powerful parole board, they were the gods in the correctional system. I had been in jail for almost fifty months, and I'd been thinking of what I was going to say to the parole board for at least a year. The main thing was to tell them that I'd learned my lesson.

"A parole board can come to a number of decisions: They can immediately release an inmate. They can turn him down. And they can tell him to reapply in another six months or two years or whatever. Whenever an inmate returns from an interview with the parole board he's immediately bombarded with questions as soon as he shows his face in the yard. What was their decision? What had they asked him? What were his answers? What was their mood?

"I was so nervous before my interview that I couldn't eat for two days. I put on a brand-new T-shirt (that immediately got soaked through with my own sweat), my gray institutional pants were perfectly pressed, my shoes were spit-shined, I was clean-shaven, and my hair was cut short. The interviews usually lasted anywhere from twenty minutes to a half hour, and there was a long line of inmates waiting to be interviewed. I waited on line the entire day without my turn coming up, so I was taken back to my cell and carefully removed my clean clothes. I couldn't eat, I couldn't sleep. I just lay on my bed thinking, going over my presentation, trying to anticipate any problems or difficult questions they'd ask me.

"I'd certainly had some terrible moments in my life, the worst being when the mother pulled the little kid away from me in the train station in Ossining.

When I got the ten-to-fifteen bit from Judge Sarafite I'd been stunned and hollowed out. But I'd never been so nervous before. There was also a certain amount of fear. I felt like a man who was crawling through the desert and dying of thirst. Suddenly he sees an oasis and he knows that his life could be saved. But he's also aware that the oasis might be a mirage. In the same way, the parole board could either save my life or condemn me to another five years in Attica.

"I finally had my interview the next day and when I walked into the room my hands were sweating so much that I had to hide them in my pants pockets. There were three members of the board—C. H. Reynolds, Robert L. Wright, and Aaron L. Jacoby—and my file had been assigned to Reynolds, who acted as the primary prosecutor and would ultimately make the final decision. Then the questions started coming.

"They asked me if I thought I could adjust to normal life. That was a standard question and an easy one to handle. They said that they were bothered by my previous associations with the Mafia and wondered if I'd be tempted to resume my involvement with them. I assured them that this would never happen. In my answers, I made sure to express my opinion that my sentence had been extraordinarily severe for my crimes. They nodded their heads but didn't otherwise respond.

"Then they asked me about Ellen (because she'd visited me several times) and if I was planning to marry her. I said that I didn't think so, but marriage was a possibility.

"Where was I going to live? With my parents. Where was I going to work? Although I had nothing specific lined up, I'd be willing to work at any kind of job that would be acceptable to the parole board. I thought I was making a good impression, but their faces were impassive.

"Then they asked me if I was guilty of the crimes of which I'd been convicted. I said yes for two reasons: Number one, I *was* guilty and there was nothing to be gained by denying this. Two, the reading I'd done indicated that the first overt sign of an individual's rehabilitation was being able to admit his guilt.

"Things got a little more lighthearted when I was queried about the five arrests I'd suffered in Attica. 'You pleaded guilty four times,' the questioner said, 'but you pleaded not guilty once. Tell us about your arrests.'

"'Gentlemen,' I said, 'I was arrested for violations like walking too fast, using the wrong broom, and leaving a crust of bread on my tray. While I realize they were all violations of the rules, I'm sure if a guard wants a certain inmate to be arrested he can always find some sort of infraction.'

"They asked if I knew the difference between a straw broom and a push broom. 'I'll know the difference,' I said, 'until my dying day.'

"They laughed after I'd said this, but I warned myself that their laughter didn't necessarily mean anything. I'd heard that parole boards could be very hostile, but also that a friendly reaction was meaningless.

"'You realize, Jack, that because of your being disbarred not only can't you practice law, but we won't allow you to even work in a law office in any capacity.'

"'I do realize that,' I said.

"They said that being a teacher in the prison school was a plus for me. 'Lending my efforts toward the rehabilitation of other inmates' was how they put it. Then one of them asked me this: 'While you've been here, have you ever prepared any legal writs for any inmates?'

"This was a double-edged sword because they knew the truthful answer was 'yes,' and they also knew the rules dictated that my answer should be 'no.' I decided that they were more concerned with whether or not I'd been rehabilitated than they were with whether or not I'd violated the rules, so I simply said, 'Yes.' They each responded with a half-smile and didn't pursue the subject. And that was that.

"When I got back to my gallery, the other inmates had the same questions for me: What mood was the board in? What did they ask you? How did you answer? Who was on the board?

"Later that evening, a runner who was friendly with the prison typist came by my cell to say, 'Jack, you made it.' But I still wouldn't believe the good news until I saw it in writing. Twenty-four hours later the verdict was official—'Paroled to your old job.' This was a standard code that meant that I had to get an acceptable job before I'd be allowed to go free.

"Before I could even figure out where I could find myself any kind of work that would satisfy the parole board, I got a letter from Ellen's father. He had already contacted the board, offered me a job at his printing business—the Record Press—and the job had been accepted. Hallelujah!"

Molinas was released from Attica on July 2, 1968, and flew from Attica into LaGuardia Airport, where Julie was waiting for him. Their reunion was surprisingly subdued. "I drove us both back to the city," Julie said, "with Jack repeatedly complaining that I was driving too fast and asking me to slow down. In reality, Jack was completely acclimated to the very slow pace of prison life and I was taking pains to drive no faster than forty-five miles per hour."

"I'm free!" Molinas kept repeating. "I'm free!"

And he swore to himself that he'd never go to prison again. Whatever he wound up doing, they'd never catch him!

The rules of Molinas's parole were fairly stringent: He could neither drive nor own an automobile. He couldn't leave New York without the permission of his parole officer (Joel Horman). He couldn't vote in any kind of election. He had to be home every evening by midnight. He had to report to his parole officer once every week (later biweekly) at 11 Gold Street in lower Manhattan. But the one prohibition that really irked Molinas forbade him from "living as man and wife with anyone to whom [he was] not legally married," and also banned him from having "sexual relations" with anyone not his "lawful spouse."

For nearly two weeks, Molinas moped around his parents' apartment, refusing the overtures of his friends to go out on the town and celebrate. Louis was busy working in the Eagle Bar, but Betty didn't let her son out of her sight. She cooked him all of his favorite meals—spinach pies, red beans and rice, and steaks. At night, the family would watch TV in the living room.

When close friends visited during the day, Molinas would retreat to his room, where they'd mostly catch up on where everybody was living nowadays and what they were doing, who was married, and who had children. Molinas could only handle seeing two or three friends at a time and they found him to be rather subdued, except that he was cursing more then he used to. Also, before serving his time, Molinas favored monogrammed shirts and took pride in being dapper. Now he wore conservative button-down collared shirts and bland chino pants. When he was alone, Molinas read mostly novels—his favorite being *The Godfather*. He also kept a diary to show his parole officer that he'd been behaving.

Louis Sohn's firm dealt primarily with printing legal forms and Molinas was employed as a salesman. "It was a token job," Sohn admitted. "Hey, somebody had to vouch for him to get him out of jail. Jack was supposed to be contacting lawyers he knew and soliciting business, but I hardly ever saw him around the office. I can understand why my daughter wrote him off, but outside of the fact that he liked a fast buck, Jack was really a very nice guy."

Horman visited Sohn's printing shop on several occasions without encountering Molinas. "He's out selling," Sohn told the parole officer. Horman also made several unannounced visits to the Ocean Parkway apartment to ascertain if Molinas was indeed living there and to make sure the parolee was at home before his midnight curfew tolled. Satisfied that these conditions were being met, Horman saw no reason to continue stalking his assigned parolee.

Within a week of his release, Molinas made two extravagant purchases—a huge Magnavox color TV for his parents (the first in the neighborhood), and for himself a brand-new silver Lincoln Continental Mark III with an impressive price tag of over seven thousand dollars. His friends were impressed by the money Molinas was flashing, but he offered them no explanation about where it came from. In truth, the Mafia brass had generously rewarded Molinas for being closemouthed during his trial and his jail time.

In mid-July, Artie Tolendini threw a party for Molinas at another friend's apartment on Parsons Boulevard in Queens. There was plenty of booze, Chinese food and Tolendini also hired four prostitutes for twenty-five dolars each. Molinas was embarrassed and somewhat reluctant to join in the fun, but at 2:00 A.M., Tolendini made an announcement: "All the straight girls have got to leave now." Then the task was to get Molinas into one of the bedrooms with the hookers. Molinas resisted but eventually went along with the program. After being alone with the girls for nearly an hour, Molinas came out of the bedroom and said with a big smile, "I'm home!"

After his official coming out, Molinas went wild. In his pre-prison days, Molinas would only get involved with beautiful women—now he dated every woman who'd sleep with him and he couldn't care less if his friends called them "dogs." With Horman's permission, Molinas moved into a "bachelor pad" in Manhattan on Thirty-sixth Street and Third Avenue. Because Molinas didn't have a license, Julie and friends like Marvin Weisman and Al Seiden would chauffeur Molinas around in his new Lincoln—but once he moved into the city Molinas did his own driving. Molinas also had a hair weave and then connected with an old flame, Ann Hemlock.

"I had a house in the Hamptons," she said, "and we went there for a weekend even though I had lost all interest in him. But Jack insisted on stopping by every bar in the area and he got nutty in every one of them. Drinking too much and coming on to every woman who gave him a second look. I was trying to be nice to him after his long ordeal, but he was just too crazy."

In August, Horman's office was moved from Gold Street to 314 West Fortieth, and instead of a private room, he was assigned to a cubicle in a large room. During their interviews, Molinas told Horman that he was bored with his job in the printing shop and wanted some kind of position in the stock market. This was impossible, since it would require clearance from the SEC, which would never be forthcoming for a convicted felon. Horman also noted several other of Molinas's "grandiose schemes," such as selling the rights to his as yet unwritten biography to a major motion picture company. Molinas also wanted permission to travel to South Africa to investigate the possibilities of investing in a platinum mine. The best Horman could do was get an okay for Molinas to engage in "a legitimate business deal" as long as the details and the other principals were on the level.

Molinas did confess to "bumping into" a Mafia-sponsored bookmaker, but said nothing about his illegally owning and driving a car. Horman's own investigations did reveal, however, that Molinas had been associating with several criminal lawyers who were known to be "mob mouthpieces," and the parolee was duly warned to sever these relationships. Horman's overall impression was that Molinas would "toe the line because he was so afraid of being returned to Attica."

The proposed platinum deal involved Arnie Goldstein, one of the original Bronx Panthers. "Shortly after Jack got out of Attica," Goldstein said, "he told me about a convicted murderer he'd met there who came from a fairly well-to-do-family in South Africa. Because of this man's family connections, he was able to buy platinum at the 'mine price.' At the time, the over-the-counter market price was in excess of three hundred dollars an ounce, but could be purchased directly from the mine for less than a hundred dollars. Jack produced letters from the Barclay Bank indicating that they were prepared to deliver the platinum to Johannesburg and it would be our responsibility to ship it from there to New York. I told Jack if that was indeed the case, we should buy a substantial amount and share in the profits. However, before making the deal and investing so much money, I insisted on traveling to Johannesburg to make sure the platinum 'was for real' and I was prepared to baby-sit the platinum all the way from Johannesburg to New York. When Jack didn't object, I flew down to South Africa by myself. After spending four days in Johannesburg, I discovered that the entire transaction was fiction and that even the Barclay letters were forged. Jack's prison buddy had scammed both of us."

Molinas's financial adventures soon became an issue with his parole officer. "I knew that Molinas was doing some stock trading in his brother's name," said Horman, "for which his brother had given him a power of attorney. This was perfectly okay. What wasn't so good was that Molinas was also investing other people's money in his brother's name. The fact that he hadn't volunteered this information made it so much the worse. I told him to cease and desist immediately. There was another illegal operation transpiring, one that I never could prove and he never admitted. This was that Molinas had established the J & M Trading Company as an umbrella under which his stock market dealings took place. Molinas was a very slippery person and I never fully trusted him."

Sometimes Jack would run into ex-cons on the street. Naturally it was a tricky situation. One day while he was walking along Third Avenue, he met a guy named Stevie who he knew from Attica. Jack had been kind of friendly with him before, and even though it was a parole violation for him to talk to anybody who had a record, Stevie looked down and out, so he stopped for a chat. He'd just been recently released and the only money he had was the twenty bucks that the state gave every con when he got out. Jack gave him a hundred bucks and wished him good luck. About two months later, he heard that Stevie was back in Attica for knocking over a grocery store.

"Another guy I accidentally met on the street was none other than Willie Sutton. It turned out that Joel Horman was his parole officer, too, and that neither of us liked Horman because he always went by the book. Willie said that he was writing a book about all of his escapades, that he was on the verge of signing a movie deal, and that his agent was booking him on a bunch of TV shows. When I told him that I was trying to get the same thing happening for me, Willie wished me good luck. Then he gave me the name of his agent and said we should all get together for dinner sometime—which, of course, we never did."

Molinas was deposed in the suit Connie Hawkins brought against the NBA. When Molinas testified that the notorious two hundred dollars was in fact a loan that was eventually repaid, the NBA had no basis to continue banning Hawkins from the league. What followed was a million-dollar settlement and Hawkins's admittance in the NBA.

As summer turned into autumn, Molinas was moved to revive another aspect of his past life: Even though he weighed close to two hundred thirty pounds and hadn't touched a basketball since his early days in Attica, Molinas got the itch to start hooping again. Molinas called Allan Seiden, who always had a prime "run" scheduled somewhere or other. Sure enough, Seiden's latest game was against the Sherman White Old-Timers in Orange, New Jersey. Seiden was happy to give Molinas a rundown on the rosters: "Sherman's got his old rebounding buddy Fletcher Johnson and also Cleo Hill, who played for the St. Louis Hawks. I've got a nice squad as well with Eddie Warner and Ed Roman."

"Can I play?"

"Of course," said Seiden, "but when was the last time you touched a basketball?"

"Five years ago."

"And you expect to compete with these guys? I don't know, Jack. Why don't you show up and we'll see how it goes."

The game began with Molinas on the bench, and after ten minutes Seiden's team was down by fifteen points and "getting our ass kicked." Molinas eventually begged his way into the game. Seiden cringed when Molinas took the floor, afraid that his buddy was so out of shape he might suffer a heart attack.

Imagine Seiden's amazement when Molinas took charge of the game and rallied his team back into contention. "He was running up and down the court like a rookie," Seiden said, "and throwing in his hook shot just like he used to do. Nobody could keep Jack away from the basket and he made Sherman look as immobile as a telephone pole. In the last thirty minutes of the game, Jack scored thirty points. We ultimately lost when the hometown referees cheated and awarded two free throws to Sherman for an imaginary foul. But the story of the game was Jack. He was sensational."

Encouraged by his performance, Molinas made an effort to play regularly, becoming a fixture at pickup games organized by Seiden at Hewlett High School. Before long, Molinas was back on the hoop-time circuit, attending NBA games and betting on college games. He even deigned to be interviewed by David Wolff for an article commissioned by *Life* magazine about Connie Hawkins:

> A few weeks ago Molinas placed his glistening shoes atop his attorney's desk, puffed a thick cigar and talked about Hawkins. Wearing an expensive suit, wide paisley tie and infectious smile, Molinas was the same picture of confidence and charm he had been until the closing days of his trial. He has abandoned his pretense of innocence, but not his sense of humor. "I don't need the publicity," he joked. "What can you write about me except that I corrupted the youth of America?"
>
> "*Allegedly* corrupted," reminded his lawyer, a Runyonesque figure in sharkskin suit, pink shirt and huge purple cuff links.
>
> "Of course," said Jack, laughing.
>
> But Molinas doesn't laugh about Hawkins. "I never made any approach or gave him any reason to think games were being fixed or bets were being made," Molinas said. "As far as that $200 is concerned, Connie called me in December [1960] and said he needed a loan or he couldn't go back to school. I never expected to see the money again. Then one day, this guy walks into my office and puts $200 on the desk. He says he's Connie's brother. And that was well before the scandal broke."

At the same time, Molinas was reiterating to close friends that he'd "taken the rap for Hawkins." What was the truth? All we know is that Molinas told different groups of listeners exactly what they wanted to hear.

In late November, Molinas took Artie Tolendini to Madison Square Garden to watch a ball game and meet Don and Otto. "It was a very social evening," Tolendini said. "We drank beer, ate hot dogs and bullshitted. Jack and the two cops traded funny stories about their days and nights on the town and Jack kept repeating that he'd never told the DA's people anything they didn't already know."

The game matched the Knicks against the Phoenix Suns, whose star player was Connie Hawkins (finally admitted into the NBA after years of legal wrangling). While the teams warmed up for the second half, Molinas said this: "What do you guys think would happen if I walked on the court and handed Hawkins an empty envelope? Who would crap in his pants first? Hawkins or Podoloff?" When the laughter faded, Molinas added, "Someday I'm going to dance on Podoloff's grave."

Whenever Molinas attended a game at the Garden, fans would shake his hand, point to the players on the court, and say, "Jack, you should be out there. None of those guys could carry your jock." Molinas was also greeted by an occasional mobster who'd tell him what a good soldier he'd been. Bookmakers, too, would pay their respects: "Glad to see you back out, Jack. What do you think of the spread?"

Molinas would also take his girlfriends to Knick games. One of them was a buxom blond from Los Angeles who wore tight blouses and miniskirts. Because of her resemblance to a voluptuous cartoon character in *Playboy* magazine, she was known only as "Annie Fanny." Molinas would parade her around the court during the game and enjoy dazzling both the spectators and the ballplayers.

"But Jack," Tolendini protested, "she's ugly."

"I don't look at her face," Molinas replied. "I just look at her tits."

Increasingly concerned with his own appearance, Molinas was fastidious about maintaining his hair weave. "I went with Jack once when he got his weave tightened," said Marvin Weisman. "Jack explained that in a hair weave the fake hair was attached to what was left of his real hair, and as his real hair grew, the weave would loosen up. He paid a yearly fee that entitled him to so many tightening treatments, and for several days after he'd had it done, the weave was so tight that the skin on his face was stretched. I'd kid him about it and he'd complain that laughing made his face hurt. So what did I do? Everything I could to make him laugh. I'll say this about Jack, no matter what went down, he always had the gift of being able to laugh at himself. That's one reason why he was such great company."

One person, however, who didn't appreciate Molinas's characteristic lightheartedness was Joel Horman. In early December 1968, Horman had information that Molinas was illegally driving a car (the Lincoln) that was registered to Julie. When faced with the charge, Molinas argued that he needed to drive in order to continue his employment. Horman and his superiors were considering citing Molinas for violating his parole, but decided that the transgressions were not serious enough to have him returned to custody. Within a few days, Horman received a letter from Louis Sohn confirming Molinas's need to operate a motor vehicle in the course of his employment. In their next interview, Horman suggested that Molinas either take taxicabs or ride the subways and denied the reinstatement of his driving license. Horman did yield on one point, however, when he permitted Molinas to continue investing in the stock market on Julie's behalf.

Two months later, Horman and another parole officer staked out Molinas's apartment and personally caught him driving the Lincoln. After searching the car and then the apartment without turning up anything illegal, Molinas was let off with another dire warning. Horman noted that during his reprimand "Molinas was nervous as hell. He was like an overgrown adolescent who'd been called on the carpet." The truth was that Molinas had already concluded that Horman would never bust him for driving a car.

By now, Molinas was getting fed up with both Horman and the restrictions imposed by his parole. The slightly built Horman was just another runt trying to prove that he was a big shot, and being on parole was an extension of being in prison. Horman was a plantation owner and Molinas was a slave. Molinas's parole was scheduled to expire in October 1973, but he couldn't wait until then. Measures had to be taken as soon as possible.

Meanwhile, Molinas showed his contempt for Horman by bringing his girlfriends to the biweekly interviews. "They were showgirl types," Horman said, "and they were all dolled up like they'd just stepped off a Broadway stage. Believe me, they created quite a stir in the office. Molinas sure was a charmer, he suggested that I read *The Godfather*, and he kept trying to convince me that he'd left the life of crime behind him. But he also began inquiring about the possibility of moving out of New York. I told him that if he could secure a legitimate job in another state we would conceivably let him go."

Until then, there were enough diversions at hand to keep Molinas occupied: the stock market, betting on ball games, easy women, and high-flying social parties. The party of the decade took place on New Year's Eve in a penthouse on East Seventy-first Street. The main attraction was supposed to be Joe Namath, the glamorous quarterback of the New York Jets, but he never showed. Molinas's date was Annie Fanny, but he did his best to enliven the activities by outrageously flirting with all the other female celebrants.

From early 1970, Molinas would also travel to Milton Gross's house in Rockville Centre, Long Island, two or three times every week for a series of tape sessions that he hoped would be the basis of the book Molinas always yearned to produce. Paul Brandt gladly relinquished his contractual rights to the project because Gross was a syndicated sports columnist for the *New York Post*, who through the years had written numerous articles that were sympathetic to Molinas."

Even while he was collaborating on the taped interviews with Gross, Molinas had written his own book proposal (*Around the Rim and Out*) and showed it to an agent who had influential contacts in the film industry. The agent reported that the proposal had elicited enthusiastic responses from Warner Brothers, ABC-TV, Seven Arts, and especially from Joe Pasternak at 20th Century Fox. Harold Messing (who was an attorney for Greenbaum, Wolf and Ernst) initiated preliminary negotiations with Pasternak and obtained a letter stating the producer's willingness to meet with Molinas. In addition, Paul Brandt had recommended Molinas to a motion picture agent named Jean Loch and she'd agreed to accept Molinas as a client.

Armed with this information, Molinas showed his proposal to Horman and asked leave to visit Pasternak in Hollywood. Horman believed that most of the proposal was "science fiction," especially a section that promised to describe "how Jack was kidnapped, beaten, and threatened with death (on many occasions), and how a war erupted between a Chicago and Brooklyn 'family' over his abduction." Yet Horman granted Molinas permission to spend six days in Hollywood commencing on August 4, 1969.

Molinas's eventual encounter with Pasternak proved inconclusive, since the producer was not willing to make any sort of commitment without seeing a screenplay (which he refused to finance). If Molinas found Pasternak to be somewhat arrogant, he was impressed with Pasternak's luxurious house, with the starlets who congregated around the swimming pool, and with the glorious California weather.

While Molinas was in Hollywood, he had a visitor—Bobby Kraw. Early in his fugitive days, Kraw had been driving through the dense Los Angeles traffic one day when he saw an intriguing sign on a construction site: "This building designed by Norman Arno." Kraw liked the sound of the name and decided to take it for his own. Since then, Bobby Kraw had simply ceased to be and Norman Arno had accumulated all the necessary identification to prove his existence. Arno and Molinas had a joyful reunion—how's Joe Jalop doing? What about so-and-so?—before getting down to more immediate concerns.

Arno explained how things worked in sunny California. The Mafia families in San Francisco, Los Angeles, and San Diego were all loose operations that didn't even know what was going on in their own backyards. Moreover, instead of areas of influence being determined by geography, one family ruled the drug trade on a statewide basis, while another family controlled gambling or prostitution, and so on. The only exception was San Jose, which was completely tied up by the Cerrito family. Arno also noted that more and more Mafioso were moving their money to California—mostly into legitimate business through their connections with various labor unions. Unlike the legal hoops through which people had to jump to either form or buy into corporations back East, in California corporate ownership went unchallenged.

In New York, the Five Families had just about everything locked up, and a hardworking con man couldn't get too friendly with anyone without mortally offending someone else. "After Apalachin and Valachi and the Banana War," said Arno, "it can cost your life or your freedom just to talk to a soldier or an old friend on the street. Things out here are much more wide open." Arno strongly suggested that Molinas attempt to get his parole transferred to Los Angeles. "Not only are there fewer restrictions out here," Arno enthused, "but the probation officers are all very laid back. They're more interested in keeping their own gigs than in busting an ex-con's chops."

Molinas was convinced. Upon returning to New York, Molinas told Horman that a motion picture deal would "undoubtedly be forthcoming" and officially requested a transfer to Los Angeles. A letter from Messing reinforced the belief that a deal with Pasternak was imminent. And Molinas further legitimized his request by presenting Horman with a thousand-dollar bill (which he never paid) from Messing for work the lawyer had already completed. Molinas also produced a letter from Arno promising unspecified employment at the rate of $125 per week in a bogus film company. Since Horman considered Molinas to be a considerable nuisance, the transfer request was granted.

While Molinas waited for the paperwork to journey through the labyrinthine probation department, he continued to enjoy the high life—gambling, gamboling, and squandering lots of money, especially on clothing. No more drab grays and white for him. If making money was easy, spending it was even easier.

Molinas's transfer was finally approved in mid-February and Julie drove him to the airport on February 25. Thoroughly enjoying the long flight, Molinas couldn't help imagining what dreams would come true in the promised land. His book would be a best-seller, his movie would be boffo at the box office, he'd buy a swanky home overlooking the Pacific, beautiful starlets would compete for his favors, he'd become a Mafia chieftain, the only Jew to be "made." *California, here I come.*

Norman Arno met Molinas at LAX and Molinas was shocked at his friend's physical deterioration. Arno was overweight, almost completely bald, the skin on his face was mottled and so flaky that he couldn't stop scratching himself, his teeth were rotten, and he looked like he was seventy years old. Until Molinas had a chance to reconnoiter what he called "the LA scene," he lived in Arno's small apartment. Molinas was pleased to discover that the only food Arno ate was steak, but he was also alarmed when he realized that Arno was an alcoholic.

At the time, Arno was in a mail-order business that primarily distributed rather modest pinup photos. His biggest moneymaker, however, was the book (later a movie) *100 Ways to Turn Your Lover On*, in which all the participants wore leotards. For the next few days, Arno shepherded Molinas around town and also introduced him to the movers and shakers. These included the likes of Tony LaRosa, a self-proclaimed promoter who occasionally bankrolled one of Arno's orgiastic opuses; Joe Black, a small-time gambler and bookie; Ted Gaisworth, a two-hundred-seventy-pound producer of porno films; Joseph "Junior" Torchio, who specialized in infiltrating record companies, nightclubs, and talent agencies at the behest of one of the New York families; and scores of other frenetic sleazebags who were desperate to make money in a hurry. For starters, Molinas began bookmaking on a limited basis (handling a total of only two thousand dollars on a typical weekend's action) and also shylocking money to several of Arno's friends.

Privately, Molinas had nothing but disdain for the Californians he'd encountered. They had no "street smarts." They were "hillbillies." Hell, they didn't even know what a chocolate egg cream was. Or a Manhattan Special (a coffee soda).

Uppermost on Molinas's mind was selling the film rights to his life's story as represented by the "sci-fi" proposal he'd written himself. One of his new buddies, Tony LaRosa, bragged about his high-level connections in the movie industry and Molinas was hopeful that he could help broker a deal. LaRosa arranged an interview with super-agent Swifty Lazar (who was gruff and dismissive) and also with a producer named Marty Britt (who was polite but also not interested).

Nevertheless, Molinas would try to impress women by talking up the movie, which he claimed was "this close to going into production." By now, Molinas was cool on the idea of Elliott Gould's playing the lead, leaning more to either Clint Eastwood or Robert Redford. To a lawyer friend named Elliot Ableson, Molinas proposed that Dustin Hoffman would be perfect for the role. "But Jack," Ableson protested, "Hoffman's a midget."

"No problem," said Molinas. "These days they can do all kinds of things with trick photography."

Mike Cleary was a probation officer in Los Angeles County, who first heard that Molinas was in the area from a friend in the Intelligence Department of the LAPD when Molinas's name happened to come up during a routine check of some wiretaps connected with a gambling operation. "The authorities in New York," said Cleary, "never let us know that Molinas had been transferred to our jurisdiction. It was clear that the New York people didn't know who Arno was and didn't care. I was convinced that there was some kind of mob-related coercion that allowed the Molinas-Arno connection to be approved. At the time, a lot of organized crime people were coming out to California because of the Colombo-Gallo turmoil in New York. These guys were looking for new turf, but they were avoiding making a commitment to either Colombo's faction or Gallo's in case they wound up backing the wrong horse. What made the Molinas situation even worse was that when his parole records were eventually sent out here, they quickly disappeared. There was a whole lot of manipulation going on, both in New York and in Los Angeles. In any case, I contacted Molinas, told him that I was his new parole officer, and that I wanted to meet with him at least once a month. What kind of guy was Molinas? He had a soft heart, but he was also full of razzle-dazzle and bullshit. And when I would say to him, 'Jack, you're full of shit,' his answer was, 'Yeah, but they believe it.'"

Molinas liked Cleary because of his laissez-faire attitude. As long as Molinas wasn't caught doing something illegal, everything was cool. Molinas went out of his way to charm Cleary, believing that having a cop in his corner would keep the other cops off his back.

On the basis of the proposal written by Gross, the book (tentatively entitled *The House That Jack Built*) was sold to Bantam Books for thirty-two thousand dollars in April 1970. One clause in the contract entitled Molinas to unilaterally terminate the project for reasons that did not have to be disclosed to either Gross or the publisher.

There were other prospective problems as well: Gross knew the book had to be a truthful account, but Molinas was reluctant to offend anybody and preferred a novel. "Jack wanted Gross to skim over the unsavory events," said Marvin Weisman, "and I thought that once Jack got his cut of the advance he was just stringing Gross along. In fact, I felt sorry for Gross."

With Gross writing the book back in New York, Molinas moved out of Arno's apartment and made a deal with Annie Fanny. While she attempted to break into showbiz in New York, Molinas would live in her one-bedroom apartment on Lexington Avenue near Santa Monica Boulevard. To sweeten the agreement, Molinas not only paid the rent but sent Annie Fanny an extra twenty-five dollars every month.

Now that he was an official resident of Los Angeles, Molinas began to hunt up a competitive basketball game. He found several—at playgrounds in Barrington, Roxbury, Beverly Hills, and Pacific Palisades. The players included NBA veterans such as Jim McMillan, Jerry West, Rudy LaRusso (whom Molinas knew from Coney Island), Elgin Baylor, Wilt Chamberlain, and Guy Rodgers. Despite the presence of so many experienced performers, Molinas treated them as if they were mere hooplings. He'd instruct Baylor to set picks, Chamberlain to stop hogging the ball, and West to zig instead of zag. They all tolerated his loudmouth antics because, even at the advanced age of thirty-eight, Molinas could still control a ball game.

Arno remained Molinas's most trusted friend and in late spring of 1970 the two of them formed a film company called Jo Jo Productions. Pornography was their specialty and the inside joke was that the company's name was actually an abbreviation of "Jerkoff and Jerkoff." Their office was situated in a storefront on La Cienega Boulevard, and also on the payroll were Tony LaRosa, who was supposed to promote the films (although he functioned mainly as a gofer), heavyweight producer Ted Gaisworth, and Junior Torchio, who was the liaison between Jo Jo and the mob. Molinas was given the title of president and his primary role was to come up with plot ideas, a role he undertook on a casual and part-time basis. Arno did everything else, including telephoning Molinas dozens of times every day to ask advice or complain about the latest in a continuing series of catastrophes. Molinas told all his friends back in New York that he soon would be "the Cecil B. DeMille of porn." But he also referred to his coworkers as "the gang who couldn't think straight."

It was difficult for producers of porno films to lose money in Los Angeles. "There's a reason why pornography is where the mob has done best out here," said Clayton Anderson, the LA County assistant district attorney. "The problem is that pornography can only be deemed illegal if it violates the ethical and aesthetic standards of the particular community in which it is exhibited. Defining such standards is virtually an impossible task. The relevant statues are so vague that it's difficult to get a convicting jury. In the late sixties and early seventies, porno was easily more profitable than drugs, or gambling or prostitution."

A successful LA pornographer, Jim Mitchell, claimed that pornography "was the ultimate affirmation of the Women's Lib movement. The new attitude was 'Wanna see my pussy? Gimme a hundred bucks.' Hey, nearly every serious producer started out making sex movies. Coppola did. It's the only cheap way to make a buck up front. And I was always happy to deal with the Mafia because they were the only outfit who paid their bills on time."

Jo Jo's movies were filmed in the basement of a house into which Arno had recently moved, and their first production was *Caught in the Can* (directed by Gaisworth), which was an X-rated version of Billy Wilder's *Some Like It Hot*. A couple of dandies, desperately attempting to meet women, try on women's clothing and land in jail, where a comely prison matron obliges their every prurient interest. Molinas especially liked the title because of the fifty months he'd spent in "the can."

One of the most important statistics in the porno industry was the number of "wet shots" a film contained. A number of young studs were employed on the set of *Caught in the Can* to insure an appropriate number of ejaculations. Unfortunately, all the johns were dried up by the time the last scene was filmed and the movie was in danger of being one wet shot short. A participant described what happened next: "Gaisworth volunteered to get a blow job and everything worked out right. But a few weeks later, we had the first screening at Gaisworth's house and his wife recognized his dick. They had a huge fight and she threatened to burn the film. Jack saved the day by grabbing the film and the projector, leaping over a couch, and hightailing it out of there in a hurry."

The Periano brothers, who were backed by the mob, operated the only local laboratory that would process porno movies. From the start, there were sizable discrepancies in the bills the Perianos submitted to Jo Jo. The way Molinas resolved the problem was not to pay the Perianos anything. "This is the code of the Mafia," Molinas said. "They'll never kill because of somebody owing them money. But they will kill somebody who lies about owing them money."

According to Richard Crane, former head of the LAPD Organized Crime Strike Force, Jo Jo was financed entirely by the Mafia: "Because of the nature of the business, Molinas and Arno couldn't help but turn a profit and that alone was enough to put them in the mob's good graces. The money came from one of the New York families and their Los Angeles representative was Mickey Zaffarano."

Zaffarano had first come to Molinas's attention as the supervisor of the parking lot that was directly behind the Eagle Bar and Grill. A 1970 report from the LAPD described how far Zaffarano had come since the days when he punched parking tickets in Coney Island:

> Zaffarano is alleged to have been an underboss in the deposed Bonano family and is presently working for Joe Colombo in NYC. He is an arbiter of disputes and holds a position of respect—"capo" = "boss."
>
> Zaffarano is also involved with the operation of Revelation Film Labs in Brooklyn, NY, one of the biggest processors of sex-oriented films in the east.
>
> Zaffarano's connection with Bonano came through Rosalie, sister of Jerome Asaro.
>
> Zaffarano—dates of birth alternately given as 5-19-23 or 5-5-24—6-0, 220 heavy build, brown eyes, black-gray hair, dark complexion
>
> Activities: pornography—hit man—armed robber—hi jack—narcotics
>
> NEVER DRIVES AN AUTOMOBILE. IS CHAUFFERED EVERYWHERE BY VARIOUS PERSONS.

Zaffarano's yellow sheet included four arrests as a "delinquent child"; a three-year term in Sing Sing for "robbery in the third degree"; dismissals on charges of receiving stolen property (December 29, 1958), failing to register for the military draft (March 23, 1959); and "making a false statement to federal authorities" (April 23, 1959). He also served six years at a federal prison in Atlanta for "transporting stolen securities."

Zaffarano's friends and business associates thought him to be a solid citizen: "A hardworking guy who woke up at five-thirty every morning." "Treats people like a gentleman." "Amazing business head. Assimilates information and knows how people tick." "Overly fair-minded." "No one in the business could ever say a negative word about him." "A stubborn man who always makes his own decisions." "Mickey knew Jack for twenty-five years and was his protector." "Mickey was a fucking legend."

Milton Gross had completed the manuscript of *The House That Jack Built* in early June 1970 and sent a copy to Molinas. A straight biography, the book presented Molinas's side of every controversy. Somehow, Zaffarano found out about the book and in the middle of the month visited Molinas at his apartment.

"Jack," Zaffarano said, "my family is very unhappy with the book."

"It won't hurt anyone," Molinas said.

"It could wind up hurting you. They believe that you'd be eager to talk too much to anyone who could promote or publicize the book."

"But—"

"There's no use arguing, Jack. A mutual friend asked me to suggest that you stick to bookies and leave books to others. My own recommendation is to cancel the book, Jack, even though that would disappoint Milton Gross. You've already done a lot of stupid things, Jack. Agreeing to have the book published would be the last stupid thing you ever did."

That's why Molinas exercised the escape clause in the contract with Bantam and *The House That Jack Built* was never published.

Meanwhile, Jo Jo had purchased a low-budget (four thousand dollars) soft-core film called *Harvey*, the first work of Stu Segall, a twenty-six-year-old director from Boston who had started out as an actor in beaver films before graduating to the production end of the business. After the sale of *Harvey*, Segall began hanging around Jo Jo's office, became very friendly with Molinas, and was soon put on the payroll as an editor and producer. A mutual friend suggested that Segall exhibited two characteristics that appealed to Molinas: "Stu always agreed with everything Jack said, and Stu was also a very good liar." With Segall as producer and Molinas directing, Jo Jo's second film was *The Magic Mirror*.

On June 27, Molinas was present at the filming of Jo Jo's third feature, *Lord Farthingay's Holiday*, which was being shot at the house of a friend of Arno's up in the hills above Sunset Boulevard, and it was there that he met the last love of his life, Noelle Gordon. On the basis of her showing in a bit part in *Harvey*, Noelle had been hired as an extra by Arno. She was lounging stark-naked on a couch waiting for the next scene and leafing through a book of paintings by Salvador Dali when Molinas first noticed her.

Junior Torchio provided this professional appraisal of Noelle: "She was about five foot six and she had auburn hair and sparkling green eyes. She was only eighteen years old but she had one of the most perfect bodies I've ever seen on a girl. Even better than Annie Fanny. Noelle also had incredibly firm breasts and a slim waist, and her ass looked like it was made out of marble. Her face reminded me of Myrna Loy. She was absolutely gorgeous."

Molinas was uncharacteristically shy and asked Arno for Noelle's phone number. "Forget about her," Arno said. "I've got a hot blond I want to introduce you to."

"No, no. I don't want to meet any blond."

Later, when the filming was completed, Noelle and Molinas met in the parking lot. She was riding a Suzuki 500 motorcycle and Molinas's ride was a rented gold Cadillac he had borrowed from Torchio. Noelle jumped to the logical conclusion that Molinas was the money man behind Jo Jo and they exchanged small talk about the weather.

Two weeks later, Noelle called Molinas and asked if she could borrow two hundred dollars. Molinas was surprised by her request and asked her to stop by his apartment to talk about it. They shared a bottle of wine and some more chitchat about how phony everything was in LA, and Molinas gave her the money. When she paid him back within a week, he asked her out on a date. By the end of the summer, Noelle and Molinas were living together in Annie Fanny's apartment.

Noelle grew up in Temple Terrace, a small town of four thousand residents built around the Temple Terrace Golf Course and Country Club, on the outskirts of Tampa, Florida. She was always a rebellious child and found few if any kindred spirits in a community whose citizens were stolidly upper class and extremely conservative. Growing up during the Vietnam War, she was outspoken and radical in her political beliefs but found herself ostracized by her neighbors and most of her classmates. She was smoking marijuana by age fifteen and dropping acid at sixteen. Her drug use caused great friction in her relationship with her father, who was an alcoholic.

Within days after her graduation from high school, she left Florida and journeyed to Oakland, California, where she earned four dollars an hour posing for painters and art classes. One artist required her to hang nude from a trapeze. But modeling was difficult—she'd have to remain immobile while her muscles cramped and flies crawled on her back. In one unusually cold classroom at Diablo Valley College she feared that her breasts were on the verge of frostbite.

Through an advertisement she found in *The Berkeley Barb*, Noelle had a successful audition for a soft-core porn movie. With her voluptuous physique and open, unabashed sensuality, Noelle was a natural. Before long she had starred in fifteen of what she called "naked-bodies-rubbing-against-each-other-films." She made fifty dollars a day for a few hours in front of the camera and then spent the afternoons at her favorite nude beach. But by the winter of 1969, the Bay Area porn scene had gone hard-core, and Noelle was getting weary of living with her current boyfriend, so she moved south to Los Angeles.

In LA, she registered with an agent, Hal Guthu, who directed her to various porno filmmakers and erotic still photographers. Noelle met Stu Segall when he was still an actor in porno films—he'd also done a centerfold for *Screw* magazine with a couple of her girlfriends. Segall appreciated Noelle's physical attributes and was quick to sign her up for a bit part in *Harvey*. And when Jo Jo purchased Segall's film, Arno contacted Noelle to offer her a role in *Lord Farthingay's Holiday*.

Noelle found Jack Molinas to be utterly fascinating. She respected his intelligence, his effortless sense of humor, and his ability to outhustle everybody else. She also felt that Molinas had a lot of useful things to teach her. But when they first met Molinas had just about run through the grubstake his grateful Mafia patrons had granted him upon his release from prison, and money was scarce. So much so that Molinas was forced to borrow five thousand dollars from his brother, Julie. And with his back to the wall, Molinas set about refilling his coffers with a vengeance.

The very first scam to which Noelle was a party involved stolen credit cards. These were supplied by "Skinny" Vinny Montalto, a native of New York. Montalto would also supply weekly lists of stolen cards that had been canceled. The cards were mostly used at fancy restaurants and Molinas and Noelle would eat out almost every night. But since Molinas was so recognizable, there were some restrictions—he couldn't be George Miller one week and then return to the same restaurant as Joe Blow the next week.

Another profitable fraud involved a black box that, attached to a telephone, could guarantee a lifetime of free calls. The only catch was that none of the free calls could go beyond fifteen minutes—if more time was needed, the caller would just hang up and dial the same number again. The designer of the magic box was a French-Canadian named Gerard, who had been referred to Molinas by Mickey Zaffarano. The box sold for a thousand dollars. With Molinas's continual need to deal with bookies back in New York, he estimated that the device paid for itself in four months.

Noelle was constantly attempting to coax Molinas into changing his fusty old habits. Being extremely health conscious, she cooked two separate meals every night—vegetarian fare for herself (which Molinas called "rabbit food"), steaks and chops for him. The only meal they both ate was a fresh spinach salad with mushrooms and bacon. And at least once every week, Molinas would sneak off and have a steak or a bowl of linguini and clams at Franco's La Taverna Restaurant on Wilshire Boulevard. Noelle also disapproved of Molinas's hair weave and constantly nagged him to go natural. But the most significant problem they had was Molinas's obsolete attitude toward the male-female relationship. Like his father, Molinas wanted to be the boss and expected instant obedience from Noelle. Whenever he got too demanding, she'd just laugh at him, jump on her motorcycle, and zoom off into the night. In their honeymoon phase, however, all of their differences seemed able to be resolved by a hearty session of sex.

As secretive as ever, Molinas confessed to Noelle that he'd served time in the pen for fixing ball games, but she had to ask his friends for further information about his past. This tactic was not always fruitful, since many of Molinas's friends disapproved of Noelle. "She was half his age," said Marvin Weisman, who frequently visited Molinas in Los Angeles. "She was very self-centered and constantly craved attention by wearing low-cut blouses and skimpy halter tops. She thought of herself as a hippie and to please her, Jack grew a Fu Manchu moustache. She was always talking, always nagging Jack to buy her the biggest Harley-Davidson there was."

Noelle often told Molinas that she loved him, but Artie Tolendini (another expatriate New Yorker) never believed her. "They both fooled around with other people," Tolendini said. "Their motto was, 'It's not who you fuck that counts, it's who you love.' Once they moved in together, Jack gave her loads of spending money and the unlimited use of his credit cards, so she stopped working. Noelle was a terrific cook and she kept the house very neat and clean. I think she dug the bucks and he dug being with her because it made him feel young again."

Naturally enough, Betty didn't approve of her son's relationship with another shiksa. She only wanted him to settle down with a nice Jewish girl and make her a grandmother. Betty's only consolation was her expectation that the relationship wouldn't last.

Annie Fanny, who carried a smoldering transcontinental torch for Molinas, was also upset about his latest romance. When she found out that Noelle had moved in, Annie called Molinas and had a screaming fit. How dare he bring another woman to live in *her* apartment? And how dare he sleep with another woman in *her* bed? "There, there," Molinas would say. "We wash the sheets every week."

Following the hippie fashion, Noelle rarely wore a bra and would think nothing about being topless when Molinas had friends over to dinner. Molinas was quick to criticize what he called her "licentiousness" and they'd frequently quarrel. But Molinas was also surprisingly casual about Noelle's friends. She once brought nine members of a motorcycle gang over for dinner. They were grubby redneck-types and eight of them had recently been released from a San Francisco prison. Molinas tolerated their presence but made no effort to socialize with any of them. While Noelle and her guests were eating, Molinas retreated to the bedroom, where he was happy enough to smoke a cigar and watch a football game on TV.

Noelle wasn't crazy about Molinas's friends, either. Saturday afternoons were set aside for people like Joe Black, Junior Torchio, and Larry Shupack (fresh out of jail) to come over and watch the college football games. Molinas was constantly on the phone talking to bookies during the games, adjusting bets and making new ones. Noelle's job was to keep everybody well-supplied with coffee. When she was out of the room, she'd hear them screaming and yahooing about the latest touchdown or interception. But as soon as she came in with a fresh pot of coffee, everybody would clam up. The cheering would resume only when she was safely returned to the kitchen.

Most of their neighbors were elderly women living on social security payments or their deceased husbands' pensions. Molinas smiled politely when they passed in the hallways and everybody coexisted peacefully enough, except for one old woman who lived next door. Her constant complaint to the superintendent was that her neighbors' lovemaking was too noisy and their bed would bang against a common wall in the middle of the night. Molinas's only concession was to move the bed closer to the middle of the room.

Noelle hated living in an apartment. The idea of people living above her and below her gave her the creeps. She implored Molinas to move to a small house somewhere but he resisted, claiming that the $125 monthly rent was an irresistible bargain. To soothe Noelle, Molinas permitted her to keep a pet cat (Wisteria) and even a boa (Rosey).

Molinas finally gave in, however, when he and Noelle moved into a two-bedroom furnished house at 8408 Ridpath Drive in Laurel Canyon. The place was owned by Betty Parrimore, a divorcée renowned for her extraordinarily large breasts and also for her unwillingness to pay for whatever repairs the house required. A handyman, an electrician, and a plumber all confessed to Noelle that instead of shelling out cash for whatever labor they'd performed, the landlady would pay them with sexual favors. This barter system did have its drawbacks—when the hot-water heater broke down in the middle of winter it went unrepaired for nearly a week while Betty searched for a plumber who'd accept sex instead of money.

Molinas wanted Noelle to cook, clean, and do the laundry and be a model homemaker. That's what women were supposed to do. But Noelle grew bored with the happy housewife routine. She didn't like having to ask Molinas for a few dollars to buy herself a new dress or to get her motorcycle serviced. After a continuing round of arguments, Noelle was "allowed" to find a job as an undercover agent for a company called the Commercial Service Systems. Disguised as an ordinary shopper, she'd visit various A&P, Pathmark, and ShopRite supermarkets. She'd wait until a particular cashier was in the middle of ringing up someone else's order, then come busting to the head of the line with a can of coffee, and say to the cashier, "I'm double-parked and my baby's in the car? Could you just take this?" Then Noelle would leave the exact change on the counter before rushing off. Meanwhile, one of her supervisors would watch to see if the cashier eventually rang up the coffee money in the cash register or dropped it in her pocket. After six weeks, Noelle had enough and quit.

Molinas also found himself a new job in the law office of Leonard Kramer. "I was advertising for what was called 'a heavy law clerk,'" Kramer said, "and Jack was referred to me by Chuck Bernstein, an attorney we both knew. Jack came to me hat in hand and said that he was on parole for another two years but that this job would be a chance for him to get back into the law. He thought that if he proved himself to be upright and totally rehabilitated he might be able to take the bar exams again. He seemed very meek, so I gave him the job. Jack earned a clerk's salary of four hundred dollars a week doing research and drafting pleadings."

Molinas also hunted down people who had been involved in car accidents, getting the information from police reports in the newspapers, from ambulance drivers, and from insurance adjusters he knew. Then he'd go to the victims' houses, sign them up as clients, and take a one-third cut from whatever settlement Kramer negotiated. Molinas's efforts turned up significant profits for himself as well as his employer.

"Jack was charming and very friendly," Kramer said, "and also a very diligent worker. He gave the impression that he was completely unsophisticated and didn't have a problem in the world. But he also had a quick, retentive mind and quite possibly a photographic memory."

When Mike Cleary checked out Kramer's Wilshire Boulevard office, the parole officer deduced that Molinas was practicing law without a license but decided to let the violation slide. "Kramer was nervous as hell," said Cleary, "because he figured that he'd been fingered for using Molinas in an illegal way. When I finally walked out of the office, I could hear Kramer's sigh of relief all the way to my car."

At the same time, Molinas was involved with Jo Jo and also continued to book small-stakes bets. Inevitably, he began using Kramer's phones to contact his stable of bettors. After Molinas had been on the job for nine months, an insurance consultant named Harvey Freeman discovered what he was up to and informed Kramer. Standing only five foot three, Kramer was physically intimidated by Molinas and was afraid to fire him, so he called in Chuck Bernstein. At first Molinas casually denied the accusation. "Nah," Molinas said. "I'm not doing anything like that." But Bernstein was persistent and eventually compelled Molinas to confess. "Yeah," Molinas said, "I'm booking some action out of here, but it's only small potatoes."

The fifty months Molinas had spent in jail had only reinforced his determination to find the perfect edge. Sure, he'd made some mistakes in his day—like allowing Reed and Kaufman to tape incriminating conversations—but they'd been due to carelessness, not stupidity. And if it wasn't for being betrayed by the likes of Reed, Kaufman, Wagman, and even Stanley the Rat, Molinas would never have been nabbed. But he was not yet forty years old and there was plenty of time to prove that he was smart enough to fool all of the people all of the time.

Molinas wasn't at all concerned about losing his lucrative gig with Kramer because there were always other less strenuous ways to make money. For example, when Vinny Mantalto left for Las Vegas, Molinas found another source for stolen credit cards—an ex-boxer named Michael Santini. To Molinas's delight, Santini also let him in on another scam that began with locating a recently vacated house. Armed with someone else's credit card, Molinas would visit Robinson's, a large department store located behind the Beverly Hilton Hotel. Then Molinas would purchase a house full of furniture and major appliances, pay for them with the card, then have the merchandise delivered to the empty house. Minutes after the delivery, everything would be moved out the back door and taken to Molinas's house on Ridpath Drive. Molinas would keep what he needed, then sell the rest to Santini at a fraction of the retail value. When another vacant house was located, Molinas would have Arno or Segall make the purchases at Johnson's. This foolproof swindle was worked four or five times within a space of six months.

Molinas was as happy as he'd ever been, and living with Noelle was the topper. She'd changed his life in so many ways—getting him mildly interested in politics, teaching him how to smoke pot, and bringing him to the brink of falling in love. "I want to marry you," he told Noelle. "I want you to have my child."

Noelle, however, was still only nineteen years old and repelled by the prospect of having her freedom circumscribed by a marriage and a child. There were too many things she hadn't done and too many places she hadn't seen. Moreover, after living with Molinas for over a year, Noelle's fascination with him was slowly turning into annoyance. For Molinas, Noelle represented his last chance to start a family. Noelle's refusals to accept his insistent proposals led to periodic quarrels and seriously threatened their relationship.

Still, there were good times to be had. Noelle loved to drink wine with her meals and Molinas soon developed the same habit. On occasion he'd also dip into the Gibson's gin while Noelle was cooking up a storm. Molinas turned out to be very affectionate when he was in his cups and Noelle called him "a happy drunk." Drugs were another story.

One day Noelle and a friend named Linda made a batch of triple-dosed pot brownies. Molinas walked into the kitchen just as the brownies were being taken out of the oven. Noelle was on the telephone, so Molinas said to Linda, "Are these brownies legit?" What he meant by "legit" was "Is it okay for me to eat them or are they earmarked for a party or something else?"

To Linda, a "legit" brownie was loaded with dope. "Sure," she said.

So Molinas drank a quart of milk and ate at least half the brownies. Linda was impressed. Then he left for a screening at Jo Jo's.

Molinas returned three hours later driving his white Continental Mark III down the middle of the street at five miles per hour. He parked the car half on the sidewalk, staggered into the house, looked at Noelle, and said, "You did it to me again." Then he crawled into the bedroom and slept for fourteen hours.

Life was good and getting better every day, and Molinas loved living like a mogul. He drove a leased Mercedes 450 SL that he called "my toy," smoked only El Triunfo #1 Mexican cigars that he bought from Geryl Company in New York (and lit them with Gold Dunhill lighters that cost a hundred), and he slept with at least one famous movie star. "I'd produced a couple of shows in a theater in the round called *Melody Land*," said LaRosa, "and that's where Goldie Hawn got started. Anyway, one of these shows was *Pal Joey* starring Barbara Nichols and

Yvonne DeCarlo. Jack had seen Yvonne around at a few parties and he was interested in her. It turned out that Yvonne was also interested in Jack. His shady past and Mafia connections really appealed to a lot of Hollywood women. So I got the two of them together and she took him to Disneyland on their first date. Jack used to brag about having screwed her."

For a while, Molinas began wearing shades, silk shirts open to show his chest, and even white shoes, determined to be part of the *in crowd.* He thought he looked hot in his Fu Manchu moustache, but when Arno told him that he looked like a "spic," Molinas shaved it off. When his friends referred to his hair weave as "the Bird's Nest," Molinas would get irritated and say, "Show me a better way to cover up the bald spots."

Yet Molinas felt so secure and so expansive that he could even make wry jokes about his notoriety as a master fixer. Once, while attending a Lakers game, Molinas asked a friend to please go to the refreshment stand and buy him a hot dog. "Why don't you go yourself?" the friend asked.

"Because I'd have to pass behind the Laker bench," Molinas said, "and if I did that, it wouldn't take three seconds before the FBI would have me in handcuffs."

And he gloried in his reputation. "Jack would bet on anything," said Elliot Ableson. "He'd spot a fly perched on a windowsill and bet that the fly wouldn't move for five seconds. That was one of his favorite bets and he always seemed to win. There came a point where we just refused to bet against him because we figured that the only way Jack could win so often was to drug the flies."

Every few months, Molinas would alert his buddies to a fixed college basketball game and tell them to "bet the mortgage." Again, his friends were amazed when he never picked a loser. But Molinas rarely bet on NBA games, convinced that they were all rigged.

Molinas placed most of his bets with independent bookmakers, and on the rare occasions when he backed the wrong team (usually football or baseball), he was reluctant to pay his debts. He'd usually bet between five hundred and a thousand dollars per game, but even if the victimized bookie was operating on a narrow margin nobody dared strong-arm Molinas because of his well-known connections with organized crime. Nor could independent bookies refuse to accept Molinas's wager for fear of offending him and his patrons. (If the bookie was well-connected himself, Molinas would negotiate a deal whereby he'd repay a third to a half of what he owed.)

It was a gambler's wet dream: Collect when you win, welch when you lose.

Besides the increasing friction with Noelle, Molinas's only other source of frustration was his failure to sell his book proposal to a film company. For a while, Molinas pursued Harold Robbins to write a screenplay, but although the best-selling novelist never actually refused, neither would he make a definite commitment. Molinas also befriended another Sephardic Jew named Saul Turtletaub, who had produced the hit TV series *Sanford and Son*, eventually proposing that they coproduce a major motion picture about Molinas's favorite subject. But Turtletaub said that he didn't want to ruin their friendship by even talking about business.

When Dave Wolf published *Foul*, a nonfiction book that completely exonerated Connie Hawkins and cast the convicted fixer as the villain, Molinas threatened to sue but never did. In truth, Molinas was proud that his name appeared so frequently in such a well-received book.

Every so often, a stranger would approach Molinas in a restaurant and say, "You son of a bitch, Molinas! I bet the wrong way on one of your fixed games and it cost me ten thousand dollars!" Molinas would shrug and say, "That's the name of the game, pal. Wise men bet on sure things, but fools bet on their own foolish opinions. Now, go away and let me finish my meal in peace."

Molinas was able to repay Julie's five-thousand-dollar (interest-free) loan because the money was pouring in from his successful bets, his stock market investments (his favorite TV program was the daily stock returns on Channel Z), his assorted scams, and especially his burgeoning loan-shark business. The loans were made to local businessmen (one owned a dry-cleaning establishment, others owned delicatessens, butcher shops, or photography studios) who lacked the credit rating to deal with banks. Molinas charged them three percent a week, and rather than employing head-breakers to collect his fees, he structured the deals so that he could garnishee the cash proceeds of any business that did not meet payments. Each agreement effectively made Molinas an investor in the business, drawing a weekly income equal to the terms of the loan.

All this while, Molinas was seeing his parole officer, Mike Cleary, on many more occasions than was required. The buzz around the LA underworld was that Molinas was keeping Cleary informed of any illegal activities being committed by his own friends and colleagues. Rather than using this information to make arrests, Cleary was merely expanding the LAPD's intelligence files. "I know this was happening," said Elliot Ableson, who was Molinas's attorney for a time, "because another client of mine was meeting with Cleary for the same purpose and used as his justification that Jack was doing it, too. Jack freely admitted to me that he was conferring with Cleary, although he never confessed what they discussed. It would be typical of Jack to do anything to save his own neck."

These rumors seemed to be verified when, in October 1970, Molinas sold his interest in Jo Jo to Junior Torchio, who retained Arno as manager. (The truth was that Milton Gross had written a column in the *New York Post* revealing that Molinas was producing porno movies, and when the heat reached LA, Cleary forced him out of Jo Jo.) Without Molinas mediating between Torchio and Arno, the company began to disintegrate. "Junior was illiterate, dumb, and dishonest," said Ableson. "He was one of the current wave of Italian New Yorkers who came out to Los Angeles and pretended to be tough but were really chicken-hearted. That's not to say Junior wouldn't hire a goon to have somebody killed. He just wouldn't have the guts to do anything like that himself."

A month later, search warrants were issued by the LA Vice Squad and Jo Jo's office was tossed. After uncovering pornographic reels, loops, and mail-order materials, Arno and LaRosa (who were the only two there at the time) were arrested for violating article 311.2 of the city penal code (distributing obscene matter, a misdemeanor). "There were a couple of things going on," LaRosa said. "Evelle Younger was a conservative Republican campaigning for California attorney general and he made war on the pornographers. There was also some kind of deal going down that I never got a handle on. In any case, on a friend's recommendation I engaged a guy named Leonard Sampson to represent me and Norman. He turned out to be a stupid Jewish shyster who didn't know nothing and was later disbarred. We wanted to bring in Elliot Ableson but the judge turned us down. During the trial, Jack sat next to Sampson and told him what moves to make."

One day a court officer asked Molinas: "Are you Jacob L. Molinas?" When Molinas admitted that he was, he was also placed under arrest on the same charges. Molinas immediately claimed there was no basis for his arrest and later produced legal proof that he had sold his share to Torchio. Both LaRosa and Arno were found guilty, fined five hundred dollars each, and sentenced to six months, but their convictions were eventually overturned on appeal.

And why wasn't Torchio arrested? Because the standard operating procedure for porno movie makers was to demand cash payments up front from theaters that were either buying (as was the case with Jo Jo's 8mm and 16mm films) or renting their films. It was Molinas's brainstorm, however, to extend credit to the theaters on the promise of payment from receipts. The police had cracked down on Jo Jo at the request of the company's organized crime competitors, who didn't like being undercut by such unfair business practices. As part of the deal between the vice squad and the Mafia, Junior Torchio got a free ride. When word of this agreement reached the streets, Molinas was off the hook.

Happy to be out of the mess at Jo Jo, Molinas set up his own office at 3600 Wilshire Boulevard, Suite 1220, and attempted to develop a national sports service (a legitimate idea revived years later by other investors and turned into a moneymaking enterprise). At the time, a local radio station (KNPC) had a "Sportswire," which provided the scores of West Coast ball games free of charge. "Two-thirds of the calls," said Cleary, "were from the East Coast, and most of these were made toll-free by guys with black boxes. Molinas's idea was to set up a telephone number that provided nationwide scores to callers. The profit would come from playing commercials between batches of scores. We figured it had to be some kind of flimflam related to gambling and we shut it down before it got off the ground."

Molinas found other mini-projects to pique his interest until something more significant developed. In prison, he had learned the value of a cup of hot water, a fresh razor blade, and a phony pack of cigarettes. No edge could be considered too dull, no swindle too petty. So he'd drive his Mercedes into a gas station, turn the crank on the gas pump, and start filling the tank. Back then, before the gauges were computerized, the gas station attendants had to personally read each pump to ascertain what the charge would be. Knowing this, Molinas would wait until the attendant turned his back, turn the crank back to zero and then top off the gas tank. Instead of ten dollars, the meter would show two dollars.

Noelle couldn't believe that with all the money passing through his hands Molinas could stoop to such penny-ante tactics. "Yeah," he'd say in his high-pitched, squeaky voice, "you do whatever you can do, or else somebody's going to do it to you."

By early March 1971, Jo Jo was in turmoil again. Disregarding Arno's strenuous objections, Torchio had ordered the films forcibly removed from the projectors of theater owners whose payments were late, and also involved Jo Jo in a territorial dispute over arcade films distributed in San Diego. Mickey Zaffarano was called in to make the peace. On March 18, however, Torchio and Arno had another violent quarrel, so Torchio hired three thugs to heave Arno through the front window of Jo Jo's office. Arno later told the police it "was just an accident." Zaffarano was outraged that Torchio had not called upon him to settle this latest dispute. (Four years later, Torchio was involved in a suspicious—and fatal—car accident in Brooklyn.)

In May, Hal Guthu got Noelle a walk-on part in a legitimate film, *Hammersmith Is Out*, which starred Elizabeth Taylor, Richard Burton, and George Raft and was filmed in Acapulco. Molinas was happy that Noelle was finally getting a break, and also that he'd have a few free days to tomcat around Los Angeles.

Molinas drove Noelle to the airport, and though they were running late, he decided that he was so hungry he had to stop at a Kentucky Fried Chicken to buy a big bucket. "He was driving one-handed along the Santa Monica Freeway at eighty miles an hour," Noelle said, "and eating the chicken with his other hand. The convertible top was down on the El Dorado he'd just bought and Jack was just ripping the flesh from the bones and tossing the leftovers up into the air, leaving a trail of chicken bones all the way to the airport. Part of Jack's charm was that he was just a little nuts."

Noelle was on location for five days. She was paid two hundred dollars for the one day she worked, and twenty-two dollars per diem for the rest. In her first scene, she appeared as a dancer in a nightclub for "about one second." Her only other appearance was a short stint as a topless bartender. At the cast party, Noelle was unimpressed by Taylor, astounded at Burton's gargantuan consumption of alcohol, and annoyed by Raft. It seems that Raft repeatedly pinched Noelle's behind and asked her to dinner. Her response was to change her seat.

For the next few months, Molinas dabbled in various deals and also invited suggestions from his cohorts. "When somebody presented Jack with a proposition," LaRosa said, "he had a habit of taking the index finger of his left hand and pressing it against his forehead like *The Thinker*. You know that famous statue? Everybody would be talking, then all of a sudden Jack would say, 'No, no, noooo. Waaait a minute.' Then everybody would shut up and listen. 'You're out of your mind,' Jack would say in his high-pitched voice. 'This is the way it should be done.' And damned if he wouldn't be right ninety-nine times out of a hundred."

Molinas further amazed his friends and associates by juggling a multitude of deals without dropping one. Chuck Bernstein and Molinas were buying and selling second mortgages on residential houses. Bernstein estimated that over the course of the next two years, Molinas cleared seven hundred thousand dollars and he made three hundred thousand. (He also estimated that Molinas owed him, and never paid, one hundred and ten thousand.) Molinas put up a cash guarantee to back Michael DiGiovanna in a record store (Music King) in Costa Mesa. Then there was the manufacturing of rockets attached to balloons to be marketed as survival devices to hikers. In his spare time, Molinas also got back into the porno business.

Stu Segall left Jo Jo when Arno and LaRosa were arrested and formed his own film company, Miracle Films. According to Segall, the name of the company came from a common line used in the business—"If it's a good film, it's a miracle." In addition, Segall formed a partnership with Ted Gaiswirth and Bill Emerson (a former LA County deputy sheriff who had been bounced from the force for using excessive brutality during the Watts riots) in still another company, Capricorn Films. All of Segall's endeavors were sheltered under one corporate umbrella, Stuart Segall Associates (SSA), with offices on Beverly Boulevard. Molinas was a consultant to SSA, Arno booked the films, and the silent partner was Mickey Zaffarano. In a coup arranged by Zaffarano, SSA later obtained the distribution rights to a pair of extremely profitable feature-length films, *Deep Throat* and *The Devil in Miss Jones.*

Even though the Mafia had sicced the law on Jo Jo for extending credit, under Molinas's guidance Capricorn did the very same thing. The twist was that Capricorn accepted postdated checks, which led to Molinas setting a record in the industry by making fifty-seven sales in one day.

Molinas also set up bank accounts under fictitious names to hide his money from the Internal Revenue Service, and was so flush that he loaned seven thousand dollars interest-free to Mickey Zaffarano so that his protector could buy a restaurant in Brooklyn.

But Artie Tolendini was increasingly disenchanted with Molinas's lifestyle. He urged Molinas to get out of LA—perhaps purchase a townhouse in New York, or a condo in Miami. "With all the Jews living there," Tolendini said, "you'd be totally at home in Miami." Tolendini also warned him about the "lowlife scum" with whom he did business: "I know who those fucking people are, Jack, and there's no way you can keep on their good side for long. Sooner or later, they're gonna turn around and fuck you up."

"Don't worry about me, Artie. I'm not doing anything that's gonna get me killed. And I never will."

In early July, Noelle finally made a move on Molinas's hair weave. Molinas's scalp would perspire and then itch in the hot weather, but the hair weave would prevent him from scratching. First off, Noelle convinced him to remove the weave during the summer months. "As tall as you are," she said, "nobody can see the top of your head anyway." Then on an autumn afternoon when he was away, Noelle simply threw the weave into the fireplace. Later, when he inquired about its whereabouts, Noelle confessed what she'd done.

"That cost me five hundred dollars!" he piped.

"It's ashes now, honey," she said.

In time, Molinas became accustomed to being bald, but he couldn't bear the other marks of the aging process. He required eyeglasses to read and drive and he considered this to be a diminishment of his masculinity. When forced to drive in the company of friends, Molinas would make sure to wear lightly tinted prescription sunglasses, even at night. As he rounded the clubhouse turn on the way to his fortieth birthday, Molinas's burgeoning business interests confined his hooping to Sunday mornings. He had no interest in any other form of physical activity, but as his paunch expanded, Molinas made no effort to alter his eating habits.

By January 1972, Molinas decided that his improved income mandated a relocation into a higher-class neighborhood. Arno had been considering moving to a flashy house up in the Hollywood Hills but had changed his mind. Arno introduced Molinas to the landlord, and the two quickly came to terms. The house at 9246 Thrush Way featured a swimming pool, a glorious view of LA (on a clear day the view stretched to Santa Monica and the ocean), a patio, a redbrick barbecue, and, next to the pool, a guest house. The monthly rent was seven-fifty and Molinas had control of the two-room guest house, deciding who could live there and pocketing whatever rent monies were forthcoming. When Molinas and Noelle moved in, three drag queens were living in the guest house and, amid a great flurry of feathers, they were booted out.

While Molinas spent a few days in New York visiting his parents, overseeing several investments, and checking up on Joe Hacken (who was doing fine, thank you, and devoting most of his efforts to rigging prizefights), Noelle and her friend Linda Brauer were charged with getting the new house in order.

> 1/20/72
> My dearest Noelle,
> I'm on my way to NY & I've drunk *four* screwdrivers & I'm feeling real good!
> Let me say that I'm sitting on the plane & doing some real good thinking & I've come to the incredible conclusion that I miss you & I love you very very much—It's quite funny but I haven't seen much of you the last two days & I really missed you!...I'm sure your efforts will prove to be very fruitful, in that we'll have a very nice house—I really know that you are a good organizer & that everything will turn out the way we planned—
> I'm really glad I moved to Calif. especially since I had the opportunity to meet you—The fact that our lives touched has enabled me to experience something wonderful & probably something I'll never experience again. Only once in my life have I ever met someone like you & that was in college some 20 years ago so you see that hasn't happened too often—You're beautiful!
> You must excuse me if I appear to be cold or something less than affectionate—You see I really have a cold exterior but inside I have a warm glow for you—
> I love you so much & hope this trip ends soon so I can be home again with you—
> Lovingly,
> // Jack //

During this trip to New York, Molinas paid a visit to Allan Seiden, who had started a new business as a ticket broker. "He was the same old Jack," Seiden said. "He called California from my office and he said, 'Norman, I got the figures. We did twenty thousand dollars in gate receipts in Chicago, fifteen thousand in Miami, and forty thousand in New York. Boston was a little weak at seventy-five hundred. Hold the fort, Norman, I'll be home tomorrow night.' Then he hung up the phone and said to me, 'Al, could you lend me twenty bucks?'"

Noelle was happy for the opportunity to decorate the place according to her own taste, and Molinas liberally praised her efforts when he returned.

Both of them adored their new address. Entering the brick-and-cedar main house through the garage, Molinas's normal route took him through the paneled basement (which featured a wet bar and access to the pool), then up a flight of stairs to the living room (which was dominated by a custom-made stereo system and a pair of five-foot-high loudspeakers). The kitchen was to the left of the living room, the two bedrooms were accessed by a short flight of steps also to the left, and to the right, a sliding glass door opened onto the patio.

The new tenant in the guest house was Harvey Freeman, an insurance adjuster Molinas knew from his days working for Leonard Kramer. "After I separated from my wife," Freeman said, "Jack called me up and mentioned that he had a guest house on the property where he was now living and that I could stay there if I wanted. 'You're a nice guy, Harvey,' Jack said, 'and I know you'll take good care of the place. Pay me a hundred and a half for a year or so until you get back on your feet, and then I'll raise you to two hundred.' It was a convenient location and a beautiful spot. Stu Segall lived next door, Peter Lawford had a house down the street, and there was an unlandscaped piece of property across the road. The only trouble I had while I was there was when my three young daughters came to visit and Noelle and her friends would walk around the pool naked. But as soon as I raised the subject, Noelle quickly agreed to wear a bathing suit when the kids were around." Freeman was very well connected and whenever Molinas and Noelle were on the outs, he'd introduce Molinas to a bevy of anything-but-bashful bathing beauties.

Noelle loved animals so much that she began to hanker after a career as a veterinarian. Molinas discouraged the possibility as being a waste of time, but Noelle believed he was afraid that if she did go to school (the veterinarian training required eight years), she'd become involved in her career and would demand to be unchained from the kitchen stove.

With more space at her disposal, however, Noelle was happy to indulge her love for pets: There was a thirty-pound German shepherd mongrel named Puppy (Molinas's favorite) that Noelle had rescued from the dog pound, and her three unnamed puppies. Also a second cat (Ulysses), a borzoi that used to snarl at Molinas whenever he approached Noelle, and a great dane named Jake. Molinas had bought Noelle a BMW 2002 for her birthday, and when she wrecked it in an accident she used the insurance payments to buy a wet suit and another dog, Tavi, a purebred wolfhound.

Molinas also adopted his own strays: business associates down on their luck like Marshall Brevitts, whose claim to fame was being the ex-manager of a minor rock star named Bobby Womack—as well as unemployed actors and part-time pimps like Randy Hicks, a black man whom Molinas met when their cars bumped fenders in a parking lot on Hollywood Boulevard. Sometimes Molinas's strays stayed for a few days in the spare bedroom, but they mostly hung around the pool and cast wolfish eyes at Noelle's naked form.

One day, when Molinas went into Schwab's drugstore to buy some aspirin, he struck up a convivial conversation with a stranger about the joys of living in the Hollywood Hills. "I've got a friend who lives up there," the stranger said, "and there's a house down the hill where a bunch of girls sit out by their pool all day smoking pot in their birthday suits. And my friend's got this really powerful pair of binoculars, see? Sometimes I go up there myself and enjoy the peep show. Say, you can stop by whenever you want to." Molinas drove straight home and ordered Noelle never to sit naked at the pool ever again. She complied for a few days, but her attitude was: "I'm just laying in the sun and minding my own business. If there's some crackpot Peeping Tom up in the hills, I don't really care."

Molinas's business deals were always percolating at a frantic pace, but otherwise life was easy at Thrush Way. On Sunday mornings, he'd play basketball, then come home and simultaneously watch a pair of NFL games on his two TVs, while also listening to other games on his three radios. (Saturday afternoons were similarly devoted to college football games.) Lounging in his leather reclining chair, Molinas would be wearing boxer shorts and a cutaway T-shirt while he eyed the TVs over one of his cigars (he'd usually smoke two or three daily). When he wanted a snack, there was a freezer full of an expensive hand-packed chocolate ice cream that he bought in bulk. The phone would also be within reach so that he could call up radio stations across the country to hear the latest updates. Whenever he had a big bet on a New York Jets game and the contest wasn't on national TV, Molinas would telephone Artie Tolendini's brother, Dugie, and request a secondhand play-by-play from the local broadcast. He'd also call various bookies to make halftime changes in his bets or arrange off-the-cuff parlays. With more money burning a hole in his pockets, he'd upped the stakes to five thousand on every game he was able to watch on TV and a thousand on several others that interested him.

One Sunday, Molinas's normal routine was upset by a phone call from his mother. It seemed that Louis and Betty were embroiled in an argument about some picayune family matter and Louis had gotten so riled up that he smashed one of his wife's most treasured serving platters. Betty, whose entire life revolved around her family and her household, was enraged and for the first time in her life shouted back at her husband: "What are you doing? My mother brought that plate with her from the old country! You old fool!" Still furious, Betty called her favorite son to say that Louis was getting senile and violent in his old age. He was impossible to live with. Betty pleaded with Molinas to send her enough money so she could move to California, live with him and his shiksa, and be done with her lunatic husband. Molinas soothed and comforted his mother, then sent her a hundred dollars with instructions to buy a whole new set of dishes.

During the week, Molinas would typically come home from his day's work and nod to Noelle and her gang of unemployed vegetarians lying by the pool and rubbing vitamin E on their nude bodies. Then he'd inhale a medium-sized toke from a joint that was inevitably on hand, retreat to the living room, and examine his accounts. After dinner, when he wasn't watching a ball game, or Channel Z, Molinas would find relaxation in reading newsmagazines or books with a Horatio Alger rags-to-riches theme. (Noelle loved to watch old movies on TV, but they'd always put Molinas to sleep before the first commercial.)

Noelle was enjoying herself immensely. She convinced Molinas to hire a woman to clean the house every week, leaving Noelle free to shop, get high, and loll around the pool. And she continued to be semifascinated by Molinas. Noelle was especially amused by his New Yorkisms—a head of lettuce was referred to as "a salad"; instead of light switches being turned off and on, they were "opened" or "closed"; similarly, oranges weren't peeled, they were "opened." A cozy and comfy life all right, but there were disturbing signs in the bedroom: At the beginning of their relationship, Molinas and Noelle would have mutually satisfying sex just about every other night. By the time they moved to Thrush Way, however, months would pass between their sessions of lovemaking. For the first time in his life, Molinas was plagued with impotence and he was so embarrassed that he'd refuse Noelle's sexual overtures. Noelle realized that a gradual diminution of sexual activity was quite normal, but she also wondered if Molinas's impotence was his subconscious way of avoiding making a final commitment to her. When she gently tried convincing him to see a therapist, he refused with an outburst of indignation. Whatever the cause, the lack of sexual satisfaction made Noelle frustrated and restless.

So frustrated that when she learned Molinas was staying out all night and getting his rocks off with other women (instead of traveling to San Francisco or San Diego on business, as he'd told her), Noelle retaliated by indulging in an all-night go-round with a stranger she picked up in a bar. When she returned home in the morning, Molinas calmly told her to pack her bags and leave.

"Hey," she protested, "you've been doing the very same thing!"

Molinas grinned, said, "You're right," and let the matter drop.

Even so, Noelle tried to be optimistic. She knew that in his own way Molinas was devoted to her.

Molinas was also extremely generous to her friends. Linda Brauer was her best pal, a single parent with a seven-year-old son who had a hard life working days as a cocktail waitress and taking high school classes at night. When her boy needed emergency dental surgery after he suffered an accident riding his bicycle, Molinas immediately insisted on making her a present of the three-hundred-dollar fee. And Molinas wouldn't let Linda pay him back. Moreover, Molinas would take her son to Laker games and play basketball with him in a local park. Molinas also got Linda a job with Chuck Bernstein's company driving rental cars from one dealership to another.

Sure, he was a good man at heart. But did Molinas really truly love Noelle? He kept saying that he did. Noelle always believed that his insistent proposals of marriage were motivated more by his desire to father a child than by any sincere feeling of love. Whenever she told him "I love you," however, Molinas's answer was "Me, too." She'd laugh, knowing that the message was "Yes, I love myself also."

In March, Molinas finally flew Betty out to Los Angeles for a visit. (Louis only received halfhearted invitations that he never accepted.) Molinas was intent on showing his mother a good time, taking her out to dinner every night and buying her fashionable clothing. Because someone in the fur business owed Molinas money on a losing bet, Betty came back to Brooklyn with a custom-made fur-trimmed coat. Betty was appalled at the disparity in the ages of her son and his ladylove, but she took a liking to Noelle, anyway, and the two of them consoled each other with tales of his legendary stubbornness.

Molinas had several additional guests from New York during the spring of 1972. When Allan Seiden arrived, Molinas was proud to take him to the best runs in town—pickup games at Barrington Park with old-timers like Guy Rodgers and Wilt Chamberlain, and also scrimmages at Pauley Pavilion featuring young-legged undergraduates from UCLA. At age forty, Molinas remained an effective half-court player but was frequently left behind when the pace quickened. Unfortunately, during a fierce rebounding scrum in a game at UCLA, Molinas landed in an off-balance position and severely strained his Achilles tendon. The injury kept him on the sidelines for the rest of the year, and even when he'd healed, his trademark fastbreaking skills were completely gone.

While Molinas was recuperating, Julie paid a visit. Noelle was surprised at how different the two brothers were. Still teaching chemistry, Julie had been frugal with his money, and his primary indulgence was taking extensive summer vacations with his friends to various European and Middle Eastern locales. Compared to Jack's rather limited intellectual pursuits, Julie's travels and active curiosity marked him as cultured and well read. Julie was steady and hardworking, whereas his older brother was as wild and careless as a windstorm.

Mostly the brothers confined their discussions to the stock market, old friends, and family, and while their affection was real, it was also totally unspoken. Jack never broached any subject that even hinted of illegalities, yet the constant phone calls and ball games on TV revealed his continued preoccupation with gambling.

"My brother seemed to be a much more hardened person out in Los Angeles," Julie said. "He had this veneer of being in control of his life, and everything seemed to be very lively but very frantic. I was also taken aback by the kinds of people who were continually around the house. Seedy-looking men and marginal criminal types. Quite often Jack would sequester himself with them for hours discussing subjects I'm sure I didn't want to know about. I expressed my feelings to Noelle in a very mild, offhanded way. She was a really nice young woman and very sharp-minded, so we shared the same concerns about the kind of people Jack was hanging around with. I remembered reading a very pertinent statement somewhere that stated: 'Give me your child for the first five years of its life and I will have it for its lifetime.' Well, Joey Hacken had

Jack for much longer than that because after spending a week with my brother, I came away thinking that I really didn't know him anymore."

Mickey Zaffarano was a constant presence at Thrush Way, usually banging on the bedroom door at 7:00 A.M. and shouting, "Noelle, I want my coffee! Get up, sis!" She would indeed climb to her feet, make coffee, and then go back to sleep. Molinas, who pointedly would not open his eyes to answer the telephone or get out of bed to greet anybody else at such a godforsaken hour, always stirred himself to share Zaffarano's morning coffee. Similarly, Zaffarano was the only visitor who'd routinely be invited to spend the night.

Whenever Molinas and Noelle gave a dinner party, Zaffarano would be enlisted to cook up his specialty—baked clams *arreganato*. Molinas and Zaffarano could spend an entire day talking about business—the distribution of porno films, Mafia politics, the stock market—but Zaffarano had no interest in gambling. Aside from business, Zaffarano's only other interest was spending time with his twelve-year-old son, Johnny, on a small powerboat he owned. Noelle liked Zaffarano's sense of humor and common sense, but most of all his affection for Molinas.

One of Noelle's friends, Barry, made his living selling dope, and on one of Zaffarano's visits he placed a large order. The drugs were duly delivered, and before Zaffarano left on a trip to New York he gave Molinas the money to be passed along to Barry. But as Noelle eventually discovered, Molinas pocketed the money.

"Cheating my friend is like cheating me!" Noelle raged at Molinas. "It's even worse, because it makes me out to be a cheater, and now it's cost me a friend!"

Molinas shouted back at her: "This is my business you're talking about, not yours, and you better not interfere!"

Harvey Freeman—whom Noelle described as "a short, overweight, mediocre run-of-the-mill guy in his mid-thirties"—would show up on their doorstep to play gin rummy with Molinas. Norman Arno was another regular, one whom both Noelle and her friend Linda actively disliked. "Arno was always telling dirty jokes," Linda said, "and he was always horny. Every time Noelle or I bent down he'd be leaning over to look down our dresses. He was one of those guys you wouldn't want your mother to know you knew. A real sleaze."

Mike Cleary stopped by once every month to show Molinas a long list of people and places. "Why did you call this guy?" Cleary would ask. "What were you doing here? What about there?" The questions seemed mostly for show because Cleary never challenged any of Molinas's far-fetched rationalizations.

On May 24, Molinas accompanied a part-time bookie and porno-film peddler named Earl Byrd to Memphis, Tennessee. Byrd was one of the unaffiliated LA bookies who'd once handled Molinas's action and been burned when Molinas refused to pay for his losses. Molinas's purpose was to speak to several theater owners about the possibility of showing some of Miracle's releases, and he gave no thought to the possibility that Byrd might be setting him up. As far as Molinas knew, Byrd was delivering copies of two porno films—*Convention* and *Search*—already scheduled for presentation. At no time during the journey did Molinas handle or otherwise carry the cans containing either film. None of the theater owners responded to Molinas's pitch and he and Byrd returned to Los Angeles on May 26.

Back in Thrush Way, Molinas always tried to be an accommodating host even in the most trying conditions. "It was just before the Memorial Day holiday," said Linda Brauer, "and I had a crew of about ten bikers who I knew from high school visiting me. Jack and Noelle were planning to spend a few days at Palm Springs, so I asked if we could use their pool while they were away. Jack trusted me implicitly, even so far as giving me keys to the house, so he said, 'Sure. Bring them over.' By no means were these bikers Hell's Angels—they rode sportsters and were all gainfully employed. Turned out that Noelle had gone ahead and Jack was leaving for Palm Springs the next day. But when we showed up, Jack took me to the Hughes Market at the corner of Santa Monica and Doheny Street and spent over two hundred dollars on hamburgers, hot dogs, steaks, booze, beer, and all the trimmings. He had never met any of these guys before but he whipped up a barbecue for them on the spot. Then when he left, Jack said they could use the pool, the shower, his shaving stuff, whatever. The bikers finally left after a few days, and there was quite a racket as they revved up their machines, with all the neighbors coming down to the road to see what was going on. Just as they took off, Peter Lawford and his wife came cruising down the street in their Mercedes convertible. 'Hi,' Lawford said to my friends. 'Nice bikes you've got there.' Then at the end of the block, Lawford stopped his car, stood up, and gave everybody the finger. When Jack came back, he was pissed at Lawford and said he was going to get even. It was so cute. Jack was going to save some bikers from Peter Lawford."

Another steady visitor was Elliot Ableson, who later became Molinas's lawyer. Ableson was very taken with Noelle. "All of Jack's friends and consorts saw him as a genius, but Noelle had him wrapped around her finger. I remember coming up there one day all dressed in a business suit for a meeting with Jack, and there was Noelle and one of her girlfriends sunbathing in the raw out by the pool. Jack got all flustered and embarrassed. 'Go get some clothes on,' he said. And Noelle's response was, 'Go fuck yourself.' She was absolutely a great broad. Super independent, bright, and sexy, just everything you would want in a live-in. My feeling was that she was really a wild, sexual girl, while Jack was a big macho talker and not the sexual performer. I always thought that Jack was the type of guy who wore his boxer shorts even when he was taking a crap."

Noelle knew Ableson was "a hotshot Beverly Hills lawyer, and an excellent one." Otherwise, she "didn't think too much of him." He was kind of cute, though, and when he asked her out, she agreed. After all, hadn't Noelle heard from several sources about Molinas continuing to see other women? For the next few weeks, Noelle and Ableson would meet in various local Ramada Inns to enjoy an intriguing affair. Ableson was fortunate that Molinas never knew, nor even suspected, what was happening. Had he known, Molinas was quite capable of arranging for a goon squad to beat Ableson to a pulp.

Finally, on June 26, 1972, Noelle had enough of Molinas's womanizing, odious business dealings, jackass friends, and macho stupidity. After weeks of arguments and petty harassment—she was spending too much money on groceries, or she was spending too much money talking to her mother on the telephone—Noelle packed her bags and said, "Well, good-bye, Jack. I'm going to San Francisco."

Never willing to get embroiled in emotional scenes, Molinas merely said, "Good-bye."

In San Francisco, Noelle moved in with a drug dealer named Oliver. On the side, they hired an elderly electronics expert (at three dollars an hour!) to build more of those black boxes that cheated the telephone company of toll calls. The boxes now sold for two hundred dollars each and parts cost eighty dollars, so Noelle and Oliver knew that they'd eventually strike it rich. In the meantime, Noelle also worked as a hostess in a fancy restaurant called McArthur Park.

Four days after Noelle left, Molinas called her. July 1 was her twentieth birthday and he asked if he could come up to San Francisco and help her celebrate. Noelle knew she couldn't live with Molinas, but she did miss him, so she said, "Sure. Why not?"

From there, the relationship resumed in a much altered fashion. Every weekend (sometimes every other weekend), Noelle would travel down to LA and stay with Molinas at Thrush Way, or else he'd come see her. "As long as I was in San Fran," Noelle said, "I never lived in one place for more than two months. I got to be so good at moving that I could pack all my stuff in half a day. The main reason why I had to keep moving so much was that the people I was living with were also very transient. They were dope dealers or car thieves or smugglers who were always trying to stay one jump ahead of the cops. Jack would take these people out for a meal and they were fascinated by him—just like I'd been when I first met him. Jack and I never got along any better than we did in those days. I believed I was having a really good time in San Fran, but when I thought about it in depth I realized that maybe I wasn't having such a good time after all. I missed Jack terribly and sometimes when I was with him at Thrush Way, it was hard to come back to San Fran."

Between visits with Noelle, Molinas was absolutely certain that he was having a good time. There were parties every night and new women to impress (with dinner at the Polo Lounge in the Beverly Hill Hotel) and then screw. Eve,

Diane, Susan—they never had last names. Breakfast was steak and eggs at Ollie Hammond's on La Cienega. And the money kept rolling in.

In mid-July, Ellen Sohn decided to move back to New York and tried to sell Molinas the furniture in her LA apartment. "But Jack wasn't interested," Ellen said. "The only kind of furniture he liked had flashy gauche silver-and-gold trim and was encased in plastic seat covers. But I did meet Noelle, who was twenty years younger than Jack. He only laughed when I pointed out that Noelle had been eleven when Jack and I first started going out."

The day before she moved, Ellen received a surprise phone call from Molinas inviting her to dinner. "I wanted to be alone with Jack one more time in a romantic setting," Ellen said, "just to see if maybe I'd been fooling myself all these years, and see if maybe I really did still love him. But I was happy when I saw that I didn't."

Midway through the dinner, Molinas asked her this: "How would you like to make ten thousand dollars?"

"Sure," she said. "How do I do it?"

"Have my child and I'll give you ten thousand dollars. I'd bet anything it'll be a boy. I'm not kidding, Ellen. This is a very serious and a very sincere offer."

"Why me, Jack?"

"Because you're the special one, Ellen. Because I love you and I've always loved you."

Ellen didn't believe that he loved her now or ever. She did pity him because he wanted a son so badly, but the whole proposition was preposterous. "No, Jack," she said. "Not for a million dollars." Then she got up and left.

Miracle Films' first feature-length (seventy minutes) film, *Saddle Tramps*, was released in September. Stuart Segall and Molinas collaborated on the script following the antics of a pair of Wild West bounty hunters who shoot up a frontier town and encounter several resourceful hookers. But the film featured too much violence and not enough sex and returned only what Segall characterized as "a fair profit."

In October, Molinas played host to a pair of unusually sinister houseguests: Nicholas ("Nicky the Nut") Musolino, and Peter ("Sonny Boy") Salanardi. This was how they were described in New York Police Department reports:

> Musolino is 5 feet 7 inches, round face, slim build, fair complexion, black straight hair, small brown eyes, small nose, small narrow mouth, round chin, small ears, arched eyebrows and long sideburns. Long time association with Mafia don Aniello Della Croce.

> Salanardi is 5 feet 11, 200 pounds, light skin, kinky brown hair, brown eyes, round face, pug nose, a long wide mouth, round chin, small ears, heavy build with gruff voice. Has a tattoo on right bicep of a double heart and the word "Marie." Active in the affairs of the Evola crime family and is a prime suspect in several unsolved armed robberies in NYC.

The two men palled around with Molinas and Ted Gaiswirth and rented cars from Chuck Bernstein. During a weekend stay at Thrush Way Noelle met them but retained no lasting impressions except that they were both secretive and nervous. On October 18, Musolino and Salanardi booked round-trip tickets to New York for a rendezvous with another mob figure named Carlo Lombardi.

A narcotics dealer and strong-arm hoodlum, Lombardi usually confined his nefarious operations to New Jersey. He was apparently also a lone wolf out to establish a reputation with the New York families. Accordingly, during the evening of August 1, 1972, Lombardi had been in New York, firing four shots into the Ravenite Social Club on 247 Mulberry Avenue in an attempt to assassinate Della Croce. He'd returned to the club seven days later, this time armed with a machine gun, which he aimed point-blank at Della Croce. But the weapon jammed and Lombardi fled, going into hiding with his girlfriend in Secaucus, New Jersey. Musolino and Salanardi had been hired by Della Croce to terminate Lombardi.

Tipped off to Lombardi's whereabouts, Musolino and Salanardi showed up in Secaucus and somehow managed to convince their prey that they'd been sent to relocate him to a safer situation in upstate New York. Lombardi and his girlfriend were driven to Old Route 17, just two miles outside of the town of Monticello, in Sullivan County, and then shot. The girl friend was only wounded in the neck and feigned death until Musolino and Salanardi left the scene, but Lombardi was dead. Immediately after the murder, Musolino and Salanardi flew back to Los Angeles and remained another few days at Thrush Way.

Musolino was eventually arrested in a Brooklyn apartment by the FBI on April 11, 1973, but Salanardi was never found. When word of all this finally reached Mike Cleary, he immediately called on Molinas to inquire why he hadn't told his parole officer that he'd hosted two underworld figures. Molinas's answer was typical: "Because you didn't ask." Even though Molinas's parole would be in effect for another seven months, Cleary let him slide again.

By his harboring Musolino and Salanardi, Molinas had proved that Zaffarano's patronage had been justified. Molinas was a good soldier. Zaffarano's bosses quickly assigned Molinas another task, one that would ultimately produce disastrous consequences.

Bernie Gussoff was born in Brooklyn in 1922 and grew up with a basketball in his hand. Good enough to become the captain of the Brooklyn College team in 1943, Gussoff knew that hoop heroes were more authentic celebrities than Hollywood stars. Naturally, Gussoff closely followed the career of Jack Molinas and was eager to meet him but never had the chance. "My father liked to be in the limelight,"said his son, Stuart, "and it gave his ego a big boost whenever he could hook up with someone who had a notorious background."

Gussoff studied the fur business in Brooklyn under Nathan Farber, one of the most successful furriers on the East Coast. Gussoff learned his lessons so well that he was allowed to marry the boss's daughter, Susan. Always ambitious and yearning to outdo his father-in-law, Gussoff went into the fur business for himself (and with considerable financial help from his mother) immediately after his discharge from the army after World War II. (Some of Farber's employees, however, believed that Gussoff had "embezzled a million dollars from the old man.") On his own, Gussoff's edge was to globalize his business by importing materials from Europe and the Far East. At first, the business boomed and he was able to buy a home in upscale Scarsdale.

Because animal pelts were extremely perishable, the fur business was a precarious one, and Gussoff's habit of buying millions of dollars of furs at auctions was always risky. If the furs didn't move quickly, he was stuck with huge storage bills and would be forced to take out sizeable loans. At its peak, Gussoff's personal income approached two hundred thousand dollars a year, not nearly enough to satisfy him, but he was greatly admired by his competitors for the vast sums of money that flowed through his hands. Generally, he was considered to be an honest man who nevertheless lacked the sophistication necessary to maintain a consistent level of success in the fur business. Gussoff simply took too many chances.

Through all the vicissitudes of his business affairs, Bernie Gussoff was always a very debonair man, standing five feet ten inches, with a slim athletic body. His pants were always creased, every hair on his head was artfully slicked into its proper place, but his reserved manner concealed a highly competitive spirit.

When the national economy deflated in the late fifties, expensive fur coats lost much of their appeal and Gussoff couldn't keep pace with his creditors. By 1962, Gussoff owed over two million dollars and was forced to declare bankruptcy. Shortly thereafter, Susan filed for divorce. "The loss of both his emotional and financial support was a very big blow to my father," said Stuart. "I don't think he ever recovered from either one, not even after he moved to California determined to start all over."

Because of the milder climate, the fur business in California was always on shaky grounds. By the time Gussoff moved to Los Angeles, the business was mostly controlled by Greeks who were extremely jealous of one another and suspicious of outsiders. He soon established Western Furs Incorporated with a partner named Ted Rosenbaum. Gussoff also established a romantic relationship with Georgie White, who was a former Miss Florida and fashion model. To augment the sale of furs, Gussoff made numerous trips to Japan and West Germany and bought large quantities of leather coats. Before long, the stylish leather coats were outselling the furs. Yet the sagging economy eventually caught up with him so that by the beginning of 1973 he once again found himself on the verge of bankruptcy.

That's when Zaffarano's overlords had Junior Torchio arrange an "accidental" meeting between Molinas and Gussoff. "When my father first met Jack," said Stuart Gussoff, "he couldn't believe his good fortune. As a lifelong basketball nut, my father certainly knew all about Jack's history, but he said that Jack had paid his debt to society, was living clean, and had made a killing in the stock market. Jack claimed he could secure some hefty loans and was willing to go into the fur business with my father. My father always wanted to be a big wheel and throw the bucks around. Jack, and the money at his disposal, represented an opportunity for him to make this dream come true. I always thought that my father would have gone ahead and worked with Jack even if he'd known that Jack was so tightly connected with organized crime. My father used to say that he'd never work *for* anybody else as long as he lived."

Did Gussoff have any prior connection with the mob? Nobody knows for sure. But one of Georgie's friends remembered her mentioning having to go over to someone named "Junior's" house to pick up a document for Gussoff. Georgie knew the address but no other name than Junior. When a woman answered the doorbell, Georgie called her "Mrs. Junior."

In January 1973, Gussoff and Molinas formed Berjac, which was ostensibly a fur business. To keep goods moving over the counter, the company was also involved in wholesaling leather jackets and women's clothing (with a specialty in pantsuits). Because the nature of the business was to overpurchase stock, Berjac was taking out loans (from legitimate sources) within three months. According to an LAPD confidential report, however, Berjac's primary business was "selling hot furs."

Sidney J. Knuckles was a member of the LAPD intelligence department and revealed the hows and whys of the Mafia's interest in Berjac. "The mob liked to set up guys like Jack by giving him some front money and having him buy into a fur business. Sure, the business was an outlet for their stolen furs, but they were also out to bleed the company dry and then let it die an unnatural death. The trouble was that with the mob's money in his pocket, Gussoff was acting like too much of a big shot. He'd go off on business junkets to China and Japan and buy more pelts than he could possibly sell. Gussoff was just frittering away all the money and there wasn't enough coming in for the mob to siphon off. It eventually got to be a big problem for Gussoff and also for Molinas."

Meanwhile, Gussoff's original enthusiasm had also infected Molinas. He invested a hundred thousand dollars of his own money when the business slumped, and the more involved he became with Berjac, the more Molinas was overwhelmed by the sheer volume of work required to keep the business functioning. He complained to Noelle that the time needed to manage the letters of credit, the buying and shipping, the importing and exporting cut into his gambling activities.

Shortly after Molinas and Gussoff became business associates their trust in one another faded and the friendship began to dissolve. Molinas's idea of saving money was to hook a black box up to the telephone in the office, a deed that sent Gussoff into a rage until it was removed. When proposed that Berjac hire two workers who happened to be Italians from New York and ex-cons to boot, Gussoff raised a stink. Molinas threatened to tie a knot in the purse strings and Gussoff eventually yielded. The two ex-cons were overpaid for doing manual labor, but their real job was to report back to the Mafia moneymen.

Another source of antagonism between the nominal partners was Georgie, who immersed herself in the company and insisted on having a say in every important decision. Even though she proved to be a highly efficient and boundless source of information, Molinas never liked her. In his mind a woman had no business running a business.

Molinas always found time to explore the possibilities of a movie deal based on his story, but when all his wheedling and boasting turned up nothing more than vague interest, he turned his attention to promoting another book. He'd been somewhat dissatisfied with Gross's efforts; the sportswriter had not presented Molinas in a very flattering manner. After Zaffarano had "suggested" that Molinas exercise his contractual right to halt the publication of *The House That Jack Built*, Bantam demanded that the thirty-two-thousand-dollar advance be returned. But Molinas balked. He told Bantam that he was displeased with Gross's work, even accused his old champion of incompetence. Bantam threatened legal action, but Molinas bought time with the dubious promise that he'd find another writer and deliver a better book.

For a while, Molinas snagged the interest of Richard Warren Lewis, who was then writing for *Playboy*. Molinas's first burst of enthusiasm propelled Lewis into writing a treatment. "But Jack didn't give Lewis much cooperation once they got started," Noelle said. "Jack just kind of sloughed off the whole project. What Jack really wanted was for someone to do all the work and for him to make all the money."

Even Julie tried his hand at writing a fictionalized version of his brother's days and ways. *Around the Rim and Out* was the resurrected title and the names of the characters were altered—Jack Molinas became Jack Moreno, Joe Hacken was Benny Lazarus—and the narrative concluded with Molinas in the Tombs. In February, Tony LaRosa introduced Molinas to still another literary agent, R. Smith Kiliper, and on April 27, 1973, Kiliper was officially empowered to represent Molinas.

Kiliper's strategy was to write a proposal for an article that might be accepted by some slick magazine. Surely, after Molinas's story appeared in a legitimate publication, the movie companies would be bidding against one another to option the rights. Again, working largely without his client's full cooperation, Kiliper produced a nine-hundred-word proposal the beginning of which was neither flat nor colorless:

> It's Sunday afternoon at a playground in the affluent Los Angeles suburb of Brentwood, but the squeak of sneakers, smell of sweat and dervish thrusts of motion are typical of three-man basketball as it's played on gritty asphalt surfaces all across America, from Harlem ghetto schoolyards to Catskill resorts to Kansas wheat fields. Waiting on the sidelines to take on the winners are a motley score of athletes, dressed in everything from football jerseys to sawed-off Levis, a number of them bearded and braided. Five of the six players grunting, snorting and zigzagging across the court are the usual collection of teenaged hotshots still perfecting their one-handed jumpers and overaged jockstraps three years out of college whose lack of conditioning is betrayed by too many Budweiser six-packs bloating their waist lines. It's not only his six-foot-six-inch height that distinguishes the sixth player from the others. Nor is it the bald spot beginning to appear on the crown of his $20 haircut or the deep circles of middle age beneath his eyes. The difference occurs when the ball is thrown to Jack Molinas, who is crouched like an arthritic on the pivot line. As his long-sideburned head bobs back and forth, his stinging elbow imperceptibly jabs into the soft underbelly of a defender, who is further thrown off-balance by a bump from Molinas' hip. At 40, several steps slower than when he was named to the National Basketball Association All-Star team, he now must resort to a deliberate, but subtle violation of the rules—in order to make the basket. The disoriented defender falls back awkwardly, watching the gracefully moving body and windmill of Molinas' arms that propels the ball through the metal hoop, whose strands snap in appreciation.

But Kiliper's efforts went unappreciated and ignored.

On January 9, 1973, Molinas was indicted by a Tennessee grand jury on a charge that he "knowingly and willingly did cause, counsel, induce, aid, and abet Earl Byrd to knowingly transport in interstate commerce, for the purpose of distribution, from Los Angeles, California, to Memphis, Tennessee, one copy each of obscene, lewd, lascivious, and filthy motion pictures entitled *Convention* and *Search*, in violation of Title 18, United States Code, #1465, and Title 18, United States Code, #2." Conviction of the charge would result in a minimum sentence of five years in prison, or a five-thousand-dollar fine, or both. There were no charges filed against Byrd.

Molinas, of course, was afraid that his parole would be instantly revoked and that he'd be remanded to Attica until his new trial convened. He hired Ableson to represent him, who immediately sought and received permission to interview Byrd. "When I spoke to Byrd," Ableson said, "he told me that the reason he sang against Jack was because Jack beat him on money he owed on losing bets."

In seeking the charge against Molinas, the Memphis DA had granted Ted Gaiswirth immunity in exchange for his testimony before the grand jury. The line of questioning attempted to link Molinas with the production of over one hundred porno films, but despite the DA's prodding, Gaiswirth never incriminated Molinas. When he appeared before the court in Memphis, Molinas was released on a ten-thousand-dollar bond, and after a series of delays and maneuverings his trial was set for mid-August. Jack was positive that he'd never be convicted.

But there was more legal trouble brewing. On February 20, the IRS subpoenaed Molinas's record of accounts with the Bank of America to substantiate their suspicion that he'd been guilty of tax fraud. In fact, the tax returns that Molinas had filed since his arrival in California reported annual income of between twenty-two thousand and twenty-four thousand dollars.

The first person Molinas sought out was Mike Cleary, but the parole officer had no juice with the IRS. Only then did Molinas turn to Elliot Ableson. "Jack," the lawyer said, "your returns are ridiculous. If the IRS ever investigates your lifestyle, you're a dead duck." Ableson recommended that Molinas immediately enlist the services of Sid Ermis, the best tax lawyer in the state.

Molinas made an appointment with Ermis and was very impressed by him until Ermis asked for a ten-thousand-dollar retainer. "I would certainly like to be your friend," Molinas responded, "but that's too much money to spend on a tax case. I would never spend that kind of money even if, God forbid, I was ever charged with murder."

Ableson then referred Molinas to a less expensive attorney, Bruce Hochman. The result was that Molinas filed amended returns for 1971 and 1972 showing an income of a hundred fifty thousand per year. That did the trick, and after paying his back taxes, Molinas was never investigated or penalized in any fashion.

In late February, Noelle unexpectedly informed Molinas that she'd decided to return to Thrush Way for good. Molinas was decidedly blasé at first. He enjoyed freelancing his way around the swinging singles scene, and he still resented Noelle for not marrying him and then leaving him. "I don't know if I want you to live at the house," he said. "Maybe you could stay there until you got your own place."

Noelle was more than willing to accommodate his wishes, but then he came home late one night and was incredibly horny. After they'd made love until the sun came up, Molinas changed his tune, saying, "It's really nice having you here, Noelle. Please don't leave." Which was also fine with her, even though Molinas didn't touch her again for another month.

And the same old problems remained unresolved: the incompatibility of their respective friends; Molinas's nagging about Noelle's wasteful spending; her hippie lifestyle versus his macho fascism. One new wrinkle was Molinas's installing Noelle in the office at Berjac. "I worked there from nine to five," she said, "answering the telephone, keeping track of the inventory, and whatever. Jack had the habit of giving away mink coats to any of his friends who were married or had girlfriends. He gave me about five or six of them, too, but I never liked the idea of an animal being killed just so somebody could have a fancy coat, so I gave them all away."

Noelle was more and more distressed by Molinas's frequent inability to perform sexually. Surely it had to be her fault! When Noelle tried discussing the problem, Molinas refused to participate. Noelle began to question her own sexuality, and she'd often break down and cry for days. She even tried to stimulate him by staging various fantasy sex situations, but he failed to respond. Their sexual relations were soon reduced to an obligatory coupling once a month.

"I was a very affectionate person," Noelle said, "and if I wasn't getting satisfied in one place, then I was going to look for it someplace else. Which I did. I found a very nice boyfriend who was married and also happened to be Jewish. And I started staying out maybe one or two nights every week."

On the ides of March, however, Molinas and Noelle traveled to New York to attend Julie's wedding. When the family was posed for a formal picture, Noelle was reluctant to be included.

"C'mon," Julie urged her. "You're practically family, anyway."

"Yes," Betty said. "It's a happy occasion."

In private, Betty told her eldest son that his entire life would have been brighter had he married Peggy Eisenhower. "For discouraging you like he did," she said, "I'll never forgive your father."

After the wedding, Noelle was in a sentimental mood and cuddled up to Molinas to say that she was willing to marry him after all. "Forget it," he said brusquely. "Now I'm the one who's not ready. Let's wait and see what happens."

While they were in New York, Betty also prepared several meals for her Jackie and his shiksa—all of her specialties, like Spanish rice, stuffed grape leaves, stews of lamb and beans. "She flavored everything with lemons and chicken fat," said Noelle, "and it was all delicious. She was always trying to stuff more food into Jack's face. 'Here,' she'd say, 'I got something in the refrigerator that I know you like. Let me warm it up in the oven.' Jack gained at least five pounds in the few days we were there."

While back in New York, Molinas also cruised over to Coney Island to see how his fondly remembered buddies were doing. "For a couple of days," said Hyman Silverglad, "Jack hung around Kaiser Park, around the bars and street corners, and regaled us with stories of how he was sleeping with so many movie stars. He mentioned Yvonne DeCarlo and Terri Moore. And he'd say that so-and-so was a nymphomaniac and such-and-such liked to take two guys on at one time. We put it all down as the same Molinas bullshit we'd heard for so many years."

Molinas also brought Noelle to meet Joe Hacken. "We had lunch in a coffee shop in Greenwich Village," Noelle said, "and I was impressed with his intelligence. Joe was obviously well read and he had very perceptive opinions about politics and everything else that was going on in the world. Things Jack was totally oblivious to. Yes, Joe was a nice man, friendly and polite, but his skin was kind of chalky, his eyes were runny, and he didn't look like he was very healthy."

When Molinas returned to Los Angeles, he learned that Berjac was in much worse shape than he realized. In the early spring of 1973, Gussoff gambled that the country's economic slump would soon end, so he bought more furs than Berjac could afford. He was soon proved wrong and the value of the furs plunged. With a refrigerated warehouse full of furs, Gussoff was forced to discount his goods and take a dramatic loss just so that Berjac could pay off the interest on its loans. Rather than dip into his own resources to save the company, Molinas borrowed twenty thousand dollars from the Bank of America, then sixty thousand from City National. When that wasn't enough, Molinas turned to Junior Torchio for assistance.

Torchio was on the payroll of Bryanston Incorporated, Louis Periano's film distribution company, which was headquartered in New York. It was Louis's father who'd been the original angel for *Deep Throat*, and both Perianos were associated with the powerful Profaci family. A loan was arranged, payable through Bryanston, for $247,000. But one of the loan conditions was that Molinas and Gussoff were required to take $250,000 life insurance policies on each other's lives. No problem.

Molinas contacted a reputable insurance agent in LA named Allan Rabins. "Molinas said that he wanted to take out 'keyman' insurance on his partner,"

Rabins recalled, "whereby one partner buys insurance on the other. This was a standard type of policy used to prevent a business from collapsing if an important member of the firm were to die. Molinas was a very sharp man who certainly knew the pertinent legalities. The beneficiary of the short-term policy wasn't Molinas himself, which was nothing out of the ordinary, either. The beneficiary was Chuck Bernstein, whom Molinas represented as another partner in the business. In the event of Bernard Gussoff's death, the policy, guaranteed by Massachusetts Indemnity, would pay three hundred thousand dollars."

For his cooperation, Molinas agreed to pay Bernstein ten thousand dollars should Gussoff's policy ever be cashed. "I trusted Jack," said Bernstein, "even when he put a bunch of documents in front of me and told me to sign them. I did so without reading them. I also found out later that my name was forged on several other papers. Anyway, Bernie also took out the same kind of insurance policy on Jack's life for just about the same kind of money, and I was the beneficiary of that one, too."

Why was Bernstein the beneficiary? Because he worked for Torchio, who, in turn, worked for Periano. So, both Molinas and Gussoff were officially on notice that the mob could make sure their loan to Berjac would get repaid by snuffing either (or both) of the partners.

Even with the policies in force, Berjac was supposed to be making monthly repayments to Bryanston, which they never did. "The Perianos wanted their money when it was due," said Mike Cleary, "and they were getting impatient. They had Torchio constantly putting pressure on both Molinas and Gussoff for a payback. Since Torchio had brought Berjac to Bryanston, his ass was also grass if there were any problems with the loan. Molinas and Torchio were arguing all the time about this."

If Berjac was not repaying the loan, Molinas made sure to make timely payments on Gussoff's life insurance policy. Gussoff, on the other hand, paid little attention to Molinas's policy and only paid two or three premium installments. By the summer, Massachusetts Indemnity terminated Molinas's policy.

Invigorated by the loan, Molinas and Gussoff investigated new markets and new sources of pelts. In June, Noelle accompanied Molinas on a short business trip to Hong Kong. "I mostly sat around the hotel while Jack met with other businessmen," said Noelle. "It was pretty boring. The only excitement we had was when we spent a day gambling in Macao, a Portuguese colony off the coast of China."

When they returned, Noelle learned she was pregnant and quickly had an abortion. "It was definitely Jack's child," Noelle said, "and he was so upset about my abortion that he didn't speak to me for a couple of weeks. Typical of Jack, he never directly mentioned what was bothering him, but resorted to indirect psychological attacks instead. Like not giving me any money. Like letting Puppy in the house but keeping my dogs outside. Whenever I tried to raise the subject of my abortion, he'd say in a very calm voice, 'I don't want to talk about it.' After that, things got very tense between us. He'd say he would be out late on business, then he'd get home at three o'clock in the morning smelling from perfume. Jack could really be a jerk. Then a few days later I was driving down Santa Monica Boulevard and I saw Jack's car exiting from a car wash, so I drove over to say hello. Then I saw a girl sitting next to him, a girl who was a friend of Linda's and whom I knew to be a hooker. I just gave Jack a dirty look and said, 'Well, I guess you're caught again.' When he came home after he dropped off the girl, we had an all-night shouting match."

Enough was more than enough, so Noelle moved out once more. This time she remained in LA and found a small garage apartment on Melrose Avenue. To avoid a scene, Noelle waited until Molinas returned to New York on another business trip before she packed her things and left Thrush Way. She kept her job at Berjac but also worked as a cocktail waitress at the Rainbow Bar and Grill, a private club on Sunset Boulevard. "I liked eating in good restaurants," she said, "wearing nice clothes, and living in a nice place. I also needed money for the wine I liked to drink, the pot I liked to smoke, and an occasional snort of coke. So I was willing to work very hard to get all of these things. I may have been a lot of things but I was never afraid of hard work."

It wasn't long before Noelle had a new boyfriend. "He owned and operated a hot dog stand in downtown LA," she said, "and his name was Hot Dog. We lived together on Melrose Avenue for a while and I really liked him a lot. He was a good Jewish boy, a little dense, but very good in bed. The trouble with Hot Dog was that he was insanely jealous. I couldn't go to lunch with a girlfriend without facing a third degree when I got home. After a couple of months, he came back from work one night to find that I'd thrown all his stuff onto the sidewalk, and that was the end of him."

On the rebound, Noelle began dating Molinas again. "That lasted," she said, "until I rolled into Thrush Way one night and found him lying on the couch with some girl. Jack was fully dressed, but her blouse was undone and her makeup was smeared all over her face. What had obviously happened was that he'd gotten his dates mixed up and invited the two of us over on the same night. I was furious. 'What are you going to do with two girls in one night?' I said to him. 'You can barely handle one at a time.' He didn't know what to say to that. So I just left."

With Noelle out again, Molinas could resume his unrestrained partying. Despite Berjac's financial struggles, Molinas's pockets were always bulging with crisp new bills wrapped inside a funky old rubber band. When dining with a friend who casually mentioned having mortgage troubles, Molinas tossed several hundred-dollar bills on the table and said, "Pay it back when you have it." He deliberately owned nothing of value to hide his true assets. He leased his new model gray Mercedes through Berjac. Afraid that the IRS was monitoring his business ventures, Molinas rarely committed anything to paper and carried all his dealings in his head.

Each of his friends knew a girl he *had* to meet. He met every one and *had* most of them. His favorite playground was the Thunderbird in Las Vegas, and he beamed when each new girl he brought there attracted hungry stares from even the most jaded casino chieftain. The best thing about the Thunderbird was that it was owned by the Mafia. That meant that he collected his winnings at the blackjack table and his losses were added to some chimerical tab.

He bought season tickets on the fifty-yard line to the Rams games and routinely bet five thousand on every game he attended. An old friend and marginal actor named Vic Morrow was Molinas's constant companion there. (Morrow grew up near Creston Avenue in the Bronx and was later killed in a tragic helicopter accident on the set of a movie as it was being filmed.) Molinas also boasted about being buddy-buddy with Warren Beatty. Even Molinas's cigars made the jump to the big leagues. His Mexican panatelas were abandoned for Partigas that were smuggled in from Cuba.

But even as Molinas was living the life of Riley, there was always another sticky predicament just waiting to blindside him. When Noelle left Thrush Way the second time, Molinas gave her the use of his El Dorado convertible. "There was a guy named Mike who was a regular customer at the Rainbow Bar and Grill," said Noelle. "One night while he was there I watched Mike take too many downs and I knew that if he tried to drive himself home he'd never make it. Turned out that Mike was a drug dealer, so I drove him home, stayed overnight, and then he drove me back to the club the next day to pick up his car, which was a Mercedes. We became really friendly after that. Anyway, I liked driving his Mercedes and he liked driving the El Dorado, so just for one day we decided to swap cars. At the time I was doing some part-time work for Chuck Bernstein. His company was called Roadrunner Driveaway Service and among his customers were people who were going on vacation or moving or something like that, and wanted their own cars waiting for them at their destination without having to drive the cars themselves. So the day after I switched cars with Mike, I was on the road making a delivery for Bernstein. When I got back to Los Angeles, I found out that the cops were all over Berjac looking for me and quizzing Jack. It seems that while Mike was driving the El Dorado, he'd gotten involved in a shootout and killed a cop named Blackie Sawyer. The El Dorado, of course, was registered in Jack's name, and there was hell to pay. Jack and I were questioned but never charged with anything and Mike was sent to prison for a long time. Jack was pissed, not at me and not that the cop was killed, but because he was afraid that his parole might be revoked for nothing that he had done wrong. He kept on saying that life wasn't fair. We both had to testify at

Mike's trial as witnesses for the prosecution and Jack believed it was his cooperation that kept his parole intact."

For several weeks, however, the LAPD kept Molinas under surveillance. One day Molinas was driving to meet some friends at a restaurant and as always speeded up through every intersection, forcing the detectives who were trailing him to run several red lights. Finally, Molinas pulled over to the curb, got out of his car, and walked over to the detectives' vehicle. "Look," Molinas said to the detectives, "let me give you the address of where I'm going so you won't have to take any chances and wind up in an accident. Okay? I'll see you fellows later."

Molinas's parole finally ended on October 20, 1973. To celebrate, Molinas took Noelle to dinner.

Many of Molinas's boyhood chums found their way to Los Angeles sooner or later and were eager to renew their acquaintance. One of these was Bob Santini, whose friendship with Molinas dated back to the first grade and continued through furious games of one-on-one in the Creston Avenue school yard. "Jack seemed different in Los Angeles," Santini said, "much more nervous and preoccupied. He still projected an air of confidence just like he did when he was younger, but it just didn't ring as true as before. Something wasn't quite right and it was like he was looking over his shoulder all the time. Jack never talked about his business dealings, but the impression I got was that, whatever he was into, he was involved with dangerous people."

Except for a newly discovered interest in the military history of World War II (encouraged by Artie Tolendini), it was business as usual for Molinas. For every deal that was initiated there were dozens that went nowhere. "There were often ten months of dialogue about these proposed deals—gold mines, silver mines, imported shrimp, reconditioned Jeeps," said Stuart Segall. "Jack was tempted by any kind of action as long as there was a lot of money in the offing and he would have the controlling interest. He liked to be thought of as a wheeler-dealer who had the Mafia behind him. He loved to play on other's people's greed. He was very perceptive when it came to other people's business. Jack's only blind spot was himself."

As ever, Molinas made sure that he was always the center of attention. "He couldn't walk into a room or a restaurant without making noise," said Segall. "He especially liked to impress women. Whenever we were at a restaurant, he talk loud enough for the broads at the next table to hear him. 'Hey,' he'd say to me, 'you want to use the Ferrari or the Porsche?' Jack really believed that everybody liked whatever he liked."

Despite his customary braggadocio, Molinas did understand that somewhere deep within his psyche there was a fragile, wounded place that made him much more vulnerable than he'd ever dare admit. He was not the macho superstud that he wished himself to be. On December 31, 1973, Molinas and Noelle drove to Las Vegas to celebrate New Year's Eve at the Dunes Hotel. During their attempted lovemaking, Molinas proved incapable of getting an erection. Certainly not a new problem, but this time Noelle was determined to try to find a solution. "Jack was only impotent with me," she remembered, "and that devastated me. So I spent the entire holiday weekend crying and pleading with Jack to get somebody to help him straighten out his own mind. It was very difficult for Jack to express what he was feeling. But for the first time since we'd been together, he was willing to talk about the problem and after a few days he said that he was willing to start seeing a psychiatrist. But, of course, he never did." However, Molinas's rare admission that he might benefit from some professional help so impressed Noelle that she moved back into the house on Thrush Way.

Meanwhile, there was increasing pressure for Berjac to start repaying the Bryantson loan. The life insurance policies were due to lapse on December 1, so something had to be done in a hurry. Junior Torchio would call the office every day and try to squeeze some money out of Molinas. When that ploy proved unsuccessful, Torchio began showing up at Berjac every week. He and Molinas would then harangue each other behind closed doors. Threats were made, excuses were offered, and the arguments invariably ended with Molinas making promises that neither of them believed.

On April 16, Noelle was at home preparing a dinner party to mark Molinas's forty-second birthday. She was in the kitchen at 7:00 A.M., cooking a variety of gourmet courses—beef in wine sauce, pork loin simmered for hours, scalloped potatoes, broccoli with Hollandaise sauce, and Dutch chocolate cake for dessert. One of the guests was Tony Mascolo, who years ago had tried to drug a friend's racehorse and ended up killing the animal. Mascolo seemed even more old-fashioned and square in the hip LA environs. After dinner, Molinas and Noelle began smoking a joint. "Wow," Molinas said after a few tokes, "I'm really wrecked."

Mascolo was genuinely frightened. "My God," Mascolo said. "Look at this! You guys are junkies!"

"Relax, Tony," Molinas said. "It's only pot. Here, have a toke."

"Get that dope away from me! I always thought you were smart, Jack. Don't you know that smoking marijuana leads to doing other drugs? Like, God forbid, cocaine and heroin?"

"That's right, Tony," Molinas said with a broad wink that everybody registered except Mascolo. "And I'm putting the word out that you're the one that got us hooked."

"Jack! Are you crazy?"

"Tony," said Molinas. "I think you must've watched that movie *Reefer Madness* too many times."

Barely three weeks later, Molinas sold his interest in Berjac to Gussoff for a hundred thousand dollars. When Molinas had left Jo Jo, he'd never bothered to make sure that his name was officially removed from the relevant legal papers—an oversight that resulted in his brief arrest during the trial of Norman Arno and Tony LaRosa. This time Molinas hired Sidney Rose, a corporate attorney from Century City, to ensure that Gussoff was now the sole owner of Berjac. The split was at least superficially amicable, and the two ex-partners continued to socialize with each other.

If Molinas always found a reason not to repay his bona fide debts to various bookies, and even to Bryantson, he never failed to pay the premiums on Gussoff's life insurance policy. And now, when Torchio hounded him to start repaying the loan, Molinas would point out that the money had been lent to Berjac. "I'm out of it and I've got the papers to prove it," Molinas said. "Gussoff's the one who owes you, not me."

Molinas soon got involved with Leonard Martinet, a financial advisor who put together syndicates that bought, built, or managed apartment houses, shopping centers, and ranches. Introduced by a mutual friend, Molinas was interested in purchasing a cherry orchard in Ripon County and sought Martinet's counsel. Martinet felt that the proposed deal was "too loose" and Molinas abandoned the project. "After that," said Martinet, "Jack came by my office a couple of times pressuring me to let him get involved in any kind of business deal that promised to make a lot of money. Before long we started up an import business. The company didn't really have an official name and we imported nuts, screws, and bolts from India and Taiwan. We also opened up a liquor store in downtown LA. All of our mutual projects did rather well."

Molinas was always very secretive about his financial resources and wanted everybody to think they were virtually unlimited, but Martinet believed he knew the truth: "I figured out that Jack had about five hundred thousand dollars at his disposal, and his trick was to maneuver this money constantly. He'd have money in one bank, then take it out and invest it in the stock market, then put all of it into another account at another bank. He once swindled the Bank of America out of sixty thousand dollars by moving his money out of there before a check cleared. Jack was always juggling checks."

One day Molinas and Martinet were meeting with a vice president of the Manufacturer's Bank in LA, trying to negotiate a six-hundred-thousand-dollar letter of credit. "Jack had the habit," said Martinet, "of suddenly changing the topic of conversation. In the middle of the meeting, Jack suddenly reached into his briefcase, pulled out a thick stack of checks, and handed them to the vice president, saying, 'Here, cash these for me, will you?' We had to stop our own discussion while the vice-president inspected every one of the checks. All of them were made out to Jack and most of them were from out of state. The amounts ranged from twenty-five dollars to maybe four thousand, and they added up to about thirty grand. 'Where did you get these checks from?' the banker asked. 'My associates sent them to me,' Jack said. A few days later, the banker, Jack, and I went out for dinner and then went over to the banker's house for drinks. After a while, the banker said that he was tired and wanted to go to bed, so Jack left, but the banker wouldn't let me go. The banker was an old man, a European Jew who didn't speak English very well. He told me that he'd run a full financial check on Jack and hadn't found where he worked or what kind of business Jack was in. All they'd found was that Jack had a certain amount of money in certain banks. 'I don't understand this man,' the banker said to me. 'There's something about him I don't like. He's got driver's licenses in California, Nebraska, and Pennsylvania. Be very, very careful with him, Leonard. His money is funny.'"

Martinet's advice soon became indispensable. "I steered Jack away from buying a racehorse," said Martinet. "I also discouraged him from investing in a cattle-feed deal. I did join him in a deal that sold sugar grown and harvested in the Grand Cayman Islands to England. Jack was so familiar with all the banks in the Bahamas that he must have been down there many times. We also formed a partnership to open another liquor store—that deal cost Jack thirty thousand up front. What was unusual about Jack was that he could come up with significant amounts of cash on a half hour's notice, even on Saturdays. His ability to do that told me he had money stashed in safe deposit boxes. I was always amazed at how well Jack could keep track of his own money because I never saw him write any figures down or consult any papers."

But the wheel was spinning faster and faster, the center was a blur, and there wasn't even a recognizable spoke to which Molinas could cling. There was nothing to prove anymore. Nobody to convince of anything. No goal beyond the accumulation of money. No reinstatement to win. No freedom to regain. Not even any debts to repay. (That was Gussoff's problem!) He was forty-two years old and no longer a boy wonder. The only thing that mattered was the next meal, the next dame, the next deal.

Noelle moved out for good on August 4. "It was the same stuff all over again," she said. "Jack's staying out all night with other women. His harassing me for spending too much money. His overall secretiveness and his stodgy ideas. It was okay for a man to have affairs, but not for a woman. But the big blowup came when my friend Oliver got out of jail. Oliver had been busted for selling drugs, but before he got nabbed he'd made a deal with Jack. Oliver had given Jack fifteen thousand dollars to be invested in whatever business venture Jack chose. The agreement was that, after a year, Oliver would get a guaranteed return of twenty-two thousand five hundred dollars. Jack had invested Oliver's money in Capricorn Films, an outfit operated by Jack, Ted Gaiswirth, and Mickey Zaffarano. At the end of the year, Zaffarano had given Jack the guaranteed money for Oliver, but Oliver was still in jail, so Jack just kept the money. Jack even had the balls to tell Zaffarano that, yes, he'd settled up with Oliver. At the time, I didn't know that Zaffarano had given Jack Oliver's money. All I knew was that Oliver was out of jail and was calling me and asking for his payoff. When I asked Jack where Oliver's money was, he told me to mind my own business. So in my desperation, I told Zaffarano that Jack hadn't paid my friend Oliver. Zaffarano flipped and he really chewed Jack out. I mean, there was a serious argument between them because not only had Jack shafted Oliver, but in effect he'd also stolen Zaffarano's money. Jack eventually agreed to make monthly payments to Oliver, but of course he never did. It wasn't a question of outsmarting somebody anymore—Jack had just turned into a greedy, tightfisted Scrooge. The upshot of the entire situation was that Jack became pissed at me. It was all my fault for not keeping my mouth shut and for butting into Jack's business. That was the last straw for me. It was crazy of me to think that Jack and I could ever work our thing out."

Molinas's fondest dream got a reprieve in the fall of 1974 when he was approached by a freelance writer named Bruce Kaiden. "Jack told me," said Kaiden, "that he didn't like Milton Gross's book, *The House That Jack Built*, because Gross did a 'bad job.' In my opinion, the book was poorly written but Jack's objections had to do more with the way he'd been portrayed—an unsympathetic wise guy. Anyway, I had my own connection with an outfit that was more a bunch of entrepreneurs at large than book publishers. They'd buy a building one day, a bankrupt business the next day, and then a book the day after that. Jack got fifteen thousand up front for the book and I got five thousand. The agreement was that I'd also get more money after I turned in each chapter. It was a straight biography and Jack and I taped a series of question-and-answer sessions. Jack was fairly cooperative, and I also did some research on my own, but the book was never completed."

In addition to the book and the several projects he was doing with Martinet, Molinas designed his most ambitious deal so far—a five-million-dollar jewel heist. His plan was to have somebody impersonate a prospective buyer of jewelry, replete with false credentials and references, then approach a big-time New York jewelry dealer. A standard practice at the time enabled a legitimate buyer to take whichever jewels he might be interested in purchasing to be evaluated by his own appraiser. Of course the plan was that Jack's phony buyer would simply take the jewels and scoot out of town. Molinas enlisted several partners in this scenario and they were only days away from setting the scam in motion, but the partners couldn't agree beforehand on their respective shares of the take and the plan was ditched at the last minute.

Molinas was annoyed at the avarice of his putative partners in crime, particularly now that Torchio's insistence that the Bryantson loan be repaid were joined by Zaffarano's not-so-gentle reminders. "Jack," said Zaffarano, "who the hell do you think you're dealing with? Certain people are getting very nervous. It would be to your benefit, Jack, to at least make some kind of repayment. Even a small one—say, ten thousand—would show them that your intentions are on the level."

"You're right, Mickey, and thanks for the tip. I'll get something done right away."

Instead of making a token installment on his debt, however, during the first week in November, Molinas made a phone call to Chuck Bernstein: "Geez, I've got to talk to you about something big. Let me buy you dinner."

But Bernstein was skeptical: "If you've got some kind of con in mind, Jack, don't bother."

"Nah, nah. It's nothing like that. Don't worry, it's legit."

At dinner that evening, Molinas introduced the subject of Bernie Gussoff's life insurance policy, saying that there'd been a "mistake" in the paperwork. Molinas offered Bernstein five thousand dollars, plus a large interest-free loan, if Bernstein would sign over the beneficiary rights on the policy to him. Bernstein agreed, but asked for a ten-thousand-dollar fee. They haggled for several hours until, worn down by Molinas's persistence, Bernstein finally agreed to accept five thousand. And it was done—in the event of Gussoff's death, Molinas would collect three hundred thousand dollars.

"You won't be sorry, Chuck," Molinas said afterward, "because this is the right thing to do. Believe me, Gussoff is one of the worst characters I've ever met. He's stiffed people all over town, and he's even screwed me out of a bundle that he owed me. A lot of people are pissed at Gussoff and, one of these days, he's going to get what he deserves."

In addition to nagging Molinas about the outstanding loan, Torchio also stepped up his hounding of Gussoff and began making explicit threats on his life. Berjac owed the Perianos $247,000, and since Molinas was officially out, Gussoff was on the hook for the entire sum. A few days after Bernstein signed the life insurance policy over to Molinas, Bernie Gussoff's mother died. "My father totally broke down at the funeral," said Stuart Gussoff. "He was yelping and crying like a baby. I just sensed that his reaction was caused by something more than the death of his mother. I think he was already mourning his own death."

On October 1, Gussoff picked a fight with his live-in girlfriend, Georgie, stormed out of the house, and moved into the Oasis Motel on Olympic Boulevard. His friends said that he did this deliberately, because he believed his life was in danger and he wanted to protect Georgie and her three children.

Gussoff also had trouble sleeping. He'd wake up at 3:00 A.M. and go for long drives. He was also unusually short-tempered with his son. "My father was running around like a scared man," said Stuart. "So I sat him down and said that I knew something was wrong. When I asked him to tell me what was bothering him, he just couldn't get it out."

Stuart dropped into Berjac's office at 5:00 P.M. on Friday, November 15, to find his father in a desperate state. "He was finagling the books," said Stuart, "trying to come up with fifty thousand dollars. That was the figure he kept repeating. 'I've got to have it,' he said. 'I've got to have it.' When he wasn't going through the books, he was on the phone trying to arrange a fifty-thousand-dollar loan. I overheard him saying to someone he was calling, 'You don't know what pressure is until the mob pressures you.' It was all very frightening."

Later that evening, Gussoff and Georgie had a dinner date at the Luau on La Cienega with another couple and a friend named Harry Rabinoff. They were both concluding their business day at the office and had their own cars parked nearby. "Bernie," said Georgie, "I'll go over to the motel with you so you can shower and change your clothes, then you can drive me home and I'll change."

"No," said Gussoff. "You go home by yourself and I'll pick you up when I'm done."

The dinner date was for 7:00 P.M., and Georgie was upset when Gussoff didn't show up. When he didn't answer the phone at his motel room, she became even more aggravated because she remembered Harry Rabinoff saying to Gussoff, "To hell with dinner, Bernie. Let's you and me go out and have ourselves a wild time on the town." She called Gussoff every ten minutes until eleven o'clock, then she got undressed and went to bed. That selfish bastard must've gone off with Rabinoff.

Meanwhile, Molinas and a date were having dinner at the Polo Lounge along with Bernstein, Segall, and their dates. "The place was full of movie stars," Bernstein said, "and there was big Jack, with his white shoes and his cigar, trying to impress everybody within hearing range with his usual bullshit about this million-dollar deal and that one. It was typical Jack Molinas that night. We stayed until ten o'clock."

The next morning, Georgie tried calling Gussoff's hotel room again but he still wasn't answering the phone. She was taking her eldest daughter, Stacey, for breakfast at a diner near the Berjac warehouse, when Georgie saw several men running from the warehouse carrying various appliances—typewriters, copying machines, TV sets. Georgie immediately called the police and then went in for breakfast.

After eating, she thought she'd call the hotel one last time. "You'd better get over here," the desk clerk told her. "Mister Gussoff's been badly beaten." In fact, he was already dead.

The LAPD death report concluded that Gussoff had been murdered:

Georgeanna White states while calling subject's tel. no., she was informed by motel mgr., Russell Green, that the maid found subject in his room, lying on the floor apparently beaten. Subject was wearing a white shirt and black-and-white checkered trousers.

Ambulance #R.A. 13 at scene pronounced subject dead at 1335 hours on 11-16-74.

Death appears to be a homicide as decedent lying face down on floor in large amount of blood from hole in back of skull and ligature around neck.

There was no evidence of forced entry. No weapon found. [The coroner's report later concluded that the hole in Gussoff's skull had been caused by an ice pick.]

At three o'clock that afternoon, Bernstein got a call from Molinas: "Chuck, guess what happened? Bernie Gussoff, my ex-partner, was killed. I knew that no-good son of a bitch would get it. What goes around, comes around."

Molinas stayed away from Thrush Way all day, knowing the LAPD would be looking for him. He had an airtight alibi, but he still wanted to put off talking to the police.

There were several theories as to why Gussoff had been whacked. According to Mike Cleary, "The primary reason was to get the message across to Jack Molinas that he'd better come up with the dough he owed. Molinas did get the message, but he continued to believe that nothing similar could ever happen to him." Stuart Gussoff had a very different take on the homicide: "I think Molinas hired somebody to kill my father so that he could collect the insurance money."

The LAPD contacted Massachusetts Indemnity to delay payment of the insurance money as long as possible. "Whatever money Jack got from Gussoff's insurance," said Sergeant Knuckles, "he was supposed to give to the mob. Our official stance was that any insurance payments would be held up until we completed our investigation of the homicide. We also knew the mob would be pushing Jack and we just wanted to see what the delay would lead to. Being an ex-lawyer, Jack knew that the insurance company couldn't withhold the money any longer than forty-five days, but in the meantime he sent dozens of letters to them and dozens of letters to us. We also told Massachusetts Indemnity to notify us as soon as they released the money to Jack."

While he was waiting for his biggest payday ever, Molinas connected with an old friend from the Bronx and made a comeback on the basketball court. "When Jack first became a lawyer," said Dr. Richard Fishman, "he handled my sister's divorce and that's how we got to know each other. We met again out in Los Angeles and I'd do little things for him like writing out a prescription if he wasn't feeling well. One time he came to my office in Pico Rivera and I removed a small mole from his face. I would never think of charging him for my services because we were pretty close friends by then. Years later, I was sponsoring a basketball team in the Bellflower Recreation League and when I asked Jack if he'd like to play with us, he said that he'd be delighted."

Molinas was forty-two, Fishman was forty-three, a forty-seven-year-old attorney played center, and the remainder of the roster was comprised of minimally talented thirtyish blue collar workers. "There was an A league for the best players," said Fishman, "and then a step down to a B league. Our team was called the Chiefs and we played in the C league. We had a ball game every Tuesday night and there were never more than thirty people in the stands. Jack easily scored about twenty-five points a game and won several games single-handedly, yet he never threw his weight around. That hook shot of his was still deadly and if he couldn't run the floor he never wasted a step. We called him the Gentle Giant. After the game, the whole team would go over to a restaurant called Stox and Jack would always order a vanilla milkshake and a piece of Hawaiian strawberry pie. We all loved being around Jack on and off the court."

With his body rounding into shape and his chops up, Molinas also played in a higher caliber game on Saturday mornings at Santa Monica High School. The players there were mostly black, and knowing exactly who Molinas was, they tried with all their might to make a good showing against him. They had young legs, but Molinas took advantage of their wild-eyed exuberance with his crafty moves and was hailed as the best player on the court—except when Wilt Chamberlain made a rare appearance. After going head-to-chest against the seven-foot-one inch Chamberlain, Molinas would brag to his buddies that not even Wilt the Stilt could block his hook shot.

On December 18, Noelle returned from Ohio, where she had been working, to spend the holiday season with Molinas. "It was a very pleasant break for me," she said. "We spent New Year's in Las Vegas with Doctor Fishman and his wife, and although nothing special happened it was a very mellow time. In a certain way, it was very tempting for me to go back and live with Jack. Despite all our problems, it was comfortable and stable, and a lot easier than working for a living. But it was also living in a rut and as long as I was with Jack my life wasn't going anywhere. Jack was a bad habit I had to quit. After the holidays I moved back to Columbus."

While he waited for his insurance money, Molinas continued playing his favorite game—Deals-A-Plenty, most of which were legitimate. He bought into a firm that sold Belgian waffles at state fairs. He set up a system to bill the California Medicaid system on behalf of participating druggists in return for nine percent of the action. He bought cheap cement in the Bahamas. ("I think Jack stashed a lot of his own money down there," said Chuck Bernstein, "because he was always talking about a bank he was going to buy in the Bahamas.") He went into a partnership with Bernstein in the liquidating assets business. ("We'd pay twenty cents on the dollar for the merchandise of a business that was going under," said Bernstein, "then sell the merchandise for whatever we could. We bought up shoes, pots and pans, dresses, and the most lucrative deal we did involved buying nails.") He set up a TV store in Omaha. He flew to Mazatlan in Mexico to arrange for the importation of fish (after conferring in San Diego with the mob to obtain their permission to move the fish through there, and insuring that the shipments would be unloaded immediately upon arrival).

Along with two mobsters of his acquaintance, Molinas also formed the Ocean Garden Products Company, which bought shrimp from Australia and India and misrepresented itself as a Mexican entity. The trick here was that they'd pay for a few small loads in cash and then have a phony Mexican address billed for a large order. On his only trip to India, in January 1975, Molinas was astounded by the extravagant nature of the tourist hotels. "Meanwhile," he wrote on a postcard to Noelle, "people on the street are eating garbage. It's awful."

Molinas's dealings in India soon attracted the interest of a major film studio, Paramount, which had forty million dollars frozen there because of the country's political turmoil. Molinas's idea was to convert the money into a commodity (like shrimp) that India routinely exported. The shrimp could then be shipped to the United States and sold there. Paramount was impressed by Molinas's suggestion, but their negotiations came to an abrupt end when he insisted on being paid fifty percent of the proceeds.

In mid-March, Molinas finally got his insurance money. Not willing to take a chance with the U.S. mail, he traveled to the home office of Massachusetts Indemnity in Boston, cashed the check in their bank, and brought the money back to Los Angeles in a suitcase.

The Perianos, however, were not aware that Bernstein had signed away his rights to the money. "Right after Gussoff's murder," said Bernstein, "two boys from San Diego came calling on me to demand the money from the policy. When I told them what had gone down, they didn't believe me. One of them said to me, 'We're going to twist your prick with a pair of pliers until you tell us the truth.' They backed off when I stuck to my story, but they followed me around for several months. Jack owed a lot of money and he was stiffing the wrong people."

Once the mob learned that Molinas had collected on Gussoff's policy, Torchio was dispatched to tighten the screws. "Jack," said Torchio, "you haven't made a payment on the loan for over a year. If you had any sense, you'd fill up a suitcase with all of the two hundred and forty-seven thousand dollars and let me take it down to San Diego. Believe me, Jack. That's the only way to go. Don't mess with these guys, Jack. I've told you that a thousand times."

"And I've told you a thousand times," Molinas replied, "Berjac borrowed the money and I haven't been connected with Berjac for nearly a year. Go get the money from Gussoff's estate. I hear he owned some land in Canada."

What did Molinas do with the three hundred thousand dollars of insurance money? He paid fifty-four thousand in cash for a Rolls Royce convertible from a dealer in Las Vegas. "You only live once," Molinas liked to say. "If you do it right, once is enough."

When Sergeant Knuckles was told of Molinas's latest purchase, he laughed. "This guy's life," Knuckles said, "isn't worth a quarter."

But Molinas was unafraid. He reasoned that only fools would murder somebody who owed them money, because dead men never paid their debts. And he envisioned himself at age sixty sitting in an easy chair and smoking a cigar while he petted a dog and had a woman rub his legs.

3/31/75
Dear Noelle,

Here it is one a.m. and I just got up from a nap (6 p.m–1 a.m.)— Pretty good nap, eh?

...Big news is that I just picked up my new car & to tell you the truth, I'm quite excited over it—A Rolls convertible in Mediterranean blue with a beige top & interior—A real beauty—Had some pix taken; when I get them I'll send you one—Guess I was destined to get it— You'd be real proud of me—

On the other side of things, Mickey is due here tonight and should be here for a week—You know what that means— (up @ 7 a.m.) ...

Hope everything going fine & please keep in touch—

Love always

// Jack //

But not even Zaffarano's pleas could move Molinas to settle up the Bryantson loan. "The only money I really and truly owe is to a couple of casinos in Las Vegas," Molinas said. "Otherwise my hands are clean, Mickey."

And the wheel was spinning faster and faster. Stashed in various lots around LA, Molinas had two hundred orange-painted Jeeps equipped with English-style wrong-sided steering wheels just waiting for the right mechanic to convert them. Molinas was also importing mass-produced leisure suits from India, as well as seeking financial backing to construct a series of shopping malls in several suburbs of Los Angeles. In addition, he was meeting with a group of wealthy investors about the possibility of a scheme that would, if successful, corner the world gold market. Molinas also revived his signal-balloon project—"Every hiker, every skier, every camper will want one," he said, "and it's small enough to carry in a backpack. All you have to do is press a button and this big balloon made of glow-in-the-dark material and carrying flares goes up." But he couldn't attract any other investors.

One enterprising businesswoman tried to entice Molinas into backing her greeting card business. She was rather good-looking, and to seal the deal she offered to sleep with him. "I'm not going to invest twenty grand just to get laid," Molinas said, but he tried (unsuccessfully) to bed her down with vague promises.

Molinas consummated enough of these deals to seriously consider purchasing the house on Thrush Way. He and his landlord agreed on a price—seventy-five thousand—and while negotiations continued, Molinas hired a contractor to renovate the house. Ah, life was good. With the Rolls parked in the garage, and Puppy on guard against intruders, Molinas would sprawl on the living room couch, smoke a Cuban cigar, look out at the glittering city below, and listen to his favorite song playing on his expensive custom-made stereo—Harry Neilson's rendition of *As Time Goes By*.

Only Noelle was missing. She was living in Columbus, managing the Garden Theater, a burlesque house, and still threatening to enroll in veterinary school. Molinas convinced himself that all he had to do was turn on the charm and she'd jump at the chance to marry him. Sure that she wouldn't refuse him, he bought $367.35 worth of glassware, blankets, sheets, towels, and other housewares from the Broadway, a department store. Then, while he was on another business trip in Mexico, he sent her a letter stating his intentions in a surprisingly vague fashion:

> 4/11/75
> Dear Noelle,
> ...It's really romantic here & that's why I think of you.... You know, I was thinking, love isn't all sex—I guess it's a combination of many things, especially digging each other & doing things together. If I had any guts, I'd invite you here, but then again, I'm leaving tomorrow. I was thinking who I'd like to be here with most, & of course you won hands down—
> When you left me this last time I felt I lost something that was part of me! With all our differences we still had something precious—not too easy to find—I'd still like to know if you feel going to school for eight years is really your answer to life—You don't have to prove a thing—You're still tops—And don't worry, I'm a pretty good judge—School would be a waste of time—Too many other things more important to do—
> Well, I guess I'll say goodnite & take a tip & read your fortune—You might be spending Xmas in Acapulco on your honeymoon—A thought, eh?
> Love always,
> // Jack //
> P.S. Just read this letter & it really doesn't sound like me—Guess this atmosphere with no phones lets your mind play & roam—

What did Noelle make of the letter? "I'd told Jack many times how much I liked Acapulco," she said, "and I guess that his intentions were for us to get married at Christmastime and then go there for our honeymoon. That was Jack's way of proposing to me. He couldn't just come out and say, 'Let's get married.' But before I even received the letter, he called me up from Mexico. 'I wrote you a letter,' he said, 'and asked you something. After you get it and read it, I'd like a reply. Just call me back and tell me what you think.'"

Noelle decided to play dumb and pretend that she never received the letter. Just to see how he'd react. Of course, by now, the last thing she wanted to do was marry Jack. Her ploy resulted in Jack's sending her another missive, dated April 27, in which neither a marriage nor Acapulco nor a prospective honeymoon was mentioned. Instead, he promised (again) to give Oliver "some cash" and concluded with this: "Real sorry my letter from Mazatlan appears to be lost—Probably the most sentimental letter I ever wrote!!!"

Molinas and his Mafioso partners had big plans for his Western TV store in Omaha and another one he'd set up in Los Angeles. "The scam was to set up a phony line of credit," said Mike Cleary. "Then they'd keep buying TVs and moving them from one store to the other. In fact, Jack was looking to establish several other TV stores in other cities. The deal they offered their customers was a dollar down and a dollar a day. This enabled Molinas and his partners to go to their suppliers and say that they were doing a huge volume. Then they'd say that several of their stores were short on product and they'd arrange for thousands of TVs to be shipped. The scam was to take the TVs, not pay the bills, and disappear into the night. But the plan never worked out. For one thing, the only company that would sell them TVs was Toshiba. And for another, on May 8, while Jack was on the phone talking to the clerk, a tornado hit Omaha and wiped out the store.

And Molinas made what he believed to be a major concession in another nebulous pitch to Noelle:

> 6/10/75
> My dear Noelle,
>
> I'm really sorry I haven't written sooner but I'm really jammed—Got so many things to do I'm really pissed- It's because I've gotten involved in so many situations; not that they're bad, but you know me, I don't trust anyone to administer my investments!
>
> ...Planning to take some time off & really have a vacation—Acapulco for Xmas—one week—& Brazil in Feb '76 for ten days—...That trip is for two—...You're invited both times if you like—
>
> I guess I really miss you & all the arguments we had—Really a pleasure, believe it, or not! Hope you decide to come back to Calif. Where you'll certainly be wanted—Think about school, if you still want to do that from here it wouldn't be bad—
>
> Redecorating the house—Paneled the back wall behind the bed in red oak & did my closet in aromatic cedar—
>
> Love always—
> // Jack //

Molinas would spend at least one weekend every month at the gaming tables in Las Vegas. During a late-June sojourn at the Tropicana, he gambled away a twenty-five-thousand-dollar line of credit on Friday, then another twenty-thousand-dollar line of credit on Saturday. On Sunday he asked for and received another twenty thousand worth of credit, but this time his luck made an about-face and he walked away from the craps table with fifty thousand dollars. Instead of stopping at the cashier's office to repay the money he'd been advanced,

Molinas went straight to his room. That evening, one of the casino's managers came to his room and asked for restitution of their loans.

In his playing days, Molinas's game plan was "The best defense was a good offense," so he blithely told the manager that he'd met a hooker at the casino's bar and taken her up to his room, where she'd lifted all of his money. "In fact," said Molinas, "I'm holding the casino responsible."

On other visits to Las Vegas, Molinas would drive back to Los Angeles immediately after losing several thousand of the casino's money. The next morning he'd invariably get a call from a casino manager, saying, "You owe us some money from the weekend, Jack. How do you want to handle this?"

"Handle what?" Molinas would say. "I don't owe you anything."

And the casino operators were afraid to go after him because of Molinas's mob connections.

For Molinas not even losses were losses. He ignored what he could and denied the rest. He left no paper trail, and kept the money moving to baffle lenders and the law alike. But some of his debts he could do nothing to erase. It was a grim accounting:

1. Despite his severance from Berjac, the Periano family had specifically made a loan of $247,000 as a gesture of goodwill to Molinas and his patrons in organized crime. So far, none of the money had been returned. To add insult to injury, Molinas had bought a Rolls Royce with a life insurance windfall.

2. Molinas owed more than $100,000 to various mob-backed Las Vegas casinos.

3. In LA alone, Molinas had stiffed hardworking bookies for over $50,000.

4. During his association with Jo Jo, Miracle, and Capricorn, Molinas ran up a $250,000 bill with several mob-controlled film-processing companies.

5. Molinas had horned in on the mob's porno film interests run by Johnny "Bump" Bompenciero in Los Angeles. This may have been his most damning offense.

6. Molinas was suspected of ratting out some of his business associates to Mike Cleary, his parole officer.

7. The suspicion also lingered that while Molinas was in the Tombs cooperating with the district attorney on the Mays case, he had given up some names in the harness racing fixes.

On the flip side, as far as the mob was concerned Molinas did have several factors working in his favor. When he was booted from the NBA, he never publicly gave up the names of other NBA players who were doing business with mob-connected bookies. Ditto for his time in the joint. He had some credit in the Gambino family for sheltering Musolino and Salanardi during their rubout of Carlo Lombardi. And he had long been under the protective custody of Mickey Zaffarano, a soldier who was widely respected on both coasts.

But Molinas already had been amply rewarded for his deeds; the debts were all that was left. He owed so much, and had for so long, that there was only one way he could ever pay.[1]

NOTE

1. For a fictionalization of the mob's role in Molinas's death see *The Great Molinas*, pp. 247, 253, 259.

Molinas had two more visitors at Thrush Way in the last week of July. The first was his mother, who was also in California to see her cousin, Morris Levy, and his wife, Linda. Molinas doted on Betty. As on her earlier visit years before, he took her to only the fanciest restaurants, bought her expensive clothing, and this time even accompanied her on an excursion to San Simeon, William Randolph Hearst's palatial residence-cum-museum.

Stuart Segall had this observation about the latest mother-and-son reunion: "Jack was a cold motherfucker, but with his mother he was a pussycat. She always called him 'Jackie' and she'd say, 'Jackie, do this,' or 'Jackie, do that,' and he'd jump to do her biding. When he was with his mother, Jack was like a nine-year-old."

Molinas's other visitor was an old girlfriend from Brooklyn, Shirley Marcus. He'd first met her at a bar in Coney Island twenty years ago and they'd dated for only a few weeks. But Shirley claimed that she'd been nursing a crush on him for all these years and when she discovered his Los Angeles address, she sent him a glossy eight-by-ten photograph and asked leave to come to California to see him. Shirley was now thirty-five, twice divorced and the mother of a nine-year-old boy. A brief phone call interested Molinas to the point where he made arrangements for her to fly to the coast. He figured if she turned out to be a drag, he could always turn her over to Harvey Freeman.

According to a confidential LAPD report:

> Shirley Marcus is a call girl who hangs out with the mob and is well-known in New York.... It is believed that she was sent to Los Angeles to set Molinas up for a hit.

On the evening of July 29, Molinas called his friend Dr. Fishman. "My youngest daughter's fifth birthday was a week away," said Fishman, "and Jack called to say he was really looking forward to coming to the party. In the past, he'd gotten wonderful birthday presents for all of my children—like a TV, a piano, and a jukebox. And he was very excited about the newest present he'd come up with. Jack was such a nice man."

The guest house where Harvey Freeman lived was broken into on the evening of August 2. "The cupboards were left open," Freeman said, "and some of the dresser drawers were as well. But nothing was taken. When I told Jack, he just laughed it off and said, 'Don't worry about it.' In retrospect, I believe that somebody wanted to see who lived there, what kind of view the place had of the main house, and, most importantly, did I have a gun."

On Saturday, August 3, Molinas was in contact with another old flame—Ellen Sohn. "I happened to be in Los Angeles at the time," she said, "in the company of my aunt. We were both staying with a friend in Santa Monica and for some reason I could never explain, I called up Jack on the morning of August 3. He said that he had a girl with him but that I should come over that evening and pay him a visit. It was a very hot day and he said we could sit around his pool and talk about the old days. He even said that he'd send a car to come and pick me up. I was very anxious to go over there, but the friend I was staying with had his own plans for the evening and my aunt didn't want to be left alone. I argued with her a little and she said, 'After what you've been through with Jack, why do you want to have anything at all to do with him?' So I decided that she was right and I stayed home to keep her company."

Saturday night, Molinas dined with a casual date and his mother at one of his favorite spots, the Luau. After dinner, he took his date home, then drove his mother to the Levys' house in Montebello. From there, Molinas met Shirley Marcus at Los Angeles International when her flight from New York arrived at 1:00 A.M. and then drove her to Thrush Way. "On the way to his house," she said, "we reminisced and had a wonderful time." Molinas knew that his nearest neighbor, Stuart Segall, was away for the weekend in Palm Springs, and as he steered his beloved Rolls up the driveway, he noted that the lights were out in Segall's house. Shirley further reported that Molinas's garage door opened electronically, and after he parked the car, they entered a patio that separated the garage from the house. From there, he guided her to the end of the patio to show her the view. It was now about 2:15 A.M.

Molinas's last words were these: "Isn't this the most beautiful place you could live, compared to Brooklyn?"

While Molinas praised the view, a twenty-eight-year-old truck thief named Eugene Connor was hiding behind a restraining wall that separated Segall's property from Molinas's. That's when Connor rose up from his hiding place, steadied his long-barreled .22 caliber pistol on top of the wall, and fired five shots in rapid succession. Two hit a window sash, one hit Shirley, one hit Puppy in a front paw, and one hit Jack Molinas in the back of his neck. He fell face up on the patio's cement floor.

Shirley, bleeding from a wound on the left side of her neck, was knocked to her knees and almost toppled over the patio's low railing. When she recovered her footing, she stumbled into the living room to summon help. As she talked to the police on the telephone, a knock sounded on the front door. The officer on the wire instructed her not to respond. Then Shirley heard the person at the door take off and run down the street. This was Joseph Ullo, a building subcontractor who had organized the hit at the bequest of the mob in order to acquit himself of sizeable gambling debts. There were two other accomplices—Robert Zander, who was paid two hundred dollars to serve as an armed lookout, and Craig Petzold, who drove the getaway car. Ullo had come to the front door intent on entering the house to make sure that Molinas was dead, and was unaware of Shirley's presence.

In the guest house, Freeman was half-asleep, and assuming that the noise he heard was a stray cat scavenging inside a garbage can, he turned over to go back to sleep. Moments later, at 2:18 A.M., he was reawakened when Ullo shouted out from Molinas's driveway, "Who called the police?"

Freeman jumped out of bed and hurried to the main house. Inside was a woman he didn't recognize, who was dazed and bleeding. She asked him for a cigarette, and when he handed one to her, he caught a glimpse of a man lying on the patio. He knew without taking a second look that Jack Molinas was dead.

The first policemen on the scene were Patrolmen A. Williams and G. Punchar, who officially pronounced Molinas dead at 2:47 A.M. Shirley Marcus was then taken to the UCLA Medical Center, where she was treated by Dr. Pius Baggenstos, a neurosurgeon, who reported that no stitches were required to close the wound because the bullet traveled so fast through her neck that it only opened a tiny hole. Marcus was then released to the police for questioning.

By the time the coroner received Molinas's body at 10:00 A.M. the next morning, several large bills (totaling at least a thousand dollars) had been removed from Molinas's wallet, leaving only $43.33. A Dr. B. Ship performed the autopsy. His report stated the following: "The body is well-developed, muscular, and well-nourished. The vital statistics are 80", 250 lbs, brown hair, brown eyes, balding. Immediate cause of death was a gunshot wound in head. The bullet entered 6-3/4 inches below top of head just below left ear. The bullet traveled upward at a 10-degree angle from front to back and exited just about even with the right earlobe. A look at the brain revealed a normal amount of gray and white matter."

The LAPD pegged the homicide as the work of a professional killer. The .22 caliber bullet was certainly indicative of the mob's favorite device, and the muffled thud that Marcus heard was also evidence of a silencer. On the other hand, would a mob-trained killer have left a live witness? According to Mike Cleary, the chance of a professional hit being solved was one in two hundred thousand. "If it was a pro job," Cleary said, "it might have been dressed up to look amateurish."

Another member of the LAPD said this: "The same imbeciles who fucked up the Manson murder investigation with sloppy, stupid, and inefficient work were put in charge of Molinas's murder." In any case, Harvey Freeman was never questioned.

Leonard Martinet was in Palm Springs when Molinas was murdered: "The LA cops had received an anonymous phone call saying that I had Jack's money, and after Gussoff and Jack, that I was next. So I was literally taken off the street and brought back to LA. I assured the cops that not only didn't I have any of Jack's money, but I had no idea where it was. They took me home, and I left the country that very same day."

Julie was on vacation with his wife, Jennie. They arrived at a hotel in Bar Harbor, Maine, at about 11:00 P.M., following an eighteen-hour boat ride from Halifax, Nova Scotia, and heard the news on a local TV broadcast. "The Los Angeles police are looking for clues in the murder of former basketball player Jack Molinas..." There was no telephone in the room and before he went out to locate one, Julie opened a bottle of Crown Royal whiskey purchased in Canada and drank a small portion—the only time in his life he'd ever had whiskey straight. Julie was devastated and wept for days afterward.

Noelle didn't hear anything until her mother called her in Columbus on Tuesday morning.

Betty received word at 4:00 P.M. on Sunday. "They should've killed me," she said through her tears, "not my Jackie."

When cornered by the media back in Brooklyn, Louis could only say, "To me it was a shock. I was so shocked that I couldn't talk. I have no idea why this happened to Jackie. "

But there was no shortage of theories. Elliot Ableson believed that Bernie Gussoff's family had contracted the killing.

Mickey Zaffarano told the press, "This wasn't the work of the Mafia because no self-respecting mobster would ever shoot a man in the presence of his woman, and also because there's no such thing as the Mafia."

Years later, Julie felt that the slaying had been done by a young mobster out to make a reputation.

Sergeant Knuckles had his own version: "This guy Ullo was a half-assed bookmaker who'd handled some of Jack's action. Jack owed Ullo ten grand and naturally wouldn't pay him. The mob had nothing to do with it."

For Ellen Sohn, the murder was connected to the Mays case. "All the people that Jack fingered went to jail," she said. "But they nursed a grudge and had him killed when they got out."

An open-coffin service was held at a synagogue in Los Angeles. Among the mourners paying their last respects was Tony LaRosa: "I went to see Jack's body in the coffin and the thing that struck me was how angry he looked. When he got it, Jack must have said, 'I've got a whole life to live and enjoy. How could they do this to me?' Poor Jack. Whatever else he was, he was certainly an unforgettable character."

Betty flew back to New York with the body and was met at LaGuardia Airport by Louis, Julie, and Jennie. According to Jewish law, burial must be within twenty-four hours of the death, but because the body had to be sent to the East Coast this was impossible. The funeral wasn't until Wednesday, August 7, at the Beth-El Cemetery in Paramus, New Jersey.

On the morning of the funeral, Julie looked carefully at his wardrobe. He knew that whatever he chose to wear would never be worn again. That evening after the funeral, when he returned to his apartment in Queens, Julie would shred the dark blue suit he'd worn, the shirt, the necktie, the socks, even the underwear, and along with the shoes throw everything down the incinerator.

As the coffin was being lowered into the yawning grave, Julie was possessed by what he knew to be an illogical question: "If I had been born first, would I now be lying there instead of him?"

According to the probate report, Molinas's assets amounted to $479,000, which included the value of a 160-acre fruit ranch in San Jacinto, an uncollected $104,000 loan to Martinet, and an uncollected $15,000 loan to another business partner. His debts included outstanding bank loans and a payment due for damage done to cars he'd leased. They totaled $210,318. The probate report, of course, didn't tally the $650,000 Molinas owed to mob-sponsored sources.

There were rumors, however, that Molinas had millions secreted away in Swiss banks, in the Bahamas, and in numerous dummy bank accounts all over the United States. Despite a long-term and concerted effort by Paul Brandt and Julie, none of this money was ever recovered. The mob, too, tried to find Molinas's "lost" money, going so far as to threaten Chuck Bernstein again, but their search also came up empty.

"When Jack died," said Elliot Ableson, "he was also due at least a million dollars in loans out on the street. This was from his loan-sharking deals. When he was rubbed out, there were a lot of smiles everywhere."

Barely three weeks after Molinas's death, on August 26, two men approached Junior Torchio in a threatening manner on a Las Vegas street. When Torchio saw them, he bolted into passing traffic, where a car driven by a sixty-seven-year-old resident of Las Vegas knocked him down and killed him.

Shirley Marcus never recovered from the shock of the murder. After spending several months in a mental institution, she died in 1978 of a drug overdose.

Molinas's killers were apprehended three years after the deed. "This is the way it went down," said Sergeant Knuckles. "Eugene Connor had a married brother and when Connor started screwing his brother's wife, the brother turned him in." Just prior to his arrest, Connor tried to commit suicide by inhaling the exhaust fumes from a running car. He wound up with significant brain damage and testified at the trial that he had only fired one shot at Molinas, a shot that missed its mark. The real killer jumped up from behind a different section of the patio wall and fired his gun at the same moment Connor fired his. Connor received a life sentence.

The same jury acquitted Joe Ullo, on a paucity of evidence.

Craig Petzold and Robert Zander both admitted they were accessories to the murder, but turned state's evidence and were given one-year suspended sentences.

Louis Molinas died in 1978, heartbroken to the end. After her husband's death, Betty enrolled in Touro College and received a BA degree in 1984. She passed away in 1993, still mourning her "favorite son." Julie retired from teaching in 1994, and he lives in Queens with his wife, Jennie.

Noelle changed her name, moved back to San Francisco, and is currently enrolled in a nursing school.

Little is known of the whereabouts of the survivors of Fixers Incorporated. Joe Green vanished. Aaron Wagman is said to be somewhere in Europe. And Joe Hacken was rumored to be dying of diabetes in a Los Angeles old-age home.

Ellen Sohn currently lives in Los Angeles with her mother. And Ellen vividly remembered the ceremony at the Beth-El Cemetery when the tombstone marking Molinas's grave was unveiled: "I didn't go to the funeral because nobody told me about it. I've never told this to anybody, but I was actually happy at the unveiling. Why? Because I no longer had to wake up in the middle of the night and worry about where he was and what kind of trouble he was getting himself into. I was happy because it was all over, at last. But then Jack's mother got hysterical when she saw me and she started screaming, 'You're the only one my Jackie ever loved! You're the only one who stuck by him!' When she did that, my sense of well-being vanished and I wanted to die. I still wasn't free of him and I never would be."

Overtime

Perhaps Molinas did indeed cause Bernie Gussoff to be murdered. Perhaps not. But the enduring question for those who knew Molinas, or knew of him, is, How could someone who was so smart, so able, and with such a bright future, lead himself down the self-destructive path that he did?

Some may blame his growing up in the West Bronx and in Coney Island, where (and when) betting on the game at hand was thought to be proof of enlightenment and sophistication.

Some may rationalize that Molinas happened to be one of the finest basketball players in the country at a time when the game was rife with players doing business.

And still others may cite Jack's father's Old World consciousness with having thrust Molinas into the crooked arms of Joe Jalop.

In the final analysis, however, it appears that Jack's misdeeds were fueled by that most ancient and universal of sins, hubris. He was too smart. Too smart to think that the rules applied to him. Too smart to even imagine that he could ever get caught.

The truth is that like Dillinger, Jack Molinas was a villain who had a heroic quality.

Most of us succeed by trudging off to work so that we can pay the rent that's due on our lives. We are heroes because we strive to help our children achieve better lives than our own; because we love as best we can, and can also be loved.

Jack Molinas simply measured success on a different scale. He wanted to control the course of human events—and for a while, he could. Call him ambitious. Call him amoral. But perhaps Jack Molinas's wildly adventurous life continues to haunt so many people because when we take our faces off at midnight, Jack Molinas is, in some ways, who we really want to be, who we are afraid to be. And maybe, in our worst nightmares, Jack Molinas is who we fear we really are.

Bibliography

Berger, Phil, and Stu Black. "Who Killed Jack Molinas?" *New York Post*, 1–8 August 1977.

Breslin, Jimmy. "The Untold Facts Behind the Basketball Scandals." *Sport*, November 1962.

Bridgwater, William, and Seymour Kurtz, eds. *The Columbia Encyclopedia: Third Edition.* New York & London: Columbia University Press, 1967.

Brown, Lou, as told to Dick Herbert. "I Worked With Basketball's No. I Briber." *Look*, 27 February 1962.

Cohane, Tim. "Behind the Basketball Scandal." *Look*, 13 February 1962.

Hoffman, Paul. *What the Hell is Justice?* Chicago: Playboy Press, 1974.

Hollander, Zander, ed. *The Modern Encyclopedia of Basketball.* New York: Four Winds Press, 1973.

Isaacs, Neil D. *The Great Molinas.* Bethesda, Md.: WID Publishing Group, 1992.

_______. *Vintage NBA: The Pioneer Years.* Indianapolis: Masters Press, 1996.

Koppett, Leonard. *24 Seconds to Shoot.* New York: Macmillan, 1968.

Menville, Chuck. *The Harlem Globetrotters.* New York: David McKay, 1978.

Nelson, Rodger. *The Zollner Piston Story.* Fort Wayne: Allen County Public Library Foundation, 1995.

Peterson, Robert W. *Cages to Jumpshots.* New York: Oxford University Press, 1990.

Rosen, Charley. *Scandals of '51.* New York: Seven Stories Press, 1999.

Tax, Jeremiah. "The Facts About the Fix." *Sports Illustrated*, 27 March 1961.

Wolf, David. "The Exile of Connie Hawkins." *Life*, 16 May 1969.

Index

Also by Charley Rosen

FICTION

Have Jump Shot Will Travel (1975)
A Mile Above the Rim (1977)
The Cockroach Basketball League (1992)
The House of Moses All-Stars (1997)
Barney Polan's Game: A Novel of the 1951 Basketball Scandals (1998)

NON-FICTION

Maverick with Phil Jackson (1976)
Scandals of '51: How the Gamblers Almost Killed College Basketball (1978)
God, Man and Basketball Jones (1979)
Players and Pretenders (1981)
More Than a Game with Phil Jackson (2001)

About the Author

Dr. Shandler is president of Shandler Associates, a consulting firm that focuses on managing and motivating Millennials and assisting technical experts in transitioning into management and leadership roles. He has extensive experience working with multigenerational learners and knowledge workers in corporate, government, university, and association settings.

Holding a Ph.D. from Ohio State University, Shandler serves on the Board of Directors for the Northern Virginia Workforce Investment Board, the Greater Reston Chamber of Commerce, and the University of Maryland, Baltimore County, Instructional Systems Design Graduate Program. He is an alumnus of Leadership Fairfax and a recipient of the 2009 Outstanding Committee Chairperson Award from the Greater Reston Chamber of Commerce.

Previous books include *From Technical Specialist to Supervisor, Reengineering the Training Function: How to Align Training with the New Corporate Agenda,* and *Competency and the Learning Organization.* Further, he has presented seminars and speeches on these and other relevant topics nationwide.

Dr. Shandler encourages readers to share their organizations' challenges and solutions in motivating Millennials through his blog posted on www.motivatingmillennials.com. He is available for keynote speeches, executive briefings, and workshop presentations. He can be reached by e-mail at don@shandlerassociates.com or donaldshandler@comcast.net or by phone at 703.674.6800.

Acknowledgements

Special appreciation is extended to the Contributing Experts and their respective organizations for their efforts in helping me identify the key Millennial motivational factors that drove the contents of this book. Their willingness to share relevant practices and strategies enriched each chapter. In addition, I would like to thank Hector Velez for introducing me to many of the Contributing Experts, Shira Harrington for reviewing and commenting on each chapter, and finally, Monica Montoya for creating the Motivational Factors Survey Analysis, which harnessed data that influenced the structure of the book.

Further, I must acknowledge the outstanding research and publication efforts of the authors quoted in this book and whose names appear in the bibliography. They have created a significant and growing body of generational literature.

Last, I extend my sincerest appreciation to Axzo Press. Their editors and team of marketing and production professionals have helped bring this project from concept to print.

Contributing Experts

Lesley N. Channell
Assistant Vice President, Human Resources
HCA Northern Virginia Market
Dominion Hospital & Center

Lesley Channell is the assistant vice president of Human Resources at Reston Hospital Center and provides support for HCA's Northern Virginia market. Lesley has worked in healthcare for the last 16 years, with 13 years' experience in human resources. Lesley received her bachelor's degree from Ithaca College in Ithaca, New York, and earned her master's degree in business administration/human resources management from Iona College in New Rochelle, New York. She has been certified as a professional in human resources by the Society for Human Resource Management.

Jennell Evans
President and CEO
Strategic Interactions, Inc.

Jennell Evans is co-founder, President, and CEO of Strategic Interactions, Inc., an award-winning performance improvement firm in Vienna, Virginia. Jennell specializes in innovative corporate initiatives involving change communications, leadership development, and creative strategic planning.

She holds a BFA from Virginia Commonwealth University, a Certificate of Instructional Design, and a Masters of Organizational Development from Marymount University. Jennell is also certified to administer the Emotional Competency Inventory (ECI) and the Myers-Briggs Type Inventory (MBTI).

In addition to her work with clients, Jennell is actively engaged in community leadership programs and is Vice Chair of Leadership Fairfax, Inc.

Erin Nicole Gordon
Systems Integration
Accenture

Erin Nicole Gordon is a business analyst with the Reston, VA, office of Accenture. Involved in systems and integration technology consulting, Erin focuses on program management, proposal development, and SAP application solutions. She has muralled professionally and leads nonprofit efforts for numerous organizations, leading a missions teams internationally in 2009.

Her educational accomplishments include earning a B.S. in Commerce (International Business and Marketing concentrations) from the University of Virginia McIntire School of Commerce, and degrees in Spanish and Studio Art from the University of Virginia. Erin is a member of the National Scholars Honor Society.

Nicole Hardin
Managing Director
HireStrategy

Nicole Hardin is currently the Managing Director for HireStrategy. HireStrategy provides human capital solutions. HireStrategy, an *Inc.* 500 company, is ranked by *The Washington Business Journal* as the #1 regional staffing firm in the Greater Washington area.

Nicole has nine years' experience in assisting emerging-growth, mid-market, and *Fortune* 500 organizations build their human capital infrastructure and in managing the technology practice. For the past six years, she has assisted leading technology organizations in the D.C. community and been ranked in the top two technology recruiters from 2003 through 2005. Before working for HireStrategy, Nicole was the leading recruiter for NRI Staffing and Glotel, an international staffing firm.

Shira Harrington
Director, Professional Search
Positions Inc.

Shira Harrington, Director, Professional Search, at Positions Inc., is a frequent keynote speaker on managing the multigenerational workforce. As an outgrowth of her successful recruiting career, she brings her real-world perspective to help executives maximize the competencies of all four generations in order to create harmonious and robust workplaces. Shira's work has been published in monthly association magazines, and she has been profiled in the *Washington Business Journal*. An avid volunteer in the local HR community, she has served as VP of Programs for DC SHRM, is Programs Chair for the HR Leadership Forum, facilitates a monthly brown-bag meeting for Washington, D.C.–area HR professionals, and leads an executive peer roundtable for small-staff association executives. She earned her Masters in Public Relations from the University of Maryland at College Park.

Deborah K. Hoover
Director, Human Resources
The Urban Institute

Deborah K. Hoover, SPHR, is currently the Director of Human Resources for The Urban Institute, a Washington D.C. policy research institution. Ms. Hoover has worked within the nonprofit, academic, and research sectors for many years and is an active member of the HR professional community. She has served on the boards of the Human Resources Leadership Forum and the Washington Area Compensation and Benefits Association, and she participates in several HR-related work groups in the D.C. metro area.

Rick Humphress
Public Sector, Human Capital Management
Oracle Corporation

Rick Humphress has nearly 25 years' experience serving in a variety of individual contributor roles at such companies as Xerox, Motorola, INTERSOLV, and Oracle. He currently serves as an Oracle Human Capital Management specialist, advising international, federal, state, and local public-sector organizations on talent management issues. Rick has published articles on human performance improvement and competency modeling. He received a BA from Stanford and an MBA from Portland State, and he is working on a PhD from Walden University in Public Policy and Administration.

Kris T. Jensen
Vice President, Corporate Services
Wisdom Worker Solutions

Kris Jensen is the Vice President of Corporate Services for Wisdom Worker Solutions. She joined this startup in 2007 after eight years as the Senior Vice President of Human Resources for The Weitz Company, a $1.5 billion national commercial contractor. Before that, Kris spent 18 years with The Principal Financial Group, an international $45 billion financial services firm. She began her career there as a Life and Health Underwriter, but honed her craft as a human resources professional by assuming the leadership of Principal's employment, administrative, succession planning, training and development, Affirmative Action, and diversity functions.

Kris holds a Bachelors degree in Industrial Administration, Behavioral Management, from Iowa State University.

Peter W. Kennedy
Principal
The PRM Consulting Group

Peter Kennedy has had over 25 years of experience in conducting and managing compensation consulting projects for a variety of employers in the private, nonprofit, and public sectors. Peter has been a frequent speaker and panelist and has published numerous articles on the subject of compensation. He is the outgoing President of the Capital Area Chapter of the National Association of Corporate Directors.

Peter is a graduate of Oberlin College (BA in Government, 1975, with Honors) and the Sloan School of Management, M.I.T. (M.S.M. degree in economics and industrial relations, 1980).

Stacey Kessel
Senior Career Planning Manager
Booz Allen Hamilton

As the Senior Career Planning Manager at Booz Allen Hamilton, Stacey Kessel is responsible for delivering career planning resources and tools to employees and managers. Before joining Booz Allen, Stacey was the Associate Director of Career Services at Harvard Business School, where she counseled MBA students on their career searches. Stacey graduated from Colby College and has an MBA from the Kellogg Graduate School of Management at Northwestern University. Stacey has been interviewed by CNN, *Forbes*, and National Public Radio regarding the job search process.

Robert McGovern
CEO and Founder
Jobfox

Rob McGovern is a 20-year technology and media-industry veteran with a passion for helping people find careers they love. Before founding Jobfox, McGovern was the founder and former CEO of CareerBuilder. He grew CareerBuilder into a profitable $150 million company with more than 400 employees. His new venture, Jobfox, is already the fastest growing career site on the Web with precision matching and new Jobfox Intros™ services—the first online networking tools that make personal introductions between top-rated candidates and corporate recruiters.

McGovern is the author of a best-selling career advice book: *Bring Your "A" Game: The 10 Career Secrets of the High Achiever*. His expert career advice has been featured on numerous television and radio programs and in print and online publications throughout the world.

Before founding CareerBuilder, McGovern was vice president and general manager at Legent Corporation, the world's seventh-largest software company. He began his professional career at Hewlett Packard, where he rose through the sales and marketing ranks in both the United States and Europe.

Sue McLeod
Senior Consultant
Hay Group, Inc.

Sue McLeod started with a math degree and a job programming computers. In 22 years of working in technology consulting, she held various positions ranging from individual contributor to senior leader. Along the way, her interest in technology was eclipsed by a passion for helping people be more effective in organizations. Her second career in leadership development, assessment, and coaching allows her to fulfill those passions.

Sue works for Hay Group, Inc., in Arlington, Virginia. She lives with her partner, Ed, and her two Millennial-generation daughters. She knits compulsively in her spare time and dreams of ocean kayaking.

Kitty Nix
Director, Strategic Development
Helios HR

Kitty Nix's consulting and human resources experience spans 13 years, including leadership and management positions in two consulting firms. She is responsible for human resources and strategic development and was actively involved in business development, marketing, and daily operations for the consulting business. Kitty's technical HR expertise includes strategic planning for HR and organizational development. She holds an M.S. in Organizational Development from George Mason University and a B.S. in Computer Information Systems from James Madison University. She is certified as a Senior Professional of Human Resources (SPHR), received her Executive Leadership Coaching certificate from Georgetown, and was awarded one of the six 2007 HR Leadership Awards of Greater Washington.

Marcia Riley
Vice President, Talent Management and Human Resources
ESI International

In January 2008, Marcia B. Riley accepted the position of Vice President, Talent Management and Human Resources, at ESI International in Arlington, Virginia. Before joining ESI International, Marcia served as Assistant Vice President, Talent Management, and Chief Learning Officer for Inova Health System in Northern Virginia. Before that, she served as Senior Training and Development Executive for Sallie Mae.

Marcia's more than two decades of talent management experience also include leading her own consulting practice, which served a range of industries and organizations, including the U.S. Senate Office of Education and Training, The Nature Conservancy, Noblis, the Society of periOperative Registered Nurses, VeriSign, The American Press Institute, and The American Society of Training and Development. Marcia lives in Silver Spring, Maryland.

Shaara Roman
Director, Human Resources
CGI Federal

Shaara Roman is the Director of Human Resources for CGI Federal, a leading IT systems-integration and managed-services provider to the federal government and a wholly owned U.S. operating subsidiary of CGI Group, Inc. Ms. Roman is responsible for providing strategic HR direction and ownership of all HR functions for the 1700-member organization.

Ms. Roman honed her HR expertise over the past 15 years in varied corporate leadership roles in public and private organizations within the financial services and IT industries. Ms. Roman received her MBA in International Business from Georgetown University in Washington, D.C.

Christopher R. Ryan
Deputy General Counsel
K12 Inc.

Christopher R. Ryan currently serves as Vice President and Deputy General Counsel of K12 Inc., a leading provider of virtual education products and services. Prior to K12, Mr. Ryan served as General Counsel and Vice President of Human Resources at Everest Software, as Deputy General Counsel at CareerBuilder, and as Branch Chief at the SEC. Mr. Ryan earned a JD from American University, an MBA from the Smith School of Business at the University of Maryland, College Park, and a BA from Wake Forest University. Mr. Ryan is also a contributor to the book *The Worst-Case Scenario Survival Handbook: Work* by Joshua Piven.

Neil Sawyer
Senior Director of Human Resources
The Campagna Center

Neil Sawyer serves as Senior Director of Human Resources for The Campagna Center, a nonprofit organization serving the families and community of Alexandria, Virginia. He received his Masters in Human Resources Management from Marymount University. Neil has over 16 years of HR expertise in a wide variety of industries, including technology, construction, manufacturing, nonprofits and associations, and publishing. He is former President of the Washington, D.C., chapter of SHRM, and he remains active in HR lobbying and in mentoring new arrivals to the profession of human resources.

Kurt Schlimme
Project Management Office Director
The College Board

Kurt Schlimme is a business and technology executive with 15 years of managerial experience. Currently, Kurt is the Project Management Office Director at The College Board, overseeing the development of processes, practices, standards, and tools related to the execution of project-based work in IT. Before coming to The College Board, Kurt held the position of Vice President of Professional Services for iBasis Speech Solutions. Kurt was also a co-founder and Vice President of Strategic Solutions for the NDC Group, a management consulting firm that was purchased by PSInet in 2000, after growing from 10 to 350 employees.

Mark Steffanina
Director, Organizational Effectiveness
Holy Cross Hospital

Working with people in organizations large and small, ranging from the arts and human services to manufacturing, has fueled Mark's fascination with human behavior in the workplace. His diverse experiences share a common pursuit—improving work-life and organizational performance by leveraging human talent, perspective, and motivation. Mark's approach, a unique blending of continuous improvement and organizational development methodologies, has been recognized in forums sponsored by the Manufacturers Alliance for Productivity Improvement, Michigan State University, and others.

Mark holds a masters degree in business administration and is currently pursuing a doctoral degree in organizational psychology.

Hector Velez
Executive Vice President
HireStrategy

Hector Velez, a recognized thought leader in the human capital field, is Executive Vice President of HireStrategy, an *Inc*. 500 firm that provides integrated staffing solutions to organizations in the technology, media, financial services, public, and nonprofit sectors. His role is to design and execute winning strategies in business development, sales, branding, technology, and customer delight. Hector is President of the HR Leadership Forum. He also serves on the board of directors of The SkillSource Group and The Northern Virginia Workforce Investment Board.

Stuart H. Weinstein
Senior Managing Consultant
IBM Global Business Services

Dr. Weinstein has 37 years of professional experience in designing, developing, and delivering instructional products for dissemination via the Internet, computer, satellite, videotape, videodisc, radio, broadcast television, CD-ROM, and classroom for military, civilian government, and commercial clients. He specializes in business process reengineering, strategic and tactical communications planning, management and leadership curricula, and change management. Additionally, he serves as a subject matter expert in attracting graduate students to IBM Learning Solutions careers. Dr. Weinstein earned a BA in Mass Communications and a M.Ed. in Education in Instructional Media from the University of Miami. He holds a Ph.D. in Instructional Systems from Florida State University.

Learning Objectives

Complete this book, and you'll know how to:

1) Implement proactive strategies that address the Millennials' need for increased flexibility and work/life balance.
2) Provide Millennials with multidimensional growth opportunities that meet both their and their organizations' intellectual capital needs.
3) Expand workplace fun and social interaction opportunities that motivate Millennials.
4) Address the Millennials' need to make and be recognized for their contributions to their workplaces and society.
5) Establish and sustain effective communication as a shared responsibility of Millennial and manager.
6) Identify those unique generational factors that influence the importance of recognition, reward, and respect as Millennial motivators.
7) Make the most of Millennials' unique learning preferences with technology-mediated learning methods.
8) Employ strategies that provide financial rewards for knowledge and move beyond the traditional concept of the performance appraisal.

Workplace and Management Competencies mapping

For over 30 years, business and industry has utilized competency models to select employees. The trend to use competency-based approaches in education and training, assessment, and development of workers has experienced a more recent emergence within the Employment and Training Administration (ETA), a division of the United States Department of Labor.

The ETA's General Competency Model Framework spans a wide array of competencies from the more basic competencies, such as reading and writing, to more advanced occupation-specific competencies. The Crisp Series finds its home in what the ETA refers to as the Workplace Competencies and the Management Competencies.

Motivating the Millennial Knowledge Worker covers information vital to mastering the following **Management** competencies:

- Supporting Others
- Motivating & Inspiring

For a comprehensive mapping of Crisp Series titles to the Workplace and Management competencies, visit www.CrispSeries.com.

A Note to Instructors

We've tried to make the Crisp books as useful as possible as classroom training manuals. Here are some of the features we provide for instructors:

- PowerPoint presentations
- Answer keys
- Assessments
- Customization

PowerPoint Presentations

You can download a PowerPoint presentation for this book from our Web site at www.CrispSeries.com.

Answer keys

If an exercise has specific answers, an answer key will be provided in the appendix. (Some exercises ask you to think about your own opinions or situation; these types of exercises will not have answer keys.)

Assessments

For each 50-Minute Series book, we have developed a 35- to 50-item assessment. The assessment for this book is available at www.CrispSeries.com. *Assessments should not be used in any employee-selection process.*

Customization

Crisp books can be quickly and easily customized to meet your needs—from adding your logo to developing proprietary content. Crisp books are available in print and electronic form. For more information on customization, see www.CrispSeries.com.

Understanding the Millennial Knowledge Worker

The intended audience of this book is the line manager and human resources professional faced with the responsibility of understanding and motivating the Millennial worker in the "New Economy." This is an economy, described by Anthony Patrick Carnevale in his book *America and the New Economy*, that has central flexible and information-based technologies. This technology raises the potential for higher quality, productivity, customization, convenience, variety, and timeliness. And the Millennial knowledge worker is quickly emerging as a key driver of this New Economy and our national competitiveness.

Recommendations for Using this Book

This book is the result of a collaborative effort between the author, the publisher, and twenty-one contributing experts. Your understanding of the following five building blocks that serve as the framework of this book will enable you to apply motivational strategies for Millennial knowledge workers. The building blocks are as follows:

- **Understand that motivating Millennials is challenging.**

  This book addresses the specific challenge of motivating the fastest growing segment of the workforce—the Millennial knowledge worker. According to the broadest definition of this term, as presented by Cara Spiro in the article "Generation Y in the Workplace" (*Defense AT&L*, Nov-Dec, 2006), this group numbers almost 80 million Americans born between 1977 and 2000, and accounts for approximately 21 percent of the overall workforce. Other researchers narrow the "anchor years" (explained later in this Introduction) to 1981–1999 (Lancaster and Stillman), while other writers reduce the size of the population (Howe and Straus). This book narrows its focus to college-educated Millennial knowledge workers. Understanding and motivating this newest segment of the workforce is now challenging most human resources professionals.

- **A need exists for an immediately usable tool for motivating Millenials.**

  As both an educator and a consultant, I would be the first person to encourage individuals to address the challenge of motivating Millennial knowledge workers by using resources other than this book. Opportunities may exist to hire a generational consultant, reexamine or restructure the human resources management systems (still in some cases a remnant of a post-industrial era), or at the very least, read a more thorough resource on the subject. However, as a realist and practitioner, I often meet individuals just like you who need an immediate and effective strategy to address the challenge of motivating the Millennial knowledge worker. That need has influenced the content and format of this book.

- **A broad continuum of strategic Millennial motivators is desirable.**

  The parts that follow present discussions of several research-based motivational factors, and strategic examples provided by many Contributing Experts. As you probably know, when it comes to motivation, one size does not fit all. Both the line manager and the human resources professional must develop a broad range of Millennial motivators.

- **The organizational experiences of a variety of contributing experts are invaluable.**

  This book is the result of moving the responsibility for generating the contents of the book from a single author to a team of subject matter experts. This methodology benefits the reader/practitioner in several ways. First, the group of carefully assembled Contributing Experts helped shape the contents of the book by their participation in creating, distributing, and collecting information, using a research-based Millennial Motivational Factors Survey. Second, a synthesis of this survey, discussed in the next chapter, with the experts' experiences results in presenting best-of-class Millennial motivators. These examples drive each chapter, with usable resources in the form of checklists, models, surveys, and tested motivational strategies.

- **There is value in surveying the rapidly growing body of Millennial literature.**

  Each part of this book acknowledges the rich body of literature that currently exists. The research efforts of other authors and consultants are employed to support the strategies and tactics presented throughout this book. This approach has enabled the author and Contributing Experts to narrow the focus of this book to application-oriented strategies that specifically address the motivational needs of the Millennial knowledge worker.

Millennials Defined

"Millennial," as most readers are already aware, is the most commonly used term to describe the subjects of this book. As Neil Howe and William Strauss write in their book *Millennials Rising: The Next Generation,* "For decades Americans have been wishing for a youth generation that would quit talking and start doing… The rising generation will introduce itself to the nation and push the nation into a new era." The authors go on to write that "Once this new youth personnel begins to focus on convention, community and civic renewal, America will be on the brink of becoming someplace very new, very 'Millennial' in the fullest sense of the word."

This book will quote authors of other books that describe our Millennials as "Generation Y," "Gen-Y," "Generation Why," "Echo Boomers," "Generation Next," and other labels. However, "Millennials" has clearly emerged as the preferred name.

It may be worthwhile to take a moment to position the Millennials in a multigenerational perspective. As Carolyn A. Martin and Bruce Tulgan write in *Managing Generation Y: Global Citizens Born in the Late Seventies and Early Eighties*, "Demographers have been unable to agree on the new generation's parameters." There are slight differences in the labels used by different researchers and authors to describe generations. But they all agree on one critical fact. There are currently four generations in the workforce, and there are more similarities in classification than differences. The following table shows three relevant examples.

Model One	Model Two	Model Three
Veterans (b. 1922–1943), Silent	Silent, 62+	Traditionalists (1900–1945)
Baby Boomers (b.1943–1960)	Young/Older Boomers, 45–61	Baby Boomers (1946–1964)
Generation X (b. 1960–1980)	Gen-X , 27–44	Generation Xers (1965–1980)
Nexters (Millennials) (b. 1980–)	Millennials under 26	Millennials (1981–1999)

Again, the focus of this book is on college-educated Millennials who are also knowledge workers. As Ron Alsop writes in *The Trophy Kids Grow Up*, "In addition to more frequent and detailed performance assessments, Millennials want companies to nurture their career development. They are clamoring for more coaching, training, and mentoring programs."

Knowledge Workers

Line managers and human resources professionals—many still using antiquated, post-industrial human resource management systems—not only have to learn how to more effectively identify, understand, and motivate the Millennial, but also must recognize and address the comparable challenge of identifying, understanding, and motivating knowledge workers. When you recognize that Millennial knowledge workers constitute an increasingly larger segment of the workforce, you can see why both managers and human resources professionals face an extraordinary management and development challenge.

Knowledge Worker: Definition and Key Characteristics

In *Managing Knowledge Workers*, Frances Horibe defines "knowledge workers" and summarizes the challenge of managing and motivating knowledge workers.

> ***"[A]t its simplest, knowledge workers are people who use their heads more than their hands to produce value. They add value through their ideas, their analyses, their judgment, their syntheses, and their designs. They still use their hands, of course, but it's more likely to be [for] inputting [information] into a computer than lifting a 50-pound sack."***
>
> **–Frances Horibe**

Horibe talks about the knowledge worker as being the driver of the previously described New Economy, "where a flood of information is coming at lightning speed, changing almost everything." The author further states that in this new economy we find ourselves questioning "how we buy, how we sell, what we make, when we make it, what we value, and where we live. Information is the new driver of wealth creation and those who have it (knowledge workers) are the keys to this new way."

Not only will managers and human resources professionals have to learn how to motivate the Millennials (address their internally driven needs, wants, and desires), but they will also have to learn how to address the human resource development and management challenge of a new economy that is increasingly more characterized by a Millennial knowledge workforce.

To help encapsulate the many challenges of managing and motivating knowledge workers, complete the following inventory, which is based on material appearing in Frances Horibe's book, *Managing Knowledge Workers*.

HR Challenges: An Inventory

Review each of the following challenges and indicate if you agree or disagree with the statement. Also, at the end of the inventory, indicate how you address and support these challenges.

Challenge	Agree	Disagree
1. The driver of success in the New Economy is knowledge.	❑	❑
2. Demand for knowledge workers is great and growing.	❑	❑
3. A knowledge worker is one who uses his/her head more than his/her hands to produce value.	❑	❑
4. About 60 percent of jobs are knowledge based. Managing the human dimension of knowledge workers is the most important job a manager has.	❑	❑

As a manager or human resources professional, I address and support these challenges by:

____

____

____

Motivating people, especially the Millennial knowledge worker, requires identifying strategies that address the needs of a particular segment of the workforce. Managers and human resources professionals cannot overlook the distinct motivational needs of each individual. But for the moment, we will look at motivation from the broader perspective of generational personalities.

> ***"[P]rofessionals... [especially knowledge workers] are best motivated by intangible rewards, such as peer recognition, learning opportunities, opportunities for more independence, and so on."***
>
> **– Karl Erik Sveiby, *The New Organizational Wealth***

Emergence of Generational Personalities

The importance of the notion of generational personalities was first introduced in 1991 when William Strauss and Neil Howe published the now classic book *Generations*, which was later followed by *13 Generations*. Since that time, a number of human resources practitioners have applied this concept to the world of work. In its simplest form, for those readers not familiar with the generation concept, the following three-step generational pattern is generally recognized and accepted.

1. Generations are defined as those Americans born in a twenty-year range between two specific "anchor years." For example, the Baby Boomer generation is widely considered to consist of those people born between 1946 and 1964. These are the anchor years. Other researchers suggest 1943 and 1960 as the generational frame of reference for the same group. The concept remains the same—anchor years within a twenty-year range define a generation.
2. Major events in society that occurred in the formative years of those generations contribute to shaping the personality of these age cohorts, which stays with them throughout life.
3. The differences between generations are claimed to be a major diversity factor affecting American business, human resources development, and management systems.

This concept of generational personalities will be shown to be a driver of motivating the Millennial knowledge worker. Employee productivity is the key to success in the New Economy, and the ability to motivate increasingly determines employee performance and retention.

In fact, understanding multigenerational differences in the workplace can mean the difference between economic success or failure. This is a well-documented return-on-investment case and not a mere human resources issue. It has emerged as a critically important business challenge that has resulted in an explosion of "generational" training programs, videos, articles, and books.

Behavioral Challenges of Millennials

The following quotes help demonstrate that motivating the Millennial knowledge worker is increasingly more challenging for the manager and human resources professional. Which of the following four quotes are most relevant to your challenges in motivating the Millennial knowledge worker?

> ***"The Millennials represent the largest, healthiest, and most cared for generation to ever enter the workforce. This also is a generation with very little real work experience."***
>
> **–Mary Crane, "Mentoring Millennials,"** ***Training Magazine***

> ***"They are independent, techno-savvy, entrepreneurial hard workers who thrive on flexibility. They take these qualities to new heights or transform them."***
>
> **–Carolyn A. Martin and Bruce Tulgan,** ***Managing Generation Y***

> ***"Millennial professionals are multi-taskers, have fast minds, are confident, [are] goal oriented, like balance, and have a strong individual spirit."***
>
> **–Lisa Orrell,** ***Millennials Incorporated***

> ***"They are questioning all the rules, all the time-honored institutions, and all the previously unanswered questions—and they are doing it loudly."***
>
> **–Eric Chester,** ***Employing Generation Why?***

If these behavioral challenges suggest that effective managers and human resources professionals must become more like social scientists, career researchers, or psychologists, you may be right. The new reality for those charged with recruiting and managing Millennials revolves around motivating and retaining the Millennial knowledge worker.

Millennials: A Research and Survey Perspective

Graduates of programs in applied behavior sciences understand that behavior is observable, measurable, predictable, and often, we hope, changeable. This Introduction provides a multidimensional perspective on understanding the behavioral challenge of motivating Millennials. This is accomplished by examining current research and demographical Millennial profiles, reviewing Millennial myths and realities, and sampling the research conclusions of an international human resources management consulting firm.

A Research and Demographical Perspective

In her article titled "Boomers, Xers, and Millennials: What They Really Want from Continuing Higher Education," Cathy Sandeen, Dean of Continuing Education and Extension at the University of California-Los Angeles, presents a demographical snapshot of Millennials. She states that "The Millennial generations (born between 1982 and 2003) experience a shift back to a child-centered social context. This time period represented the lowest child-to-parent ratio in American history." Some highlights of her discussion follow, in the format of a behavioral quiz.

Did You Know?
A Millennial Behavioral Quiz

Identify the five Millennial behavioral characteristics most relevant to your organization. Discuss these challenges with your colleagues, and generate strategies to address the behavioral legacies that Millennials bring to the workplace.

____ 1. Concern with quality of education emerged, and standardized test scores began to increase.

____ 2. Parents of Millennials seemed obsessed with preparing their children for the future.

____ 3. Millennial children began building their résumés in preschool, attending the best schools and participating in a plethora of extra-curricular activities.

____ 4. They are a pressured and achieving generation.

CONTINUED

CONTINUED

____ 5. Millennials are trusting of their parents and other authority figures.

____ 6. Millennials are team-oriented, confident, and optimistic.

____ 7. They grew up with computers; they experienced the rapid adoption of the Internet, cell phones, and other mobile devices.

____ 8. They are a highly networked, connected generation and tend to be completely immersed in technology.

____ 9. Millennials are graduating from college and entering graduate school.

____ 10. They tend to be very career oriented and expect rapid advancement and perks.

____ 11. Millennials appreciate feedback, having been graded, evaluated, and ranked throughout their lives.

____ 12. Because of their skill at multitasking, Millennials are likely to want to build parallel careers, not focusing on one job or profession at the exclusion of another.

____ 13. Multitasking may ultimately take the form of continuous job-changing for Millennials.

____ 14. Because of their community orientation, they tend to appreciate mission-driven organizations.

____ 15. They are motivated by helping others, improving the environment, and making the world a better place.

Millennial Myths and Realities

Robert Half International, one of the world's first and largest specialized staffing firms, and Yahoo! HotJobs present still another study of Millennials, entitled *What Millennial Workers Want: How to Attract and Retain Gen Y Employees*. The following information was based on a survey of 1,007 people between the ages of 21–28 who are employed full-time or part-time and have college degrees or are attending college. This survey revealed five Millennial myths and facts. The following quote from the study sets the stage for them.

> ***"In reality, our survey results point to an ambitious, highly motivated generation that shares many of the same concerns as their predecessors. In fact, the survey respondents appear more attuned to issues such as saving for retirement, having good health care benefits, and balancing work and personal obligations than might be expected of those who are relatively new to the workforce. Much of this may be due to the fact that they've witnessed significant uncertainty in their lifetimes, making security and stability increasingly attractive, both in their personal lives and on the job."***
>
> ***What Millennial Workers Want: How to Attract and Retain Gen Y Employees***

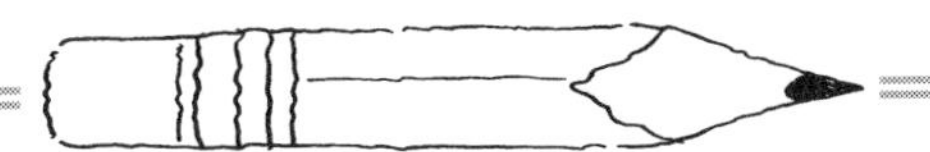

TEST YOUR ASSUMPTIONS

Read and discuss each of the following five Millennial myths with your fellow managers and human resources professionals before reviewing the corresponding facts.

Myth One: Generation Y (Millennials) lives in the moment and would rather play than work.

Myth Two: Generation Y expects instant gratification.

Myth Three: This generation slacks off at work to take care of personal matters.

Myth Four: Generation Y workers can't take direction.

Myth Five: Generation Y employees have a sense of entitlement.

After discussing each of the above myths with your colleagues, reconcile your answers with the facts.

Fact One: Millennials are most concerned about supporting themselves and their families, saving enough money, finding and keeping a job, and having career satisfaction.

Fact Two: They're focused on the future and worried about funding their retirement.

Fact Three: Seventy-three percent worry about balancing professional and personal obligations.

Fact Four: They want frequent communication with their bosses.

Fact Five: They expect to pay their dues in different ways.

At *www.rhi.com*, you can read the entire article that these five "Millennial Myths and Facts" were selected from; it might provide additional insights into motivating the Millennial knowledge worker.

Sharing Responsibility for Motivating the Millennial Knowledge Worker

Managers and human resources professionals face the challenge of reconciling the expectations of employee and employer. As one component of an employment contract, they must not overlook the importance of the physical, psychological, and social aspects of the environment.

The Three E's: Employee, Employer, and Environment

Jeffrey Zaslow's article "The Most Praised Generation Goes to Work," which appeared in *The Wall Street Journal* (April 20, 2007), discusses three specific challenges of dealing with "the Über-stroked kids reaching adulthood." He makes two important statements:

> **"*Childhood in recent decades has been defined by stroking—by parents who see their job as building self-esteem, by soccer coaches who give every player a trophy, by schools that used to name one student of the month and these days name 40.*"**

> **"*Now, as the greatest generation grows up, the culture of praise is reaching deeply into the adult world. Bosses, professors, and mates are feeling the need to lavish praise on young adults, particularly twenty-somethings, or see them wither under an unfamiliar compliment deficit.*"**

Zaslow outlines three employer/employee concerns relevant to motivating the Millennial knowledge worker:

1. Praise inflation
2. Modern pressures
3. No more red pens

The following Agree/Disagree inventory, based on his article, summarizes these concepts and provides a tool you can use with your colleagues to assess the impact of these behaviors on motivating and managing Millennials.

AN INVENTORY FOR MILLENNIAL MANAGERS

Indicate whether you agree (A) or disagree (D) with each of the following motivational factors, and discuss these items with your colleagues.

Praise Inflation	A	D
1. Employers say the praise culture can help them with job retention.	❑	❑
2. People's positive traits can be exaggerated until the words feel meaningless.	❑	❑
3. It's important to make at least five positive statements for each negative one.	❑	❑
4. Many managers are joining "America's excessive praise parade" to hold onto young workers.	❑	❑
5. Workers under 40 require more stroking and rewards and want more constant feedback.	❑	❑
Modern Pressures	**A**	**D**
1. Heightened pressure to perform in today's demanding firms has created a culture where you have to give instant feedback or you will fail.	❑	❑
2. Gen Y-ers don't just say they want feedback. They are also saying they require it.	❑	❑
3. One company encourages managers to start every meeting with informal recognition.	❑	❑
4. Managers need to get a sense of how Millennials like to be praised—in public or one-on-one in the office.	❑	❑
5. Organizations should be encouraged to develop formal mechanisms. One is called "S.A.Y. It" cards: "someone appreciates you."	❑	❑

CONTINUED

CONTINUED

No More Red Pens	A	D
1. Some young adults are consciously calibrating their dependence on praise—they are on the border of the Millennial generation that requires over-praise and a thirtysomething generation that is less addicted to praise.	❑	❑
2. University professors have attended seminars to learn techniques of supportive criticism. You need to throw away your red pens to avoid intimidating students.	❑	❑
3. When people are lousy, they need to be told that. Ego-stroking may feel good, but it doesn't lead to happiness.	❑	❑
4. We need to declare a moratorium on meaningless and baseless praise that often begins in nursery school. "I am special, look at me."	❑	❑
5. Organizations should follow the Scooter Stores model and hire "celebration assistants," charged with throwing confetti, filling balloons, and showing up at employees' desks to offer high-fives.	❑	❑

The Employer's Perspective: New Work Rules for Millennials

Rob McGovern, CEO of Jobfox, brings a unique employer perspective to the challenge of motivating Millennials. He has worked for several well-known companies, including Hewlett-Packard, Disney, and IBM. He also founded and later sold his company, CareerBuilder. At the age of 30, he wrote the book *Bring Your "A" Game: The 10 Career Secrets of High Achievers*, targeted at Gen X and Gen Y people. From this multidimensional perspective, he wrote what has come to be a Millennial mantra: "Companies must learn to hire, appreciate, and motivate younger workers, or they will perish."

An Employer's Portrait of Millennials

Rob McGovern writes that Generation Y is the most educated and most technologically savvy generation ever. Yet companies continue to have biases against younger workers. In a Jobfox poll of more than 200 recruiters, 63 percent rated Baby Boomers as "greater" performers in their organizations. This compares to 58 percent who rated Gen X as greater performers, 20 percent for Gen Y, and 25 percent for our older workers, the Traditionalists.

In short, Rob McGovern states that "companies don't think highly of Gen-Y (or older workers). I think it's because companies don't understand them. But those that do will gain a competitive advantage. Just as there were workplace changes made to accommodate Baby Boomers and Gen-Xers, I foresee changes ahead as Gen-Y grows in the workplace."

Having interviewed hundreds of younger workers for *Bring Your "A" Game*, Rob McGovern learned a few things about Generation Y:

1. **They crave stability.**

   The Gen Y world is full of instability. Ask them about the world and they might talk about hurricanes, tsunamis, 9/11, Code Orange alerts, three wars, and AIDS. They live in a world with a constant "News Alert" crawling at the bottom of their TV monitors. They watched their parents turn the word "downsized" into a verb. With this set of experiences as a frame of reference, Gen Y would like to think of a company as a refuge. If we can meet their other needs, which I will discuss next, I think we'll see tenure begin to rise again in the decades ahead.

2. **They want balance.**

   Younger workers play for different rewards. With Baby Boomers, all you had to do was wave $10,000 more and a promotion in front of them and they were on their way. Gen Y doesn't want this. Gen Y, instead, wants a little balance to go with the American dream. Give flexible hours. These workers just don't understand the rigidity of the world that the Baby Boomers have created. "Why can't I work 12 hours a day, three days a week? Why does it have to be your way?"

3. **They want to take charge.**

   Gen Y doesn't want to be a junior anything. This is the generation that looked out the car window past the "Baby on Board" sign. This is a generation with helicopter parents who told them every day that they are "special and entitled to speak up to make something of themselves." This is a generation that believes everyone deserves a trophy, win or lose. So, here comes a big corporation. What do we do? We put them in a sea of look-alike cubicles and tell them to learn the ropes if they want to make something of themselves.

   They want to make a contribution on the first day. As companies, we need to do a better job of addressing their sense of contribution. Gen Y will not be satisfied working inside the machine. We need to work with them to help them see how their actions are connected to organizational goals.

> ***"If we went into a time machine today and went forward in time, I would not be surprised to see companies with three-day work weeks, addressing new Gen-X/Gen-Y learning styles. It's going to happen. Especially as younger workers inherit leadership roles, giving them a place where they feel like they belong."***
>
> **–Rob McGovern, "Attracting and Retaining Young Professionals"**

The Millennial Workers' Environment

Neil Sawyer introduces the last of the "Three E's"—Environment. The company that he has had experience with earned a place on the "Best Places to Work for" list published by *Publishers Executive Magazine*. The organization, a leading publisher in Washington, D.C., is referred to as "Leading Publisher" in this Introduction. The company's Web site states that "The company hires professionals who are smart, competitive, and fast." Sawyer presents the following case for the appropriate Millennial environment. How does your organization meet these needs?

The Leading Publisher's employee population has a large portion of young employees (between 22 and 33 years old). These employees fill a wide range of job functions, including, but not limited to, graphic artists, print and online editors, Web designers, IT professionals, and administrative support personnel.

Three Unique Environmental Factors: The Leading Publisher prides itself on its unique corporate culture. While embodying many of the mainstream philosophies, it seeks to include younger employees and promote a workplace that is not stereotypical. Three aspects show this deviation from the "corporate American" feel.

1. **The architecture and workspaces of the Leading Publisher's offices:**

   All offices of the Leading Publisher are designed and decorated with respect given to "what would an energetic, style-conscious, young employee want to see in his/her workplace?" The CEO's personal art collection graces the hallways on three floors of the corporate headquarters, and the furniture is hand-picked for its trend-setting style.

2. **The relaxed dress code at the Leading Publisher:**

   Employees are told from their first day on the job that there is no dress code. The philosophy is that we are adults who can make our own choices regarding what is appropriate attire. While some employees prefer to wear shorts and flip-flops during the summer months, others opt for business casual, and to date, no employee has ever needed to be counseled on their attire choices.

3. **The open-door policy of the CEO:**

   Employees are told during the orientation luncheon with the CEO that if they ever have a question or concern about the company or its practices, they may come see him personally. Younger employees routinely take him up on his offer. The CEO doesn't just listen to the concerns of these employees; he acts on them. Human Resources has in the past been tasked to do research and suggest alternative ways of conducting aspects of the business, based on these informal conversations with staff.

There is no magic formula for creating an effective Millennial culture for each organization. The environment is influenced by the company's products and services. However, the three previously outlined environmental factors clearly enhanced the Millennial culture of the Leading Publisher in Washington, D.C.

Millennial Motivational Issues

The goal of the author and Contributing Experts has been to create an immediately usable resource that identifies those specific Millennial motivators, and provides strategies and tactics to address them.

A variety of checklists, inventories, and assessments are presented throughout the book. These are helpful resources for immediate application of strategies and are designed to achieve the following objectives:

- **Acknowledge broader issues related to motivating Millenials.** While the focus of this book is specifically on motivating Millennial knowledge workers, the reader/practitioner should also be aware of broader human resource management issues that also affect Millennials.
- **Present multiple perspectives on Millennials.** Effectively motivating Millennials requires an understanding of how different stakeholders view the Millennial. With this in mind, four Contributing Experts present their perspective on Millennials; the experts are a Millennial, a recruiter, a human resource manager, and a workforce consultant.
- **Explain the research-based methodology that generated sixteen Millennial motivators.** Through the use of research and survey methodologies, and the active involvement of the twenty-one Contributing Experts featured in this book, sixteen Millennial motivators were identified. These motivators drive the following eight parts of the book.

Motivating Millennials

As we seek to understand Millennial motivational issues, it's important that we examine several global workforce issues that have dramatically changed the way in which organizations manage their human capital.

The following list of four broad Millennial motivational issues will provide you with an opportunity to assess and rank the issues that affect your organization. The checklist may also serve as a discussion resource for various business units and workgroups.

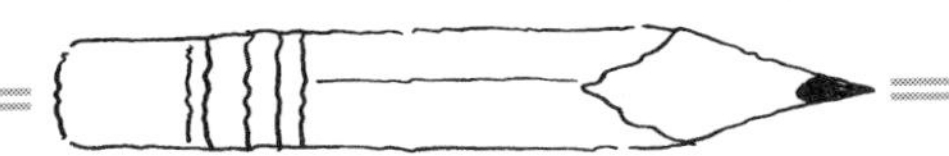

Four Millennial Motivational Issues

Review each of the following items and rank the importance of each one, using a scale of 1–5 (with 5 the highest). Discuss these items with your business unit and/or workgroup.

____ 1. **The emergence of a global economy has created a workforce crisis.** The current concern for recruiting, retaining, and motivating Millennials is rooted in a much broader issue—the emergence of a highly competitive global workforce.

Thomas Friedman reinforces this reality in *The World is Flat* by stating, "Cheap ubiquitous telecommunication has finally obliterated all impediments to international competition," and "American workers should be prepared to create value with leadership and sell personality."

The challenge is how to keep workers engaged and loyal to your firm.

____ 2. **Learning is not only a Millennial motivator, but also a link that is connected to business strategies.** Peter M. Senge's 1990 book, *The Fifth Discipline: The Art and Practice of the Learning Organization,* formalized the concept that "In the long run, the only sustainable source of competitive advantage is your organization's ability to learn faster than its competition."

An organization that promotes learning and then "stands ready to quickly capitalize on that information" will be the type of organization that will move forward successfully into the next decade (Michael J. Marquardt, *Building Learning Organizations*).

Providing Millennials with career development opportunities through continuous learning is not only a motivator for them, but also has a critical return-on-investment factor.

Given the increasing pressures of global demographic shifts, economic challenges, and the complexity of retaining talent, more companies are turning to learning and development as a way to improve performance, improve motivation, develop required skills, and sustain productivity.

CONTINUED

CONTINUED

____ 3. **Generational issues are business issues.** Today's employers are faced with managing a multigenerational workforce.

Carolyn A. Martin, Ph.D., and Bruce Tulgan address this issue at the beginning of their book *Managing the Generation Mix: From Collision to Collaboration,* stating:

- Generational problems are important reflections of critical business issues facing organizations that are transitioning from a workplace of the past to that of the future.
- Your challenge as a manager of a workplace mix of four generations (also called Gen Mix) is to steer your multi-generation team members off the rigid course of "business as usual" into an open field of innovation, productivity, and learning.
- Many organizations have finally figured out how to recruit young talent, only to watch them drive down a collision course with seasoned employees over issues of work ethics, respect for authority, dress code, and every work arrangement imaginable.

____ 4. **Technology and demographics are on a collision course.** Not only is there a challenge in managing a mix of four generations in the workforce, but now there is the additional challenge of managing across the technology gap.

In his book *Generation Blend: Managing Across the Technology Age Gap*, Rob Salkowitz presents the following points to reinforce the importance of this challenge:

- Generational attitudes toward technology affect issues as diverse as recruitment and retention, employee training, management decision making, collaboration, knowledge sharing, work/life balance, and ordinary work habits.
- Organizations are scrambling to unlock the talents of a multigenerational workforce in a connected world.
- The retirement of the Baby Boomers, the arrival of the Millennials, and the impact of Web 2.0 create unprecedented complexity for employers and workers in the 2010s and beyond.

The issues and challenges are to identify what initiatives can be launched to bridge the divide in work styles and technological skills that separates veterans from newcomers to the workforce.

Generational Strategies vs. Workforce Talent Management

There's no doubt that the concept of a generational approach to human resource management is an improvement over the more traditional one-size-fits all HRM system of recruiting, selecting, managing, motivating, developing, and retaining employees. However, a more sophisticated and effective strategy should also be considered. Rick Humphress, a Contributing Expert for this book, makes the case for moving beyond a simple generational strategy to employing a more comprehensive four-stage strategy for managing workforce talent.

The Four-stage Talent Management Strategy

Rick Humphress, Public Sector HCM Specialist
Oracle Corporation

Public- and private-sector organizations use talent management practices to increase the productivity and reduce the costs associated with the workforce. Typical talent management practices include succession and career planning, strategic staffing, pay for performance, training, and performance management. These talent management practices are evolving through four stages as they are applied to the workforce.

First, organizations apply talent management practices uniformly through the employee population without regard to any differences or distinctions. This one-size-fits-all approach is easy to implement, administer, and maintain. However, it is difficult to adapt to changing conditions and it generates high employee turnover.

Next, organizations apply talent management practices differently based on sociological differences between generations—Traditionalists, Baby Boomers, Generation X, or Gen Y (Millennials). Although it's an improvement over the homogeneous approach, the generational approach is still rather broad since it divides 150 million workers into just four categories. Talent management practices are still blunt instruments without any individual precision.

Next, organizations apply talent management practices differently based on specific worker temperaments or types (e.g., the Myers-Briggs Type Indicator, or MBTI). This approach divides the worker population into several categories (sixteen in the case of MBTI) to which talent management practices can be adapted.

Finally, at the finest level of granularity, talent management practices can be precisely tailored to meet the needs of each individual. A talent-management rules engine can interact with each individual employee profile to generate a deeply personalized and unique performance improvement plan for each person.

The driving force behind progressing through these four stages of talent management deployment is computer automation. Manual systems promote homogeneous practices because it is just too difficult to create multiple talent management approaches. Achieving deeply personalized talent management, however, takes more than software and hardware.

First, the talent management rules must be established. Second, the employee profiles must be in a centralized HR database. Third, the various talent management practices must be integrated applications and not isolated information silos. Finally, the organization must be willing to make a commitment to a holistic view of HR as a complex system that can be continuously improved.

Four Portraits of Millennials

Here, we introduce four perspectives on Millennials: those of a Millennial, a recruiter, a human resources manager, and a workforce consultant. As you read each of the following four portraits, consider jotting down your thoughts, observations, and lessons learned on the worksheet that follows the last perspective.

A Millennial's Self-Portrait

Erin Nicole Gordon
Accenture

Raised by the Baby Boomers, we emerge on the scene as "high maintenance" with our laptops and continual texting. We are "Millennials"—often characterized as demanding, inflexible, inexperienced, gregarious, and even loud. However, these descriptions don't fit all Millennials. In contrast to the typical Millennial profile, the Millennial knowledge worker, with which I identify, represents a high-performing, task-oriented group with a high capacity to learn and grow.

In portraying the Millennial knowledge worker, I suggest a subset of adjectives introducing thoughtful contradictions to stereotypes and highlighting our potential. These adjectives set the stage for factors motivating the Millennial knowledge worker and describe how I personally identify with the group addressed in this book. Attributes revealing how best to strategically motivate the Millennial knowledge worker will be discussed in the snapshot to follow. These characteristics include: independent or do-it-yourself (DIY), engaged, ambitious, innovative, and compassionate. Each attribute acknowledged and thoughtfully considered will serve to realize the possibilities of a Millennial knowledge worker.

Flexibility and Work/Life Balance. As an independent worker, I value the flexibility to work where and when best fits my schedule. Moreover, I prefer to work when maximum levels of productivity are possible, and that certainly does not conform to the 8 a.m.–5 p.m. norm of conducting business. The flexibility component in scheduling work also offers me the authority to choose my priorities, whether work or activities beyond my career. By providing flexibility, my employer addresses the factor of work-life balance, another quality of work I value highly. Like most Millennial knowledge workers, I pursue life outside of work and dedicate much of my time to interests outside my career. While work is a priority, I prefer a balance and the freedom to seek that balance. As I am given the flexibility to work independently, I become increasingly more productive and am more likely to collaborate with others given the new time created by flexible parameters.

Recognition. When graduates seek employment after college, common assumptions often set expectations. Whether the assumption results from teaching, observation of parents' experiences, or mere perceptions, I recall most classmates, myself included, acknowledging "serving time" in our first positions as a requirement. This meant succumbing to the requests of an employer in return for the willingness to meet personal needs for a short period of time, namely, earning the respect needed to work independently.

A second assumption makes clear why numerous Millennial knowledge workers expect respect quickly. We assume that our first job's purpose is only to prepare us for the next career move, which should occur in three years at most. We anticipate moving on almost immediately, gaining the mutual trust and respect necessary to succeed. The do-it-yourself, independent nature of the Millennial knowledge worker creates needs for employment to be flexible, allowing the option to seek an appropriate work/life balance if expectations for productivity are well-defined from the beginning.

Multidimensional Millennial Growth Opportunities. Recognizing independence by offering flexibility and work/life balance is essential to motivating the knowledge worker. Further still, a focus upon the engaged, ambitious attitude of this group is at the heart of motivating Millennials and retaining high-quality resources. Growth opportunities coupled with ways to actively contribute fuel the fire of ambition in many Millennials. College recruitment efforts with my current employer demonstrate the continual demand for growth opportunities in coming generations; candidates often request models for career development or program overviews to indicate how career advancement may be achieved. I interviewed with a variety of employers, inquired about developmental opportunities, and turned away all employment not exhibiting a clear path for advancement with fast-paced progression.

The Millennial knowledge worker seeks multidimensional growth opportunities that may be found through mentorship, executive/client interaction, or simply rich, informal relationships. From a team perspective, group projects to gain exposure or introduce challenges with problem-solving elements present engaging activities with added social benefit. Other developmental prospects include networking engagements, community involvement, and nonprofit work. Any opportunity allowing leadership or service involvement typically wins the interest of a Millennial. Because contribution is no longer defined as merely increasing profit, these diverse growth opportunities allow for both development and uniquely individual ways to contribute in an organization.

Purpose, Contribution, and Challenging Work. Like many Millennial knowledge workers, I seek a sense of purpose in my career; knowing that I make an identified difference in my work is a significant reward. In the past, growth was measured by promotions or titles, but recognition for contributions no longer means monetary gains or a corner office. I personally find more motivation in being extended the opportunity to give back to the community than in increased pay.

The ability to give back to the community in some way while working will ultimately make most menial tasks worthwhile to a Millennial knowledge worker because the societal contribution seems to matter more in the long run than any slight promotion received to advance a career.

Fun and Social Interaction. As already implied, there is an element of compassion that characterizes the Millennial knowledge worker. This compassion often combines with fun and social interaction, all of which motivate high-performing workers. Whereas there once existed clearly defined times for work and play, these distinctions fade for a Millennial. We work and play simultaneously, just as we choose when and where we do so. Similarly, we find no differentiation between work and community service. As evidenced by the many corporate initiatives and missions that now include developmental and service-oriented relationships (working and being involved all at once), there is a clear effort to engage the cause-oriented Millennial knowledge worker like myself. We use these opportunities to exercise our creativity and leverage our innovative, tech-savvy capabilities to maximize our work around the clock. We have no bounds and only need continual support to continually deliver high performance.

As I observe various projects and find a myriad of twenty-somethings tucked into cubicles, I see that this firm "gets" the Millennial knowledge worker. Kudos to corporate efforts—we must recognize that our employers are aware and willing to work with these and all differentiating attributes we bring to the table in order to keep us motivated. We possess the potential to sustain competitive advantages sought in the corporate setting—just ensure that we do not lose wireless access!

A Millennial Recruiter's Perspective

Nicole Hardin
HireStrategy, Inc.

Over the past several decades, the relationship between employer and employee has been evolving, and with the overwhelming number of Millennials joining the workforce, it is likely that we will see a new paradigm created. The expectations of the Millennial worker are distinctly different from those of their older counterparts already in the workforce. Key criteria that Millennials are using to decide where they will be working include the following:

- **They want to work with their friends.** This generation is evaluating their future employers by how they envision their relationships with co-workers. It is a given that Millennials expect to work with people who are as bright, capable, and driven as they are. In addition, however, they expect that they will make social connections, to some degree, with their team members.
- **They expect a coach/mentor, not a boss.** They have been coached their whole lives and they expect nothing different from their direct manager. It is important to keep in mind that many Millennials view their parents as friends and will expect the same kind of mentor relationship from their boss.

- **They are passionate about developing, evolving, and being rewarded.** This is the generation that seeks instant gratification, and they want an environment where they are reminded (constantly) that their work matters and they are making a difference. The good news is, they aren't as driven by jumps in compensation or meaningless promotions. Their focus is much more on learning new skills and knowing that their work is making a real impact.

- **They want to be part of something "bigger than themselves."** This may be one of the most socially aware generations ever. Millennials will be partial to a company that has a mission that benefits society. The good news is that they are excellent team players, and when they feel like part of a mission, this skill is further enhanced.

- **They, more than any other generation in the past, have a very clear picture of what they want, and they feel entitled to it now.** They see no reason to pay their dues or work somewhere they don't like in order to gain valuable experience. They want good experience in a good environment and are unlikely to make many compromises.

- **Their parents will be integral in their decisions about where they work.** Millennials have always looked to their parents as partners in life decisions, and this decision is no different.

As a result, many companies have responded to these Millennial requirements with the following strategies:

- **Most companies have done a lot of work to develop their corporate cultures.** They have recognized that throwing a ping-pong table in the break room isn't, in itself, a culture, and they have invested time and resources into making it a real part of the organization. Furthermore, most companies have become much better at marketing their cultures to prospective employees. In the past, it was enough to say "we are a great place to work." Companies are now demonstrating why they are a great place to work.

- **Companies have worked to create smaller steps in career paths** to keep employees engaged and feeling rewarded more regularly.

- **We have seen a rise in corporate events** (usually smaller, informal gatherings) to promote the social component that this generation craves.

- **Companies have put a lot more emphasis on their recruiting processes.** This is no longer just a focus for HR. Companies are investing time and training with not only their managers but also their team leads and anyone who is involved in the interview process. There has been a shift to ensure that the interview not only evaluates the candidate's skills but also sells the candidates on investing their talents in this organization.

Those strategies are a good start, but there are some additional steps that can bridge the Millennial/employer gap even further. For example:

- **The key to securing and retaining the Millennial generation is their manager.** They need to have a manager who is open to constant communication and regular praise. They want to constantly be gaining new responsibilities and taking on more and more meaningful work. They need a manager who has bought into "them," not just "the work they do." Millennials need to believe that their manager has a strong commitment to their development, and need to see their manager demonstrate this on a daily basis through mentorship.
- **Companies need to get better at demonstrating how what they do affects society and showing that they are socially conscious.**
- **It would behoove many companies to start working on a plan for how they can influence the parents in the recruiting process.**
- **The more clearly companies can lay out a development program, the more likely a Millennial will be to make a commitment to the organization.** The plan doesn't have to show all upward mobility. It's important to remember that this generation is accustomed to constant motion, so put some ability for them to move horizontally into their development plan. They want to learn and be challenged, and you can do that without making them managers.

Three Recurring Themes

Shaara Roman, HR Director
CGI Federal

In my dealings with Millennials as an HR executive, I have experienced three recurring themes, and offer the following advice to managers of Gen Y employees:

1. **Provide a learning environment.** Millennials want an environment in which they can constantly learn and be mentored. They want to have access to information when they need it, and they want training accessible 24/7. They want opportunities to explore different roles and career paths, and they want an organization that will allow them to advance in their career.

   Provide a clear career path: Manage the employee's impatience to get to the next level by being concrete and deliberate in creating a path to get there. Share your expectations of specific behaviors, experiences, or deliverables that are needed before the employee can get to the next level.

   Be supportive of your employees, engage in dialogue, and be supportive of their decisions and choices. Show that you will actively work with an employee and champion his choice for career growth, even if it is not with your team. Provide direct and constructive feedback, but be open to receiving feedback yourself.

2. **Provide a social environment.** Our Gen Y employees repeatedly cite our company-funded social club as a benefit they value greatly. It also gives them the sense that the organization is committed to meeting their needs. In addition to having formal opportunities to socialize with co-workers, Millennials want to know that they are working with people who could be friends. They want to be able to relax and go to happy hours, sporting events, and so on with their work colleagues.

   Chill a little. As a manager, try to provide an environment that is friendly and relaxed. Every now and then, when possible, build in some downtime, whether it's in a team meeting once a quarter or a happy hour. Celebrate birthdays and service anniversaries. Allow opportunities for team members to recognize each other. On occasion, grab a coffee with your employee or walk to the sandwich store together.

3. **Provide a flexible environment.** I envy Millennials because they have a life! Gen Y-ers are vocal about expressing their thoughts—which are really not that much different from ours. They are not clock-watchers, and they are de-motivated by having to adhere to what may seem like an arbitrary schedule. While work is not the number-one priority, Millennials will work hard to accomplish what needs to be done.

   Manage by outcomes. I would suggest revisiting the notion of hard and fast start and end times for the work day. Instead, pick "core hours," such as 10 a.m. to 3 p.m., when everyone is expected to be in the office. The most effective way to manage Millennials in a professional setting is to provide a deliverable and a deadline. How and when the work gets done is really up to the individual. The individual will almost always come through. The flexibility and autonomy to set their schedule makes Millennials feel respected and valued for their contributions. I find that if you give a little, you will get a lot in return.

Portrait of a Millennial

Kris T. Jensen, Vice President, Corporate Services
Wisdom Worker Solutions

As each generation enters the workforce, its behaviors are shaped by the realities currently evident in the world. While some realities may be held in common, Millennials who came of age in the 1990s will have experienced slightly different world realities than those who just started turning 16 in 2009. With that in mind, consider the following:

- **A skill package versus a profession**

  Millennials recognize that versatility both reinforces their value to their current employer and increases their marketability to any organization. Consequently, rather than being categorized by a profession or an industry, they focus on obtaining a comprehensive set of skills that employers identify as critical to success in the workplace.

Millennials are often self-confident, resourceful, collegial, open, expressive, and direct. However, they will need development in interpersonal skills, basic English writing, coping skills, and critical thinking skills.

- **A global tribe**

Shifting socio-economic factors worldwide have given Millennials the opportunity to grow, learn, and live with more diverse people. This openness to diversity has also contributed to the redefinition of the nuclear family. Parents, who have highly active roles in Millennial lives, have solicited their input on a variety of family decisions, leading Millennials to expect to be consulted in the workplace and to exercise their personal choice. Concerns about their personal safety in schools, organizations, and in public have led some sociologists to acknowledge that Millennials may have a polarized view of the world. (Studies conducted by the Center for Creative Leadership have identified few behavioral differences among generations from country to country.)

- **Virtually real**

Millennials have been raised in the virtual world. Documenting the most intimate details of their lives in videos, in photos, and on social networking Web pages, they have a broader sense of their virtual reality, which redefines privacy. This 24/7 lifestyle has some believing that while Millennials have greater work/life balance, they might need to be "unplugged" from time to time to forestall burnout and related health issues. Immersion in technology should not be confused with competence, as not all Millennials are technically adept to the same degree. Most, however, have an understanding of how technology has the "power to personalize." Those who work diligently to protect those of us surfing in the virtual world suggest that Millennials may be naïve and too trusting of those they find online.

- **A growing conscience**

Ultimately Millennials will reach and overtake the footprint of the Baby Boomers. As they grow into their size, there is a corresponding social awareness rising, much as the Boomers heralded a period of great social change. Millennials recognize the world realities they may be inheriting, including a burgeoning federal debt, significant unemployment, and an impaired planet. Generational scholars state that every fourth generation represents a period in which society redefines its nature and purpose. Protected as children, Millennials will likely return to being institutionally driven with a trust in authority, making them powerful elders that will provoke the conscientious change typically instigated by a fourth generation.

PORTRAITS OF A MILLENNIAL: LESSONS LEARNED

Now that you have reviewed the four Millennial portraits, identify the lessons gleaned from each perspective.

Lessons learned from the Millennial's perspective:

Lessons learned from the Millennial recruiter's perspective:

Lessons learned from the human resources manager:

Lessons learned from the Millennial-workforce consultant:

Summary

This introduction had three main objectives: first, to acknowledge issues related to motivating Millennials; second, to present four perspectives of Millennials; and third, to explain the research-based methodology that produced the sixteen Millennial motivators that appear in this book:

- Flexibility and work/life balance
- Multidimensional Millennial growth opportunities
- Fun and social interaction
- Purpose, contribution, and challenging work
- Establishing and sustaining excellent communications
- The three R's: recognition, respect, and rewards
- Learning, training, and technology
- Pay for performance

As you begin to use this book as a resource to motivate your Millennial knowledge workers, you can do so sequentially or by selecting those sections most relevant to your immediate needs.

PART 1

Flexibility and Work/Life Balance

"Kids in their twenties are all about figuring out how to find balance and not being stuck in a career path that shoots straight to the top. What is more important is that they do something that is valuable and meaningful."

–New Options, New Talent: The Government Guide to the Flexible Workforce

In this part:

- Getting Started
- Flexibility and Work/Life Balance: Not New Concepts
- Perspectives on Flexibility and Work/Life Balance
- Proactive Strategies Supporting Flexibility and Work/Life Balance
- Flexibility and Work/Life Balance: Examples

Getting Started

Each of the eight parts of this book focuses on one or more "Millennial motivators." These were identified, as described in the Introduction, through the use of research and survey methodologies and the active involvement of the twenty-one Contributing Experts featured in this book. Sixteen Millennial motivational factors were identified and are now presented.

It was not surprising that flexibility emerged at the top of the list in the Motivational Factors Survey, with over 80 percent of the respondents ranking it as the most important motivator. Work/life balance also made it to the top-ten list. As the research and writing process progressed, it became apparent that flexibility and work/life balance are interdependent factors in meeting the motivational needs of Millennial knowledge workers. Part 1 builds on this conclusion by addressing the following four objectives:

- Understanding that flexibility and work/life balance are not new concepts
- Appreciating that the current workforce crisis is driving the need for flexible work arrangements
- Recognizing the need to take a closer look at Millennials and their need for increased flexibility and work/life balance
- Implementing proactive strategies in support of flexibility and work/life balance

Flexibility and Work/Life Balance: Not New Concepts

Although flexibility and work/life balance have emerged as important motivational factors for Millennial knowledge workers, these concepts are certainly not new to the workplace or workforce. Human resource managers, researchers, and employers have addressed this issue, as the following brief discussion summarizes.

Work/Life Balance

The concept of work/life balance is not new. During past decades, both here in the United States and in other countries, employees have been working harder and working longer hours, and as the research indicates, often feel that they don't have enough time for their spouses, their children, and themselves. What is unique, according to Erica D. Chick, writing in *Fundamentals of Work-Life Balance*, "is that the role of work itself has changed from a matter of survival to a matter of personal satisfaction. People often work more to achieve success in their personal lives."

While implementing a plan for work/life balance has been a "desirable" for the past generation, it is now a well-documented "essential" for Millennial knowledge workers. They ask themselves and their employers, "How do I balance competing demands to ensure that I am spending my time most effectively in areas that are of value to me?" Later in this part, recommendations will be made to help Millennials address this concern.

Flexibility

The motivational factor of flexibility is not an exclusively Millennial issue. It is, in the broadest sense, part of an employee-employer equation that has the potential to satisfy the needs and suit the lifestyles of each generation in the workplace. However, as with work/life balance, for the Millennial knowledge worker, flexibility is not merely desirable, but rather is essential.

According to Ken Dychtwald, Tamara J. Erickson, and Robert Morison, authors of *Workforce Crisis: How to Beat the Coming Shortage of Skills and Talent,* three components of flexibility are required to create a customized "employment deal." These components are flexible work arrangements, flexible learning opportunities, and flexible compensation and benefits. The following short exercise, based on material selected from their book, is presented in the form of an inventory to further explore the concept of flexibility.

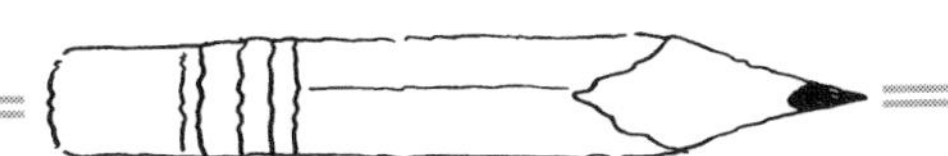

THE FLEXIBLE EMPLOYMENT DEAL

Identify which of the following flexibility components characterize your organization's or business unit's current strengths, and identify any areas that require further development.

1. **Flexible work arrangements.** Does your organization:
   - ❑ Customize work schedules, locations, and formats to engender productivity and loyalty?
   - ❑ Enable teleworkers and other flex workers to stay connected with the organization, both socially and electronically?

2. **Flexible learning opportunities.** Does your organization:
   - ❑ Adopt multiple learning methods to meet the needs of diverse learners?
   - ❑ Use learning experiences to bring groups together?
   - ❑ Leverage the learning potential and efficiency of information technology?

3. **Flexible compensation and benefits.** Does your organization:
   - ❑ Enable employees to achieve better work/life balance by making compensation and benefits clear, accessible, manageable, and valuable?
   - ❑ Make compensation part of a larger performance management system that motivates each employee to work toward high performance and business results?

Perspectives on Flexibility and Work/Life Balance

The challenge of balancing the needs of employee and employer has been addressed from many perspectives in the past. However, the emergence of a fiercely competitive, rapidly changing global economy and the growth of a Millennial workforce have increased the focus on this subject.

William Bridge's book, *JobShift: How to Prosper in a Workplace without Jobs,* raised some provocative and significant issues. The following points reflect the changing perspective on flexibility and work/life balance:

- **Traditional jobs are disappearing.**

  The traditional concept of a "job," with an eight-hour day, is quickly disappearing. A new organizational structure is emerging, based on projects that can often be completed without a traditional workday schedule and that might not even require "going to work."

- **We will all have to learn new ways to work.**

  Although the new ways of working will sometimes require new technological skills, they will more often require something more fundamental: the skill of finding and doing work in a world without clear-cut and stable jobs. Today's worker needs to look for work that needs doing.

- **Millennial workers are starting their careers with work/life plans in place.**

  People who are working on more than one project are already dividing their jobs into several pieces. The old policy of jobs—and job sharing—will be put into the Policy Museum as an artifact of a bygone age, and people will get on with doing the work that needs doing.

Alternative Work Schedules Are Now Required

In her book *Work Concepts for the Future: Managing Alternative Work Arrangements*, Patricia Schiff Estess addresses a basic yet underutilized concept: Has your organization moved from a more flexible scheduling strategy—often hush-hush in implementation—to chiseling formal, written policies on alternative work schedules into the corporate mission? As Estess states, "Even without a detailed cost-benefit analysis, alternative work arrangements that provide greater flexibility in the workplace and the hours people work have gone on for decades. Organizations know it is smart business to keep good employees by accommodating schedules as much as possible."

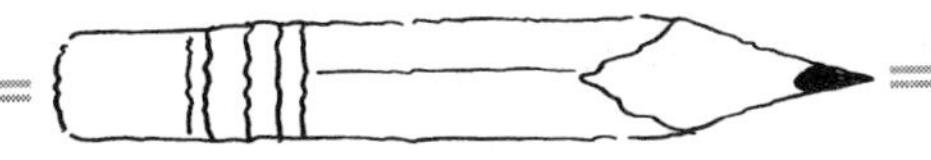

ALTERNATIVE WORK SCHEDULES: MILLENNIAL MOTIVATORS

Indicate which of the following statements (if any) are true.

Our organization has formally embraced the following flexible and alternative work schedules or policies:

____ 1. We embrace flextime as a win-win strategy for employer and Millennial.

____ 2. We achieve greater performance and productivity by condensing work into a compressed work week.

____ 3. Telecommuting is endorsed and encouraged.

____ 4. Job sharing has emerged as a viable and productive staffing structure.

____ 5. Reducing the work week has been introduced as a way of more effectively balancing work and personal life.

Millennials Are Starting Their Careers with Work/Life Plans in Place

The challenge of motivating the Millennial knowledge worker is not limited to private-sector corporations. Rather, this challenge has just as much of an impact on the public sector. As an example, the National Academy of Public Administration addressed this challenge in its 1998 publication titled *New Options, New Talent: The Government Guide to the Flexible Workforce*. It states that "Today's young workers are starting their careers with work/life balance in place. As a result … they want to spend more time with their families and realize the importance of having a life outside of work."

Recommendations for Action by Agencies and Their Managers

The authors of *New Options, New Talent*, while focusing on government organizations, provide recommendations for motivating the Millennial knowledge worker in both the public and private sectors, as follows.

1. **Think of the workforce as a multifaceted whole.**

   This approach requires that results-oriented strategic plans focus on all of the work to be accomplished, rather than on the number of workers.

2. **Use results rather than resources to measure performance.**

   The private and public sectors are moving toward a focus on results, rather than on the number of employees or equivalent managers. Refocus attention from headcounts to results.

3. **Identify a single official responsible for workforce policies and procedures.**

   Respond to the needs of the New Economy, which is characterized by more competitive, information-technology-driven services. This strategy requires a broader organizational and leadership commitment, coordination of organization policies, and cooperation of HR professionals and senior management.

Flexible Work Arrangements and Large-Scale Business Benefits

Addressing the motivational needs of Millennial knowledge workers through increased emphasis on flexibility and work/life balance is not a single workforce issue. Rather, it needs to be put into a broader perspective. As the authors of *Workforce Crisis* write, "There is a big difference between offering flexible arrangements to some workers and implementing flex work on a large scale that reaps business benefits."

Workforce Crisis Drives the Need for Flexible Work Arrangements

In his book *Generation Blend: Managing Across the Technology Age Gap*, Rob Salkowitz documents the convergence of three intriguing factors related to our evolving workforce and evolving work:

- A generational shift is underway across most of the developing world, as the cohort born after the end of World War II approaches retirement and a new generation of Millennials prepares to make its mark on the world.
- Experts predict that the demographic shift will make it more difficult for employers to find skilled workers to fill critical jobs.
- The ubiquity of technology raises the bar even higher. It means that workers will need to have deep knowledge of software, computers, and communication devices, even in jobs and industries that traditionally did not require those skills.

Salkowitz aptly describes the challenges that generational differences can and will make in a new world of work. And managing the different outlook of the tech-savvy Millennial college graduate can be a challenge. The freewheeling Millennial personal networking and communication style might have to be reconciled with more structured workplace requirements.

A Closer Look at Millennials and Their Need for Flexibility and Work/Life Balance

Today's Millennials are starting work with work/life balance in place and a pronounced need for flexibility. They have clearly developed motivational drivers that are critically important to them. These behavioral preferences will continue to challenge employee retention, recruiting, and management.

The following evaluation items are culled from Cam Marston's book, *Motivating the "What's In It for Me?" Workforce*, which reveals a broad spectrum of Millennial behavioral preferences that reinforce the importance of addressing flexibility and work/life balance and the need for proactive strategies.

A FLEXIBILITY AND WORK/LIFE BALANCE CHECKLIST

Identify which of the following behaviors characterize your Millennial knowledge workers' needs for flexibility and work/life balance.

____ 1. Millennials often measure an effective work ethic by whether they get the job done on time, not by how many hours they work each week.

____ 2. Technology is a freedom tool. It enables workers to complete their jobs faster and more easily, so they can get back to what's important—their lives outside the office.

____ 3. Gen X-ers say, "Get a life." New Millennials say, "I have a life. Work comes second."

____ 4. Millennial professionals like balance. These young adults value the good life, like their parents do, but are not willing to sacrifice time with family and friends to achieve it.

____ 5. Millennials are likely to want to build parallel careers, not focusing on one job or profession at the exclusion of others.

____ 6. Data consistently show that balance and flexibility are critical priorities for Millennials entering the workforce.

____ 7. Flexibility in planning a career around major life events is the most important element for achieving a good balance between a career and one's personal life.

____ 8. Work/life integration adds another dimension—not just the ability to do work from a life setting (e.g., at home or while doing life- and family-oriented activities), but the ability to participate in life from a work setting.

____ 9. Gen Y-ers are independent, techno-savvy, entrepreneurial hard workers who thrive on flexibility, and take these qualities to new heights or transform them.

Proactive Strategies Supporting Flexibility and Work/Life Balance

Flexibility and work/life balance are clearly interdependent Millennial motivators. However, in an effort to heighten the application potential for you, our reader/practitioner, the following discussion treats them separately. A combination of research-based recommendations and examples from our Contributing Experts further highlights selected concepts.

Flexibility: The Single Most Important Millennial Motivator

Contributing Expert Christopher R. Ryan, Deputy General Counsel, K12 Inc., captures the importance of this motivator in the following statement:

"Millennial workers came of age in a world free from the previous time and space limitations on learning and working. Millennials seek flexibility in various dimension of their work life: in work hours (enable them to pursue outside interests), in work locations (e.g., telecommuting), and in the overall way that work fits into their lives. The concept that one can only be productive in the office between the hours of 9:00 AM and 6:00 PM is alien to Millennials. Facebook has replaced 'face time.' In order to attract and motivate Millennials, employers and managers must change their options on work and productivity and they must provide the necessary technology to enable this balance and flexibility."

A Continuum of Flexibility Strategies

More specifically, there clearly appears to be a continuum of flexibility opportunities that line managers and human resources professionals can implement. These opportunities are presented in the following inventory, which you can use to identify your organization's current strengths and areas requiring further development.

1. **Flexibility in attendance and punctuality**

   Eric Chester, in *Employing Generation Why? Understanding, Managing, and Motivating Your New Workforce*, suggests that this generation isn't known for being punctual. And rather than lamenting about individuals arriving late and leaving early, you might do better to look both at corporate policies and at your personal work philosophy. In simplest terms, as our Contributing Experts also recommend, figure out what you really need from your employees. Often there are more opportunities for flexibility to be inserted into the workplace schedule.

2. **Implementing flexible work**

   Flexible scheduling is just a single component, or a tactic, of a much broader flexible work program. The authors of *Workforce Crisis* suggest the broader strategy of implementing a flexible work program in your organization. More specifically, they identify four key variables and suggest looking for situations in which all four variables are favorable. The four key variables are:

   - ▷ **The nature of the work** — How elastic is the work itself? Must it be performed at specific times or in specific places?
   - ▷ **Flexible-time programs** — Evaluate which positions are right for flexible hours and shifts. Define core business hours and the earliest start times and finish times.
   - ▷ **Reduced-time programs** — Evaluate which positions are right for reduced hours. Can you redistribute or reschedule work across existing resources, ensuring that workloads mesh with work times?
   - ▷ **Flexible-plan programs** — Evaluate which positions are right for mobile work or telecommuting. Can you install collaboration tools and ensure communication and connectedness for those people working off-site?

3. **Technology as a resource for Millennial flexibility and work/life balance**

   The growth of Millennial literature, research, and training programs parallels the rapid growth of this important workforce generation. Rob Salkowitz's recent book, *Generation Blend: Managing Across the Technology Age Gap,* presents a compelling case for technology further supporting the Millennials' priorities of flexibility and work/life balance. He states, "Millennials seek remote access and mobility, access to personal networks at work; standard accessible technology; two-way channels of internal communication; blogs and other channels of personal expression."

   The Millennials' use of technology to address both work and personal priorities on and off the job, while at times frustrating to managers, is emerging as a mutually beneficial resource.

Flexibility and Work/Life Balance: Examples

The motivational strategies and tactics presented in each part of this book are not mere academic recommendations. Rather, they are reflections of best-of-class practices. The following examples highlight the value of moving from concept to actual practice. They include a list of best practices, worker testimonials, and a final inventory of best practices.

The first snapshot of flexibility and work/life balance strategies and employee testimonials is just one example of the value of proactively addressing this motivational factor. The second short example highlights the importance of addressing the needs of working parents and other employees.

Creating an Environment Where People Come First

Shaara Roman, Director, Human Resources
CGI Federal

At CGI, we work together to create an environment where our people come first. We call our employees "members" to reinforce that all who join our team are, as owners, empowered to participate in the challenges and rewards that come from building a world-class company. We are one of the largest independent IT and business process services firms in the world, and our members are the key element of our continued success.

- **Telecommuting and flexible work schedules**

  To help employees save on travel costs and balance work and family, we offer our employees the opportunity to telecommute, as well as flexible work schedules. Both benefits are consistently praised by employees in our annual satisfaction survey. Part-time work arrangements and job sharing are also supported.

- **Member testimonials**

  We receive an overwhelming number of comments on CGI's commitment to work/life balance in our member satisfaction survey. For example:

  "I appreciate the flex time and how supportive managers are of staff utilizing flex time and vacation time to maintain work/life balance."

  "The freedom to work from where I need to when I need to is very important to me. The fact that I am able to remotely log into all my files and applications is important when I am traveling, as well as when I just have an idea at 8 p.m. at home and want to record it or send an email."

"When life happens, I've always been able to adjust my work hours to accommodate it."

"The ability to partially telecommute significantly increases my ability to help look after family members who have special needs."

Working Moms and Other Employees

Hector Velez, Executive Vice President
HireStrategy

First of all, we offer up to twelve weeks of maternity leave. Then, we encourage working mothers to telecommute at least one day a week. We have found that this has done wonders for morale and retention. Doing this cuts down on commuting time and allows the employee valuable time with her family. Another key to the success of this program has been the unconditional top-down support from the executive team. This support helps to alleviate the "guilt" factor that tends to seep into the employee's consciousness. From flextime and telecommuting to parental leave, we also try to expand the concept of family-friendly benefits to make sure they cover adoptive parents, fathers, and grandparents, as well as working mothers.

In addition, all HireStrategy employees are entitled to 120 hours (15 days) of leave each calendar year, which will accrue, pro-rated starting from the date of hire. Employees are encouraged to use their vacation each year; however, if they're unable to do so, up to one week can be carried over to the following year.

Finally, to enhance flexibility and productivity, we have created Web-enabled CRM technology so work can be done from any location with Internet access. We encourage employees to use the technology so that during off hours and when they're away from the office, they are "connected" and can maximize their performance.

Inventory of Flexible Workplace Policies

Kitty Nix, Director, Strategic Management
Helios HR

There are number of factors that are critical to building a culture focused on results while still encouraging flexibility and success for each employee. These factors include: a leadership team that models the way; business processes that focus on institutionalizing efficient product development and delivery models; and policies that reinforce the desire to provide flexibility while ensuring results. Following is a sample of some of these best-practice policies.

- **Management by Objectives (MBOs) performance metrics**

  Does your organization set individual objectives for all employees? Ideally, these objectives should stem from the organization's strategic plan. For example, for organizations providing professional services, does every employee have individualized utilization targets? These objectives should serve as the basis to hold employees accountable for results.

- **Core business hours**

  Does your business have core business hours? For example, do you mandate that all employees be accessible in person, via e-mail, or via cell phone between the hours of 9:30 to 4:30, but allow flexibility for some to work 7:30 to 5:00 while others work 9:30 to 6:00?

- **Paid time off**

  Do you group leave benefits into one bucket to maximize flexibility for employees? For example, do you have one policy that includes holidays, vacation time, and sick leave? This policy and the core-business-hours policies not only accommodate individual priorities, such as the need to celebrate different holidays, but also actually benefit the business by increasing customer access to your workforce.

- **Cell phone and data service reimbursement**

  Do you provide reimbursements for cell phones and data services so employees can be accessible while not in the office, such as for client meetings or for attending to personal business during the day?

- **Laptops**

  Do you provide laptops for all of your employees? You will find that employees are much more likely to go above and beyond the call of duty if they are equipped with tools that foster flexibility and allow them to work wherever they want.

- **Telecommuting, compressed work week, and job sharing**

  Do you encourage unique and individualized work arrangements that allow employees to address their non-work priorities? Many employees are interested in serving their community or actively participating in family responsibilities. Creating an environment that allows employees to reduce work hours, work remotely, or work fewer days can create employee loyalty that money cannot buy.

Not only do these policies foster a flexible environment, which helps to attract and retain the 21–30-year-old knowledge worker, but they also offer the opportunity to increase customer service. After all, happy employees are best equipped to serve customers.

Strategies for Work/Life Balance

The Millennial motivational factor of work/life balance is clearly a companion to the motivational factor of flexibility. It is one of the most significant priorities of the Millennial worker. There is, in fact, a clear generational progression in the importance of this motivational factor from Traditionalists to Boomers to Generation X to Millennials.

In the past, Traditionalists viewed work as the center of their life. The Boomers, while still influenced by the Traditionalist workaholic legacy, sought more balance in their lives. Generation X progressed further, as Rob Salkowitz states in *Generation Blend*, in "working to live, prioritizing lifestyle over career choices." And, finally, Millennials, accustomed to multitasking, simply view work as just one more thing to fit into their schedules.

The following model of previous generations' work/life relationships illustrates how work was viewed as the center of a worker's life in the past. Everything else (family, friends, entertainment, chores, vacation, community service, hobbies) merely revolved around the periphery.

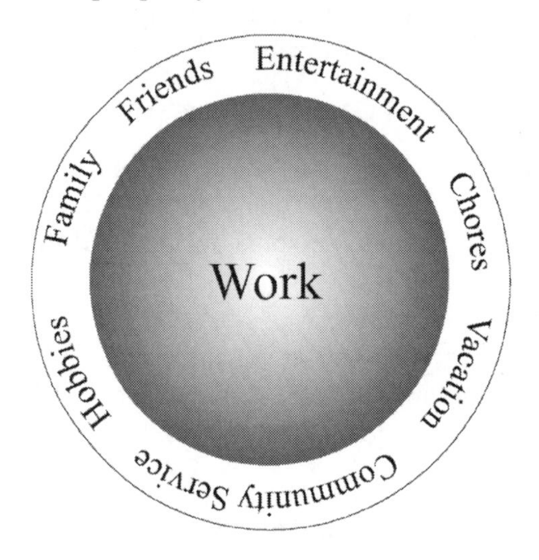

Previous generations' work/life balance[1]

Work is Viewed Differently By Today's Workers

New Options, New Talent: The Government Guide to the Flexible Workplace, by the National Academy of Public Administration, discusses Gen X workers in the federal sector and describes a set of worker behaviors that clearly set the stage for Millennials moving work/life balance into their top-ten list of motivational factors. As an example, consider how many of the following Gen X preferences are now priorities for your Millennial workforce.

[1] Source: *New Options, New Talent: The Government Guide to the Flexible Workplace*, by the National Academy of Public Administration

- Today's workers no longer find security in a "lifetime" employer.
- "Work" and "lifetime employment" are no longer one and the same.
- Individuals have a different perspective on a one-employer career.
- Instead of finding security in an employer, people find security within themselves.
- Today's workers want to continue to learn in order to expand their skills, improving their marketability.
- For Generation X and Millennial workers, expanding their skills is comparable to purchasing disability insurance as a protection against accident or illness.

The employer- or work-centric model has been transformed, first by Boomers, then Gen Xers, and finally, Millennials into a balancing of work and life. As the following model illustrates, Work and Life now appear on a scale with emphasis on balance.

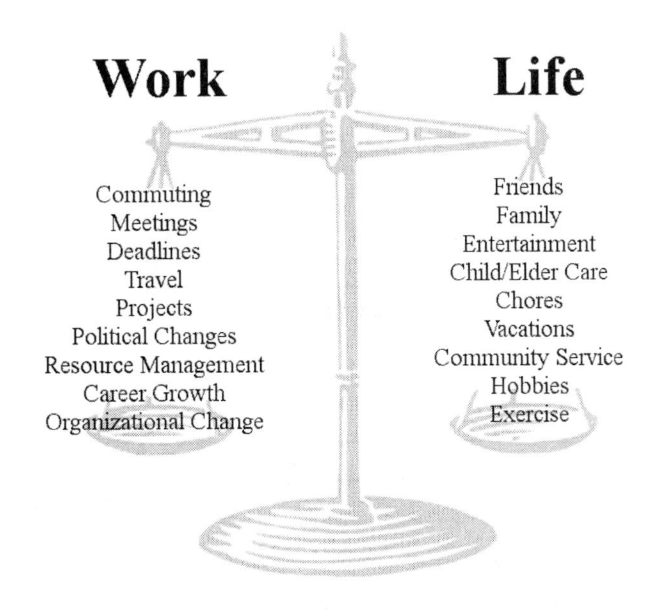

Younger generations' work/life balance[1]

The concept of "The Balance Scale" has been embraced and modified by organizational effectiveness and human resources professionals. Cam Marston, in *Motivating the "What's In It For Me? Workforce,* suggests an interesting application of the concept. He presents a scale with two components: "Employee" on one side and "Company" on the other. He suggests using it as a motivational and communication tool between employee and manager. A short summary of his suggested application of this tool follows.

[1] Source: *New Options, New Talent: The Government Guide to the Flexible Workplace*, by the National Academy of Public Administration

The Employee and Company Scale: A Proactive Millennial Resource

In his book *Motivating The "What's In It For Me?" Workforce*, Cam Marston makes an important recommendation for managers of new Millennial employees. "As a manager, the thing to do is negotiate with your employees." More specifically, he introduces the concept of using the following Balance Scale to reconcile and balance Millennials' work/life needs with those of the organization.

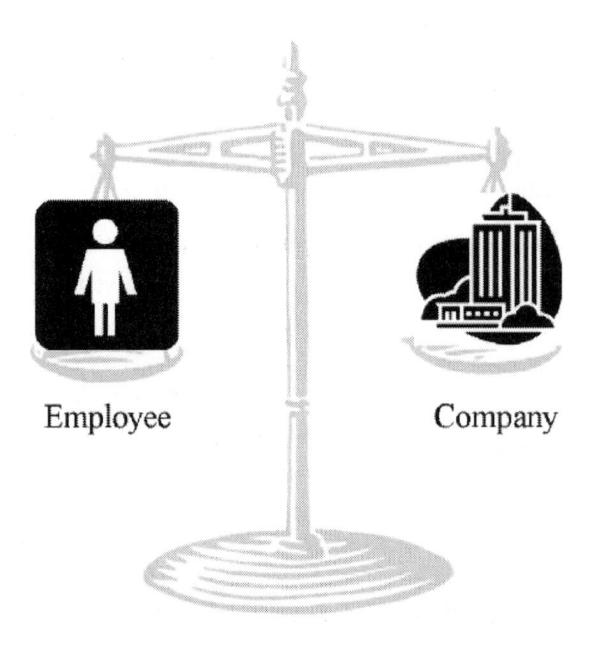

To effectively use the Employee and Company Scale, he makes the following recommendations.

- Give some thought to drawing this scale on paper when you talk with employees.
- Use it as a visual guide to show them how their needs must be balanced by the company's needs.
- Let employees see that the scale must remain level in order to serve customers, keep the company running, and allow everyone to be happy.
- Explain that employees become valuable when they are willing to work with their employer to keep the scale in balance.

The use of the scale will provide an opportunity to reconcile company needs with those work/life balance needs of the Millennial. This scale will also provide an opportunity for each individual to identify his or her own motivational and performance needs. It also provides an excellent opportunity to communicate with, negotiate with, and motivate the Millennial.

Further Discussion

Shira Harrington, Director, Professional Search Positions, Inc.

If we were to peer into the near future, we might be surprised to see the fulfillment of William Bridges' predictions that "Traditional jobs are disappearing." With the prevalence of remote technology, teleworking models, and the increased use of virtual communication, that day might come sooner than we think. There are two primary challenges, however, that must be overcome for this futuristic concept to become a reality: 1) a revamping of government and corporate regulations; and 2) a changing of old mindsets.

Revamping of Government and Corporation Regulations

Our current labor force is guided by restrictive, albeit often necessary, government regulations, such as the Fair Labor Standards Act, which mandates such distinctions as exempt vs. non-exempt employees. To retain the Millennial knowledge worker who, for example, may be classified as non-exempt but wants the flexibility to work creative (or even longer) hours, this can hinder a manager's ability to customize alternative working arrangements. Although created to protect workers during the industrial age, when hourly abuses were the norm, today these types of restrictive measures can impede employers from fostering an employee-centric talent management model. Advocacy organizations such as the Society for Human Resource Management should be encouraged to lobby for the repealing or revising of such laws in an effort to increase the opportunities for retaining a changing workforce.

Changing of Old Mindsets

Yet even with more flexible government and corporate policies in place, old mindsets must be changed as well. What originally generated a fascination in generational and age diversity was the struggle of older professionals to appreciate today's young workers' attitudes toward work-life integration, which are quite different from those of people who entered the workforce in the 1960s, '70s, and '80s. Further study should be conducted into ways that Veterans and Boomers can be sensitized not only to accept but also to champion flexible work arrangements without harboring a sour-grapes mentality because they were not afforded those opportunities when they were in their 20s. Although diversity training has been a good first step in creating awareness of the need for such accommodations, we are now ready for these older generations to embrace a complete shift of the mind, and of the heart, to engage an ambitious and demanding young workforce who must be retained in order for the company to remain competitive.

Summary

Millennials are keenly aware of the importance of flexibility and work/life balance. As Lisa Orrell writes in *Millennials Incorporated*, "They expect their manager and company to support and respect their lives outside of work." However, as managers address this pronounced need for work/life balance, they must also reconcile the organization's need to remain profitable in an increasingly competitive global economy. In addition, the Millennials' additional requirement for multidimensional growth opportunities, as discussed in the Part 2 of this book, further increases the challenge of meeting their motivational needs.

P A R T **2**

Multidimensional Millennial Growth Opportunities

> ***"** They [the Millennials] are looking for opportunities that empower them to use… time, tools, and their remarkable talents to build a better life… to have a job that means more than a paycheck and a life that really matters."*
>
> **–Eric Chester, *Employing Generation Why?***

In this part:

Getting Started

A wide variety of responses resulted from a Contributing Expert–assisted preliminary survey of Millennial motivational factors. These included "career advancement, "challenging work," "fast cycle work environment," "quick promotions, and "personal goals." In addition, "learning, "training" and "technology" emerged high on the list of frequent responses. After an analysis of this data, some results were combined when definitions of similar factors emerged. The final Survey Analysis resulted in our creating eight parts of this book to discuss sixteen prominent motivational factors. Part Two, Multidimensional Growth Opportunities, is the result of this process. Emphasis is placed on the following four objectives:

- ▶ Appreciate that multidimensional growth opportunities are non-negotiable Millennial requirements
- ▶ Provide opportunities to reconcile Millennials' growth opportunities and the intellectual-capital needs of knowledge organizations
- ▶ Examine and apply Contributing Experts' strategies for implementing multidimensional growth opportunities
- ▶ Identify potential Millennial leaders through multidimensional growth opportunities

Multidimensional Growth Opportunities as Non-Negotiable Requirements

A theory of adult development pioneered by psychoanalyst Erik H. Erikson describes three stages of adulthood: intimacy (ages 21–35), generativity (ages 35–55), and integrity (age 55+). As Harry Levinson writes in "A Second Career: The Possible Dream" (in *Harvard Business Review On Work and Lift Balance*), Daniel Levinson's studies of executives "indicate that at about age 37, the adult throws off the guidance or protection of older mentors or managers and takes full charge of himself." Daniel Levinson calls this "the BOOM [becoming one's own man] effect," and it can drive people to seek new careers.

By curious counterpoint, our Millennials "want it all now." As Martin and Tulgan write in *Managing Generation Y*:

> ***"Organizations that can't—or won't—customize training, career paths, incentives, and work responsibilities need a wake-up call."***

They further state:

> ***"This generation won't be lured by promises of climbing ladders, paying dues, and cashing out at retirement. They want to know:***
>
> ***— What value can I add today?***
>
> ***— What can I learn today?***
>
> ***— What will you offer me today?***
>
> ***— How will I be rewarded today?"***

A quick review of current Millennial literature indicates a recurring priority: Millennials have a strong need for ongoing multidimensional growth opportunities.

How Does Your Organization Meet Millennials' Growth Needs?

Identify which of the following motivational needs your organization addresses effectively, and which ones require more attention.

____ 1. "The Millennial Professional tends to be very demanding (of themselves and others) and understands that it is their responsibility to work hard to get what they want... This ambition and desire for 'success and rewards' has been in them from birth, with Boomer or Gen-X parents telling them they can do anything they put their minds to." (*Millennials Incorporated*)

____ 2. "For them [Millennials], life is an all-you-can-eat buffet offering unlimited choice, few rules, and a pay-as-you-go system... [T]hey believe in their ability to leapfrog over the painstaking cultivate/plant/fertilize parts and go directly to the harvest." (*Employing Generation Why?*)

____ 3. "Because Gen Yers grew up with interactive media that combined education with fun, they expect learning to be part of their daily lives. They want to experience clear connections between the skills they learn today and the skills they will use tomorrow." (*Managing Generation Y*)

____ 4. "Leaders with a knowledge perspective can see alternative career patterns for professionals, patterns that often involve new experiences, travel, and changes of work—including changing career tracks. Successful knowledge organizations know their professionals so well that they can plan this kind of career for them." (*The New Organizational Wealth: Managing and Measuring Knowledge-based Assets*)

If there is one assumption that line managers and human resources professionals must unequivocally embrace, it is that multidimensional opportunities are non-negotiable Millennial requirements.

Reconciling Millennial Growth Opportunities with Knowledge Organizations

A variety of strategic initiatives appear to be coming together that not only leverage the talent of a multigenerational workforce, but also propel the "new Millennials" as an emerging component of a responsive "New Economy." As the authors of *Workforce Crisis: How to Beat the Coming Shortage of Skills and Talents* recommend:

> **"*What many young people need most to feel happy in a company is the continuous opportunity to learn and grow through frequent changes in roles, responsibilities, and programs."***

The authors go on to state:

> **"*Challenge them, stretch them, stimulate them, let them try new things, allow them to learn by doing and failing—if you can do these things, you will keep more of the young talent you have."***

Interestingly, there is increasingly more evidence that the growth opportunities for both Millennial knowledge workers and their respective organizations can employ complementary strategies. Several conceptual building blocks are discussed next, followed by examples of multidimensional growth opportunities provided by our Contributing Experts.

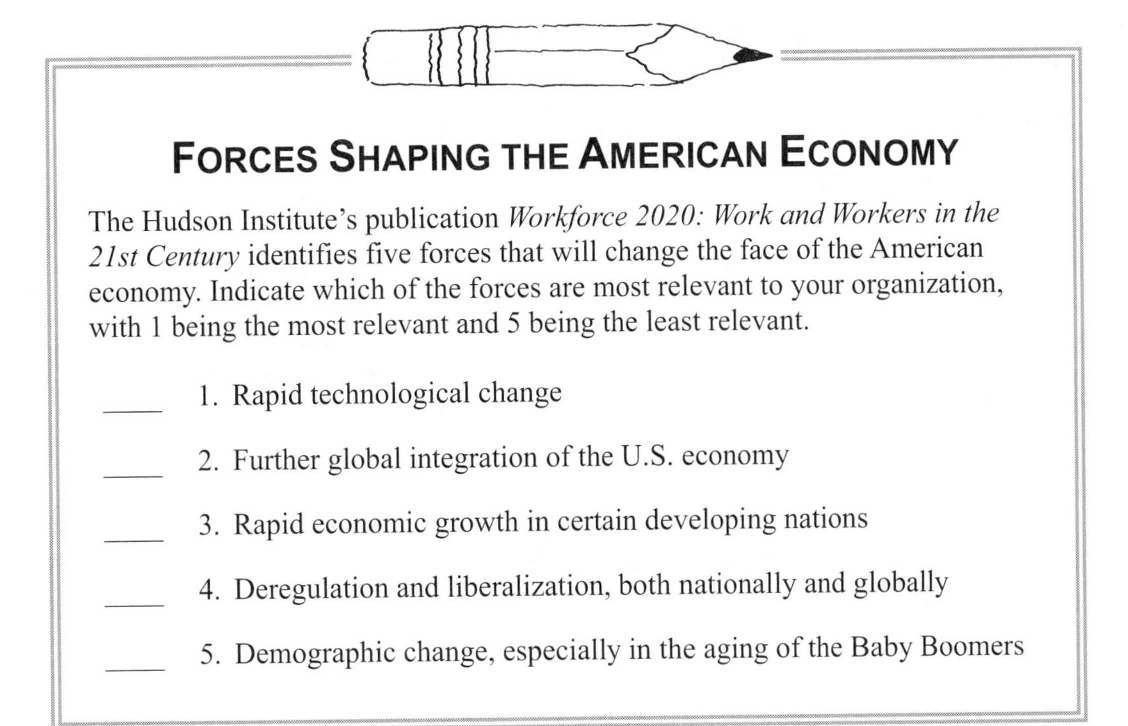

FORCES SHAPING THE AMERICAN ECONOMY

The Hudson Institute's publication *Workforce 2020: Work and Workers in the 21st Century* identifies five forces that will change the face of the American economy. Indicate which of the forces are most relevant to your organization, with 1 being the most relevant and 5 being the least relevant.

____ 1. Rapid technological change

____ 2. Further global integration of the U.S. economy

____ 3. Rapid economic growth in certain developing nations

____ 4. Deregulation and liberalization, both nationally and globally

____ 5. Demographic change, especially in the aging of the Baby Boomers

Clearly, rapid technological change, especially during the aging of the Baby Boomers, will create both winners and losers among industries, companies, and occupations. The growing number of Millennial knowledge workers will be willing to job-hop for better positions to remain on the winning side of the employment equation.

The New Economy as a Knowledge Economy

Frances Horibe, writing in *Managing Knowledge Workers: New Skills to Unlock the Intellectual Capital in Your Organization*, describes the New Economy as a "…flood of information coming at lightning speed" that is "changing almost everything. How we buy, how we sell, what we make, when we make it, what we value, and where we live." As she concludes the preface to her book, she makes five key points that are directly relevant to the Millennial knowledge worker:

- "The driver of success in the New Economy is knowledge."
- "Demand for knowledge workers is great and growing."
- "A knowledge worker is one who uses her head more than her hands to produce value."
- "About 60 per cent of all jobs are knowledge-based."
- "Managing the human dimension of knowledge work is the most important job a manager has."

The Millennials and Organizational Learning

Becoming a learning organization benefits all employees regardless of their generation, occupations, and education. However, as many of our reader/practitioners appreciate, organizations must expand the scope of learning. In the 1990s, organizations emphasized getting out of the "business of training" and into the "business of learning and performance." Now, as the authors of *Workforce Crisis* remind us, "Learning isn't a specialist activity in HR—it's a core management issue, a leadership responsibility, and an employee responsibility."

In a learning organization, learning takes place on a 24/7 basis, up, down, and across the organizational ladder, in classrooms, in hallways, online, and over a cup of coffee. Dychtwald, Erickson, and Morison suggest that organizational learning can be thought of as a three-legged stool. This concept is most relevant to the learning needs of Millennial knowledge workers.

ORGANIZATIONAL LEARNING

Indicate which of the following motivational needs your organization addresses effectively, and which require more attention.

My organization:

____ 1. Realizes individual career and growth plans, orchestrating work assignments (especially stretch assignments) and training experiences to accomplish them.

____ 2. Ensures the right mix of skills and the right behaviors for learning company wide.

____ 3. Establishes connections among people who can productively teach, learn from each other, and share information with one another.

____ 4. Progresses from passive directories of expertise and experience to active "communities of practice."

____ 5. Improves individual and network knowledge and capability.

____ 6. Delivers useful content and experience to develop specific capabilities.

____ 7. Provides courses conducted in person or virtually, plus on-the-job instruction and certification.

Multidimensional Growth Opportunities at CGI Federal

Shaara Roman, HR Director
CGI Federal

At CGI, we strive to create an environment that promotes the professional development of our members and facilitates and encourages the exchange of expertise among them. This enables us to continue to meet the quality needs of the marketplace. CGI understands the need to maintain and enhance our members' technical and managerial knowledge and skills on an ongoing basis. Our training and professional development programs ensure that this need is met.

Members of CGI are responsible for setting their career objectives and pursuing their professional development in a manner consistent with the company's goals and objectives. We recognize that an employee's growth and development comprise a combination of ongoing project opportunities, formal training programs, and coaching and mentoring.

Ongoing Project Opportunities

CGI is in the business of delivering projects, which afford our members unlimited opportunities to develop skills and pursue career advancement. Most members are part of project teams that are structured to provide support and training from teammates at all levels. In addition, our employees have the opportunity to work on numerous projects throughout their careers, with each project providing its own opportunities for learning. A significant percentage of our members begin at the ground level of project work and advance up the management ladder as they gain skills and experience.

Formal Training Programs

We offer a variety of professional, technical, and leadership training to employees within our company.

- **CGI 101**

  An intensive four-day leadership training seminar that covers CGI from A to Z, including the company's philosophy, values, business methodologies, and frameworks. Attendees have an opportunity to meet CGI's senior executives, listen to presentations from leaders of key operational areas, learn CGI's management processes, and network. This program is currently available to managers and above when they join CGI or are promoted, but will soon be made available to all CGI members.

- **Project Leaders Development Track**

  This comprehensive training course educates members on all aspects of successful project delivery with the goal of increasing CGI's success rate in delivering projects on time, on budget, and in line with client expectations.

- **Guided Tour**

  This e-learning tool provides members with a virtual tour of CGI as a whole, including our operations, practices, and culture. It also points members to a variety of resources on our enterprise portal. The tool also features a feedback mechanism, allowing members to ask questions and offer suggestions.

- **Personal Development Kiosk**

  More than 29,000 hours of classroom instruction were delivered to CGI members in 2008. Each employee has a key to a Personal Development Kiosk, which provides 24/7 access to an extensive library of business and technical courses and publications. Employees can integrate training and information access into their workout routines or commutes by downloading courses to an MP3 player for training on the go.

- **Next-Level Leadership Program**

  We understand that a large part of a member's satisfaction and engagement rests in the hands of his or her leaders. To promote better leadership, we offer a learning cohort training program to help up-and-coming executives "step up" to the next level by learning how to empower their teams, communicate a vision, and broaden their footprint in the organization. We have seen how this program benefits not only our future leaders, but also the teams they work with.

- **Tuition Reimbursement**

  We provide tuition reimbursement to members with outstanding performance who are building their careers at CGI. This reimbursement can range from a select course to the pursuit of a degree.

Mentoring/Coaching

The third element of a member's growth and development comes from informal and formal mentoring/coaching programs. All new employees are assigned a mentor for their first year to enhance the integration and assimilation process. We have also recognized the value of a formal mentoring/coaching program to help our employees navigate their careers and get guidance and informal learning from someone other than their manager. In the CGI Federal Business Unit, we are preparing to launch a formal mentoring program to provide mentoring relationships that will focus on specific development needs identified by the employee.

Multidimensional Growth Opportunities at The Urban Institute

Deborah K. Hoover, HR Director
The Urban Institute

At The Urban Institute, we have worked hard over a number of years to provide a culture of support that recognizes young professionals' needs and desires for growth, accomplishment, and responsibility. This is most particularly true for policy researchers, the core of our workforce. Whether straight out of academic programs or after a few years of experience, our recruits have several things in common—they are highly accomplished, they possess high levels of intrinsic motivation, and they want to make a difference at work and beyond very quickly. In many ways, they are the very model of the Millennial knowledge worker.

Due to the researchers' centrality to our mission, our human resources policies and programs, our managerial practices, and the organizational culture as a whole have developed in such a way as to feed the very needs for which Millennials are known. Outward signs of our support for their needs can be found throughout the organization. The following table provides numerous examples of our approach to job, career, professional, and personal growth. Throughout, we underscore the continuing need for learning and application of knowledge, support and rewards for growth and accomplishment, and the idea that responsibility includes leadership. By maintaining high expectations and establishing clear indicators of accomplishment, we give Millennial staffers a clear sense of the "Urban" experience—what they must give and what, in turn, they will take away from this experience.

A Multidimensional, Integrated Approach to Growth

	Programs and policies include:	Effective supervisors and managers provide:	How an organization's culture reflects attitudes on growth
Job growth	Best-in-class tuition assistance program Financial support for conference attendance, outside seminars, and professional association memberships In-house learning communities Brown-bag seminars	Mentoring Opportunities to work in small teams Exposure to multiple projects	Adjectives used to describe the environment: collegial, collaborative, decentralized "My job is as big as I want it to be." Multidisciplinary teams
Career growth	Written standards for performance, promotion, and salary determinations Open job search process A formal salary and promotion process Staff-wide announcements of promotions	Opportunities to collaborate meaningfully with senior scholars Authority and responsibility for project deliverables Expectation of greater independence over time Exposure to external stakeholders	Recognized research career ladder that is consistent with sister research institutions Pragmatic policy interpretation that recognizes unique circumstances and individuals Managerial willingness to coach and explain
Professional growth	Formal committees responsible for reviewing individual accomplishments Access to leadership training opportunities Participation in organizational decision-making through employee committees Annual "Best-in Class Research Awards" Employee-led "RAA Discussion Series"	Facilitation of external relationships with funders, outside scholars, government representatives, and other stakeholders Opportunities to lead project teams Financial support and paid time for professional development activities	Statements from staff, e.g., "To get ahead in research, you really need an advanced degree." Physical office space supports small and large conferences, enabling researcher participation at all levels In-house research library services UI Summer Academy for Public Policy Analysis & Research
Personal growth and social interactions	In-house personal development seminars Employer-sponsored parties, networking, and recreational activities Employer-sponsored charitable activities supporting the larger community In-house workout facility Alumni network	Role-modeling through attendance and participation in all activities	From several exit interviews, "The thing I've liked the best about my time here is that I've grown up." Physical office space includes many small and less formal group spaces where staff chat, read, and eat lunch An open-door policy all the way to the executive suite Very few "employee class" distinctions Annual team building allowance for each work group

The Booz Allen Hamilton Career Planning Services Model

Stacey Kessel, Career Planning Senior Manager
Booz Allen Hamilton

Booz Allen Hamilton's career planning services serve more than 18,000 employees worldwide. Given the diversity of needs, we designed service offerings that could be self-directed and accessed via a website. We also offer enhanced and customized career planning and mentoring services for strategic employee groups such as staff with highly marketable skills.

Model Development

The model design was validated through benchmarking, internal surveys, interviews, and focus groups. A broad representation of leaders across the firm collaborated on the design. Client staff as well as people-services colleagues (HR, Recruiting, and Learning and Development) provided input that helped shape the services model.

Managers' self-assessments of skills, attitudes, and actual behavior on career development gave us their perspective on their responsibilities and ways to successfully support them. For example, managers said they did not want to attend training to build their career coaching skills, but rather would benefit from hearing about their peers' best practices. In focus groups with top-performing employees, we heard a consensus that successful employees take responsibility for driving their own careers.

The Career Planning Services Framework

Taking into consideration both manager and employee perspectives, we framed our Career Planning Services as a means to strengthen the partnership between employees and managers, and we offer services and support tailored to both groups. Additionally, to facilitate the sharing of best practices, we have leveraged technology (website, blogs, wikis, etc.) and developed online tools that allow managers to collaborate with each other regarding people development. In this online environment, managers can collaborate and share best practices. As noted, Career Planning Services reaches all of the firm's 18,000 employees. While the resources and tools are accessible to staff at all levels, they are particularly geared to administrative professionals up to director-level staff.

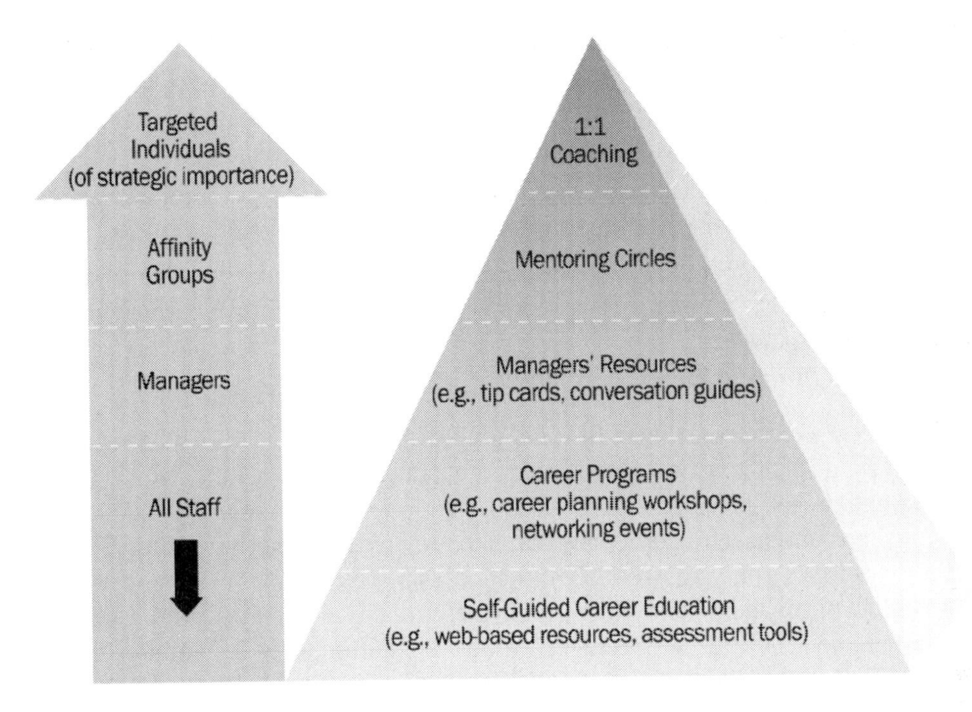

The Career Planning Services framework at Booz Allen Hamilton

Innovative Services

Our Career Planning Services are innovative in terms of balancing the business needs of our firm with the individual career interests, goals, and passions of our employees. Traditionally, candid career discussions of "Where do you see yourself in five years?" occur solely in the interview phase. Our firm-wide "Take 5" campaign encourages managers and employees to dedicate time for ongoing discussions on career development, and encourages the development of multiple mentoring relationships to support career planning goals. The objective is that as employees' interests and plans grow and develop, managers can adapt and integrate information about business direction to ensure that careers are aligned with the firm. The results are stronger connectivity between employees and managers, an improved sense of clarity regarding career options within the firm, and ultimately, improved engagement levels.

Beyond "Career Pathing"

In addition, our practice goes well beyond "career pathing" by encouraging employees to explore all of their interests, both those directly related to their day jobs and others that could be considered extracurricular. We have adopted a philosophy of "job sculpting" and coaching employees on how to "mold" their current positions to better reflect their interests. This concept, created by Dr. James Waldrop and Dr. Timothy Butler of Harvard Business School, is an innovative approach to career development in the context of the employee-employer setting.

Response to Changing Demographics

Lastly, our service offerings meet the changing demographic needs of the firm. Because a significant number of staff work on location at client sites, we developed a suite of online, self-directed career planning and mentoring tools and resources (vs. workshops and coaching sessions that need to be delivered in person). We offer three courses in a virtual-classroom setting accessible by staff across the world to facilitate networking across the firm's many offices and client sites. And each course is targeted for different segments of our population: Gen X/Y and/or those with significant work experience.

Multitude of Learning Solutions and Delivery Services

Our Career Services Model reflects a careful balance of employee and manager needs, the best interests of the firm, and best practices in the industry. Tailoring the services to our culture, the model incorporates a multitude of learning solutions and delivery methods. It provides:

- A framework of services driven by customer needs analysis
- A vehicle to educate employees on career opportunities within the firm
- A host of resources for managers to engage in effective career conversations with staff
- A program for enhancing the culture of mentoring throughout the firm

Millennial Leadership Opportunities and Multidimensional Career Growth

Providing multidimensional growth opportunities for Millennials benefits both individual and organization. In addition, evidence from an increasingly greater number of researchers indicates that multidimensional career growth opportunities for a new "hero" generation will benefit society at large.

Generational Personalities

William Strauss's and Neil Howe's now classic book *Generations: The History of America's Future* introduced the concept of generational personalities and went on to develop a methodology for assessing, explaining, and forecasting the ways that generational factors can and will influence future historical events. The authors take this concept a step further in suggesting that predictable cycles of social dynamics will repeat themselves.

Almost a decade later, Strauss and Howe published *Millennials Rising: The Next Great Generation*. Their enthusiasm for this group, often called the new "hero" generation, is apparent in the following statement:

> ***"As a group, Millennials are unlike any other youth generation in living memory. They are more numerous, more affluent, better educated, and more ethnically diverse... Over the next decade, the Millennial Generation will entirely recast the image of youth from downbeat and alienated to upbeat and engaged—with potential seismic consequences for America."***

Meeting the multidimensional career needs can benefit society and the New Economy on a variety of levels. Most important, "When Millennials hit the workforce in significant numbers, they are going to shake things up with their numbers, their collective purpose, and their global perspective; they can't help but transform the workplace and the world" (*Generation Blend*).

Investing in Millennial Leadership Potential

Investing in developing Millennial leadership potential has emerged as a clearly defined body of literature. A new book, *Millennial Leaders: Success Stories From Today's Most Brilliant Generation Y Leaders,* by Bea Fields, Scott Wilder, Jim Bunch, and Rob Newbold, present well-documented case histories of the proven leadership track record of the new "hero" generation.

Sue McLeod, a Hay Group, Inc., Contributing Expert, presents the following research-based summary, which points out the importance of multidimensional career growth opportunities for Millennials. More specifically, Hay Group, Inc., has identified four growth characteristics of people with high potential for leadership positions. This short summary captures still another important Millennial dimension.

Investing in Potential

Sue McLeod, Senior Consultant
Hay Group

We know that it pays off to develop your high-potential employees and do what you can to keep them. And we know that the younger generation wants continuous development and increasing challenge. But how can you tell which employees are high potentials, worthy of your investment? Our research identified four growth characteristics of people with potential for leadership positions:

- Social understanding and empathy
- Curiosity and eagerness to learn
- Emotional balance, resilience, and realistic optimism
- Thinking beyond the boundaries—a disposition to look beyond their role and make connections between their ideas and others.

There are also factors that are often used to assess leadership potential, but are, in fact, not such good indicators:

- Being the very best performer in the current job
- Expressing great personal ambition and drive

Further Discussion

Shira Harrington, Director, Professional Search Positions, Inc.

Several important issues remain that merit further consideration.

How do smaller organizations tackle the challenge of providing ongoing learning opportunities when financial and staff resources do not allow for corporate universities or even a human resources staff to design comprehensive learning and development programs?

What are the practical implications of these learning opportunities? Are employees given sufficient working hours to participate in these programs, or are they required to use personal learning time? Millennials will generally push back if asked to use their free time for work-related activities.

How receptive are supervisors to being trained on coaching and mentoring methods? In particular, Generation X managers tend to be adverse toward coaching and mentoring Millennial workers since they generally reject such performance management for themselves.

Will corporations utilize virtual learning models such as Second Life, which are currently being implemented by such progressive companies as IBM and Microsoft, in order to facilitate collaboration and learning between remote locations?

As Millennials age and change their marital and/or family status, how will this affect their ability to take advantage of training programs that may require them to learn during their personal time? Generation X knowledge workers are well aware of this challenge, as they are now of the age to have families themselves.

How are employers using their learning programs to develop succession planning models in light of the short tenure of Millennials, which averages 18 months according to the Bureau of Labor Statistics? What implications does this have for their future growth into executive leadership?

What types of courses are being designed to shore up basic competencies such as writing, oral communication, problem solving, and conflict resolution, since these are areas in which Millennials are generally weak?

Finally, how are organizations developing pairing models in their mentoring programs? Are they teaming retiring Veteran and older Boomer populations with Millennials, who tend to be hungry to learn from their "elders"? Are employers capitalizing on the institutional knowledge of these seasoned employers to stave off the inevitable brain drain?

Summary

Part Two objectives focused on appreciating that multidimensional growth opportunities are non-negotiable Millennial requirements; providing opportunities to reconcile these growth opportunities and the knowledge organization's intellectual capital needs; examining and applying Contributing Experts' strategies for providing multidimensional growth opportunities; and identifying potential Millennial leaders through these growth opportunities.

As we move on to Part Three, Fun and Social Interaction, we have an opportunity to further discuss a significant Millennial motivational factor. For the Millennial, there is a clear and concurrent blending of advancing one's career, learning new competencies and skills, and having fun in a highly social setting at the same time. This is a fascinating generation that has moved work/life balance from a desirable to an essential attribute of the new workplace.

P A R T **3**

Fun and Social Interaction

> ***"Virtually every piece of research about Generation Why (Millennials) highlights the importance they place on fun. What may be surprising is the extreme importance Generation Why places on having fun on the job."***
>
> **–Eric Chester,** ***Employing Generation Why?***

In this part:

- Getting Started
- Fun and Social Interaction: Important Motivational Factors
- Managers and HR Professionals Need to Employ "Millennial Fun" Strategies
- Managers and HR Professionals Need to Increase Millennial Social Interaction
- Fun and Social Interaction: Examples

Getting Started

As with previous parts of this book, this part is driven by our survey of Millennial motivational factors. Responses that are relevant to this part include the value Millennials place on "managers' treatment of Millennials as colleagues," "interest in employees," "enjoyment," "humor," flexibility," and "growth." After analyzing the data, we combined similar factors. "Fun" received the fifth highest frequency of responses, and "social interaction" was close behind, as the seventh most important motivational factor. As a result, these two companion motivational factors were combined into this section.

This part focuses on the following four objectives:

- Recognize that fun and social interaction are significant motivational factors that must be acknowledged and valued as a human capital asset.
- Encourage managers and human resources professionals to incorporate strategies for the motivational factor of fun into the workplace.
- Identify organizational opportunities for incorporating technology-based and non-technology-based social interaction strategies into the workplace.
- Provide Contributing Experts' best-of-class strategies for expanding opportunities for fun and social interaction.

Fun and Social Interaction: Important Motivational Factors

As Rebecca Huntley writes in *The World According to Why: Inside the New Adult Generation,* "In order to understand why they are who they are, we need to understand their past, the world they were born into and grew up in." And while the focus of this book does not allow for a more historical generational analysis, we can look forward and describe select behaviors of what is clearly the largest youth generation in history, encompassing more than 80 million people in the United States.

They are described, in part, as adaptable, innovative, efficient, resilient, tolerant, and committed. Eric Chester, writing in *Employing Generation Why?,* states that "Ready or not, here comes Generation Why. And they're not politely knocking—they're breaking down the door. They are entering the workforce—and society—with a whole new set of attitudes, values, and beliefs."

Furthermore, Millennials expect their work environment to be fun and to provide them with a continuum of varied social interactions and even, as Martin and Tulgan write, "infinitely thrilling opportunities."

The Role and Responsibility of Managers and Human Resources Professionals

Gaining an appreciation of the importance of the motivational factors of fun and social interaction is a shared responsibility of manager, human resources professional, Millennial, and organization. There are obviously a variety of ways we can learn from each other.

From my perspective as educator and consultant, I find that Millennials are helping us rediscover what we once experienced in childhood. When you observe children at play, you become aware that in one sandbox or school-yard experience, they combine learning, play, creativity, and fun. Unfortunately, as many of us grew up—certainly the older generations—we came to understand that we "learned" in school, "played" in the park," and "had fun" in still another location.

In contrast, Gen Yers grew up with interactive media combining education and fun, so they are accustomed to learning as part of their daily lives. They are used to having unlimited options and few rules. They want high levels of fun and social interaction now, on the job, and 24/7.

In taking a closer look at the previously described set of Millennial expectations, we can see that there is actually a positive and productive correlation between Millennials' need for immediate fun and social interaction and an organization's performance expectations. A review of the following organizational inventory reinforces this observation.

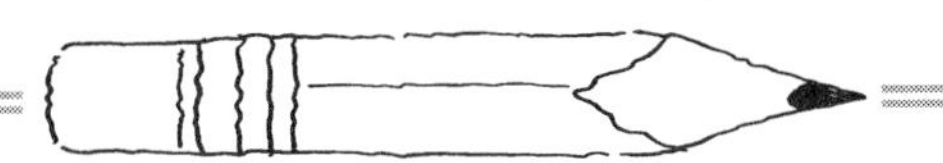

Fun and Social Interaction: An Organizational Inventory

Indicate which Millennial motivational factors your organization currently recognizes and supports, and which factors require more attention.

____ 1. "Generation Why doesn't just love fun; they are addicted to it… There is absolutely no doubt that Gen Why has no interest in a working environment that is not heavy on fun." (From *Employing Generation Why?*)

____ 2. "There's virtually no limit to what organizations will do to energize their teams with fun—and usually low-cost activities." (From *Managing the Generation Mix*)

____ 3. "If you can create an environment which is always pushing the envelope, gives people a fair amount of autonomy, involves them in decisions that affect them, and make it a fun place to work, you can create a center of excellence." (From *Managing Knowledge Workers)*

____ 4. "Human capital is the ultimate business asset. The organization with the better workforce wins. But don't equate better with skills and expertise. Human capital has three dimensions, all of which factor in the performance equation."

- Intellectual capital is what people know and learn.
- Social capital is how people form connections and share.
- Emotional capital is how much people are committed to the organization and how much of themselves they're willing to invest in its success. (From *Workforce Crisis*)

Fun and social interaction will be shown to be critically important Millennial motivational factors. In addition, they will be presented as readily accessible resources for line managers and human resources professionals. Remember, "The organization with the better workforce wins."

The Manager's Role as "Ringmaster of Fun" or "Millennial Empowerer"

While there is no doubt that Millennials place great emphasis on having fun in the workplace, "fun provider" might not be an easy leadership role for all managers to support. From a generational perspective, we know that Boomers (those individuals approximately 45–61 years old), according to Eric Chester, "believe that work is a sacrifice you make in order to enjoy life away from work. Boomers are willing to work long hours, to struggle to succeed, and to take pride in the status of difficult, involving, and high-paying jobs."

In addition, Rick Humphress, a Contributing Expert for this book, reminds us that we should also be cautious about generalizing about generational behavioral differences, when examining sociological differences is only one method of viewing behavior. He further states that when organizations apply broader talent management practices based on specific worker temperaments or types (e.g., the Myers-Briggs Type Indicator), the worker populations can be divided into sixteen categories. Taking the concept a step further, instead of thinking in terms of four generational classifications, we can suggest that there may be as many as sixteen behavioral types for each generational classification.

The point in presenting this concept is take the pressure off of managers so they don't have to think of themselves, as Eric Chester describes, as "having to be the guru of workplace fun." Instead of serving as the "guru" or "ringmaster," the manager can serve as an "empowerer of Millennials" to set the scene for incorporating fun in the workplace. The following inventory provides an opportunity for reader/practitioners to identify their own strengths and areas for development as empowerers of Millennials.

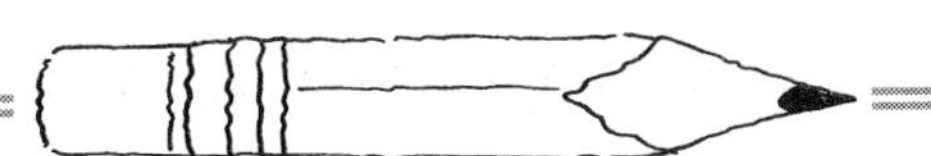

MANAGERS WALK THE "FUN" TALK: AN INVENTORY

Indicate which of the following behaviors you personally model for your Millennial workers, and which behaviors require more attention.

____ 1. "[I know that] in the eyes of the Millennial Professional, [my] credibility and respect level will skyrocket if [I] not only manage them with friendliness, but [manage] with a sense of humor (and humanness), as well." (From *Millennials Incorporated*)

____ 2. "[I] help Gen-Yers find the fun in work, such as learning new skills, building relationships with impressive people, and achieving tangible results they can put their name on." (From *Managing Generation Y*)

____ 3. "[As an] effective manager I search for innovative ways to incorporate fun into their workplace, realizing that this serves them well on several fronts." (From *Employing Generation Why?*)

____ 4. "[I] find ways to recognize and reward desired behaviors and then celebrate them." (From *Motivating the "What's in it for Me?" Workforce*)

____ 5. "[I recognize that] centers of excellence are almost always fun places to be—not just exciting work environments—but actually fun. So how do you do it?" (From *Managing Knowledge Workers*)

____ 6. "[I understand that] Millennials just want to have fun—at work... They look to the workplace as a social organization, not just a job." (From *The Trophy Kids Grow Up*)

Managers and HR Professionals Need to Employ "Millennial Fun" Strategies

The following three strategies range from the most basic to the more comprehensive. Each strategy is followed by specific tactics that you can select and employ as relevant to your needs. A final Action Plan appears at the end of this section to further heighten application potential.

Strategy One: Establish a Climate for Fun and Social Interaction

The following recommendations, from *Managing Generation Y*, offer a good starting point for the manager wanting to enhance a climate of fun and social interaction.

▶ **Create a comfortable, low-stress environment.**

There is absolutely no question, based on solid research, that Millennials find as the primary cause of stress, not the work itself, but the non-collegial management style of their supervisor. Proven "Millennial de-motivators" are managers who yell (hard to believe,) treat them as kids (unforgiveable,) and make unreasonable demands (poor management skills.) A comfortable, low-stress environment can be created by a manager providing feedback in a constructive way, making the Millennial feel comfortable, and in general presenting an easygoing and laid-back interpersonal style.

▶ **Focus on work, but be personable and have a sense of humor.**

Contrary to misconceptions, Millennials do not want an all-fun, no-work environment. On the contrary, they respect a manager who can be serious and professional about work, but at the same time have a sense of humor, risk vulnerability, and maintain a creative and upbeat environment.

▶ **Spend time getting to know your team and their capabilities.**

Managing knowledge and human capital is not a mere systems process, but rather is part of a broader human equation. While the following recommendations may appear to be drawn from a Basic Supervision 101 training course, they are nonetheless too often overlooked.

- ▷ Capitalize on informal "getting-to-know-you timeouts." Get ready for spontaneous brainstorming or coaching sessions.
- ▷ Encourage staff members to talk about what's important to them, what's on their minds.

- ▷ Plan one-on-one meetings on a consistent basis (weekly or at least biweekly).
- ▷ Encourage Gen Yers to create and maintain an achievement file or career portfolio. This is not only a great morale booster for them, but a useful tool for you.

In summary, providing opportunities to get to know your Millennial staff as colleagues, team members, and unique individuals is a sound basis for establishing a climate for fun and social interaction.

Strategy Two: Having Fun Can Start Small

For some readers/practitioners, it may be easier to recognize and appreciate the importance of the Millennial motivation factors of fun and social interaction than to implement an actual strategy. However, "having fun" in the workplace does not have to be an elaborate or complicated process. In *Managing Knowledge Workers*, Frances Horibe describes several rules of thumb that Barb MacCallum of Careerware put in place, which increased both employee retention and customer satisfaction. Here are her simple and effective suggestions:

- ▶ **Find a fun person to put in charge of events.**

  By identifying the right person to provide leadership for this initiative, you not only lighten your work load; you are also giving the task to someone who may be better suited to create fun and excitement.

- ▶ **Use the employees' standard of fun, not the manager's.**

  Even a fundamental understanding of generational attributes will quickly delineate differences in the core values, assets, and work styles of Boomers, Generation Xers, and Millennials. What may be fun for a Boomer may not be fun for a Millennial.

- ▶ **It doesn't have to be big or expensive, but it does have to include everyone.**

  Initiating a variety of corporate fun initiatives does not have to be a resource-intensive activity (time, budget, etc.). But as Contributing Expert examples will soon suggest, there needs to be a broad variety of fun and social interaction activities that are modest in cost. The activities should also be ones that everyone not only can participate in, but also want to participate in.

The previous three suggestions are presented as an accessible starter kit. It is intended as a low-risk, high-reward Millennial motivational strategy.

Strategy Three: Implementing a Multidimensional Fun Strategy

The Motivational Factors Survey that was used to shape the contents of this book clearly placed "fun" in the top-ten list of Millennial motivators. And the fact that almost any book on Millennials, knowledge workers, and managing the mix of generations addresses the subject of fun further reinforces the importance of this motivational factor.

Perhaps the most thorough and strategic treatment of the subject appears in Eric Chester's book *Employing Generation Why? Understanding, Managing, and Motivating Your New Workforce*. In his book, he states, "Generation Why doesn't just love fun; they're addicted to it… For them, work is no different from going to school or a friend's house or even an amusement park." Here are Chester's three suggestions:

1. **"Make fun through competition."**

   "Appeal to the game playing nature of Gen Y. They absolutely love to compete, especially when the winner is recognized and rewarded." However: "Be leery of contests where employees continually compete against each other for a single prize. Instead, get them to support each other by pitting them against a very achievable goal where everyone eventually does the victory dance."

2. **"Make fun through participation."**

   "When Generation Why is participating, they're engaged. When they're not, they're disengaged. It's that simple. Companies that learn how to appeal to their innate desire to express themselves through creative participation in the process … find that they can capture the soul and release the imagination of a very inventive resource." Eric Chester adds, "Find a way to point a spotlight in their direction, and you'll get a command performance."

3. **"Make fun through interaction."**

   "Today's … members of Gen Why are starting to demand social interaction. … As a result, Generation Why is trying to compensate by seeking jobs where they can work alongside their friends and where social interaction isn't penalized." "Instead of being the ringmaster, empower your young employees to create their own fun by simply providing an atmosphere conducive to social interaction."

Continuing Expert best-of-class examples and research suggest that when a sense of fun and social interaction is introduced into a workplace, and this is balanced with a clear delineation of roles and responsibilities, both Millennials and their organizations benefit.

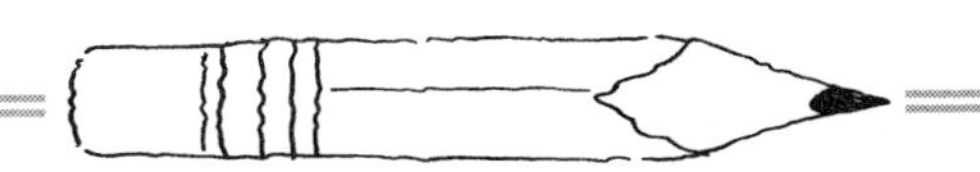

A "Fun" Action Plan

Review each of the following nine tactics and indicate which are the most relevant to your organization's efforts to employ fun and social interaction as motivators.

____ 1. Create a comfortable, low-stress environment.

____ 2. Focus on work, but be personable and have a sense of humor.

____ 3. Spend time getting to know your team members and their abilities.

____ 4. Find a "fun" person and put him or her in charge of events.

____ 5. Use the employees' standard of fun, not the manager's.

____ 6. It doesn't have to be big or expensive, but it does have to include everyone.

____ 7. Create fun through competition.

____ 8. Create fun through participation.

____ 9. Create fun through interaction.

There is an infinite number of ways to enhance the "Fun Factor." The most important concept is that you are embracing the concept as a strategy that not only enhances the quality of the workplace, but also unlocks the intellectual capital of your organization. This turns impending demographic challenges—a deficit of younger workers—into a managerial opportunity.

Managers and HR Professionals Need to Increase Millennial Social Interaction

While results from the Millennial Motivational Factors survey and related examples demonstrate fun and social interaction as integrated motivators, further discussion of social interaction is warranted.

A Portrait of Millennials: Social Interaction

Millennials do not just want their job to be fun; they want their workplace to be a social organization. The examples of our Contributing Experts, as well as dozens of books, research studies, and recruitment campaigns, all reinforce this accelerating trend. Ron Alsop, writing in *The Trophy Kids Grow Up,* states that "Some companies are helping young employees find opportunities to socialize together both at work and after hours. Such activities build camaraderie as employees get better acquainted with each other and learn about common interests."

Social Interaction and Technology

Much of this part outlines the Millennials' high need for social interaction. However, we cannot overlook the fact that Millennials are described as "growing up digital," with computer games, cell phones, and the Internet as a given.

In *Workforce Crisis*, Dychtwald, Erickson, and Morison state that "For them, technology is not an occasional tool, but a constant extension of themselves. They are accustomed to instant communication and long-distance collaboration. For many purposes, they prefer phone contact, email, or instant messaging to face-to-face communication."

The ability to increase social interaction through technology has enormous potential for the Millennial knowledge worker. In *Generation Blend: Managing Across the Technology Gap,* Rob Salkowitz illustrates how technology and generational differences are on a collision course. However, he also proactively provides solutions to reconciling the best that younger and older workers have to offer. In his discussion of Millennials in the workforce, he makes several points related to technology and the motivational factor of social interaction.

- **Raised to collaborate**

  Millennials have been raised to collaborate. And an ever-expanding constellation of technology (including social networking sites) allows for self expression, instant person-to-person contact, and communal activities around shared interests.

- **Global orientation**

  The Millennials' world is far more expansive than previous generations'. Through online social networks, they can reach beyond the confines of geography to establish relationships with others.

- **Personal networks at work**

  Not only do Millennials require remote access and mobility, but they also require access to personal networks at work.

- **Positive social interactions**

  The technological aspects of Millennial work styles have positive social and organizational implications. Collaboration tools can be used to create cross-disciplinary communities, communities of expertise, and systems to discover new people with whom to collaborate.

Part Three of this book began by identifying Millennials as collaborative by nature, thriving on continuous feedback, supporting open communication, and seeking out social networks. Logically, they also seek out technology-driven communication and collaboration systems, portals, workspaces, and teamware. These tools not only add fun and social interaction to the workplace, but also advance organizational performance.

Fun and Social Interaction: Examples

In this section, several Contributing Experts provide examples of introducing fun and social interaction into the workplace to advance organizational performance.

Fun and Social Interaction at The Urban Institute

Deborah K. Hoover, HR Director
The Urban Institute

Whether it's the annual holiday party, a summer picnic, a softball team, or more serious research-oriented staff activities, Institute staff enjoy interacting with their colleagues. Without question, exit interview responses to the question about "What staff liked best" are resoundingly "the people."

The RAA Discussion Series is a particularly good example of how Millennials have serious fun at work. The discussion series began as an attempt by management to integrate young researchers more into the intellectual life of the Institute. However, over time the discussion series has morphed into a social and learning community that is self-governed and led by the participants. The group, which consists primarily of researchers in their early to late 20s, meets monthly with senior leadership and senior research staff. At these gatherings, junior researchers hear from nationally known experts in their policy fields and have the opportunity to network with the experts and their colleagues from other research programs.

In addition, the group hosts social functions (happy hours, outings in D.C., etc.) and organizes an annual Institutional charitable activity serving the larger D.C. metropolitan community. This group addresses several motivational factors particularly relevant to Millennials. In all, it is a blend of fun, socializing, and learning that speaks to employees across levels as they share ideas, argue policy, and get to know each other as people.

Creating an Enjoyable Work Environment

Kitty Nix, Director, Strategic Development
Helios HR

The following quiz will help you assess your organization's progress in creating a work environment that Millennials are likely to enjoy.

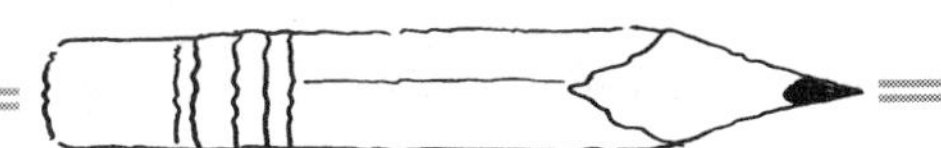

Is Your Workplace Fun?: A Quiz

Select a colleague with whom you work closely and discuss each of the following items. At the end of the discussion, see if you can reach consensus regarding whether your workplace provides a "fun" environment.

	Yes	No
1. Can you think of a time when you saw the CEO or a member of the senior management team laugh?	❑	❑
2. Does your organization have regular social events such as family picnics, holiday parties, or social hours?	❑	❑
3. Do groups of people regularly go out to lunch together?	❑	❑
4. Does your organization publicly recognize individual and team contributions?	❑	❑
5. Does your office have a place for employees to gather informally, such as a break room or lounge?	❑	❑
6. Does your employer encourage employees, including recent hires and junior employees, to generate creative ideas for having fun?	❑	❑
7. Does your organization celebrate individual milestones such as anniversaries, birthdays, weddings, babies, and so forth?	❑	❑
8. Does your company have a regular newsletter that includes humorous articles?	❑	❑

Action Plan: What recommendations can you and your colleague make to increase the fun in your workplace? How would it increase social interaction? Productivity? Retention?

____

____

____

____

____

Fun and Social Interaction: Four Examples

Neil Sawyer, Senior Director of Human Resources
The Campagna Center

With many companies experiencing lean times, my experiences with one organization in particular demonstrate the Millennial motivators of fun and social interaction. The organization put together an informal program of social events, excursions, and community outreach initiatives that are low cost and employee driven.

Habitat for Humanity

One program provides paid time off for employees who volunteer for Habitat for Humanity. The initial thought was to give employees incentives to take an active part in an outreach program that is related to our industry. Employees can take hours off or a full day. The company goes a step further by making a matching contribution to Habitat for Humanity. This appeals to many younger employees who are socially conscious and eager to be involved at a grassroots level. Employees are encouraged to make monetary contributions throughout the year with matching funds being given by the company.

Low-Cost Trips and Social Events

This company has held many low-cost trips and social events. Employees are often willing to pay their own way for social events and excursions as long as the planning is done and in place. Weekend day trips to New York or Atlantic City have been very successful. The company rents the tour bus, offers a discounted rate for employees, and provides convenient pickup/drop-off times and places. Employees like the convenience of being able to pay and go.

The value in this strategy is that employees get to do things that they might not do if the planning was entirely their own. The company benefits by the increased interactions between employees who might not have any contact during a workday. It is simple to put together—the company provides the place or means of travel, the employees provide the rest. After years of doing this, we have never had an employee express anything but gratefulness for the generosity of the company for providing the outlet for socializing.

Partnering with Local Businesses

Another way we have brought discounted outings to employees is to partner with local businesses. Newly established businesses are often looking for endorsements from companies with name recognition. In exchange for the right of the business owner to say that our company is a valued customer, he or she will offer (sometimes deep) discounts to our employees. Everything from Paintball excursions to dining to rentals and hotel stays have been discounted to staff on a regular basis. To many of the younger and lower-paid employees, this is a valuable perk of the job.

A Free Day Off

One of our biggest perks comes in the form of a free day off. This day is usually around an established holiday but is not always linked to it. The CEO of the company is the sole determiner of what days they will be. There is seldom any significant advance notice. The CEO will send out an e-mail message about some aspect of life or an amusing story to all staff. At the end of the message, he will tie it into a good reason to take the day off. Employees have come to enjoy his writings as much as having the free day off.

Fun and Social Interaction: From Google to Online Recruiting Company

Christopher R. Ryan, Deputy General Counsel
K12 Inc.

Google's Headquarters and Satellite Offices

The media regularly report on leading work environments that provide amusing and entertaining opportunities for their employees, fueling Millennials' expectations that work will also be fun. Reports on the work environment at Google's headquarters and satellite offices almost sound too good to be true: gourmet cafeterias; not just a foosball table but complete game rooms; relaxation "pods"; on-site masseuses; slides instead of stairwells; a bring-your-pet-to-work policy—these are just a handful of examples.

Unfortunately, most companies aren't as fortunate as Google to have a market capitalization of over $100 billion and over $15 billion in cash on hand. Google also has the advantage of being a technology company that adopted an offbeat and fun culture at the time of its founding, achieved tremendous success very quickly, and managed to maintain its original culture. As a result of Google's unusual situation, it is impossible for companies to simply adopt the Google model; however, there are things that every company can do to foster fun and frivolity.

An Online Recruiting Company

For example, an online recruiting company I worked for cultivated a fun work environment as a way to attract, motivate, and retain its young workforce. A company-sponsored softball team welcomed players of all abilities and held post-game celebrations—win or lose, of course. The kitchen area featured satellite televisions with remote controls. Employees did not spend hours during the day watching their favorite shows, but they did enjoy the brief escape that the television provided as they heated up their lunch in the microwave or took a short break. There was also a foosball room, which was most frequently occupied long after the close of business by software developers who needed a diversion from a long day of coding.

Upon closing a deal, members of the sales department were encouraged to hit a full-size gong that resonated throughout the entire floor to announce their achievement. While a loud gong sound was admittedly a bit distracting at times, it was also an important reminder that the company had obtained a new customer and additional revenue to fuel the company's operations and future growth. Additionally, each department had its own "break out" room that department members designed themselves, within a specified budget.

Despite, or possibly because of, this concentration on fun, the company was very successful and was able to attract a steady stream of new workers as it grew. While a traditional manager or employer might have viewed these fun activities as counterproductive distractions, companies have to adapt to the expectations and work habits of Millennials.

Today's Millennial workers, at least the realistic ones who are in the majority, understand that they cannot expect to work in an environment that is as fun and whimsical as the "Googleplex" (Google even has a fun name for their headquarters building). At the same time, any initiatives that a company can take to inject a little entertainment and amusement into the workplace will satisfy Millennials' expectations for fun and should result in higher job satisfaction, lower attrition rates, and therefore more productivity from this next generation of workers.

Fun and Social Interaction at HireStrategy

Hector Velez, Executive Vice President
HireStrategy

HireStrategy goes beyond the simple balance of the professional and the personal. HireStrategy espouses and acts on a philosophy of not only balance, but integration as well. Our exceedingly dedicated staff members, due to their work ethic and business demands, already make work part of their personal lives. It only makes sense that there is some *quid pro quo*. HireStrategy supports the insertion of employees' personal lives into the workplace. For example, an individual who is "plugged in" 24/7 should have, and does have, the flexibility to leave "early" to attend a child's soccer practice.

In addition to our annual performers club trip to a sunny locale, HireStrategy holds both offsite Annual Kick-Offs and Quarterly Meetings. These meetings include team-by-team reporting on business results, analysis, and plans. But they also include a fun outing. Examples of fun outings range from a day at Dave & Busters to a day at Strike Bethesda. In between, we also have team-building exercises such as "Positive Flooding." Every employee gets an opportunity to hear all of his or her colleagues articulate positive attributes about them!

HireStrategy's annual holiday party includes the employees along with their spouses/partners or significant others. Every party has a different theme. Last year we had a Casino Night, complete with a Pit Boss and croupiers/dealers at the different tables.

Other fun activities include:

- Bagel Wednesdays (free bagels for the staff)
- Monthly all-hands meetings (recognitions of birthdays, HireStrategy anniversaries, and so on)
- Outings to live performances
- Happy hours
- Sports (tag football, softball, etc.)

Most important, "fun" and "social interaction" are not extraneous organizational activities, but are rather a fluent extension of the HireStrategy culture. It is not by accident that employees can be heard saying "This is a great place to work."

Further Discussion

Shira Harrington, Director, Professional Search Positions, Inc.

Contributing Expert Christopher Ryan aptly notes, "While a traditional manager or employer might have viewed these fun activities as counterproductive distractions, companies have to adapt to the expectations and work habits of Millennials."

This concept of creating a fun workplace to accommodate Millennials can be a source of contention for many older workers, particularly Boomers and Veterans, who don't believe that this type of fun has any place in a serious work environment. Many corporate cultures are not nearly as progressive or Millennial-friendly as Google. In fact, some in corporate America have not even adopted any sort of flexible scheduling, let alone days off for volunteer activities. The challenge for many employers will, again, be overcoming old mindsets with relation to incorporating fun into the workplace.

Many Boomer (and even older Gen X) managers struggle with the seemingly ongoing social interactions that many Millennials engage in throughout the day. What was once the occasional "water-cooler talk" for older workers has become an elongated social bonding between Millennials that can cause their managers to believe (rightly or wrongly) that work is simply not getting done.

Although for many Millennials, work and social interaction are one and the same, perception can be reality when it comes to performance management. How do employers change the mindsets of seasoned professionals when it comes to *how* and *when* work gets done? How do we truly move beyond face time and allow Millennials needed fun time in the workplace?

Summary

This part focused on four key points. First, fun and social interaction are significant motivational factors that must be acknowledged and valued as human capital assets. Second, managers and human resources professionals must incorporate strategies to integrate fun in the workplace. Third, opportunities for incorporating technology- and non-technology-based social interaction strategies must also be incorporated into the workplace. Finally, Contributing Experts provided a variety of examples of how fun and social interaction meet Millennial motivational needs.

The authors of *Workforce Crisis* state, "What many young people need most to feel happy in a company is the continuous opportunity to learn and grow through frequent changes in roles, responsibilities, and programs." The opportunity to work for an organization that reflects their personal values and beliefs provides a variety of platforms to make a significant contribution and is almost an extension of their need for on-the-job fun and social interaction.

PART 4

Purpose, Contribution, and Challenging Work

> *"Generation Y employees [Millennials] bring specific values and ideals to the business world that ultimately will alter workplace policies and management strategies. Companies that make an effort to understand and act upon these professionals' viewpoints will find themselves with a dedicated and ambitious group of workers."*
>
> –from *What Millennial Workers Want: How to Attract and Retain Gen Y Employees*

In this part:

- Getting Started
- New Rules for Employment: Placing Millennials in Perspective
- The Millennials' Need to Make and Be Recognized for their Contributions
- The Manager's Role in Motivating Millennials as Contributors
- Challenging Work: Global, National, and Organizational Issues

Getting Started

As with previous parts of this book, this part is driven by our survey of Millennial motivational factors. Responses that are relevant to this part include the value Millennials place on "purpose," "contribution," "challenging work," "passion for work," "fast cycle work environment," "accomplishment," and "pride in work environment." After analyzing the data, we combined similar factors. Since "purpose," "contribution," and "challenging work" appeared in the top eleven frequencies of responses and are closely interrelated as motivational factors, they were combined and emerged as Part Four: Purpose, Contribution, and Challenging Work.

Common themes that appear in a variety of Millennial books, research studies, and the workplace are the Millennials' sense of purpose, the desire to contribute, and the need for challenging work. For a variety of reasons, Millennials begin work by setting tremendous goals for themselves. As Cam Marston states in *Motivating the "What's in it for Me?" Workforce*, "They know what they want to do and where they want to be." He goes on to say, "They have no idea how to get there, mostly because they lack sufficient experience to create the blueprint that will get them from where they are today to their goals. And that is where their bosses come into the picture."

Cam Marston's statement reinforces the objectives of this part. Helping the Millennial knowledge worker to find purpose, opportunities to contribute, and challenging work is a shared, collaborative responsibility of the Millennial, the manager, and the organization. This premise drives the objectives of this part:

- Recognize that Millennials have a strong sense of purpose that drives their careers and lives. They expect their employer to provide flexible opportunities to meet this need.
- Acknowledge that Millennials have a profound need to be recognized for the contributions they make to their workplaces and society.
- Understand that Millennial knowledge workers are high-achieving multitaskers requiring a variety of challenging assignments and projects.

New Rules for Employment: Placing Millennials in Perspective

The challenge of motivating Millennial knowledge workers is significantly influenced by a trend that started well over a decade ago. It has been exacerbated by current economic conditions, requiring organizations to reinvent themselves in order to address a global economic crisis.

More specifically, William Bridges wrote, as far back as 1994, that "the old rules [of employment] are gone. Finished. Disappeared and left no forwarding address." These "old rules," which, fortunately, Millennials and Gen Xers have little knowledge of, were built on the following four-point paradigm. Quoting Bridges directly (from *JobShift*):

> ***Yesterday's organizations, built on the job paradigm,***
>
> — ***'located' the employee at a particular level on a vertical hierarchy, responsible to the person above and responsible for the people (if any) below;***
>
> — ***'located' the employee horizontally, as well, in a department or functional unit that was responsible for some particular kind of work, for example, engineering, accounting, or sales;***
>
> — ***gave each employee a well-defined area of responsibility, which was formalized in a job description;***
>
> — ***laid out before ambitious employees "career paths" that they could aspire to follow upward through the hierarchy ... —a stepping-stone path of jobs toward greater power and financial reward.***

As previously stated, these old rules are gone. Interestingly, the "new rules" for employment, outlined by Bridges in 1994, are remarkably similar to the Millennial knowledge workers' need for their organizations to help them find a sense of purpose through flexible employment opportunities and work assignments. The following organizational assessment is based on material appearing in *JobShift*.

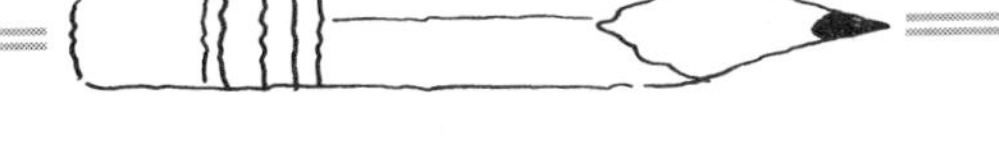

New Rules for Employment and Millennial Motivational Needs

Review each of the following statements and identify those strategies and tactics your organization currently embraces in support of the motivation factor of purpose. Also, identify those that need more attention.

New Employment Rules	Currently Supports	Needs Attention
1. Everyone is a contingent worker. Everyone's employment is contingent on the results the organization can achieve.	❑	❑
2. Recognizing the turbulence in the business environment, Millennials need to regard themselves as people whose value to the organization must be demonstrated in each successive situation they find themselves in.	❑	❑
3. Workers need to develop a mindset, and a way of managing their own careers, that is more like an external vendor than like a traditional employee.	❑	❑
4. Companies will work with these new-style workers collaboratively to make the relationship as mutually beneficial as possible.	❑	❑
5. Workers must be able to switch their focus rapidly from one task to another, to work in situations where the group is the responsible party and the manager only a coordinator, to work without clear-cut job descriptions, and to work on several projects at a time.	❑	❑
6. Ultimately, it is the Millennials who must manage their careers and lives.	❑	❑

As a result of completing the previous assessment, I have identified the following strategy to utilize the motivational factor of Purpose:

____

____

____

Reconciling Millennials' and Managers' Expectations

For the purpose of this part, the Millennial motivational factors of purpose, contributions, and challenging work are treated separately. This approach allows for the presentation of a broad variety of strategies and examples. However, in reality, managers and human resources professionals will find that they will be required to address all three motivational factors concurrently.

Millennials' Purpose Expectations

- Work that is personally stimulating
- Work that makes a true impact on social issues, the environment, labor standards, globalization, diversity, and corporate citizenship
- Work that is of demonstrable value to their organization, clients, and community

Managers' Purpose Expectations and Strategies

- Manage Millennials' expectations in a way that pays off for both employee and employer
- Show new hires how their work makes a difference and why it is valuable to the organization
- Offer a rich variety of opportunities to advance their careers
- As a boss, inspire Millennials in their work and lead them
- Engage in the types and frequency of communication that Millennials prefer
- Provide challenging work that is purposeful and really matters
- Ensure that Millennials know why they are doing whatever it is they are doing
- Communication "just in time" and "all the time"

Communicating Purpose

The previous discussion works with the assumption that Millennial knowledge workers have a desire to do purposeful work and to make a significant contribution to their organization and, most often, society. A recurring theme in reconciling Millennial and manager expectations is the mutual responsibility to collaborate and communicate. Contributing Expert Sue McLeod of Hay Group takes these concepts a step further in sharing the importance of leadership style as a strategy to communication purpose.

Practice What You Preach

Sue McLeod, Senior Consultant
Hay Group

Hay Group's research into effective leaders shows that there are six basic leadership styles, and successful leaders use them all—in the right situation.

The younger generation's desire to do purposeful work and to make significant contributions requires their leaders and managers to use a Visionary Leadership style. You're using the Visionary Leadership style when you:

- Communicate your organization's goals, mission, and strategy, including the contribution to your customers and society.
- Explain why a project, job, or task is important to achieving the mission.
- Remind employees how their contributions (no matter how small) make a difference to the organization, the customer, and their colleagues.

There are also styles that will diminish employee engagement over time, especially with employees who want to understand their purpose and feel like part of the team. Be careful if you find yourself using the Directive style, which is focused on immediate compliance, uses "directives" (often referred to as the "command and control" style), and motivates with the threat of negative consequences. You're using the Directive style when you:

- Tell employees what to do and how to do it.
- Finish your instructions (either out loud or in your head) with some variation of "Or else…."
- Answer "Why?" with some variation of "Because I said so."
- Closely monitor your employees, ready to give another directive (or threat) if they deviate from the defined task.

The Millennials' Need to Make and Be Recognized for their Contributions

In *Millennials Rising: The Next Great Generation*, Neil Howe and William Strauss state, "The Millennial future is what America is destined to become—and soon… With Millennials rising, America needs to start thinking bigger. Test them. Challenge them. Put difficult tasks before them, and have faith that they can do themselves and their nation proud." This enthusiastic statement, made in 2000, has become today's reality. And it is not a coincidence that the Motivational Factors Survey resulted in "Contributions" being ranked high on the list. Perhaps the most effective way to discuss the motivational factor of contribution is to view it through the twin lenses of Millennial and manager.

Millennials as Visionary Contributors

Rob Salkowitz's recent book *Generation Blend* captures the ultimate power of the Millennials' potential contribution to the workplace in Chapter Eight, titled "Ambassadors of the Future: Turning to Younger Workers for Strategic Insights." He begins and ends the chapter with research-based statements that I am taking the liberty of reformatting as a "Declaration of Intent."

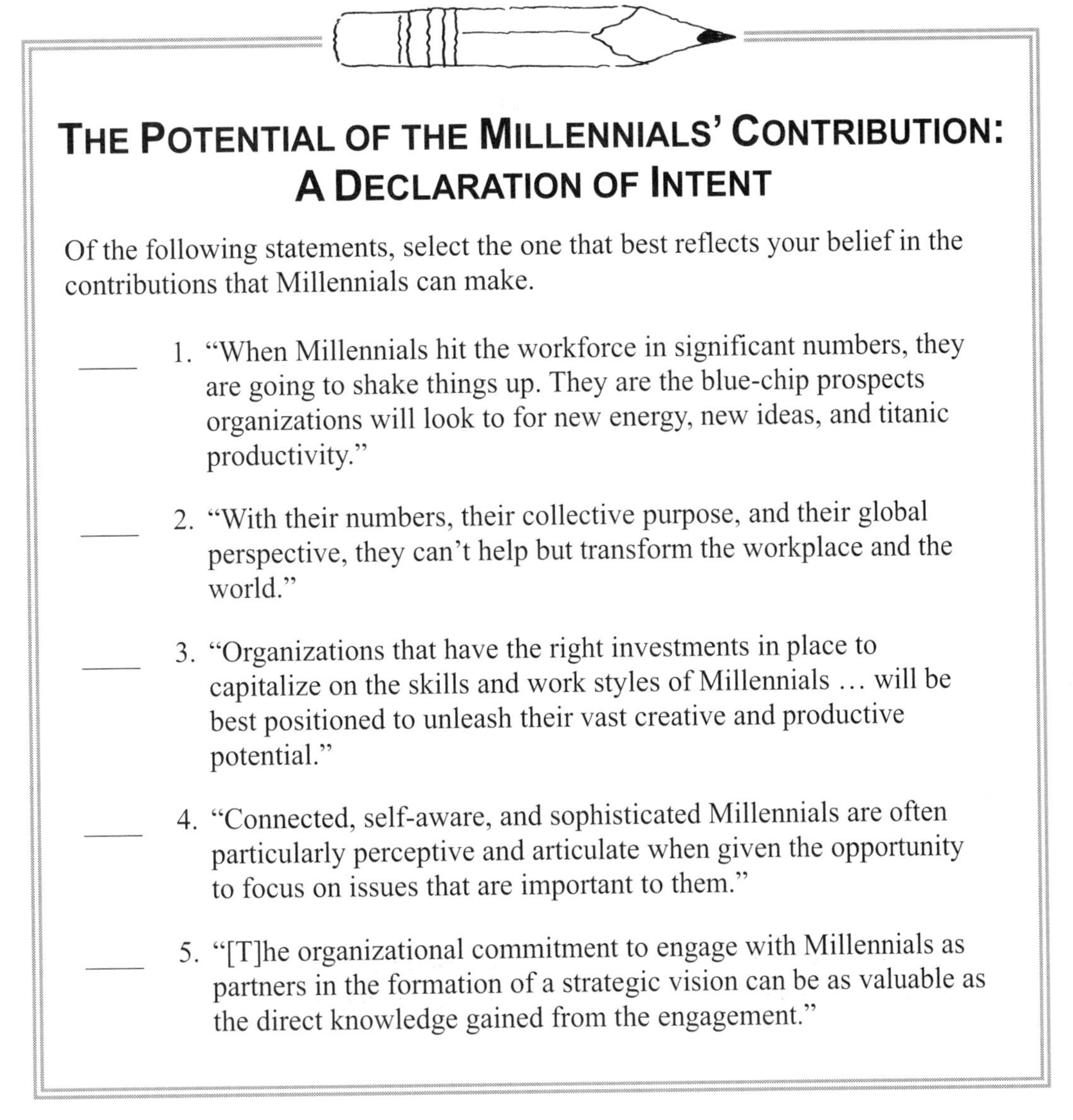

The Potential of the Millennials' Contribution: A Declaration of Intent

Of the following statements, select the one that best reflects your belief in the contributions that Millennials can make.

____ 1. "When Millennials hit the workforce in significant numbers, they are going to shake things up. They are the blue-chip prospects organizations will look to for new energy, new ideas, and titanic productivity."

____ 2. "With their numbers, their collective purpose, and their global perspective, they can't help but transform the workplace and the world."

____ 3. "Organizations that have the right investments in place to capitalize on the skills and work styles of Millennials … will be best positioned to unleash their vast creative and productive potential."

____ 4. "Connected, self-aware, and sophisticated Millennials are often particularly perceptive and articulate when given the opportunity to focus on issues that are important to them."

____ 5. "[T]he organizational commitment to engage with Millennials as partners in the formation of a strategic vision can be as valuable as the direct knowledge gained from the engagement."

There is no doubt that Millennials bring a set of very special strengths to the workplace. They are, as the previous statements suggest, adaptable, creative, independent thinkers, and quick learners. And they seek opportunities to contribute right away. With this appreciation of the rich contributions that Millennials can make, the question to answer is how managers motivate and engage Millennials so they actually contribute.

Millennials as Contributing Leaders

As many of our reader/practitioners know, you do not have to be a manager to be a leader. In fact, many Millennials would suggest that their manager might not be a leader. At the same time, as there is increasingly greater professionalization of the workforce—knowledge workers—and a corresponding flattening of organizational management levels, there is a tremendous opportunity for Millennials to emerge as leaders. This is what Jennell Evans, Contributing Expert, describes in the following example.

The Emerging Leaders Institute

Jennell Evans, President and CEO
Strategic Interactions

In addition to contributing to their employers' goals, Millennials seek opportunities to serve in their community, which connects to their desire for work/life balance. A great example of this is the overwhelming successful Emerging Leaders Institute, an initiative of Leadership Fairfax, Inc., headquartered near Tyson's Corner, Virginia.

Founded in 2003, the Emerging Leaders Institute (ELI) is an application-based program that brings together participants from all kinds of private, public, and nonprofit sectors in the Washington D.C. metro area. This nine-month program, dedicated to "inspiring, developing, and connecting young community leaders," provides opportunities for hands-on community service projects like renovating group homes or organizing food banks.

Relationships are forged through shared experiences such as group skills training, community service projects, and preparation to serve on nonprofit boards. Millennials get to see the impact of their community service work and see how they can make a difference in their own backyards.

The program has built-in feedback (Millennials love this!), with coaches and a mentor (usually a Leadership Fairfax Institute alum) assigned to each person attending the program.

Another cornerstone of the program is leadership skills training. Millennials tend to seek more responsibility and leadership opportunities earlier in their careers than did previous generations. As participants in the ELI program, they learn critical communication skills such as conflict management and negotiating.

The Manager's Role in Motivating Millennials as Contributors

There are no shortcuts to effectively manage others regardless of the generation of manager or employee. In essence, "being a good manager" means "being a good manager." But as the authors of *What Millennial Workers Want: How to Attract and Retain Gen Y Employees* state, "[F]or Millennials, having a good boss is particularly important. This is a group that has high expectations for authority figures and craves continued feedback and reinforcement. Pairing these staff members with your best managers will go a long way toward keeping these employees satisfied and productive."

Before examining specific strategies and tactics that managers can employ to maximize the contribution they make to an organization, an opportunity is presented for you to assess yourself as a Millennial "dream boss." The following assessment is based on *What Millennial Workers Want: How to Attract and Retain Gen Y Employees*, a report of survey findings by Robert Half International and Yahoo! HotJobs.

A Millennial's Portrait of a Dream Boss: A Self-Assessment

Indicate your greatest strengths and areas requiring further development. Share the results of this self-assessment with a colleague and staff member and seek feedback. Are your views of your strengths and areas to improve in concurrence with your colleague's or staff's feedback? If you want to go for bonus points, ask your Millennials to provide their feedback.

Current Strength	Future Goal	Aspects of a Dream Boss
❑	❑	Skillful manager, advisor, and supporter
❑	❑	Pleasant and easy to get along with
❑	❑	Understanding and caring
❑	❑	Flexible and open-minded
❑	❑	Respects/values/appreciates employees
❑	❑	Good communication skills

Motivating Millennials as Contributors by Understanding Millennials as Contributors

Ken Blanchard, whom you may know as the originator of the concept of the One-Minute Manager, once stated that "What motivates people is what motivates people." Building on his riddle-like statement, we can say, "Motivating Millennials as contributors begins by understanding Millennials as contributors." This requires that we understand Millennials as both Millennials and knowledge workers.

The behaviors and characteristics of the four generational groups have been influenced by a variety of events and environmental factors. This has led to the methodology of generational analysis. Since the 1991 publication of William Strauss and Neil Howe's book *Generations*, there has emerged a methodology for attracting, recruiting, managing, motivating, and retaining Millennials. While I personally agree with Contributing Expert Rick Humphress that this may be a simplification of a way to understand human behavior, the concept of generational analysis does provide a basic frame of reference.

With this concept of generational analysis as an acceptable methodology, we can move forward and describe several of the behavioral characteristics of Millennials as contributors. Lisa Orrell writes in *Millennials Incorporated*, "Although the Millennial Generation is said to be the brightest and best educated generation our country has ever seen, and even though they typically far surpass their Gen X and Boomer bosses and co-workers in the area of being tech-savvy, this unique group of young adults certainly isn't arriving to the professional world without their fair share of 'baggage.'"

MILLENNIALS AS CONTRIBUTORS: CHALLENGES AND STRATEGIES FOR THE MANAGER

Select a challenge that you face to further maximize your Millennials' contributions. Then select one or more managerial strategies to motivate Millennials and maximize their contributions.

Behavioral Challenges

____ 1. While very independent and bright, Millennials need to be given a clear path and a plan for accomplishing a task.

____ 2. They are willing to work hard and make creative contributions while "on the job," but want respect for their time outside of work with friends, family, and interests.

____ 3. There is no doubt that Millennials are goal oriented and highly productive. However, they want to know the reason for a delegation or assignment and its ultimate goal.

____ 4. They want to be free to ask questions and to share their feelings and ideas, and they want constant feedback and recognition for their contributions.

Managerial Strategies

____ 1. Establish a communication environment, in informal hallway conversations, before meetings, and during meetings, that encourages participation and contribution.

____ 2. Consider, as mentioned earlier in the book, the power of the environment. Provide open and informal spaces for collaborative engagement.

____ 3. Create a culture of continuous learning, introduction of new ideas, and a variety of assignments that provide opportunities to encourage contribution.

____ 4. Challenge and delegate nonstop. As Lisa Orrell writes, "They want to make a difference and have an unlimited capacity to contribute."

Opportunities to maximize Millennial contributions are unlimited. However, as Contributing Expert Rick Humphress previously pointed out, we must be cautious in using generations as the single differentiator of behavior. He reminds us that on an individual level, one Millennial can be quite different from another. Nonetheless, we can generalize, based on research, that Millennial knowledge workers are entrepreneurial hard workers who are techno-savvy and thrive on flexibility.

Organizations, managers, and human resources professionals can maximize Millennial contributions by customizing work responsibilities, designing flexible and responsive career paths, and providing education and training opportunities. Maximizing Millennial contributions depends on being able to answer the questions that Millennials typically ask, as presented in *Managing Generation Y*:

- What value can I add today?
- What can I learn today?
- What will you offer me today?
- How will I be rewarded today?

Understanding Millennials as Knowledge Workers

In the broadest sense, Millennials are defined by anchor years that identify an age cohort ranging from 19 to 30 years of age. As discussed earlier in the book, different researchers differ slightly in defining the age range. However, the focus of this book is not on Millennials who can work in a variety of service, manufacturing, or technology industries. This book focuses on Millennial knowledge workers, who are defined by Frances Horibe as those "who [use their] head more than their hands to produce value" and most likely are college educated.

In order to maximize the Millennials' contributions to the workplace, one must also understand this Millennial knowledge worker. This group includes a broader population than just computer programmers. As Frances Horibe writes in *Managing Knowledge Workers*, "knowledge workers are not just employees in high-tech companies. People in advertising agencies, consulting companies, financial institutions—anyone who uses their head more than their hands to create wealth—are all knowledge workers." From this perspective, then, it's clear that additional strategies are needed.

Consultation and Involvement: Strategies for Engagement

In order to maximize the hard-working, achievement-oriented attributes of Millennial knowledge workers, organizations must embrace strategies of consultation and involvement to increase engagement. Following is a brief explanation of each strategy and its advantages, and an application exercise.

Engagement Strategy One: The Consultation Process

In *Managing Knowledge Workers*, Frances Horibe provides us with a formal definition of the consultation process and the advantages of using it as a strategy to heighten knowledge workers' contributions:

> ***"Consultation is a process by which management seeks the opinion of employees on important issues of the day. It is primarily about testing the waters since, with consultation, the right to decide the issue is with management. Consulting allows employees to express an opinion about their future."***

According to Horibe, the following are the advantages of using the consultative strategy to increase contribution:

- Employees will contribute their intellectual capital only if they believe their opinion counts.
- One way to show employees that their opinions matter is to consult them on corporate issues.
- Issues on which employees are consulted must be both substantive and amenable to influence.
- Employees must understand that they are being consulted, not asked to approve a decision, and that a consensus is not necessary.

The Consultation Process: An Application Opportunity

1. Does a consultation strategy appear relevant to increasing your Millennial knowledge workers' contributions?
2. If so, indicate how you apply it.

   Specific individual ______________________________

   Corporate issue ______________________________

   When used______________________________

   How implemented______________________________

   Anticipated outcome ______________________________

Engagement Strategy Two: Involvement

Frances Horibe introduces another strategy to increase knowledge worker contributions by tapping the organization's intellectual capital through involvement. A definition of involvement, a list of advantages of using it, and another application opportunity follow.

The involvement process is a strategy that asks individuals to decide or recommend on major challenges. "Not only will this approach bring to light more of the implicit knowledge people have of what might work, [but] it will also challenge their creativity and reinforce their belief that you value their opinions and knowledge" (Horibe). As a reader/practitioner, you can appreciate this strategy's potential to increase the Millennial knowledge worker's contributions.

According to Horibe, the following are the advantages of using the involvement strategy to increase contributions:

- Involvement will increase knowledge workers' commitment to the organization, though it will take some time.
- It demonstrates that the employees' opinions count.
- To help the process, a person should be appointed to challenge a function, and all team members should be briefed on the complexities of the issues they are tackling and be trained on how to work as a team.
- While this process doesn't necessarily produce better decisions, it does produce ones to which employees are more committed.

INVOLVEMENT: AN APPLICATION OPPORTUNITY

1. Does an involvement strategy appear relevant to increasing your Millennial knowledge workers' contributions?
2. If so, indicate how you apply it.

   Specific individual ______________________

   Corporate issue ______________________

   When used ______________________

   How implemented ______________________

   Anticipated outcome ______________________

Both the consultation and involvement strategies have the potential to increase the employee's engagement in the workplace. Each strategy has its own advantage. However, as Horibe states, "Involvement changes not merely how work is accomplished, but how completely the heart and brain are involved in the company's business." This is clearly a motivational factor.

Structure, Direction, and Deadlines

There is no doubt that understanding Millennials as contributors and engaging them through consultation and involvement strategies can motivate them. The previously presented strategies provide an opportunity to show that their work makes a difference and is of value to the organization. In addition, it provides an opportunity for the Millennial knowledge worker to participate in work that is stimulating and challenging. And finally, the use of these strategies demonstrates that their work clearly benefits internal and external customers and at times even the community at large.

However, there is also a potential challenge in employing these strategies with Millennials. Research indicates that Millennials require structure and supervision. A review of Millennial research results in the following recommendations.

- Millennials require "regular checking in" by their supervisors to assist with obstacles, answer questions, and to provide guidance.
- Millennial professionals ask "why?" a lot. They want to know a reason for the request, the purpose, and the ultimate goal.
- Nothing should be assumed. Lay out the big picture in clear terms.
- Millennials require careful handling when their performance is not up to par.
- Managers need to provide Millennials with an unusual amount of handholding, reminding them of project deadlines.

In an effort to maximize the Millennials' contributions to the workplace, they need structure and explicit direction. The recommendation to give them a checklist and then be sure that they get the job done appears in a variety of books and studies.

Managers also need to provide specific and frequent clarification of project deadlines. Millennials require encouragement to take some chances and learn from their inevitable mistakes. Finally, managers can teach Millennials to break problems into more manageable units and determine which data are most relevant to the solution.

The manager who recognizes the Millennials' need for structure, direction, deadlines, and clarity can meet not only individual needs, but also organizational needs.

Challenging Work: Global, National, and Organizational Issues

Recent events dramatize a problem far more critical than simply addressing the need to provide Millennials with challenging work. *Workforce 2020: Work and Workers in the 21st Century*, published by the Hudson Institute over a decade ago, predicted the global and national economic challenges we are now facing. It emphasizes the following three principles—not just for motivating Millennials, but for America to maintain its position in a fiercely competitive global economy:

- "The journey to Workforce 2020 is a journey to an uncertain destination. "
- "America must adapt the institutions shaping its labor force to new circumstances. We cannot produce twenty-first-century knowledge workers in nineteenth-century public schools, early-twentieth-century higher education institutions, or mid-twentieth-century federal job training programs."
- "Society-wide solutions will not address America's workforce challenges adequately. … Individual and local experimentation is the order of the day to provide competition in some instances and increase knowledge in others."

Creating a 21st-Century Workplace

Those of us who see the Millennials as the hero generation that will help lead us forward as knowledge workers and become a new breed of leaders recognize that the ultimate and more inclusive solution to creating a twenty-first-century workforce is, as Cam Marston writes in *Motivating the "What's In It For Me?" Workforce,* the need for our organizations to become "fast, functional, and multigenerational." Marston makes a simple, and most critical, point in stating that "Age diversity among employees will be a thorny issue for the foreseeable future. … You'd like to know how to get consistently high performance from *all* your employees." While space does not allow the necessary discussion of a four-generation workforce, the following steps are worth reviewing.

From *Motivating the "What's In It For Me?" Workforce,* here are the four steps for maximizing the productivity of a multigenerational workforce:

1. Identify the problem areas.
2. Rate your success in hiring the best talent.
3. Now that you've got them, learn how to keep your Gen X and new Millennial employees. (Related fact: According to the Bureau of Labor Statistics, the average mid-twenties employee leaves his or her job every 1.3 years.)
4. Spend time getting to know your employees.

Meeting the Contribution Needs of Millennials

Motivating the Millennial Knowledge Worker places emphasis on providing the reader/practitioner with relevant motivational strategies and tactics. This part concludes by presenting recommendations from Contributing Experts.

Provide Challenging Work that Really Matters

Those organizations that want to become a Millennial "employer of choice" must recognize that Millennials have well-documented workplace expectations. And number one, according to *Managing Generation Y* by Carolyn A. Martin, Ph.D. and Bruce Tulgan, is providing challenging work that really matters. Completing the following exercise will provide you with an opportunity to assess your organization's effectiveness in meeting this Millennial expectation.

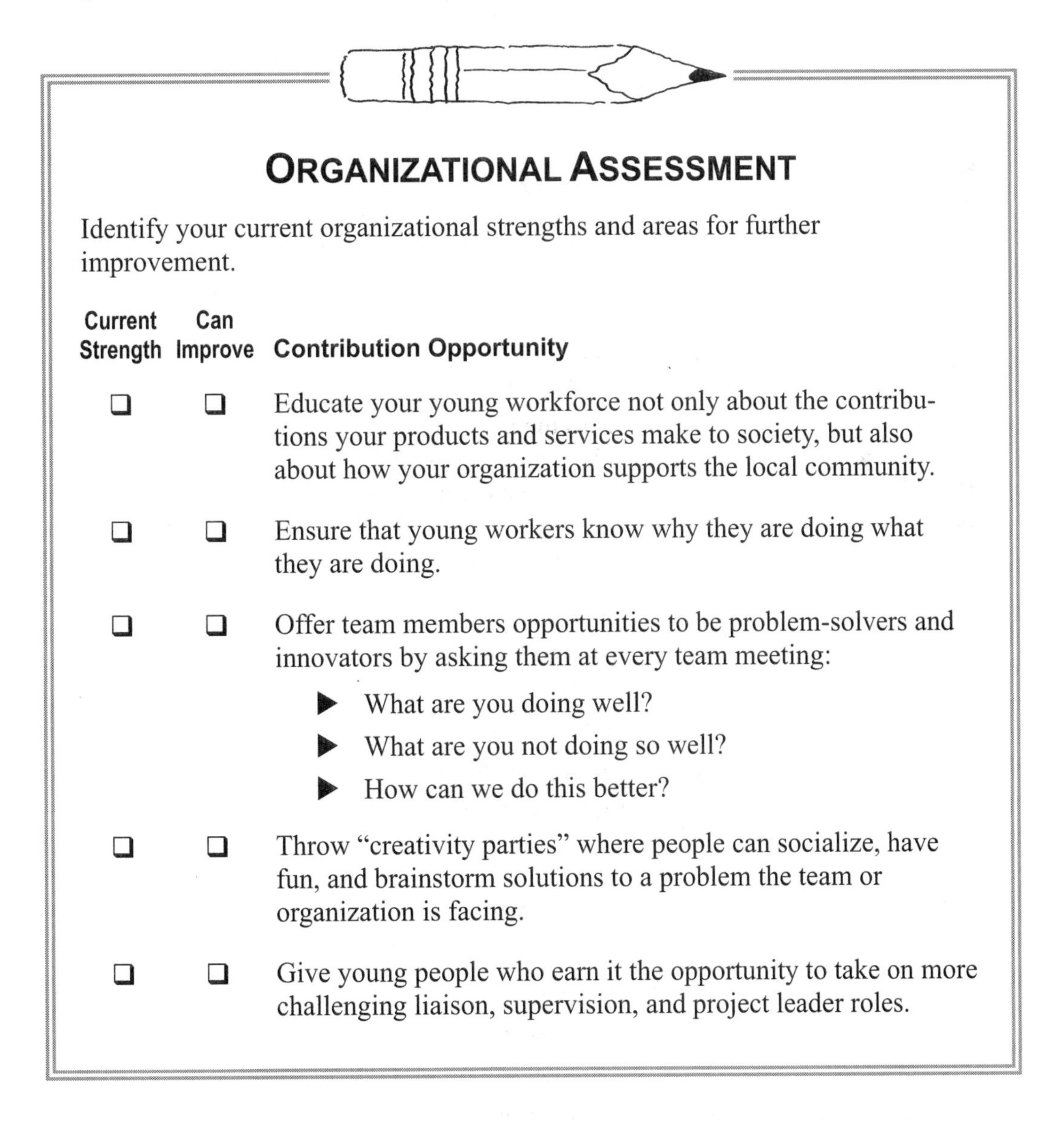

ORGANIZATIONAL ASSESSMENT

Identify your current organizational strengths and areas for further improvement.

Current Strength	Can Improve	Contribution Opportunity
❑	❑	Educate your young workforce not only about the contributions your products and services make to society, but also about how your organization supports the local community.
❑	❑	Ensure that young workers know why they are doing what they are doing.
❑	❑	Offer team members opportunities to be problem-solvers and innovators by asking them at every team meeting: ▶ What are you doing well? ▶ What are you not doing so well? ▶ How can we do this better?
❑	❑	Throw "creativity parties" where people can socialize, have fun, and brainstorm solutions to a problem the team or organization is facing.
❑	❑	Give young people who earn it the opportunity to take on more challenging liaison, supervision, and project leader roles.

Provide Meaningful Work and Engage Workers

The authors of *Workforce Crisis: How to Beat the Coming Shortage of Skills and Talents* present a fascinating recommendation that is especially relevant to motivating the Millennial knowledge worker. They suggest that "You can completely overhaul the 'employment deal' to provide flexible work arrangements, learning opportunities, and compensation and benefits, but your best employees will still leave if their work neither stimulates them nor brings out their best talents."

While common characteristics of "interesting work" are relevant to all generations, they are specifically important to the Millennial knowledge worker. I have taken the liberty of paraphrasing material that appears in *Workforce Crisis* to create the following Millennial Inventory.

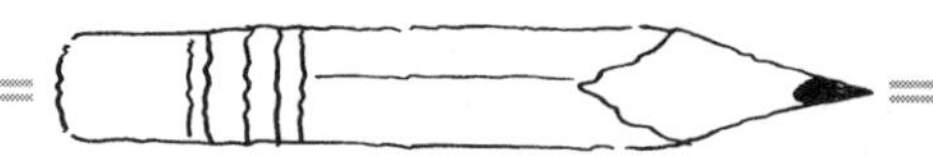

Do I Find My Work Interesting? A Millennial's Perspective

Consider distributing and discussing this exercise at your next one-on-one Millennial mentor meeting. Identify ways you can make improvements.

I find that my work provides opportunities for:

Yes	No	Sources of Interest
❑	❑	Stimulation
❑	❑	Variety
❑	❑	Edification
❑	❑	Increasing connections
❑	❑	Control
❑	❑	Value

Next, the supervisor discusses the following question with a Millennial.

My work would be more interesting if my supervisor:

____

____

____

____

Enhancing the Contribution of Senior Research Staff

Deborah Hoover
The Urban Institute

Millennial researchers often want opportunities to step out from behind those with more experience and to choose for themselves the work relationships and projects that meet their own needs for a sense of purpose and challenging work. Senior research staff can no longer simply lay out all of the design elements of a research project and then task Millennials without consideration of their wants and needs, because they just will not stand for it.

Millennials ask why things matter, why we don't do things differently, and suggest (sometimes quite strongly) alternative approaches. They are far less hesitant to turn down an assignment if they don't see it as a "true opportunity," and they simply quit if they don't see their needs being met. Whereas other employees may see some assignments as the "dues that must be paid," Millennials often decline assignments that don't meet their own personal needs and seek out those that do—even in circumstances in which management is unsupportive and/or punitive.

Managers and supervisors who link work with a sense of purpose, and challenge these bright young people early on, are clearly the most successful in terms of recruitment and retention. Unfortunately, some supervisors simply don't get it. A case in point is illustrated next:

Exit Interview

Audrey was a fabulous researcher; she was extremely accomplished, well connected, and passionate about her work and that of her staff. She recruited only the best and the brightest young researchers, but she just could not keep them. The complaints started as "grapevine" gossip and over time evolved into a dull roar. Exit interview comments include the following:

"I wanted more responsibility, more contact from my boss, and I was bored."

"The general environment—there are a lot of smart, nice people here, but not enough opportunities to bring it out of them."

"I don't feel like I'm having an impact."

And yet, in other parts of the organization, it's clear that supervisors can and do make a huge difference when they understand and work with Millennials in the ways that appeal to them:

"I was trusted with the work and given a lot of responsibility from the beginning."

"I liked the freedom I got, even at the lower level, in terms of pursuing the job I loved doing and the respect I received, even as a new employee."

Enhancing the Contribution of the Financial Services Investment Department

Kris T. Jensen, Vice President, Corporate Services
Wisdom Workers

Faced with the task of retaining and challenging administrative employees, the management team in the investment department of a global financial services giant created self-directed support teams for hundreds of real estate underwriters and investment executives. Team members were carefully selected for their willingness to make decisions, collaborate, and communicate effectively, along with their attention to detail and quality orientation.

While most employees were young and were not college graduates, older long-term employees also became part of the teams, though not always in the team leader role. Employees who were concerned about their ability or desire to work in a participative, self-directed structure were re-assigned to other areas of the company.

To align all the work groups to execute business strategies effectively, we gave each team extensive training to help them understand each other's work styles and learn how to collaborate without management intervention. Because investment employees were located on four floors, a team of service and support employees was assigned to each floor and given budget and service authority to perform on behalf of their internal "clients."

All four teams also had to coordinate assignments from one floor to another in order to keep their workloads even; e.g., when a team on one floor had more work than they could process, they could use the other three teams to supplement their staff. The teams had to negotiate and renegotiate their own clients' priorities, along with assisting a sister team.

Under the direction of the senior manager, who was ultimately responsible for the entire service system, team members participated in hiring and firing as well as in providing individual employee performance feedback. All employees were held accountable for problem solving, production, and innovation, consulting with the senior manager only when they could not identify an optimal solution or service offering.

Management focused on establishing and maintaining a work environment that assured competent teams, along with creating communication processes for regular debriefings, information exchange, and mediation processes when the teams ran into disputes they couldn't resolve themselves.

Because employees had tremendous control over their work and participated in key operational decisions while being highly accountable for products and services, this team structure allowed management to recruit and retain high-performing multigenerational employees with no turnover. Additionally, fewer than 30 employees could support more than 500 professionals.

Enhancing Contributions of Registered Nurses

Lesley Channell, Assistant Vice President of Human Resources
Dominion Hospital and Reston Hospital Center

Healthcare is not immune from having a workforce comprising four generations of workers. Over the years, there has been a lot of discussion about not "eating our young" when it comes to the orientation of new Registered Nurses. In-services on this topic have been given to our Nursing Directors and are incorporated in our Charge Nurse workshop in an effort to embrace all ages of workers. The level of technology proficiency is very high for the 21–30-year-old workers. They are very easy to train, but the Nursing Directors have noticed that these workers need a lot of reassurance and praise on a frequent basis.

The Director must be two steps ahead of young workers, thinking of projects to keep them engaged because they can become easily bored. This age group is constantly looking at ways to fix and upgrade processes. We know that an employee who has a friend at work is usually a more engaged employee. This group seems to require friends at work, versus other age groups that see that as a nicety. Working in groups provides a better work environment for them than does working alone. This group prefers a collaborative approach to working with physicians and other members of the healthcare provider team.

New grad RNs don't view being a nurse as the final destination of their career path. They typically don't want to "just be a nurse," so they are focused on obtaining a masters degree and becoming certified in their field. However, climbing the ladder cannot occur at the expense of an imbalance between work and life needs.

Further Discussion

Shira Harrington, Director, Professional Search Positions, Inc.

Jennell Evans made an excellent comment about Millennials when she aptly wrote, "As participants in the Emerging Leader Program, they learn critical communication skills such as conflict management and negotiating." Many Millennials, having been raised by doting parents who showered, and continue to shower, frequent praise on their children, are not accustomed either to receiving constructive—let alone outright negative—feedback from their bosses or to dealing with interpersonal conflicts.

In addition, with the advent of Internet search engines, many Millennials believe that if the researched information is not on Google, it must not exist. (Robert Wendover, President of Generation Trends, calls this phenomenon "menu-driven thinking," referring to the drop-down menus used in the Help function of software programs.) This, along with the trend of most Millennials having been raised in team environments, both in school and in extracurricular activities, has led to a lack of individual problem-solving abilities and strategic thinking. This is notwithstanding that they are still young and relatively inexperienced.

As a result of these variables, employers should make a concerted effort to create challenging work assignments not only to appeal to Millennials' desire for stimulating and creative work but also to purposely mentor them in resolving conflicts and thinking strategically. Future discussions should be had around specific strategies to engage and train Millennials in these two areas, because they have been socialized in such a way as to be significantly lacking in these skills, more so than other generations.

Summary

Part Four's objectives focused on three key points. First, Millennials have a strong sense of purpose that drives their careers and lives. They expect their employer to provide flexible opportunities to meet this need. Second, Millennials have a profound need to make and be recognized for the contributions they make to their workplaces and to society. And third, Millennial knowledge workers tend to be high-achieving multitaskers who require a variety of challenging assignments.

From Part Four: Purpose, Contribution, and Challenging Work, we move on to Part Five: Establishing and Sustaining Effective Communication. The manager who demonstrates the ability to understand and respond to the Millennials' communication expectations will find that he or she is also reinforcing and recognizing the importance that Millennials place on purpose, contribution, and challenging work.

PART 5

Establishing and Sustaining Effective Communication

"One of the most profound impacts of networked information and communication technology is the way it reduces—and potentially eliminates—the need for concepts such as the workplace and the workday." "The ability to manage in this kind of information-rich environment is often cited as one of the critical differences in generational workstyles."

–Generation Blend: Managing Across the Technology Age Gap

In this part:

- Getting Started
- The Importance of Establishing and Sustaining Effective Communication
- Strategies and Tactics
- Collaboration Technologies

Getting Started

As with previous parts of this book, this part is driven by our survey of Millennial motivational factors. Responses that are relevant to this part include "understanding," "treatment as colleagues," "interest in employees," "humor," "communication all the time," and "frequent feedback." Similar descriptors of motivational factors were combined, and Part Five, Establish and Sustain Effective Communication, emerged.

Further research and Contributing Experts' recommendations resulted in this part's focus on the following four objectives:

- Review the "Portrait of a Millennial" (in this book's Introduction) to reinforce the importance of establishing and sustaining effective communication.
- Acknowledge that establishing effective communication is a shared responsibility of Millennial and manager.
- Identify strategies and tactics that managers can use to establish and sustain effective communication with Millennials.
- Understand why collaborative technologies are not only promising new information tools for the enterprise, but a critical communication tool for Millennials who are highly networked on and off the job.

The Importance of Establishing and Sustaining Effective Communication

The "Portrait of a Millennial" (in this book's Introduction) is relevant as we discuss the motivational factor of establishing and sustaining effective communication. Integrating what has been described as the most demanding and coddled generation in history into the workplace is a challenge. To what degree their behavior has been shaped by the driven Baby Boomer generation, new Web 2.0 technologies, and an unpredictable and volatile global economy are all moot points.

What is relevant is an understanding of a collective portrait of Millennials as it relates to communication. The following Millennial Communication Portrait is presented as a frame of reference for this part.

MILLENNIAL COMMUNICATION PORTRAIT: 13 KEY BEHAVIORS

Select those behaviors that influence your ability to establish and sustain effective communication with Millennials.

____ 1. Millennials are trusting of their parents and other authority figures.

____ 2. Millennials are team-oriented, confident, and optimistic.

____ 3. They are a highly networked and connected generation.

____ 4. They are accustomed to receiving recognition for practically every achievement, no matter how trivial.

____ 5. They expect to be treated as special and receive constant feedback.

____ 6. Their self-esteem is most important.

____ 7. They require a comfortable, low-stress environment.

____ 8. They appreciate a manager who has a sense of humor.

____ 9. They want to respect their manager and in turn be respected.

____ 10. They desire consistent mentoring and constructive feedback.

____ 11. They are inclusive by nature.

____ 12. The content of communication is less important than the act of communicating.

____ 13. They are eager to please.

Identify those unique Millennial behaviors that you need to give further consideration in an effort to establish and sustain effective communication.

Establishing and Sustaining Effective Communication is a Shared Responsibility of Manager and Millennial

There are two major reasons that communication, negotiation, motivation, and other competency strategies often fail. First, a manager may diligently initiate an effective strategy in an effort to improve the manager/employee relationship and assume that this is all that is needed. Wrong. What is needed is ongoing and varied follow-up to sustain and support the process. Second, communication is not thought of as a shared responsibility between two individuals, most often a manager and an employee. With this shared-responsibility concept in mind, let us now take a look at the Millennials' and managers' communication needs and responsibilities.

Millennials' Communication Expectations and Responsibilities

Millennials have been described as a self-reliant generation comfortable with themselves and others. Jean M. Twenge, author of *Generation Me,* also describes them as confident, assertive, and entitled. She labels them as "Generation Direct." The following quote from her book sets the scene for our next point.

> ***"Some older business managers complain that young people are too blunt. These managers say that young employees ask for instant feedback that's straightforward and uncomplicated, and give it in return. Some managers are surprised at young people's willingness to critique the performance of older workers."***
>
> **–Jean M. Twenge**

The implications of Generation Direct's communication preferences have a clear impact on the discussion, in *What Millennial Workers Want: How to Attract and Retain Gen Y Employees,* of the Millennials' perspective on "The Boss Factor" and "The Coworker Factor." Let us begin with "The Boss Factor."

The Boss Factor and Millennial Communication Expectations

Millennials are accustomed to direct, ongoing supervision from parents, teachers, and other authority figures. They seek a similar relationship with their bosses, looking to them for constant feedback.

The following exercises are based on *What Millennial Workers Want: How to Attract and Retain Gen Y Employees*, a report by Robert Half International and Yahoo! HotJobs.

THE BOSS FACTOR: A MANAGER'S SELF-ASSESSMENT

Evaluate your strengths and any areas that require further development. Also consider distributing this form to your Millennials and seeking their feedback.

Are you…	Yes	No
1. A skillful manager, advisor, and supporter?	❑	❑
2. Pleasant and easy to get along with?	❑	❑
3. Understanding and caring?	❑	❑
4. Flexible and open-minded?	❑	❑

Remember, Millennials as a group crave continual feedback and reinforcement. The previously listed managerial tactics that will help you meet requirements of the "boss factor" communication needs will also help to improve Millennial performance.

Recommendations to Meet Millennials' "Boss Factor" Communication Needs

After considering the previously listed expectations that Millennials have of their bosses, identify one or more of the following recommendations that can help you meet their needs.

____ 1. Don't wait for the annual performance review to provide feedback—give spot reviews as tasks and projects are completed.

____ 2. Be a fair-minded manager who dispenses advice, provides support, and then gives them space to do their jobs their own way.

____ 3. Provide open responses that are honest.

____ 4. Model the communication practices that you expect in others.

____ 5. Acknowledge your Millennials as both professionals and individuals. Recognize that they have lives outside of work.

____ 6. Acknowledge their ideas and encourage them to approach you with their thoughts.

What other recommendations would you make to meet the Millennials' communication needs?

____

____

____

____

The Coworker Factor and Millennial Communication Expectations

Robert Half International and Yahoo! Hot Jobs commissioned a national survey of more than a thousand adults, ages 21–28; the survey sampled an equal number of men and women. The findings were reported in *What Millennial Workers Want: How to Attract and Retain Gen Y Employees*. As the study reveals, while Internet technology has been fairly ubiquitous for this group, we are reminded not to assume that it is the Millennial's communication method of choice. Millennials are a highly social generation, accustomed to doing things as part of a group since their years in daycare and preschool. Two interesting findings from the study:

- Two-thirds of survey respondents selected in-person conversation with their coworkers as their preferred communication method.
- Only one in five would rather communicate by e-mail.

Communication Implications for Managers of Millennials

While effective management is both an art and a science, there are also research-based recommendations that can help meet Millennial communication needs. Here are four for your consideration.

1. Make sure your workplace is structured to encourage plenty of "face time," which Millennials enjoy.
2. Arrange workgroups in open, connected seating areas that facilitate face-to-face communication.
3. Create opportunities for employees to socialize during and after work (remember Part Three: Fun and Social Interaction).
4. The more Millennials feel connected to their co-workers, the more they are likely to be satisfied with their jobs and stay with your organization.

As we assess Millennial communication expectations, we find some interesting paradoxes. While Facebook may be a preferred way of social networking, face time emerges as a workplace communication preference. Just as Millennials demonstrate an impressive set of communication strengths, they also have their own set of skill deficits.

Millennial Communication Deficits

Here are a few examples of potential Millennial communication deficits that would profit from the manager and mentor's coaching.

- While "Generation Direct" can be an asset, as previously discussed, any strength can also be a weakness. Millennials could increase their communication effectiveness by being a little more cautious, politically aware, and sensitive in the way they respond.
- Millennials are excellent multitaskers. However, too much multitasking can undermine the effectiveness of interpersonal communication. Reading and responding to e-mail while talking to a colleague on the phone or face to face results in ineffective communication. In *The Trophy Kids Grow Up*, Ron Alsop writes, "Some critics even consider the Millennials' extreme multitasking a manifestation of an attention disorder and have labeled them the Ritalin Generation."
- Written communication in the form of memos, compelling documents, and letters appear to require remediation for Millennials, according to studies conducted by The Conference Board. Ron Alsop makes another compelling statement that "Employers are finding that this e-literate generation is barely literate in other forms of communication."

Strategies and Tactics

There is an infinite variety of strategies and tactics that a manager can use in establishing and sustaining effective communication. This section offers two sets of recommendations. First, a series of research-based recommendations by other authors and researchers is presented. Second, four best-of-class recommendations are presented by our Contributing Experts.

Research-based Strategies and Tactics for Effective Communication with Millennials

The title of this book should not imply that motivation is a separate competency that stands alone. Often, in one informal hallway meeting with a Millennial, a manager may find that he or she has to communicate, motivate, delegate, and perhaps resolve a conflict. However, by studying and mastering specific strategies and tactics of each critical managerial competency—especially communication—the manager can increase his or her effectiveness.

Research-Based Strategy One: Surefire Ways to Connect to Millennials

In virtually every study of Millennials, communication emerges as a dominant theme. Eric Chester, in *Employing Generation Why?,* stresses the importance of building an effective, ongoing communication relationship with Millennials. I have selected five relevant communication strategies for this part.

- **Keep positive today and be optimistic about tomorrow.**

  Both the United States and our broader global economy are rallying to respond to challenges that have not been experienced in decades. While it would be naïve to suggest that a manager present a distorted view of a severe workplace/workforce situation, he or she can certainly avoid appearing to be a prophet of doom. Rather, the manager has an opportunity to generate both physical and psychic energy by the words and actions presented each day. By presenting opportunities for Millennials to solve problems and to develop creative ideas, individuals and teams can generate psychic income.

- **Know the why; show the way.**

  While "Millennials" has come to be the most generally accepted term to describe what is now the twenty-something population, other authors and researchers have coined different labels. Eric Chester chooses to label the post–Generation Xers (born after 1980) as "Generation Why?" His reason, to quote him directly, is "Although they are better educated, more techno-savvy, and quicker to adapt than those who have come before them, they refuse to blindly conform to traditional standards and time-honored institutions. Instead, they boldly ask Why?"

With this explanation of "why," it is beneficial to respond to questions about the logic and reasoning of a manager's actions. In addition, the manager of Millennials can meet their employees' communication needs by anticipating and inviting questions.

- **Tell the truth.**

  This has been—and continues to be—a period of accelerated mergers, acquisitions, and business closures. Public- and private-sector leaders have been tried for fraud, misconduct, and a variety of other criminal acts. The Millennial generation, described by some as our hero generation, has great pride in their country, concern for the community, and respect for the environment. They value honesty and integrity.

  The more opportunities you seek to share timely, relevant information with Millennials, the more you can build trust in yourself and your organization.

- **Get to know them.**

  The bedrock principle of effective communication begins by understanding yourself. A corollary principle is "empathic communication." Stephen R. Covey wrote in *The Seven Habits of Effective People* that your effectiveness as a communicator is based not merely on communicating information, but also on an appreciation of how others will respond to the information. This principle takes on added value when you plan to delegate, motivate, and negotiate.

  How much do you know about your Millennials—not just their skill sets, but their interests, hobbies, and values? Do your management style and team structure provide opportunities for you to get to know employees and for them to get to know you and each other?

- **Be an example.**

  Historically, one career-related problem for knowledge workers has been the absence of leader/technologist role models. This is of increasing importance as Millennial knowledge workers identify the leader/mentor as a significant motivational factor. No longer is "Do as I say, not as I do" an acceptable response. Millennials thrive with leaders who model the behaviors they strive to achieve. In addition to seeking out a collegial relationship founded on respect, they crave that leader whom Warren Bennis describes as "the individual who will take you places that you would not have gone on your own."

  In addition, Millennials seek out leaders who can give and receive effective feedback—the heart of establishing and sustaining effective communication. Many technically educated knowledge workers are promoted into management positions because of their technical skills. If you happen to fall into this category, you may find the Interactive Behavioral Simulations® developed by Strategic Interactions, Inc., to be of value. Contributing Expert Jennell Evans of Strategic Interactions, Inc., presents this learning methodology later in this part.

Research-based Strategy Two

You may have attended supervisory or management development courses in the past. Perhaps you even taught a course to your colleagues. You probably have a fundamental appreciation of the following basic supervisory techniques:

1. Effective communication with others begins with understanding yourself.
2. Getting to know your colleagues and employees as unique individuals is invaluable.
3. Creating a comfortable and low-stress work environment reaps multiple rewards.
4. Communication is not a just-in-case situation, but an all-the-time need.
5. Developing others is significantly enhanced by effective delegation and mentoring.

And of course, the final test of your basic supervisory effectiveness is meeting the needs of both individuals and the organization. Authors Carolyn A. Martin, Ph.D., and Bruce Tulgan present a series of Communication Best Practices in their book *Managing the Generation Mix: From Collision to Collaboration*. These practices are relevant to establishing and sustaining effective communication not just with Millennials, but with your entire multigenerational workforce.

Martin and Tulgan make two important points:

1. As a manager, you can create the expectation that even in a hectic environment, communication on all projects, assignments, and important issues will be just in time, all the time.
2. Help teams create easy-to-use communication systems that facilitate good communication.

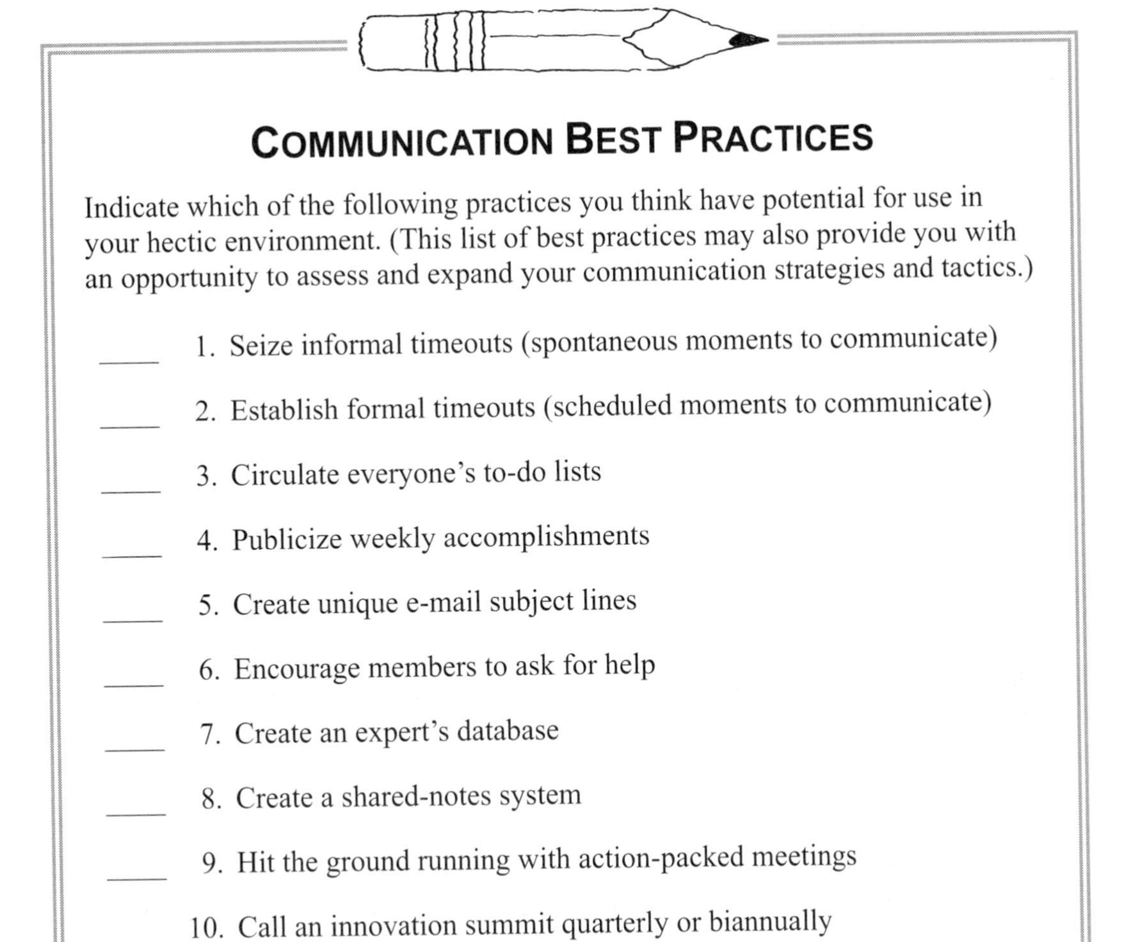

Communication Best Practices

Indicate which of the following practices you think have potential for use in your hectic environment. (This list of best practices may also provide you with an opportunity to assess and expand your communication strategies and tactics.)

____ 1. Seize informal timeouts (spontaneous moments to communicate)

____ 2. Establish formal timeouts (scheduled moments to communicate)

____ 3. Circulate everyone's to-do lists

____ 4. Publicize weekly accomplishments

____ 5. Create unique e-mail subject lines

____ 6. Encourage members to ask for help

____ 7. Create an expert's database

____ 8. Create a shared-notes system

____ 9. Hit the ground running with action-packed meetings

____ 10. Call an innovation summit quarterly or biannually

Practice What You Preach: Communication Strategies

The following list of best practices provides examples of how four organizations address the issue of establishing and sustaining effective communication with Millennials. Each strategy presents a different perspective that should enhance your resources.

Practice What You Preach

Sue McLeod, Senior Consultant
Hay Group

The younger generation like structure to understand the rules—what's expected to succeed now? What does it take to get ahead?

Clarify the rules

- Define the behaviors you need your employees to demonstrate.
- Define how behavioral expectations change with different levels or roles.
- Communicate these behaviors through the organization.
- Connect the behaviors to your organization's business, mission, and goals.

Younger employees pick up the difference between words and actions—and these disparities fuel their cynicism. They are also quick to call "foul" when they see that there are different rules for different people. These rules need to be woven into your "people processes"—evaluations, training and development, and recruitment—and they need to be applied consistently.

Walk the talk

- Include information about your expectations in the recruiting process.
- Use interview techniques that screen job candidates' behaviors as well as their skills and experience.
- Ensure that managers communicate expectations and give frequent feedback to reinforce the desired behaviors.
- Incorporate behavioral expectations into formal performance reviews.
- Provide opportunities for employees to develop and demonstrate new behaviors needed for advancement, through coaching, mentoring, training, and new work assignments.
- Hold everyone accountable for demonstrating important behaviors.

Interactive Behavioral Simulations®

Jennell Evans, President and CEO
Strategic Interactions, Inc.

Millennials want consistent feedback on "how they are doing," "how they can improve," and "how they can move up" more frequently than any other generation. Their desire for sustained communication can create challenges with co-workers and managers less inclined to take time to give feedback or share information in general. The reality is that Millennials expect their manager to take the time to give feedback, or they may seek a different employer who understands how important it is to provide this kind of communication.

A lot of workplace research confirms that the primary reason most people leave their jobs is that they do not have a good relationship with their managers. Because excellent communication is key to good relationships, it is important that organizations give people the tools and resources (i.e., communication skills training) to successfully manage relationships in the workplace.

One of the fundamental responsibilities of a manager is to give feedback to those he or she supervises. At Strategic Interactions, we worked with an organization that wanted to provide feedback skills training to managers, most of whom supervised younger workers. The client's data from exit interviews confirmed that the organization was losing young talent because managers did not give them feedback, or when they did, it was not specific or timely.

Most people avoid giving feedback because they do not know how to do it, especially if they know the person needs to be doing something better. People need to learn *how* to give feedback through real-life experiences, so they understand their own responses in feedback situations, as well as understanding what the person receiving the feedback may be experiencing.

To help this client stop the loss of young talent, we designed a simulation-based half-day workshop to demonstrate the behavioral aspects of giving feedback, and we included information about generational diversity. This highly experiential workshop allowed the managers (engineers) to practice giving feedback without any risk of "saying things the wrong way" and potentially damaging the relationship. In essence, we created a "learning lab," where managers could observe how to give feedback and try out different strategies within their own comfort zone. One specific simulation involved a Boomer giving feedback to a Millennial. The simulation allowed the Boomer to better understand the Millennial's perspective regarding feedback, as well as learn skills in giving feedback that the Millennial could understand and make a plan to improve.

The client validated through internal measures that the managers who attended the training had significantly higher retention rates than managers who had not attended the training.

Effective Recruiting, On-boarding, and Assimilation Examples

Marcia Riley, Vice President, Talent Management and Human Resources
ESI International

When I received a job offer from John Elsey, President and CEO of ESI International, I hesitated because of the long commute from Silver Spring to Arlington each day. He actually did some research for me. He got in his car and drove several routes and e-mailed me with the fastest route. It was an exceptional and thoughtful "best practice" that took my breath away. I accepted the position!

While I was serving at Inova Health System as their very first Chief Learning Officer, we hired two individuals who had not yet met and who would be working very closely together. I suggested that they meet for breakfast or lunch at the company's expense before they started, so that on day one they would have a friend and begin working as a team. Both stayed with Inova for many years and were key contributors during their tenure at the organization. To this day, I get calls from them telling me how much that meeting mattered to their on-boarding at Inova. They always remembered how special that was, and they were an outstanding team for many years.

When we hire new employees at ESI, we check in with them at 45 days. Many organizations check in with managers to see how their new employees are doing. At ESI, we believe that work is about trust and open communication. As the vice president of Talent Management and Human Resources, I sit down with every new employee to make sure that we are living up to our promises as their new employer. We do not have an issue with turnover because we keep in touch with our employees and they know that their satisfaction with our organization is important to us.

Member Partnership Management Framework (MPMF)

Shaara Roman, Director of Human Resources
CGI Federal

To help managers communicate better, CGI's ISO-9001 certified Member Partnership Management Framework (MPMF) establishes communication channels and processes between management and members that the management team of each business unit is accountable for following. In fact, their compensation is tied to their MPMF compliance.

Through a prescribed set of activities, including new employee orientation and integration, performance and career management, and ongoing one-on-one and team meetings, we build strong and long-term relationships with our members. The MPMF provides for ongoing measurement and improvement processes where members, as owners, are inspired to grow the company and are empowered to build a challenging and rewarding career.

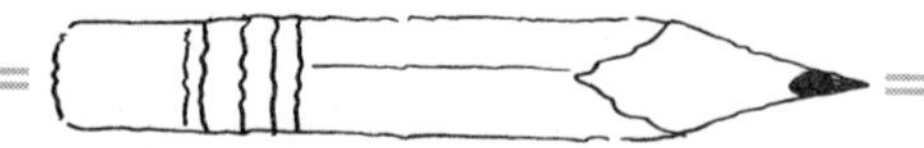

MANAGER APPLICATION EXERCISE

Based on your review of the previous Contributing Expert strategies, specify those concepts most relevant to your establishing and sustaining effective communication with your Millennials.

1. ______________________________
2. ______________________________
3. ______________________________
4. ______________________________
5. ______________________________

Collaboration Technologies

Each new Millennial study, publication, and performance improvement program provides a different perspective on how to motivate the Millennial knowledge worker and improve performance. The most recent of these studies and books clearly address the importance of understanding these new "digital natives" and "technophiles." The following quote from Ron Alsop's book *The Trophy Kids Grow Up* captures the unique, critically important, and dominant Millennial characteristic.

> ***"Millennials are so tied to technology tools that they may be 10 feet away from you but still send a text message or e-mail rather than simply call out to you. Millennials have even been known to quit their jobs by e-mail. Yet as many impatient Millennials might say, e-mail is sooo dead. It's the new snail mail. Millennials expect rapid-fire feedback and get bored in a New York minute. No, make that a nanosecond… Now, texting on cell phones, instant messaging, and sending messages on social networking sites have become their preferred modes of communication."***
>
> **–Ron Alsop**

While this quote may capture a unique behavioral communication characteristic of Millennials, Rob Salkowitz takes this a step further. His book *Generation Blend: Managing Across the Technology Age Gap* addresses a critical point. "The arrival of the Millennials and the impact of Web 2.0 technology in the enterprise create unprecedented complexity for employers and workers in the 2010s and beyond." In Salkowitz's discussion of Millennials in the workforce, he demonstrates the interplay of Millennial characteristics, priorities, work styles, and of course, technology.

Technology Implications of Millennial Characteristics, Priorities, and Work Styles

Millennials see technology as a tool to provide:

- Social networks and contact management tools
- Real-time communication
- Open communication and information channels
- Expertise location systems
- Two-way channels of internal communication
- Blogs and other channels for personal expression
- Remote access and mobility, and access to personal networks at work
- Communication and collaboration systems, portals, workspaces, or teamware
- User environments that allow for shifting context

As Rob Salkowitz points out, "the generational personality of Millennials and their close relationship with technology has several implications for their future as participants in the workforce." However, many organizations still function with traditional channels of communication. These traditional channels do not meet the Millennials' need to be heard on the job and to receive frequent and useful feedback. The following statement is a wake-up call for all managers and human resources professionals: "Since they [Millennials] tend to be tribal and socially networked, they want sociable workplaces; they want to connect with others (including mentors)."

Further Discussion

Shira Harrington, Director, Professional Search
Positions Inc.

The author, in describing why communication strategies often fail, makes a profound point when he says, "What is needed is ongoing and varied follow-up to sustain and support the process." He goes on to note that the second reason communication fails is that it "is not thought of as a shared responsibility between two individuals, most often a manager and an employee."

Looking beyond generational diversity for a moment, we could see truly effective communication as the essence of harmony in the workplace (and in the world, for that matter). When we focus on two-way communication—i.e., when both parties ask thought-provoking, non-judgmental questions, receive constructive feedback, and share suggestions aimed at mutual benefit—productivity naturally increases because the goal is success, not control over an individual.

Even discussing this concept is a paradigm shift from the business practices of the Veteran generation, who used a command-and-control style of supervision to cajole—or even force—performance out of their direct reports. Now that Baby Boomers have instituted a more collaborative style of performance management, the challenge is to arrive at a level of communication that moves beyond top-down management and includes Millennials (and all generations) as partners in corporate achievement.

While the topic of business communication is not a new one, using generational diversity as a "back door" training technique with managers could be a novel approach, such as that instituted by Strategic Interactions, Inc., in its simulated-feedback learning labs. We know that when placed in positions of leadership, most people either shy away from giving feedback or feel the need to assert their authority. Since neither tactic will work effectively with Millennials, now is the time to focus on unique strategies that will allow managers to safely explore ways to bring out the best performance in their young partners.

Thinking longer term, future research should address the coaching of Millennials who have already entered into management positions. Many of these ambitious protégés have been creating a unique challenge for their direct reports (who could be of any generation) due to their tendency to collaborate endlessly without making authoritative decisions. Compounded by their general avoidance of conflict, this generation has an even greater need for effective communications training.

Whether 75 years old or 25 years old, all employees could use extra learning support in the area of communication. We would do well to put into practice the famous axiom, "Seek first to understand before seeking to be understood."

Summary

Part Five's objectives focused on four key points. First, a review of a "Portrait of a Millennial" reinforced the importance of establishing and sustaining effective communication. Second, establishing and sustaining effective communication was presented as a shared responsibility of manager and Millennial. Third, strategies and tactics that managers can use to establish and sustain effective communication were emphasized. Fourth, collaboration technologies were described as promising new information tools for enterprises and critically important communication tools for Millennials.

PART 6

The Three R's: Recognition, Reward, and Respect

> *"Meet Generation Y, the most high-maintenance workforce in the history of the world. It is also a generation that we desperately need to be creative, productive, and efficient in these challenging times."*
>
> –**Bruce Tulgan,** *Not Everyone Gets a Trophy*

In this part:

Getting Started

As with previous parts of this book, this part is driven by our survey of Millennial motivational factors. Responses that are relevant to this part include "recognition," "treatment as colleagues," "interest in employees," "respect," "personal goals," "generous time off, "rewards," "promoted quickly," and "comprehensive benefits." After the data were analyzed, similar descriptors of motivational factors were combined, and recognition, reward, and respect emerged as compatible motivational factors.

Further research and Contributing Experts' recommendations result in this part's focus on the following four objectives:

- Identify those unique generational factors that influence the importance of recognition, reward, and respect as Millennial motivators.
- Appreciate the importance of appropriate recognition for the Millennial knowledge worker.
- Establish an organizational and managerial climate to apply reward strategies.
- Develop a mutually beneficial climate in support of respect.

Generational Factors

There is substantial research to support the statement that unique generational factors have influenced the importance of recognition, reward, and respect as Millennial motivators. Since William Strauss and Neil Howe introduced the concept of generational personalities with their now classic 1991 book, *Generations: The History of America's Future, 1584-2069,* a well-documented body of literature has suggested that methods of generational analysis can be applied to organizations as a system to attract, recruit, develop, manage, motivate, and retain all generational cohorts.

A casual review of the events and factors that have shaped the behaviors and values of the Millennials demonstrates why they value recognition, reward, and respect.

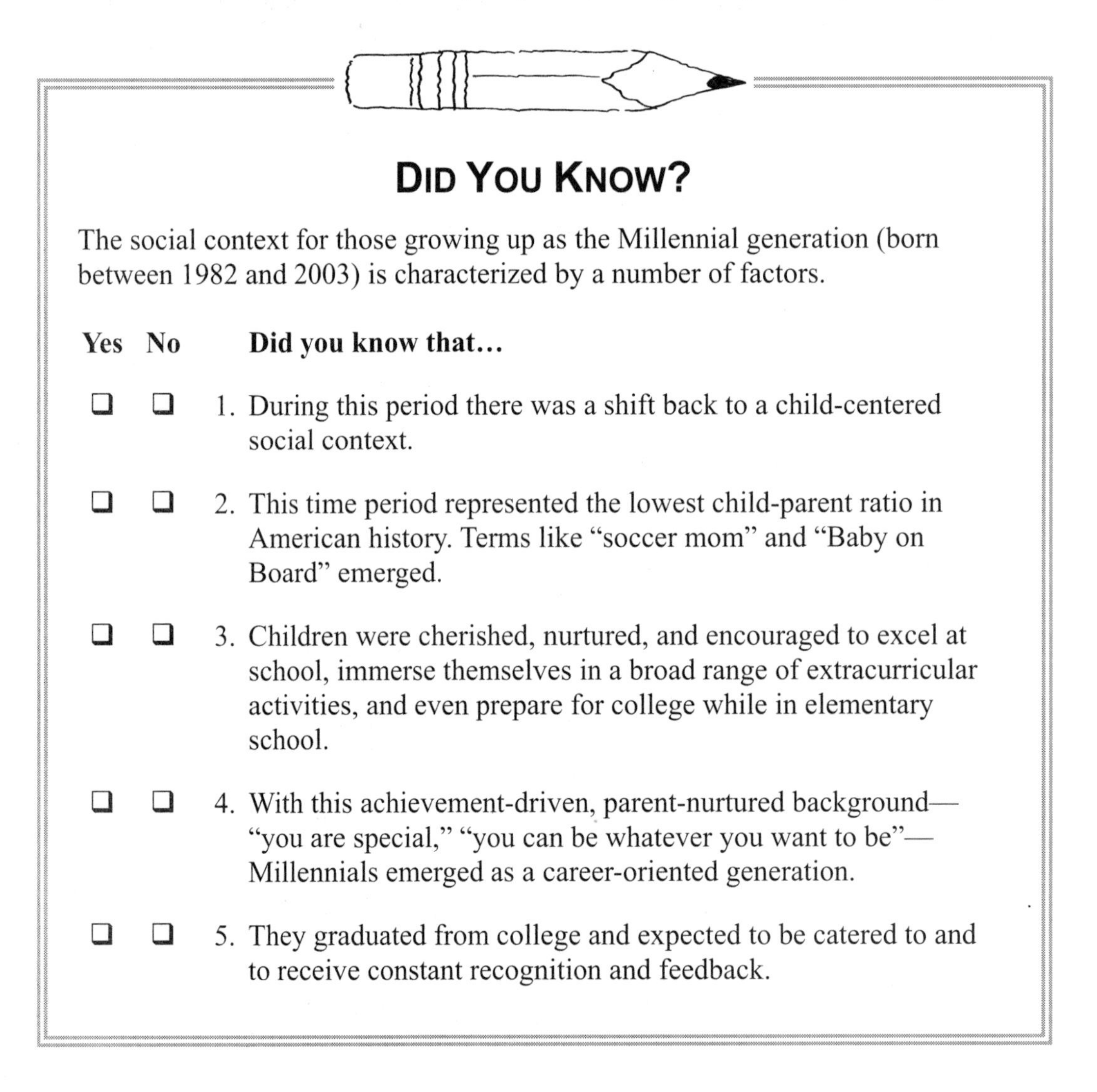

DID YOU KNOW?

The social context for those growing up as the Millennial generation (born between 1982 and 2003) is characterized by a number of factors.

Yes	No	Did you know that…
❑	❑	1. During this period there was a shift back to a child-centered social context.
❑	❑	2. This time period represented the lowest child-parent ratio in American history. Terms like "soccer mom" and "Baby on Board" emerged.
❑	❑	3. Children were cherished, nurtured, and encouraged to excel at school, immerse themselves in a broad range of extracurricular activities, and even prepare for college while in elementary school.
❑	❑	4. With this achievement-driven, parent-nurtured background—"you are special," "you can be whatever you want to be"—Millennials emerged as a career-oriented generation.
❑	❑	5. They graduated from college and expected to be catered to and to receive constant recognition and feedback.

Neil Howe and William Strauss wrote in their 1991 book, *Millennials Rising*:

> ***"They're the most watched over generation in memory. Each year, adults subject the typical kid's day to ever more structure and supervision, making it a nonstop round of parents, relatives, teachers, coaches, baby-sitters, counselors, chaperones, minivans, surveillance cams, and curfews."***

It is apparent why recognition, reward, and respect are important to Millennials. It is not surprising that titles such as *The Trophy Kids Grow Up: How the Millennial Generation Is Shaking Up the Workplace* are appearing. A chapter in Bruce Tulgun's new book, *Not Everyone Gets a Trophy,* suggests that leaders and human resources professionals must practice "*in loco parentis* management."

Recognition for the Millennial Knowledge Worker

In the dictionary, "recognize" is defined as "to acknowledge or to take notice of in some definite way." Recognition is also part of a continuous retention system described, in *Workforce Crisis*, as "Attentive management, where the direct manager not only appreciates employees' points of view [and contributions], but also attends to the employee's needs and progress and explicitly encourages—and is accountable for—retention." Taking the definition a step further, recognition, rewards, and respect are part of a broader motivational and retention strategy that links the human resources workforce plan to tangible business outcomes. It is all part of a comprehensive strategy that helps management avoid excessive costs, optimize productivity, and beat the competition to market.

While the early part of this chapter discusses the Three R's—recognition, reward, and respect—separately, they are actually concurrent motivational factors. Perhaps another way to view these components is as an equation:

Recognition + Rewards + Respect = Repeated High Performance

Strategies to Meet the Recognition Needs of Millennial Knowledge Workers

The earlier description of Millennials suggests that they expect their managers to be similar to their parents, teachers, and coaches. Millennials have been described as "crying out to management" to recognize and praise them. They are drawn to organizations and managers that offer frequent recognition. They are quick to leave those that don't give it. The positive aspect of this need for recognition is that when they receive it in a timely and authentic manner, they have a proven track record of exceeding normal expectations.

The Four P's of "Wise Recognition and Rewards"

Earlier discussion suggests that opportunities to meet the Millennials' needs for recognition, rewards, and respect often occur concurrently. From this perspective, Eric Chester, in his book *Employing Generation Why? Understanding, Managing and Motivating Your New Workforce*, presents four criteria for "wise recognition and rewards."

1. **Personal**

   ▷ The perceived value of recognition or a reward escalates when it is individualized.

   ▷ Look for formal and informal opportunities to get to know what employees like to do in their personal time away from work.

   ▷ Demonstrate this knowledge when you customize the recognition or rewards you give.

2. **Proportionate**

   ▷ A reward or recognition should match the level of performance being recognized.

   ▷ Plan your recognition and reward program to make certain that it includes various levels of achievement.

   ▷ Avoid heaping praise on minor task assignments that are a routine part of the job.

3. **Punctual**

   Millennials live in the moment. As a manager or human resources professional, you know that the closer to the accomplishment that recognition or a reward is given, the more effective it is. With this in mind, you are encouraged to:

   ▷ Develop a recognition and reward inventory that is ready to be used at the appropriate time (gift cards, tickets to sporting events, time off, etc.).

   ▷ Prepare to give unscheduled spot awards to enhance your unit's motivational climate.

   ▷ Deliver the recognition or reward today, rather than promise it for tomorrow.

4. **Public**

   "Praise in public, censure in private" is a Supervision 202 principle. Yet often it is not practiced to the degree it should be. Here are three recommendations.

   ▷ Present recognition and rewards in the presence of the employee's peers. This will multiply the value exponentially.

   ▷ Consider sharing the news of recognition or rewards in an e-mail message or on a website.

   ▷ Take advantage of coffee breaks, luncheons, or dinners to "seize the moment" to announce an unanticipated act of recognition or reward.

The Four P's of Wise Recognition and Rewards are sound management practices that are especially relevant to meeting the motivational needs of the Millennial knowledge worker, who thrives on spontaneity, positive feedback, and social work environments.

Application Exercise: The Four P's of Recognition and Rewards

Select one tactic from each of the Four P's of Recognition and Rewards that you will apply to improve your Millennial recognition and reward strategies. Record your tactics in the action plan below.

1. Personal: ______________________________

 ____

2. Proportionate: ______________________________

 ____

3. Punctual: ______________________________

 ____

4. Public: ______________________________

 ____

Make note of another recognition and reward tactic from your own experiences that is especially relevant to the Millennials.

____

____

____

____

Contributing Experts: Two Perspectives

The contents of this book have been significantly shaped by the expertise, interest, and guidance of Contributing Experts. At this point in the part, two Contributing Experts are featured. The first, Shaara Roman, provides a unique description of a multilevel corporate recognition program. The second, Rick Humphress, presents best-of-class practices and a recognition checklist. He then introduces a research-based recognition model that serves as a framework for application and further discussion.

Each organization has an unlimited opportunity to initiate a comprehensive recognition program. Often a program's strategies and tactics were initiated at different times in response to different needs in terms of corporate communication, organizational development, and motivation. In addition, a recognition program may respond to local, regional, and national needs. The examples presented by Shaara Roman showcase such a model.

A Multilevel Corporate Recognition Program

Shaara Roman, Director, Human Resources
CGI Federal

CGI Federal provides a number of recognition and reward programs for our members.

- **The Builders Award program** — Members who have contributed significantly to the growth of our company are recognized via our annual Builders Award program. They are invited to an awards ceremony held during our annual Vice Presidents Conference and are presented with a commemorative plaque by our founder, Serge Godin, and our CEO, Michael E. Roach. A framed photograph of each honoree is also displayed at a local office of his or her choice, as well as in our corporate headquarters in Montreal. Approximately ten people are chosen for this prestigious award each year.
- **The Excellence in Innovation Awards program** — This annual awards program recognizes members who have developed tools, frameworks, methodologies, or processes that benefit the company or our clients in some major way. Significant cash prizes are awarded, including a $10,000 prize for the winning individual submission, and a $25,000 prize for the winning team submission (split among team members). The winners, the number of which varies from year to year, are presented with an engraved award and cash prizes by senior management during our Member Annual Tour.

- **The Service Recognition program** — Through this program, CGI recognizes important milestones in a member's career at CGI, including his or her third, fifth, tenth, fifteenth, twentieth, twenty-fifth, and thirtieth anniversaries. Ceremonies are held during the regular team meetings within each business unit so that members can be recognized by their peers. Members are also recognized during our Member Annual Tour and in company publications. The program also provides a choice of gift, the value of which varies according to the number of years of service. In addition, members completing 25 years of service are awarded a one-time bonus of five extra vacation days.
- **Above & Beyond, and the CGI Showcase** — Stories of members who have excelled in their work are featured regularly in the Above & Beyond and CGI Showcase sections of our global member newsletter, as well as in a news section on our enterprise portal. Members are invited on an ongoing basis to submit stories.
- **The CGI Federal Recognition program** — The Stars program gives members an opportunity to nominate their colleagues for recognition. Those chosen for recognition receive a commemorative gift and a gift card. They also receive coverage in local publications and are eligible for an annual award.
- **The Member Partnership Management Framework** — In addition to our formal recognition programs, CGI's ISO-9001 certified Member Partnership Management Framework encourages informal recognition of members during quarterly "All Hands" team meetings.

Best-of-Class Practices, a Checklist, and a Model

Rick Humphress, Public Sector, Human Capital Management
Oracle Corporation

A preliminary review of Contributing Experts' Motivational Indicators outlines three interrelated and significant Millennial Motivational Factors. A direct quote of several statements captures the importance of this part. First, Millennials expect appreciation and recognition for their efforts and ideas. Their expectation is that this recognition is frequent and often presented in front of their peers. One form of recognition that is especially meaningful is recognition from senior management and increased visibility in the organization.

Along with the importance of recognition is the importance of respect. As one Millennial stated, "Ask me for my input and listen to my ideas." Respect for ideas is a critical motivator. The recognition and respect equation is further reinforced by a variety of diverse and timely rewards. As one important example, Millennials view increased responsibility as a reward. They clearly and aggressively seek greater responsibility as a reward for accomplishment. And the range of rewards varies with the individuals. In addition to salary, they seek a diverse menu of rewards that can be tailored to their individual motivational profile. A quick promotion and change of job title or the opportunity for accelerated learning may be examples of "one size does not fit all."

Perhaps one of the greatest Millennial motivational challenges is reconciling the business needs of the organization and the motivational preferences of Millennials. The desire to be treated as respected colleagues—despite age, position title, and responsibility—is a key driver of the Millennial motivators of recognition, respect, and rewards.

Best-in-Class Practices

Recognition is a form of appreciation that gives people a positive attitude about their ability to contribute to a team or organization. Research in industrial psychology shows that by setting, achieving, and recognizing goals and goal achievement, organizations will be more successful. The following represents a set of best-in-class practices and considerations that an organization can use to guide the implementation of a recognition program to benefit all employees regardless of their sociological grouping (Traditionalists, Baby Boomers, Gen Xers, or Millennials).

- **First, do no harm.** Organizations should examine their practices and methods of delivering recognition and should stop de-motivating activities.
- **Everyone can be praised.** Recognition should be awarded on a straight-line basis: set criteria and reward everyone who meets them. Do not set up a win-lose culture by recognizing only the top performance.
- **Recognition must be motivational.** It should be fair, consistent, timely, specific, and intermittent. Otherwise, it may become an expected entitlement and lose its motivational qualities.
- **Tailor recognition.** Based upon age, employees belong to broad sociological groups associated with specific characteristics. However, each of these employees also has an individual personality, and recognition should be tailored to the needs of the individual for it to be truly motivational.

- **Differentiate incentive programs from recognition programs.** Incentive programs publicly identify in advance precise behaviors rewarded with specific rewards. Recognition programs reward specific desirable behaviors after the fact.

- **Public recognition is not always best.** Since good performance is an exceptional event (a unique person performing a certain behavior at a specific time), it should be recognized in a private, one-on-one setting. One notable exception is group recognition.

- **Encourage positive gossip.** When a peer employee or a manager in another division compliments superior performance, use this as the basis to recognize an employee. It will be perceived as more genuine and it will promote social cohesion because an employee cannot help but feel closer to a person who genuinely praises him or her.

- **Train employees how to give recognition.** Keep the praise simple, and any rewards, symbolic. Sandwiching corrective feedback between two slices of recognition can work very well because it softens the blow. Many Millennials are very sensitive to any corrective feedback, so managers need to be delicate in how they deliver it.

- **Train employees how to receive recognition.** Employees need to engage in behaviors that encourage managers to give recognition, including avoiding disclaimer statements, showing sincere appreciation, valuing the recognition, and giving reciprocal recognition for the praise.

Checklist

To implement a best-in-class recognition program:

- ❑ Examine existing recognition practices and eliminate those that do not produce any motivational benefits or are de-motivating.
- ❑ Clearly articulate the organizational differences between an incentive program (known rewards, known time frame) and recognition (unknown rewards, unknown time frame).
- ❑ Determine criteria or standards of behavior worthy of recognition.
- ❑ Determine what kind of recognition would uniquely motivate each employee.
- ❑ Train recognition givers and receivers on optimal methods to give and receive rewards.
- ❑ Track recognition and performance appraisals to determine the impact of recognition on job performance.

Models

Organizations give recognition to motivate employees and to encourage productive work behaviors. Recognition is a primary positive reinforcement because it strengthens an existing behavior. The question arises of what pattern of recognition delivers the highest motivation, as measured by the number of positive work behaviors. Research shows that the best recognition would occur not after every positive instance, but rather after a variable number of positive instances. A variable ratio schedule of VR-10, for instance, means that on average, recognition follows every tenth instance of good work behavior. Variable recognition keeps the employee guessing when the next payoff of praise will occur. This schedule of recognition generates the highest rate of response of any alternative.

	Ratio	Interval
Variable	**VR:** The number of positive work behaviors required before recognition occurs varies from one period to the next. VR-10 indicates that recognition is given, on average, after every tenth positive work behavior.	**VI:** After a variable period of time (interval), the first positive work behavior is recognized. VI-10 indicates that recognition is given immediately after an average of ten units of time have passed.
Fixed	**FR:** The number of positive work behaviors required before recognition occurs is a fixed number. FR-10 indicates that recognition is given after every tenth positive work behavior.	**FI:** After a fixed time interval, the first positive work behavior is recognized. FI-10 indicates that recognition is given immediately after ten units of time have passed.

Additional Recognition Strategies

A broad variety of recognition strategies are available to meet the motivational needs of Millennials. In addition to those previously presented, the following examples are provided. As Ken Blanchard, known for his situational leadership methodology, suggests, "One size does not fit all." He once said that "What motivates people is what motivates people." This concept is especially important in selecting the appropriate recognition strategy for your Millennials, while recognizing that within their generational band, there are opportunities to customize and tailor strategies and tactics to meet individual needs. With this concept in mind, the following recognition strategies are presented. Select those that are most appropriate for the individual Millennial whom you have identified to recognize.

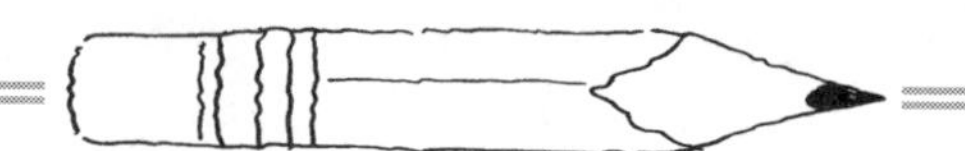

Millennial Recognition Strategies

Identify a specific recognition strategy that would be most appropriate for an individual member of your team.

____ 1. **Recognize the whole person.** As Part One: Flexibility and Work/Life Balance stressed, Millennials place considerable importance on a balanced life, in which work is only one component of their "get a life" portfolio. Work is a means to an end; it is not an end in itself. One way to recognize this healthy priority is to gain a deeper and more detailed understanding of your individual Millennials. A sincere and appropriate interest in an employee's personal life can create a bond and trust, which benefit both individual and organization.

____ 2. **Promote and reinforce excellence.** Many Millennials work in rapidly changing, high-productivity, task-driven environments. Individuals who demonstrate skill in multitasking often work on concurrent projects with multiple formal and informal reporting lines. In this environment, managers may miss—and underestimate—the value of promoting and reinforcing excellence on a continuous basis. This form of recognition, "psychic income," can range from a formal, scheduled event to more informal and spontaneous recognition. This could be done through e-mail, a website, a meeting announcement, gift certificates, or an electronic scorecard that reinforces organizational values.

____ 3. **Recognize and address Millennial generational priorities.** Author Rob Salkowitz discusses this concept as it relates to generational technology implications. However, the concept also applies to other workplace and Millennial cultural implications. The following two examples are presented as potential Millennial generational recognition motivators.

Example 1: Millennials value gaining approval and recognition. This requires providing more hands-on management with direct communication and feedback.

Example 2: Millennials value making a difference. This requires providing more opportunities for participation in shaping policies.

Applying Reward Strategies

Motivating Millennial knowledge workers through the use of recognition, reward, and respect strategies is not a tedious managerial task. In *Motivating the "What's In It For Me?" Workforce,* Cam Marston makes this very point in stating that "One way to create the behavior you're looking for is to find ways to recognize and reward the desired behaviors in your workforce and then to celebrate them."

The importance of rewards is not new. Virtually every basic management or organizational behavior book presents the concept of rewards. It is, as defined in *Understanding People: Models and Concepts*, "the means and methods a manager uses for rewarding (or punishing) employees for their behavior, including strategies he/she uses, if any, for motivating them and the atmosphere he/she establishes, which lead employees to anticipate being rewarded or punished for certain kinds of behavior." While the importance of rewards has not changed, what has changed is the type of reward each of the four generations identifies as being of unique importance to them.

Portrait of Millennials: A Behavioral Review

A review of select Millennial behavioral characteristics highlights the relevance and importance of recognition and reward strategies.

- Millennials tend to be very career oriented and expect rapid advancement and perks.
- Millennials appreciate feedback, having been graded, evaluated, and ranked throughout their lives.
- They want frequent communication from their boss.
- They are motivated to contribute beyond what is expected of their formal position.
- They believe that the better the performance, the better their opportunity for advancement.
- Managers need to get a sense of how Millennials like to be praised—in public, in team meetings, or one-on-one in the office.
- They want to take charge. They believe they deserve a trophy, whether they win or lose.
- They want to add value through their ideas, their analyses, and their judgment.
- They are independent, techno-savvy, entrepreneurial hard workers who thrive on flexibility.

What Do Millennial Knowledge Workers Want from their Jobs?

We are focusing on Millennials who are also knowledge workers. I have daily contact with this group, as I write this book from the Greater Washington D.C. area, where Millennial knowledge workers are sought after despite a national economic downturn. I agree wholeheartedly with the research-based Millennial expectations that follow.

Millennial Expectations

Among the nine expectations presented in "What Do Young Workers Expect from Work?" and "What Matters to Young Workers?" in *Workforce Crisis* are the following relevant Millennial motivational factors of rewards, recognition, and respect. One definition of motivation is meeting the individual's desires, wants, and needs.

- "Individual responsibility, freedom to make decisions"
- "Opportunities to learn and grow"
- "Team-based work, collaborative decision making"
- "Lots of feedback, frequent and constructive reviews"
- "Work that is personally stimulating and enjoyable"
- "Work that is worthwhile to society"

Millennial Knowledge Workers and Rewards

As there is a growing body of literature about Millennials, there is a corresponding body of literature about knowledge workers. With these resources available, there is a rich library of reward strategies and tactics to employ. Opportunities exist to customize motivational strategies to meet the needs of each Millennial. The following discussion of rewards combines recommendations of a noted author and Contributing Experts.

An Author/Researcher's Perspective

Frances Horibe, writing in *Managing Knowledge Workers,* raises several questions that the reader/practitioner needs to address. She discusses how organizational rewards contribute to employee satisfaction and retention. She also delineates three types of rewards—money, personal awards, and awards programs—as they relate to the motivational needs of knowledge workers. Strategies and tactics have been selected from her book to create the following organizational inventory.

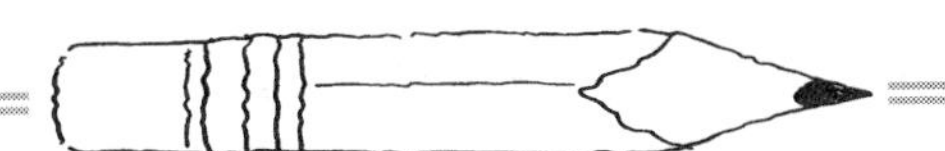

How Do You Reward Knowledge Workers: An Organizational Inventory

Indicate which of the following reward tactics you currently use or should use.

Money: This includes bonuses, incentive programs, profit sharing, stock options, and salary.

____ 1. Competing on price. Do you pay competitive salaries? Does it enable you to increase the service you provide in support of existing production and innovations?

____ 2. Diminishing returns. Does money, in the form of increased salaries, maintain its motivational value? Or are there other factors equally or more critical to retaining your Millennial knowledge workers?

____ 3. Is money the best way to recruit and maintain your intellectual capital?

____ 4. Be-all and end-all. Money isn't the driver many people think it is. Your competitive edge is considering other rewards to recruit, reward, and retain Millennial knowledge workers.

Personal: Frances Horibe introduces praise as a motivational strategy relevant to knowledge workers, and provides examples of praise. Here are six types for your consideration.

____ 1. Praise something the employee cares about.

____ 2. Praise patterns as well as extraordinary efforts.

____ 3. Praise the characteristic or trait, not just the activity.

____ 4. Praise only what you believe is important.

____ 5. Separate praise and opportunities for improvement.

____ 6. Tell the person how you really feel about their work.

CONTINUED

CONTINUED

Award Programs: Award programs go beyond personal recognition given as a reward and become a more formal part of the organizational culture. However, they are often a collection of activities that individually and collectively lose their potential. As Horibe writes, "Unless formal recognition programs help people stand a little taller and prouder, they have no value."

There are three ways to strengthen your organization's award program for knowledge workers. They are:

____ 1. Decide what you want from the award program.

____ 2. Maximize your success in designing award programs for knowledge workers that are clearly valued.

____ 3. Appreciate that creating new knowledge is an important motivator for knowledge workers. Their need for external awards is not as great as for other types of workers.

Critical Factors for Reward Program Success

Sue McLeod, Senior Consultant
Hay Group

Our research shows that the most successful reward programs work because they have been well implemented, rather than neatly designed. This implementation requires a strong partnership between Human Resources and line managers. We've identified six key rules that organizations should follow when putting their reward programs in action:

1. Don't leave the job of implementing reward programs solely to HR.
2. Use line managers to communicate the intent and rationale of the reward program to employees.
3. Ensure that HR makes the goals of the reward program clear and easy to understand.
4. Communicate the total value of the organization's reward program by using individualized total reward statements.
5. Encourage line managers to make use of the entire palette of your rewards, including intangible rewards, to motivate employees.
6. Make sure that HR provides line managers with the necessary tools and backup to help them effectively communicate the benefits of the program to employees.

A strategy or tactic, no matter how well designed, is only as effective as its implementation. And in the previous case, it requires a collaborative effort between the line manager and the human resources professional—the target audiences for this book.

Millennial Reward Assumptions: A Shared Responsibility

Many of our reader/practitioners are familiar with the concept of employee contracts. In many cases, the concept is limited to a letter of employment, much like a prenuptial agreement, that spells out the terms of employment and includes the familiar clause stating that both employer and employee can part ways at any time without an explanation. However, in more sophisticated organizational cultures, and under the leadership of the human resources professional and senior management, the "social" and "psychological" contracts are discussed and initiated that enable the employee to feel more part of the organization and its respective culture.

The Millennial Reward Contract

It has become quite apparent, based on numerous research studies, books, and the work of consultants, that Millennials have a set of clearly defined reward expectations. And while there is no proven formula that works in all organizations or for all professionals, in general the following three Millennial reward assumptions deserve consideration.

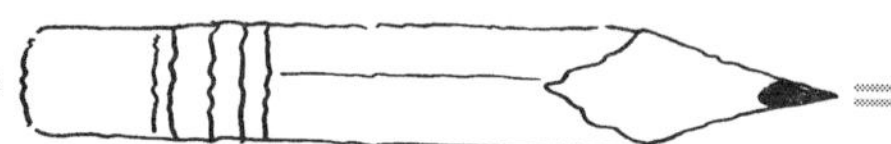

Three Assumptions about Rewards for Millennial Knowledge Workers

Indicate how well you and your organization effectively meet the following three assumptions.

❑ 1. **The Millennials' high expectations**

For a variety of reasons discussed in previous parts of this book, one of the most noticeable characteristics of Millennials is a strong sense of entitlement. This "What's In It for Me?" generation begins employment with each new job with extremely high expectations. Virtually every book or study on the topic describes their desire for fast promotions and frequent performance feedback, while prioritizing their need for work/life balance and participation in community service. In fact, the traditional concept of work/life balance has taken on an expanded meaning for Millennials. They now think in terms of "work-life integration." More specifically, they view work and life as a blend. Personal life comes into work, and work comes into personal life. This is a new reality for the Millennial.

CONTINUED

CONTINUED

- ❑ 2. **The manager's role in outlining goals and rewards**

  The concept of introducing a performance management model is not new or novel. Basic Supervision and Introduction to Management courses include a model that begins by stressing step one as setting goals and communicating expectations. However, this concept is even more important for Millennials. Lisa Orrell, in *Millennials Incorporated,* states, "Clearly outline goals and rewards for everything. Be very clear on what you want done and what they will get when it's done."

- ❑ 3. **Rewarding work behavior—the manager's roles**

  Abraham Maslow wrote extensively about motivation. One observation he made was that most employees want to do a good job and like to be told when they have done a good job. Unfortunately, many managers do not provide this positive feedback often enough. Rewarding good performance and providing consistent positive feedback takes on critical importance to a generation used to instant feedback and gratification from parents, teachers, coaches, and community.

Application Exercise

After reviewing the three previous assumptions, I can better meet the reward motivational needs of Millennial knowledge workers by:

____

____

____

____

Three Reward Strategies Beyond Money

Salary cannot be dismissed as a critically important recruiting and retention tool for Millennial knowledge workers. In a survey commissioned by Robert Half International and Yahoo! HotJobs, with results published in *What Millennial Workers Want: How to Attract and Retain Gen Y Employees*, employees ranked salary a 9.5 in importance on a 1-to-10 scale, with 10 being the most important. However, most experienced managers and HR professionals also know that it is one of the most short-lived motivators unless a balanced portfolio of reward strategies exists. In fact, many of us already know that some of the important Millennial reward strategies may cost the least and benefit Millennials and the organization the most. Here are two critically important reward strategies and several examples for each category for your consideration.

Make Increased Responsibility a Reward

Every behavior can be viewed as both a strength and a weakness. For example, Millennials have high expectations for fast promotions and frequent feedback. They have also been described as multitaskers with an insatiable appetite for increased responsibility. The opportunity to maximize this behavioral trait is further reinforced by an examination of terms appearing in the Motivational Factors Survey that shaped this book. Those behavior preferences included:

Career advancement	Fast-cycle work environment
Challenging work	Accomplishment
Passion for work	Trail blazing
Immediacy	Quick promotions
Adaptability	Empowerment
Accomplishment	Treatment as colleagues

As Lisa Orrell suggests in *Millennials Incorporated,* "New challenges and constant stimulation keep them motivated. This doesn't mean constantly having to promote them! Find ways to challenge them within their current positions until they deserve to be promoted."

Learning as a Reward

An organization's building intellectual capital and managing knowledge workers implies opportunities for continuous learning where there is a tendency to consider learning itself as a reward. In fact, an organization's ability to manage knowledge and meet Millennials' learning needs has become a predominant characteristic to be considered. Michael J. Marquardt, author of *Building Learning Organizations,* reinforces this point in stating that "To succeed in the fast-changing globally competitive business environment of today, an organization must have the capacity to continually learn from its experiences … and translate that knowledge into improved performance." Several of his strategies use learning to motivate Millennial knowledge workers. The following exercise is based on material in Marquardt's book, *Building Learning Organizations*.

Motivating Millennial Knowledge Workers: A Strategies Checklist

Indicate which of the following strategies you currently employ and which strategies you might employ in the future.

Currently Use	Should Use	
❑	❑	Recognize and reward learning
❑	❑	Build learning into all operations and activities
❑	❑	Intertwine and align organizational learning with business and personal success
❑	❑	Set aside time for learning
❑	❑	Measure and broadcast the impact and benefits of learning
❑	❑	Maximize learning on the job

As a result of providing increased responsibility and learning as rewards, I will apply the following strategy:

___

___

___

Rewarding Performance

While rewarding performance is a recommended and accepted practice in managing and supervising others, the generational literature suggests that rewarding the "most coddled generation in history" requires special attention. Contributing Expert Rick Humphress has previously suggested that treating each generation with "generalized motivational strategies" may overlook the individual differences that often exist within the same generation.

Contributing Expert Sue McLeod presents Hay Group's research-based recommendation of rewarding Millennial performance. She writes:

The younger generation may be used to "everyone gets a trophy," but you know that won't help your organization succeed. Treating everyone the same can demoralize the best and create a sense of entitlement for the rest.

On the other hand, Millennials are used to being graded, getting feedback, and knowing where they stand against standards of performance. At the same time, they have a strong desire to get ahead and want support and encouragement along the way.

Our research shows that a work climate that rewards people based on their performance differentiates outstanding performance from average or poor performance. This helps to create engaged employees—those who are willing to put extra effort into improving their performance.

To increase your focus on rewards that motivate:

- Look for opportunities to praise good performance.
- Recognize and reward people on a timely basis for the level of their job performance.
- Reinforce outstanding performance.
- Ensure that recognition and encouragement greatly outweigh constructive criticism and negative feedback.
- Develop creative and flexible ways to recognize and reward individual and group performance.
- Celebrate individual, unit, department, division, and corporate accomplishments.
- Use the promotion system to help the best rise to the top.

The Third R: Respect

Effectively motivating the Millennial knowledge worker requires both individual and manager to enter into a behavioral contract in support of shared respect. While we all would like to embrace the golden rule of "treating others as you would like to be treated," a generational challenge appears to exist in this area. The following short discussion addresses this challenge and presents select strategies to address it.

From a review of Millennial literature and the Motivational Factors survey that shaped this book, it is quite clear that Millennials want to be treated as colleagues, they want their leader to have strong character, they want to work in an ethical environment, and they take pride in their work. Furthermore, there is research-based data to indicate that Millennials have respect for authority—as they have had for their parents and teachers. However, there are some generational differences that are not just behavioral differences, but critically important business issues.

Several authors address the motivation factor of respect. All have studied this challenge and made recommendations. In an effort to engage our reader/practitioner, I am presenting these recommendations in the form of a quiz. The following exercise is based on material appearing in *Generation Blend* by Rob Salkowitz and *Managing the Generation Mix: From Collision to Collaboration* by Carolyn A. Martin and Bruce Tulgan.

A Respect for Authority: Did You Know?

Directions: Indicate whether you were aware of the following respect factors.

	Yes	No
1. It's a curious paradox that the generation that questions everything is nevertheless more respectful of individuals and institutions who have earned their trust.	❑	❑
2. The track record shows that Millennials get along better with their parents, teachers, and much older workers than do Boomers or Gen Xers.	❑	❑
3. Many experts suggest that mentoring programs may be an especially effective way of integrating Millennials into the culture of the organization and bringing them up to speed on the formal and informal knowledge they need to be effective.	❑	❑
4. Millennials are well regarded by their elders, especially in the area of technology prowess.	❑	❑
5. Generational issues are important reflections of critical business matters that every organization is now experiencing as it transitions from the workplace of the past to the workplace of the future.	❑	❑
6. An organizational and managerial responsibility exists to create an environment that encourages courtesy, kindness, and respect.	❑	❑
7. Shared responsibility and mutual respect are exhibited through thoughtful, kind, and courteous behaviors.	❑	❑
8. Millennials claim that the relationship they have with their immediate boss is a critical factor in whether they stay or leave a job. They are certain at an early age about what they want that relationship to be.	❑	❑

As a manager, I can help further improve our "culture of respect" by:

____

____

____

Further Discussion

Shira Harrington, Director, Professional Search Positions, Inc.

It is a commonly accepted truism that people are motivated differently. In the case of Millennials, however, we should be encouraged to focus on the conditions under which a manager should feed this motivation through rewards. The author points out that many Millennials "believe they deserve a trophy, whether they win or lose." This is a recurring theme in generational literature that should be researched more intensively as Millennials move through management and beyond.

The author quoted Eric Chester, who noted that managers should "avoid heaping praise on minor task assignments that are a routine part of the job." While this seems like a simple enough concept, it should not be glossed over. For a generation that was given an "A for effort," recognition for simply showing up to work on time may be an expectation for some Millennials. Where does a manager draw the line in deciding what performance to reward? The author rightly suggests that we should "promote and reinforce excellence." Yet how does one define excellence for Millennials?

As the body of performance management literature evolves, we would benefit from a narrowly focused discourse on how to set clear expectations for Millennials that distinguish between minimum acceptable standards (not worthy of rewards) versus those behaviors that truly go above and beyond. While some managers may choose to reward the lowest common denominator, forward-thinking coaches will find a way to raise the bar to bring out the very best ingenuity from these young professionals. This competitive advantage will in turn serve the ultimate goal: to increase the bottom line.

Summary

This part focused on four key points. First, it identified those unique generational factors that influenced the importance of recognition, rewards, and respect as Millennial motivators. Second, it stressed the importance of appropriate recognition for the Millennial knowledge worker. Third, it presented concepts enabling the application of reward strategies. Fourth, it focused on strategies for developing a mutually beneficial climate in support of respect.

Part Seven: Learning, Training, and Technology now addresses the motivational importance that Millennials and their organizations place on the capacity to continually learn and remain competitive in a rapidly changing and fiercely competitive global economy.

P A R T 7

Learning, Training, and Technology

"There is absolutely no question that America's economic leadership and the increasingly more competitive global economy will be influenced by the growing importance of our Millennial knowledge workers. 'Learning organizations,' 'managing human and intellectual capital,' and 'lifelong learning' are now common drivers of performance in any responsive organization."

–Rick Humphress, Oracle Corporation

In this part:

- Getting Started
- The Forces Shaping America's Economy
- Knowledge Has Become the Important Factor in Economic Life
- A Paradigm Shift From 20th-Century Training to 21st-Century Learning
- Millennials and Their Unique Learning Preferences
- Learning and Training Recommendations

Getting Started

The research that has led to writing this part positions the Millennial knowledge worker as a seminal force, a centerpiece, of the new economy. This strategic positioning of the Millennial knowledge worker is the result of a fortuitous combination of events. First, knowledge is the new wealth of organizations, and effectively managing this knowledge has become critical to our economic life. Second, technology has changed and will continue to change how we work. And this has also significantly altered the way we learn. In short, the knowledge economy has increased the importance of the learning organization. This dynamic has created the need for knowledge workers to learn faster and more effectively. Finally, the unique learning preferences of a generation that has "grown up digitally" directly support their comfort level with technology-mediated learning methods. The following four objectives support this assumption.

Research and Contributing Experts' recommendations resulted in this part's focus on the following four objectives:

- Understand the forces shaping America's economy and their implications for work and workers in the twenty-first century.
- Appreciate that knowledge has become the most important factor in economic life.
- Recognize that a paradigm shift from twentieth-century training to twenty-first-century learning has taken place.
- Recognize that unique Millennial learning preferences directly coincide with the rise of technology-mediated learning methods.

The Forces Shaping America's Economy

The importance of identifying strategies and tactics to motivate Millennial knowledge workers cannot be fully appreciated without understanding the forces shaping the American economy. Perhaps the best way to create an understanding of the forces—directly relevant to this book—is to examine select trends presented by authors Richard W. Judy and Carol D'Amico in the Hudson Institute publication *Workforce 2020: Work and Workers in the 21st Century.* Concepts from this publication—a sequel to the Hudson Institute's landmark study, *Workforce 2000*—establish an excellent platform for Part Seven.

Trends Shaping the American Economy

- **Rapid technological change as the seminal force influencing the American and global economy**

  The pace of technological change is accelerating. And in this rapidly changing environment there will be winners and losers among industries, companies, occupations, and individuals. This scorecard of "winners" and "losers" has taken shape faster than anyone imagined as the result of the global recession we are now experiencing.

  More specifically, rapid technological change alters the productive process, i.e., the way work is done, as well as the products themselves. And unlike the technological changes that underlay the earlier growth of assembly-line manufacturing that once increased the demand for unskilled labor, today's technological changes in America have tended to require more highly skilled workers, but fewer low-skilled ones. Enter the Millennial knowledge worker.

- **Further global integration of the U.S. economy**

  Global integration is the second force shaping the American economy, as documented in *Workforce 2020*. Quite simply, distance is no longer a communication challenge. By the late 1990s, the marginal costs of communicating globally via the Internet had plunged to zero for most users. Compared to the rest of the world, America enjoys a relative abundance of highly skilled workers in specialized sectors such as Information Technology. This is a global competitive advantage. Again, enter the Millennial knowledge worker.

▶ Diminishing monopolies and intensifying competition

The protection once provided by geography and the unavailability of satisfactory substitutes is fast disappearing for more and more producers. And as the Hudson Institute report states, "because companies face increasing competition, they must live with unrelenting pressure to become more efficient and respond quickly to changing technological and market conditions." To survive and thrive in the twenty-first century, individual Americans need to manage their most important assets—their workplace skills. Enter the career-driven Millennial knowledge worker.

▶ America's emerging high-tech and global economy

The Millennial knowledge worker is well positioned to respond to America's swiftly developing technologies, which will increase the demand for highly skilled and well-educated workers. Furthermore, as earlier portraits of Millennials have indicated, a profile of their important motivational factors makes them a perfect "behavioral fit" for a rapidly changing and more entrepreneurial economy that places a premium on adaptability and flexibility. Simply put, workers able to master technology and cope with change will have an advantage. Enter the Millennial, yet again.

▶ Implications for America's workforce

Becoming a productive worker in America's fast-paced, rapidly changing, technology-driven, globally competitive economy will not be easy. But the Hudson Institute's report, *Workforce 2020*, while not directed at Millennials, clearly positions Millennials as the perfect candidates to help shape America's economy. Quoting the report directly:

> ***"Workers will change jobs more often. Rapid change dictated by competitive pressures will force companies to evaluate their staffing needs constantly, which will lead to frequent 're-sizing' of their workforces. As a result, workers will change jobs, employers, and even occupations more often than in the past. Moreover, workers in all occupations will need to prepare themselves mentally and professionally for this uncertainty."***
>
> ***–Workforce 2020: Work and Workers in the 21st Century***

Once again, the Millennial knowledge worker appears well positioned for these changes.

Knowledge Has Become the Important Factor in Economic Life

The previous discussion establishes a framework for the importance of the knowledge economy and the compatible and important role of the Millennial knowledge worker in this economy. The following discussion goes a step further and reinforces the link between the knowledge economy, the emergence of the learning organization, continuous learning, and a new Millennial career model.

The Knowledge Economy, Organization, and Worker

Working with the assumption that knowledge has become the most important factor in economic life—the one indispensable asset of the organization—it is worth taking a moment to discuss each of the interrelated components. A select summary of key points presented by author Thomas A. Stewart in *Intellectual Capital: The New Wealth of Organizations* helps to establish the importance of understanding why "learning," "opportunities for growth," and "rapid advancement" are among the top Millennial motivational factors.

The Knowledge Economy

The case has been made, and will continue to be reinforced, that knowledge has become an organization's preeminent resource. Managing intellectual capital has become an organization's first priority. Thomas Stewart asserts that it is "more important than raw material, money, automobiles, oil, steel or any other products of the Industrial Revolution." The knowledge economy, often described as an Information Revolution, is currently driving the reinvention of business, economic life, and society. It has quickly become apparent that a new knowledge-based economy will require the need for new skills, organizational structures, management, and leadership strategies—and yes, new workers, knowledge workers, and even more specifically, Millennial knowledge workers.

The Knowledge Organization

Virtually every organization has become "information intensive." Organizations are dependent on knowledge as a source of what attracts customers and clients and as a means of running the place. According to Thomas Stewart's research, a "knowledge organization" is defined by three factors:

- The enormous growth in the sheer information it handles
- What the organization does with the information and how they use it to replace inventories, warehouses, and other physical assets, saving both money and time
- How knowledge-intensive organizations are structured differently than traditional companies.

An ultimate goal of the knowledge organization is to move beyond using knowledge to improve productivity in our old business—or doing the same with less. Tomorrow, the shift is in using knowledge as a form of competitive advantage—generating new business.

The Knowledge Worker

Thomas Stewart makes a simple yet critical point in stating, "the notion of a knowledge economy and a knowledge company has a bit of the abstract about them, but there is nothing abstract about 'knowledge.'" In the same way we have generated profiles of Millennials, we can also generate a profile of the knowledge worker—often our very same Millennial. Several characteristics of the knowledge worker follow:

- Information is the most important material used on the job.
- Information and knowledge are both the raw material of labor and its product.
- Knowledge workers experience an increase in the knowledge content of their work.
- Better-educated workers are being hired to perform knowledge-intensive tasks.
- The education premium provides the growing role of knowledge in creating value and wealth.
- Knowledge workers, alone or in teams, plan, organize, and execute many aspects of their own work.

While not all knowledge workers are Millennials, the previously presented profile directly parallels their employment and learning preferences.

This brief summary of the emergence of the knowledge economy, organization, and worker clearly creates a case that the Millennial knowledge worker, the fastest growing segment of our workforce, is well positioned to support the growth of the competitive economy.

An Organizational Assessment

Based on the previous profile of the knowledge economy, organization, and worker, briefly describe how you would assess your organization's strengths and areas needing more development for each factor.

Knowledge economy: ______________________________

____

____

Knowledge organization: ______________________________

____

____

Knowledge worker: ______________________________

____

____

The End of the Beginning

In the conclusion of her book, *Managing Knowledge Workers: The Skills and Attitudes to Unlock the Intellectual Capital in Your Organization*, Frances Horibe includes the statement quoted below. It not only summarizes the previous discussion, but sets the scene for the emergence of the learning organization.

> ***"Knowledge is now the coin of the realm, and the knowledge worker is the most important source of wealth in an organization. Companies are coming to terms with this and starting to assess how to leverage their intellectual capital. … [T]rying to introduce changes to use your intellectual capital to its best advantage is a daunting task. It will require not simply changing what we do but [also changing] what we think and how we relate to each other."***

The Emergence of the Learning Organization

During the past decade, an interesting commonality of interests has emerged between the academic and corporate communities—one that is a perfect fit for motivating the Millennial knowledge worker. Universities have embraced more business-like practices common to corporations. In fact, the explosive and successful growth of nonprofit universities has provided best-of-class models of applying business practices to education. Second, organizations—increasingly more knowledge driven—have launched their own "corporate universities" that enable the alignment of business and educational needs. And both universities and corporations have moved to competency-based, outcome-driven, and even employer-centric educational strategies.

Taking this a step further, we now talk, as part of our common vocabulary, about the "learning organization" and the "corporate university" as components of the responsive knowledge organization. This strategic approach to "just-in-time" and "on-the-job" "continuous learning directly parallel the Millennial motivation factors." "Growth opportunities," "learning," and "training/lifelong learning" were all in the top ten responses to the Motivational Factors Survey.

An entirely new Millennial mindset has emerged regarding not only "work and life" balance, but also "work and learning" balance. In short, learning must take place almost as a byproduct of people doing their work—in contrast to acquiring knowledge before performing a particular task.

Michael J. Marquardt, writing in *Building the Learning Organization*, presents a brief description of the "new learning organization." A brief organizational assessment based on Marquardt's book is presented for you to measure your organization's strengths as a learning organization. This is obviously a major recruitment and retention tool for Millennial knowledge workers.

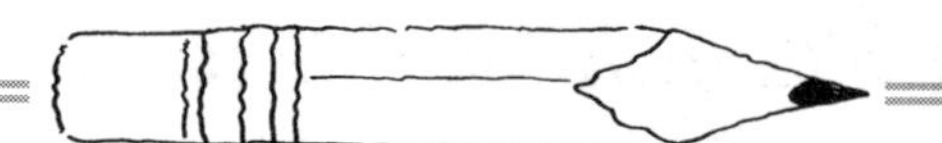

Is Your Organization a "Learning Organization"?

Review each of the following five characteristics of a responsive learning organization and identify your organization's current strengths and areas for development.

Current Strength	Should Improve	Characteristics
❑	❑	1. Learning is performance based (tied to business objectives).
❑	❑	2. Importance is placed on the learning process (learning how to learn).
❑	❑	3. The ability to define learning needs is as important as the answers.
❑	❑	4. Organization-wide opportunities exist to develop knowledge, skills, and attitudes.
❑	❑	5. Learning is part of work, a part of everybody's job description.

We can become a more effective learning organization by:

____

____

____

Implications of the Knowledge Economy and Learning Organizations for Millennial Knowledge Workers

Several positive characteristics quickly emerge from the previous discussion of the knowledge economy and the learning organization. These terms are a perfect match for meeting the Millennial motivational needs. They are "empowering," "sharing," "enabling," and "encouraging people to learn." Here is a short description of the importance of each characteristic as it relates to the Millennial motivational factor of learning.

Strategies to Address the Millennial Desire to Learn

Encourage Millennials to Learn: A common theme in almost every book on managing human and intellectual capital, workforce development, employee acquisition and retention, and the learning organization itself is that there is a new workplace competency. It is encouraging people to learn. This major motivational factor is most likely one of the reasons why your Millennials have joined your organization. It's not what the Millennial knows now but what they want and need to know for tomorrow. As Frances Horibe states, "To continue to create wealth through knowledge, people themselves must be up-to-date. Without a continual replenishment of the well of knowledge, it will eventually run dry."

In order for an organization to go beyond offering random training events and on-site college courses, it needs to consider establishing a formal, structured learning program for all levels of the organization. This program would include the following components:

- Formal training, learning, and development programs
- Encouraging informal learning
- Rewarding learning

Empower and Enable People to Learn: Perhaps one of the most effective sources of power a manager or leader can demonstrate is not "positional power," but "empowering others" to learn, take leadership, and assume responsibility for their projects and tasks. Empowering and enabling high-achieving, self-directed Millennial knowledge workers to learn offers a fluent extension of this process. It is also a direct fit for their motivational profile. While there are a wide variety of strategies to empower and enable people to learn, several that are especially relevant to knowledge workers appear below. How well does your organization do in meeting these learning needs?

The following strategies for empowering and enabling Millennials (or anyone) to learn are from *Building the Learning Organization:*

1. Institute personnel policies that reward learners.
2. Empower employees to learn and produce.

3. Balance the learning and development needs of the individual and [the organization.
4. Invite leaders to champion learning processes and projects.
5. Maximize learning from alliances and joint ventures.
6. Encourage leaders to model and demonstrate learning.

Encourage Knowledge Sharing and Demonstrations of Learning: One career commandment suggested by Michael K. Badawy, author of *Developing Managerial Skills in Engineers and Scientists*, is to delegate those things that you do best to allow time for you to learn new things. This delegation also allows you to monitor the performance of the individual to whom you delegate the assignment. Ironically, the opposite often happens in technology-driven knowledge organizations, where technical experts may hoard knowledge. One characteristic of the learning organization and managing of knowledge is establishing the strategy of learning from each other.

The New Millennial Career Model and Learning

An interesting confluence of the changing nature of work, worker, and learning has resulted in a new career model for the Millennial knowledge worker.

Earlier I referred to William Bridges' book *JobShift: How to Prosper in a Workplace Without Jobs.* More than ten years ago, he documented the disappearance of the regular concept of a 40-hour-a-week job with a routine day, familiar tasks and assignments, and actually "going to work" at a physical location. He talked about the changing and flexible nature of business needs that would require an equally flexible workforce.

In addition, instead of jobs, he suggested that projects have emerged as the predominant component of an organization's structure. And as many of us know, projects are usually time-limited and defined by parameters of schedule, budget, and quality. Leap forward ten years, and we see organizations responding to the needs of a rapidly changing, competitive global economy by embracing a project-driven model of organization and structural change. And this trend coincidentally parallels the Millennials' motivation needs for "flexibility," "growth opportunities," social interaction," "fast work cycle," and "changing and challenging work."

This book has drawn heavily from two separate but overlapping bodies of literature: understanding generational differences and appreciating the need to effectively manage knowledge workers. And Thomas A. Stewart formalizes the integration of these two disciplines in his book *Intellectual Capital: The New Wealth of Organizations*, in Chapter 12, "Your Career in the Information Age." The statements in the following exercise are from Stewart's book.

Career Strategies in the Information Age: A Checklist

Imagine that you're meeting with a new Millennial knowledge worker who is seeking guidance on how to manage his/her career in your organization. The Millennial is asking you to identify those strategies that would increase his/her knowledge of how to stay motivated and advance his/her career. Indicate which of the following strategies you would share with him/her.

- ❑ 1. "A career is a series of gigs, not a series of steps."
- ❑ 2. "Project management is the furnace in which successful careers are [forged]."
- ❑ 3. In the new organization, "[p]ower flows from expertise, not from position."
- ❑ 4. "Most roles in an organization can be performed by either insiders or outsiders."
- ❑ 5. "Careers are made in markets, not hierarchies."
- ❑ 6. "The fundamental career choice is not between one company and another, but between specializing and generalizing."
- ❑ 7. "Intellectual capital is the source of wealth for individuals as well as for organizations—and it is held in common between them."

I have selected the following strategies to coach my Millennials:

____

____

____

I would also add to the list of strategies the following career recommendation based on my own experiences as a manager:

____

____

____

A Paradigm Shift From 20th-Century Training to 21st-Century Learning

The paradigm shift from the "business of training" into the "business of learning" is not new to many of our reader/practitioners. From my experience working with our Contributing Experts, I am well aware that most organizations have made this shift. However, since publishing my book *Reengineering the Training Function: How to Align Training with the New Corporate Agenda* a number of years ago, I continue to find organizations that have not fully made this paradigm shift. It is a critical one to consider in meeting the Millennial motivational need of learning. The following is a brief summary of this concept from my book.

Traditional Corporate Perspective	The New Corporate Realities
Static or steady business and organizational development processes do not require an accountable and responsive training initiative.	Rapidly changing business trends directly impact organization and the need for continuous learning.
A traditional training department supports tightly focused HRD initiatives.	Training becomes one component of the Continuous Learning Organization.
Classroom-based, instructor-led training delivers limited courses in few locations on a regular basis.	Just-in-time competency-based training must now be available in diverse instructional formats and locations.
Little accountability for transfer of training and strategic impact on business and organizational development initiatives.	Considerable emphasis is placed on improving performance, return on investment through benchmarking, and continuous process improvement.

Ideally, we would like to work with the assumption that all organizations have moved in the direction of becoming responsive learning organizations. But classroom-based training is alive and "unwell" in many organizations. And the Millennials, as our new "digital natives," are the first to describe it as ineffective.

It quickly becomes apparent in the following discussion that organizations must change both pedagogical and methodological strategies. We recognize that this need for change is driven by a variety of factors, including the need to create a competitive workforce, employ new information technology learning systems, and generate return on investment. But perhaps an equally important driver of the need to improve our learning systems is the workforce itself—the Millennial knowledge workers. It would not be unrealistic to suggest that they are, at the very moment you are reading this page, participating in multiple social media networks, and blogs, Twitters, and tweets, and of course, Facebook or whatever happens to be the popular social media network at the time. Placing Millennials in a traditional classroom with notebooks and PowerPoint slides may be a fast track to the Help Wanted column.

Technology Changes Work

It is interesting to note that although we are currently enjoying the light-speed impact of new technologies changing how we work, the concept of technology in the workplace is not new. Books written about sociotechnical systems decades ago addressed the issues of how technology changes work and, as will be discussed in just a few pages, how it changes learning. In order to put this broader concept of technology changing work in perspective, a brief review of our critical assumptions is presented. The parallel to Millennial motivational needs is striking. The following short section is based on information appearing in *Sociotechnical Systems: A Source Book* by William A. Pasmore and John J. Sherwood.

Organizations as Sociotechnical Systems

In practice, working toward the joint optimization of the social and technological systems of an organization is a comprehensive process that requires a thorough understanding of an organization, including:

- The social processes that occur in organizations and the variety of theories and methods for making more effective use of human resources
- The technological processes used by the organization and the constraints that it places on the design and operation of the social system
- The theory of open systems, because no two organizations are exactly alike or are faced with the same environmental demands
- The mechanics of change, both in the execution of the initial sociotechnical system design and in provision for the continual adaptation of the organization to new environments.

Technological Changes in Work Parallel Millennial Motivators

An interest coalescing of technology and forces in human resources is taking place. These forces include the accelerating ways that technology has transformed work and the rapid growth of Millennial knowledge workers. While some technologies merely improve the existing ways of working, the emergence and widespread application of connected information work software is actually changing work itself. And as we briefly review four ways that technology changes work, we cannot help to think that these changes directly parallel the previous documented motivational needs of the Millennial knowledge worker.

The following list is based on material appearing in *Generational Blend* by Rob Salkowitz.

Four Ways Technology Changes Work

1. **Technology makes work collaborative.**

   The tools for collaborative technologies are, according to Rob Salkowitz, "getting better: more relevant, more contextual, less disrupting and better integrated into the information work environment." Interestingly, the Millennial motivational factors include "collaboration," "social interaction," "communities of interest," and "open communication with teams." These behavioral technology preferences directly parallel the Millennials' use of Blogger, LinkedIn, Facebook, and other Web 2.0 technologies.

2. **Technology collapses time and space.**

   As we know, appreciate, and even seek out for ourselves, technology has significantly redefined the concept of the workplace and workday. As Salkowitz points out, networked information and communication technology offers the ability to connect and secure voice and data networks anywhere and anytime, and provide a high-quality experience for accessing data, applications, and services. Coincidentally, our Millennial knowledge worker has clearly prioritized "flexibility" as the top motivational factor, followed by others relevant to communication technology, including "open communication with teams," "communities of interest," and "work and life balance."

3. **Technology makes work transparent.**

   Many of us remember, or are still experiencing, a work environment that requires going to the same place of work on a daily basis and working eight to ten hours under the physical supervision of a manager. For a number of reasons, especially the omnipotent presence of technology, the concept of the workplace has become—and will continue to develop into—a flexible and virtual relationship between employer and employee. Desks, file cabinets, and individual hard drives are no longer the home for reports, documents, and project updates.

   Organizations are now using Enterprise Resource Planning (ERP) systems and Manufacturing and Supply Chain Management systems to coordinate supply networks. In addition, the Internet, e-mail, text messaging, and voice mail have resulted in technology-based collaborative workspaces. And ironically, as Salkowitz points out, rather than having a boss physically watch over you, "the net result of these developments is that workers and their work products are more visible, accessible, and accountable than ever before." Transparency is now a face of the 21st-century workplace.

   And once again, coincidentally, Millennials who blog, Twitter, tweet, and manage their Facebook accounts find this new transparent work environment desirable, as it meets their bimodal needs. First, they do not necessarily take privacy for granted. Second, technology allows them to maintain compliance with organizational processes.

4. **Technology amplifies the potential of people.**

   When we reexamine the result of the Millennial Motivational Factors Survey and review the Portraits of Millennials, we find priorities placed on "career advancement," "challenging work," "treatment as colleagues," "social interaction," and "growth opportunities.

These motivational needs are now being met, in part, as connected information systems become smarter and more sophisticated. Several select attributes of the new technology amplify the potential of people, including small teams who can now perform tasks that previously required large numbers of people; more knowledge and job-specific functions will be embedded into software sharing information, previously limited and accessible only to experts. In addition, workers can visualize data in richer ways, and it pushes exceptional responsibility and competence onto the shoulders of our high-achieving Millennials.

Rob Salkowitz summarizes the implication of technology amplifying the potential of people as it specifically relates to Millennials in his statement, "What younger workers know is how to find information they need when they need it, using search engines, social networks, data visualization applications, and person-to-person communication tools." This combined new Millennial skill has been uniquely labeled "just-in-time comprehension."

Millennials in the Technology-Driven Workplace

It is important not to use "generational generalizations" to characterize each group and their attitudes towards technology and their learning style. However, there is a growing body of literature and research that describes Millennials not only as techno-savvy workers, but also as especially well suited to the needs of the new technology-driven workplace. The following checklist of Millennials' competitive advantages in the workplace is provided as a fluent transition to the final section of this part, "Millennials and Their Learning Preferences."

MILLENNIALS IN THE TECHNOLOGY-DRIVEN WORKPLACE: A CHECKLIST OF ATTRIBUTES

Research and Contributing Expert input have identified the following "technology attributes" that Millennials bring to the workplace. Identify which of the following best characterize Millennials that you supervise, and indicate if there are others that you would add to the list.

- ❑ 1. They have never known a life without a computer—through the use of technology, they can take in 20 hours of information in seven hours.
- ❑ 2. Millennials eagerly embrace technology in its many permutations and combinations.
- ❑ 3. They are independent and highly networked, both personally and technologically.
- ❑ 4. They are the first entirely technology-savvy generation to enter the workplace.
- ❑ 5. They appreciate continuous learning opportunities.
- ❑ 6. Technology is not an occasional tool, but a constant extension of themselves.
- ❑ 7. They want all the education that they can get on the job.
- ❑ 8. They excel at multitasking and building parallel careers—not focusing on one job at the exclusion of others.

CONTINUED

CONTINUED

- ❑ 9. They are accustomed to instant communication and long-distance collaboration.
- ❑ 10. Technology to them is a freedom. It is a tool that enables them to complete their jobs faster and easier.

Action Items:

The technology-driven attributes that characterize Millennials that I supervise are:

____

____

____

Other technology-driven attributes my team possesses include:

____

____

____

Millennials and Their Unique Learning Preferences

The following discussion serves as an internal summary, transitioning the reader into the final section of this part.

Millennials' Insatiable Appetite for Learning

Rick Humphress
Oracle Corporation

There is absolutely no question that America's economic leadership, in an increasingly competitive global economy, will be influenced by the growing importance of our Millennial knowledge workers. "Learning organizations," "managing human and intellectual capital" and "lifelong learning" are now common drivers of performance in any responsive organization.

More specifically, success at motivating the 21–30-year-old knowledge worker is anchored to three key drivers, presented by Contributing Expert Kitty Nix. First, Millennials are knowledge seekers with an insatiable appetite for relevant learning opportunities. Their loyalty is no longer anchored to their organization, but is anchored to their academic discipline and their very own knowledge portfolio, which they aggressively manage. Second, they seek continuous, just-in-time opportunities to learn and grow. Their learning preference is often on-the-job—having a need to learn what they need when they need it—and competency-based learning—relevant to their increasing their professional effectiveness. Third, while our emphasis is on the acquisition of knowledge, we should not overlook the importance of training, which provides a shorter-term solution to developing job-related skills. "Just-in-time" vs. "just-in-case" training is a critical Millennial motivational indicator.

An important component of developing learning organizations and human capital is technology. And the Millennial brings to the workplace "maximum" technology expectations as essential to their learning and career growth. As Contributing Expert Chris Ryan recommends, "an organization needs to provide the technological tools such as a laptop (that can be taken home for work after-hours), special software, instant messaging, and access to social networking websites. The Millennial knowledge worker is motivated by gaining access to new technologies as they become available to both keep their skills current and maintain their perceived 'edge' over the more senior coworker."

On-the-job sponsored learning and training and attractive office space with up-to-date technology and resources are now minimum requirements for motivating the Millennial knowledge worker.

Making a Case for Millennial Adult Learners: Coinciding Forces

There is a tendency to treat Millennial learners differently than other generational groups. This overlooks two key points. First, Millennials as digital natives are attracted to, and most comfortable with, technology-mediated methods of learning; yet these new learning technologies are of value to all generational cohorts. Second, in our enthusiasm to focus on Millennials' learning preferences, the key concepts of Malcolm Knowles's theory of andragogy—teaching adult learners—should not be overlooked.

Millennial as Digital Natives Gravitate to Technology-Mediated Learning

Rick Humphress states that a premise of this part is that learning should be different for the four broad sociological groups that include Traditionals, Baby Boomers, Gen Xers, and Millennials. However, he suggests that Millennials have unique needs associated with learning methods and the use of technology. In his research of adult learning theory, he has been unable to find a study that makes a distinction between adults based on age. Indeed, he argues, Knowles and others implicitly state that adult learning theory applies to all adults. From his perspective, his only meaningful differentiation between the various groups is the amount of life experience members of each group bring to training.

Even then, a Millennial could have more germane experience than a Baby Boomer depending on the area of inquiry. Therefore, it is apparent that the factors imputed to the Millennials are in fact important to all sociological classes, since they are important to all adults. In fact, Rick Humphress suggests that the trend to be noted is that the constantly changing knowledge economy has placed a premium on effective training for all workers. This has led to an improvement in technology-mediated learning methods for all users. It just happens to coincide with the rise of technology-focused Millennials in the workforce.

Malcolm Knowles's Theory of Andragogy: Assumptions

Anyone having the slightest experience teaching adult learners has formally or informally come to understand that adults learn differently than younger students. Knowles's theory of andragogy, discussed in his now classic book, *The Adult Learner*, addresses a variety of learning preferences that are relevant to all four generational groups.

- Adults need to know why they need to learn something before undertaking to learn it.
- Adults have a self-concept of being responsible for their own decisions, for their own lives.
- Adults come into an educational activity with both a greater volume and a different quality of experience than children do.
- Adults become ready to learn those things they need to know and to be able to do in order to cope effectively with their real-life situations.
- Adults are not subject-oriented but life-centered in their orientation to learning.
- Adults are motivated more by intrinsic motivators (self-esteem, job satisfaction, improved life quality, etc.) than by extrinsic motivators (bonuses, salary increases, promotions, etc.).

These concepts deserve our consideration as a platform to understand Millennial comfort with technology-mediated learning and with basic concepts of adult education.

Millennial Learning Preferences: Four Perspectives

A variety of educators and consultants have identified the unique learning preferences of Millennials. Each of the following four individuals offers specific observations and recommendations on how to support the Millennial motivational factor of learning. Let's begin with an academic perspective first.

A University and Research Perspective

Dr. Cathy Sandeen is Dean of Continuing Higher Education at the University of California-Los Angeles. In her article, appearing in the *Continuing Higher Education Review,* Vol. 72, 2008, she presents a comprehensive generational perspective on learning. It is entitled "Boomers, Xers and Millennials: What Are They and What Do They Really Want from Continuing Higher Education." It is a rigorously researched and well-documented article that addresses issues beyond the context of this book. However, there are two sections especially relevant to this part.

Based on her research and university administration and teaching experience, Sandeen draws the following conclusions:

- Boomers, Gen Xers, and Millennials are expert multitaskers and résumé-builders, and they are technology-immersed, networked, and connected.
- They are success-oriented and status conscious.
- Topics likely to appeal to them, in part, include new technology and basic job skills (presentations, finance, spreadsheets, career information).
- Because of their immersion in technology, they are likely to prefer distance learning.
- Due to their experience with traditional education, they continue to be drawn to classroom-based experiences as well.
- The opportunity to receive education via wireless devices is appreciated.
- They expect their educational experience to be highly customized.
- They expect 24/7 access to instructors and student services staff.
- Finally, and most interestingly, facilities that can create a Starbucks-like multitasking environment will be a big hit.

Millennial Learner Hypothesis: Program Selection, Format, Marketing

Dean Cathy Sandeen's research and analysis also generated a series of hypotheses about the needs or preferences of adult learners by generations. While you are encouraged to read her entire article for this broader perspective, those hypotheses which are specifically relevant to Millennial learners follow. Millennials will tend to:

- Show interest in career-related programs
- Show some interest in graduate school or degree preparation
- Prefer online formats over classrooms
- React positively to career relevance in marketing messages
- Appreciate the ability to sample a program prior to enrolling
- Show greater preference for electronic channels
- Show interest in social networking as a marketing channel

Not only have organizations moved out of "the business of training" and into "the business of learning," but they now find that they need to address both the learning preferences of Millennials and the challenges of teaching multigenerational audiences.

Learning Along with the Millennials

There is no doubt that organizations have embraced pedagogical and methodological concepts in the design and delivery of training. There is clear evidence that these changes have included moving beyond training as an activity—complete with small group activities, flipcharts, PowerPoint presentations, and refreshment breaks. And while globalization and information technology have, in general, improved training and education delivery, Russ Eckel, Founder and President, Nommos Group and Generations at Work, writing in his article "Learning Along with Millennials," makes a key point:

> ***"Important as these factors [globalization, information technology] are, there is another reason why almost all aspects of training [and education] must change—the workforce. To be specific, young workers, indeed the Millennials, have arrived. With them comes a whole new way of working and learning. Therefore, to understand your organization's future training [and education] needs lies in your understanding and integration of Millennial learning style."***
>
> **–Russ Eckel**

Russ Eckel introduces the concept of "Millennial modes of learning" by citing the work of Christopher Dede, a professor at Harvard University School of Education. He is an expert on learning technology and educational pedagogy. He identifies the following five elements, which together constitute the Millennial generation's preferred modes of learning.

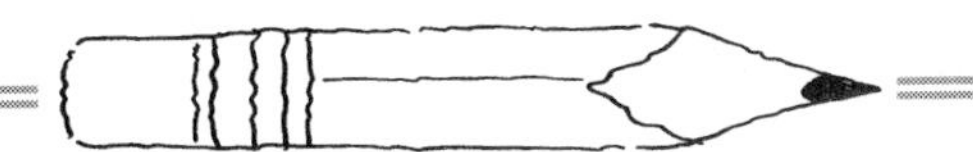

Five Elements Constituting Millennial Modes of Learning

Identify which of the following elements you are currently using in your Millennial training and education programs. Also identify which element(s) you are not using, but should consider employing.

Currently Using	Should Consider	
❑	❑	1. Fluency in multiple media and simulation-based virtual settings
❑	❑	2. Communal learning involving shared experiential knowledge
❑	❑	3. A balanced amount of experiential learning, guided mentoring, and collective reflections
❑	❑	4. Expression through nonlinear associational webs
❑	❑	5. Co-creation of learning experience

Based on review of the previous listed five Millennial learning modes, I have identified the following strengths and areas for improvement:

___

___

___

When you compare the previously presented five elements constituting Millennial modes of learning with earlier profiles of Millennials, you can see a match between motivation factors and learning styles. Those behavioral characteristics included "multitasking," "being connected," "using a broad range of communication technology to share experiences," and "the desire to create their own learning experience." Learning for Millennials has more in common with their social networking practices, involving collaboration with friends, students, mentors, the ubiquitous presence of computers, and of course, an extraordinary array of technologies, now including vlogs (video logging) and microblogging (short blog posts under 140 characters).

Portfolio of Training Media

In the same way Millennials have moved away from developing traditional résumés and toward creating portfolios of life and work experience, their learning preferences gravitate toward a wide variety of training media. Russ Eckel, President Nommos Group and Generations at Work, credits Suzanne Roberts, a senior IBM learning specialist, with developing a wide portfolio of training media that constitutes the "Neo-Millennial Learning System." The mix of media includes:

- Self-study, Web-based training
- Web-based discussion groups
- Online workshops
- Mobile wireless courseware
- Face-to-face workshops

For those of us involved with graduate and certification programs for working professionals, we refer to this learning portfolio as "blended learning." This "Neo-Millennial" learning system also parallels the Millennial motivational factors presented earlier in the book. These include "state-of-the-art technology," "social interaction," and "communities of interest." The parallel between social networking and co-creating a shared learning experience is strikingly similar. Interestingly, major corporations are now encouraging and even requiring managers to actively engage in social networking as part of the organization's efforts in recruiting, managing, and motivating the workforce.

New Training Techniques Needed for Millennials

John Ambrose, Vice President of Strategy, Corporate Development and Emerging Business, Skillsoft, makes an important statement in his article "New Training Techniques Needed for Millennials," which sets the scene for his specific and relevant recommendations. He states:

> ***"Today's graduates—dubbed "Millennials"—are a completely new breed of workers compared with their predecessors. They have a different take on what makes a desirable work environment. The new generation coming into the workforce expects ongoing enrichment and challenges. We can't train this new generation the same way we did employees five or ten years ago."***
>
> **–John Ambrose**

He makes an important point that training (learning) will be seen as a benefit only if it is approached correctly. From his perspective as Senior Vice President of Skillsoft, he has the unique advantage of working with a wide variety of public- and private-sector organizations. And from this broad perspective he makes a number of recommendations that I have taken the liberty of presenting in the form of an organizational assessment.

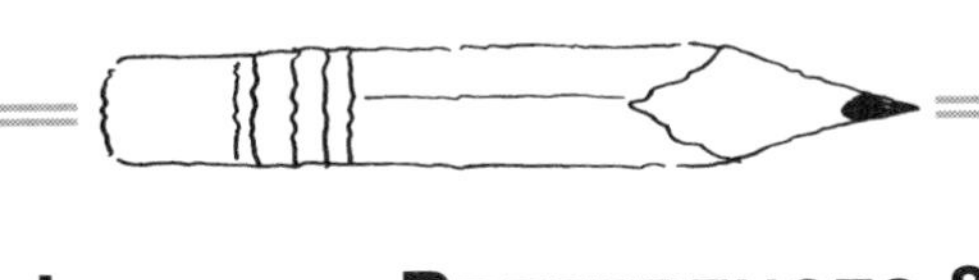

Millennial Learner Preferences & Practices

Identify those Millennial learning practices that your organization is currently employing, and provide specific applications. Also, identify several Millennial learning practices that you are currently not employing but that have the potential to enhance your programs.

____ 1. Young professionals want to know that what they learn today will help them in their long-term career.

____ 2. Learning should be made part of the daily workflow rather than being relegated to training sessions that take them away from their jobs.

____ 3. New hires are accustomed to a very interactive digital lifestyle.

____ 4. Millennials, often described as "digital natives," are accustomed to receiving and disseminating information from multiple sources simultaneously.

____ 5. Millennials expect engaging learning experiences, whether they take place in the classroom or online.

____ 6. They presume that employers will communicate via highly produced, entertaining media.

____ 7. Millennials, raised on video games, gravitate toward multipath gaming techniques that put them in control.

____ 8. Virtual classrooms can be used to bring together groups of learners to interact and discuss topics that have been covered in online self-study.

____ 9. Interspersing multimedia learning that incorporates audio and video will keep their attention from waning.

____ 10. Millennials used to a 24/7 work and life balance can take advantage of digestible learning experiences on demand via mobile learning devices.

Even a quick review of the previous ten Millennial learning preferences and recommendations reinforces the importance for organizations to move continuous learning out of an isolated classroom, with PowerPoint presentations and printed handouts, and move to a learning platform that embraces the potential of podcasts, laptops, and MP3 players. "Learning anytime, anyplace, any way" is quickly replacing "just-in-case training."

Learning and Training Recommendations

This part has presented a broad variety of Millennial learning strategies and tactics. When employed, they will also lend support to the learning motivational needs of Millennials. A final set of recommendations is now presented by contributors to reinforce the application potential of these concepts.

Best-of-Class Practices

Rick Humphress
Oracle Corporation

- Scheduled training should be set so that it is more accessible to employees.
- Scheduled training should be revised to include more information germane to the employee's work setting and must elicit the learner's participation.
- Scheduled training should be taught by qualified trainers who understand the principles of adult learning and how to engage adult learners.
- Managers should have responsibility for the learning and development of their employees built into their job descriptions.
- Managers should have a subset of the adult learning skills demanded of training instructors.
- Managers should be evaluated on how well they develop the competencies of their employees.
- Organizations should provide and publicize learning centers (physical or virtual) that employees can access.
- Organizations should train employees on research methods to help them learn on their own.
- Organizations should actively "mine" employees for relevant data that can be placed in a data store that is available to all employees. One modern variant of this idea is the "wiki."

Checklists

The following steps should be taken in order to institute a learning environment that will meet the needs of all adult learners. The checklist items start at the highest strategy level and descend to the lowest tactical learning level:

- Do I have executive management support and direction? Executive management must establish a supportive environment for learning that encourages employees to participate and guides training in the task of providing learning and development.
- Have I engaged the learner in analysis? Instructional designers must involve the learners in the design of the training curriculum by forming planning committees or learning task forces.
- Have I empowered the learner to participate in the training? When analyzing the needs of a training program (using the ADDIE or some such model), you must be sure to leave room for an individual diagnosis of the needs of the particular learners attending each unique session of training.
- Have I aligned the course objectives with learner needs? Instructional designers and trainers must translate the competencies to be learned into a set of materials that will effectively transmit these competencies to the learner.
- Have I gathered learner-centric course evaluations? While Kirkpatrick, Philips, and others stress the financial impact of training programs, it is important to understand what personal value the training had for individual learners.

Learning and Training Recommendations

Kris Jensen, VP, Corporate Solutions
Wisdom Workers Solutions

Although the idea of lifelong learning was "pioneered" by Generation X, all generations have adopted their wisdom by recognizing that an employee's marketability hinges on lifelong learning. However, distrust in Corporate America's long-term promises by the youngest generations keeps them focused on short-term transactional arrangements. To enhance retention efforts, one top-twenty construction company opted to turn skeptics of long-term promises into committed employees by communicating a concrete picture of career potential with the firm. The company created a "womb to tomb" (entry level to senior executive) curriculum, tailored to each job group (i.e., Accounting, Project Management, etc.). A detailed role profile served as the foundation of the program, giving each employee a framework for their success on the job, including their job description, career path, training and development required, and business outcomes expected. These outcomes then became a clear set of measures by which to evaluate the employee's performance.

Competency models outlining the success factors required of leaders, managers, and employees provided a roadmap for training and development, and criteria for hiring and promoting employees, aligning individual talents and interests to the work. The curriculum outlined activities that would appeal to various learning styles and fit different locations and time availability. Managers and employees in each discipline confirmed the definition and scope of the jobs.

Additional programs were created to support employees as they progressed through their careers. A Peer Advisor program provided one-to-one on-boarding assistance by partnering one- and two-year employees with new hires to help them acclimate to the company and teach them the "unwritten" rules of the road, ultimately evolving into a longer-term mentoring relationship. An intensive, year-long leadership development program offered high-potential employees an entrée into high-performing upper management and executive levels. Designed to develop and maintain a pipeline of leaders for organizational sustainability, the program was based on the five prongs of the company's leadership competency model and included thought leadership in each component, along with hands-on practice in each competency area. Candidates were selected from the company's talent pool through formal talent reviews and succession planning processes.

Learning and Training Recommendations

Hector Velez, Executive VP, Business Development
HireStrategy

HireStrategy training program comprises the following elements: textbook training, quarterly company-wide training sessions, classroom training, and on-the-job (OTJ) training. Our program is designed as a road map to move our Associates into a successful career with HireStrategy as quickly and efficiently as possible.Several people contribute to our Associates' SmartStart training experience. SmartStart is facilitated by the Managing Director and others who may have responsibilities to familiarize new Associates with the HireStrategy environment. However, as they progress through each phase, they will recognize that, by design, they gradually take on greater responsibility for their own progress.

Starting a new job with a new organization is a critical time. We want our employees' transition into HireStrategy to be a positive experience with a positive outcome. After all, SmartStart exists due to the natural disorientation that comes from entering new surroundings. To assist new Associates, the Managing Director, and others who may help new employees settle into their new job, we designed checklists of actions and experiences to expose them to specific information, office layouts, equipment, hardware/software applications, work processes, and business systems important to their early development. These checklists are an integral part of our manual. Aside from guiding them through SmartStart, the process further integrates the new employees into the HireStrategy team.

Learning and Training Recommendations

Christopher R. Ryan, Deputy General Counsel
K12 Inc.

Technology is changing society and the work environment at a dizzying pace, especially for those who can remember work before e-mail or even computers. From its invention until the beginning of the 1990s, the personal computer was extremely expensive, making it unavailable for most users outside of an office environment or computer laboratory. Personal and work computers during this time were also not interconnected. This all changed with the advent of advances in technology, less expensive computers, and the commercialization of the Internet.

Today's Millennial workers represent the first group of workers who grew up in an Internet world. Indeed, the speed of change and pervasiveness of technology is second nature to them. As a result, businesses must support and nurture the need for Millennials to be "plugged in" and to have access to the technology they need to do their jobs. For example, a company I worked for gives employees the choice of a desktop or laptop computer. Millennials usually favor laptop computers because they provide flexibility in when and where work is performed. Instant messaging is a communication tool that some companies prohibit on their networks due to security and productivity concerns, but Millennials rely upon "IM" extensively to interact with others and fulfill their responsibilities. Another tool that Millennials rely upon to do their jobs is collaboration software, such as Microsoft SharePoint. Collaboration software enables users to post documents and comments asynchronously in a shared environment.

Staying current with technology is even becoming a necessary tool for attracting and interviewing Millennials. For example, the *Wall Street Journal* has reported on the increased use of the online virtual-reality platform "Second Life" as an interviewing tool with Millennials. Prospective employers invite candidates to meet them in a virtual office within Second Life, and each party selects an avatar to represent them in the interview. Today's employers must adapt and rise to the challenge of relating to and supporting Millennials' use of technology.

Further Discussion

Shira Harrington, Director, Professional Search Positions Inc.

In the beginning of this part, the author quotes Frances Horibe, who makes a point that may be a touchstone in unlocking what triggers the Millennial knowledge worker:

> ***"Knowledge is now the coin of the realm, and the knowledge worker is the most important source of wealth in an organization. Companies are coming to terms with this and starting to assess how to leverage their intellectual capital."***

In recent years, the term "human capital" has become an "in" phrase among savvy business executives. In an attempt to describe the people part of the organization in a way which shows they are the key drivers to success, management may be treading on delicate waters when it comes to motivating their key knowledge worker Millennials, especially in the area of learning.

The question becomes, how do you integrate a company's need to build ROI with a Millennial worker's need for personal fulfillment, including learning and development? While an organization exists first and foremost to be profitable, with the lack of corporate loyalty in Millennials, any attempt to treat them as a number or a statistic may have the reverse effect of retaining them and making them feel like valuable, individual contributors.

This dichotomy is one that needs to be addressed in future research. It is true that engaged employees drive corporate capital; however, if Millennials feel that they are simply a data point in a human capital metric, they will be less motivated to participate in, let alone absorb, the learning that is needed to enhance their performance. At the end of the day, Millennials choose to engage in learning and development activities to enhance their own personal and professional development, not necessarily to drive corporate profits. Finding equilibrium between these competing objectives will determine how much Millennials allow their employers to leverage their human capital potential.

Summary

Part Seven had four key objectives. First, it explained that the forces shaping America's economy have implications for work and workers in the 21st century. Second, it stressed the importance of knowledge becoming the most important factor in economic life. Third, it documented that a paradigm shift from 20th-century training to 21st-century learning has taken place. Fourth, and finally, it demonstrated that the Millennials' unique learning preferences coincide with the rise of technology-mediated learning methods.

Part Eight: Pay for Performance takes on the challenge of demonstrating that an organization's efforts to meet the Millennial motivational factors discussed throughout the book will result a greater return on investment. It is the final piece of the human resource management continuum of recruiting, selecting, managing, motivating, and rewarding—not just with the previously presented "rewards and recognition" strategies, but with one of the Millennials' top motivators: money.

PART 8

Pay for Performance

"Flexible pay-for-performance initiatives that can be implemented and adapted to shorter time frames—12, 24, or 36 months, very much like emerging prenuptial agreements—are now needed for Millennial knowledge workers."

–Rick Humphress, Oracle Corporation

In this part:

- Getting Started
- Money as a Driver of Superior Performance
- Beyond the Performance Appraisal
- Identifying Strategies for Providing Financial Rewards for Knowledge
- A Pay-for-Performance Initiative

Getting Started

This part focuses on four objectives. Contributing Experts have provided pay-for-performance strategies that enhance the relevance and application of the following four objectives.

- Seize the opportunity to build on the foundation of intangible rewards and recognition motivators presented in Part Six to now include the tangible motivator of money as a driver of superior performance.
- Move beyond the traditional concept of a performance appraisal in order to implement a pay-for-performance system.
- Identify and employ strategies for providing financial rewards for knowledge.
- Implement a pay-for-performance system in shorter time frames of 12, 24, or 36 months.

Money as a Driver of Superior Performance

Part Six: Rewards, Recognition, and Respect focused on four key points. First, it identified those unique generational factors that influence the importance of recognition, reward, and respect as Millennial motivators. Second, it stressed the importance of appropriate recognition for the Millennial knowledge worker. Third, it presented concepts enabling the establishment of an organizational and managerial climate to apply reward strategies. Fourth, it focused on developing a mutually beneficial climate in support of respect.

Examples of the importance of Millennial knowledge worker reward, recognition, and respect strategies selected from Part Six include:

- The Millennial age cohort places considerable importance on the motivational factors of recognition, reward, and respect.
- Millennials are drawn to organizations and managers that offer frequent recognition.
- When Millennials' need for recognition is met in a timely and authentic manner, they go to the next step and exceed normal expectations.
- Millennials have a set of clearly defined reward expectations, including increased responsibility, opportunities to learn, and frequent praise and feedback for performance.
- Effectively motivating Millennial knowledge workers requires both individual and manager to enter into a behavioral contract in support of respect.

Money as a Motivator

Money is not a prime motivator, and in most cases, it starts to lose its value as a motivator at a certain point. However, when tied to a well-designed pay-for-performance system and comprehensive benefits package, it meets a variety of Millennials' tangible and intangible motivational needs.

Most experienced managers and human resources professionals know that money is one of the most short-lived motivators. We also know that it does not have as much power to attract and retain Millennial knowledge workers as many think it does. However, money is an important part of a balanced portfolio of reward strategies. In a survey commissioned by Robert Half International and Yahoo! HotJobs, with results published in *What Millennial Workers Want: How to Attract and Retain Gen Y Employees*, respondents ranked salary as 9.5 in importance on a 1-to-10 scale, with 10 being the most important. An opportunity exists to build on the foundation of intangible rewards and recognition to now include the tangible motivator of money as a driver of superior performance.

Beyond the Performance Appraisal

To implement an effective pay-for-performance system, you need to go beyond the traditional concept of a "performance appraisal." The implementation of an effective pay-for-performance initiative, designed to meet the needs of the Millennial knowledge worker, requires a systems view of performance management. This includes building upon a foundation of reward, recognition, and respect; going beyond traditional performance appraisals; and, finally, rewarding knowledge.

The knowledge and experience of Contributing Expert Peter W. Kennedy, Principal, PRM Consulting Group, and his associate, Sandy Grogan Dresser, are now drawn upon to address this challenge. Their discussion sets the scene for this part's discussion of pay for performance. Their contributions to this chapter have been selected from articles that they wrote for the *Compensation of Employee Benefits Journal,* which is no longer in print.

Appraising and Paying for Performance: Another Look at an Age-Old Problem

Peter W. Kennedy, Principal
PRM Consulting Group

Why is the relatively simple notion of improving performance through management and appraisal so difficult to successfully implement in practice? The reasons are unfortunately numerous enough to consume entire textbooks on the subject. For the most part, however, they relate to simple human weaknesses: fear, pride, impatience, lack of candor or discipline, procrastination, and poor communication skills. But most of all, even reasonable people don't necessarily agree. We simply don't come to the business at hand with the same expectations; each of us brings with us our own set of values and beliefs, with resulting differences in what we deem acceptable, outstanding, marginal, or dare I say, just plain old good.

The most common complaints are that appraisals:

- Take too much time
- Are too subjective
- Are all the same
- Make distinctions without a real difference
- Are not timely enough
- Belittle people
- Ignore the system
- Are used for too many purposes which often conflict

The purpose of this part is not to instruct our readers on how to address and resolve each of the previously listed performance appraisal complaints. Rather, it is to suggest that few would disagree with the contention that performance appraisals have been, for the most part, a resounding failure in corporate America. Surveys indicate, time and again, the widespread dissatisfaction with formal, written performance appraisals, both for employees who are subjected to the annual ritual and for the supervisors who are required to conduct them.

Other Approaches to Consider

The widespread dissatisfaction with traditional appraisals and merit pay has spawned a number of alternative approaches, which are not necessarily mutually exclusive. Each has its own advantages and disadvantages. Success with any single approach depends on an organization's ability to articulate and stick to the approach's central purpose and then implement and maintain it consistently over time.

Management by Objectives (MBO)

A common component of what we consider to be a traditional performance appraisal, MBO is worth mentioning not only because it remains widespread, but also because it explicitly recognizes the need for performance planning, not just appraisal. Where work is not routine, MBO can be and is used by supervisors, in consultation with those they supervise, to establish worthwhile and meaningful work goals at the beginning of the year. Performance is then appraised at the end of the year, based on how well the goals were achieved.

If done correctly, MBO helps to control the element of surprise in year-end appraisals, gives employees some constructive influence over what is to be appraised, and is more likely to result in a common understanding and agreement as to what was actually achieved at year end.

Total Quality Management (TQM)

W. Edwards Deming called performance appraisal one of the seven deadly diseases. Among other criticisms, he indicated that the traditional performance appraisal discourages risk-taking, leaves people depressed and bitter, and is unreliable and inconsistent as a measurement tool.

Deming's prescription for total quality management is to get rid of performance appraisals altogether. Instead of grading everyone, the organization should emphasize pride in workmanship and treat everyone the same within certain control limits. The call to abandon the formal performance appraisal as we know it in the name of total quality management and improvement is compelling given the success of Deming's methods.

Multi-Source Assessment

Where Deming's clear goal is the improvement of company performance through the careful management of product quality, the focus in multi-source assessment (or 360-degree feedback) is on obtaining a more complete understanding of all of the employee's performance successes and setbacks by getting feedback from as many people who interact with the employee as possible. Rather than getting just one assessment from the direct supervisor, organizations that use multi-source assessment typically find the aggregate result to be more a more thorough and therefore more accurate and reliable assessment of individual performance.

A typical approach might involve six to ten raters for each person. Finding enough individuals familiar with each person's work can be a problem, unless work is very much centered in teams. A similar issue can be the selection of the raters. A good management information system is necessary to report and administer the multiple ratings. Raters can be trained to develop their rating abilities; the rating results can be used to provide feedback on rating consistency.

Assessing Individual Competencies

While definitions of the term may vary, the basic concept of a competency is any individual attribute that can help ensure organizational success. Competencies include knowledge, skills, abilities, behaviors, other personal attributes, or even values that people bring to their work. The term is intentionally broad so as to capture important personality traits, such as integrity, initiative, optimism, energy, and honesty.

The rationale for including competencies in performance appraisals is that they build a stronger, more flexible workforce driven by customer focus, guided by a global competitive strategy, focused on learning as a competitive advantage, and supportive of worker mobility within and between companies. Each of these rationales is especially relevant to motivating the Millennial knowledge worker.

Identifying Strategies for Providing Financial Rewards for Knowledge

This book is not just about motivating Millennials, but is more specifically about Millennial knowledge workers. This raises the bar for identifying motivational strategies to address the specific motivational needs of knowledge workers as they relate to pay for performance. More specifically, the following brief discussion acknowledges the need to:

- Identify organizational processes that reward intellectual capital
- Implement systems capable of managing intangible assets
- Develop flexible compensation and benefits systems

Identify Organizational Processes that Reward Intellectual Capital

There is no doubt that an ever-growing percentage of individuals are now described as "knowledge workers." In simplest terms, this means that information and knowledge are the raw materials of their labor and its products. This had led to the concepts of a "knowledge economy," a "knowledge organization," and an organization's "intellectual capital."

Thomas A. Stewart, writing in *Intellectual Capital: The New Wealth of Organizations,* states that "Every organization houses valuable intellectual materials in the form of assets and resources, tacit and explicit perspectives and capabilities, data, information, knowledge, and maybe wisdom." Intellectual capital is strategically located in an organization's people, structure, and customers.

Paying for Intellectual Capital

There is no question that intellectual capital is a valuable asset to an organization. In simplest terms, smart workers work smarter. There is documented evidence that a relationship exists between a worker's education and productivity. However, Thomas Stewart raises an important point, especially relevant to motivating Millennial knowledge workers: Organizations and managers have had a hard time distinguishing between the cost of paying people and the value of investing in them.

Tools for Measuring and Managing Intellectual Capital

The following assumptions suggest the need to identify tools and processes that reward knowledge workers.

- The number of knowledge workers—a large percentage, Millennials—is rapidly increasing.
- A need exists to not only attract and recruit Millennial knowledge workers, but also identify strategies to motivate, retain, and develop them.
- There is a difference in the cost of paying people and the value in investing in them.
- A need exists to identify tools to measure human capital.

Thomas A. Stewart concludes his book, *Intellectual Capital*, with a variety of strategies and tools to measure and manage intellectual capital. As one example, he indicates that while answering the following questions won't yield quantitative data about human capital, it will yield a rich harvest of qualitative information.

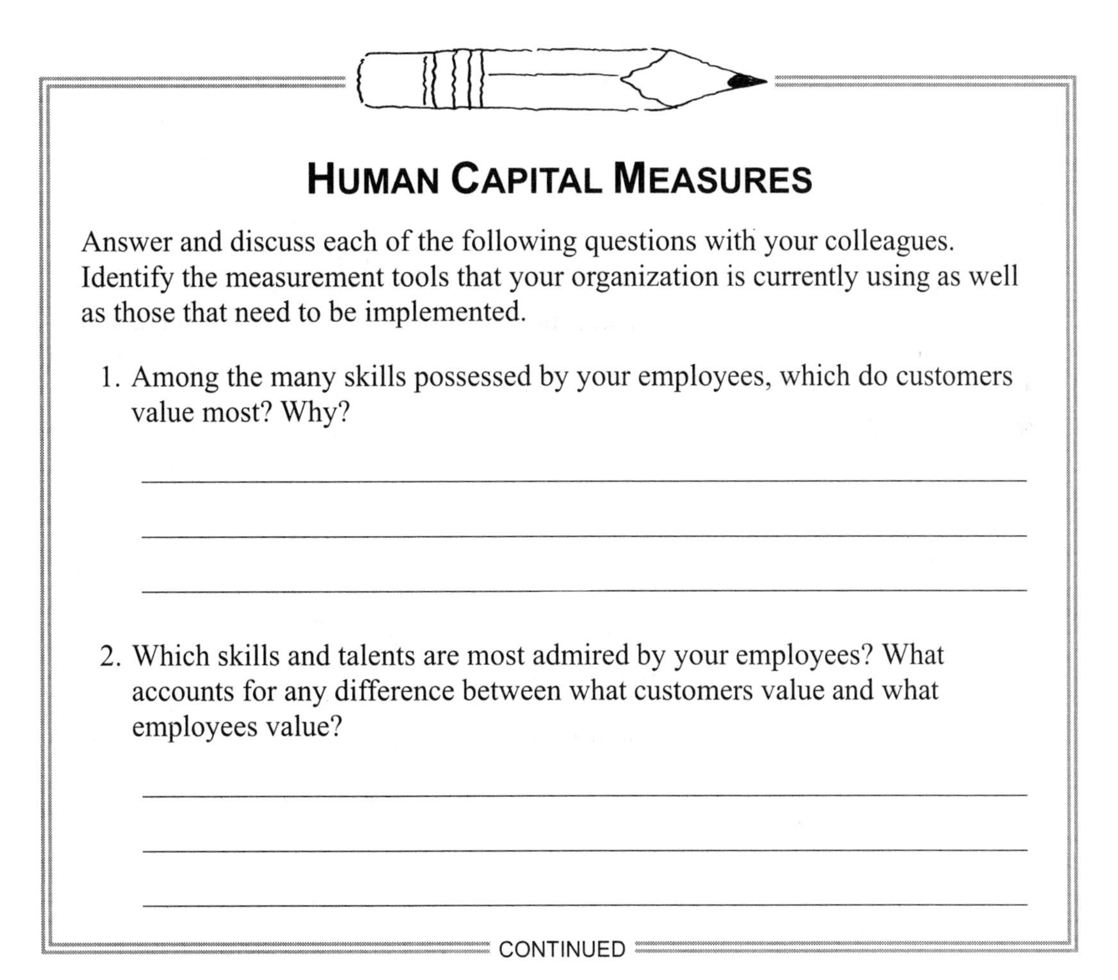

HUMAN CAPITAL MEASURES

Answer and discuss each of the following questions with your colleagues. Identify the measurement tools that your organization is currently using as well as those that need to be implemented.

1. Among the many skills possessed by your employees, which do customers value most? Why?

   ____

   ____

   ____

2. Which skills and talents are most admired by your employees? What accounts for any difference between what customers value and what employees value?

   ____

   ____

   ____

CONTINUED

CONTINUED

3. What emerging technologies or skills could undermine the value of your proprietary knowledge?

____

____

____

4. Where in your organization do high-potential managers most want to be assigned? Where do they least want to work? How do they explain their preferences?

____

____

____

5. What percentage of managers has completed plans for training and developing their successors?

____

6. What percentage of all employees' time is spent in activities of high value to customers? What percentage of expert employees' time is spent in activities of low value to customers?

____

____

7. When competitors are hiring, do they hire from you?

____

____

8. Why do people leave you to accept jobs elsewhere?

____

____

____

CONTINUED

CONTINUED

9. Among experts in your labor market—including headhunters—what is your company's reputation vis-à-vis its competitors?

___

___

___

Application Exercise: Based on your answering and discussing each of the previous questions, identify the following.

A current measurement our organization is using: ___

___

___

A measure that we need to implement: ___

___

___

Flexible Compensation and Benefits

There is common agreement among economists, business leaders, and politicians that the driver of success in "The New Economy" is knowledge. The demand for knowledge workers is great and growing, with an estimated 60 percent of all jobs now knowledge-based. Those organizations that survive and thrive in a fiercely competitive global economy will have to rethink their workforce strategies and transform their management and human resource practices to attract, retain, engage, and develop workers of all ages.

However, the Millennial offers a special challenge. In particular, the Millennial knowledge workers realize that they are an attractive commodity in the competitive labor market and have demonstrated the ability to effortlessly job-hop for better opportunities. In order to meet their motivational needs, as addressed in previous parts, organizations need to provide not only innovative learning opportunities and flexible work arrangements, but also creative and responsive compensation and benefits programs. "Pay for performance" quickly emerges as a driver of this employee attraction, engagement, and retention strategy.

A Pay-for-Performance Initiative

A pay-for-performance initiative, implemented in shorter time frames of 12, 24, or 36 months, is required to effectively motivate Millennial knowledge workers. Before the presentation of pay-for-performance motivational strategies, the following two important assumptions must be examined. They are especially relevant to Millennials. First, a human resources professional will quickly suggest that the behavior that is recognized and rewarded is the behavior that is repeated. Second, as stated earlier in this part, a survey commissioned by Robert Half International and Yahoo! HotJobs found that employees ranked salary as 9.5 in importance on a 1-to-10 scale. In short, while all previously discussed Millennial motivators are important, let us not overlook money.

Paying for Performance: An Overview

Rick Humphress
Oracle Corporation

We begin by addressing and responding to a variety of assumptions necessary to establish a relevant pay-for-performance system. This includes, in part, removing politics and "perceptional" elements from reward systems and instead having rewards linearly tied to performance. In addition, a comprehensive benefits package will provide opportunities to customize financial motivators for not only Millennials, but a variety of age cohorts. In many cases, generous time off and flexible schedules in support of work/life balance carry as much weight as competitive salaries.

Many Millennial knowledge workers have experienced mergers, acquisitions, and significant organizational changes. Products and services have been outsourced, insourced, or simply eliminated. As a result, Millennials have become behaviorally conditioned to perceive themselves as replaceable and driven by competitive market conditions. Flexible pay-for-performance initiatives that can be implemented and adapted to shorter time frames—12, 24, or 36 months, very much like emerging prenuptial agreements—are now needed.

Best-of-Class Practices

In order for a pay-for-performance system to be effectively implemented, the following conditions must be met. These conditions flow from Vroom's Expectancy Theory Model, discussed below.

- Employees trust management.
- Management has implemented a valid job evaluation system.
- Management has established clear performance factors.
- Management adequately funds the system.
- Management has implemented an accurate appraisal system without forced distribution models.

Consider pay for performance as one of a number of coordinated efforts rather than as a single silver bullet for increased performance. Research literature cannot identify a single pay-for-performance system implemented as the sole solution for improved productivity that has ever succeeded.

Checklist

Pay-for-performance perversions to eliminate:

- ❑ Too much focus on the short term at the expense of the long term. If your pay-for-performance plan sacrifices the long term for short-term benefits, it may fail to achieve the desired results.
- ❑ Setting limits on expectations encourages mediocrity. If your pay-for-performance plan defines minimal expectations too low, it may erode overall performance.
- ❑ Too much emphasis on the individual destroys teamwork. If your pay-for-performance plan rewards the individual without recognizing the role of the team, it could discourage collaboration.
- ❑ Too much internal competition reduces productivity. If your pay-for-performance plan pits individuals against one another for scarce rewards, they may engage in counterproductive activities that improve their changes for reward—but not organizational effectiveness.

The Vroom Expectancy Theory

Pay for performance will work only if each of the following causal links is strong:

1. Employees attach value to the desired result of higher pay (valence).
2. Employees believe that rewards will actually be provided as a consequence of high performance (instrumentality).
3. Employees believe that they can actually accomplish the task that will lead to the reward of higher pay (expectancy).

The ASPIRE Model

Motivating people through higher pay is only one of several methods for improving worker performance. The ASPIRE human performance improvement model identifies five factors:

- **Actuate** — Understand how positive and negative motivators affect worker performance.
- **Skills** — Analyze, design, develop, implement, and evaluate training solutions to increase worker performance.
- **Power** — Understand how job design affects an individual's ability to perform the job.
- **Information** — Understand the design of process documentation and job aids (employee performance support systems) for improved worker performance.
- **Resources** — Identify and quantify the gaps in the deployment of necessary resources, tools, and environmental support.
- **Expectations** — Understand how such factors as self-esteem, work ethic, values, and quality orientation affect job performance, in order to better match the worker to the work being performed.

Millennial Expectations: Compensation and Benefits

Money can take on a variety of forms within an organization's compensation system. In simplest terms, it is thought of as salary. However, it can also include bonuses, profit sharing, incentive programs, and even stock options. However, while too often it is thought of as the major source of employee satisfaction, it is only one component of how an organization rewards its employees. In addition to money, many organizations have a full range of employee awards programs. Finally, the human element in the personal touch, ranging from a simple pat on the back to public and private praise, completes the reward equation. Frances Horibe, in *Managing Knowledge Workers,* sums it up in stating, "When the money is taken for granted and the plaques gather dust, these [personal touches] are remembered. It is a powerful motivator in and of itself and gives meaning to the money and the awards."

Money as a Means to Freedom

Both the formal Motivational Factors Survey and a review of Millennial literature generated similar conclusions. The very same generational cohort that wants "fun and social interaction," "flexibility and work/life balance," and "recognition, respect, and rewards" also wants security, compensation, and benefits. What may initially appear a bimodal set of wants quickly becomes clear when Millennial priorities are examined.

When we examine Millennial priorities of wanting greater integration between work and life at the workplace, the desire to develop portable skills, a concern with making a difference in the community, environment, and world, money becomes a means to an end. More specifically, Millennials view money as a means to achieve freedom, to have a choice about their lifestyle and when and where they work.

Paying for Performance: Implementation Challenges and Leadership

To be successful, pay for performance requires the organization, human resources professionals, and managers to address and overcome a variety of challenges. Presented quotes from Peter Kennedy's article "Appraising and Paying for Performance: Another Look at an Age-Old Problem" help to put the challenges and opportunities into perspective.

Pay-for-Performance Challenges

Peter W. Kennedy
PRM Consulting Group

The Zero-Sum game

In order to fully understand the issue of paying for performance, we must first recognize that money is a limited resource. In a typical zero-sum game, one individual's gain is another's loss. Most pay-for-performance systems have this unfortunate attribute, at least to some extent. Merit pay, which always purports to pay for performance by determining salary increases based on performance appraisal results, is almost always doomed by this fundamental constraint.

Plain old recognition, with no monetary component, has no such constraint. Its supply is essentially unlimited. Paying for performance sets up winners and losers. Recognizing performance, on the other hand, is purely win-win.

Motivation and Money

If performance appraisals do not seem to motivate people, but recognition does, what about money? Well, let's try to be reasonable about the response: of course it does! But only to a point.

Aon Consulting used to conduct an annual study titled "United States@Work," which correlated numerous variables to a set of six questions intended to reflect employees' commitment to the organization: pride in the work (willingness to refer company's products and services or the company itself as a place to work); productivity (ability and desire to work with others); and tenure (predisposition to leave, and how much of a pay increase this requires). Pay, as a driver of commitment in these studies, is consistently ranked high, but not in the top ten factors that respondents say is most important in reinforcing their commitment to their employer.

[This is in contrast to other survey results, such as the Millennial Motivation Factors Survey, which found pay for performance ranked within the top ten, and the previously cited Robert Half International survey, which ranked money as 9.5 on a scale of 1 to 10.]

Some critics of pay-for-performance systems have pointed out that money, in and of itself, particularly when tied to the achievement of particular goals, can have the effect of redirecting one's attention away from the task at hand to the monetary incentive to be gained. In other words, the acquisition of money becomes the end in itself, sometimes to the detriment of the work itself, even possibly degrading the quality of work and/or encouraging purely self-serving individual behavior. This observation became abundantly clear in the fall of 2008 as the financial sector collapsed but many executives were paid handsome bonuses that encouraged overly risky behavior.

The Element of Surprise

Which leads to a crucial, but often overlooked point: money is more effective when it is used as a reward rather than an inducement. Reward, in the meaning intended here, is a retrospective assessment and acknowledgement (with a significant monetary value). It is most effective when there is an element of surprise. It is the unanticipated award that tends to reinforce behavior and results without detracting from one's interest in the work at hand.

Performance Appraisals and Pay

So, should performance appraisals be tied to pay? In my opinion, they should provide information that leads to basic decisions over time about which employees to terminate, retain, or promote. They should not be used to make miniscule distinctions in pay adjustments. Let's keep the focus of performance appraisals squarely on simple communication about what needs to happen on the job.

Courage and Commitment

Sue McLeod, Senior Consultant
Hay Group

Why worry about paying for performance? Our research shows that the #1 reason for voluntary attrition of high performers is compensation. And you do want to keep your high performers, don't you? Think your Millennials (and other employees) won't find out where they stand compared to their peers? Think again. Remember, this is a generation that is highly connected, thinks they should have access to all important information, and shares with people they barely know.

How do you know if your compensation truly pays for performance? There are two simple tests:

- Do your highest performers consistently receive significantly higher rewards?
- Do your poorest performers consistently receive the lowest rewards?

Your managers are the front line of your pay-for-performance system. They need courage and commitment to succeed.

- Share your commitment. Give managers the tools they need to make tough decisions, communicate consistently, and send the right messages about superior performance.
- Bolster their courage with training, coaching, and support.
- Keep the focus. Measure results and give managers feedback and more training or coaching if needed.

Internal Freelancers and Spot Bonuses

Neil Sawyer, Senior Director, Human Resources
The Campagna Center

Older workers probably grew up with the philosophy instilled in them that they must give their life to the company, and for whatever the company gives them back, they should be grateful. Young workers don't seem to have this presumption. They expect to be paid for work done and are not shy about asking for it.

Freelancers

Most leading publishing companies I am familiar with make use of internal freelancers. These are regular full-time staff members who contract to do work in other departments or divisions of the company on their own time. These are employees who usually have a valued, specific skill set and are typically younger and more eager to get extra money. The company benefits because the excess work would have to be farmed out to a contractor, or temp help would have to be brought in to complete it. Having an employee do the work gives a sense of corporate insider knowledge that is often valuable and can actually decrease the amount of time it takes to get an assignment done. All work to be freelanced in-house must be approved in advance, and a rate of pay that would be higher than the hourly wage of the employee but less than a contractor must be agreed upon. This work must be done at home and not with company equipment—a requirement that younger employees don't mind.

Spot Bonuses

The same organization uses another form of payment for piece work. This is the use of "spot bonuses" for employees who contribute in a significant way to a major project or who have gone above and beyond their normal duties for an extended period of time. These bonuses can range from $500 gross to $5000 net, depending on the scope of the particular project.

Further Discussion

Shira Harrington, Director, Professional Search Positions, Inc.

In his checklist of "pay-for-performance perversions to eliminate," Rick Humphress points out two related issues that should be expanded upon in future research and writing. He notes, "Too much emphasis on the individual destroys teamwork," and "Too much internal competition reduces productivity." As we contemplate ways to motivate Millennials, more consideration needs to be given to the value of rewarding the group, beyond the individual contributor.

Most Millennials were raised in a culture that rewarded teamwork. From "No losers in Little League" to being given group projects throughout their schooling, Millennials appreciate the value of teamwork more so than most generations. As a result, many are more motivated when they know that their team has done a good job and moreover, when rewards are fair.

Equity is a concept that is not lost among this generation, which often wants to equalize rewards rather than recognize the lone superstar. While certainly the latter motivation exists, employers will find that a team-based, project-based reward system, in conjunction with a well-designed individual-based performance plan, will go a long way to building a sense of cohesion and, dare I say, family among this peer-seeking cohort. Sharply contrasted with the motivators of their elder siblings, Generation X, which often seeks rewards for individual entrepreneurial prowess, Millennials will frequently flock toward collaborative achievement. As Millennials continue to grow into the ranks of management, performance measures are likely to evolve into an appreciation of the power of "we" versus "me."

Summary

Part Eight's objectives focused on four key points. First, an opportunity exists to build on the foundation of intangible rewards and recognition motivators presented in Part Six to now include the tangible motivator of money as a driver of superior performance. Second, in order to implement an effective pay-for-performance system, organizations must go beyond the traditional concept of a "performance appraisal." Third, strategies for providing financial rewards for knowledge were identified. Fourth, a pay-for-performance initiative, implemented in shorter time frames of 12–36 months, is required to effectively motivate Millennial knowledge workers.

APPENDIX

Appendix Overview

Motivating the Millennial Knowledge Worker has been designed as both a resource for the individual reader and a classroom training manual. This Appendix provides reader and trainer with further application resources.

The first section outlines suggestions for implementing your action plan. It continues with the book's Contributing Experts identifying and addressing specific Millennial motivational changes. It concludes with a Chapter Checklist: Designing Your Action Plan.

The second section provides a unique organizational assessment tool. The TIP'M© Methodology, developed by Contributing Expert Mark Steffanina, provides both tactical and strategic approaches to building a pro-Millennial workplace by using the Team Improvement and Prioritization Matrix©. Further information about the implementation of this copyrighted tool is available from the author.

Implementing Your Action Plan

Motivating the Millennial knowledge worker is not a passing human resources management fad. Rather, it is now a workforce necessity for organizations seeking to respond to an increasingly more competitive global marketplace, economic challenges, and rapidly changing technologies. Earlier in this book, Millennials were described as the fastest growing segment of the workforce. Further defining this population to focus on Millennial knowledge workers—those individuals who use their heads more than their hands to produce value—identified a segment of the workforce that will drive America's New Economy. As previously quoted, Neil Howe and William Straus describe the impact of the Millennials this way: "This rising generation will introduce itself to the nation and push the nation into a new era." A need has emerged for highly interactive "performance partnerships" between Millennial, manager, and human resources professional.

This appendix presents three application tools for reader and trainer:

- An opportunity is presented to review Contributing Experts' final recommendations addressing specific Millennial motivational challenges.
- A review of each part's learning objectives is presented in a checklist format, allowing the reader to identify those specific behaviorally based Millennial motivational challenges relevant to their workforce.
- A motivational factors survey is introduced, providing readers with an opportunity to implement an organizational Millennial motivational assessment.

Millennial Motivational Challenges: Expert Strategies

Over twenty Contributing Experts have been involved with this book from start to finish. It is appropriate to include examples of how they have addressed specific Millennial motivational challenges. Our experts' biographical sketches appear in the Introduction of the book.

The Importance of the Generational Perspective

Jennell Evans, President and CEO
Strategic Interactions, Inc.

The North American workplace today is the most age-diverse workforce that we have known since the Industrial Revolution. At no other time in history have so many and such diverse generations worked together side by side. There have been multiple generations in the workforce before, but the organizational hierarchy of the manufacturing economy mostly segregated them from one another.

Today, those social and physical separations exist to a much lesser extent. The new, flatter organizational structures and the need for teamwork are creating a generational mix that we have never experienced before, with four generations now in the workforce. This remarkable mix of perceptions and values can foster incredible creativity or, if not managed properly, can lead to intergenerational conflict and high turnover.

To motivate Millennials, the youngest of the four generations in the workforce, leaders of organizations will benefit by cultivating the following two strategies:

1. Embrace social responsibility from the top down:

    - Organizations that authentically and visibly "walk the walk" on social responsibility will attract, engage, motivate, and retain Millennial talent. In 2007, Deloitte & Touche USA conducted a survey and found that two-thirds of the 18- to 26-year-olds responding said that they would prefer to work for companies that allow them to contribute to nonprofit organizations.
    - Since 86% of all U.S. high schools provide community service experiences, Millennials enter the workforce understanding how they can have a positive impact by doing something they feel passionate about, and this is very important to this generation of workers.
    - With the highest rate of volunteerism ever in the U.S., employers who embrace social responsibility as a core value will not only attract "the best and the brightest," but will most likely be better positioned to retain this talented generation and create a pipeline of future leaders.

2. Embrace diverse work/life balance strategies.

    Millennials are committed to work/life balance, and for many, that balance includes opportunities to do things other than work, and to connect with people through volunteer activities, which become part of their identity and their social networking in person and online.

Don't Stereotype Us!

Erin Nicole Gordon, Systems Integration and Technology
Accenture

Contrary to the plethora of negative stereotypes surrounding the twenty-something young professional, Millennial knowledge workers can be successfully motivated. By identifying common attributes (including independent or do-it-yourself, engaged, ambitious, innovative, and compassionate) and successfully providing opportunities that engage these attributes in the workplace, an employer can retain and fully realize the potential of the Millennial knowledge worker.

- As I am given the flexibility to work independently, I become increasingly more productive and am more likely to collaborate with others, given the new time frames created by flexible parameters.
- Growth opportunities coupled with ways to actively contribute fuel the fire of ambition in many Millennials. These opportunity offerings motivate best if they are multidimensional.
- Most menial tasks may be worthwhile to a Millennial knowledge worker if there is an identifiable contribution to society.
- With many corporate initiatives and missions now including developmental and service-oriented relationships (working and being involved all at once), there is a clear effort to engage cause-oriented Millennial knowledge workers, like me.

The Millennial knowledge worker must recognize that employers are aware and willing to work with our differentiating attributes in order to keep us motivated. We possess the potential to sustain the competitive advantage sought in the corporate arena.

Develop Each Individual Employee

Nicole Hardin, Managing Director
HireStrategy

The most important steps any organization can take in developing a sustainable strategy for motivating and retaining Millennials is committing to their employees through strong management, focusing on the development of each individual. This generation craves responsibility and the ability to make an impact on the world around them. Ways to accomplish this include:

- Management that understands that their mission is to facilitate a meaningful relationship with these workers while leveraging their motivation and technical abilities.
- Strong organizational values, complemented by being socially conscientious and mission driven, will not only attract these workers but also earn their loyalty.
- It cannot be over-emphasized how critical it is that companies develop a transparent commitment not just to business values, but to society. It isn't enough anymore to "do no harm"; it is essential to be proactive in positive contribution to society.

This generation is looking for authenticity in all of the actions above, making the full commitment of the organization necessary to successfully motivate the Millennials.

Researchers Have Unique Needs

Deborah K. Hoover, Director of HR
The Urban Institute

It's really no secret—in our best young researchers, their motivation comes from within themselves.

- Avoid de-motivating them with heavy-handed supervision.
- Put your own ego aside and give true responsibility for a project.
- Teach and mentor by helping define problems and assignments.
- Relate real-world conditions to their work assignments.
- Listen, and employ patience.

Nurture the Millennial knowledge workers and get out of the way. They will make you proud and produce truly exceptional ideas and organizational results.

Pull Back the Motivational Lens and Manage Talent

Rick Humphress
Oracle Corporation

Organizations need to adapt their current talent management practices to accommodate Millennial employees. Leaders should:

- Create adequate career and succession plans that give Millennials a clear view of advancement.
- Recruit Millennials by using social networking methods, backed by a strong organizational brand and a streamlined staffing process.
- Motivate Millennials through a combination of monetary and non-monetary rewards that are tailored uniquely for each person.
- Develop Millennials using andragogical training delivered just in time as employees need them to be successful.
- Evaluate Millennials frequently and make the feedback bi-directional.

If organizations improve talent management along these lines, they will provide a smoother transition with a richer transfer of knowledge between generations.

Maximize Productivity and Commitment

Kris T. Jensen, VP Corporate Services
Wisdom Worker Solutions

In these competitive times, organizations are increasingly in need of a highly skilled but adaptable workforce. To develop the resources they require, leaders can influence Millennials' productivity and commitment by:

- Acknowledging their contributions and letting them participate in meaningful work projects that are aligned to the organization's mission and vision.
- Evaluating their performance based on business outcomes and results rather than on "face time"; allowing them to pioneer flexible alternatives to existing processes, schedules, and locations; and fearlessly innovating products and services.
- Communicating performance feedback, development activities, and career options on an informal, just-in-time basis.
- Leading from a position of influence, created through expertise, charisma, or information, rather than asserting organizational authority that will likely lead to compliance and resistance rather than engagement.
- Creating an employee value proposition that builds individual commitment to the organization long-term or welcomes them back when circumstances temporarily suspend the relationship.
- Modeling high-integrity business behaviors.

Imbued with confidence throughout their lives, Millennials will continue to push their environments to transition from control-based to freedom-based accountability and to share a mentality of free agency.

Understand that Millennials Play by Different Rules

Robert McGovern, CEO and Founder
Jobfox

Gen Y plays for a different set of rewards. Understanding this is the first step in motivating the Millennial knowledge worker:

- **More than money** — Gen Y isn't motivated by monetary rewards as much as older workers are. Young workers often value leisure time and flexible work schedule benefits, for example, more than money.
- **Experimentation** — Millennials are able to rapidly adapt to technology change via sophisticated trial-and-error learning styles. Employers must learn to accommodate and create organizational growth opportunities from these "learn-as-I go" approaches, across all business settings.
- **Contribution** — Top-down management hierarchies are foreign to the "Baby-on-Board" generation. From day one, corporate leaders must include Gen Y workers as significant participants in the establishment of business objectives and the roles to be played in meeting important corporate goals.
- **Stability** — Gen Y workers have grown up in a world filled with rapid change. As a result, they seek work as a refuge. However, very few companies are viewed as safe havens by Millennials.

This could be the most committed group of workers ever, I believe, but only for the companies that understand how to create favorable work environments for this new generation.

Learn from Millennials

Sue McLeod, Senior Consultant
Hay Group

The Millennial generation challenges the adult world they are joining because of their different approaches to work and their lives. We need to look beyond these challenges to see that these young people also have a lot of strengths, including their energy, education, and willingness to commit and work hard when the right situation is presented. The Millennial generation has a lot to offer, a lot to teach us, and a lot to learn. But didn't we all when we were their age? And more profoundly, don't we all, at every age?

By demanding (through their words and actions) more engaging work environments and more meaningful work, the Millennials are asking us to step up our leadership.

They come into work with the expectation that we will put the best practices into practice, rather than just paying lip service. The secret, though, is that the best practices will work for all of us, not just the Millennials.

By stepping up our leadership, we will also be teaching the Millennial generation how to lead. This will be a great gift to them and to the world, because the challenges they will face in their adult lives will be great—a changing economy and a changing global business landscape—and they'll eventually be leading the generations that follow them.

Provide Opportunities for Employee Growth

Kitty Nix, Director, Strategic Development
Helios HR

Millennials are often seeking employee development as a significant part of their employee/employer relationship. High-potential employees in this age group have increased expectations regarding their career growth and the responsibilities of their employers to provide appropriate opportunities. When motivating and working to retain Millennials, leaders must address these expectations and communicate the organization's plans and strategy in this area. Motivating this segment of your workforce through employee growth and development may include:

- Providing readily available, company-sponsored training and educational opportunities to keep skills sharp and current.
- Creating a well-defined career trajectory with both technical and management tracks that provide clear steps in career progression.
- Increasing communication between managers and employees regarding individual interests, future goals, and growth opportunities.

- Providing recognition for a job well done, a competitive salary that recognizes accomplishments, and identification of new challenges.
- Instituting a mentor program, providing coaching, and continually giving constructive feedback throughout the year.
- Ensuring that employees know how their contributions fit into the larger mission of the organization so they are not just executing a job description in isolation.
- Including Millennials in charting their own growth path, working to accommodate both personal and business goals.

Motivation for these individuals includes a partnership with an employer that is focused on experiential learning, continued skill growth, and a defined career path. The number-one priority of our Millennial workforce is being provided with multiple opportunities and avenues to develop to their full professional potential.

Customize the Employment Experience

Marcia Riley, Vice President, Talent Management and Human Resources
ESI International

I've learned from experience that it really is about creating a customized employment experience for everyone who joins your team. I try to treat my employees like valued *internal customers,* and the resulting ROI in loyalty and contribution is remarkable!

- The recruiting and on-boarding of Millennials begins at the interview. Once you know that you intend to make an offer, find out what the Millennial values in the arena of creativity, contribution, coaching, recognition, etc. Build choices into the way they get work done, and try to meet their needs from day one. Check in with them frequently about what is working and not working in their new position.
- Have them mentored by someone their age who has already made a successful transition into your organization. The research about employee engagement indicates that having even one friend at work increases the possibility that new employees will stay with the organization.
- Don't hover or micromanage; focus on results and deliverables.

In closing, remember that Millennial employees grew up in a different world than you did, but that world is just as real and critical to them as your world is to you. Recognize and respect their differences, and you'll have a wonderful new member of your multi-generational workforce.

One Size Does Not Fit All

Christopher R. Ryan, Deputy General Counsel
K12 Inc.

It is a mistake to apply a one-size-fits-all approach to motivating workers, especially Millennials. The key is to avoid the trap of assuming that what motivates you will apply equally to the employees you manage regardless of their age or function.

- New generations seek to distinguish themselves from prior generations to establish their own identity, and the Millennial generation of workers is no different.
- However, technology and the associated pace of change have made it more challenging for managers to adapt to and determine how to motivate this new group of workers.
- Today's manager needs to venture beyond his or her comfort zone to become more perceptive and open minded about meeting the needs of Millennial workers.
- Otherwise, it will be difficult to motivate and retain this group of workers, who are needed to perform staff work in the short term and who will become mid-level and senior managers in the long term.

Given the rapid growth of numerous economies through globalization, the future competitiveness of the United States depends on our ability to adapt to and leverage this next generation of workers.

Final Recommendations for Motivating Millennials

Kurt Schlimme, Project Management Office Director
The College Board

The new workforce of Millennials offers unknown potential related to performance, productivity, creativity, and innovation within their organizations. Managers must learn to harness this new potential through their management techniques.

- Defining specific work outcomes and time expectations in relation to assignments or deliverables allows Millennials to use their thought processes and work patterns in creative and effective manners.
- Letting them take ownership of the work products but governing the work products via constraints and expectations allows for the development of a natural mentoring relationship.
- Shifting managerial focus from "direct and control" to "observe and support" engages the workers' sense of commitment and contribution.

Millennials will be the new work force. Organizations that can adapt their cultures and management to optimize and motivate Millennial performance will be successful. Moreover, managers who can harness their potential and optimize Millennial performance will be highly recognized within their own organizations.

Address the Challenge of Motivating Millennial Knowledge Workers

Shira Harrington, Director, Professional Search Positions, Inc.

At the initial drafting of this book, our country had yet to be hit with the global economic recession we are currently facing. The impact of this downturn has been felt by most every worker, including Millennials. What was once the generation of What's-In-It-For-Me may be evolving into the generation of How-Do-I-Land-An-Unpaid-Internship?

The classic Howe and Strauss book *Generations* contends that every four generations we see the same generational traits recycle. This may be poignantly true for the Millennial generation, who, like their WWII elders, are learning to appreciate the little things once again. It will be interesting to watch the evolution of this generation, some of whom were in the workforce before the recession, some of whom are in college and facing an uncertain job market, and some of whom are sitting in classrooms and around the dinner table being prepared by their teachers and parents for a world with fewer pearls in their oysters.

All of that said, certain generational traits were imbued from an early age into the Millennials, and taught them that they could do anything they set their hearts and minds to and should settle for nothing less than the best in their careers. Blending their parental encouragement from the past with the financial uncertainty of the future should yield some interesting behavioral and motivational results for employers.

Hopefully, the lesson learned is that neither employer nor employee should take each other for granted any longer. Economic winds, societal events, and parenting styles may change, but we must learn to recognize that at the end of the day, businesses need to turn a profit and workers want to be appreciated for their contribution to the bottom line. Focusing on what motivates every employee makes good sense for Wall Street—and for Main Street.

Leverage Unique Motivators

Mark Steffanina, Director of Organizational Effectiveness
Holy Cross Hospital

Leveraging the unique motivations of Millennial knowledge workers fosters their engagement, providing an environment conducive to eliciting their discretionary effort. Consequently, engaging environments that draw on knowledge worker motivations fuel outcomes such as employee satisfaction, retention, and productivity.

- Understand and recognize that knowledge worker motivational factors can serve as keys to unlocking performance potential.
- Use the Team Improvement and Prioritization Matrix (TIP'M) methodology to involve twenty-something knowledge workers in evaluating their workplaces.
- Employ the completed TIP'M to identify misalignment between motivational factors and workplace characteristics.
- Encourage knowledge worker participation in action plan development and implementation to realize the latent opportunities identified by the TIP'M.

Having twenty-something knowledge workers contribute to building their motivation-leveraging workplace will provide not only a satisfying working environment but also improved organizational performance.

Foster Employee Commitment and Engagement

Hector Velez, Executive Vice President, Business Development
HireStrategy

Employers in the Washington, D.C. metro area, one of the most vibrant employment markets in the country, look to HireStrategy as a value-added resource in order to design and implement their human capital initiatives. This has opened a privileged window into the inner workings of some of the great places to work and some of the not-so-great places to work in our country. Those great places to work have definitely figured out how to create the conditions that allow their staffs to succeed and achieve their professional, financial, and personal goals. The following includes some of our observations.

Employee commitment and engagement are key to any organizations success. The Millennial generation requires that management rethink their leadership styles and focus. Now, more than ever, leaders need to:

- Create a culture where everybody is a customer who needs to be delighted; "everybody" includes employees, support staff, paying customers, job applicants, and the community at large.
- Demonstrate a strong sense of humility (the era of know-it-alls is over).

- Communicate with total transparency, from the strategic to the tactical, within all functional areas, especially the financial (the era of surprises is over).
- Avoid delusional optimism or the purposeful ignorance of the facts, which will be counterproductive when the realities of the business world and the economy at large inevitable disrupt a company's "hockey stick" growth curve!
- Lead by example in order to create and promote a culture of complete trust and confidence where employees are treated like mature professional adults (the era of micromanagement is over).
- Avoid overreliance on managing to quarterly earnings, which has hollowed out organizations' leadership ranks. Hopefully we are entering a new era of truly enlightened organizational design and economic vibrancy.

Organizations—whether private-sector firms, publicly traded firms, government agencies, or nonprofits—need to embrace a paradigm shift from managing by numbers to managing talent.

Use Technology Challenges as Motivators

Stuart H. Weinstein, Ph.D, Senior Managing Consultant
IBM

Motivation for 21–30-year-old knowledge workers is no longer merely grounded in their potential salary, long-term commitments to an employer, or assurances of sequential progression in a specific field. It's critical to recognize that:

- Technology challenges, the potential to be "special," and opportunities to contribute generate motivation within the employee and spark enthusiasm in the job environment, which is rewarding when it spreads to others at any age.
- At high-tech firms, satisfaction often comes from Millennials' personal accomplishments and the ability to experiment with new ideas and products that are perceived as a vision for their future.
- Technology and innovation may not permit "seasoning" of their ideas, but rather require rapid adoption.
- Employers should harness the excitement that the Millennials feel and encourage them to communicate it to those who are entering the workforce.

The ability of the Millennials to be unconstrained by tradition, and allowed to explore new ideas and combinations of ideas that have never been considered, encourages them to influence what is yet to be our future.

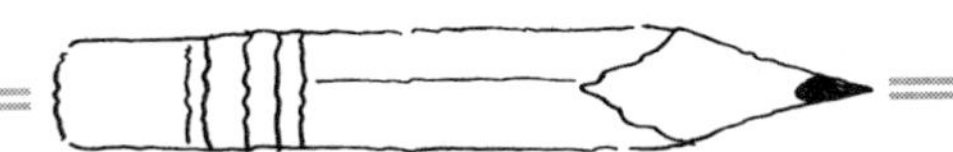

Chapter Checklist: Designing Your Action Plan

The following learning objectives appeared in previous chapters. Review and select those that are relevant to designing your own plan for motivating Millennials.

Introduction: Understanding the Millennial Knowledge Worker

- ❑ 1. Review five recommendations for using this book effectively.
- ❑ 2. Gain an understanding of the Millennial knowledge worker.
- ❑ 3. Share responsibility for motivating the Millennial knowledge worker.

Introduction: Millennial Motivational Issues

- ❑ 1. Acknowledge broader Millennial motivational issues.
- ❑ 2. Appreciate four portraits of Millennials from Contributing Experts' perspective.
- ❑ 3. Understand the critical Millennial motivational factors that drive this book.

Part 1: Flexibility and Work/Life Balance

- ❑ 1. Acknowledge the importance of flexibility and work/life balance.
- ❑ 2. Explore flexible work arrangements driven by the current workforce crisis.
- ❑ 3. Take a closer look at Millennials' need for flexibility and work/life balance.
- ❑ 4. Develop proactive strategies in support of flexibility and work/life balance.

CONTINUED

CONTINUED

Part 2: Multidimensional Millennial Growth Opportunities

- ❑ 1. Recognize that multidimensional growth opportunities are non-negotiable Millennial requirements.
- ❑ 2. Reconcile growth opportunities of Millennials and the intellectual-capital needs of knowledge organizations.
- ❑ 3. Consider the multidimensional Millennial growth opportunities presented by Contributing Experts.
- ❑ 4. Identify Millennial leadership opportunities through growth opportunities.

Part 3: Fun and Social Interaction

- ❑ 1. Harness the importance of fun and social interaction as a significant Millennial motivational factor as well as a valued human capital asset.
- ❑ 2. Encourage managers and human resources professionals to incorporate strategies for adding fun into the workplace.
- ❑ 3. Identify opportunities to incorporate social interaction into the workplace.

Part 4: Purpose, Contribution, and Challenging Work

- ❑ 1. Provide flexible opportunities to meet Millennials' need for career and life purpose.
- ❑ 2. Recognize the contribution that Millennials make to their workplaces and society.
- ❑ 3. Address Millennials' need for challenging work that addresses global, national, and organizational issues.

Part 5: Establishing and Sustaining Effective Communication

- ❑ 1. Establish and sustain effective communication that meets Millennial motivational needs.
- ❑ 2. Acknowledge that effective communication is a shared responsibility of manager and Millennial.
- ❑ 3. Employ a variety of relevant communication strategies and tactics.

CONTINUED

CONTINUED

Part 6: The Three Rs: Recognition, Rewards, and Respect

- ❑ 1. Identify the unique generational factors that influence the importance of recognition, rewards, and respect as Millennial motivators.
- ❑ 2. Appreciate the importance of appropriate recognition for Millennial knowledge workers.
- ❑ 3. Establish an organizational and managerial climate to apply reward strategies.
- ❑ 4. Develop a mutually beneficial climate in support of respect.

Part 7: Learning, Training, and Technology

- ❑ 1. Understand the forces shaping America's economy and their implications for work and workers in the 21st century.
- ❑ 2. Recognize that knowledge has become the critically important factor in economic life.
- ❑ 3. Respond to the paradigm shift from 20th-century training to 21st-century learning.
- ❑ 4. Appreciate the Millennials' unique learning preferences.

Part 8: Pay for Performance

- ❑ 1. Include the tangible motivator of money as a driver of superior performance.
- ❑ 2. Move beyond the traditional concept of a performance appraisal to implement a pay-for-performance system.
- ❑ 3. Identify strategies for providing financial rewards for knowledge.
- ❑ 4. Implement pay-for-performance initiatives in shorter time frames (12–36 months).

An Organizational Millennial Motivational Assessment

The primary focus of this book has been encouraging individual managers and human resources professionals to assume responsibility for developing and motivating Millennial knowledge workers. In Appendix 2, Contributing Expert Mark Steffanina presents a methodology that provides an opportunity for organizations to take responsibility for conducting a motivational factors survey to effect broader change. First, an explanation of the Team Improvement and Prioritizing Matrix methodology is presented. Second, examples of its application are presented to illustrate its effectiveness.

Introducing the TIP'M Methodology

Mark Steffanina, MBA, Director of Organizational Effectiveness,
Holy Cross Hospital

Disciplined problem solving, continuous improvement, and data-driven decision making form an integral part of organizational development activity, particularly as they provide for the weaving of unique human insights into the fabric of organizational functioning. One approach, both tactical and strategic, to build a pro-Millennial workplace is to use a disciplined technique known as the Team Improvement and Prioritization Matrix (TIP'M) methodology. The TIP'M methodology uses motivational criteria to assess organizational health by performing a gap analysis of the organization's current state and one that encourages Millennial motivation.

The TIP'M enables organizational development practitioners to transform the workplace into one that is Millennial oriented by maximizing and leveraging their unique motivational factors. Leveraging the factors of Millennial motivation in organizational design fosters Millennial recruitment, development, and retention—strategic objectives pursued by many organizations interested in human capital. Moreover, using Millennial motivational factors to shape the Millennial workplace ultimately pays dividends to the organization in terms of improved outcomes attained through encouraging Millennial performance and productivity.

The TIP'M methodology also serves as a tactical device, directly engaging and involving Millennials in the process of organizational development. In so doing, the TIP'M methodology is an empowering tool, facilitating Millennial participation in workplace improvement. Engaging Millennials in a direct manner, making them collaborators in the enhancement of workplace functioning, serves to engender a sense of ownership among them and fosters their connection to the organizational enhancements that will result from the use of the methodology. In addition, by engendering ownership, the TIP'M methodology leads to the promotion of Millennial discretionary effort, driving their retention and further encouraging their performance and productivity.

Determining Priorities

Social psychological factors, group dynamics, and organizational culture and health all affect the way in which Millennials perceive their motivational factors. The first stage in building a Team Improvement and Prioritization Matrix (TIP'M) is to determine how the Millennials in a particular organization perceive the priority of the various Millennial motivational factors. These priorities will serve the organizational development practitioner by indicating the degree of influence that each factor has on the organization's Millennial workforce. Pursuant to building a working environment that facilitates Millennial motivation, these factors become characteristics or necessary criteria of a motivational workplace. Consequently, the priority that a particular Millennial subgroup places on one factor over another becomes a rather important key to an organizational development practitioner.

There are many ways to determine the priorities that a particular Millennial group places on various motivational factors; the critical aspect of ranking the factors is the engagement of the Millennials in the activity. If it is possible to physically assemble the group, then brainstorming, multi-voting, Crawford slips, and nominal group techniques can be used to involve the Millennials in ranking their motivational factors. In organizations with a technological orientation, online surveys, shared databases, virtual bulletin boards, e-mail, or even text messages can be used to collect input from the Millennial subgroup and rank their motivational factors.

The ranked motivational factors form the left, or vertical, axis of the TIP'M (Figure 1) and will be used as weighted criteria against which the organization will be assessed. These will ultimately direct an organizational development practitioner to the gaps between the organization's current state and one that promotes Millennial motivation.

The factors may be prioritized in various ways. Perhaps the easiest approach may be to have each Millennial rank the factors in order from most significant to least so the organizational development practitioner can aggregate and weight them accordingly. Another method may involve the use of a Likert scale, having each Millennial provide his or her perception of the degree of influence that each motivational factor has in order for the organizational development practitioner to subsequently use the average response for each motivational factor's weight.

Describing the Organization within a TIP'M

The second stage in building a Millennial-focused workplace with the TIP'M methodology is the construction of the top, or, horizontal axis of the matrix (Figure 1). Along the horizontal axis are descriptors, characteristics, activities, or features of the workplace in its current state. These descriptive characteristics of the current workplace may include, for example, flexible scheduling, weekly staff meetings, on-site educational opportunities, recognition events, merit compensation increases, and so on, depending on the organization. Refer to the end of this section for examples of workplace features used to construct Team Improvement and Priority Matrices.

Assessing Organizational Characteristics Against Motivational Factors

The third stage in developing a TIP'M and using it for workplace transformation is to assess each of the organizational characteristics against the Millennial motivational factors. This stage involves the Millennials in evaluating their workplace in terms of its ability to respond to their motivational factors. The Millennials will compare each characteristic of their workplace against their motivational factors and will assign a rating indicating how well the workplace characteristic responds or supports each motivational factor.

A rating system of some sort is employed to describe these relationships; variations may include scales of 1–3 (corresponding to ordinal responses such as Low, Medium, or High), or gradients of 1–5 or 1–10; and 0 for no relationship or support at all. Common among these rating systems is that the higher number corresponds to a greater link between the workplace feature or characteristic and the motivational factor.

For example, should flexible scheduling be a feature of a particular workplace, each Millennial would evaluate it against each motivational factor, expressing his or her perspective by using the defined scale. One would expect an organizational characteristic such as flexible scheduling to be highly responsive to the Millennial motivational factor of flexibility. However, if this characteristic is perceived by the particular group of Millennials as something other than highly responsive, such feedback would be an important cue to the organizational development practitioner of an opportunity in distributive, procedural, or transactional justice or some other issue that may impede flexible scheduling.

Just as with engaging the Millennial subgroup in ranking their motivational factors, having them assess features of their workplace may be done in a wide variety of ways. Some organizations may prefer assembling their Millennials together in a focus group, while others may prefer to collect each individual Millennial's response in the form of an online or paper survey. Of course, if some survey method is used, the organizational development practitioner will have to aggregate the responses in some manner. No matter how the Millennials are engaged in the process, the organizational development practitioner will benefit from their insight, feedback, and ownership in honing their workplace into an environment that contributes to their motivation.

Completing the TIP'M

The fourth stage in employing the TIP'M methodology and transforming the workplace into one supporting Millennial motivation is the completion of the matrix. The weights assigned by the Millennials to each of their motivational factors are considered against their ratings of each workplace feature. Although there are several ways to compare the workplace features and corresponding motivational factors, one robust approach is to represent the weight of each motivational factor relative to the responsiveness of each workplace feature by the product of the two measures. In other words, the matrix is completed by multiplying each motivational factor's rank by each corresponding workplace feature's rating, indicating the product in the cell adjacent to the feature's rating, as shown in Figure 1.

Team Improvement and Prioritization Matrix©

Relative Rank	**Motivational Factors**	Workplace Feature 1	Workplace Feature 2
(Slightly Motivating = 1 Highly Motivating = 10)	Evaluate each workplace feature against these motivational factors below on a 1 - 10 scale in terms of how well they respond to each motivational factor. 1= Little responsiveness, 10= High responsiveness. Use '0' to indicate no responsiveness whatsoever.	Flexible Scheduling	Weekly Staff Meetings
10	**Flexibility**	10 / 100	3 / 30
9	**Fun**	2 / 18	6 / 54
8	**Rewards and Recognition**	2 / 16	6 / 48
7	**Challenge**	0 / 0	1 / 7

Figure 1: Sample matrix view

The TIP'M is completed by calculating the sum of the products of each column and row. In the previous example, the sum of the products in the Flexible Scheduling column is 134, and the sum of the products in the Weekly Staff Meetings column is 139. Comparing the sums of all the columns will help you understand which workplace features tend to provide greater support for Millennial motivation over others. Similarly, the row sums may also be calculated to provide insight into how the motivational factors are encouraged by the workplace features.

Analysis of the Completed Matrix

The fifth stage in using the TIP'M method to improve organizational functioning by leveraging Millennial motivations is to analyze the completed matrix. Having engaged the Millennial subgroup in the process of developing the TIP'M, the organizational development practitioner has rich feedback to guide organizational improvement. The completed matrix may be used in several ways; among the most obvious is to note the cells with the highest and lowest products. In the Figure 1 example, Flexibility relative to Flexible Scheduling received the highest rating, suggesting its high relative responsiveness to the Millennial motivator of flexibility. Conversely, Challenge relative to Flexible Scheduling received the lowest rating, signifying a lack of responsiveness between the workplace feature, Flexible Scheduling, and the Millennial motivator, Challenge. It is important to note that this lack of responsiveness may not necessarily be a negative aspect of organizational functioning (as perhaps the two cannot, or should not, be related). However, these relationships are noteworthy when the entire matrix is viewed from a broad perspective rather than a cellular one.

One broader perspective is to analyze these results across each motivational-factor row. In Figure 1, doing so might suggest that the Challenge motivational factor is not well addressed by the workplace features in general, receiving only "0" and "1" for a row sum of "7" from the Millennial subgroup.

The results of tallying the high and low aggregate ratings given by the Millennials provide a sense of what generally responds to their motivating factors and what does not, another way to consider the results. No matter which analytical perspective or combination thereof is used, the results of the TIP'M methodology are helpful in guiding future organizational development efforts aimed at bolstering Millennial motivation.

Sharing Results

A final stage in the use of the TIP'M methodology, as with any disciplined improvement method that engages people in the improvement process, is to share the results with the Millennials involved and suggest subsequent next steps. Since the Millennial subgroup was actively involved in the process of creating the TIP'M, they rightly deserve a review of the finished product. Sharing subsequent next steps to be taken organizationally in response to their input into the TIP'M will further promote their ownership of the improvements to come, increasing their motivation to contribute.

Team Improvement and Prioritization Matrix©

Relative Rank (Slightly Motivating = 1 Highly Motivating = 10)	Motivational Factors Evaluate each workplace feature against these motivational factors below on a 1 - 10 scale in terms of how well they respond to each motivational factor. 1= Little responsiveness, 10= High responsiveness. Use '0' to indicate no responsiveness whatsoever.	Workplace Feature 1 Flexible Scheduling	Workplace Feature 2 Weekly Staff Meetings	Workplace Feature 3 Monthly Service Awards	Workplace Feature 4 Onsite Training	Workplace Feature 5 Quarterly Teambuilding Event	Total	Factor Responsiveness Quotient
10	**Flexibility**	10 / 100	3 / 30	4 / 40	6 / 60	3 / 30	260	52%
9	**Fun**	2 / 18	6 / 54	8 / 72	8 / 72	10 / 90	306	68%
8	**Rewards and Recognition**	2 / 16	6 / 48	10 / 80	5 / 40	8 / 64	248	62%
7	**Challenge**	0 / 0	1 / 7	1 / 7	6 / 42	9 / 63	119	34%
6	Pay for Performance	3 / 18	3 / 18	4 / 24	5 / 30	2 / 12	102	34%
5	**Respect**	5 / 25	8 / 40	9 / 45	7 / 35	8 / 40	185	74%
4	Communication	8 / 32	10 / 40	3 / 12	6 / 24	8 / 32	140	70%
3	Social Interaction	2 / 6	7 / 21	9 / 27	5 / 15	9 / 27	96	64%
2	Purpose and/or Contribution	5 / 10	7 / 14	8 / 16	4 / 8	9 / 18	66	66%
1	Technology	8 / 8	3 / 3	3 / 3	9 / 9	2 / 2	25	50%
	Total	233	275	326	335	378		
	Feature Responsiveness Quotient	45%	54%	59%	61%	68%		

M. Steffanina, 2008

Figure 2: Team Improvement and Prioritization Matrix, Sample 1

TEAM PRIORITIZATION AND IMPROVEMENT MATRIX©		Sporting Events	Career Development Planning	Staff Meetings	Performance Reports	Educational Programs	Quarterly Goal Celebrations	Holiday Celebrations	Fitness Program		Responsiveness Quotient
MOTIVATING FACTORS	Relative Importance	Responsiveness for each feature above (scale: L for Low, M for Medium, H for High)									
Respect	8.8	M	M	L	L	M	M	L	L		0%
Communication	8.1	L	L	H	H	M	L	L	L		25%
Social Interaction	7.8	H	L	L	L	L	H	H	M		38%
Purpose and/or Contribution	7.6	L	M	M	L	L	H	H	L		25%
Rewards and Recognition	7.4	L	L	L	L	L	H	H	L		25%
Challenge	7.3	H	L	L	L	H	L	L	M		25%
Fun	7.2	H	L	L	L	L	H	H	M		38%
Flexibility	7.2	L	L	L	L	L	L	L	L		0%
Pay for Performance	6.3	L	M	L	M	M	L	L	L		0%
Technology	6.0	L	M	L	L	M	L	L	L		0%
Total Low		6	6	8	8	5	5	6	7	Total Responsiveness Quotient	
Total Medium		1	4	1	1	4	1	0	3		
Total High		3	0	1	1	1	4	4	0	18%	
Aggregate Responsiveness		-3	-6	-7	-7	-4	-1	-2	-7		

M. Steffanina, 2008

Figure 3: Team Improvement and Prioritization Matrix, Sample 2

Team Improvement and Prioritization Matrix©	Factor Rank	Staff Development Opportunities	Factor Weight	Comp Time	Factor Weight	Support from Supervision	Factor Weight	Interaction with co-workers	Factor Weight	Interaction with scholars	Factor Weight	Total Characteristic Score	Factor Weighted Responsiveness Ratio
Communication	10	3	30	3.5	35	4.5	45	3.5	35	4	40	185	74%
Respect	9	4	36	3	27	3.5	31.5	3.5	31.5	4.5	40.5	166.5	74%
Pay for Performance	8	2	16	1.5	12	1.5	12	1.5	12	1.5	12	64	32%
Purpose and/or Contribution	7	2.5	17.5	2.5	17.5	2.5	17.5	3.5	24.5	5	35	112	64%
Social Interaction	6	1.5	9	3.5	21	3.5	21	3.5	21	5	30	102	68%
Learning	5	2.5	12.5	2	10	2.5	12.5	4	20	5	25	80	64%
Challenging Environment	4	4	16	3.5	14	4.5	18	3	12	4.5	18	78	78%
Flexibility	3	3.5	10.5	4	12	4	12	4	12	5	15	61.5	82%
Technology	2	4	8	2	4	3.5	7	3	6	5	10	35	70%
Fun	1	3.5	3.5	4	4	4	4	3.5	3.5	5	5	20	80%
Total Aspect Score		30.5	159	29.5	156.5	34	180.5	33	177.5	44.5	230.5	**66%**	
Responsiveness Ratio		61%		59%		68%		66%		89%		**Factor Weighted Assessment Score**	

M. Steffanina, 2008

Figure 4: Team Improvement and Prioritization Matrix, Sample 3

Additional Reading

Books

Alsop, Ron. *The Trophy Kids Grow Up: How the Millennial Generation Is Shaping Up in the Workplace.* San Francisco, CA: Jossey-Bass, 2008.

Bridges, William. *JobShift: How to Prosper in a Workplace without Jobs.* New York, NY: Perseus Books, 1995.

Carnevale, Anthony. *America and the New Economy.* San Francisco, CA: Jossey-Bass, 1991.

Chester, Eric. *Employing Generation Why? Understanding, Managing, Motivating Your New Workforce.* Lakewood, CO: Tucker House Press, 2002.

Chick, Erica D. *Fundamentals of Work-Life Balance.* Alexandria, VA: InfoLine, August, 2004.

Dychtwald, Ken, Tamara J. Erickson, and Robert Morison. *Workforce Crisis: How to Beat the Coming Shortage of Skills and Talents.* Boston, MA: Harvard Business School Press, 2000.

Estess, Patricia Schiff. *Work Concepts for the Future.* Crisp, 1996.

Friedman, Thomas. *The World is Flat: A Brief History of the Twenty-first Century.* New York, NY: Picador, 2005.

Judy, Richard W. and Carol D'Amico. *Workforce 2020: Work and Workers in the 21st Century.* Indianapolis, IN: Hudson Institute, 1999.

Horibe, Frances. *Managing Knowledge Workers: New Skills and Attitudes to Unlock the Intellectual Capital of Your Organization.* New York, NY: John Wiley & Sons, 1999.

Howe, Neil and William Strauss. *Millennials Rising: The Next Great Generation.* New York, NY: Vintage Books (Random House), 2000.

Howe, Neil and William Strauss. *Generations: The History of America's Future, 1584-2069.* 1992.

Howe, Neil and William Strauss. *13 Gen: Abort, Retry, Ignore, Fail?* New York, NY: Vintage Books (Random House), 1993.

Marquardt, Michael J. *Building Learning Organizations: Mastering the Five Elements for Corporate Learning.* New York, NY: The McGraw-Hill Companies, 1996.

Martin, Carolyn A. and Bruce Tulgan. *Managing Generation Y: Global Citizens Born in the Late Seventies and Early Eighties.* Amherst, MA: HRD Press, Inc., 2001.

Martin, Carolyn A. and Bruce Tulgan. *Managing the Generation Mix: From Collision to Collaboration.* Amherst, MA: HRD Press, 2002.

McGovern, Rob. *Bring Your "A" Game: The 10 Career Secrets of High Achievers.* Sourcebooks, Inc., 2005.

Marston, Cam. *Motivating the "What's In It for Me?" Workforce: Manage Across the Generational Divide and Increase Profits.* San Francisco, CA: John Wiley & Sons, 2007.

National Academy of Public Administration. *New Options, New Talent: The Government Guide to the Flexible Workforce.* Washington, D.C.: National Academy of Public Administration, HRM Series IV, August 1998.

Orrell, Lisa. *Millennials Incorporated.* Intelligent Women Publishing (Wyatt-Mackenzie), 2007.

Pasmore, William A. and John J. Sherwood, ed. *Sociotechnical Systems: A Source Book.* San Diego: University Associates, 1978.

Robert Half International and Yahoo! HotJobs. *What Millennial Workers Want: How to Attract and Retain Gen Y Employees*. 2008.

Salkowitz, Rob. *Generation Blend: Managing Across the Technology Gap.* Hoboken, NJ: John Wiley & Sons, Inc., 2008.

Senge, Peter M. *The Fifth Discipline: The Art and Practice of the Learning Organization.* New York, NY: Currency Doubleday, 1994.

Stewart, Thomas A. *Intellectual Capital: The New Wealth of Organizations.* New York, NY: Currency Doubleday, 1997.

Sveiby, Karl Eric. *The New Organizational Wealth: Managing and Measuring Knowledge-Based Assets.* San Francisco, CA: Berrett-Koehler Publishers, Inc., 1997.

Twenge, Jane M. *Generation Me: Why Today's Young Americans Are More Confident, Assertive, Entitled—and More Miserable.* New York, NY: Free Press, 2006.

Tulgan, Bruce. *Not Everyone Gets a Trophy: How to Manage Generation Y.* San Francisco, CA: Jossey-Bass, 2009.

Articles

Crane, Mary. "Mentoring Millennials," *Training Magazine* (TrainingMag.com). January 17, 2008.

Levinson, Harry. "A Second Career: The Possible Dream," *Harvard Business Review on Work and Life Balance*. Boston: Harvard Business Press, 2000.

Sandeen, Cathy. "Boomers, Xers, and Millennials: Who are They and What Do They Really Want from Continuing Higher Education?" *Continuing Higher Education Review*. The Journal of the University Continuing Education Association, Volume 72, Fall 2008.

Spiro, Cara. "Generation Y in the Workplace," *Defense AT&L*, Nov-Dec, 2006.

Zaslow, Jeffrey. "The Most Praised Generation Goes to Work," *The Wall Street Journal*. April 20, 2007.

50-Minute™ Series

If you enjoyed this book, we have great news for you.
There are more than 200 books available in the
Crisp Fifty-Minute™ Series.

Subject Areas Include:

Management and Leadership
Human Resources
Communication Skills
Personal Development
Sales and Marketing
Accounting and Finance
Coaching and Mentoring
Customer Service/Quality
Small Business and Entrepreneurship
Writing and Editing

For more information visit us online at

www.CrispSeries.com

VERS